Lecture Notes in Computer Science   **10160**

Commenced Publication in 1973
Founding and Former Series Editors:
Gerhard Goos, Juris Hartmanis, and Jan van Leeuwen

More information about this series at http://www.springer.com/series/7408

Thomas Gibson-Robinson · Philippa Hopcroft
Ranko Lazić (Eds.)

Concurrency, Security, and Puzzles

Essays Dedicated to Andrew William Roscoe
on the Occasion of His 60th Birthday

Springer

Editors
Thomas Gibson-Robinson
University of Oxford
Oxford
UK

Ranko Lazić
University of Warwick
Coventry
UK

Philippa Hopcroft
University of Oxford
Oxford
UK

ISSN 0302-9743   ISSN 1611-3349 (electronic)
Lecture Notes in Computer Science
ISBN 978-3-319-51045-3   ISBN 978-3-319-51046-0   (eBook)
DOI 10.1007/978-3-319-51046-0

Library of Congress Control Number: 2016960194

LNCS Sublibrary: SL2 – Programming and Software Engineering

Cover illustration: Self-portrait of the honoree.

Printed on acid-free paper

This Springer imprint is published by Springer Nature
The registered company is Springer International Publishing AG
The registered company address is: Gewerbestrasse 11, 6330 Cham, Switzerland

Bill Roscoe working in University College, Oxford in 1979.
Taken by Coby Roscoe.

Preface

This volume contains papers written in honour of A.W. Roscoe, better known as Bill Roscoe, on the occasion of his 60th birthday. Bill was born in Dundee and went on to read Mathematics at University College, Oxford (Univ) in 1975, achieving the top first. Bill's main tutors at Oxford were Michael Collins and Gordon Screaton, both of whom have had huge influences on his life and career. Remarkably, Bill has never left Univ, and is currently a Senior Research Fellow at the college, having previously been a College Lecturer and a Tutorial Fellow.

After completing his undergraduate degree, Bill completed a DPhil at Oxford under the supervision of Professor Sir Tony Hoare. Bill's thesis was on the mathematical foundations of Communicating Sequential Processes (CSP), a topic to which he has become synonymous and that has come to dominate his research career. His early work on CSP in the 1980s, together with Steve Brookes and others, focused on formally defining the mathematical foundations of CSP, and resulted in the development of the form of CSP used today. More widely, Bill has made huge contributions to the understanding of concurrency, as demonstrated by the fact that his first textbook on the subject, *The Theory and Practice of Concurrency*, has over 2,000 citations. He is undoubtably one of the leading figures worldwide in the area of process algebras. Bill's research interests are not only confined to Computer Science; he also published a number of papers on topology, leading to an Erdös number of 2.

Bill has been the driving force behind the development of FDR, the CSP refinement checker, since its inception in the early 1990s. This also involved the setting up of the first company that he was involved in, Formal Systems (Europe) Limited. Bill is not only the most ardent user of FDR but has also made considerable contributions to the ideas behind FDR; most notably in determining how to efficiently perform refinement checking, and to FDR's compression functions. He has also built various tools to translate other languages into CSP for analysis using FDR, including one for analysing simple imperative programs, and another for analysing Statecharts.

Bill's passion for theory is matched with an equal desire to see his research make an impact in practice by solving industrial challenges. One of Bill's (many) remarkable qualities is his ability to deal with the details of analysing a horrendously combinatorially complex system in his head, even while performing at a board. He became known by some of his industrial partners as the "Professor of Difficult Sums", as he is the go-to person for fiendish challenges! Bill has enjoyed numerous fruitful collaborations with industry partners and government agencies throughout his career; for example, with Draper, Inmos, U.S. Office of Naval Research, and QinetiQ (and its previous versions). One of his early collaborations with Inmos on the verification of the floating-point unit on the T800 transputer, led to a Queen's Award in 1990. These collaborations have proven to be a stimulating influence on Bill's research over the years, as is demonstrated to this day by his exciting research projects, which combine theory and practice in order to tackle the escalating costs of software development.

Bill is known for his love of solving puzzles using CSP and FDR. One of Bill's first papers was on this topic, and involved solving the so-called trains problem, where trains have to be moved to the correct sheds over a predetermined configuration of tracks. He later wrote a practical to accompany the undergraduate course in Concurrency at Oxford that required students to solve this problem, which is still in use today. He is particularly proud of the fact that FDR managed to find a shorter solution than previously known to a variant of the puzzle. Bill's passion for solving puzzles using CSP and FDR extends over many well-known examples and has become so well-established that they are now used as standard benchmarks for FDR. Indeed, he evaluates all of his new hardware on the basis of how quickly it can master his standard peg solitaire script!

In the mid-1990s Bill became involved in using CSP to analyse the security properties of systems. He first worked on analysing security protocols using CSP and FDR, along with Gavin Lowe amongst others. This work led to FDR becoming widely used as a protocol analysis tool, and also led to many advances in FDR particularly enhancing its scalability. He also worked on information flow, and developed one of the few definitions of non-interference that deals adequately with refinement. Lately, Bill has worked on human-interactive security protocols that allow secure networks to be established using non-fakable information that can be exchanged between humans. This technology has industrial applications such as mobile payments, medical data exchange, and telephony.

Bill's research record is matched by an astonishing track record of leadership and administration within the University of Oxford. Bill took over as Head of the Computer Laboratory at Oxford in 2003, and over a ten-year period led the department to nearly triple in size. His ambitions for the department were perhaps best illustrated in 2011, when he oversaw the change in name of the department, from the Computer Laboratory to the Department of Computer Science. This change in name clearly signalled to the world that the department was now intent on being a world-leading department of computer science — a status that has subsequently been confirmed by many third-party rankings. (Just before we went to press, the *Times Higher Education* published its first ever ranking of worldwide computer science departments, placing Oxford third in the world overall, and first in the UK.) In terms of scale and breadth of research interests, the present Department of Computer Science bears very little resemblance to the Computer Laboratory that Bill joined nearly 40 years ago; but in terms of quality, as these rankings clearly testify, the Department remains world class.

Bill has also been involved in the administration of Univ since he was appointed a tutorial fellow in 1983. Notably, he was appointed as a tutorial fellow in Computer Science two years prior to the degree launching! Bill therefore taught Mathematics for the first two years of his fellowship, which was a major contributor to the cohesion between Computer Science and Mathematics at Univ, something that continues to this day.

No account of Bill would be complete without the mention of his wife Coby, whom he met during his student days at Univ. Their story began in college over a computer and an accounting system in need of some software. The rest is history, filled with amazing stories of their travels around the world together.

November 2016

Thomas Gibson-Robinson
Philippa Hopcroft
Ranko Lazić

Bill Roscoe, on His 60th Birthday

Tony Hoare

Microsoft Research, Cambridge, UK

Happy Birthday, Bill! And many happy returns of the day! And not just of today. I wish you also many returns of the earlier happy days that you and I have spent together as friends and colleagues. For the benefit of our more recent mutual friends and colleagues assembled here, may I recall with gratitude and pleasure some of your notable earlier contributions to the development of Computer Science at Oxford?

In 1978, Bill was awarded the Junior Mathematical Prize for top marks in the Final Examination of his Bachelor's degree at Oxford. Nevertheless, he bravely registered as a Doctoral student in the Programming Research group (PRG), which was then populated by just two academics (Joe Stoy and myself) and two programmers (Malcolm Harper and Andrew Newman). Together with a fellow student Steve Brookes, he embarked on a search for a formal semantics for Communicating Sequential Processes (CSP). This was a new theoretical concurrent programming language which I had designed and published before arrival at Oxford. Indeed, the formalisation of its semantics was a strong part of my motive for moving to Oxford.

An early assignment that I gave to Bill and Steve was to formalise the algebraic laws which governed reasoning about programs expressed in CSP. The next week they came back to ask a question: What were the laws that I wanted? I had no idea how to answer that question. So I threw it straight back at them, as their next assignment, to tell me what laws I should be wanting. To do that we started on an investigation into a mathematical model (then known as a denotational semantics) which the laws would have to satisfy.

On the basis of this model, Bill and Steve proved a highly elegant collection of algebraic laws, entirely to my satisfaction. Bill also formalised and proved the correctness of an abstract implementation of the language, using Gordon Plotkin's notion of a Structural Operational Semantics. The proof of the consistency of a model with its algebraic laws and its operational implementations has been the inspiration for my own life's work on Unifying Theories of Programming right up to the present day.

On graduation in 1982, Bill obtained an IBM Research Fellowship of the Royal Society, and continued work of the CSP model and its applications. At the same time he pursued his previous interest in Topology. In 1983, he accepted the offer of a University Lectureship in Computation at the PRG. He immediately established a close collaboration with David May, the Chief Designer of the Inmos Transputer and its assembly language occam. He led a joint project to check the design of the Inmos floating point unit for their transputer chip, whose architecture was explicitly based on CSP.

This project won, jointly for Inmos and the PRG, the Queen's Award for Technological Achievement, 1990. The award was an enormous boost for the PRG, as a counterbalance to its established reputation as one of the most theoretical Computer Science Departments in the UK. Further boosts were Bill's success between 1985 and

1994 in winning research grants totalling around \$1.5 million in research grants from US sources, and about £0.25 million from UK sources.

I am delighted to exploit this occasion to acknowledge in public my deep personal gratitude for all Bill's help to me personally in fulfilling my duties and achieving my aims for the development of Computer Science at Oxford. And on a more personal level, he was the organiser of my own 60th birthday party, and my retirement symposium in 1999, and another symposium organised jointly with Cliff Jones and Ken Wood for my 75th birthday in Cambridge. He edited the proceedings of the two symposia, and they were presented to me as festschrifts.

Let me conclude by turning again to the earlier days. When Bill's external examiner Peter Cameron received a copy of Bill's Doctoral Thesis, he phoned me with the rueful comment that it contained sufficient material to fill three successful theses of the more normal kind. I was able to console him that he needed to examine only one of them, and he could select whichever one he wished.

Now it is my rueful comment that Bill's lifetime achievement would be enough to fill three normal lifetimes; and in this address, I have selected only on the early years of just one of them. They have given me a lot to thank him for. During this symposium, I greatly look forward to hearing more up-to-date accounts of the many facets of his later achievement.

A Tribute to Bill Roscoe, on the Occasion of His 60th Birthday

Stephen Brookes

Department of Computer Science, Carnegie Mellon University, Pittsburgh, USA

I first met Bill Roscoe as an undergrad at University College in 1975. We were both studying Mathematics, and began to gravitate towards Logic and Computer Science in our second and third years. Later we became graduate students together, and we have known each other as friends and colleagues for over 40 years.

At Univ Bill came across initially as a rather shy and enigmatic Scotsman, but we became friends soon, despite his insistence on introducing me to the Poetic Gems of William McGonagall, oft cited as the "worst poet in the world" and (like Bill) hailing from Dundee. Bill has a warm sense of humor (I have lived in the USA long enough that my spell checker no longer corrects back to UK spelling) and I'm sure he agrees with the general assessment of McGonagall's (lack of) talent. Bill also turns out to have a highly competitive (not to say vicious) approach to croquet, which we discovered on the lawns of Logic Lane and Stavertonia. He is also an excellent chef, although he does tend to use every pot and pan in the kitchen.

Academically, it soon became clear that Bill was a star: in 1978 he achieved the top all-round university-wide score in Finals. We both stayed on for graduate studies at the Programming Research Group, where we got started with Tony Hoare, who was looking for a mathematical semantics for CSP. Looking back, I would characterize those years at the PRG as an incredibly satisfying and formative period for both of us. Under Tony's gentle guidance, we began to find our own feet as researchers. This was a time marked by failures and divergences, as we tried out ideas, learned what worked and what did not. Our dissertations emerged from this collaborative effort, culminating in our first journal paper ("A Theory of Communicating Sequential Processes", known to us as HBR, published in J. ACM, July 1984). This work also led ultimately to the foundations of the FDR model checker, which Bill and his team developed into a highly effective tool with many practical applications. We also travelled together to attend our first international conference, (ICALP, Noordwijkerhout, July 1980). Building on our Ph.D. foundations, Bill and I organized a research conference (Seminar on Concurrency, July 1984), together with Glynn Winskel. The failures/divergences model, CSP, and FDR form a lifelong thread connecting us, even as our own research paths diverged into many new directions. It is always rewarding to look back on past achievements and reflect. It is especially pleasing to recall many happy days of working with Bill (and Tony), and to realize that those early days were when we found our own voices and learned to explore and experiment.

As grad students we both enjoyed a couple of years as Lecturers at Univ. In the following years, I moved abroad and Bill travelled briefly across the High to St. Edmund Hall, then back to Univ. Bill came to Florida for my wedding (to Lynn) in 1984, and

Lynn and I came back to Oxford a few years later, when Bill and Coby got married. We have remained fast friends and colleagues. Bill has had an outstanding career and he continues to shine as a researcher, author, advisor, and even administrator. His many graduate students have gone on to establish themselves in academia and industry. He can look back proudly on his own achievements and those of his advisees.

Bill never ceases to remind me that I am older than he is (albeit by less than a month), and that my own hair became grey faster than his. So it is appropriate for me to welcome Bill to the over-60's generation, even though he'll always be a couple of weeks behind me. I look forward to many more years of research, and may more years of friendship. I end with the following paraphrase in echo of McGonagall:

This is Bill's first 60th Birthday year,

And will be the only one, I rather fear:

Therefore, sound drums and trumpets with cheer,

Until the echoes are heard o'er land, sea, email and Twitter.

Herding Cats, Oxford Style

Michael Wooldridge

Department of Computer Science, University of Oxford, Oxford, UK

Managing academics, so the saying goes, is like trying to herd cats. Academic departments, by and large, are not like closely managed small businesses, but more like a collection of cottage industries, each only dimly aware that they are part of a larger activity (the university). It often comes as a complete surprise to outsiders, who imagine that as employees of a university will naturally owe their allegiance to their employer, but the nature of academic life is such that many academics feel their primary allegiance is not to their university, but to their discipline (maths, physics, computer science, and so on). And as if this situation were not strange enough, at Oxford, we have colleges thrown in the mix as well. Academic freedom means that we feel entirely comfortable saying "no" to those who, technically speaking, are our bosses. For good measure, we often like to point out the foolishness of their ways in detail, perhaps in the hope that they will not bother us again. Those benighted souls who agree to be the head of an academic department are burdened with responsibility by the bucketload, but precious little actual power to effect change. Little wonder that many academic heads retreat to their offices, keep their heads down, and try to get through their sentence creating as little fuss as possible.

I have been a member of the UK academic community for more than a quarter of a century. I have spent a great deal of time over that period studying the dynamics of UK computer science departments. Over that period, there has been a lot of change. Some small departments have grown big; some weak departments have grown strong; and some formerly strong departments have plummeted in quality. Naturally, I am curious about what drives the successes, and what factors lead to the failures.

The recipe seems to be relatively simple, but surprisingly difficult to get right. It certainly isn't corporate management techniques that drives academic excellence. Key performance indicators, extensive documentary paper trails, strategic planning away days, and all the rest of it certainly has its place, but you can diligently do all that stuff and more, and still remain resolutely mediocre. There is plenty of evidence of that, not just in the UK academic sector, but in universities across the world.

So what is it, that drives success? Colleagues who have read so far will no doubt be pleased to hear my firm rejection of the culture of managerialism, but they may be less pleased to hear what I am about to say next. Success stories in academia, as elsewhere, don't happen by accident. Wherever I see success, I see evidence of *leadership*.

Leadership and management, of course, are *not* the same thing; academic leadership is hard to define. But it certainly involves having a clear and realistic vision of where you are going; a balanced understanding of your weaknesses, and those areas that you can realistically make progress; the ability to make your case, and have difficult conversations with those who don't get the point; a clear understanding of academic excellence, and a willingness to support it; and above all, a determination to keep hold of what universities are really all about: research and teaching.

Which brings me to Oxford, and to Bill Roscoe.

It is approaching 15 years since Bill took over as Head of Department of Computer Science at the University of Oxford. He certainly did not take over a weak department: there was excellence aplenty. But, I think it is fair to say, the department at that time was relatively small, and narrowly focussed. Bill took on the challenge of transforming the department in terms of its scale and breadth of activity. Transformative change is not an easy thing to accomplish, even under the best of circumstances. But the nature of Oxford as a collegiate university makes it tremendously difficult to effect transformative change quickly. Decisions at Oxford usually require broad consensus from large and diverse constituencies, and computer science as a relatively new subject has relatively little presence in the colleges and ancient decision-making bodies of the university.

Bill's achievements as Head of Department are, therefore, genuinely remarkable. Oxford's computer science department has grown at a phenomenal rate, and now counts nearly 75 academics in its roster of full-time academic staff. In 2003, the department graduated just three DPhil students; this year we will graduate nearly 50. In the academic year 2014–2015, the department generated more research grant income than in the entire period 2001–2008; we have grown from a pool of about 20 post-doctoral researchers to nearly 150 currently. On every meaningful metric that I can think of, the department has surged ahead.

As an outsider, I watched Oxford's growth with interest, and was deeply impressed. I wanted to join the party, and was fortunate enough, in 2012, to be able to join the fun. This change did not happen by accident. It was not handed to us on a plate. It was not easy. It was not simple. It did not happen overnight. It was the result of a committed, decade-long process, under which the department had determined, focussed leadership, driven to build and improve. It was a tiring, and I daresay at times dispiriting business. It would have been very easy to walk away. But the results, I believe, speak for themselves. Bill was not the father of the Department of Computer Science, but he is, I believe, the father of the department as it stands today – and the department is, I honestly believe, the most exciting place in Europe to be a computer scientist right now. Those of us in the department, and the University of Oxford itself, owe Bill a tremendous debt. The department is clearly a labour of love for Bill; and even ignoring all Bill's other work as a researcher and entrepreneur, it would be a fitting legacy for a career.

Contents

Stealthy Protocols: Metrics and Open Problems

Olga Chen, Catherine Meadows[✉], and Gautam Trivedi

U.S. Naval Research Laboratory, Code 5540, Washington, DC 20375, USA
{olga.chen,catherine.meadows,gautam.trivedi}@nrl.navy.mil

Abstract. This paper is a survey of both methods that could be used to support stealthy communication over both wired and wireless networks and techniques for evaluating them. By stealthy communication we mean communication using channels that guarantee that the nature of the communication, or even the fact that communication is taking place at all, is hidden. Although stealthy communication and information hiding have been studied from a number of different points of view, e.g. image steganography, network covert channels, and covert wireless communication, not much has been done to tie these different threads together and attempt to see how the different branches of stealthy communication research can inform each other. In this paper we take the first steps to remedying this deficiency. We identify open problems, point out gaps, and indicate directions for further research.

1 Introduction

Over the years, there has been a substantial amount of research on hidden communication in computer systems. This started with the study of covert channels within computer systems, in particular multi-level secure systems, and has continued in such areas as image steganography, network covert channels, and covert wireless communication. This raises the question: how feasible is *stealthy communication*? By stealthy communication we mean communication that is sent over *channels* in a way only detectable by the intended recipient. By channel we mean any means of communicating information using any layer of a protocol stack. This is closely related to information hiding and indeed can be considered a subset of it. However, we concentrate on using features of communication protocols as the cover source, thus ruling out areas such as image steganography.

The first thing needed in order to build stealthy communication tools, or to detect stealthy communication, is a good understanding of the channels available to us. What properties are required in order for channels to support stealthy communication? Can we detect when a channel is no longer suitable? Conversely, if we want to detect stealthy communication, how can we take advantage of the characteristics of the channels being used?

Obtaining an answer to these questions requires a careful study of available stealthy channels and their properties. For this we can take advantage of the research that has gone before. However, one thing needed is methods for comparing different channels that may make use of different communications media.

© Springer International Publishing AG 2017
T. Gibson-Robinson et al. (Eds.): Roscoe Festschrift, LNCS 10160, pp. 1–17, 2017.
DOI: 10.1007/978-3-319-51046-0_1

Unfortunately, there has not been much cross-fertilization between the different areas of research, perhaps because of the very different natures of the different media used. This makes it difficult to compare the features of different channels or to determine what general principals apply. Thus in this paper we provide the groundwork for such cross-fertilization by exploring the various techniques available for stealthy communication, identifying the issues that affect it, and finally, using our observations to identify areas where further research is needed.

The paper is organized as follows. We first recall the basic framework used to reason about stealthy communication, a slightly modified version of the framework developed at the first Information Hiding Workshop. We then give a brief overview of the known techniques for stealthy communication. We next give an overview of metrics for stealthy communication, and discuss the different types of stealthy technologies with respect to these metrics. We then discuss various features of cover and stego channels that can affect stealthy communication, and use this to suggest desired features of potential future metrics. We also discuss results concerning metrics for image steganography and other applications could be useful if they were also found to hold for network channels. We conclude with a list of open problems.

2   General Framework

We use the general framework developed during the first Information Hiding Workshop [35], with some minor modifications. This involves a communication channel and three principals:

- **Alice**, who is sending information over the channel;
- **Bob**, who is receiving information over the channel from Alice, and;
- **The Warden**, who is watching the channel and is attempting to determine whether or not Alice is transmitting any information to Bob. An *active* warden may try to interfere with the communication by adding noise, whereas a *passive* warden can only watch the communications without altering them in any way [46].

Alice and Bob could act as originators of the communication or could possibly manipulate an already-existing overt communication channel between unsuspecting parties.

Alice communicates with Bob by modifying a set of variables that both Bob and the Warden may observe. The Warden's job is to determine whether or not Alice is sending data to Bob. Bob's job is to determine the information that Alice is sending to him (the question of Bob's determining *whether* Alice is sending is another problem outside the scope of this framework).

There are also several types of sources:

- **Cover source.** This is the source without any encoded data from Alice.
- **Stego source.** This is the result of embedding Alice's information in the cover source.

There are also two types of *noise*. Both are added to the stego source after it leaves Alice. One is added to the channel between Alice and Bob. The other is added to the channel between Alice and the Warden. Note that some of the noise on the channel between Alice and Bob may have been added (at least partially) by the Warden. In this paper we will generally assume that the Warden does not add noise, as we are more interested at this point in the stealthy techniques themselves than in countermeasures.

3 Overview of Methods

Network covert channels can occur at all layers of the protocol stack. At the higher layers, covert channels can occur in any type of protocol, but at the lower layers, in particular the physical layer, work has concentrated mostly on wireless protocols. Here the complexity of management of the physical layer appears to offer more opportunities for exploiting covert channels. Thus, in this section we consider higher layer and physical layer protocols separately.

3.1 Higher Layer Network Covert Channels

Covert channels are traditionally divided into two types: *storage channels*, in which Alice sends information to Bob by modifying the attributes of the data she sends along the legitimate channel, and *timing channels*, in which she modifies the timing of the events that Bob observes. Both types of channels occur in higher layer protocols, and we consider them below.

Exploiting Storage Channels. Protocols often carry random or unpredictable information as part of their metadata. In this case it may be possible to hide data in these fields. If the metadata is random one can replace it with encrypted data, which may be assumed to be indistinguishable from random. If it is not completely random, the problem becomes somewhat harder; one must determine the probability distribution of the metadata, and replace it with (encrypted) data whose distribution is indistinguishable from that of the genuine metadata.

Storage covert channels can utilize *unused fields or bits* in the packet headers. For example, Fisk et al. in [14] suggest using reserved bits and data fields when $RST = 1$ in TCP packets as potential covert channels. They also suggest that data can be hidden in timestamp, address flag or unnecessary fields (such as TOS or DF) of IP packets or in the code field (when sending just the type) and unused bits of ICMP packets.

Padding TCP or IP headers to 4-byte boundaries [14] as well as padding IPv6 headers can be used as potential covert storage channels.

Some protocols, such as IPv6, also contain *header extensions*. Lucena et al. [28] show that these extension fields, such as Authentication Header (AH) or Encapsulating Security Payload (ESP), can be used for this purpose.

Storage covert channels can also utilize *existing, currently-used fields* in packet headers. Fisk et al. [14] suggest a method of using TCP initial sequence number field as well as the checksum field in both TCP and UDP as covert channels. IP's Time To Live (TTL) field as well as the equivalent IPv6 Hop Limit field [28] can serve as additional examples of storage covert channels where information is hidden in the metadata. The DNS protocol also has several fields that can be used to send covert data. According to Davidoff et al. [12], such fields as NULL, TXT, SVR, or MX could serve as excellent covert data sources. Van Horenbeck [19] also presents a covert channel approach by integrating the covert data into the HTTP request string.

Information can also be encoded in the length of the packets that Alice sends to Bob. However, such techniques are vulnerable to deep packet inspection, and so proper precautions must be taken. For example, Girling [17] proposed to modify lengths of link layer frames in order to transmit covert data, but a similar technique has also been proposed for TCP/IP/UDP packets by Lucena et al. [28].

Exploiting Timing Channels. Timing channels involving varying the time it takes for bits to reach the receiver have many attractive features from the point of view of stealthy communication. The delays can be made small enough so that they do not affect the timing signature of a protocol, timing delays are surprisingly robust against noise arising from further delays as traffic travels along the internet, and the fact that the modified parameter, time, has only one dimension makes it tractable to reason about timing channels mathematically, and thus to develop detectors and tests for stealthiness.

Hiding Information in Packet Round Trip Delays. Some of the earliest work on timing channels involved measurement of round trip delays between an inquiry by Bob and a response by Alice. For example, Brumley and Boneh [7], showed that timing channel attacks on cryptosystems can be performed over a network. That is, the delays in response caused by side channels in cryptographic algorithms are relatively unaffected by network noise. Since round trip measurements require a challenge from Bob for each transmission by Alice, they are not really appropriate for the sending of very long messages, but they point out that timing delays can be a robust method for transmitting information, even over the Internet.

Hiding Information in Inter-Packet Arrival Times. The most popular timing channel from the point of view of stealthy communication is the inter-packet arrival channel, in which information is encoded in the length of the time between packet arrivals. Unlike round-trip times, measuring inter-packet arrival delays does not require further communication between Alice and Bob, thus increasing both stealthiness and throughput.

Inter-packet arrival channels have appeared in various applications. They have been proposed for the use in watermarking techniques both for intrusion detection [44] and breaking anonymous communication systems [43]. The idea is to attack schemes that hide the passage of packet streams through the Internet. The attacker first watermarks the stream by altering the times between the packets according to some chosen pattern. The attacker can then trace the stream as it travels through the Internet by checking the watermark. This watermark turns out to be surprisingly resistant to noise introduced as it travels through the network. Research on both defeating and hardening watermarking techniques has led to a greater understanding of inter-packet arrival channels.

Inter-packet arrival times have also been studied from the point of view of covert transmittal of information. In [38], Gaura, Molina, and Blaze show how passwords gleaned via keyboard monitoring can be transmitted via inter-packet arrival times and describe a tool, Jitterbug, that implements this. No attempt however is made to provide stealthiness against a warden who is monitoring the channel for covert inter-packet arrival time communication. This sparked an interest in the exploitation of inter-packet arrival times as a stealthy form of communication, and considerable work followed both on new schemes exploiting inter-packet arrival times, as well as methods for detecting such covert communication.

In general, inter-packet arrival time schemes have been classified into two types: *passive schemes*, in which modifications to the timing are made to a sequence of received packets, and *active schemes*, in which an entirely new sequences of packets are created. For the most part, active schemes have been preferred to passive ones. This is because a passive scheme puts a time constraint on Alice. If she takes too long to produce a modified sequence, she will slow down the delivery of the packets, and thus might be detected. Thus Jitterbug, a passive scheme, uses a very simple encoding method in which inter-packet arrival times are only increased. On the other hand, with an active scheme, it is possible to create sophisticated schemes that use the inverse distribution function to map an encrypted steganographic message to a sequence of inter-packet arrival times whose distribution can be made identical to a given i.i.d. distribution. This approach is used, for example, by Sellke et al. [37] and Ahmadzadeh and Agnew [2]. Methods that fall somewhere between the two extremes are also available. For example, in Cabuk's time-replay channel [8]. a sequence of packets is captured, and the median 9f the inter-arrival times is sampled. The sequence is then divided into partitions that are replayed, with a 1 encoded as an interval between partitions above the median and a 0 encoded as an interval below the median. As in Jitterbug, a real sequence in modified, but as in methods based on the inverse distribution function, the sequence is sent all at once, instead of times being modified as packets are received.

3.2 Wireless Physical Layer Channels

Wireless covert communications channels have been present and utilized long before the advent of the Internet. In particular spread spectrum communications techniques have been studied and implemented for over one hundred years [1]. The original intent of spread spectrum techniques such as Frequency Hopping Spread Spectrum (FHSS) and Direct Sequence Spread Spectrum (DSSS) was to ensure resilient radio communications in the presence of interference and jamming. Spread spectrum techniques rely on spreading a signal of a given bandwidth over a much greater bandwidth. Such techniques result in a signal being transmitted with a lower Signal to Noise Ratio (SNR), than would normally be required, thus resulting in a signal with Low Probability of Detection (LPD) characteristics, assuming the signal has been sufficiently spread [40]. We do not address the specifics of spread spectrum systems as we do not consider these techniques applicable to stealthy protocols for the purpose of this paper.

Apart from traditional spread spectrum communications techniques, which are widely utilized in military communications, there are several other techniques that can be used to covertly carry information. These techniques can utilize physical layer characteristics (i.e. waveform and/or modulation) or link layer protocols to hide information. As an example of the former, consider Orthogonal Frequency Division Multiplexing (OFDM). In practical implementations of OFDM waveforms, such as WiMAX and Long-Term Evolution (LTE), unused blocks of subcarriers may be used to covertly carry information [18]. Such techniques take advantage of white-spaces in the radio frequency (RF) spectrum to carry information that only the intended recipient can detect. As an example of the latter, specific fields of link layer protocols, such as IEEE 802.11 Wireless Local Area Networks (WLAN) can be used to covertly carry data. Examples of such covert channels are described in [15,36].

Other physical layer techniques have also been explored. In [45] the authors propose an authentication scheme that superimposes a secret modulation on waveforms without requiring additional bandwidth which in effect results in a covert channel. A radio frequency watermarking scheme for OFDM waveforms is proposed in [25]. The authors introduce the concept of constellation dithering (CD), where watermark bits are mapped to a QPSK watermarking constellation and spread using a Gaussian distributed spreading code, and baud dithering, where a watermark is introduced by positive and negative cyclic time shifts over the transmitted symbols. The authors proceed to derive the performance of such schemes in Additive White Gaussian Noise (AWGN) channels.

In general, implementing covert communications over wireless communications channels presents a different set of advantages as well as disadvantages over wired communications networks. In wired networks, care must be taken to ensure that channels are not disrupted by network devices that lie in between the two end points for the covert channel. In wireless covert channels, the range between the two end points is limited only by the transmit power of the originating end point and by the receiver. In wired networks, however, bit error rates can be negligible. The probability of the distant end successfully receiving data transmitted by the originator is therefore quite high, if no intermediate nodes disrupt the communications channel. In wireless communications channels, however, various types of noise and interference (i.e., low SNR) can severely degrade channel capacity. Indeed, one only has to refer to the Shannon-Hartley theorem to understand the adverse impact of low SNR on channel capacity. The covert channel capacity is thus highly dependent on the dynamic nature of wireless channels, where frequency-selective fading channels can greatly impact the SNR.

3.3   Characteristics of Network Covert Channels

Noise. We say that a channel is *noisy* if Alice's communications to Bob can be affected by noise on the channel. This is the case, for example, for methods based on packet inter-arrival times. These inter-arrival times may change as the packets travel through the network, thus adding noise to Alice's signal.

We say that a method is *noise-free* if we assume that there is no noise on the channel between Alice and the Warden (other than noise added by Alice herself). Methods that hide information in channels whose integrity is protected by other means, e.g. error-correcting codes, can be considered noise-free. Such is the case, for example, for methods that hide information in protocol metadata.

We say that a method is *noise-dependent* if the security of the encoding against the Warden depends (at least partially) on the noise in the channel between Alice and the Warden. In many cases (e.g. packet inter-arrival times and many of the physical layer covert channels), Alice's ability to hide the fact that she is communicating to Bob may depend on her ability to make her alterations to the channel look like noise to the Warden. If the channel was typically not noisy, it would be harder for Alice to take advantage of this.

Discrete vs. Continuous. A method is discrete or continuous depending upon whether the channel Alice is exploiting is discrete or continuous. Methods based on altering protocol metadata are generally discrete, and methods based on timing channels are generally continuous. Continuous methods have the potential advantage that Alice can convey additional information by varying the power of her signal, and evade detection by the Warden by keeping the power of her signal below a certain threshold. The method described by Lee et al. in [26] is an example of the latter. Alice and Bob are assumed to have access to specialized hardware that allows them to generate and detect extremely low-power signals (that is, extremely small variations in timing) that are undetectable by the Warden.

4   Stealthiness Metrics

In this section we consider the various metrics that can be used to evaluate stealthy protocols. Since we are not only interested at the rate at which stealthy protocols can deliver this information, but the degree to which they can do this without being detected, we discuss not only traditional metrics for throughput and capacity, but metrics for detectability as well. We also discuss how these metrics can be combined.

In this section we draw heavily on previous work in image steganography. Although the conditions found and methods used in image steganography differ from those in network covert channels, image steganography is the area where the most progress in metrics has been made. Thus we pay close attention to results in this area and review them from the point of view their applicability to network covert channels.

4.1 Throughput and Capacity

The definition of throughput and capacity for stealthy channels is the same as that for regular communication channels. However, the metrics used to approximate them may depend on specific features of stealthy channels.

We define the *throughput* after time t as $B(1 - BER)/t$, where B is the number of bits Alice sends from time 0 to time t, and BER is the bit error rate. Probably the first to develop a throughput metric for stealthy protocols was Girling [17], for noiseless storage channels. Assuming that 1 bit is encoded in each B-byte block sent, the time to send a block is T, the time used by the software independent of block size is S, the network protocol overhead per block is N bytes, and the network speed is V bits per second, then the bandwidth of the channel is $V/(64(B + N) + S \cdot V)$.

We can also define the *capacity* of the channel between Alice and Bob in the usual way, as the supremum over all possible distributions of Alice's input into the channel of the mutual information between Alice and Bob. Thus work has been done on computing the capacities of different types of covert channels, motivated originally by interest in managing covert channels in multi-level secure systems, and more recently by concern about reducing side channels in hardware and software. This is usually based on abstract models of the channels that can be instantiated in a number of different ways. Research in this direction began with Millen [29] who developed a formula for a simple model of a storage channel where the data passed along the channel consisted of overt and covert bits. Moskowitz and Miller computed bounds for noiseless timing channels where the alphabet consists of times of different lengths [32], and for a noisy timing channel whose alphabet has only two symbols [31]. Of particular interest is the *timed Z- channel* whose capacity was estimated by Moskowitz et al. [30]. This is a noisy channel whose alphabet consists of two time intervals, with noise that can only increase the size of the interval, that is, to change a zero to a one, but not vice versa. Such a scenario is of interest because it appears in many realistic covert channel scenarios; indeed the NRL Pump [21] was designed to mitigate a channel of this type.

4.2 Detectability

Detectability metrics measure the vulnerability to detection by the Warden of a given embedding method. The *detectability* of an embedding method measure the probability that the Warden guesses correctly, at a given point in the communication, whether or not Alice is transmitting along the channel. That is, it is $\alpha + \beta$, where α is the probability of a true positive given the best possible detector, and β is the probability of a true negative. There are several ways that we can measure this.

For empirical studies, one can estimate a lower bound on detectability by running experiments with different detectors. The following two methods, discussed in [24], are considered standard.

1. Compute the area under the Receiver Operating Characteristic (ROC) curve
   of a binary classifier for the presence or absence of payload (AUR), unnor-
   malized so that AUR = 0.5 corresponds to a random detector and AUR = 1
   to perfect detection. The ROC curve is obtained by plotting the true positive
   rate against the false positive rate at various threshold settings.
2. Compute $1 - P_E$, where $P_E = \frac{1}{2}min(\alpha + \beta)$ is minimum sum of false positive
   and false negative rate errors for a binary classifier for the presence or absence
   of payload.

It is also possible to use more sophisticated metrics based on experience with
multiple detectors. These metrics may not be efficient enough to use as real-time
detectors, but nevertheless may be practical for estimating the detectability of
an embedding method. Consider, for example, the Maximal Mean Discrepancy
(MMD) test in [24] to estimate the detectability of various embedding methods
of image steganography, based on the ratio of the size of the payload to the
size of the cover source. This test takes as input various features of the images
that have been useful in the past for steganalysis, thus allowing one to take
advantage of the history of the behavior of different kinds of detectors. MMD
is not efficient enough to serve as a detector itself, but still can be useful in
measuring detectability.

In Cachin's seminal paper [10] on "An Information- Theoretic Model for
Steganography", the probability of the Warden's guessing correctly whether or
not Alice is transmitting is estimated using the relative entropy between the cover
and the stego source. This is used, in particular, to prove results about perfectly
secure steganographic systems. However, according to an analysis by Pevný et al.
in [34] none of the metrics derived from relative entropy appear to suitable for
evaluating experimental results from image steganography. According to [34],
this is a result of the high dimensionality d of the data and relatively small
sample size D. They note that the k-nearest-neighbors (kNN) algorithm [6,41]
is the only relative entropy estimator that generally scales well for the high
dimensions required for image steganography, but it turns out to be inaccurate
for large d and small D due to difficulty in estimating cross-entropy.

However, relative entropy does appear to be a useful source of metrics for
network timing channels, as we shall see below.

Detectability Metrics for Network Timing Channels. Although their has been a
substantial amount of work on detectability and detectors in image steganography, much less work has been done in network covert channels. However, there
has been a number of detectors proposed for methods based on inter-packet
arrival times, which we discuss here.

The earliest work on inter-arrival times metrics were not necessarily intended
for general use, but were intended to show how it could be possible to detect
some of the earlier, and simpler, embedding methods that were first proposed,
such as Jitterbug.

The regularity test was proposed as a metric for network timing channels by
Cabuk et al. in [9]. It measures the degree to which the variance of the source

is generally constant. Its rational is based on the fact that many embedding schemes produce results with low variance. In [16] this was found to do a poor job as a detector, mainly because noise on the channel increases the variance of the cover source, thus making the variance of cover and stego source appear similar.

The Kolmogorov-Smirnov (KS) Test, proposed as a metric for network timing channels by Peng et al. [33], was investigated in [16], and found to have difficulty dealing with stego source whose distribution was very similar to that of the cover source. This is because the KS test measures the maximal distance between the distributions of two empirical distribution functions. If the changes made by the stego source to the distribution are small enough so that they fall within the natural variance of the cover source, then KS will not detect a difference.

In their influential paper [16] Gianvechhio and Wang consider distinguishers for network covert timing channels, based on statistical estimators. They wind up recommending two measures of empirical probability distributions (actually a series of measures) computed from covert timing channel data: the *first order entropy*, and the *corrected conditional entropy* (CCE), which is defined as

$$CCE(X_m|X_{m-1}) = H(X_m|X_{m-1} + \text{perc}(X_m) \cdot H(X_1)$$

where $X_1, \ldots, X_m$ is a sequence of random variables, $\text{perc}(X_m)$ is the percentage of unique patterns of length m with respect to the set of patterns of length m. One can use this to estimate the entropy *rate*, which is the limit $\lim_{m \to \infty} H(X_m|X_1, \ldots, X_{m-1})$, by taking the minimum of CCE over different m. Estimates of entropy and entropy rates, once computed, are then compared for both cover and stego traffic.

The idea behind the use of entropy and corrected conditional entropy is that they test for different things. Entropy is good for detecting small changes in the distribution of a single random variable, and thus is useful for detecting steganographic techniques that alter that distribution. However, if the distribution is kept unchanged, but the correlations between variables are altered, CCE provides the better detection mechanism. The metrics also have the advantage that they can be computed using a relatively small number of samples, a constraint that is likely to hold for network covert channel traffic, especially when they are used as detectors. This combination of entropy and CCE is probably the most commonly used metric in current research on covert timing channels.

More recently work has begun to appear on using anomaly detection methods to assist in detecting exploitation of covert channels. Liu et al. [27] describe a metric that divides timing data into different scales using a wavelet transform and then compares pairs from different flows using relative entropy. They compare their techniques experimentally with existing detection techniques and show favorable results. Their system is specifically designed for cloud storage environments, but the metrics should be applicable elsewhere as well.

There has also been work on investigating the limitations of these types of metrics. For example, a possible weakness lies in the reliance of many methods (e.g. the Gianvechio-Wang method) on computing statistical behavior of strings of bounded length. This is sufficient for certain types of distributions, such as Markov distributions, but not for others. Some work has already been done on this problem. For example, in [11] Crespi, Cybenko, and Giani show how, given an integer k, it is possible create a steganographic source that has the same statistics as the cover source for k-length strings, but differs from for $k+1$-length strings. That is, the steganographic information is encoded in the distribution of the k-length strings. The amount of computation used to apply Crespi et al.'s algorithm for evading detection grows according to a factor of σ^k, where σ is the size of the alphabet, so this limits how far Alice can go in this way. A study of the complexity of both detectors and evasion techniques would be of interest.

4.3 Putting It All Together: Steganographic Capacity and Asymptotic Bounds

So far, there are two important aspects of metrics for stealthy communication that remain to be addressed. One of these is how to bring together the various different performance requirements of stealthy communication methods: throughput, low detectability, and robustness, under one metric. The other is how to measure the performance over time, which can often be done by studying the asymptotic behavior of the communication.

To our knowledge, such combined metrics for stealthy communication over networks and the asymptotic behavior of such metrics have not been studied until relatively recently. However, this question *has* been studied in the related area of image steganography. This is the *square root law* which says that, if the distribution of the stego channel differs from that of the cover channel (i.e. Alice has made a wrong guess about the distribution of the cover channel), then, if she attempts to transmit more than $O(\sqrt{(n)})$ bits of payload using an n-bit cover source, the Warden can detect her communication with arbitrarily low probability of error as n approaches infinity. However, if she transmits $o(\sqrt{n})$ bits of payload the stegosystem can be made arbitrarily secure by choosing sufficiently large n, and if $\lim_{n \to \infty} \frac{P_n}{\sqrt{n}} = \epsilon$ for some positive ϵ, where P_n is the size of the payload for cover source of size n, then the security of the stegosystem asymptotically approaches a constant positive value r. Thus we can define the *steganographic capacity* of a channel to be $r\sqrt{n}$, where n is the size of the cover source.

This has been proved in the case in which the cover source is a stationary Markov chain (a relatively simple but still non-trivial case), by Filler, Ker, and Fridrich, in [13]. But it has also been validated experimentally by Ker et al. in [24]. In these experiments, for different types of cover images, steganographic techniques, and detection techniques, behavior consistent with the square root law was consistently observed. Moreover, it did not require enormously large cover images to produce this behavior: the cover image size runs from 0 to 60,000–150,000 pixels or 0 to 30,000–50,000 nonzero DCT coefficients, depending upon the stenography method.

The next problem is computing the steganographic capacity. In [22] Ker argues for the use of a metric based on estimating the asymptotic behavior of relative entropy as the ratio of payload to cover size tends to zero. Although relative entropy itself appears to be too unstable to supply a suitable metric in this case, Ker provides an estimator based on the the Fisher information, which, for well-behaved distributions, is equal to the quadratic term of the Taylor expansion around zero. SFI has some drawbacks for image steganography though, in that like most other methods for estimating conditional entropy, it is difficult to compute for large dimensions. Thus in order to make it practical to compute, it is necessary to compute it over groups of pixels instead of individual pixels. This means that a certain amount of information is lost. Thus, as Ker points out, while SFI can be useful in comparing embedding techniques, it should probably not be used as the sole means of evaluating an embedding method.

Research in steganographic capacity opens up questions as to how this could be applied to other types of covert channels, e.g. network timing channels or wireless channels. The probability distributions of the cover sources, although not trivial to estimate, are in general easier to estimate than those of the cover channels in image steganography. However, the channels, especially wireless channels, are likely to be noisy, which is less often the case for image steganography. That this noise can result in a similar square root law is shown by Bash, Goeckel, and Towsley in [4], in which the channels between Alice and Bob and between Alice and the Warden are both subject to additive white Gaussian noise (AWGN). Similar to the square root law for image stenography, if Alice attempts to transmit more than $O(\sqrt{(n)})$ in n uses of the channel, then either the Warden can detect her with arbitrarily low probability of error, or Bob can not decode her message reliably; that is, the probability that he decodes it incorrectly is bounded below by a non-zero constant. Analogous results to the steganographic laws are also shown for the cases in which Alice transmits at rates at and below $O(\sqrt{(n)})$. More recently, these results have been extended to optical channels (with experimental validation) [3], arbitrary discrete memoryless channels [5,42] and general memoryless classical quantum channels [39].

4.4 Desirable Metrics for Variables and Cover Sources

The behavior of the variables and cover sources used in stealthy communication is of great importance to the usability and security of that method, and generally is a factor deciding which method to use. However, metrics for stealthy communication do not generally take them into account, and indeed they may be hard to quantify. Here we present some properties of variables and cover sources for which in many cases metrics do not yet exist, but would be useful to have. We also give suggestions for metrics where appropriate.

Footprint and Keyboard. We define the *footprint* of an embedding method to be the set of variables observable by the Warden that are modified by Alice in order to communicate with Bob. We note that not all of these variables need to be observable by Bob. They may have simply been modified by Alice in the process of altering other variables that *are* observable by Bob.

Conversely, we define the *keyboard* to be the set of variables observable to Bob that Bob reads in order to obtain the message from Alice. Again, these variables may or may not be observable by the Warden.

The concepts of footprints and keyboards are intended to give an indication of the types of risks and advantages that may result from employing a method that results in the modification of variables that one may not have complete control over. In general, a large footprint with highly correlated variables may serve to alert the Warden that Alice is communicating. The larger the size the more data the Warden can observe, and the higher the correlation the less freedom Alice has in modifying the different variables in order to pass under the Warden's radar. For example, consider protocol emulation, a form of covert communication in which, the nature, not the existence, of the communication is masked by emulating some other, more innocuous protocol than the one actually being used. Protocol emulation generally has a large footprint, since the variables Alice must modify include every feature of the protocol being emulated. As pointed out in [20], this makes this method vulnerable even to a very weak, local warden who observes such features such as presence of certain types of messages, packet sizes, packet timing and rate, periodic messages exchanges, and the use of TCP control channels. Packet length modification has a smaller footprint, but notice that it is still nontrivial, since modification of a packet's length requires modification of its contents too. In particular, these contents must be modified carefully to avoid detection via deep packet inspection.

Conversely, a larger keyboard whose variables are only weakly correlated can be an advantage to Alice, since she can spread her message over several variables, thus increasing the capacity of the channel. For example, in the packet length channel discussed above, Alice could encode information not only in the length of the packets but in the bits that she adds to the packets.

Finally, encoding information via inter-packet arrival times seems to have the smallest footprint, as well as the smallest keyboard. We note however the size footprint of an active embedding methods may vary, depending on whether a network flow is constructed by repeating an existing flow with some changes as in [9] or built from scratch. Moreover, the size of the keyboard can be increased by using smaller increments of timing intervals to encode information.

Confidence and Mutability. The *confidence* in the cover source is the degree to which we trust our estimate of its probability distribution. This can be estimated using statistical methods for estimating confidence intervals.

The *mutability* of the cover source is closely related to the confidence we may have in it. It is the degree to which the cover source may change and will need to be remeasured in order to ensure that covert communication is not detectable by the warden. For example, the cover source for protocol emulation is highly mutable, since protocols are constantly updated and reimplemented in different ways. Likewise, the cover source for channels based on network traffic behavior (e.g. inter packet arrival times) are be highly mutable, since network traffic behavior can change over time. Most mutable are wireless channels, since their behavior can change based on not only on network traffic but external conditions like the weather. Even in the case in which the cover source appears relatively static, this might not be the case in reality. For example, in the case of storage channels, a protocol field that is supposed to be random may or may not be treated that way by the implementors, or may be repurposed in later versions. Mutability has an effect on how often and thoroughly statistical properties of cover traffic and noise need to be monitored in order to ensure robustness and non-detectability.

5 Open Problems

One of the surprising things that we have discovered in this survey is a lack of cross-fertilization between different areas. For example, image steganography and covert communication via network timing channels appear to have much in common, but in only a very few cases do results in one area appear to have had influence on research in another area. That is unfortunate, because research in image steganography appears to be much further advanced than other areas, and lessons learned from there, when they are applied to other areas, could easily save much work and time. In particular, the following work needs to be done:

We need better understanding of the square root law, in particular experimental validation of results for noisy channels (e.g. [4]) as they apply to network timing channels. We may develop strategies for evading it by varying channels and encoding schemes, or concentrating on cover sources whose statistical behavior is well understood. We are helped in this by the fact that there are many possible different types of channels to take advantage of, not only different types of network timing channels but storage channels as well.

We also need a more thorough understanding of the metrics available. Nobody appears to have done a thorough survey and evaluation of all the metrics available for measuring the distance between two probability distributions in terms of the applicability to stealthy communication. Instead, the studies we have seen focus on evaluating metrics that have previously been proposed for the particular stealthy communication problem area under study (although the work of Liu et al. [27], which uses techniques from anomaly detection, is an exception). A thorough study of the various features of channels and algorithms and how they relate to methods for estimating the distance between two probability distributions would be useful.

In particular, we need a better understanding of where our detectors and the metrics they are based on can fail, in order that they can be refined and improved. As we have noted, some theoretical work does already exist on this problem. But although methods have been discovered for evading the most commonly used metrics, they require a considerable computational investment on the part of the transmitter. Is this computational burden inherent, or can it be decreased? Moreover, what are the practical implications? According to [23], there is a considerable gap between theoretical and experimental behavior of detectors for image steganography, and their effectiveness in actual practice. Is the same true for covert channels in other media, and if so, how can methods be improved?

In addition, better methods for estimating throughput and capacity of encoding techniques are needed. Current work mostly relies on experimental results, and it is not always clear how to generalize it. However, we may be able to combine this experimental work with work on measuring the capacity of abstract channels to better our understanding.

References

1. Dixon, R.C.: Spread Spectrum Systems with Commercial Applications, 3rd edn. Wiley, Hoboken (1994)
2. Ahmadzadeh, S.A., Agnew, G.B.: Turbo covert channel: an iterative framework for covert communication over data networks. In: Proceedings of the IEEE INFOCOM 2013, Turin, Italy, 14–19 April 2013, pp. 2031–2039 (2013)
3. Bash, B.A.: Fundamental Limits of Covert Communication. Ph.D. thesis, University of Massachusetts Amherst, Februrary 2015
4. Boulat, A.B., Goeckel, D., Towsley, D.: Limits of reliable communication with low probability of detection on awgn channels. IEEE J. Sel. Areas Commun. **31**(9), 1921–1930 (2013). Selected Areas in Communications
5. Matthieu, R.: Bloch: covert communication over noisy channels: a resolvability perspective. IEEE Trans. Inf. Theory **62**(5), 2334–2354 (2016)
6. Boltz, S., Debreuve, E., Barlaud, M.: High-dimensional statistical distance for region-of-interest tracking: application to combining a soft geometric constraint with radiometry. In: IEEE Conference on Computer Vision and Pattern Recognition, CVPR 2007, pp. 1–8. IEEE (2007)
7. Brumley, D., Boneh, D.: Remote timing attacks are practical. Comput. Netw. **48**(5), 701–716 (2005)
8. Cabuk, S.: Network Covert Channels: Design, Analysis, Detection, and Elimination. Ph.D. thesis, Purdue University, December 2006
9. Cabuk, S., Brodley, C.E., Shields, C.: IP covert timing channels: design and detection. In: Proceedings of the 11th ACM Conference on Computer and Communications Security, pp. 178–187. ACM (2004)
10. Cachin, C.: An information-theoretic model for steganography. Inf. Comput. **192**(1), 41–56 (2004)
11. Crespi, V., Cybenko, G., Giani, A.: Engineering statistical behaviors for attacking and defending covert channels. IEEE J. Sel. Top. Sig. Proces. **7**(1), 124–136 (2013)
12. Davidoff, S., Ham, J.: Network Forensics: Tracking Hackers through Cyber Space. Prentice-Hall, Upper Saddle River (2012)
13. Filler, T., Ker, A.D., Fridrich, J.: The square root law of steganographic capacity for Markov covers. In: Proceedings of SPIE, Media Forensics and Security, SPIE 2009, vol. 7254 (2009)
14. Fisk, G., Fisk, M., Papadopoulos, C., Neil, J.: Eliminating steganography in internet traffic with active wardens. In: Petitcolas, F.A.P. (ed.) IH 2002. LNCS, vol. 2578, pp. 18–35. Springer, Heidelberg (2003). doi:10.1007/3-540-36415-3_2
15. Frikha, L., Trabelsi, Z., El-Hajj, W.: Implementation of a covert channel in the 802.11 header (2008)
16. Gianvecchio, S., Wang, H.: Detecting covert timing channels: an entropy-based approach. In: Proceedings of the 14th ACM Conference on Computer and Communications Security, pp. 307–316. ACM (2007)

17. Girling, C.G.: Covert channels in LAN's. IEEE Trans. Soft. Eng. **13**(2), 292–296 (1987)
18. Hijaz, Z., Frost, V.: Exploiting OFDM systems for covert communication. In: IEEE Military Communications Conference (2010)
19. Van Horenbeck, M.: Deception on the network: thinking differently about covert channels. In: Proceedings of the 7th Australian Information Warfare and Security Conference. Edith Cowan University (2006)
20. Houmansadr, A., Brubaker, C., Shmatikov, V.: The parrot is dead: Observing unobservable network communications. In: 2013 IEEE Symposium on Security and Privacy (SP), pp. 65–79. IEEE (2013)
21. Kang, M.H., Moskowitz, I.S.: A pump for rapid, reliable, secure communication. In: Proceedings of the 1st ACM Conference on Computer and Communications Security, pp. 119–129. ACM (1993)
22. Ker, A.D.: Estimating steganographic fisher information in real images. In: Katzenbeisser, S., Sadeghi, A.-R. (eds.) IH 2009. LNCS, vol. 5806, pp. 73–88. Springer, Heidelberg (2009). doi:10.1007/978-3-642-04431-1_6
23. Ker, A.D., Bas, P., Böhme, R., Cogranne, R., Craver, S., Filler, T., Fridrich, J., Pevný, T.: Moving steganography and steganalysis from the laboratory into the real world. In: Proceedings of the First ACM Workshop on Information Hiding and Multimedia Security, pp. 45–58. ACM (2013)
24. Ker, A.D., Pevný, T., Kodovský, J., Fridrich, J.: The square root law of steganographic capacity. In: Proceedings of the 10th ACM Workshop on Multimedia and Security, pp. 107–116. ACM (2008)
25. Kleider, J.E., Gifford, S., Churpun, S., Fette, B.: Radio frequency watermarking for OFDM wireless networks, vol. 5, pp. 397–400 (2004)
26. Lee, K.S., Wang, H., Weatherspoon, H.: Phy covert channels: can you see the idles? In: 11th USENIX Symposium on Networked Systems Design and Implementation, NSDI14. USENIX (2014)
27. Liu, A., Chen, J.X., Wechsler, H.: Real-time timing channel detection in an software-defined networking virtual environment. Intell. Inf. Manage. **7**(06), 283 (2015)
28. Lucena, N.B., Lewandowski, G., Chapin, S.J.: Covert channels in IPv6. In: Danezis, G., Martin, D. (eds.) PET 2005. LNCS, vol. 3856, pp. 147–166. Springer, Heidelberg (2006). doi:10.1007/11767831_10
29. Millen, J.K.: Covert channel capacity. In: 1987 IEEE Symposium on Security and Privacy. IEEE Computer Society (1987)
30. Moskowitz, I.S., Greenwald, S.J., Kang, M.H.: An analysis of the timed Z-channel. In: Proceedings of the 1996 IEEE Symposium on Security and Privacy, pp. 2–11. IEEE (1996)
31. Moskowitz, I.S., Miller, A.R.: The channel capacity of a certain noisy timing channel. IEEE Trans. Inf. Theory **38**(4), 1339–1344 (1992)
32. Moskowitz, I.S., Miller, A.R.: Simple timing channels. In: Proceedings of the IEEE Computer Society Symposium on Research in Security and Privacy, pp. 56–64. IEEE (1994)
33. Peng, P., Ning, P., Reeves, D.S.: On the secrecy of timing-based active watermarking trace-back techniques. In: 2006 IEEE Symposium on Security and Privacy, p. 15. IEEE (2006)
34. Pevný, T., Fridrich, J.: Benchmarking for steganography. In: Solanki, K., Sullivan, K., Madhow, U. (eds.) IH 2008. LNCS, vol. 5284, pp. 251–267. Springer, Heidelberg (2008). doi:10.1007/978-3-540-88961-8_18

35. Pfitzmann, B.: Information hiding terminology. In: Anderson, R. (ed.) IH 1996. LNCS, vol. 1174, pp. 347–350. Springer, Heidelberg (1996). doi:10.1007/3-540-61996-8_52

36. Rezaei, F., Hempel, M., Peng, D., Qian, Y., Sharif, H.: Analysis and evaluation of covert channels over LTE advanced. In: IEEE Wireless Communications and Networking Conference (WCNC) (2013)

37. Sellke, S.H., Wang, C.-C., Bagchi, S., Shroff, N.B.: TCP/IP timing channels: theory to implementation. In: 28th IEEE International Conference on Computer Communications, Joint Conference of the IEEE Computer and Communications Societies, INFOCOM 2009, Rio de Janeiro, Brazil, 19–25 April 2009, pp. 2204–2212 (2009)

38. Shah, G., Molina, A., Blaze, M., et al.: Keyboards and covert channels. In: USENIX Security (2006)

39. Sheikholeslami, A., Bash, B.A., Towsley, D., Goeckel, D., Guha, S.: Covert communication over classical-quantum channels. In: IEEE International Symposium on Information Theory, ISIT 2016, Barcelona, Spain, 10–15 July 2016, pp. 2064–2068 (2016)

40. Simon, M., Omura, J., Scholtz, R., Levitt, B.: Spread Spectrum Communications Handbook. McGraw-Hill Inc., New York (1994). Revised edition

41. Singh, H., Misra, N., Hnizdo, V., Fedorowicz, A., Demchuk, E.: Nearest neighbor estimates of entropy. Am. J. Math. Manag. Sci. **23**(3–4), 301–321 (2003)

42. Wang, L., Wornell, G.W., Zheng, L.: Limits of low-probability-of-detection communication over a discrete memoryless channel. In: IEEE International Symposium on Information Theory, ISIT 2015, Hong Kong, China, 14–19 June 2015, pp. 2525–2529 (2015)

43. Wang, X., Chen, S., Jajodia, S.: Network flow watermarking attack on low-latency anonymous communication systems. In: IEEE Symposium on Security and Privacy, SP 2007, pp. 116–130. IEEE (2007)

44. Wang, X., Reeves, D.S., Felix Wu, S., Yuill, J.: Sleepy watermark tracing: an active network-based intrusion response framework. In: Proceedings of the 16th International Conference on Information Security: Trusted Information: the New Decade Challenge, Sec 2001, pp. 369–384. Kluwer (2001)

45. Yu, P.L., Baras, J.S., Sadler, B.M.: Physical-layer authentication. IEEE Trans. Inf. Forensics Secur. **3**(1), 38–51 (2008)

46. Zander, S., Armitage, G., Branch, P.: A survey of covert channels and countermeasures in computer network protocols. IEEE Commun. Surv. Tutorials **9**(3), 44–57 (2007)

A Specification Theory of Real-Time Processes

Chris Chilton[1], Marta Kwiatkowska[1], Faron Moller[2], and Xu Wang[2(✉)]

[1] Department of Computer Science, University of Oxford, Oxford, UK
[2] Department of Computer Science, Swansea University, Swansea, UK
xu.wang.comp@gmail.com

Abstract. This paper presents an assume-guarantee specification theory (aka interface theory from [11]) for modular synthesis and verification of real-time processes with critical timing constraints. Four operations, i.e. conjunction, disjunction, parallel and quotient, are defined over specifications, drawing inspirations from classic specification theories like refinement calculus [4,19]. We show that a congruence (or pre-congruence) characterised by a trace-based semantics [14] captures exactly the notion of substitutivity (or refinement) between specifications.

Dedication: I would like to thank Prof. Bill Roscoe for leading me into the fascinating world of concurrency and nurturing my appreciation for simplicity and elegance in theories of relevance. —— Xu Wang

1 Introduction

Modular synthesis and verification of *quantitative aspects* (e.g. real-time, probability, reward, etc.) of computational and physical processes (e.g. cyber-physical systems) is an important research topic [5].

In this programme of quantitative study, a specification of components consists of a combination of *quantitative assumptions* and *quantitative guarantees*. A refinement relation captures the *substitutability* between quantitative components, adhering to the so-called *contra-variance* principle: refinement implies the relaxation of assumptions as well as the strengthening of guarantees.

As one step of the programme, this paper targets component-based development for real-time systems with critical timing constraints. We propose a complete timed specification theory based on a framework of *minimal extension of timed automata* [1], which is endowed with the operations of *parallel composition* for structural integration, logical *conjunction/disjunction* for viewpoint fusion and independent development, and *quotient* for incremental synthesis. The operations in some sense can be regarded as the concurrent and real-time incarnations of similar operations from refinement calculus [4,16,17,19] (i.e. *sequential composition, angelic choice, demonic choice,* and *pre-post specification*).

The refinement relation is defined relative to the notion of *incompatibility error* (aka *contract breach* [4]). That is, mismatch of the assumptions and

© Springer International Publishing AG 2017
T. Gibson-Robinson et al. (Eds.): Roscoe Festschrift, LNCS 10160, pp. 18–38, 2017.
DOI: 10.1007/978-3-319-51046-0_2

guarantees between components *composed in parallel* gives rise to errors (aka *abort* [4,19] and denoted $\bot$). Refinement means error-free substitutivity.[1]

Previously, based on this framework, [9] introduced a compositional linear-time specification theory for real-time systems, where the substitutive refinement is the weakest pre-congruence preserving incompatibility errors and characterisable by a finite double trace semantics. A key novelty of [9] lies in the introduction of an explicit *timestop* operation (denoted by $\top$) that halts the progress of the system clock, which, remarkably, corresponds to a timed incarnation of *miracle* or *magic* in refinement calculus[2].

While timestop is appropriate for a restricted class of applications, there are common cases where the operation of stopping the system clock is not meaningful or implementable (aka *infeasible* [19]). Hence, it is desirable to consider systems without explicit or implicit timestops, which we call *realisable systems*.

For realisable systems, components, not substitutively-equivalent according to [9], can become equivalent under realisability due to the environment losing the power to observe the timing difference in error occurrences. Thus, we need a new substitutive equivalence as a coarsening of the congruence in [9].

To best characterise the coarsening, our theory requires a shift of focus to a more game-theoretical treatment, where the coarsening constitutes a reactive synthesis game, called *normalisation*, that collapses erroneous behaviours in a specification. Normalisation is strictly more aggressive than classical timed reactive synthesis [3,7], which enables us to achieve the weakest congruence results.

Furthermore, in a similar vein to timed concurrent games [12,13], where one of the key concerns is the removal of time-blocking strategies by applying blame assignment, the composition of realisable systems (e.g. conjunction or quotient) in our framework generates new unrealisable behaviours, which have to be removed. Rather than employing blame assignment, our framework, reduces the problem to another timed synthesis game that turns out to be precisely the dual game of normalisation called *realisation*, again re-confirming the duality between contract breach and infeasibility of refinement calculus.

Finally our theory presents a trace-semantics characterisation of the refinement and operators, which supports the explicit separation of assumptions and guarantees, and integrates well with automata learning techniques.

Our trace-semantics can be regarded as a timed extension [21] of Dill's trace semantics [14], who first used untimed double-trace semantics for asynchronous circuit verification, i.e. a set of *success traces* and a set of *failure traces*, which, in turn, are inspired by earlier trace theory of asynchronous circuits [15,23] and CSP process algebra [22].

---

[1] Note that the existence of incompatibility errors does not mean that the composed system is un-usable; an environment can still usefully exploit the system by only utilising the part of the system that is free of the incompatibility errors, as has been well explained in [11].

[2] It were Carroll Morgan and Joseph M. Morris who first added miracle to refinement calculus.

Previously, trace semantics has been the basis of our untimed specification theory [8], which supports all four operators and the weakest congruence preserving substitutivity. We have also connected double-trace semantics with CSP model checking [22] in [26], which can potentially be further extended to connect our timed theory with timed CSP model checking [2].

2 Minimal TA Extension for Timed Specification

Our theory builds on *timed I/O automata* and *timed I/O transition systems*.[3]

2.1 Timed I/O Automata (TIOA)

Clock constraints. Given a set X of real-valued clock variables, a *clock constraint* over X, cc: $CC(X)$, is a boolean combination of atomic constraints of the form $x \bowtie k$ and $x - y \bowtie k$, where $x, y \in X$, $\bowtie \in \{\leq, <, =, >, \geq\}$, and $k \in \mathbb{N}$.

Definition 1. *A TIOA is a tuple* $(C, I, O, L, l^0, AT, Inv, coInv)$, *where:*

- $C \subseteq X$ *is a finite set of clock variables (ranged over by x, y, etc.)*
- $A = I \uplus O$ *is a finite alphabet (ranged over by a, b, etc.) consisting of the input actions I and output actions O*
- L *is a finite set of* locations *(ranged over by l, l', n, n', etc.) while $l^0 \in L$ is the initial location*
- $AT \subseteq L \times CC(C) \times A \times 2^C \times L$ *is a set of* action transitions
- $Inv : L \to CC(C)$ *and* $coInv : L \to CC(C)$ *assign invariants and co-invariants to states, each of which is a downward-closed clock constraint.*[4]

    In the rest of the paper we use $l \xrightarrow{g,a,rs} l'$ as a shorthand for $(l, g, a, rs, l') \in AT$. g: $CC(C)$ is the enabling guard of the transition, $a \in A$ the action, and rs the subset of clock variables to be reset.

    Our TIOAs are an extension of timed automata [1], distinguishing *input from output* and *invariant from co-invariant*. The *semantics of TIOAs* is an extension of timed transition systems (TTSes) called Timed I/O Transition Systems.

2.2 Timed I/O Transition Systems (TIOTSes)

Plain states. A plain state is a pair drawn from $P = L \times \mathbb{R}^C$ (i.e. a location and clock-valuation pair). A *clock valuation* (drawn from $\mathbb{R}^C$) is a map that assigns to each clock variable x in C a real value from $\mathbb{R}^{\geq 0}$.

Definition 2. *A TIOTS is a tuple* $\mathcal{P} = \langle I, O, S, s^0, \to \rangle$. $S = P \uplus \{\bot, \top\}$ *is a set of states*, $s^0 \in S$ *is the designated initial state, and* $\to \subseteq S \times (I \uplus O \uplus \mathbb{R}^{>0}) \times S$ *is the action- and time-labelled transition relation which is time-additive.*[5]

---

[3] Our timed framework originally appeared in [9]. However, the version presented here contains important technical extension as well as presentational improvements.

[4] Invariants and guards on output actions are constraints on the *system* (aka guarantees) whereas co-invariants and guards on input actions are constraints on the *environment* (aka assumptions).

[5] $\mathcal{P}$ is *time-additive* providing $p \xrightarrow{d_1+d_2} s'$ iff $p \xrightarrow{d_1} s$ and $s \xrightarrow{d_2} s'$ for some $s \in S$.

Notation. In the rest of the paper we use p, p', p_i to range over P while s, s', s_i range over S. Furthermore we define $tA = I \uplus O \uplus \mathbb{R}^{>0}$, $tI = I \uplus \mathbb{R}^{>0}$, and $tO = O \uplus \mathbb{R}^{>0}$. Symbols like α, β, etc. are used to range over tA.

A *timed trace* (ranged over by tt, tt', tt_i etc.) is a finite mixed sequence of positive real numbers ($\mathbb{R}^{>0}$) and visible actions such that *no two numbers are adjacent to one another.*

For instance, $\langle 0.33, a, 1.41, b, c, 3.1415 \rangle$ is a timed trace denoting the observation that action a occurs at 0.33 time units, then another 1.41 time units elapse before the simultaneous occurrence of b and c, which is followed by 3.1415 time units of no event occurrence. The empty trace is denoted by ϵ. An infinite timed trace is an infinite such sequence.

We use $l(tt)$ to indicate the duration of tt, which is obtained as the sum of all the reals in tt, and use $c(tt)$ to count the number of action occurrences along tt. Concatenation of timed traces tt and tt', denoted $tt \frown tt'$, is obtained by appending tt' onto tt and coalescing adjacent reals (summing them). For instance, $\langle a, 1.41 \rangle \frown \langle 0.33, b, 3.1415 \rangle = \langle a, (1.41 + 0.33), b, 3.1415 \rangle = \langle a, 1.74, b, 3.1415 \rangle$.

Prefix/extension are defined as usual by concatenation. We write $tt \upharpoonright tA_0$ for the projection of tt onto timed alphabet tA_0, which is defined by removing from tt all actions not inside tA_0 and summing up adjacent reals.

Non-zenoness. For a TIOTS $\mathcal{P}$, we use $p \overset{tt}{\Rightarrow} p'$ to denote a finite execution starting from p that produces trace tt and leads to p'. Similarly, we can define infinite executions which produce infinite traces on $\mathcal{P}$. An infinite execution is *zeno* iff the action count is infinite but the duration is finite.

We say a TIOTS $\mathcal{P}$ is *non-zeno* providing no plain execution is zeno. $\mathcal{P}$ is *strongly non-zeno* iff there exists some $k \in \mathbb{N}$ s.t., for all plain executions $p \overset{tt}{\Rightarrow} p'$, it holds that $l(tt) = 1$ implies $c(tt) \leq k$. Here, we say a finite or infinite execution is a *plain execution* iff the execution only visits plain states.

Assumption on TIOTSs. We only consider non-zeno time-additive TIOTSs in this paper. For technical convenience (e.g. ease of defining time additivity and trace semantics), the definition of TIOTSs requires that $\top$ and $\bot$ are *chaotic states* [22], i.e. a state in which the set of outgoing transitions are all self-loops, one for each $\alpha \in tA$.

The strong non-zenoness is not an assumption of our theory. But with this additional requirement we can show that the synthesis and verification theory in this paper is fully automatable.

2.3   A Game-Based Interpretation

The derivation of TIOTSes from TIOAs is more or less standard, extending the one from TAs to TTSes. Here we just give an intuitive explanation using games. The formal definition can be found in [9].

TIOAs are designed as *mixed assume/guarantee specifications* of timed components. Their semantics is best illustrated by interpreting TIOTSes as timed game graphs. The game has three players: environment, system and coin. The environment controls *input actions* and *delays* while the system controls *output actions* and *delays*. The game has *two game-ending states*: $\top$ (system losing) and $\bot$ (environment losing). States other than $\top$ and $\bot$ are plain states. The coin serves as a tie-breaker for symmetric moves proposed by the other two players.

The environment must respect the constraints on input and delay, i.e. *input guard* and *co-invariant*, which constitutes the assumption half of the specification. *Guard-violating input* and *coinvariant-violating delay* are mapped to $\bot$.

The system must respect the constraints on output and delay, i.e. *output guard* and *invariant*, which constitutes the guarantee half of the specification. *Guard-violating output* and *invariant-violating delay* are mapped to $\top$.

Since delay is controlled by both sides, there exists a contention between invariant and co-invariant violations. If a delay exceeds the *upper bound* of one[6] before exceeding that of the other, the violation of the former will pre-empt the violation of the latter. If a delay *exceeds the upper bounds of both simultaneously*, the invariant violation will be pre-emptive and the delay mapped to $\top$.[7]

On top of game graphs, system and environment, assisted by coin, play a concurrent timed game based on delayed actions:

- A delayed action is either (d, a) or $(\infty, -)$, where $d \in \mathbb{R}^{\geq 0}$ and $a \in I \cup O$.
- Given a current state, each player proposes a delayed action under their control at that state,
  - The delayed action with *strictly smaller delay* will be chosen.
  - If the two delays *tie* (i.e. equal), it will be resolved by *tossing a coin*.
- Fire the chosen delayed action and transit to the destination state.

TIOAs do not have explicit $\top$ and $\bot$. But a $\bot$-location equates to having *true* as invariant and *false* as co-invariant. Dually, we have a $\top$-location. Together, they are reminiscent of abort and magic in their predicate forms [4,19].

2.4   Conventions on Disabled Transitions

In presenting TIOAs and TIOTSes, one often needs to be economical in drawing transitions. So a convention on disabled transitions is required.

1. a disabled input at a plain state is equivalent to an input transition to $\bot$.
2. a disabled output at a plain state is equivalent to an output transition to $\top$.

---

[6] Note that invariant and co-invariant are downward-closed. Thus, the only way to violate them is to exceed their upper bounds.

[7] One further case missing above is that, for an action transition, there is possibility that its guard is respected but the invariant/co-invariant of its destination (say l) is violated. In such situation, a state (l, t) is treated (1) as $\top$ if t violates the invariant in location l and (2) as $\bot$ if t violates the co-invariant in l while the invariant holds.

Our TIOTSes, on the other hand, disallow *disabled delay transitions*. So the delays enabled at each plain state are *unbounded*, leading to either consistently other plain states or a mixture of plain states with $\top/\bot$ *separated by a finite bound*. The convention induces some semantic-preserving transformations on TIOTSs.

$\top/\bot$ *completion*. The $\bot$-*completion* of a TIOTS $\mathcal{P}$, denoted $\mathcal{P}^\bot$, adds an a-labelled transition from p to $\bot$ for every $p \in P$ $(= L \times \mathbb{R}^C)$ and $a \in I$ s.t. a is not enabled at p. The $\top$-*completion*, denoted $\mathcal{P}^\top$, adds an a-labelled transition from p to $\top$ for every $p \in P$ and $a \in O$ s.t. a is not enabled at p.

Similarly, we can define $\top/\bot$ completion on TIOAs. We say a TIOA, $\mathcal{P} = (C, I, O, L, n^0, AT, Inv, coInv)$, is $\top$-completed iff, for all $a \in O$ and $l \in L$, we have $\bigvee\{g_k \mid l \xrightarrow{g_k, a, rs_k} l'_k \in AT\} = true$. We say $\mathcal{P}$ is $\bot$-completed iff, for all $a \in I$ and $l \in L$, we have $\bigvee\{g_k \mid l \xrightarrow{g_k, a, rs_k} l'_k \in AT\} = true$.

$\top/\bot$ *removal* The inverse operations of $\top/\bot$ completion, called $\top/\bot$ *removal*, are also semantic-preserving transformations. For instance, $\top$-removal removes all output transitions from plain states to $\top$ in a TIOTS. We leave it as an exercise for the readers to define $\top/\bot$ removal for TIOAs.

2.5   Liveness and Safety

The constraints in TIOAs can be classified as either *safety* constraints or *liveness* constraints. The former are the guards on transitions while the latter are the invariants/co-invariants on locations.

Example. Fig. 1 depicts a job scheduler together with a printer controller. The invariant at location A of the scheduler forces a *bounded-liveness guarantee* on outputs in that location: as time must be allowed to progress beyond $x = 100$, the *start* action must be fired before x exceeds 100. After *start* being fired, the clock x is reset to 0 and the scheduler waits (possibly indefinitely) for the job to *finish*. If the job finishes, the scheduler expects it to take place at a time point satisfying $5 \leq x \leq 8$ (i.e. a *safety assumption*).

The controller waits for the job to *start*, after which it will wait exactly 1 time unit before issuing *print* (forced by the invariant $y \leq 1$ on state 2 and the guard $y = 1$ on the *print!* transition, acting together as a combined liveness and *safety guarantee*). Then, the controller requires the printer to acknowledge the job as having been *printed* within 10 time units (i.e. co-invariant $y \leq 10$ in state 3 acting as a *bounded-liveness assumption*). After receiving it, the controller must indicate to the scheduler, within 5 time units, that the job has *finish*ed.

2.6   Specification Composition: Generic Synchronised Product

This paper introduces a series of four operators for specification composition: $\parallel$ for parallel composition, $\wedge$ for conjunction, $\vee$ for disjunction and $\%$ for quotient. At the core of these operators is a generic synchronised product $\prod_\otimes$ operation, where $\otimes$ ranges over the set $\{\parallel, \vee, \wedge, \%\}$. After instantiation, $\prod_\otimes$ produces

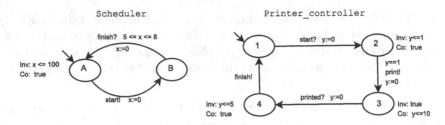

Fig. 1. Job scheduler and printer controller.

four variants ($\prod_\|$, $\prod_\wedge$, $\prod_\vee$ and $\prod_\%$), each of which needs further add-on transformations in order to define the four specification composition.

In order to obtain a modular and factored structure, we adopt a two-step approach to defining $\prod_\otimes$. In the first step we define, for each $\otimes \in \{\|, \vee, \wedge, \%\}$, a state composition operator $\otimes$ and an alphabet composition operator $\otimes$ (i.e. $\otimes$ is polymorphic). In the second step, we use $\prod_\otimes$ to lift the state/alphabet composition to the process composition.

We say (I_0, O_0) and (I_1, O_1) are $\|$-*composable* if $O_0 \cap O_1 = \{\}$, are $\wedge$- *and* $\vee$-*composable* if $(I_0, O_0) = (I_1, O_1)$, and are $\%$-*composable* if (I_0, O_0) *dominate* (I_1, O_1), i.e. $A_1 \subseteq A_0$ and $O_1 \subseteq O_0$. Then, assuming $\otimes$-composability on alphabet pairs, we can define the alphabet composition operations $(I_0, O_0) \otimes (I_1, O_1)$ as follows: $(I_0, O_0) \| (I_1, O_1) = ((I_0 \cup I_1) \backslash (O_0 \cup O_1), O_0 \cup O_1)$, $(I_0, O_0) \wedge (I_1, O_1) = (I_0, O_0)$, $(I_0, O_0) \vee (I_1, O_1) = (I_0, O_0)$ and $(I_0, O_0) \% (I_1, O_1) = (I_0 \cup O_1, O_0 \backslash O_1)$.

The definition of $s_0 \otimes s_1$ is supplied in Table 1.[8] Intuitively $\bot$ is equated to an *erroneous specification* while $\top$ is equated to *timestop*, i.e. the operation of stopping the system clock or freezing the global time.

Thus, $\top$ represents the *magic moment* from which the whole system stops running and freezes, eliminating, once and for all, all subsequent possibility of reaching the erroneous state. This gives rise to a *refinement ordering* over states, whereby $\top$ refines plain states, which in turn refine $\bot$.

Timestop can explain the behaviour of $\top$ in parallel composition: the equation $\bot \| \top = \top$ holds because time stops exactly at the moment of reaching the erroneous state, so the resulting state is a timestop, rather than $\bot$.

It is also easy to see that *state conjunction* ($\wedge$) and *disjunction* ($\vee$) operations in Table 1 follow the intuition of the join and meet operations.

The *state quotient* ($\%$) operation is harder to explain. But some intuition can be recovered from the *derivation* of $\%$ based on $\|$ and $\neg$, i.e. $s_0 \% s_1 = (s_0^- \| s_1)^-$, where *state mirror* ($\neg$) behaves like negation (c.f. Table 1).

State-to-process lifting. Given two $\top/\bot$ completed TIOTS, $\mathcal{P}_i = \langle I_i, O_i, S_i, s_i^0, \rightarrow_i \rangle$ for $i \in \{0, 1\}$, s.t. $S_0 \cap S_1 = \{\bot, \top\}$ and (I_0, O_0) and (I_1, O_1) are $\otimes$-composable, $\mathcal{P}_0 \prod_\otimes \mathcal{P}_1$ gives rise to a new $\top/\bot$ completed TIOTS $\mathcal{P} = \langle I, O, S, s^0, \rightarrow \rangle$ s.t. $(I, O) = (I_0, O_0) \otimes (I_1, O_1)$, $S = (P_0 \times P_1) \uplus P_0 \uplus P_1 \uplus \{\top, \bot\}$,

---

[8] For $i \in \{0, 1\}$ and $p_i = (l_i, t_i)$, $p_0 \times p_1 = ((l_0, l_1), t_0 \uplus t_1)$ ($t0$ and t_1 are clock-disjoint).

Table 1. State composition operators.

$\|$	$\top$	p_0	$\bot$
$\top$	$\top$	$\top$	$\top$
p_1	$\top$	$p_0 \times p_1$	$\bot$
$\bot$	$\top$	$\bot$	$\bot$

$\wedge$	$\top$	p_0	$\bot$
$\top$	$\top$	$\top$	$\top$
p_1	$\top$	$p_0 \times p_1$	p_1
$\bot$	$\top$	p_0	$\bot$

$\vee$	$\top$	p_0	$\bot$
$\top$	$\top$	p_0	$\bot$
p_1	p_1	$p_0 \times p_1$	$\bot$
$\bot$	$\bot$	$\bot$	$\bot$

$\%$	$\top$	p_0	$\bot$
$\top$	$\bot$	$\bot$	$\bot$
p_1	$\top$	$p_0 \times p_1$	$\bot$
$\bot$	$\top$	$\top$	$\bot$

$\neg$	
$\top$	$\bot$
p	p
$\bot$	$\top$

$s^0 = s_0^0 \otimes s_1^0$ and $\to$ is the smallest relation containing $\to_0 \cup \to_1$,[9] and satisfying the rules:

$$\frac{p_0 \xrightarrow{\alpha}_0 s_0' \quad p_1 \xrightarrow{\alpha}_1 s_1'}{p_0 \otimes p_1 \xrightarrow{\alpha} s_0' \otimes s_1'} \qquad \frac{p_0 \xrightarrow{a}_0 s_0' \quad a \notin A_1}{p_0 \otimes p_1 \xrightarrow{a} s_0' \otimes p_1} \qquad \frac{p_1 \xrightarrow{a}_1 s_1' \quad a \notin A_0}{p_0 \otimes p_1 \xrightarrow{a} p_0 \otimes s_1'}$$

Remark. Note the subtlety in the transition rules of $\mathcal{P}_0 \prod_\wedge \mathcal{P}_1$ and $\mathcal{P}_0 \prod_\vee \mathcal{P}_1$. If we have $p_0 \xrightarrow{\alpha} p_0'$ in $\mathcal{P}_0$ and $p_1 \xrightarrow{\alpha} \top$ in $\mathcal{P}_1$, then we have $p_0 \times p_1 \xrightarrow{\alpha} p_0'$ in $\mathcal{P}_0 \prod_\wedge \mathcal{P}_1$. That is, process $\mathcal{P}_1$ is discarded after the transition and the rest of the execution is the solo run of $\mathcal{P}_0$.[10]

We can also lift the state mirror operator $\neg$ to process level by defining the *pre-mirror* operator $\neg_0$; $\mathcal{P}^{\neg_0}$ interchanges $I_\mathcal{P}$ and $O_\mathcal{P}$ as well as $\top$ and $\bot$ in $\mathcal{P}$.

The definition of parallel synchronised product can be lifted to TIOAs. Given two $\otimes$-composable $\top/\bot$-completed TIOAs with disjoint clocks ($C_0 \cap C_1 = \{\}$), $\mathcal{P}_i = (C_i, I_i, O_i, L_i, n_i^0, AT_i, Inv_i, coInv_i)$ for $i \in \{0,1\}$, their synchronised product gives rise to another TIOA $\mathcal{P} = \mathcal{P}_0 \prod_\otimes \mathcal{P}_1$:

- $C = C_0 \cup C_1$, $(I, O) = (I_0, O_0) \otimes (I_1, O_1)$, $L = L_0 \times L_1$ and $n^0 = n_0^0 \times n_1^0$;
- AT is the least relation that contains AT_0, AT_1 and $\{l_0 \times l_1 \xrightarrow{g_0 \wedge g_1, a, rs_0 \cup rs_1} n_0' \times n_1' \mid l_0 \xrightarrow{g_0, a, rs_0} n_0' \in AT_0 \wedge l_1 \xrightarrow{g_1, a, rs_1} n_1' \in AT_1\}$
  $\cup \{l_0 \times l_1 \xrightarrow{g_0, a, rs_0} n_0' \times l_1 \mid l_0 \xrightarrow{g_0, a, rs_0} n_0' \in AT_0, a \in (A_0 \backslash A_1)\}$
  $\cup \{l_0 \times l_1 \xrightarrow{g_1, a, rs_1} l_0 \times n_1' \mid l_1 \xrightarrow{g_1, a, rs_1} n_1' \in AT_1, a \in (A_1 \backslash A_0)\}\}$;
- and $(Inv(l_0 \times l_1), coInv(l_0 \times l_1)) = (Inv_0(l_0), coInv_0(l_0)) \otimes (Inv_1(l_1), coInv_1(l_1))$.

We define the invariant/co-invariant composition operation $\otimes$ as follows[11]:

- $(Inv_0, coInv_0) \| (Inv_1, coInv_1) = (Inv_0 \wedge Inv_1, coInv_0 \wedge coInv_1)$
- $(Inv_0, coInv_0) \wedge (Inv_1, coInv_1) = (Inv_0 \wedge Inv_1, coInv_0 \vee coInv_1)$
- $(Inv_0, coInv_0) \vee (Inv_1, coInv_1) = (Inv_0 \vee Inv_1, coInv_0 \wedge coInv_1)$
- $(Inv_0, coInv_0) \% (Inv_1, coInv_1) = (Inv_0 \wedge coInv_1, coInv_0 \wedge Inv_1)$

The pre-mirror ($\mathcal{P}^{\neg_0}$) of a TIOA $\mathcal{P}$ interchanges $I_\mathcal{P}$ and $O_\mathcal{P}$ as well as the invariant and co-invariant for each location of $\mathcal{P}$.

---

[9] Containment of $\to_0 \cup \to_1$ is not required for parallel composition, but is necessary for conjunction and disjunction.

[10] The technique was inspired by a discussion with Roscoe on angelic choice in CSP.

[11] Note that the above definition exploits the fact that the addition or removal of *false*-guarded transitions to AT will not change the semantics of the automata.

3   Parallel Composition, Refinement and Determinisation

We define the parallel composition of specifications as $\mathcal{P}_0 \parallel \mathcal{P}_1 = \mathcal{P}_0^{\perp} \prod_{\parallel} \mathcal{P}_1^{\perp}$, since $\prod_{\parallel}$ can be extended without modification to work on $\perp$-complete TIOTSs.

Informally, we say one specification is a refinement of another if the former can replace the latter in all closed contexts. A *closed context* of a specification $\mathcal{P}$ is another specification $\mathcal{Q}$ s.t. (1) $\mathcal{P}$ and $\mathcal{Q}$ are $\parallel$-composable and (2) $I_{\mathcal{P}} \subseteq O_{\mathcal{Q}} \wedge I_{\mathcal{Q}} \subseteq O_{\mathcal{P}}$.

Definition 3 (Substitutive Refinement [9]**).** *Let* $\mathcal{P}_{imp}$ *and* $\mathcal{P}_{spec}$ *be TIOTSs with identical alphabets. We say* $\mathcal{P}_{spec} \sqsubseteq \mathcal{P}_{imp}$ *iff for all closed contexts* $\mathcal{Q}$, $\mathcal{P}_{spec} \parallel \mathcal{Q}$ *is* $\perp$-*free implies* $\mathcal{P}_{imp} \parallel \mathcal{Q}$ *is* $\perp$-*free. We say* $\mathcal{P}_{spec} \simeq \mathcal{P}_{imp}$ *(i.e. substitutively equivalent) iff* $\mathcal{P}_{imp} \sqsubseteq \mathcal{P}_{spec}$ *and* $\mathcal{P}_{spec} \sqsubseteq \mathcal{P}_{imp}$.

A first observation of the refinement definition is that each specification has a deterministic counterpart to which it is substitutively equivalent. The counterpart can be constructed by a modified determinisation procedure.

Determinism. A TIOTS is *deterministic* iff there is no ambiguous transition, i.e. $s \xrightarrow{\alpha} s' \wedge s \xrightarrow{\alpha} s''$ implies $s' = s''$. A TIOA is *deterministic* iff, for each $l \in L$ and $a \in A$, l has a pair of distinct a-transitions $l \xrightarrow{g_1, a, rs_1} l_1$ and $l \xrightarrow{g_2, a, rs_2} l_2$ implies g_1 and g_2 are disjoint.

We define the *determinisation* $\mathcal{P}^D$ of $\mathcal{P}$ as a modified subset construction procedure on $\mathcal{P}^{\perp}$: given a subset S_0 of states reachable by a given trace, we only keep those which are minimal w.r.t. the state refinement ordering.[12]

Proposition 1 ([9]**).** *Any TIOTS* $\mathcal{P}$ *is substitutively equivalent to the deterministic TIOTS* $\mathcal{P}^D$.

From a game theoretical perspective, our modified determinisation procedure converts an imperfect-information game into a perfect-information game.

On the level of TIOAs, strongly non-zeno TAs are known to be determinisable with a symbolic procedure [6], based on which we can implement our procedure (say $DET(\mathcal{P})$) to determinise TIOA $\mathcal{P}$.

In the sequel we focus on deterministic TIOA/TIOTS, i.e. *interfaces*.

4   A Story of Two Games

Our realisability theory will build on a pair of two-player games dual to each other: *normalisation* and *realisation*. They are derivatives of the three-player game in Sect. 2. In all three games, the system tries to steer the game play clear of $\top$ while the environment tries to steer clear of $\perp$.

We give the technical definition of the games in this section, deferring the provision of intuition and *their uses in specification theories* to the next section.

---

[12] The modified determinisation procedure first appeared in the Definition 4.2 of [26], which is for the untimed case.

4.1   Timed Strategies

An interface $\mathcal{P}$, being a game graph, encodes a set of strategies for each of the three players. We give a formal definition of (timed) strategies below:

- A *system strategy* $\mathcal{G}_s$ is a deterministic tree TIOTS[13] s.t. each plain state p in $\mathcal{G}_s$ is ready to accept all possible inputs by the environment (i.e. a is enabled for all $a \in I$), but allows a single move by the system.
  The system move (denoted $mv(p)$) can be a delayed output (d, a) for some $a \in O$ and $d \in \mathbb{R}^{\geq 0}$ or an infinite delay $(\infty, -)$.[14]
  Dually, we can define *environment strategies* (e.g. $\mathcal{G}_e$). A system strategy is a $\perp$-complete TIOTS while an environment strategy is $\top$-complete.
- Given TIOTSs $\mathcal{P}$ and $\mathcal{P}'$ with *identical alphabets* (i.e. $O = O'$ and $I = I'$), we say $\mathcal{P}$ is a *partial unfolding* [25] of $\mathcal{P}'$ if there exists a function $f : S_{\mathcal{P}} \to S_{\mathcal{P}'}$ such that (1) f maps $\top$ to $\top$, $\perp$ to $\perp$ and plain states to plain states, and (2) $f(s_{\mathcal{P}}^0) = s_{\mathcal{P}'}^0$ and $p \xrightarrow{\alpha}_{\mathcal{P}} s \Rightarrow f(p) \xrightarrow{\alpha}_{\mathcal{P}'} f(s)$.
- We say a TIOTS $\mathcal{P}$ *contains* a strategy $\mathcal{G}$, denoted $\mathcal{G} \in \mathcal{P}$, if $\mathcal{G}$ is a partial unfolding of $(\mathcal{P}^{\perp})^{\top}$. We say there is a strategy $\mathcal{G}$ *at state* p in $\mathcal{P}$, if $\mathcal{G} \in \mathcal{P}(p)$, where $\mathcal{P}(p)$ is the TIOTS $\mathcal{P}$ re-initialised to state p.

The coin is treated as a special player. A strategy of the coin is a function h from tA^* to $\{0, 1\}$. We denote the set of all possible coin strategies as H.

Strategy composition. A composition of a set of three strategies, denoted $\mathcal{G}_s \times_h \mathcal{G}_e$, will produce, according to the timed concurrent game rules defined in Sect. 2, a simple path which is a partial unfolding of both $\mathcal{G}_s$ and $\mathcal{G}_e$. The simple path can be either *finite and ending in* $\top/\perp$ or *infinite*.

4.2   Two Games

Normalisation game. In the normalisation game, the system forms a coalition with the coin to play against the environment and seek $\perp$-reachability.

Given an interface $\mathcal{P}$, we say a system strategy $\mathcal{G}$ at p and a coin strategy $h \in H$ is *winning* at p iff $\mathcal{L} \times_h \mathcal{G}$ ends in $\perp$ for all possible environment strategies $\mathcal{L}$ at p. Then we say a plain state p in $\mathcal{P}$ is $\perp$-*winning* iff the system and the coin have a winning strategy at p.

---

[13] We say an acyclic TIOTS is a *tree* if (1) there does not exist a pair of transitions in the form of $p \xrightarrow{a} p''$ and $p' \xrightarrow{d} p''$, (2) $p \xrightarrow{a} p'' \wedge p' \xrightarrow{b} p''$ implies $p = p'$ and $a = b$ and (3) $p \xrightarrow{d} p'' \wedge p' \xrightarrow{d} p''$ implies $p = p'$.

[14] For the former, $\mathcal{G}_s$ generates exactly a time interval $(0, d]$ of delays from p, after which $\mathcal{G}_s$ arrives at another plain state with a enabled. For the latter, an infinite time interval $(0, \infty)$ of delays are enabled at p. The delays either all lead to plain states or $(0, \infty)$ can be further partitioned into two intervals s.t. the delays in the first interval lead to plain states while those of the second lead to $\top$ or $\perp$.

Conversely, we say an environment strategy $\mathcal{L}$ at p is a *normalising strategy*[15] at p iff $\mathcal{L}$ from p can steer the game play clear of $\bot$, i.e. for all coin strategies $h \in H$ and system strategies $\mathcal{G}$ at p, $\mathcal{L} \times_h \mathcal{G}$ produces either a finite play ending in $\top$ or an infinite play.

Interestingly, an environment strategy is normalising iff it is *normalisable*, i.e. it is free of $\bot$. Thus, a state is a $\bot$-winning state iff it contains no normalisable (or normalising) environment strategy.

Synthesis of game winning states is a central problem of the game-theoretical research. To synthesise $\bot$-winning states in interfaces, we focus on the two *representative subclasses* of $\bot$-winning states: auto-$\bot$ and semi-$\bot$ states.

Auto-$\bot$ and semi-$\bot$. Given a $\top/\bot$ complete interface, we say a plain state p is an *auto-$\bot$ state* iff $p \xrightarrow{a} \bot$ for some $a \in O$. We say a plain state p is a *semi-$\bot$ state* iff (1) all input transitions in p or any of its time-passing successors lead to $\bot$, and (2) there exists $d \in \mathbb{R}^{>0}$ s.t. $p \xrightarrow{d} \bot$. For a general interface $\mathcal{P}$, we say p is an auto-$\bot$ (or semi-$\bot$) state in $\mathcal{P}$ iff it is an auto-$\bot$ (or semi-$\bot$) state in $(\mathcal{P}^\top)^\bot$.

For auto-$\bot$ and semi-$\bot$ states, system (and coin) has a one-step winning strategy to reach $\bot$, which are a delay move and an output move resp. The absence of semi-$\bot$/auto-$\bot$ states characterises the absence of $\bot$-winning states.

Lemma 1. *An interface is free of $\bot$-winning states iff it is free of semi-$\bot$ and auto-$\bot$ states.*

Hence we can *find and remove* all $\bot$-winning states in an interface by finding and removing all auto-$\bot$ and semi-$\bot$ states in it.

Normalisation. The normalisation of an interface $\mathcal{P}$, denoted $\mathcal{P}^N$, is obtained by collapsing all $\bot$-winning states in $\mathcal{P}$ to $\bot$, which can be implemented by a $\bot$-*backpropagation* procedure that repeatedly collapses semi-$\bot$ and auto-$\bot$ states in $\mathcal{P}$ to $\bot$, until semi-$\bot$ and auto-$\bot$ freedom is obtained. Normalisation returns a *normalised interface*, which is either the $\bot$-*TIOTS* (i.e. a degenerated TIOTS with $\bot$ as the initial state) or a TIOTS free of $\bot$-winning states.

On deterministic TIOAs, we can implement $\bot$-backpropagation procedures by fixpoint calculation via constraint backpropagation (based on weakest precondition calculation), denoted as $BP(\mathcal{P}, \bot)$.

Realisation Game. In the realisation game, the environment forms a coalition with the coin to play against the system and seek $\top$-reachability. By duality we obtain the definition of $\top$-*winning*, auto-$\top$ and semi-$\top$ states.[16]

---

[15] We choose not to call it a winning strategy as it serves additional purpose for our paper.

[16] Given a $\top/\bot$ complete interface, we say a plain state p is an *auto-$\top$* iff $p \xrightarrow{a} \top$ for some $a \in I$; a plain state p is a *semi-$\top$* iff (1) all output transitions in p or any of its time-passing successors lead to the $\top$ state, and (2) there exists $d \in \mathbb{R}^{>0}$ s.t. $p \xrightarrow{d} \top$.

We say a system strategy is *realising* iff it can steer the realisation game play clear of $\top$, which is equivalent to being *realisable*, i.e. free of $\top$. Obviously a state is a $\top$-winning state iff it contains no realisable or realising system strategy.

Lemma 2. *An interface is free of $\top$-winning states iff it is free of semi-$\top$ and auto-$\top$ states.*

Similarly we can *find and remove* all $\top$-winning states in an interface by a *realisation* operation.

Realisation. The realisation of an interface $\mathcal{P}$, denoted $\mathcal{P}^R$, is obtained by collapsing all $\top$-winning states in $\mathcal{P}$ to $\top$ (implementable by a dual $\top$-*backpropagation* procedure on TIOTSes or a constraint-backpropagation procedure $BP(\mathcal{P}, \top)$). Realisation returns a *realised interface*, which is either the $\top$-*TIOTS* (i.e. with $\top$ as the initial state) or a TIOTS free of $\top$-winning states.

Interference between the two games. Note that a state in an interface can be simultaneously $\bot$- and $\top$-winning (e.g. simultaneously auto-$\top$ and auto-$\bot$). The anomaly arises due to the coin being shared by both coalitions.

Since coin can only be on one side at a time, this implies that the two games must be played *one-at-a-time* rather than simultaneously.

Hence, in our realisability theory it is meaningless to have states that are both $\bot$- and $\top$-winning. In the sequel we will apply realisation and normalisation operations *alternatingly* to ensure all generated interfaces are *well-formed*, i.e. having no state simultaneously $\bot$- and $\top$-winning.

We say a state is a *neutral states* iff it is neither $\top$-winning nor $\bot$-winning. An interface free of $\top$-winning and $\bot$-winning states is called a *neutral interface*.

The *fundamental principle of interfaces* is to *ensure that all interactions between the system and environment stay in neutral states*.

5   Realisable Specification Theory

When a component, specified by an interface $\mathcal{P}$, interacts with an environment, it plays a game with the environment. This game on a closer look, however, is not identical to the game defined (on the game graph $\mathcal{P}$) in Sect. 4. The component strategies in the new game is still constrained by $\mathcal{P}$ (i.e. as it is for the system strategies contained by $\mathcal{P}$ in the old game). But the environment is entirely un-constrained, which may choose from all strategies definable by its alphabet. Thus, the environment can be extremely powerful in such game interactions, especially when it is further equipped with the timestop operation.

Previously [9], we have developed a specification theory for such systems, where $\simeq$ gives rise to a weakest congruence w.r.t. $\prod_{\parallel}$, $\prod_{\wedge}$, $\prod_{\vee}$ and $\prod_{\%}$ operations of this paper. It results in a greatly simplified theory without the need for timed game synthesis.

In this section we are going to remove the timestop and its related time-blocking behaviours from both components and environments, and develop a new specification theory for realisable components.

For a proper treatment of un-constrained strategies, we need first to define a notion of *aggressiveness*.

Comparing strategies. Different strategies vary in their effectiveness to steer the interaction clear of $\top$ or $\bot$. Such effectiveness can be compared if two strategies closely resemble each other: we say $\mathcal{G}$ and $\mathcal{G}'$ of the same player are *affine* if $s_{\mathcal{G}}^0 \stackrel{tt}{\Rightarrow} p$ and $s_{\mathcal{G}'}^0 \stackrel{tt}{\Rightarrow} p'$ implies $mv_{\mathcal{G}}(p) = mv_{\mathcal{G}'}(p')$. Intuitively, this means $\mathcal{G}$ and $\mathcal{G}'$ propose the same move at the 'same' states.

Given two affine strategies $\mathcal{G}$ and $\mathcal{G}'$, we say $\mathcal{G}$ is *more $\bot$-aggressive* than $\mathcal{G}'$, denoted $\mathcal{G} \preceq \mathcal{G}'$, if (1) $s_{\mathcal{G}'}^0 \stackrel{tt}{\Rightarrow} \bot$ implies there is a prefix tt_0 of tt s.t. $s_{\mathcal{G}}^0 \stackrel{tt_0}{\Rightarrow} \bot$ and (2) $s_{\mathcal{G}}^0 \stackrel{tt}{\Rightarrow} \top$ implies there is a prefix tt_0 of tt s.t. $s_{\mathcal{G}'}^0 \stackrel{tt_0}{\Rightarrow} \top$. Intuitively, it means $\mathcal{G}$ can reach $\bot$ faster but $\top$ slower than $\mathcal{G}'$. $\preceq$ forms a partial order over the set of strategies possessed by a player. Dually, we can define $\mathcal{G}$ being *more $\top$-aggressive* than $\mathcal{G}'$ as $\mathcal{G}' \preceq \mathcal{G}$.

'Representative' winning strategies. We say an environment strategy $\mathcal{G}_e$ is a *winning strategy* in the interaction with component $\mathcal{P}$ iff $\mathcal{G}_s \times_h \mathcal{G}_e$ does not end in $\bot$ for all coin strategies h and all system strategies $\mathcal{G}_s \in \mathcal{P}$.

Of all environment winning strategies against component $\mathcal{P}$, the subset of minimally $\top$-aggressive ones can *fully* represent the whole set (by an upward-closure operation on $\preceq$), since the capability of a less aggressive strategy in steering clear of $\bot$ implies the same capability for more aggressive ones.

Thus, our theory can focus mainly on 'representative' environment winning strategies, which, by the magic of mirror, have already been encoded in $\mathcal{P}$.

Lemma 3. $\mathcal{G}_e$ *is a minimally $\top$-aggressive environment winning strategy in the game with component $\mathcal{P}$ iff $\mathcal{P}^{\neg 0}$ (i.e. pre-mirror of $\mathcal{P}$) contains $\mathcal{G}_e$.*

In another word, an interface $\mathcal{P}$ encodes both a set of component strategies (say SG) and a 'representative' set of environment winning strategies (EG), which are resp. the component guarantees and environment assumptions of the interface.

5.1   Unrealisability

The timestop operation $\top$ freezes the global time by halting the progress of the system clock. In general, such capability is too powerful to be realistic. Thus, a (component or environment) strategy containing timestop is *unrealisable*, and a state possessing no realisable component strategy is an *unrealisable state*.

According to Sect. 4, unrealisable states are exactly $\top$-winning states. Realisation operation is equivalent to removing all unrealisable system strategies from an interface.

Lemma 4. *Given an interface $\mathcal{P}$, the set of realisable component strategies of $\mathcal{P}$ is exactly the set of component strategies of $\mathcal{P}^R$.*

5.2 Incompatibility

Given two interfaces $\mathcal{P}$ and $\mathcal{Q}$ with *complementary* alphabets (i.e. I and O interchanged), their parallel composition calculates the intersection of $SG_{\mathcal{P}}$ and $EG_{\mathcal{Q}}$ as well as that of $SG_{\mathcal{Q}}$ and $EG_{\mathcal{P}}$. That is, the guarantees provided by one interface will be matched against the assumptions required by the other.

For a general component $\mathcal{P}$, both $SG_{\mathcal{P}}$ and $EG_{\mathcal{P}}$ may contain unrealisable strategies. For a realisable component $\mathcal{P}$, only $EG_{\mathcal{P}}$ may contain unrealisable strategies. In a specification theory, environments are also components. If all components are realisable, the unrealisable part of $EG_{\mathcal{P}}$ becomes irrelevant. For instance, if $EG_{\mathcal{P}}$ consists of only unrealisable strategies, it is equivalent to being empty.

In the process of fulfilling assumptions with guarantees, if there is a match (i.e. non-empty realisable intersection), assumptions will be absorbed by guarantees and disappear since $\mathcal{P} \parallel \mathcal{Q}$ forms a closed system. Otherwise (i.e. empty realisable intersection), it gives rise to the so-called *incompatible states*, i.e. states in which all 'representative' environment winning strategy are unrealisable.

A state p in $\mathcal{P}$ is incompatible implies p in $\mathcal{P}^{\neg o}$ is unrealisable, which in turn implies (by duality) p in $\mathcal{P}$ is *un-normalisable*, i.e. a state containing no normalisable environment strategy. According to Sect. 4, un-normalisable states are exactly $\perp$-winning states.

In assume-guarantee specification theories, auto-$\perp$ and semi-$\perp$, as members of incompatible states, are endowed with specialised interpretations, capturing resp. safety mismatch errors (aka *exception*) and liveness mismatch errors (aka *time-out*).

Exception. The arrival of an input at a location and time of a component when it is not expected (i.e. the input is disabled at the location and time) triggers an exception in the parallel composition. Exception is captured by auto-$\perp$ states.

Figure 2 shows the parallel composition of the job scheduler with the printer controller. In the transition from $B4$ to $A1$, the guard combines the effects of the constraints on the clocks x and y. As *finish* is an output of the controller, it can be fired at a time when the scheduler is not expecting it, meaning that an exception is raised due to safety errors. This is indicated by the transition to $\perp$ when the guard constraint $5 \le x \le 8$ is not satisfied.

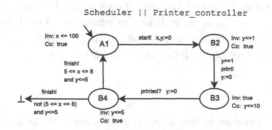

Fig. 2. Parallel composition of the job scheduler and printer controller.

Timeout. The non-arrival of an expected input at a location of a component before the expiration of its co-invariant triggers a *bounded-liveness error* (aka timeout) in the parallel composition.

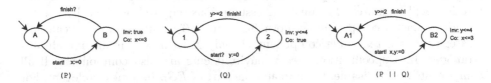

Fig. 3. Bounded liveness error.

Figure 3 shows an example for bounded-liveness errors. In the closed system $P \parallel Q$, at location $B2$ the system is free to choose either output *finish* after $y \geq 2$ or delay until $x > 3$. If it chooses the latter, P component will time out in location B and the system will enter $\perp$. Note that the timeout here is due to the fact that the urgency requirement at location 2 of Q (i.e. $y <= 4$) is weaker than the timeout bound set at location B of P (i.e. $x <= 3$). (If it is otherwise, the invariant at $B2$ will preempt the co-invariant at $B2$ and eliminate the possibility of timeout.)

5.3   Realisable Specification and Coarsened Refinement

Now let us start to move back to specifications by defining realisable specifications, which will give us the advantage of the closure under hiding and renaming operations.[17]

We first notice that the definition of auto-$\top$ and semi-$\top$ can be extended to specifications. Then we say a specification is *realisable* iff it is free of both auto-$\top$ and semi-$\top$. Due to the preservation of auto-$\top$ and semi-$\top$ freedom by determinisation, we have:

Lemma 5. *Given a realisable specification P, P^D is a realisable interface.*

Recall that P and P^D are substitutively equivalent according to the finest $\simeq$, in which the timestop operations greatly increase the distinguishing power of the processes, enabling it to tell two interfaces apart by examining the *timing difference* in error occurrences as well as the *existence* of such occurrences.[18]

After the removal of timestop and restricting to realisable specifications, however, the substitutive equivalence is coarsened to be $\simeq_r$.

---

[17] We omit the two operators in this paper due to space limitation.

[18] That is, they can distinguish the $\perp$ state from the $\perp$-winning states by stopping time immediately.

Realisable refinement. Let $\mathcal{P}$ and $\mathcal{Q}$ be realisable specifications with identical alphabets. $\mathcal{P}$ *realisably refines* $\mathcal{Q}$ (i.e. $\mathcal{Q} \sqsubseteq_r \mathcal{P}$), iff, for all realisable specification $\mathcal{R}$ that is a closed context of $\mathcal{P}$, $\mathcal{Q} \parallel \mathcal{R}$ is $\bot$-free implies $\mathcal{P} \parallel \mathcal{R}$ is $\bot$-free. We say $\mathcal{Q} \simeq_r \mathcal{P}$ (*realisably equivalent*), iff $\mathcal{P} \sqsubseteq_r \mathcal{Q}$ and $\mathcal{Q} \sqsubseteq_r \mathcal{P}$.

It is obvious that $\simeq_r$ is the weakest equivalence preserving incompatible states (over realisable specifications). In the sequel we show that $\simeq_r$ is a congruence w.r.t. the parallel $\parallel$, conjunction $\wedge$, disjunction $\vee$ and quotient $\%$ operators.

Note that, even though the sequel focuses on realisable specifications which are closed under all four operations, we still need unrealisable specifications as a detour to simplify operator definitions like quotient and conjunction, since realisable specifications are not closed under $\prod_\wedge$ and $\prod_\%$.

Lemma 6. *Given a realisable specification $\mathcal{P}$, $\mathcal{P} \simeq_r \mathcal{P}^D \simeq_r (\mathcal{P}^D)^N$.*

6   Conjunction, Disjunction and Quotient

In this section we will present the operational definition of conjunction, disjunction and quotient operators[19], building on top of the generic synchronised product operator in Sect. 2.

Desiderata of the operators. Let us first describe the desired effects these operators aim to achieve before the formal development.

Over the set of realisable specifications, e.g. $\mathcal{P}$, $\mathcal{Q}$ and $\mathcal{L}$, and with respect to the substitutive refinement $\preceq_r$: (1) $\mathcal{P} \vee \mathcal{Q}$ gives rise to the *strongest* realisable specification that are *weaker than both $\mathcal{P}$ and $\mathcal{Q}$*; (2) $\mathcal{P} \wedge \mathcal{Q}$ gives rise to the *weakest* realisable specification that are *stronger than both $\mathcal{P}$ and $\mathcal{Q}$*; and (3) $\mathcal{P} \% \mathcal{Q}$ gives rise to the *weakest* realisable specification $\mathcal{L}$ s.t. $\mathcal{L} \parallel \mathcal{Q}$ *is stronger than $\mathcal{P}$*.

Thus, conjunction and disjunction calculate the meet and join w.r.t. $\preceq_r$, whilst quotient synthesises a controller to interact with the specification and steer its execution away from incompatible states.

Operational definitions. The definition of $\prod_\wedge$ can be extended without modification to work on $\bot$-complete TIOTSs.[20] The definitions of $\prod_\vee$ and $\prod_\%$ do not extend to $\bot$-complete TIOTSs.

We define $\mathcal{P} \vee \mathcal{Q} = \mathcal{P}^\top \prod_\vee \mathcal{Q}^\top$ and $\mathcal{P}^\neg = ((\mathcal{P}^D)^N)^{\neg 0}$. We define the other two operators by a three-step recipe: $(((\mathcal{P}^D)^N)^\top \prod_\otimes ((\mathcal{Q}^D)^N)^\top)^R$. We start with normalisation, go on with applying the $\prod_\otimes$ operators (after $\top$-completion), and finish with realisation. It is easy to verify that realisable specifications are closed under all three operators.

We can verify that $\mathcal{P}_0 \% \mathcal{P}_1 \simeq_r (\mathcal{P}_0^\neg \parallel \mathcal{P}_1)^\neg$. This is a lifting, from the state level to the process level, of a corresponding equation in Sect. 2.

---

[19] It is easy to verify that realisable specifications are closed under $\parallel$ defined in Sect. 3 since $\parallel$ preserves auto-$\top$ and semi-$\top$ freedom.

[20] With the extension, blocked synchronisation, i.e. an action being enabled on one process but not so on the other, becomes possible.

7 Declarative Theory of Contracts

We now present a timed-trace semantics to all the operators defined in this paper. For this purpose we adopt the *contract* framework promoted in [5,20][21], which has the advantage of explicitly separating *assumptions* from *guarantees*.

Given a specification $\mathcal{P} = \langle I, O, S, s^0, \rightarrow \rangle$, three sets of traces can be extracted from $((\mathcal{P}^\perp)^\top)^D$:

- TP is a set of timed traces leading to plain states
- TF is a set of timed traces leading to the erroneous state $\perp$
- TM is a set of timed traces leading to the timestop state $\top$.

TF and TM are extension-closed due to the chaotic nature of $\top$ and $\perp$, while TP is prefix-closed. Since $TF \uplus TP \uplus TM$ gives rise to the full set of timed traces (i.e. tA^*), we need only two of the three sets to characterise $\mathcal{P}$.

In a system-environment game play, TF is the set of behaviours that the environment tries to steer the play away from, whereas TM is the set of behaviours that the system tries to steer the play away from. Thus, TF and TM characterise resp. the assumptions AS and guarantees GR of the specification.

Definition 4 (Contract). *A* contract *is a tuple* (I, O, AS, GR), *where AS and GR are two disjoint extension-closed trace sets. The contract of* $\mathcal{P}$ *is defined as* $TT(\mathcal{P}) := (I, O, TF, TM)$.

We say the contract of a specification $\mathcal{P}$ is *realisable* iff $\overline{GR}$ in $TT(\mathcal{P})$ is *I-receptive*. A trace set TT is *I-receptive* iff, for each $tt \in TT$, we have (1) $tt^\frown \langle e \rangle \in TT$ for all $e \in I$ and (2) $tt^\frown \langle d \rangle \notin TT$ for some $d \in \mathbb{R}^{>0}$ implies there exists some $0 \leq d_0 < d$ and $e_0 \in O$ s.t. $tt^\frown \langle d_0, e_0 \rangle \in TT$.

We say the contract of a specification $\mathcal{P}$ is *normalisable* iff $\overline{AS}$ in $TT(\mathcal{P})$ is *O-receptive*. A trace set TT is *O-receptive* iff, for each $tt \in TT$, we have (1) $tt^\frown \langle e \rangle \in TT$ for all $e \in O$ and (2) $tt^\frown \langle d \rangle \notin TT$ for some $d \in \mathbb{R}^{>0}$ implies there exists some $0 \leq d_0 < d$ and $e_0 \in I$ s.t. $tt^\frown \langle d_0, e_0 \rangle \in TT$.

We can lift the realisation and normalisation operations to contracts:

Definition 5 (Realisation). *The realisation of a contract is* $(I, O, AS, GR)^R = (I, O, AS \setminus GR^R, GR^R)$, *where GR^R is the least extension-closed superset of GR s.t. no $tt \in \overline{GR^R}$ is an auto-$\top$ or semi-$\top$.*

We say a trace $tt \in TT$ is an *auto-$\top$* iff $tt^\frown \langle e \rangle \notin TT$ for some $e \in I$. A trace $tt \in TT$ is an *semi-$\top$* iff there exists some $d \in \mathbb{R}^{>0}$ s.t. $tt^\frown \langle d \rangle \notin TT$ and $tt^\frown \langle d_0, e_0 \rangle \notin TT$ for all $0 \leq d_0 < d$ and $e_0 \in O$. It is easy to verify $\overline{GR^R}$ is I-receptive and $TT(\mathcal{P})^R = TT(\mathcal{P}^R)$.

Dually, we can define a trace $tt \in TT$ being an *auto-$\perp$* or *semi-$\perp$*.

Definition 6 (Normalisation). *Given a contract* (I, O, AS, GR), *we define* $(I, O, AS, GR)^N = (I, O, AS^N, GR \setminus AS^N)$, *where AS^N is the least extension-closed superset of AS s.t. no $tt \in \overline{AS^N}$ is an auto-$\perp$ or semi-$\perp$.*

It is easy to verify that $\overline{AS^N}$ is O-receptive and $TT(\mathcal{P})^N = TT(\mathcal{P}^N)$.

---

[21] Bertrand Meyer [18] and Ralph Back [4] first coined the terminology of *contract* in the context of programming languages.

The theory of realisable contracts. A realisable specification gives rise to a realisable contract. Over realisable specifications, our contract theory, with the assistance of normalisation operation, provides an alternative characterisation of $\simeq_r$, which says that a realisable specification $\mathcal{P}$ is a refinement of another one $\mathcal{Q}$ iff $\mathcal{P}$ has less assumptions and more guarantees than $\mathcal{Q}$.

Definition 7 (Neutral contract). *A contract* $(I, O, \overline{AS}, \overline{GR})$ *is neutral iff* $\overline{AS}$ *is O-receptive and* $\overline{GR}$ *is I-receptive.*

The neutral contract of the above $\mathcal{P}$ is defined as $CT(\mathcal{P}) := TT(\mathcal{P})^N$.

Theorem 1. *Given realisable specifications* $\mathcal{P}_0$ *and* $\mathcal{P}_1$ *with* $CT(\mathcal{P}_0) = (I, O, AS_0, GR_0)$ *and* $CT(\mathcal{P}_1) = (I, O, AS_1, GR_1)$, $\mathcal{P}_0 \sqsubseteq_r \mathcal{P}_1$ *iff* $AS_1 \subseteq AS_0$ *and* $GR_0 \subseteq GR_1$.

Based on neutral contracts, we present the trace semantics of the parallel, disjunction, conjunction and quotient operations. The core part of the operations is based on a set of patterns originally presented in [20]. The specialisation required for the timed theory lies in the application of closure conditions like normalisation, realisation and *alphabet enlargement*.

Alphabet enlargement. Given a set Δ of actions disjoint from $I \cup O$, we define $(I, O, AS, GR)^\Delta := (I \cup \Delta, O, AS^\Delta, GR^\Delta)$, where $TT^\Delta := \{tt : (tA \cup \Delta)^* \mid tt \upharpoonright tA \in TT\} \cdot (tA \cup \Delta)^*$.

In the rest of the section we consider two realisable specifications $\mathcal{P}_i$ for $i \in \{0, 1\}$ with $CT(\mathcal{P}_i) = (I_i, O_i, AS_i, GR_i)$ and $\bar{i} = 1 - i$.

Proposition 2 (Parallel Composition). *If realisable specifications* $\mathcal{P}_0$ *and* $\mathcal{P}_1$ *are* $\|$-composable, *then* $CT(\mathcal{P}_0 \parallel \mathcal{P}_1) = (I, O, (AS_0^{\Delta_0} \cup AS_1^{\Delta_1}) \backslash (GR_0^{\Delta_0} \cup GR_1^{\Delta_1}), GR_0^{\Delta_0} \cup GR_1^{\Delta_1})^N$, *where* $I = (I_0 \cup I_1) \backslash O$, $O = O_0 \cup O_1$, $\Delta_0 = A_1 \backslash A_0$ *and* $\Delta_1 = A_0 \backslash A_1$.

Intuitively, the above says that the composed guarantees are the union of component guarantees, whilst the composed assumptions are the union of component assumptions *with those fulfilled by the composed guarantees deducted.*

Proposition 3 (Disjunction). *If realisable specifications* $\mathcal{P}_0$ *and* $\mathcal{P}_1$ *are* $\vee$-composable, *then* $CT(\mathcal{P}_0 \vee \mathcal{P}_1) = (I, O, AS_0 \cup AS_1, GR_0 \cap GR_1)^N$, *where* $I = I_0 = I_1$ *and* $O = O_0 = O_1$.

Disjunction places union over assumptions but intersection over guarantees.

Proposition 4 (Conjunction). *If realisable specifications* $\mathcal{P}_0$ *and* $\mathcal{P}_1$ *are* $\wedge$-composable, *then* $CT(\mathcal{P}_0 \wedge \mathcal{P}_1) = (I, O, AS_0 \cap AS_1, GR_0 \cup GR_1)^R$, *where* $I = I_0 = I_1$ *and* $O = O_0 = O_1$.

Conjunction places union over guarantees but intersection over assumptions.

Proposition 5 (Quotient). *If realisable specifications* $\mathcal{P}_0$ *and* $\mathcal{P}_1$ *are* %-*composable, then* $\mathcal{CT}(\mathcal{P}_0 \% \mathcal{P}_1) = (I, O, AS_0 \cup GR_1^{\Delta_1}, (GR_0 \backslash GR_1^{\Delta_1}) \cup (AS_1^{\Delta_1} \backslash AS_0))^R$, *where* $I = I_0 \cup O_1$, $O = O_0 \backslash O_1$ *and* $\Delta_1 = A_0 \backslash A_1$.

The composed assumptions of quotient is the union of $\mathcal{P}_0$-assumptions and $\mathcal{P}_1$-guarantees, whilst the composed guarantees is the union of (1) $\mathcal{P}_0$-guarantees outside of $\mathcal{P}_1$-guarantees and (2) $\mathcal{P}_1$-assumptions outside of $\mathcal{P}_0$-assumptions.

Mirror. The operation simply interchanges assumptions and guarantees.

Proposition 6. $\mathcal{CT}(\mathcal{P}^\neg) = (O, I, GR, AS)$.

Based on the above theorem we can prove the congruence result.

Theorem 2. $\simeq_r$ *is a congruence w.r.t.* $\|$, $\vee$, $\wedge$ *and* %, *subject to composability.*

8   Comparison with Related Work

Our framework builds on the timed specification theories of [12,13] and [10], albeit with significant differences.

Formalism. All three theories are based on variants of Timed I/O Automata. Our variant, like that of [12,13], uses two invariants (aka *input/output invariants* in [12,13]) in order to recover the duality between assumptions and guarantees; whereas the TIOAs in [10] possess no such duality. Our TIOA semantics, on the other hand, differs from those of [12,13] in the formulation of timed games and adoption of $\top/\bot$, which enable us to reduce the two transition relations in [12,13] to the one relation of Sect. 2.

Timed Game. Both [12,13] and [10] use two-player games, whereas our theory uses a three-player game (with a coin), which is crucial for uncovering the interference between the dual pair of two-player games, normalisation and realisation.

Even with the reduction to two-player games, our treatment of timed games is still different. In comparison with [12,13], our games require that *in each move a finite delay is followed by an action*. Therefore, a play cannot have consecutive delay moves and the possibility of zeno plays (i.e. an infinite play generating a finite trace) is ruled out. Furthermore, finite plays ending in timestop or timelock (i.e. semi-$\top$) can also be removed since we have the realisation game.

In comparison with [10], which is based on the timed game framework of [3,7], our games are strictly more aggressive in classifying winning states. For instance, [3,7] do not classify auto-$\top/\bot$ as winning states.

Linking with refinement calculus. The introduction of $\top$ and $\bot$, inspired by *abort* and *magic* of refinement calculus, significantly simplifies our theory (esp. the operator and refinement-relation definitions and the duality of games), in addition to pointing towards future theory unification.

In contrast, without $\top$ and $\bot$ the pursuit of duality in [12,13] does not end with a simplified theory[22]; especially it misses the second game in duality.

---

[22] [12,13] focuses on the definition of one operator, parallel composition, which is of considerable complexity.

On the other hand, [10] makes no attempt to link with refinement calculus.

Linear-time and Non-determinism. [10] and [11–13] uses timed alternating simulation as refinement, which (1) does not admit the weakest precongruence and (2) restricts [10,12,13] to consider only deterministic timed systems.

In contrast, we use linear-time semantics that gives rise to both the weakest precongruence and a $\top/\bot$-sensitive determinisation procedure, enabling us to handle non-deterministic timed systems.

Untimed theories. Finally, we remark that our linear-time specification theory owes much to the pioneering work on trace theories for asynchronous circuit verification, especially Dill's trace theory [14]. It is from this community that we take inspiration for the notion of game synthesis, double-trace semantics, auto-$\bot$ (aka auto-failure) and the derivation of quotient from mirror.[23]

In comparison with untimed theories, where only one game with auto-$\bot$ is required,[24] the timed theory requires timestop, two games *in duality*, three players and the new notion of semi-$\top/\bot$. Furthermore, with the use of invariants and co-invariants in timed specifications, timed theory can give a systematic treatment to liveness based on finite traces.

9   Conclusion and Future Work

We have devised a fully compositional specification theory for realisable real-time components. The linear-time theory enjoys strong algebraic properties, supports a full set of composition operators, and admits the weakest substitutive precongruence preserving safety and bounded-liveness error freedom.

Acknowledgments. We benefit from discussions with Prof. David Dill and Prof. Jeff Sanders on *timed extension of trace theory* and *refinement calculus*.

References

1. Alur, R., Dill, D.L.: A theory of timed automata. Theor. Comput. Sci. **126**, 183–235 (1994)
2. Armstrong, P.J., Lowe, G., Ouaknine, J., Roscoe, A.W.: Model checking timed CSP. In: A Festschrift on the Occasion of H. Barringer's 60th Birthday (2014)
3. Asarin, E., Maler, O., Pnueli, A., Sifakis, J.: Controller synthesis for timed automata. In: IFAC Symposium on System Structure and Control, Elsevier (1998)
4. Back, R.J., von Wright, J.: Refinement Calculus: A Systematic Introduction. Springer, New York (1998)
5. Benveniste, A., Caillaud, B., Nickovic, D., Passerone, R., Raclet, J., Reinkemeier, P., Sangiovanni-Vincentelli, A., Damm, W., Henzinger, T., Larsen, K.: Contracts for systems design. Technical report RR-8147, S4 team, INRIA, November 2012

---

[23] The mirror-based definition of quotient (for the untimed case) was first presented by Verhoeff as his Factorisation Theorem [24].

[24] Composition of untimed specifications will not generated new unrealisable behaviours.

6. Bertrand, N., Stainer, A., Jéron, T., Krichen, M.: A game approach to determinize timed automata. In: Hofmann, M. (ed.) FoSSaCS 2011. LNCS, vol. 6604, pp. 245–259. Springer, Heidelberg (2011). doi:10.1007/978-3-642-19805-2_17
7. Cassez, F., David, A., Fleury, E., Larsen, K.G., Lime, D.: Efficient on-the-fly algorithms for the analysis of timed games. In: Abadi, M., Alfaro, L. (eds.) CONCUR 2005. LNCS, vol. 3653, pp. 66–80. Springer, Heidelberg (2005). doi:10.1007/11539452_9
8. Chilton, C., Jonsson, B., Kwiatkowska, M.: Compositional assume-guarantee reasoning for input/output component theories. Sci. Comput. Program. **91**, 115–137 (2014). Part A
9. Chilton, C., Kwiatkowska, M., Wang, X.: Revisiting timed specification theories: a linear-time perspective. In: FORMATS 2012 (2012)
10. David, A., Larsen, K.G., Legay, A., Nyman, U., Wasowski, A.: Timed I/O automata: a complete specification theory for real-time systems. In: HSCC 2010 (2010)
11. de Alfaro, L., Henzinger, T.A.: Interface automata. In: ESEC/FSE 2001 (2001)
12. de Alfaro, L., Henzinger, T.A., Stoelinga, M.: Timed interfaces. In: EMSOFT 2002, vol. 2491, pp. 108–122 (2002)
13. de Alfaro, L., Stoelinga, M.: Interfaces: a game-theoretic framework for reasoning about component-based systems. Electron. Notes Theoret. Comput. Sci. **97**, 3–23 (2004)
14. Dill, D.L.: Trace theory for automatic hierarchical verification of speed-independent circuits. In: ACM Distinguished Dissertations. MIT Press (1989)
15. Ebergen, J.C.: A technique to design delay-insensitive VLSI circuits. Technical report CS-R8622, Centrum voor Wiskunde en Informatica, June 1986
16. He, J., Hoare, C.A.R., Sanders, J.W.: Data refinement refined. In: Robinet, B., Wilhelm, R. (eds.) ESOP 1986. LNCS, vol. 213, pp. 187–196. Springer, Heidelberg (1986). doi:10.1007/3-540-16442-1_14
17. Hoare, C.A.R., He, J., Sanders, J.W.: Prespecification in data refinement. Inf. Process. Lett. **25**(2), 71–76 (1987)
18. Meyer, B.: Design by contract. In: Advances in Object-Oriented Software Engineering. Prentice Hall (1991)
19. Morgan, C.C.: Programming from Specifications. Prentice Hall International Series in Computer Science, 2nd edn. Prentice Hall, UK (1994)
20. Negulescu, R.: Process spaces. In: Palamidessi, C. (ed.) CONCUR 2000. LNCS, vol. 1877, pp. 199–213. Springer, Heidelberg (2000). doi:10.1007/3-540-44618-4_16
21. Reed, G.M., Roscoe, A.W., Schneider, S.A.: CSP and Timewise Refinement, pp. 258–280. Springer, London (1991)
22. Roscoe, A.W.: The Theory and Practice of Concurrency. Prentice Hall, UK (1998)
23. van de Snepscheut, J.L.A.: Trace Theory and VLSJ Design. LNCS, vol. 200. Springer, Heidelberg (1985)
24. Verhoeff, T.: A Theory of Delay-Insensitive Systems. Ph.D. thesis, Dept. of Math. and C.S., Eindhoven University of Technology, May 1994
25. Wang, X.: Maximal confluent processes. In: Haddad, S., Pomello, L. (eds.) PETRI NETS 2012. LNCS, vol. 7347, pp. 188–207. Springer, Heidelberg (2012). doi:10.1007/978-3-642-31131-4_11
26. Wang, X., Kwiatkowska, M.Z.: On process-algebraic verification of asynchronous circuits. Fundam. Inform. **80**(1–3), 283–310 (2007)

Towards Verification of Cyber-Physical Systems with UTP and Isabelle/HOL

Simon Foster and Jim Woodcock[✉]

Department of Computer Science, University of York, York YO10 5GH, UK
{simon.foster,jim.woodcock}@york.ac.uk

Abstract. In this paper, we outline our vision for building verification tools for Cyber-Physical Systems based on Hoare and He's Unifying Theories of Programming (UTP) and interactive proof technology in Isabelle/HOL. We describe our mechanisation and explain some of the design decisions that we have taken to get a convenient and smooth implementation. In particular, we describe our use of lenses to encode state. We illustrate our work with an example UTP theory and describe the implementation of three foundational theories: designs, reactive processes, and the hybrid relational calculus. We conclude by reflecting on how tools are linked by unifying theories.

1 Introduction

Cyber-Physical Systems (CPS) are networks of computational devices that interact with the world through an array of sensors and actuators, and combine discrete computation with continuous physical models of their environment. For example, automated, driverless vehicles that are required to sense their environment, construct a real-time model of the present situation, make decisions about developing scenarios, and respond within a sufficiently short amount of time to ensure the safety of its passengers and other road users. Engineering such systems whilst demonstrating their trustworthiness is a major challenge. CPS engineering involves a wide range of modelling and programming paradigms [10], including concurrency, real-time, mobility, continuous variables, differential equations, object orientation, and diagrammatic languages. These aspects are represented by a variety of domain-specific and general-purpose languages, such as Simulink, Modelica, SysML, Java, and C, and thus engineering trustworthy CPS requires that we semantically integrate models in a consistent way, and then form arguments that the system as a whole exhibits certain properties.

Semantic integration has been made possible using the industry-developed standard FMI [5] (Functional Mockup Interface), which describes a CPS using a network of FMUs (Functional Mockup Units) that represent components or constituent systems. An FMU exposes a number of observable continuous variables that characterise the state of the individual model at a particular instant. Variables can either be of type input, output, or state, depending on whether they are

---

This paper is dedicated to Bill Roscoe on the occasion of his 60th birthday.

© Springer International Publishing AG 2017
T. Gibson-Robinson et al. (Eds.): Roscoe Festschrift, LNCS 10160, pp. 39–64, 2017.
DOI: 10.1007/978-3-319-51046-0_3

under the control of the FMU or the environment. FMUs can be stepped forward in time, which will cause these variables to evolve. A requested time step may be rejected and require curtailing if an event, such as a zero-crossing, occurs in the meantime, since the other FMUs may need to be notified. A master algorithm manages stepping the individual FMUs forward, and distributing information in between time steps. Aside from this minimal operational interface, each FMU is treated as a black box. An FMU can correspond to an abstract model of behaviour, an implementation of a particular component, or even a physical piece of hardware, which allows for Hardware in the Loop (HiL) simulation and testing. FMI thus allows one to describe heterogeneous multi-models that are described in different notations, and with different underlying semantic models, but are nevertheless integrated through a common operational interface.

Though FMI provides the necessary operational interface between different models and programs, it alone does not provide enough semantic information to verify them. In order to achieve that, we need a way of tackling the inherent semantic heterogeneity of the multi-model, for which we use Hoare and He's *Unifying Theories of Programming* [8,24,39] (UTP), which is a long-term research agenda to describe different computing paradigms and the formal links between them. It allows us to consider the various semantic aspects of a heterogeneous multi-model as individual theories that characterise a particular abstract programming or modelling paradigm. Hoare and He [24] show how the alphabetised relational calculus can be applied to construct a hierarchy of such theories, including simple imperative programs (relations), designs that correspond to pre- and postcondition specifications, and various theories of concurrent and parallel programs, including the process algebras ACP, CCS, and CSP [23]. Since the advent of UTP, a host of additional UTP theories have been developed that variously tackle paradigms like real-time programming [34], object-oriented programming [32], security and confidentiality [3], mobile processes [33], probabilistic modelling [6], and hybrid systems [15]. Moreover, the FMI API itself has been given a UTP-based semantics [9] that can be used as an interface to the semantic model of individual FMUs, and also allows a network of FMUs to be verified at this level using the FDR3 refinement checker [18]. The UTP approach allows computational theories to be formalised and explored as independent theories, and then later integrated to provide heterogeneous denotational semantic models. This can either be done directly through theory combination, or where theories are not directly compatible, such as in the case of discrete and continuous time, through the use of Galois connections that characterise best approximations.

In order to make UTP theories practically applicable to program verification, tool support is needed, and so we are also developing a theorem prover for UTP based on Isabelle/HOL [28], which we call *Isabelle/UTP* [16,17]. Isabelle is a powerful proof assistant that can be used both for the mechanisation of mathematics, and for the application of such mechanisations to program verification, which is famously illustrated by the seL4 microkernel verification project [26]. Another excellent example is the use of Kleene algebras to build program verification tools [1], from which Hoare logics, weakest-precondition calculi, rely-guarantee calculi, and separation logics have been created. Specifically of interest for CPS, there has also been a lot of recent work on formalising calculus, analysis, and ordinary differential equations (ODEs) in Isabelle [25], which can then be applied to verification of hybrid systems. Similarly, we are also building a mechanised library of UTP theories[1], including associated laws of programming and verification calculi.

Crucial to all of these developments is the ability to integrate external tools into Isabelle that can provide decision procedures for specific classes of problems. Isabelle is well suited to such integrations due to its architecture that is based on the ML and Scala programming languages, both of which can be used to implement plugins. Isabelle is sometimes referred to as the *Eclipse* of theorem provers [37]. The *sledgehammer* tool [4], for example, integrates a host of first-order automated theorem provers and SMT solvers, which often shoulder the burden of proof effort. *Sledgehammer* is used, for example, by [1], both at the theory engineering level, for constructing an algebraic hierarchy of Kleene algebras, and also at the verification level, where it is used to discharge first-order proof obligations. For verification of hybrid systems, it will also be necessary to integrate Isabelle with Computer Algebra Systems (CAS) like Mathematica, MATLAB, or SageMath, to provide solutions to differential equations, an approach that has been previously well used by the KeYmaera tool [30, 31].

Our vision is the use of Isabelle and UTP to provide the basis for CPS verification through formalisation of the fundamental building-block theories of a CPS multi-model, and the integration of tools that implement these theories for coordinated verification. This is, of course, an ambitious task and will require collaboration with a host of domain experts. Nevertheless, the vision of UTP is to provide a domain in which such cooperations can be achieved.

This paper gives an overview of the state of our work towards verification of CPS in UTP. In Sect. 2, we describe our approach to mechanising UTP in Isabelle/HOL, including its lens-based state model, meta-logical operators, and the alphabetised relational calculus. In Sect. 3, we show how an example theory can be mechanised and properties proved in *Isabelle/UTP*. In Sect. 4, we give an overview of the UTP theories of CPS that we have mechanised so far. In Sect. 5, we conclude.

2 Algebraic Foundations of Isabelle/UTP

In this section we summarise the foundations of *Isabelle/UTP*, our semantic embedding of the UTP in Isabelle/HOL, including its lens-based state model, meta-logical functions, and laws. *Isabelle/UTP* includes a model of alphabetised predicates and relations, proof tactics, and a library of proven algebraic laws. Following [11, 12], our predicate model is a parametric Isabelle type α upred $\widehat{=} \alpha \Rightarrow bool$ where α is the domain of possible observations, that is, the alphabet.

---

[1] This library can be viewed at github.com/isabelle-utp/utp-main.

The predicates-as-sets model is standard for most semantic embeddings of UTP, both deep [16,29,40] and shallow [11,12], and means that the predicate calculus operators can be obtained by simple lifting of the HOL equivalents. This means that we can automatically inherit the fact that, like HOL predicates, UTP predicates also form a complete lattice. Moreover, this facilitates automated proof for UTP predicates, which we make available through the predicate calculus tactic *pred-tac*, which can be used to discharge a large number of conjectures in our UTP theories.

A major difference between *Isabelle/UTP* and the deep embeddings is that we use Isabelle types to model alphabets, rather than representing them as finite sets. Use of types to model alphabets has the advantage that the type checker can be harnessed to ensure that variables mentioned in predicates are indeed present in the alphabet. What the predicate model lacks *a priori* though, is a way of manipulating the variables present in α; for this we use lenses.

2.1 Lenses in Brief

UTP is based on the paradigm of predicative programming, where programs are predicates [22]. This view results in a great simplification, with much of the machinery of traditional denotational semantics swept away, including the brackets mapping fragments of syntax to their denotation, as well as the environment used to evaluate variables in context. As an example of the latter, $x := 1$ is just another way of writing the predicate $x' = x + 1$. This simplified view of an environment-free semantics is difficult to maintain when thinking about more sophisticated programming techniques, such as aliasing between variables. See, for example a UTP semantics for separation logic [38], where environments are reintroduced to record variables stored on the heap and the stack. This raises the general methodological question of what is the most convenient way of modelling the state space for a UTP theory? The answer to this is especially important for our mechanisation in Isabelle, if we are to provide a generally reusable technique.

Rather than characterising variables as syntactic entities [16], we instead algebraically characterise the behaviour of variables using lenses [14,17]. Lenses allow us to represent variables as abstract projections on a state space with convenient ways to query and update in a uniform, compositional way. Variables are thus represented by regions of the state space that can be variously related, namelessly and spatially; these regions can be nested in arbitrary ways. Lenses are equipped with operators for transforming and decomposing the state space, enabling a purely algebraic account of state manipulations, including consistent viewing, updating, and composition. Importantly, the theory of lenses allows us to formalise meta-logical operations in the predicate calculus, such as freshness of variables and substitution of expressions for variable names.

A lens X from a view type V to a bigger source type S is a function $X : V \Longrightarrow S$ that allows us to focus on V independently of S. The signature of a lens consists of two functions:

get : $S \rightarrow V$
put : $S \rightarrow V \rightarrow S$

Consider as an example, a record lens. For the record

$(\!|\, forename : String, surname : String, age : Int \,|\!)$

there are seven lenses (the record has three components, so there are $2^3 - 1$ ways of decomposing it). Other examples include product, function, list, and finite map lenses. A number of algebraic laws might be satisfied by a particular lens:

$$\begin{aligned} \text{get}\,(\text{put}\, s\, v) &= v & \text{(PutGet)} \\ \text{put}\,(\text{put}\, s\, v')\, v &= \text{put}\, s\, v & \text{(PutPut)} \\ \text{put}\, s\,(\text{get}\, s) &= s & \text{(GetPut)} \end{aligned}$$

Lenses that satisfy combinations of these laws are classified in different ways [14,17]:

Well-behaved lenses	PutGet + GetPut
Very well-behaved lenses	addition of PutPut
Mainly well-behaved lenses	PutGet + PutPut

The majority of laws in *Isabelle/UTP* require variables to be modelled as mainly well-behaved lenses of type $\tau \Longrightarrow \alpha$, where τ is the variable type, though some laws depend on them being very well-behaved. From these axiomatic bases we define operations for querying and composing lenses. These include independence $(X \bowtie Y)$, sublens $(X \subseteq_L Y)$, equivalence $(X \approx_L Y)$, composition $(X \,;_L Y)$, and summation $(X +_L Y)$. All of these operations can be given denotations in terms of the get and put [17]; here we focus on the intuition and algebraic laws.

Independence, $X \bowtie Y$, describes when lenses $X : V_1 \Longrightarrow S$ and $Y : V_2 \Longrightarrow S$ identify disjoint regions of the common source S. Essentially, this is defined requiring that their put functions commute. In our example, the *forename* and *surname* lenses can be updated independently and thus *forename* $\bowtie$ *surname*. Lens independence is thus useful to describe when two variables are different. The sublens partial order, $X \subseteq_L Y$, conversely, describes the situation when X is spatially within Y, and thus an update to Y must affect X. From this partial order we can also define an equivalence relation on lenses in the usual way:

$$X \approx_L Y \;\hat{=}\; X \subseteq_L Y \wedge Y \subseteq_L X$$

Lens composition $X \,;_L Y : V_1 \Longrightarrow S$, for $X : V_1 \Longrightarrow V_2$ and $Y : V_2 \Longrightarrow S$, allows one to focus on regions within larger regions, and thus allows for state space nesting. For example, if a record has a field that is itself a record, then lens composition allows one to focus on the inner fields by composing the lenses for the outer with those of the inner record. Lens composition is closed under all the algebraic lens classes. We also define the unit lens, $0_L : unit \Longrightarrow S$, which has an empty view, and the identity lens, $1_L : S \Longrightarrow S$, whose view is the whole source. Both of these lenses are also very well-behaved.

Lens sum, $X +_L Y : V_1 \times V_2 \implies S$, parallel composes two independent lenses $X : V_1 \implies S$ and $Y : V_2 \implies S$. This combined lens characterises the regions of both X and Y. For example, the lens $forename +_L age$ allows us to query and updates both fields simultaneously, whilst leaving $surname$ alone. Finally, the associated lenses $\mathrm{fst}_L : V_1 \implies V_1 \times V_2$ and $\mathrm{snd}_L : V_2 \implies V_1 \times V_2$ allow us to view the left and right elements of a product source-type.

Our lenses operations satisfy the following algebraic laws, all of which has been mechanised [17], assuming X, Y, and Z are well-behaved lenses:

Theorem 1. *Lens algebraic laws*

$$X \mathbin{;}_L (Y \mathbin{;}_L Z) = (X \mathbin{;}_L Y) \mathbin{;}_L Z \tag{L1}$$

$$X \mathbin{;}_L \mathbf{1}_L = \mathbf{1}_L \mathbin{;}_L X = X \tag{L2}$$

$$X \bowtie Y \Leftrightarrow Y \bowtie X \tag{L3}$$

$$X +_L (Y +_L Z) \approx_L (X +_L Y) +_L Z \qquad X \bowtie Y, X \bowtie Z, Y \bowtie Z \tag{L4}$$

$$X +_L Y \approx_L Y +_L X \qquad\qquad X \bowtie Y \tag{L5}$$

$$X +_L \mathbf{0}_L \approx_L X \tag{L6}$$

$$X \subseteq_L X +_L Y \qquad\qquad X \bowtie Y \tag{L7}$$

$$\mathrm{fst}_L \bowtie \mathrm{snd}_L \tag{L8}$$

$$\mathrm{fst}_L \mathbin{;}_L (X +_L Y) = X \qquad\qquad X \bowtie Y \tag{L9}$$

$$X \bowtie (Y +_L Z) \qquad\qquad X \bowtie Y, X \bowtie Z \tag{L10}$$

The majority of these laws are self explanatory, however we comment on a few. Sum laws like L4 use lens equality rather than homogeneous HOL equality since the left- and right-hand sides have different types. Law L9 shows how the fst_L lens extracts the left-hand side of a product. Interestingly, these laws contain the separation algebra axioms [7], where separateness is characterised by $\bowtie$, and thus shows how our lens approach also generalises memory heap modelling. Thus we have an abstract model of state and an algebraic account of variables.

2.2 Expressions

Expressions have a similar type to predicates: $(\tau, \alpha)\, \mathsf{uexpr} \,\hat{=}\, \alpha \Rightarrow \tau$, where τ is the return type and α is the alphabet. We thus harness the HOL type system for ensuring well-formedness of expressions. HOL contains a large library of expression operators, such as arithmetic, and we lift these to UTP expressions. We also introduce the following core expressions constructs:

- $e =_u f$: equality of UTP expressions.
- $\&x$: obtains the value of lens $x : \alpha \implies \tau$ in the state space.
- $«v»$: embeds a HOL expression of type τ into a UTP expression.

In general for expressions, we try to follow the standard mathematical syntax from the UTP book [24] and associated tutorials [8,39]. For example, for the predicate operators we introduce overloaded constants so that the type system must determine whether operators like $\wedge$ and $\neg$ are the HOL or UTP versions. Where this is not possible, for example equality, we add a u subscript.

2.3   Meta-logical Functions

Isabelle/UTP is based on a semantic model for alphabetised predicates, rather than syntax. Since we do not formalise a fixed abstract syntax tree for UTP predicates, there are no notions such as free variables or substitution that ordinarily would be recursive functions on the tree. Instead, we introduce weaker semantic notions that are sufficient to characterise the laws of programming:

- *Unrestriction*, $x \mathbin{\sharp} P$, for lens x and predicate P, that semantically characterises variables that are fresh.
- *Semantic substitution*, $\sigma \dagger P$, for substitution function σ.
- *Alphabet extrusion*, $P \oplus_p a$, for lens a.
- *Alphabet restriction*, $P \restriction_p a$, for lens a.

Intuitively, $x \mathbin{\sharp} P$ holds, provided that P's valuation does not depend on x. For example, it follows that $x \mathbin{\sharp} \textbf{\textit{true}}$, $x \mathbin{\sharp} «v»$, and $x \mathbin{\sharp} (\exists x \bullet x >_u y)$, but not that $x \mathbin{\sharp} (x =_u 1 \wedge y =_u 2)$. What differentiates it from syntactic freshness is that $x \mathbin{\sharp} (x =_u 0 \vee x \neq_u 0)$, because the semantic valuation of this predicate is always $\textbf{\textit{true}}$. Unrestriction can alternatively be characterised as predicates which satisfy the fixed point $P = (\exists x \bullet P)$ for very well-behaved lens x. Substitution application $\sigma \dagger P$ applies a substitution σ to P. A substitution function $\sigma : \alpha \, \mathsf{usubst} \, (\hat{=} \, \alpha \Rightarrow \alpha)$ is a mapping from variables in the predicate's alphabet α to expressions to be inserted. Substitution update $\sigma(x \mapsto_s e)$ assigns the expression e to variable x in σ, and

$$[x_1 \mapsto_s e_1, \cdots, x_n \mapsto_s e_n] = \mathsf{id}(x_1 \mapsto_s e_1, \cdots, x_n \mapsto_s e_n)$$

creates a substitution for n variables. A substitution $P[\![e_1, \cdots, e_n / x_1, \cdots, x_n]\!]$ of n expressions to corresponding variables is then expressed as

$$[x_1 \mapsto_s e_1, \cdots, x_n \mapsto_s e_n] \dagger P$$

We now present some of the proven laws of substitutions.

Theorem 2 (Substitution query laws).

$$\langle \sigma(x \mapsto_s e) \rangle_s x = e \tag{SQ1}$$
$$\langle \sigma(y \mapsto_s e) \rangle_s x = \langle \sigma \rangle_s x \qquad\qquad if\, x \bowtie y \tag{SQ2}$$
$$\sigma(x \mapsto_s e, y \mapsto_s f) = \sigma(y \mapsto_s f) \qquad\qquad if\, x \subseteq_L y \tag{SQ3}$$
$$\sigma(x \mapsto_s e, y \mapsto_s f) = \sigma(y \mapsto_s f, x \mapsto_s e) \qquad\qquad if\, x \bowtie y \tag{SQ4}$$

SQ1 and SQ2 show how substitution lookup is evaluated. SQ3 shows that an assignment to a larger lens overrides a previous assignment to a small lens and SQ4 shows that independent lens assignments can commute.

Theorem 3 (Substitution application laws).

$$\sigma \dagger \&x = \sigma(x) \tag{SA1}$$

$$\sigma(x \mapsto_s e) \dagger P = \sigma \dagger P \qquad\qquad if x \sharp P \tag{SA2}$$

$$\sigma \dagger (\neg\, P) = \neg\, (\sigma \dagger P) \tag{SA3}$$

$$\sigma \dagger (P \wedge Q) = (\sigma \dagger P) \wedge (\sigma \dagger Q) \tag{SA4}$$

$$(\exists\, y \bullet P)[\![e/x]\!] = (\exists\, y \bullet P[\![e/x]\!]) \qquad if x \bowtie y, y \sharp e \tag{SA5}$$

These laws effectively subsume the usual syntactic substitution laws, for an arbitrary number of variables, many of which simply show how substitution distributes through predicate operators.

Alphabet extrusion $P \oplus_p a$, for $P : \alpha$ upred, extends the alphabet type using lens $a : \alpha \implies \beta$: it projects the predicate's alphabet α to "larger" alphabet type β. Lens a can be seen as a coercion that shows how the original state space α can be embedded into β. Effectively alphabet extrusion retains the predicate's characteristic valuation set over α, whilst filling in the rest of the variables in source alphabet β with arbitrary values.

Alphabet extrusion can be used to map a predicate α upred to a relation $(\alpha \times \alpha)$ upred by application of the lens $\mathsf{fst_L}$ or $\mathsf{snd_L}$, depending on whether a precondition or postcondition is desired. We give these two lifting operations the syntax $\lceil p \rceil_< \,\hat{=}\, p \oplus_p \mathsf{fst_L}$ and $\lceil p \rceil_> \,\hat{=}\, p \oplus_p \mathsf{snd_L}$, respectively, where p is a predicate in only undashed variables. We similarly create the substitution extension operator $\lceil \sigma \rceil_s$ that maps all variables and expressions to relational equivalents in undashed variables. Alphabet restriction is simply the inverse of extrusion: $P \restriction_p a$, for $P : \beta$ upred and $a : \alpha \implies \beta$, yields a predicate of alphabet α. Unlike extrusion this operation can be destructive if the predicate refers to variables in β but not in α. We demonstrate the following laws for extrusion and restriction:

Theorem 4 (Alphabet laws).

$$\boldsymbol{true} \oplus_p a = \boldsymbol{true} \tag{AE1}$$

$$\langle\!\langle v \rangle\!\rangle \oplus_p a = \langle\!\langle v \rangle\!\rangle \tag{AE2}$$

$$(P \wedge Q) \oplus_p a = (P \oplus_p a) \wedge (Q \oplus_p a) \tag{AE3}$$

$$\&x \oplus_p a = \&(x \,;\, {}_L\, a) \tag{AE4}$$

$$x \bowtie a \Rightarrow x \sharp (P \oplus_p a) \tag{AE5}$$

$$(P \oplus_p a) \restriction_p a = P \tag{AE6}$$

As indicated by laws AE1 and AE2, alphabet extrusion changes only the type of predicates with no variables; the body is left unchanged. Extrusion distributes through all the predicate operators, as expected, as indicated by law AE3. Applied to a variable, extrusion precomposes the variable lens with the given alphabet lens, as law AE4 demonstrates. Law AE5 shows that extrusion yields a predicate unrestricted by any variable x in the state-space extension. Finally, AE6 shows that alphabet restriction inverts alphabet extrusion.

2.4 Relations and Laws of Programming

A relation is a predicate with a product state space: α relation $\widehat{=} (\alpha \times \alpha)$ upred. Variables of α can therefore be lifted to input or output variables by composing the corresponding lens with fst_L or snd_L respectively.

Definition 1 (Relational variables).

$$\$x \;\widehat{=}\; x \,;\, {}_L \mathrm{fst}_L \qquad\qquad \$x' \;\widehat{=}\; x \,;\, {}_L \mathrm{snd}_L$$

It is important to note that "$\$x$" is distinguished from "$\&x$": the former has a product alphabet whilst the latter has a scalar one. Thus $\&x$ is useful when writing predicates which should not contain dashed variables: $\$x =_u \&y$ will usually result in a type error. Alphabet coercion can be used to convert between relations and predicates, and in particular it follows that $\lceil \&x \rceil_< = \$x$.

We define the relational calculus operators like $P \;;\; Q^2$ and I by lifting of the constructs for HOL relations. Again, this gives us access to various built-in laws for binary relations, and allows us to produce a tactic for relational calculus, *rel-tac*. Conditional (if-then-else) is introduced using predicate operators as $P \lhd b \rhd Q \;\widehat{=}\; (b \wedge P) \vee (\neg\, b \wedge Q)$. Assignment is defined as a general construct over a state substitution: $\langle \sigma \rangle_a : \alpha$ relation updates the state by applying the substitution $\sigma : \alpha$ usubst to the previous state. The alphabet of the substitution is α rather than $\alpha \times \alpha$ as this ensures that the assigned expressions cannot refer to post variables, as usual. The unary substitution $x := e$ can then be defined as $\langle [x \mapsto_s e] \rangle_a$, and similarly for simultaneous assignment of n variables. This has the advantage that the duality between substitution and assignment is clear in the corresponding algebraic laws. We have proven a large library of laws for relations, a selection of which is shown below, accompanied by the Isabelle names.

Theorem 5. *Relational laws of programming*

$$P\,;\,(Q\,;\,R) = (P\,;\,Q)\,;\,R \qquad\qquad \text{(seqr-assoc)}$$
$$I\,;\,P = P \qquad\qquad \text{(seqr-left-unit)}$$
$$\textbf{false}\,;\,P = \textbf{false} \qquad\qquad \text{(seqr-left-zero)}$$
$$(P \lhd b \rhd (Q \lhd b \rhd R)) = (P \lhd b \rhd R) \qquad\qquad \text{(cond-shadow)}$$
$$\lceil p \rceil_< \wedge I = I \wedge \lceil p \rceil_> \qquad\qquad \text{(pre-skip-post)}$$
$$(p\,;\,\textbf{true}) = p \Leftrightarrow \mathrm{snd}_L \sharp p \qquad\qquad \text{(precond-equiv)}$$
$$P\,;\,Q = (\exists\, v \bullet P[\![\langle\!\langle v \rangle\!\rangle/\$x']\!]\,;\,Q[\![\langle\!\langle v \rangle\!\rangle/\$x]\!]) \qquad \text{(seqr-middle)}$$
$$\langle \sigma \rangle_a\,;\,P = \lceil \sigma \rceil_s \dagger P \qquad\qquad \text{(assigns-r-comp)}$$
$$\langle \sigma \rangle_a\,;\,\langle \rho \rangle_a = \langle \rho \circ \sigma \rangle_a \qquad\qquad \text{(assigns-comp)}$$

We comment on a few of these. Law pre-skip-post shows that a precondition conjoined with relational identity can become a postcondition, since all variables

---

[2] This is written as $P \;;\; Q$ in Isabelle since ; is a delimiter for assumptions.

are identified. Law seqr-middle allows us to extract the intermediate value of a single variable in a sequential composition. Constant v is not a UTP state variable, but rather a logical HOL variable indicated by use of quoting. Law assigns-r-comp is a generalised version of the law $x := v \; ; \; P = P[v/x]$—it states that an assignment of σ followed by P equates to a substitution on P. We have to extend the alphabet of σ to match the relational alphabet of P using $\lceil \sigma \rceil_s$. Finally, law assigns-comp states that the sequential composition of two assignments corresponds to the functional composition of the two substitutions. From this law we can prove the assignment commutativity law:

Theorem 6. *Assignment commutativity*

$$(x := e \,; \; y := f) = (y := f \,; \; x := e) \quad if\, x \bowtie y, x \,\sharp\, f, y \,\sharp\, e \quad \text{(assign-commute)}$$

Proof. By combination of laws assigns-comp and SQ4. $\square$

Altogether we have proven over 200 hundred laws of predicate and relational calculus, many of which can be imported either from HOL or by Armstrong's algebraic hierarchy [1]. This then gives us the foundation on which to build UTP theories for Cyber-Physical Systems.

3   Example UTP Theory

In order to exemplify the use of Isabelle/UTP, we mechanise a simple theory representing Boyle's law. Boyle's law states that, for an ideal gas at fixed temperature, pressure p is inversely proportional to volume V, or more formally that for $k = p \cdot V$ is invariant, for constant k. We here encode this as a simple UTP theory. We first create a record to represent the alphabet of the theory consisting of the three variables k, p and V.

record *alpha-boyle =*
  boyle-k :: real
  boyle-p :: real
  boyle-V :: real

For now we have to explicitly cast the fields to lenses using the VAR syntactic transformation function [11] – in the future this will be automated. We also have to add the definitional equations for these variables to the simplification set for predicates to enable automated proof through our tactics.

definition $k :: real \implies alpha\text{-}boyle$ **where** $k = VAR\ boyle\text{-}k$
definition $p :: real \implies alpha\text{-}boyle$ **where** $p = VAR\ boyle\text{-}p$
definition $V :: real \implies alpha\text{-}boyle$ **where** $V = VAR\ boyle\text{-}V$

declare *k-def* [*upred-defs*] **and** *p-def* [*upred-defs*] **and** *V-def* [*upred-defs*]
We also prove that our new lenses are well-behaved and independent of each other. A selection of these properties is shown below.

lemma *vwb-lens-k* [*simp*]: *vwb-lens k* **by** (*unfold-locales, simp-all add: k-def*)
lemma *boyle-indeps* [*simp*]: $k \bowtie p \quad p \bowtie k \quad k \bowtie V \quad V \bowtie k \quad p \bowtie V \quad V \bowtie p$
  by (*simp-all add: k-def p-def V-def lens-indep-def*)

3.1   Static Invariant

We first create a simple UTP theory representing Boyle's laws on a single state, as a static invariant healthiness condition. We state Boyle's law using the function B, which recalculates the value of the constant k based on p and V.

definition $B(\varphi) = ((\exists\ k \cdot \varphi) \wedge (\&k =_u \&p\cdot\&V))$

We can then prove that B is both idempotent and monotone simply by application of the predicate tactic. Idempotence means that healthy predicates cannot be made more healthy. Together with idempotence, monotonicity ensures that the image of the healthiness function forms a complete lattice, which is useful to allow the representation of recursive constructions with the theory.

lemma *B-idempotent*: $B(B(P)) = B(P)$ **by** *pred-tac*
lemma *B-monotone*: $X \sqsubseteq Y \implies B(X) \sqsubseteq B(Y)$ **by** *pred-tac*

We also create some example observations; the first (φ_1) satisfies Boyle's law and the second doesn't (φ_2).

definition $\varphi_1 = ((\&p =_u 10) \wedge (\&V =_u 5) \wedge (\&k =_u 50))$
definition $\varphi_2 = ((\&p =_u 10) \wedge (\&V =_u 5) \wedge (\&k =_u 100))$

We first prove an obvious property: that these two predicates are different observations. We must show that there exists a valuation of one which is not of the other. This is achieved through application of *pred-tac*, followed by *sledgehammer* [4] which yields a *metis* proof.

lemma φ_1-*diff*-φ_2: $\varphi_1 \neq \varphi_2$
  by (*pred-tac, metis select-convs num.distinct*(5) *numeral-eq-iff semiring-norm*(87))

We prove that φ_1 satisfies Boyle's law by application of the predicate calculus tactic, *pred-tac*.

lemma *B*-φ_1: φ_1 *is B* **by** (*pred-tac*)

We prove that φ_2 does not satisfy Boyle's law by showing that applying B to it results in φ_1. We prove this using Isabelle's natural proof language, Isar, details of which can be found in the reference manual [36]. The proof below is annotated with comments.

lemma *B*-φ_2: $B(\varphi_2) = \varphi_1$
proof –
  — We first expand out the definition of φ_2
  have $B(\varphi_2) = B(\&p =_u 10 \wedge \&V =_u 5 \wedge \&k =_u 100)$
    by (*simp add:* φ_2-*def*)
  — Then the definition of B
  also have ... $= ((\exists\ k \cdot \&p =_u 10 \wedge \&V =_u 5 \wedge \&k =_u 100) \wedge \&k =_u \&p\cdot\&V)$
    by (*simp add: B-def*)
  — The existentially quantifier k can be removed
  also have ... $= (\&p =_u 10 \wedge \&V =_u 5 \wedge \&k =_u \&p\cdot\&V)$
    by *pred-tac*
  — We show that $(10::'a) \cdot (5::'a) = (50::'a)$
  also have ... $= (\&p =_u 10 \wedge \&V =_u 5 \wedge \&k =_u 50)$
    by *pred-tac*

— This is then definitionally equal to φ_1
also have ... = φ_1
  by (*simp add:* φ_1-*def*)
— Finally we show the overall thesis
finally show *?thesis* .
qed

3.2 Dynamic Invariants

Next we build a relational theory that allows the pressure and volume to be changed, whilst still respecting Boyle's law. We create two dynamic invariants for this purpose.

definition $D1(P) = (($\$$k =_u$ \$$p\cdot$\$$V \Rightarrow$ \$$k\,' =_u$ \$$p\,'\cdot$\$$V\,') \wedge P)$
definition $D2(P) = ($\$$k\,' =_u$ \$$k \wedge P)$

D1 states that if Boyle's law satisfied in the previous state, then it should be satisfied in the next state. We define this by conjunction of the formal specification of this property with the predicate. The annotations $\$p$ and $\$p\,'$ refer to relational variables p and p'. *D2* states that the constant k indeed remains constant throughout the evolution of the system, which is also specified as a conjunctive healthiness condition. As before we demonstrate that *D1* and *D2* are both idempotent and monotone.

lemma *D1-idempotent:* $D1(D1(P)) = D1(P)$ **by** *rel-tac*
lemma *D2-idempotent:* $D2(D2(P)) = D2(P)$ **by** *rel-tac*

lemma *D1-monotone:* $X \sqsubseteq Y \Longrightarrow D1(X) \sqsubseteq D1(Y)$ **by** *rel-tac*
lemma *D2-monotone:* $X \sqsubseteq Y \Longrightarrow D2(X) \sqsubseteq D2(Y)$ **by** *rel-tac*

Since these properties are relational, we discharge them using our relational calculus tactic *rel-tac*. Next we specify three operations that make up the signature of the theory.

definition *InitSys ip iV*
  $= ((\text{«}ip\text{»} >_u 0 \wedge \text{«}iV\text{»} >_u 0)^\top \;;;\; p,V,k := \text{«}ip\text{»},\text{«}iV\text{»},(\text{«}ip\text{»}\cdot\text{«}iV\text{»}))$

definition *ChPres dp*
  $= ((\&p + \text{«}dp\text{»} >_u 0)^\top \;;;\; p := \&p + \text{«}dp\text{»} \;;;\; V := (\&k/\&p))$

definition *ChVol dV*
  $= ((\&V + \text{«}dV\text{»} >_u 0)^\top \;;;\; V := \&V + \text{«}dV\text{»} \;;;\; p := (\&k/\&V))$

InitSys initialises the system with a given initial pressure (ip) and volume (iV). It assumes that both are greater than 0 using the assumption construct $c^\top$ which equates to $I\!I$ if c is true and *false* (i.e. errant) otherwise. It then creates a state assignment for p and V, uses the B healthiness condition to make it healthy (by calculating k), and finally turns the predicate into a postcondition using the $\lceil P \rceil_>$ function.

  ChPres raises or lowers the pressure based on an input dp. It assumes that the resulting pressure change would not result in a zero or negative pressure, i.e. $p + dp > 0$. It assigns the updated value to p and recalculates V using the original value of k. *ChVol* is similar but updates the volume.

lemma *D1-InitSystem*: *D1* (*InitSys ip iV*) = *InitSys ip iV* **by** *rel-tac*
InitSys is *D1*, since it establishes the invariant for the system. However, it is not *D2* since it sets the global value of k and thus can change its value. We can however show that both *ChPres* and *ChVol* are healthy relations.

lemma *D1*: *D1* (*ChPres dp*) = *ChPres dp* **and** *D1* (*ChVol dV*) = *ChVol dV*
  by (*rel-tac, rel-tac*)

lemma *D2*: *D2* (*ChPres dp*) = *ChPres dp* **and** *D2* (*ChVol dV*) = *ChVol dV*
  by (*rel-tac, rel-tac*)

Finally we show a calculation for a simple animation of Boyle's law, where the initial pressure and volume are set to 10 and 4, respectively, and then the pressure is lowered by 2.

lemma *ChPres-example*:
  (*InitSys 10 4* ;; *ChPres* (−2)) = $p,V,k := 8,5,40$
proof −
  — *InitSys* yields an assignment to the three variables
  have *InitSys 10 4* = $p,V,k := 10,4,40$
    by (*rel-tac*)
  — This assignment becomes a substitution
  hence (*InitSys 10 4* ;; *ChPres* (−2))
      = (*ChPres* (−2))⟦$10,4,40/\$p,\$V,\$k$⟧
    by (*simp add: assigns-r-comp alpha*)
  — Unfold definition of *ChPres*
  also have ... = ((&p − 2 >$_u$ 0)$^\top$⟦$10,4,40/\$p,\$V,\$k$⟧
          ;; $p := \&p − 2$;; $V := \&k / \&p$)
    by (*simp add: ChPres-def lit-num-simps usubst unrest*)
  — Unfold definition of assumption
  also have ... = (($p,V,k := 10,4,40$ ◁ (8 :$_u$ *real*) >$_u$ 0 ▷ *false*)
          ;; $p := \&p − 2$;; $V := \&k / \&p$)
    by (*simp add: rassume-def usubst alpha unrest*)
  — (0::'a) < (8::'a) is true; simplify conditional
  also have ... = ($p,V,k := 10,4,40$;; $p := \&p − 2$;; $V := \&k / \&p$)
    by *rel-tac*
  — Application of both assignments
  also have ... = $p,V,k := 8,5,40$
    by *rel-tac*
  finally show *?thesis* .
qed

4   Theories of Cyber-Physical Systems

In this section we describe some the key UTP theories we have mechanised which form the basis for our future semantic model of Cyber-Physical Systems.

4.1 Designs

The simplest theory in UTP is that of a nondeterministic imperative programming language expressed in the relational calculus of alphabetised predicates arranged in a complete lattice. The ordering is refinement, which is defined as universal inverse implication: $(P \sqsubseteq Q) = [Q \Rightarrow P]$ (here the brackets are universal closure over the alphabet). The worst program, the bottom of the lattice, is abort, with semantics *true*; the best program, the top of the lattice, is miracle, with semantics *false*. This theory of nondeterministic programming is that of partial correctness, with recursion given a strongest fixed-point semantics. The choice of semantics for recursion is a very practical one to make the theory work. If the weakest fixed-point were chosen, then some desirable laws would fail to hold. For example, we'd certainly like the following law to hold: *abort* ; $P = abort$. Choosing a weakest fixed-point semantics gives us the equation (*true* ; $x := 0$) = $x := 0$, for a state with a single variable x: it is possible to recover from abort (for example, a non-termination recursion) and behave as though it had never happened. On the other hand, the choice of the strongest fixed-point would validate the law, thus: (*false* ; $x := 0$) = *false*. It turns out that the strongest fixed-point is also easier to reason with. Compare the laws defining the extreme properties of the two operators:

$$(F(P) \sqsubseteq P) \Rightarrow (\mu F \sqsubseteq P) \qquad (S \sqsubseteq F(S)) \Rightarrow (S \sqsubseteq \nu F)$$

The left-hand law states that if P is a pre-fixed-point of F, then it can't be any weaker than the weakest fixed-point. This would be useful in reasoning about a recursive specification μF of a program P. The right-hand law states that if S is a post-fixed-point of F, then it can't be any stronger than the strongest fixed-point. This would be useful in reasoning about a recursive implementation νF of a specification S. The left-hand law seems more practically useful than the right-hand one. The cost of this practical benefit is an inescapable law: $S \sqsubseteq abort$, for every specification S, since abort, with a strongest fixed-point semantics, is the top of the lattice. So the result is a theory of partial correctness: if we have $S \sqsubseteq P$, and the P terminates (that is, it is not *abort*), then P is correct. For this price, a simple rule is obtained in Hoare logic for reasoning about the (partial) correctness of loops:

$$\frac{\{\, b \wedge c \,\} \, P \, \{\, c \,\}}{\{\, b \wedge c \,\} \ \textbf{\textit{while}} \ b \ \textbf{\textit{do}} \ P \ \{\, \neg \ b \wedge c \,\}}$$

So it was that the proof rules for fixed-points determined the early emphasis of partial correctness in program verification.

UTP's theory of designs extends the treatment of the nondeterministic imperative programming language from partial to total correctness. This is done by restricting attention to a subclass of predicate for which the left and right-zero laws actually hold: (*true* ; P) = *true* = (P ; *true*). These predicates are called designs.

The insight is to capture the theory of assertional reasoning and assumption-commitment pairs as single relations by adding two observations: that a program has started ok and that a program has terminated ok'. A design is then a precondition-postcondition pair

$$(P \vdash Q) \;\hat{=}\; (ok \wedge P \Rightarrow ok' \wedge Q) \quad \text{for } P \text{ and } Q \text{ not containing } ok \text{ or } ok'$$

This is read as "if the program has started (ok) and the precondition P holds, then it must terminate (ok') in a state where the postcondition Q holds." This is clearly a statement of total correctness. Notice that, although the syntax of a design is a pair of alphabetised predicates, its meaning is encoded as a single predicate.

Designs form a complete lattice with **false** $\vdash Q$ (abort) at the bottom and **true** $\vdash$ **false** (miracle) at the top. These two definitions can be simplified as **true** and $\neg ok$, respectively. Thus, abort permits any and every behaviour, whilst a miracle, quite properly, cannot be started, and so has no behaviours at all.

A theory in UTP has three components. The first is the signature; here this is the syntax of the programming language and the syntax of a design pair. The second component is the alphabet; here this is the two boolean observations ok and ok' NS ny program variables. The third component is a set of healthiness conditions characterising membership of the theory. In the case of designs, there are two healthiness conditions, one concerning each observational variable. The first states that no observation may be made of a program before it has started. This is necessary for proper initialisation and to make sequential composition work properly.

$$\textbf{H1}(P) \;\hat{=}\; ok \Rightarrow P$$

The healthiness condition is presented as a monotone idempotent function; its fixed points are its healthy predicates.

The second healthiness condition concerns termination and seeks to eliminate the specification that would require a program not to terminate: $\neg ok'$. Refinement allows us to write a correct program that improves on what a specification requires. In our programming methodology, anything is better than nontermination, so you should not be allowed to require nontermination. The following healthiness condition formalises this:

$$\textbf{H2}(P) = P \;\Leftrightarrow\; [P^f \Rightarrow P^t]$$

where $P^f \;\hat{=}\; P[\textbf{false}/ok']$ and $P^t \;\hat{=}\; P[\textbf{true}/ok']$. Hoare and He show how to present this condition in terms of the fixed points of the monotone idempotent function **H2** [H&H]. They also shows how to characterise the space of designs in three equivalent ways: syntactically, as the fixed points of these two healthiness conditions, and as the solutions of algebraic equations (left unit and left zero). Finally, they prove that the lattice of designs is closed under the nondeterministic programming language's combinators with assignment as the basis.

The theory of designs has been mechanised in *Isabelle/UTP* and we show an excerpt from this theory. We introduce the alphabet by parametric type

$'\alpha$ *alphabet-d* [11,12] which extends the alphabet $'\alpha$ with the variable lens *ok*. Moreover, we add the useful type synonym

type-synonym $'\alpha$ *hrelation-d* = ($'\alpha$ *alphabet-d*, $'\alpha$ *alphabet-d*) *relation*

which describes a homogeneous relation with a design alphabet. We then use these to create the signature and healthiness conditions of designs in a similar way to the theory demonstrated in Sect. 3. Then many standard laws of designs can be proved automatically, as the following demonstrates.

theorem *design-false-pre*: ($false \vdash P$) = *true* **by** *rel-tac*

Of course not all properties can be proved this way, and in any case there is great value in presenting the intuition behind a theorem through proof. We demonstrate this firstly that the syntactic form of designs is equivalent to the healthiness conditions.

theorem *H1-H2-eq-design*: *H1* (*H2 P*) = $(\neg P^f) \vdash P^t$
proof −
  have *H1* (*H2 P*) = ($\$ok \Rightarrow H2(P)$)
    by (*simp add*: *H1-def*)
  also have ... = ($\$ok \Rightarrow (P^f \vee (P^t \wedge \$ok'))$)
    by (*metis H2-split*)
  also have ... = ($\$ok \wedge (\neg P^f) \Rightarrow \$ok' \wedge \$ok \wedge P^t$)
    by *rel-tac*
  also have ... = $(\neg P^f) \vdash P^t$
    by *rel-tac*
  finally show *?thesis* .
qed

This proof makes use of the auxiliary theorem *H2-split* to expand out **H2** which states that $\mathbf{H2}(P) = P^f \vee (P^t \wedge ok')$. We also show that the design identity $\mathbb{I}_D$ is a right unit of any design. We define this element of the signature as follows:

definition *skip-d* :: $'\alpha$ *hrelation-d* (II_D) **where** $II_D = (true \vdash_r II)$

The turnstile $P \vdash_r Q$ is a specialisation of $P \vdash Q$ which requires that neither P nor Q have ok, ok' in their alphabets. It use alphabet extrusion and the Isabelle type system to ensure this: $ok \vdash_r P$ entails a type error. Proof of the right unit law requires that we can calculate the sequential composition of two designs, which the following theorem demonstrates.

theorem *rdesign-composition-cond*:
  assumes $out\alpha \,\sharp\, p_1$
  shows $((p_1 \vdash_r Q_1) \mathbin{;;} (P_2 \vdash_r Q_2)) = ((p_1 \wedge \neg (Q_1 \mathbin{;;} (\neg P_2))) \vdash_r (Q_1 \mathbin{;;} Q_2))$
  — proof omitted

    This is itself a specialisation of the more complex design composition law [8] which adds the requirement that the assumption of the first design be a condition. Thus the theorem assumes $p1$ does not refer to variables in the output alphabet, $out\alpha$, which is just shorthand for fst_L. The law demonstrates the advantages of the alphabets-as-types approach: we do not require provisos that p_1, Q_1, P_2, and Q_2 do not refer to ok and ok' which greatly simplifies the theorem and its application. We can now prove the unit law, which we do in Isar.

theorem *rdesign-left-unit*:
  fixes $P\ Q\ ::\ '\alpha$ *hrelation-d*
  shows $(II_D\ ;;\ P \vdash_r Q) = (P \vdash_r Q)$
proof −
  — We first expand out the definition of the design identity
  have $(II_D\ ;;\ P \vdash_r Q) = (true \vdash_r II\ ;;\ P \vdash_r Q)$
    by (*simp add: skip-d-def*)
  — Next, we apply the design composition law above in a subproof
  also have ... $= (true \land \neg (II\ ;;\ \neg P)) \vdash_r (II\ ;;\ Q)$
  proof −
    — The assumption of identity is **true** so it is easy to discharge the proviso
    have $out\alpha\ \sharp\ true$
      by *unrest-tac*
    — From this we can apply the composition law
    thus *?thesis*
      using *rdesign-composition-cond* **by** *blast*
  qed
  — Simplification then allows us to remove extraneous terms
  also have ... $= (\neg (\neg P)) \vdash_r Q$
    by *simp*
  — Finally, we can show the thesis
  finally show *?thesis* **by** *simp*
qed

4.2   Reactive Processes

A more sophisticated UTP theory is that of reactive processes. In the reactive paradigm, a process is a pattern of behaviour expressed in terms of observable events. In general, the behaviour is as follows. The process minds its own business internally until it's ready to interact with its environment; it then pauses and waits until its environment is cooperative, whereupon it reacts and then returns to its own business; this behaviour is repeated. A reactive process characteristically has two sorts or after-states: intermediate states, where the process is waiting for interaction with its environment; and final states, where the process has reached its ultimate computation, completed its behaviour, and terminated.

We investigate this paradigm in terms of its three components as a UTP theory.

First, we consider the signature of the theory. We consider a simple extension of the nondeterministic programming language in the previous section, augmented by an operator that synchronises on an event with the environment. If P is a reactive process, then $a \rightarrow P$ is another process that first engages in the synchronisation of the event a and then behaves like the process P.

Next, we consider the alphabet of observational variables.

We can observe the sequence of events synchronised by an individual reactive process. We call this sequence a trace, and denote its before-value by tr and its intermediate or final value by tr'. It is a sequence over the set of events.

We can also observe whether a reactive process is in one of its waiting states. This is an observation that we denote by the boolean variables *wait*, in the before state, and *wait'* in the intermediate or final state.

The stability of a reactive process is described in the same way as the termination of a nondeterministic program. That is, *ok'* describes whether the reactive process has reached a stable state, whether it be intermediate or final. Thus, the combination of *ok'* and *wait'* is of interest. If $ok' \land wait'$, then the process has reached a stable intermediate state. If $ok' \land \neg\ wait'$, then the process has reached a stable final state. Regardless of the value of *wait'*, if $\neg\ ok'$, then the process is in a divergent state.

The final observation that may be made of a reactive process concerns its liveness. The process $a \rightarrow SKIP$ is waiting to perform the event a and then terminate (*SKIP*). While it is waiting, it cannot refuse to perform a. The observational variable *ref'* records this fact. We can think of the value of *ref'* as an experiment offered by the environment: will the process deadlock if we offer these events? Suppose that the universe of events is $\{a, b, c\}$. Our process will deadlock if we offer it the empty experiment $\varnothing$ (all processes have this property). It will also deadlock if we offer it either or both b or c. The maximal refusal is the pair $\{b, c\}$; note that the process will refuse any subset: *ref'* is downward closed. Now consider the nondeterministic process $a \rightarrow SKIP \sqcap b \rightarrow SKIP$. The nondeterministic choice can be resolved in two ways: if the first branch is taken, then it may refuse b; if the second branch is taken, then it may refuse a. Note that although *ref'* is downward closed, there is no maximal refusal set. Recording a refusal set is one way of capturing this kind of nondeterministic choice. Our process is then partially specified by the predicate

if *wait'* **then**
$\quad (tr' = tr) \land (ref' \subseteq \{b, c\} \lor ref' \subseteq \{a, c\}) \land ok'$
else
$\quad ((tr' = tr \frown \langle a \rangle) \lor (tr' = tr \frown \langle b \rangle)) \land ok'$

Reactive processes have three healthiness conditions. The first requires that the trace grows monotonically, so that history is never edited.

$$\boldsymbol{R1}(P) \ \widehat{=} \ P \land tr \leq tr'$$

(Here, $\leq$ denotes the sequence prefix relation.)

The second healthiness condition requires that a process P is insensitive to the trace of events that occur before P is initiated:

$$\boldsymbol{R2}(P) \ \widehat{=} \ P[\langle\rangle, tr' - tr/tr, tr'] \lhd tr \leq tr' \rhd P$$

(Here we use the sequence subtraction operator.)

Finally, sequential composition must be made to work as it does in a programming language, and not merely as relational composition. In the sequence P ; Q, if P is waiting, then Q must not be initiated. Define

$$\mathit{I\!I}_{rea} \mathrel{\widehat{=}} \textbf{\textit{R1}} \circ \textbf{\textit{H1}}((ok', wait', tr', ref', x') = (ok, wait, tr, ref, x))$$

where x is a list of the process's state variables. Our healthiness condition is

$$\textbf{\textit{R3}}(P) \mathrel{\widehat{=}} (\mathit{I\!I}_{rea} \lhd wait \rhd P)$$

For the full semantics, other healthiness conditions are needed, but almost all the process algebraic laws for CSP can be proved correct based on the semantics presented so far, providing we add two more healthiness conditions concerning ok and ok'. Fortunately, we have already presented them: they are **H1** and **H2**, simply adjusted for the larger alphabet of reactive processes.

The CSP processes are the fixed points of the montone idempotent function

$$\textbf{\textit{CSP}} \mathrel{\widehat{=}} \textbf{\textit{R1}} \circ \textbf{\textit{R2}} \circ \textbf{\textit{R3}} \circ \textbf{\textit{H1}} \circ \textbf{\textit{H2}}$$

Equivalently, by theorem *H1-H2-eq-design* every **CSP** relation can be stated as a reactive design of the form $\textbf{\textit{R}}(P \vdash Q)$, where $\textbf{\textit{R}} \mathrel{\widehat{=}} \textbf{\textit{R1}} \circ \textbf{\textit{R2}} \circ \textbf{\textit{R3}}$, and P and Q are assumptions and commitments over the trace and program variables. For example, the worst CSP process is **Chaos** $\mathrel{\widehat{=}} \textbf{\textit{R}}(\textbf{false} \vdash \textbf{true})$, which fails to satisfy its assumption and thus establishes nothing other than that the trace must increase monotonically (by **R1**). Every CSP process can be expressed as such a reactive design [8].

We have likewise mechanised the theory of reactive designs, and here show a few of the properties proved, though without proofs for reasons of space. The first property shows that **Chaos** is indeed the bottom of the lattice – every CSP process refines it. The second shows that **Chaos** is a left zero for sequential composition: since $wait'$ is always **false** the second process can never be executed.

theorem *Chaos-least*: **assumes** P *is CSP* **shows** $Chaos \sqsubseteq P$
— proof omitted

theorem *Chaos-left-zero*: **assumes** P *is CSP* **shows** $(Chaos \;;\; P) = Chaos$
— proof omitted

More laws we have proved can be found in our online UTP repository[3].

4.3 Hybrid Relational Calculus

Differential Algebraic Equations (DAEs) are often used to model the continuously evolving dynamic behaviour of a system. The theory of hybrid relations in UTP unifies discrete and continuous variables used in such models. We introduce

---

[3] github.com/isabelle-utp/utp-main/blob/master/utp/utp_reactive.thy.

a theory of continuous-time processes that embeds in the theory of alphabetised predicates trajectories of states evolving over time intervals representing piecewise continuous behaviour.

We start with the UTP theory of alphabetised relations, which therefore will not capture continuous process termination or stability. This allows us to treat the behaviour of hybrid processes as an individual phenomenon, before augmenting the theory with additional structure to capture such properties by embedding it in the theory of timed reactive designs [19,35].

Alphabet. Our theory has two variables $ti, ti' : \mathbb{R}_{\geq 0}$ that observe the start and end time of the current computation interval and its duration $\ell = ti' - ti$, as in the Duration Calculus [41]. Following [20], we classify the alphabet of a hybrid relation in three disjoint parts: input variables, $\mathrm{in}\alpha(P)$; output variables, $\mathrm{out}\alpha(P)$; and continuous variables, $\mathrm{con}\alpha(P)$ (such as $\underline{x}, \underline{y}, \underline{z}$). Continuous variables of type $\mathbb{R}$ describe a value at a particular instant of time; trajectory variables of type $\mathbb{R}_{\geq 0} \to \mathbb{R}$ describe the evolution of a value over all time (values outside $[ti, ti')$ are irrelevant).

A junction between the discrete and continuous world is established by making a discrete copies $x, x' : \mathbb{R}$ of the values of each continuous variable $\underline{x} : \mathbb{R}_{\geq 0} \to \mathbb{R}$ at the beginning and end of the interval under observation. Discrete variables that are not surrogates for continuous variables are in the sub-alphabet

$$\mathrm{dis}\alpha(P) \mathrel{\widehat{=}} \{\, x \in \mathrm{in}\alpha(P) \mid \underline{x} \notin \mathrm{con}\alpha(P) \,\} \cup \{\, x' \in \mathrm{out}\alpha(P) \mid \underline{x} \notin \mathrm{con}\alpha(P) \,\}$$

Following [13], we define a continuous variable lifting operator from a predicate in instant variables to one in trajectory variables:

$$P @ \tau \mathrel{\widehat{=}} \{\, \underline{x} \mapsto \underline{x}(\tau) \mid \underline{x} \in \mathrm{con}\alpha(P) \backslash \{\underline{t}\} \,\} \dagger P$$

In $P @ \tau$, we map every flat continuous variable (other than the distinguished time variable $\underline{t} \in [ti..ti')$) to a corresponding variable lifted over the time domain. So the new predicate holds for values of continuous variables at the instant τ, a variable that is free in P. So each flat continuous variable $\underline{x} : T$ is transformed to a time-dependent function $\underline{x} : \mathbb{R} \to T$ type. In this way, we lift time predicates to intervals.

Our hybrid theory has two healthiness conditions:

$$\textbf{HCT1}(P) \mathrel{\widehat{=}} P \wedge ti \leq ti'$$

$$\textbf{HCT2}(P) \mathrel{\widehat{=}}$$
$$P \wedge$$
$$\left(ti < ti' \Rightarrow \bigwedge\nolimits_{\underline{v} \in \mathrm{con}\alpha(P)} \left(\begin{array}{l} \exists I : \mathbb{R}_{\mathrm{oseq}} \bullet \\ \mathrm{ran}(I) \subseteq \{ti \ldots ti'\} \\ \wedge\, \{ti, ti'\} \subseteq \mathrm{ran}(I) \\ \wedge\, (\forall n < \#I - 1 \bullet \underline{v}\ \text{cont-on}\ [I_n, I_{n+1})) \end{array} \right) \right)$$

where $\quad \mathbb{R}_{\mathrm{oseq}} \mathrel{\widehat{=}} \{\, x : \mathrm{seq}\,\mathbb{R} \mid \forall n < \#x - 1 \bullet x_n < x_{n+1} \,\}$

$$f\ \text{cont-on}\ [m, n] \mathrel{\widehat{=}} \forall t \in [m, n) \bullet \lim_{x \to t} f(x) = f(t)$$

HCT1 requires that time advances monotonically. **HCT2** requires that every continuous variable $\underline{v}$ is piecewise continuous: for non-empty intervals there is a finite number of discontinuous points (the range of I) between ti and ti'. The set of totally ordered sequences $\mathbb{R}_{oseq}$ captures the set of discontinuities; the continuity of f is defined in the usual way by requiring that at each point in $[ti, ti')$, the limit correctly predicts the function.

Both healthiness conditions are idempotent, monotone, and commutative, as is their composition **HCT** = **HCT2** ∘ **HCT1**. The image of **HCT** a complete lattice.

The signature of our theory is as follows:

$$P, Q ::= \mathbb{II} \mid P \; ; \; Q \mid P \lhd b \rhd Q \mid x := e \mid P^* \mid P^\omega \mid$$
$$\lceil P \rceil \mid \langle F_n \mid b \rangle \mid P [b] Q$$

This syntax extends the signature of the alphabetised relational calculus with operators to specify intervals $\lceil P \rceil$, differential algebraic equations $\langle F_n \mid b \rangle$, and behavioural preemption $P [b] Q$. P^* and P^ω describe finite and infinite iteration, respectively. The following operators of relational calculus $P \; ; \; Q$, $P \lhd b \rhd Q$, P^*, $\mathbb{II}$, $x := v$, **true**, and **false** are **HCT** closed.

Finally, we define the interval operator from the Duration Calculus [41] and our own variant.

$$\lceil P \rceil \; \hat{=} \; \mathbf{HCT2}(\ell > 0 \wedge (\forall \underline{t} \in [ti, ti') \bullet P @ \underline{t}))$$

$$\llbracket P \rrbracket \; \hat{=} \; \lceil P \rceil \wedge \bigwedge_{\underline{v} \in con\alpha(P)} (v = \underline{v}(ti) \wedge v' = \lim_{t \to ti'} (\underline{v}(t))) \wedge \mathbb{II}_{dis\alpha(P)}$$

$\lceil P \rceil$ is taken from the Duration Calculus: it is a continuous specification statement that P holds at every instant over all non-empty right-open intervals from ti to ti'; we make it healthy with **HCT2** for piecewise continuity. $\llbracket P \rrbracket$ links discrete and continuous variables with the given property.

By making x' the limit of $\underline{x}$, rather than its value at the end of the interval, we do not constrain the trajectory valuation at ti'; so it can be defined by a suitable discontinuous discrete assignment at this final instant. Following [21], we use the interval operator to give the basis of systems of differential equations. As a result, we can refine a DAE, under given initial conditions, to a suitable solution expressed using the interval operator. Intervals satisfy a number of standard laws.

$$\lceil true \rceil = \ell > 0 \qquad\qquad \lceil false \rceil = \mathbf{false} \qquad\qquad \lceil P \wedge Q \rceil = \lceil P \rceil \wedge \lceil Q \rceil$$

$$\lceil P \vee Q \rceil \sqsubseteq \lceil P \rceil \vee \lceil Q \rceil \qquad\qquad \llbracket P \rrbracket \sqsubseteq \llbracket P \rrbracket \; ; \; \llbracket P \rrbracket$$

The evolution of a DAE system in semi-explicit form is modelled by an operator, adapted from $\mathcal{HCSP}$ [27,41].

$$\langle \underline{\dot{v}}_1 = f_1; \cdots; \underline{\dot{v}}_n = f_n \,|\, 0 = b_1; \cdots; 0 = b_m \rangle$$
$$\hat{=} \ \lceil (\forall\, i \in 1..n, \forall\, j \in 1..m \bullet$$
$$\underline{\dot{v}}_i(\underline{t}) = f_i(\underline{t}, \underline{v}_1(\underline{t}), \cdots, \underline{v}_n(\underline{t}), \underline{w}_1(\underline{t}), \cdots, \underline{w}_m(\underline{t})))$$
$$\wedge\, 0 = b_j(\underline{t}, \underline{v}_1(\underline{t}), \cdots, \underline{v}_n(\underline{t}), \underline{w}_1(\underline{t}), \cdots, \underline{w}_m(\underline{t})) \rceil$$

A DAE $\langle F_n \,|\, B_m \rangle$ consists of a set of n functions $f_i : \mathbb{R} \times \mathbb{R}^n \times \mathbb{R}^m \to \mathbb{R}$, which define the derivative of variable $\underline{v}_i$ in terms of the independent time variable $\underline{t}$ and $n + m$ dependent variables. It also contains algebraic constraints $b_j : \mathbb{R} \times \mathbb{R}^n \times \mathbb{R}^m \to \mathbb{R}$ that must be invariant for any solution and do not refer to derivatives. For $m = 0$ the DAE corresponds to an ODE, which we write as $\langle F_n \rangle$. The DAE operator is defined using the interval operator to be all non-empty intervals over which a solution satisfying both the ODEs and algebraic constraint exists. Non-emptiness is important as it means that a DAE must make progress: it cannot simply take zero time since $\ell > 0$, and so a DAE cannot directly cause "chattering Zeno" effects when placed in the context of a loop, though normal Zeno effects remain a possibility.

To obtain a well defined problem description, we require the following conditions to hold [2]: (i) The system of equations is consistent and neither underdetermined nor overdetermined. (ii) the discrete input variables v_i provide consistent initial conditions. (iii) the equations are specific enough to define a unique solution during the interval ℓ. The system is then allowed to evolve from this point in the interval between ti and ti' according to the DAEs. At the end of the interval, the corresponding output discrete variables are assigned. During the evolution all discrete variables and unconstrained continuous variables are held constant.

Finally, we define the preemption operator, adapted from $\mathcal{HCSP}$.

$$P\,[\,b\,]\,Q \ \hat{=} \ (Q \lhd b\,@\,ti \rhd (P \wedge \lceil \neg b \rceil)) \vee ((\lceil \neg b \rceil \wedge b\,@\,ti' \wedge P)\,;\,Q)$$

P is a continuous process that evolves until the predicate B is satisfied, at which point Q is activated. The semantics is defined as a disjunction of two predicates. The first predicate states that, if B holds in the initial state of ti, then Q is activated immediately. Otherwise, P is activated and can evolve while B remains false (potentially indefinitely). The second predicate states that $\neg B$ holds on the interval $[ti, ti')$ until instant ti', when B switches to a true valuation; during that interval P is executing. Following this, P is terminated and Q is activated.

Although space does not permit us to go into details, we have mechanised this theory in Isabelle/UTP[4].

5 Conclusions

In this paper we describe our work towards building a mechanised library of computational theories in the context of the UTP, including those for concurrent

---

[4] See github.com/isabelle-utp/utp-main/blob/master/utp/utp_hybrid.thy.

and hybrid systems. Our aim in the future is to use these theories to enable integration of heterogeneous multi-model semantics, as described by FMI, for the purpose of multi-pronged verification. We are currently working on integrating hybrid relations and reactive in order to mechanise *hybrid reactive designs*. A hybrid reactive design has the form $\mathbf{R}(P \wedge \llbracket R \rrbracket \vdash Q \wedge \llbracket G \rrbracket)$, where P and Q are the precondition and postcondition on the discrete state, and R and G are assumptions and commitments on the continuous variables. Such a construction will enable us to apply contractual-style program construction and reasoning to concurrent Cyber-Physical Systems. Moreover work is underway to explore other theories relevant for CPS, in particular real-time modelling and probability. Once these theories are mechanised we will also explore the links between them, in particular useful Galois connections between discrete and continuous time domains, which are practically applicable for verification.

Though our *Isabelle/UTP* theory library is a step forward, further work in needed particularly in the direction of tool integration. As Hoare and He pointed out in Chapter 0 of the UTP book [24]:

> *At present, the main available mechanised mathematical tools are programmed for use in isolation [...] it will be necessary to build within each tool a structured library of programming design aids which take the advantage of the particular strengths of that tool. To ensure the tools may safely be used in combination, it is essential that these theories be unified.*

We believe that the Isabelle framework is a significant step towards acquisition of this goal. Nevertheless, there is certainly more to be done, particularly in the area of mechanisation of continuous mathematics and application of associated computational algebra tools.

Acknowledgements. This work is partly by EU H2020 project *INTO-CPS*, grant agreement 644047, http://into-cps.au.dk/. We would like to thank our colleagues Ana Cavalcanti, Bernhard Thiele, and Burkhart Wolff for their collaboration on this work.

References

1. Armstrong, A., Gomes, V., Struth, G.: Building program construction and verification tools from algebraic principles. Formal Aspects Comput. **28**(2), 265–293 (2015)
2. Bachmann, B., Aronsson, P., Fritzson, P.: Robust initialization of differential algebraic equations. In: Fritzson, P., Cellier, F.E., Nytsch-Geusen, C. (eds). Proceedings of the 1st International Workshop on Equation-Based Object-Oriented Languages and Tools, EOOLT 2007, Berlin, Germany, 30 July 2007, vol. 24, Linköping Electronic Conference Proceedings, pp. 151–163. Linköping University Electronic Press (2007)
3. Banks, M.J., Jacob, J.L.: Unifying theories of confidentiality. In: Qin, S. (ed.) UTP 2010. LNCS, vol. 6445, pp. 120–136. Springer, Heidelberg (2010). doi:10.1007/978-3-642-16690-7_5

4. Blanchette, J.C., Bulwahn, L., Nipkow, T.: Automatic proof and disproof in Isabelle/HOL. In: Tinelli, C., Sofronie-Stokkermans, V. (eds.) FroCoS 2011. LNCS, vol. 6989, pp. 12–27. Springer, Heidelberg (2011). doi:10.1007/978-3-642-24364-6_2
5. Blochwitz, T., Otter, M., Arnold, M., Bausch, C., Elmqvist, H., Junghanns, A., Mauss, J., Monteiro, M., Neidhold, T., Neumerkel, D., Olsson, H., Peetz, J.V., Wolf, S., Clauß, C.: The functional mockup interface for tool independent exchange of simulation models. In: Proceedings of the 8th International Modelica Conference, pp. 105–114 (2011)
6. Bresciani, R., Butterfield, A.: A UTP semantics of pGCL as a homogeneous relation. In: Derrick, J., Gnesi, S., Latella, D., Treharne, H. (eds.) IFM 2012. LNCS, vol. 7321, pp. 191–205. Springer, Heidelberg (2012). doi:10.1007/978-3-642-30729-4_14
7. Calcagno, C., O'Hearn, P., Yang, H.: Local action and abstract separation logic. In: LICS, pp. 366–378. IEEE, July 2007
8. Cavalcanti, A., Woodcock, J.: A tutorial introduction to CSP in *Unifying Theories of Programming*. In: Cavalcanti, A., Sampaio, A., Woodcock, J. (eds.) PSSE 2004. LNCS, vol. 3167, pp. 220–268. Springer, Heidelberg (2006). doi:10.1007/11889229_6
9. Cavalcanti, A., Woodcock, J., Amálio, N.: Behavioural models for FMI co-simulations. In: Sampaio, A., Wang, F. (eds.) ICTAC 2016. LNCS, vol. 9965, pp. 255–273. Springer, Cham (2016). doi:10.1007/978-3-319-46750-4_15
10. Derler, P., Lee, E.A., Sangiovanni-Vincentelli, A.: Modeling cyber-physical systems. Proc. IEEE (special issue on CPS) **100**(1), 13–28 (2012)
11. Feliachi, A., Gaudel, M.-C., Wolff, B.: Unifying theories in Isabelle/HOL. In: Qin, S. (ed.) UTP 2010. LNCS, vol. 6445, pp. 188–206. Springer, Heidelberg (2010). doi:10.1007/978-3-642-16690-7_9
12. Feliachi, A., Gaudel, M.-C., Wolff, B.: Isabelle Circus: a process specification and verification environment. In: Joshi, R., Müller, P., Podelski, A. (eds.) VSTTE 2012. LNCS, vol. 7152, pp. 243–260. Springer, Heidelberg (2012). doi:10.1007/978-3-642-27705-4_20
13. Fidge, C.J.: Modelling discrete behaviour in a continuous-time formalism. In: Araki, K., Galloway, A., Taguchi, K. (eds.) Proceedings of the 1st International Conference on Integrated Formal Methods, IFM 1999, York, UK, 28–29, pp. 170–188. Springer, London (1999)
14. Foster, J.: Bidirectional programming languages. Ph.D. thesis. University of Pennsylvania (2009)
15. Foster, S., Thiele, B., Cavalcanti, A., Woodcock, J.: Towards a UTP semantics for Modelica. In: Proceedings of 6th International Symposium on Unifying Theories of Programming, June 2016. To appear
16. Foster, S., Zeyda, F., Woodcock, J.: Isabelle/UTP: a mechanised theory engineering framework. In: Naumann, D. (ed.) UTP 2014. LNCS, vol. 8963, pp. 21–41. Springer, Cham (2015). doi:10.1007/978-3-319-14806-9_2
17. Foster, S., Zeyda, F., Woodcock, J.: Unifying heterogeneous state-spaces with lenses. In: Sampaio, A., Wang, F. (eds.) ICTAC 2016. LNCS, vol. 9965, pp. 295–314. Springer, Cham (2016). doi:10.1007/978-3-319-46750-4_17
18. Gibson-Robinson, T., Armstrong, P., Boulgakov, A., Roscoe, A.W.: FDR3 — a modern refinement checker for CSP. In: Ábrahám, E., Havelund, K. (eds.) TACAS 2014. LNCS, vol. 8413, pp. 187–201. Springer, Heidelberg (2014). doi:10.1007/978-3-642-54862-8_13
19. Hayes, I.J., Dunne, S., Meinicke, L.: Linking unifying theories of program refinement. Sci. Comput. Program. **78**(11), 2086–2107 (2013)

20. He, J.: HRML: a hybrid relational modelling language. In: IEEE International Conference on Software Quality, Reliability and Security (QRS 2015) (2015)
21. He, J.: From CSP to hybrid systems. In: Roscoe, A.W. (ed.) A Classical Mind: Essays in Honour of C.A.R. Hoare, pp. 171–189. Prentice Hall, Hertfordshire (1994)
22. Hehner, E.C.R.: Predicative programming, parts 1 and 2. Commun. ACM **59**, 134–151 (1984)
23. Hoare, T.: Communicating Sequential Processes. Prentice-Hall, Upper Saddle River (1985)
24. Hoare, T., He, J.: Unifying Theories of Programming. Prentice-Hall, Englewood Cliffs (1998)
25. Immler, F.: Formally verified computation of enclosures of solutions of ordinary differential equations. In: Badger, J.M., Rozier, K.Y. (eds.) NFM 2014. LNCS, vol. 8430, pp. 113–127. Springer, Cham (2014). doi:10.1007/978-3-319-06200-6_9
26. Klein, G., et al.: seL4: formal verification of an OS kernel. In: Proceedings of 22nd Symposium on Operating Systems Principles (SOSP), pp. 207–220. ACM (2009)
27. Liu, J., Lv, J., Quan, Z., Zhan, N., Zhao, H., Zhou, C., Zou, L.: A calculus for hybrid CSP. In: Ueda, K. (ed.) APLAS 2010. LNCS, vol. 6461, pp. 1–15. Springer, Heidelberg (2010). doi:10.1007/978-3-642-17164-2_1
28. Nipkow, T., Wenzel, M., Paulson, L.C.: Isabelle/HOL: A Proof Assistant for Higher-Order Logic. LNCS, vol. 2283. Springer, Heidelberg (2002)
29. Oliveira, M., Cavalcanti, A., Woodcock, J.: Unifying theories in ProofPower-Z. Formal Aspects Comput. **25**(1), 133–158 (2013)
30. Platzer, A.: Differential-algebraic dynamic logic for differential-algebraic programs. J. Logic Comput. **20**(1), 309–352 (2010)
31. Platzer, A.: Logical Analysis of Hybrid Systems. Springer, Heidelberg (2010)
32. Santos, T., Cavalcanti, A., Sampaio, A.: Object-orientation in the UTP. In: Dunne, S., Stoddart, B. (eds.) UTP 2006. LNCS, vol. 4010, pp. 18–37. Springer, Heidelberg (2006). doi:10.1007/11768173_2
33. Tang, X., Woodcock, J.: Travelling processes. In: Kozen, D. (ed.) MPC 2004. LNCS, vol. 3125, pp. 381–399. Springer, Heidelberg (2004). doi:10.1007/978-3-540-27764-4_20
34. Wei, K.: Reactive designs of interrupts in Circus Time. In: Liu, Z., Woodcock, J., Zhu, H. (eds.) ICTAC 2013. LNCS, vol. 8049, pp. 373–390. Springer, Heidelberg (2013). doi:10.1007/978-3-642-39718-9_22
35. Wei, K., Woodcock, J., Cavalcanti, A.: *Circus Time* with reactive designs. In: 4th International Symposium on Unifying Theories of Programming, UTP 2012, Paris, France, 27–28 August 2012, pp. 68–87 (2012). Revised Selected Papers
36. Wenzel, M., et al.: The Isabelle/Isar Reference Manual. http://isabelle.in.tum.de/doc/isar-ref.pdf
37. Wenzel, M., Wolff, B.: Building formal method tools in the Isabelle/Isar framework. In: Schneider, K., Brandt, J. (eds.) TPHOLs 2007. LNCS, vol. 4732, pp. 352–367. Springer, Heidelberg (2007). doi:10.1007/978-3-540-74591-4_26
38. Woodcock, J.: Engineering UToPiA. In: Jones, C., Pihlajasaari, P., Sun, J. (eds.) FM 2014. LNCS, vol. 8442, pp. 22–41. Springer, Cham (2014). doi:10.1007/978-3-319-06410-9_3
39. Woodcock, J., Cavalcanti, A.: A tutorial introduction to designs in unifying theories of programming. In: Boiten, E.A., Derrick, J., Smith, G. (eds.) IFM 2004. LNCS, vol. 2999, pp. 40–66. Springer, Heidelberg (2004). doi:10.1007/978-3-540-24756-2_4

40. Zeyda, F., Foster, S., Freitas, L.: An axiomatic value model for Isabelle/UTP. In: Proceedings of 6th International Symposium on Unifying Theories of Programming (2016, to appear)
41. Zhou, C., Hansen, M.R.: Duration Calculus–A Formal Approach to Real-Time Systems. Monographs in Theoretical Computer Science. An EATCS Series. Springer, Heidelberg (2004)

FDR: From Theory to Industrial Application

Thomas Gibson-Robinson[1]([✉]), Guy Broadfoot[1], Gustavo Carvalho[2],
Philippa Hopcroft[1], Gavin Lowe[1], Sidney Nogueira[2], Colin O'Halloran[1],
and Augusto Sampaio[2]

[1] Department of Computer Science, University of Oxford, Oxford, UK
thomas.gibson-robinson@cs.ox.ac.uk
[2] Centro de Informática, Universidade Federal de Pernambuco, Recife, Brazil

Abstract. FDR is the most well-known verification tool for CSP. Since
its early beginnings in 1980s, it has developed into one of the world's
fastest model checking tools. Over the years, FDR has made a significant
impact across academic subject areas, most notably in cyber-security,
as well as across industrial domains, such as high-tech manufacturing,
telecommunications, aerospace, and defence. In honour of Bill Roscoe's
60th birthday, this paper provides a brief history of FDR, together with a
collection of notable examples of FDR's practical impact in these areas.

1 Introduction

FDR (or Failures-Divergences Refinement, to give it its full title) [12,13] is the
most well-known verification tool for CSP [15,29,31]. At its core, FDR is capable
of checking for refinement between CSP processes, which allows it to be used
to verify whether systems meet various specifications. Bill Roscoe has been the
driving force behind the continued advancement of FDR over the last three
decades to its impressive standing today as one of the world's fastest model
checking tools, FDR3. Over the years, FDR has enabled the exploitation of
formal verification across subject areas and industrial sectors, including cyber
security, aerospace, defence, high tech manufacturing and telecommunications.
FDR is an example of how building tooling to support academic theories, such
as CSP, is one of the essential ingredients for enabling them to be successfully
applied in practice. In turn, this has led to stimulating collaborations between
Roscoe's research group and numerous industrial partners that have inspired
new avenues of research in the theory of CSP as well as FDR itself.

In honour of Bill Roscoe's 60th birthday, this paper brings together a selection of authors who have collaborated with Roscoe and who have extensively
used FDR in practice. This is but a glimpse into the areas where FDR has been
applied and by no means intended to be complete. Following a brief overview of
the CSP notation, this paper gives a brief history of FDR and highlights some

© Springer International Publishing AG 2017 (outside the US)
T. Gibson-Robinson et al. (Eds.): Roscoe Festschrift, LNCS 10160, pp. 65–87, 2017.
DOI: 10.1007/978-3-319-51046-0_4

of the key advancements made over the years. This is followed by four sections, each summarising different application areas, where FDR has made a significant impact over a sustained period of time, in the following areas: analysis of security protocols, verification of safety critical systems in aerospace and defence, verification of embedded software systems in high-tech manufacturing, telecommunications and medical systems, and test case generation for aerospace and telecommunications.

2   Background

CSP is a *process algebra* in which programs or *processes* that communicate events from a set Σ with an environment may be described. We sometimes structure events by sending them along a *channel*. For example, $c.3$ denotes the value 3 being sent along the channel c. Further, given a channel c the set $\{|c|\} \subseteq \Sigma$ contains those events of the form $c.x$.

The simplest CSP process is the process $STOP$ that can perform no events. The process $a \rightarrow P$ offers the environment the event $a \in \Sigma$ and then behaves like P. The process $P \ \Box \ Q$ offers the environment the choice of the events offered by P and by Q and is not resolved by the internal action τ. $P \ \Box \ Q$ non-deterministically chooses which of P or Q to behave like. $P \rhd Q$ initially behaves like P, but can timeout (via τ) and then behaves as Q.

$P \ _A\|_B \ Q$ allows P and Q to perform only events from A and B respectively and forces P and Q to synchronise on events in $A \cap B$. $P \ \underset{A}{\|} \ Q$ allows P and Q to run in parallel, forcing synchronisation on events in A and arbitrary interleaving of events not in A. The *interleaving* of two processes, denoted $P \ ||| \ Q$, runs P and Q in parallel but enforces no synchronisation. $P\backslash A$ behaves as P but hides any events from A by transforming them into the internal event τ. This event does not synchronise with the environment and thus can always occur. $P[\![R]\!]$ behaves as P but renames the events according to the relation R. Hence, if P can perform a, then $P[\![R]\!]$ can perform each b such that $(a, b) \in R$, where the choice (if more than one such b) is left to the environment (like $\Box$).

Skip is the process that immediately *terminates*. The sequential composition of P and Q, denoted $P; \ Q$, runs P until it terminates at which point Q is run. Termination is indicated using a $\checkmark$: *Skip* is defined as $\checkmark \rightarrow STOP$ and, if the left argument of $P; \ Q$ performs a $\checkmark$, then $P; \ Q$ performs a τ to the process Q (i.e. P is discarded and Q is started).

Recursive processes can be defined either equationally or using the notation $\mu X \cdot P$. In the latter, every occurrence of X within P represents a recursive call.

The simplest approach to giving meaning to a CSP expression is by defining an operational semantics. The operational semantics of a CSP process naturally creates a *labelled transition system* (LTS) where the edges are labelled by events from $\Sigma \cup \{\tau\}$ and the nodes are process states. Formally, an LTS is a 3-tuple consisting of a set of nodes, an initial node, and a relation $\xrightarrow{a}$ on the nodes: i.e. it is a directed graph where each edge is labelled by an event. The usual way of defining the operational semantics of CSP processes is by presenting *Structured*

Operational Semantics (SOS) style rules in order to define $\xrightarrow{a}$. For instance, the operational semantics of the external choice operator are defined by:

$$\frac{P \xrightarrow{a} P'}{P \,\square\, Q \xrightarrow{a} P'} \qquad \frac{P \xrightarrow{\tau} P'}{P \,\square\, Q \xrightarrow{\tau} P' \,\square\, Q}$$

with symmetric rules for Q.

CSP also has a number of *denotational models*, such as the traces, stable failures and failures-divergences models. In these models, each process is represented by a set of behaviours: the traces model represents a process by the set of sequences of events it can perform; the failures model represents a process by the set of events it can *refuse* after each trace; the failures-divergences model augments the failures model with information about when a process can perform an unbounded number of τ events. Two processes are equal in a denotational model iff they have the same set of behaviours. If every behaviour of *Impl* is a behaviour of *Spec* in the denotational model X, then *Spec is refined by Impl*, denoted *Spec* $\sqsubseteq_X$ *Impl*.

CSP can also model processes with priority: $prioritise(P, \langle X_1, \ldots, X_n \rangle)$ behaves like P, except that in any state, transitions labelled with events in X_i are only permitted if no event in X_j for $j < i$ is possible.

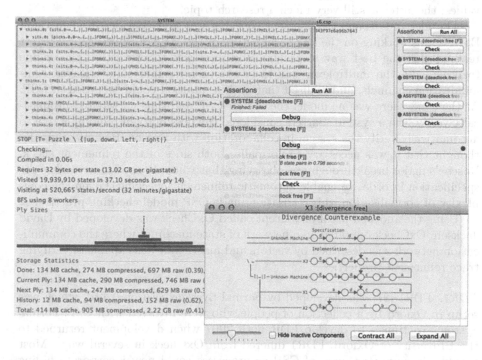

Fig. 1. Screenshots of FDR3 showing the main window, the debug prompt, and the built-in process explorer.

3   A Brief History of FDR

FDR is a *refinement checker* for CSP. As input, FDR takes in a file written in a textual form of CSP describing a number of processes, and can then verify if one process refines another, according to the CSP denotational models (cf. Sect. 2). When a refinement check fails, FDR provides a s*counterexample* that shows a behaviour of the system that violates the required refinement property. FDR is also capable of checking other properties such as deadlock freedom, determinism, and divergence freedom by automatic reduction to a refinement check. Figure 1 shows a screenshot of FDR3's debug window, showing a counterexample to a divergence assertion.

All versions of FDR have operated in a similar way, first developed by Jackson and Roscoe. In order to check if $P \sqsubseteq_X Q$ in the denotational model X, P and Q are converted into LTSs using CSP's operational semantics (the tools differ greatly in how this is represented). The refinement check is then performed by considering the product of these LTSs, and performing either a depth or breadth-first search over the product. In each state of the product, various properties are checked according to the denotational model that the refinement check is being performed in. All versions of FDR have also been explicit, in the sense that data values are explicitly represented rather than being represented by symbolic values; the latter is still very much a research topic.

The idea of automatic refinement checking was first considered when Geoff Barrett was working on the link architecture of the H1 Transputer [35]. Barrett realised that the best way of proving it correct was to prove that the engine together with the multiplexer was the same as a number of interleaved communication channels, and realised that such a question could be posed in CSP. At the time, there was no model checker for CSP and thus no way to automatically verify such a system. Barrett considered the possibility of building a tool to automatically verify the system in collaboration with Roscoe. Barrett originally thought that it was necessary to normalise both sides of the refinement check. Roscoe's major breakthrough was observing that you only need to normalise the specification in order to enable automatic refinement checking. Given the complexity of normalisation, this realisation made CSP model checking practical.

Using the above, a proof-of-concept called OxCheck was developed by David Jackson. OxCheck operated on a network of state machines where the communication network was described by vectors and masks and was capable of verifying trace refinement properties.

FDR1. FDR1 [27] was developed by Formal Systems (Europe) Ltd, which was setup in Oxford by a collection of people who were involved with CSP. Formal Systems continued to develop FDR until 2007 when development returned to the University of Oxford. FDR1 differed from OxCheck in several ways. Most notably, it supported more of CSP as processes could now incorporate hiding and renaming (at the top-level), and support was also added for the failures and failures-divergences models. FDR1 also eventually had a graphical debugger that allowed the user to inspect their processes when a refinement error was

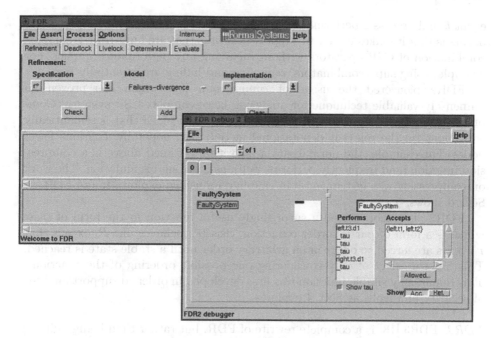

Fig. 2. A screenshot of FDR2 showing the main window and the debug viewer.

detected. This support for visualising counterexamples quickly became one of the most notable features of FDR, in contrast to most other verification tools that often lack any sort of visualisation component.

FDR2. Development on FDR2[1] [12] (shown in Fig. 2) commenced in 1994 as a joint effort between the University of Oxford and Formal Systems. At the time, Bryan Scattergood was a DPhil student of Roscoe's at Oxford, where he worked on a new input language for FDR called machine-readable CSP, or CSP_M. CSP_M combines the CSP process algebra (in an essentially general way) with a lazy functional programming language that permits general purpose models to be constructed easily. The generality of CSP_M is one of the principle strengths of FDR2, and is one of the key features that has enabled FDR to tackle the variety of problems covered later in this paper. CSP_M has had a lasting impact, as it is still in use today in the most recent versions of FDR.

FDR2 was notable for its support for *supercombinators*. These provide a general way of combining a number of LTSs using rules that indicate how transitions from different LTSs should interact. For example, a rule may specify that the supercombinator performs the event a in the case that process 1 performs the

---

[1] There were actually several major versions of FDR2 released: FDR 2.83 represented the final version that Formal Systems produced, whilst FDR 2.94 was a significant new release of FDR2 that incorporated, amongst numerous other enhancements, support for several new denotational models.

event b and process 2 performs the event c. The main advantage of supercombinators is that it makes it easy to support networks that are built from a complex combination of CSP operators without incurring any performance impact. For example, using supercombinators, renaming and hiding are essentially free.

FDR2 pioneered the usage of *compression* [33] which has proven an immensely valuable technique for analysing large complex CSP systems. Compression functions take in an LTS and return a second LTS that is semantically equivalent (in the relevant denotational model) but, hopefully, contains fewer nodes. For example, the normalisation algorithm outlined above is a compression function (and frequently performs well), as is strong bisimulation. The work on compression was instrumental in enabling industrial exploitation of FDR, as Sect. 6 shows.

FDR2 also incorporated a surprisingly useful function in the form of chase which is a form of partial-order reduction. chase(P) behaves like P, except that τ events are forced to occur in an arbitrary order until a stable state is reached. This has the effect of only considering one possible ordering of the τ actions. This remarkably simple function was first developed in order to support analysis of security protocols, as Sect. 4 explores.

FDR3. FDR3 [13] is a complete rewrite of FDR, but rather than being built by the same team as previous versions, FDR3 started life in 2010 as a side-project of Gibson-Robinson during his doctorate. During Gibson-Robinson's undergraduate, he built a CSP generator that enabled FDR2 to model check models written in other process algebras, based on work of Roscoe [30]. The CSP generator for this was rather complex, and after becoming frustrated by the number of errors FDR2 gave along the lines of <> is not a set (with no attached line number), he wrote a type checker for CSP. This type checker formed the basis of FDR3, which was then developed over the next few years, culminating in its final release in December 2013.

Compared to FDR2, FDR3's major feature is its speed: it is typically three times faster on a single core but is also capable of using multiple cores. Further, when running on multiple cores and checking models in the traces and failures models, it scales linearly [13] (i.e. twice as many cores cause FDR to take half the time). FDR3 also incorporates a cluster version that is also capable of scaling linearly as more nodes are added to the cluster [13]. Few other model checkers are capable of scaling in such ways. One particularly notable experiment involved the use of FDR3 on a cluster of 64 16-core servers running on Amazon's EC2 service, which managed to model check a problem with over 1 trillion states.

The other notable difference to users of FDR is the redesigned user interface of FDR3, as shown in Fig. 1. This is particularly noticeable in terms of the graphical debugger which now shows, at a glance, exactly how the different processes interact to produce an event. This sounds straightforward, but it turns out to be particularly difficult to compute the alignment when divergence counterexamples are found in processes that include compressions.

4   Analysis of Security Protocols

A security protocol is an exchange of messages between two or more agents, over a possibly insecure network, with a security-related goal, such as establishing a cryptographic key, or authenticating one agent to another. In the past, security protocols were very difficult to get right: many were suggested, only to subsequently be found to be insecure.

The analysis of security protocols is an area where the use of FDR has been very successful and influential. The technique has proved successful at identifying attacks upon protocols, and, in other cases, proving protocols secure. It has influenced many later techniques.

Early models. Roscoe first suggested the use of FDR to analyse security protocols [28]. The technique was subsequently developed by Lowe. This work is best known for its demonstration [17] of how it could be used to find the (now well known) attack upon the Needham-Schroeder Public Key Protocol [20]. The basic technique is outlined below, using this protocol as an example. The protocol can be described as follows. The encryption of message m by key k is denoted as $\{\!| \; m \; |\!\}_k$, and concatenation of messages is denoted using ".".

$$1. \; a \to b : \{\!| \; na.a \; |\!\}_{PK(b)}$$
$$2. \; b \to a : \{\!| \; na.nb \; |\!\}_{PK(a)}$$
$$3. \; a \to b : \{\!| \; nb \; |\!\}_{PK(b)}$$

Here a is an initiator who seeks to establish a session with responder b. a selects a nonce (i.e. a large random number) na, and sends it along with her identity to b (message 1), encrypted using b's public key $PK(b)$. When b receives this message, he decrypts the message to obtain the nonce na. He then returns the nonce na, along with a new nonce nb, to a, encrypted with a's key (message 2). When a receives this message it would seem that she should be assured that she is talking to b, since only b should be able to decrypt message 1 to obtain na. a then returns the nonce nb to b, encrypted with b's key. It would seem that b should be assured that he is talking to a, since only a should be able to decrypt message 2 to obtain nb.

The CSP models represent encryption symbolically. For example, the encryption $\{\!| \; m \; |\!\}_k$ is written as Encrypt.$k.m$. Honest agents running the protocol are modelled as CSP processes. For example, the initiator a using nonce na could be modelled by the following process.

```
Initiator (a,na) =
  InitRunning.a?b → send.Msg1.a.b.Encrypt.PK(b).na.a →
  receive.Msg2.b.a.Encrypt.PK(a).na?nb →
  send.Msg3.a.b.Encrypt.PK(b).nb → InitDone.a.b → STOP
```

This represents sending and receiving of messages in an obvious way. An initial message indicates that a intends to run the protocol with b (who might be the intruder, or might be an honest agent); and a final message indicates that she thinks she has completed the protocol with b.

Next, a model of the most nondeterministic intruder is built. The intruder can (1) overhear and/or intercept any messages being passed in the system; (2) create new messages from messages he knows, for example by encrypting or decrypting with keys he knows; (3) send messages he has seen or created to other agents, possibly using a faked identity.

In order to capture (2), above, a relation $\vdash$ can be defined, such that if S is a set of messages, and m is a message, $S \vdash m$ if m can be produced in a single step from S. The rules below capture encryption, decryption, concatenation and splitting of messages.

$$\{m, k\} \vdash \{\!| \, m \, |\!\}_k, \qquad \{\{\!| \, m \, |\!\}_k, k^{-1}\} \vdash m,$$
$$\{m_1, m_2\} \vdash m_1.m_2, \qquad \{m_1.m_2\} \vdash m_1, \qquad \{m_1.m_2\} \vdash m_2.$$

An intruder who knows the set of messages S can be defined as follows. The intruder can: hear a message m on the network and add it to his knowledge; say some message m that he knows, i.e. send it on the network; or deduce some message m from some subset S' of the messages he knows, and add m to his knowledge.

```
Intruder (S) =
  hear ? m → Intruder(S ∪ {m})
  □ say ? m:S → Intruder(S)
  □ (□ S' ⊆ S, m ∈ Msg, S' ⊢ m • deduce . S' . m → Intruder(S ∪ {m}))
```

This process can be instantiated with some initial knowledge set, for example containing all public keys and the intruder's own private key.

In practice, the above definition is impractical, because the FDR compiler would build the entire Intruder process at compile time, which would be too time consuming in most cases: if there are n facts that the intruder might learn, the process has 2^n states. A better approach is outlined below.

The intruder can be combined with the honest agents, using a combination of parallel composition and renaming, for example to create a small system, with a single initiator A and a single responder B, each running the protocol once. Each send event of an honest agent can be synchronised with a corresponding hear event of the intruder and maybe a receive event of the other honest agent, representing a message being intercepted or correctly transmitted, respectively. In addition, each receive event can be synchronised with a corresponding say event of the intruder, representing the intruder faking a message, or sending a message with his own identity.

FDR is then used to test whether the system satisfies various security properties. For example, consider the question of whether the initiator A is authenticated to the responder B. This is equivalent to saying that whenever B has apparently completed the protocol with A —modelled by the event

RespDone.B.A— A has indeed been running the protocol with B —modelled by the event InitRunning.A.B. Hence this property can be tested as follows:

AuthInit $=$ InitRunning.A.B $\rightarrow$ RespDone.B.A $\rightarrow$ STOP
assert AuthInit $\sqsubseteq_T$ System $\setminus (\Sigma - \{$InitRunning.A.B, RespDone.B.A$\})$

This refinement fails. The FDR debugger can then be used to reveal the sequence of events that led to the failure; this is the well known attack on the protocol, described below.

$$\alpha.1. \quad A \rightarrow I \quad : \{\!| N_a.A \,|\!\}_{PK(I)}$$
$$\beta.1. \quad I_A \rightarrow B \quad : \{\!| N_a.A \,|\!\}_{PK(B)}$$
$$\beta.2. \quad B \rightarrow I_A : \{\!| N_a.N_B \,|\!\}_{PK(A)}$$
$$\alpha.2. \quad I \rightarrow A \quad : \{\!| N_a.N_B \,|\!\}_{PK(A)}$$
$$\alpha.3 \quad A \rightarrow I \quad : \{\!| N_B \,|\!\}_{PK(I)}$$
$$\beta.3. \quad I_A \rightarrow B \quad : \{\!| N_B \,|\!\}_{PK(B)}$$

In run α, the initiator A runs the protocol with the intruder I. In run β, I runs the protocol with responder B, pretending to be A. The intruder uses the former run as an oracle in order to fool B in the latter run.

It is possible to capture confidentiality properties in a similar way. For example, consider the property: if the responder B completes a run with A, then its nonce Nb is secret. An event leak.Nb is introduced to indicate that the intruder knows Nb (by renaming says.Nb). The following refinement check then captures this property.

SecretNb $=$ leak.Nb $\rightarrow$ SecretNb $\square$ RespDone.B.A?Na!Nb $\rightarrow$ SecretNb'
SecretNb' $=$ RespDone.B.A?Na!Nb $\rightarrow$ SecretNb'
assert SecretNb $\sqsubseteq_T$
        System $\setminus (\Sigma - \{$RespDone.B.A.Na.Nb, leak.Nb $|$ Na $\leftarrow$ Nonce$\})$

The lazy intruder. As noted above, the previous model of the intruder is impractical. Roscoe and Goldsmith [34] developed a better approach, described below.

A set Msg is defined comprising all messages or sub-messages that the intruder could feasibly learn. Then, for each message m, a two-state process is defined, corresponding to whether the intruder knows m:

Ignorant(m) $=$
    ($\square$ S $\subseteq$ Msg, S $\vdash$ m $\bullet$ deduce.S.m $\rightarrow$ Knows(m))
    $\square$ hear.m $\rightarrow$ Knows(m)

Knows(m) $=$
    ($\square$ S $\subseteq$ Msg, m $\in$ S, m' $\in$ Msg, S $\vdash$ m' $\bullet$ deduce.S.m' $\rightarrow$ Knows(m))
    $\square$ hear.m $\rightarrow$ Knows(m)
    $\square$ say.m $\rightarrow$ Knows(m)

If he is ignorant of m, he may deduce it from some set S such that S $\vdash$ m, or hear it sent by an honest agent. If he knows it, he may use it to deduce other messages, or he may hear it again, or he may send it to another agent.

Combining the above processes together in parallel, synchronising appropriately, gives a model of the intruder equivalent to the previous one. A particular deduction deduce.S.m can happen only if the intruder knows all the messages in S, and does not know m. If there are n facts, this model can be compiled in time $O(n)$ (compared with $O(2^n)$ for the previous model).

However, this definition is still inefficient. Suppose, as a result of hearing a new message, the intruder can make k independent deductions. Then these deductions could be made in $k!$ different orders, and FDR could explore each of these. Therefore, the number of orders explored needs to be reduced. There are three important observations: all permutations of the same set of deductions reach the same state; no deduction disables a deduction of a different message; and no deduction disables the intruder's ability to send a message. Therefore, arranging for the deduction events to occur in an arbitrary order until no more are available, gives the intruder the maximum ability to send messages.

This reduction is a form of partial-order reduction. In order to support it, FDR was extended with the function chase, as described in Sect. 3: this forces τ events to happen in an arbitrary order until no more are available. Since it was introduced, chase has been used as a partial-order reduction in a number of other analyses.

Further developments. Creating CSP models of security protocols is time-consuming and error prone. In order to make CSP-based analyses more practical, Lowe developed a compiler, Casper [18], that creates the CSP model from a much simpler and more concise description. This makes the technique applicable by those with no knowledge of CSP; it has been widely used in industry and as a teaching tool.

Many encryption schemes satisfy some interesting algebraic properties. For example, if encryption is implemented as bitwise exclusive-or, then it is associative and commutative. Such algebraic properties can be captured by defining the corresponding equivalence as a set of pairs. For example, writing Xor for the bitwise exclusive-or operator, the commutativity property would be captured by including $(\mathsf{Xor}.m_1.m_2, \mathsf{Xor}.m_2.m_1)$ in this set, for each m_1, m_2, and also lifting this equivalence to all relevant contexts. For each equivalence class, a representative member can be picked; write $rep(m)$ for the representative member of the equivalence class containing m. Then each message m sent or received by an honest agent is renamed to $rep(m)$ before synchronizing the agents. This means that if m and m' are equivalent, one agent sends a message using m, and another agent receives a message using m', these two events will synchronize, via an event using $rep(m) = rep(m')$. In order to support this, FDR was extended with a function mtransclose that calculates an equivalence relation from a set of generators, and then chooses a representative member for each equivalence class.

A shortcoming of the techniques described so far is that if no attack is found upon a particular (typically small) system running the protocol, it does not mean that there is no attack upon some larger system. Roscoe and Hopcroft [32] developed a technique to simulate a system with an unbounded number of runs, although with a bound (typically one) of the number of concurrent runs that a particular agent could be involved in. The idea is to "recycle" values, such as nonces, to allow them to be reused in subsequent runs, while giving the impression that new values are used. Techniques from data independence were used to justify the correctness of this technique. In addition, the functionality of certain server processes was incorporated within the intruder. These ideas were extended in [4] by embedding arbitrary processes within the intruder, simulating an unbounded number of concurrent runs.

Many modern security protocols are layered on top of a general-purpose secure transport protocol, such as TLS, which provides authentication and confidentiality. A special-purpose application protocol builds on top of this, using the transport protocol to securely transfer individual messages. Dilloway and Lowe [11] studied different security properties that might be provided by such secure transport protocols. They also studied how to analyse the application within such a setting, abstracting away from the implementation of the secure transport protocol, and modelling just the services it provides.

Creese et al. [9] investigated *empirical channels*: typically human-mediated channels, used to transfer small amounts of data, alongside a less secure network channel. They again investigate different security properties that might be provided by such channels, and how to model them.

5   Assuring Critical Systems

During the mid-eighties the Royal Signals and Radar Establishment, RSRE, engaged with the University of Oxford about the use of CSP. For example the traces model of CSP was used as an example of a concrete category of information flow properties [22,23] now termed examples of hyperproperties [8]. The lack of tool support for CSP resulted in little application of CSP to Ministry of Defence (MOD) projects. It was not until the mid-nineties the Systems Assurance Group at the Defence Evaluation and Research Agency, DERA, (which RSRE became part of) first started to carry out research using FDR2 on security protocols in collaboration with the University of Oxford.

The success of applying FDR to security protocols led the Systems Assurance Group to speculate whether CSP and FDR could be used to provide objective information to support a safety case for launching a Tomahawk Land Attack Missile from a Royal Navy submarine. In collaboration with Formal Systems Ltd, a CSP constraint-based approach to assessing third party systems was developed. The approach required only partial information about a system, which was then checked against safety properties by the FDR model checker. The major concern of the assessment of the procured weapon system was the integration of a Unix based subsystem, known as ATWCS (Advanced Tomahawk Weapon Control System), into the Royal Navy's legacy submarine command and control system. The integrated system consisted of eight physically distinct, but communicating, subsystems. There was already sufficient information relating to the correctness and reliability of individual components obtained by detailed safety analysis, such as fault-tree analysis. However no formal analysis of the interactions between subsystems had been performed to determine whether unsafe emergent behaviour could appear.

A system-level hazard analysis had already been performed that identified a number of hazards which were then grouped into a few hazard categories. Specific questions of interest were derived from the hazard categories and were carefully formulated so that they could be conveniently expressed as CSP refinement assertions. From the viewpoint of formal analysis and model checking, the most significant feature of this modelling task was the size and complexity of the system; it was originally believed that the system would not be tractable for model checking. The initial strategy was to model as much of the system as possible and then, when the state space exceeded feasible limits, proceed by making abstractions. However, Roscoe suggested using the partial order method called chase, which was previously developed for modelling security protocols (see Sects. 3 and 4); this made the model check feasible.

The technical approach placed all the claims about a subsystem's behaviour in parallel, synchronising over common inputs and outputs. The information about a subsystem's behaviour was derived from documentation and checked with the customer and supplier. Where documentation was incomplete or ambiguous, the claim was weakened to ensure that the actual system behaviour was contained within the modelled behaviour. Although this is safe, it led to significantly more behaviours, or states, to be assessed. Separate validation took place to assess the accuracy of the modelled claims about a subsystem's behaviour. The questions formulated from the system hazard analysis and expressed in CSP were used as specifications against which the modelled behaviour of the system, expressed as a conjunction of claims about subsystem behaviour, was checked. The refinement check showed that if the subsystems behaved as expected then the system would not manifest system level hazards.

Component failures. The assumption that each subsystem functions correctly is clearly improbable; however, due to the pessimistic approach to modelling the claims about a subsystem, the model can still be accurate even though the subsystem does not function perfectly. Unfortunately this is still not good enough and the failure modes of the modelled system have to be considered. In the same way that erroneous behaviour of computer systems can be explored by means of software fault injection, the failure modes of the modelled system can be assessed by injecting faults into the subsystems in the CSP model.

The ability to inject errors into the CSP model allowed the Systems Assurance Group to deal with random or systematic failures in a subsystem to determine their impact on the system, with respect to the safety properties identified from the system hazard analysis. The results of the analysis demonstrated scenarios under which a systematic or random error in certain subsystems could give rise to a system level hazard. These scenarios were presented to the customer and system integrators in order to determine whether the identified anomaly was an artefact of the pessimistic nature of the model, or was a genuine problem.

In fact the problem arose because timing properties were not part of the model and could not be readily inferred from the system description.

Essentially the model revealed the possibility of a dangerous signal propagating through the system before any interlock could stop it. An independent model, which gave priorities to signals invoking interlocks over signals which invoke action by the system, demonstrated that the identified anomalies were due to race conditions. The CSP/FDR analysis technique was pessimistic, but counterexamples to critical properties allowed directed testing and analysis. Therefore the generated dangerous scenarios can be used to direct a testing programme to check that the race conditions are such that the system is safe.

The safety assessment showed that no single subsystem failure could give rise to a system hazard, with the caveat that there was no underlying common mode failure that would manifest itself as two apparently independent failures. Checking the validity of the models was a separate assessment concern, but the modelling provided a means of focusing the assessment of the system information and the independent models were used to cross check each other. More technical detail about this work can be found in [24, 40].

Evolution of CSP/FDR system assessment. Although the assessment of third party systems was developed specifically for the integrated Royal Navy and ATWICS subsystems, it was quite general and applied to other MOD procurement projects over a number of years. Over those years, a number of modelling patterns were identified that became a Dependability Library which could be used for modelling various system architectures. To conveniently access and scale assessments, tool support and a graphical language was developed called ModelWorks. ModelWorks evolved further in response to a number of challenges from distributed Service Oriented Architectures, automotive architectures and distributed collaborative software agents.

In a blind trial run by Jaguar Land Rover, ModelWorks, using FDR2, was successful in finding a known design flaw in a car immobiliser that comprised 13 separate software systems communicating across a CAN bus. In another experiment, ModelWorks demonstrated an indicative saving of up to 80% of the cost of developing another automotive software system. The main barrier for adoption was learning how to model systems in the ModelWorks language. The ModelWorks concept was re-developed from 2013–2016 by D-RisQ Ltd as an intermediate representation for other modelling languages, such as Simulink/Stateflow and SysML, thus obviating the need to learn a new language. ModelWorks representations are state machines, which communicate over various media, which are automatically compiled into efficient machine readable CSP models for FDR3. The size of typical subsystems within Simulink/Stateflow is now within reach of FDR3 thanks to the use of a cluster of servers, and the use of SMT solvers to limit the size of data types required. At the subsystem level the compositional properties of CSP can be used at a meaningful level for a human, as opposed to delving into a subsystem to tease out some compositional property. The technology has been taken forward through the Advance Manufacturing Supply Chain Initiative, AMSCI, in order to determine how maximum commercial benefit can be gained by an Original Equipment Manufacturer (such as Jaguar Land Rover) and its supply chain [39].

Outside of the automotive sector, ModelWorks has been applied to the development of a safety critical decision engine for an autonomous mode of an unmanned surface vehicle for over the horizon operation. A Simulink/Stateflow model of the decision engine has been verified against three criteria: that the system does what is required; that the system never does what is not required; and when something goes wrong (e.g. component failure), that the behaviour of the system under failure conditions is acceptable. The Simulink/Stateflow model has subsequently been used to automatically generate C code for integration with the rest of the surface vehicle's software for the validation of its system requirements and the development of further system requirements [1].

The application of CSP/FDR to the assessment of critical systems has spurred on research into scaling the application of FDR and the research results that continue to be manifested through FDR have spurred on the theory and practice of assessing critical systems; Roscoe has been at the centre of this interchange. More exciting theoretical and practical developments are expected over the coming few years with the challenges presented by the pervasive use of embedded devices in emerging critical applications.

6   Scalable Verification of Embedded Software

This section gives a summary of how CSP and FDR can play a pivotal role in successfully applying formal verification in the development of large complex software embedded in cyber-mechanical systems, found in domains such as high-tech manufacturing, medical systems, telecommunications, aerospace, and automotive. Such systems are characterised by being long running, event driven, reactive and concurrent, and are also often distributed over multiple processing nodes. Systems with these characteristics lend themselves to being modelled and verified in CSP extremely well. This section gives an example of how FDR was successfully integrated into a software development framework called Analytical Software Design (ASD), developed by Broadfoot and Hopcroft in the early 2000s [16,19], and subsequently used in industry.

This work was inspired from Broadfoot's original work in his MSc thesis [3] at the University of Oxford, where he realised that, in order to leverage formal approaches effectively in industry, the following two major hurdles had to be overcome. Firstly, the approach must be accessible to software engineers without specialised knowledge, otherwise the adoption barrier is too great. In addition to user notations, automation is a key part of enabling this. Secondly, it must be scalable to systems ranging from thousands to millions of lines of code. Broadfoot and Hopcroft sought to address these challenges by combining an extended version of the sequence-based specification (SBS) method developed by Poore and Prowell [25], with automated verification using CSP and FDR and automated code generation. The SBS notation provided an accessible input notation for specifying system designs whilst the automatic generation of CSP models and runtime code ensured consistency of behaviour between representations. Further, this made formal verification accessible to non-specialist users.

Component-based approach. ASD relies on a component-based approach to specify, design and implement software systems comprising of components interacting with one another via synchronous and asynchronous communication. A component is a unit of system and subsystem composition with contractually specified interfaces with its environment and explicit context dependencies. A component can be deployed independently, provides services to its environment and makes use of services provided by its environment. The conceptual boundary between a component and its environment is known as the *component boundary*. The environment comprises all other components, subsystems and systems with which a component interacts at runtime.

Every component can be specified by two types of models. A *design* model specifies the configuration of its provided and required interfaces and the structural relationships between a component and its environment. This is specified in the form of a deterministic Mealy machine using a tabular notation derived from the sequence-based specification. At runtime, this is executed according to the system's runtime semantics; these semantics are formally defined in terms of CSP. An *interface* model specifies an abstraction of the component's externally visible behaviour at the interface, and is modelled as a deterministic or nondeterministic Mealy machine.

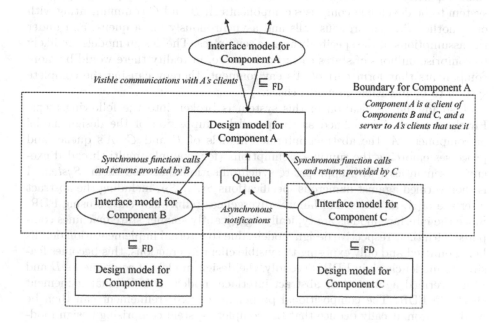

Fig. 3. A component-based architecture with compositional verification.

Figure 3 gives an overview of a component-based architecture, which is based on the client-server model. Clients can initiate synchronous function calls downwards to their servers; servers can respond with void or valued return events that correspond to the synchronous function calls, and post asynchronous notifications in the queues of its clients.

Compositional verification using CSP and FDR. Corresponding CSP models are generated automatically from design and interface models, and the component designs can be automatically verified using FDR. The CSP model not only captures the behaviour in the models as specified by the user, but also captures the properties of the run-time environment in which the generated code will be executed. For a given component X, this includes the externally visible behaviour of all of the components that X interacts with (representing its environment) and the runtime execution semantics (e.g. a multi-threaded execution semantics with the necessary queuing semantics for modelling the asynchronous notifications). The CSP models are then verified for errors such as deadlocks, livelocks, interface non-compliance, illegal behaviour, illegal nondeterminism, data range violations, and refinement of the design and its interfaces by a specification.

In practice, formally model checking the correctness of a complete system in the target domains is infeasible due to their size and complexity. To scale, it is essential to make use of abstraction and break the problem down into feasible verification steps. This is achieved by using CSP abstraction techniques and the compositional property of CSP refinement. Using the example in Fig. 3, the system to be developed comprises components A, B and C communicating with one another via synchronous calls and asynchronously via a queue, and under the assumptions of the specified runtime semantics. The design models are likely to comprise millions of states each; furthermore, in reality there would be more components that form part of A's environment, thereby causing the complete system to be infeasible to model check.

Instead, the verification of this system is broken into the following steps: Firstly, *System A* is defined as the parallel composition of the design model of component A, the abstract interface models of B and C, A's queue, and processes enforcing the runtime assumptions (for example, multi-threaded execution semantics), with appropriate synchronisations between them. *System A* is then verified against numerous specifications $S_1, ..., S_N$, including the abstract interface of A, as traces and failures-divergences refinement checks using FDR. Since the interface models are typically significantly smaller state machines compared with their respective design models, due to internal implementation details being omitted and only exposing the visible client interactions, this becomes feasible to model check in FDR. Secondly, the design models of components B and C are verified against their abstract interface models as individual refinement checks in FDR. The compositional properties of CSP refinement can then be used to automatically deduce that the complete system comprising design models of A, B and C will satisfy specifications $S_1, ..., S_N$ and interface model of A. By applying this compositional approach on industrial scale software systems, FDR proved to scale extremely well.

Industrial impact. The use of FDR within the ASD framework proved to have significant impact within industry. Examples include: Philips Health Care reported cost savings of 60 % with defects reduced by 90 % (in X-ray machines) [14]; and Ericsson produced essentially error free software, with a sevenfold increase in productivity and up to 50 % cost saving over conventional software development techniques [10]. In the period of July 2009 to July 2013, the commercial product implementing the ASD framework was used to create more than 250 million lines of executable code in C, C++, C#, and Java, with individual generated systems frequently being over 500,000 lines of code [26]. All of the models from which this code was generated had been verified using FDR.

Future developments. A component-based architecture does not imply that it is compositional for the purposes of verification using CSP refinement. Therefore, ASD imposes a strict tree architecture, as well as enforcing runtime semantics and communication patterns that are compositional. In practice, systems can rarely be partitioned in such a way completely and this has proven to be a major challenge, requiring a high level of skill and experience from the software engineers. Another interesting challenge arises when existing abstraction techniques in CSP are not able to capture certain runtime assumptions, due to the way in which CSP treats internal τ events. An example of this occurred in modelling asynchronous communication, where the runtime environment assumed that the rate of processing notifications in a component's queue far exceeded their rate of arrival. Roscoe and Hopcroft [36] made significant steps towards tackling this problem by developing a new type of abstraction, which involved introducing a new *prioritise* operator to CSP and FDR, and demonstrated how this could be applied in practice.

Enabling formal verification to be widely adopted into industrial software development environments, for the purposes of driving down cost and increasing reliability, is an active area of research within Roscoe's research group. For example, they are working on developing a new scalable model-based verification framework as part of two large research projects, in collaboration with industry partners in high-tech manufacturing, aerospace and defence. These projects seek to make it simpler to apply such frameworks in practice, as well as broaden the scope of system architectures and properties that can be automatically verified in a compositional manner.

7   Industrial Test Case Generation

In this section, a process algebraic strategy for test case generation from natural-language requirements or use cases is presented. The underlying formalism is CSP and the mechanisation of the strategy is based on (traces) refinement assertions that are verified using FDR. Variations of the strategy with two industrial applications are discussed: testing mobile device applications in the context of a partnership with Motorola, a Lenovo company; and verifying data-flow reactive systems, in the aerospace domain, via a cooperation with Embraer.

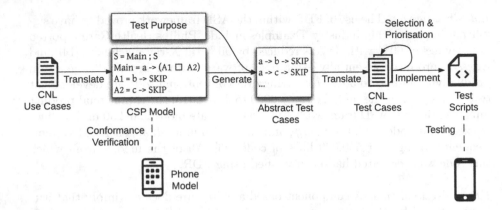

Fig. 4. Overview of the test generation strategy.

Testing mobile devices The strategy for testing mobile devices is summarised in Fig. 4. It is implemented in the TaRGeT tool [21]. The input is a use case template written in a (controlled) natural language (CNL), with a well-defined syntax. If the use case description is syntactically correct, a CSP model, say S, is automatically derived from the use cases. The test case generation can be guided by a selection mechanism known as a test purpose (say, TP), which specifies traces of interest but additionally includes marking events not in the alphabet of S. This is also described in natural language and translated into a CSP process. The model subject to test case generation is the parallel composition $STP = S \parallel_{\alpha_S} TP$.

The test purpose TP synchronises on all events of S until there are no further events to synchronise, when it communicates a marking event. Then both S and TP deadlock. This happens for all possible parallel executions of TP and S. For example, for selecting a trace $\langle a, b \rangle$ of S, TP needs to include a trace $\langle a, b, m \rangle$, for a marking event m playing the role of an annotation. Then $\langle a, b, m \rangle$ is a trace of STP. Such traces can be automatically generated as counterexamples of the refinement assertion $S \sqsubseteq_T STP$, since all traces that end with a mark (and are traces of STP) are not traces of S.

In Fig. 4, these counterexamples are the abstract test cases. They can then be translated back to construct CNL test cases used for manual execution. Alternatively, these test cases can be fed into another tool, as AutoMano [2], now called Zygon, and automatically translated into test scripts of automation frameworks like UI Automator[2]. These are then executed to test the mobile devices. If a model of the mobile device application is available, it is possible to perform conformance verification directly, by checking whether the implementation model, say I, is a refinement of S, as also illustrated in Fig. 4.

The conformance notion adopted in this approach is the relation **cspio**, intended to capture the **ioco** [38] relation in the CSP setting. However, **ioco**

---

[2] UI Automator — https://developer.android.com/topic/libraries/testing-support-library/index.html{\#}UIAutomator.

is defined in a model called suspension traces [38], which distinguishes between input and output events, and includes a special output event to represent quiescence (δ). It is possible to capture the **ioco** relation via an encoding in the standard traces model. This entails splitting the alphabet of specification and implementation models into disjoint input and output sets of events. The formulation refers only to the set of output events, which is denoted $\mathcal{O}$. The set $\mathcal{O}_\delta = \mathcal{O} \cup \{\delta\}$ additionally includes the event δ that represents quiescence.

Definition 1 (CSP input-output conformance).

$$I \text{ cspio } S \;\hat{=}\; \forall \sigma : traces(S) \bullet out(I, \sigma) \subseteq out(S, \sigma)$$

$$where\ out(R, \sigma) = \{a : \mathcal{O}_\delta \mid \sigma \,^\frown \langle a \rangle \in traces(R)\}$$

Informally, this means that after performing a specification trace, the outputs offered by the implementation must be a subset of those offered by the specification, for the same trace. In the context of mobile device applications this relation is adequate because it allows for partial specifications. The development tends to proceed on a feature basis, so it is possible, for instance, to test the properties of a specific feature against an implementation involving several other features. The following theorem [7,21] states that **cspio** conformance can be verified using FDR (as an alternative to testing, when a model of the implementation is available) in terms of traces refinement. A detailed discussion on how this can be performed in a compositional way is presented in [37].

Theorem 1 (Verification of cspio).

$$I \text{ cspio } S \;\Leftrightarrow\; S_\delta \sqsubseteq_T (S_\delta \,\triangle\, ANY(\mathcal{O}_\delta, STOP)) \underset{\Sigma_\delta}{\|} I_\delta$$

$$where\ ANY(X, R) = \Box\ a : X \bullet a \to R$$

In the above theorem the notation Σ_δ stands for $\Sigma \cup \{\delta\}$, and P_δ stands for a process that behaves as P but outputs δ in all quiescent states of P [7]; this is necessary to capture **ioco**. The annotation of quiescence can be concisely and elegantly captured using the CSP notion of priority. In this case, it is necessary only to give priority to output events over δ.

Definition 2 (Quiescence annotation).

$$P_\delta \;\hat{=}\; prioritise(P \mathbin{|||} RUN(\{\delta\}), \langle \mathcal{O}, \{\delta\}\rangle)$$

Most formal approaches to test case generation are based on operational models like labelled transition systems. A distinguishing feature of using a process algebra like CSP is that one can benefit from the rich set of operators, semantic models and tools, as well as, and most importantly, abstraction. Test generation and conformance verification, as presented here, abstract from any specific algorithm, and are characterised in terms of refinement assertions in the traces model. This strongly supports conservative extensibility when considering other

aspects like data and time, in addition to control behaviour. For example, as shown in [21], state can also be incorporated as an orthogonal aspect. A CSP process, say M, is designed to model a memory to record the state of variables. The specification, previously represented by the process S, then becomes $SM = (S \parallel M) \setminus \alpha_M$. Despite this model increment, the test generation and
$\quad\quad\quad\quad\quad\alpha_M$
conformance verification strategies are entirely preserved, using SM in place of M in the formulations. Additionally, one can now perform state based test selection. Time is addressed in the next section.

As practical achievements, the TaRGeT tool has been used in some Motorola teams that reported gains between 40% and 50% in productivity related to test case generation. Concerning the time to generate the test cases, a tool like TaRGeT is incomparably faster than designing test cases manually. Nevertheless, there are other activities in the process, beyond test design. Particularly, the inspection phase used to take a significant amount of time, and this happens regardless of whether the tests are manually designed or automatically generated.

Data-flow reactive systems. As a variation and extension of the strategy presented in the previous section, the NAT2TEST framework has been devised [5]. The input is also authored in natural language but, instead of use cases, higher level requirements are used as the basis to test generation. The output are test vectors in the form of a matrix, where each line assigns values for input and output variables, for a particular time value. The approach allows several target formalisms from which test vectors are generated. One of these options is CSP.

A conformance relation, **csptio**, has been proposed to consider timed behaviour (discrete or continuous), in addition to control and data. Again, due to the abstraction provided by a process algebraic characterisation in CSP, **csptio** is a conservative extension of **cspio**. To give an intuition, avoiding all the technical details involved [6], the relation is defined as:

Definition 3 (CSP timed input-output conformance).

$$I \text{ csptio } S \;\widehat{=}\; \forall \sigma : traces(S) \bullet out(I, \sigma) \subseteq out(S, \sigma)$$
$$\land \; elapse(I, \sigma) \subseteq elapse(S, \sigma)$$

Note that the first conjunct coincides with the definition of **cspio**. The second conjunct, significantly simplified here, captures the timed behaviour in a symbolic way. Conformance means that the possible values of the elapsed time in the implementation, after a specification trace, should be a subset of that of the specification, after the same trace. Concerning mechanised conformance verification, the first part can be checked using FDR, as already explained. The second conjunct is transformed into a constraint satisfaction problem and is verified using an SMT solver like Z3[3].

This framework is not yet deployed, but experiments with some applications provided by Embraer have shown that the strategy was able to generate the

---

[3] Z3—http://z3.codeplex.com/.

same vectors that were manually designed by domain specialists, except when there was tacit information involved. Additional and more elaborate controlled experiments are necessary to establish the precise productive gains.

Despite the several advantages of a CSP characterisation of test generation and conformance verification, there are two main potential disadvantages in this approach. One is efficiency: test generation using specialised algorithms tend to be more efficient than using a refinement checker. The second drawback is that working at the CSP level does not allow one to have access to operational model elements like states and transitions used as coverage criteria in practical testing approaches. Interestingly, however, using facilities provided by the FDR Explorer API, it is possible to obtain the LTS of a CSP model, and then devise algorithms that implement coverage criteria, as a separate concern to test generation.

8   Conclusion

The examples in this paper only scratch the surface of what has been achieved with FDR over its 25-year history. For example, FDR has also been used to analyse: unmanned aerial vehicles; fault-tolerant processors; concurrent algorithms; and numerous puzzles (thanks to Roscoe's passion for using FDR to solve such things). Without Roscoe's contributions and continued enthusiasm for FDR, it would not be where it is today.

FDR also promises to have a bright future as researchers at Oxford are working on a number of interesting extensions. For example, the use of SAT solvers for finding deadlocks, enabling FDR to analyse larger networks for deadlocks, and support for symmetry reduction, which will help FDR analyse heap structures in concurrent programs. There are also plans to create a new input language for FDR to complement CSP_M which, whilst it has shown remarkable longevity, is less ideal for certain applications of FDR.

Acknowledgements. We are hugely grateful to Michael Goldsmith for his expert memory recalling the early days of FDR.

References

1. Unmanned Safe Maritime Operations Over The Horizon (USMOOTH) (2015). http://gtr.rcuk.ac.uk/projects?ref=102303
2. Arruda, F., Sampaio, A., Barros, F.: Capture and replay with text-based reuse and framework agnosticism. In: Software Engineering and Knowledge Engineering (2016)
3. Broadfoot, G.H.: Using CSP to support the cleanroom development method for software development. MSc Thesis, University of Oxford (2001)
4. Broadfoot, P.J., Roscoe, A.W.: Embedding agents within the intruder to detect parallel attacks. J. Comput. Secur. **12**(3,4), 379–408 (2004)
5. Carvalho, G., Barros, F.A., Carvalho, A., Cavalcanti, A., Mota, A., Sampaio, A., NAT2TEST tool: From natural language requirements to test cases based on CSP. In: Software Engineering and Formal Methods (2015)

6. Carvalho, G., Sampaio, A., Mota, A.: A CSP timed input-output relation and a strategy for mechanised conformance verification. In: ICFEM (2013)
7. Cavalcanti, A., Hierons, R.M., Nogueira, S., Sampaio, A.: A suspension-trace semantics for CSP. In: Theoretical Aspects of Software Engineering (2016)
8. Clarkson, M.R., Schneider, F.B.: Hyperproperties. J. Comput. Secur. **18**(6), 1157–1210 (2010)
9. Creese, S., Goldsmith, M., Harrison, R., Roscoe, A.W., Whittaker, P., Zakiuddin, I.: Exploiting empirical engagement in authentication protocol design. In: Security in Pervasive Computing (2005)
10. de Jongh, H.: Brabantse vinding verslaat Indiase softwaremakers. http://fd.nl/entrepreneur/wereldveroveraars/634621-1211/brabantse-vinding-verslaat-indiase-softwaremakers
11. Dilloway, C., Lowe, G.: Specifying secure transport layers. In: CSFW (2008)
12. Formal Systems (Europe) Limited (2013)
13. Gibson-Robinson, T., Armstrong, P., Boulgakov, A., Roscoe, A.W.: FDR3: a parallel refinement checker for CSP. Int. J. Softw. Tools Technol. Transf. **18**(2), 149–167 (2016)
14. Groote, J.F., Osaiweran, A., Wesselius, J.H.: Analyzing the effects of formal methods on the development of industrial control software. In: ICSM (2011)
15. Hoare, C.A.R.: Communicating Sequential Processes. Prentice-Hall Inc., Upper Saddle River (1985)
16. Hopcroft, P.J., Broadfoot, G.H.: Combining the box structure development method and CSP. Electron. Notes Theoret. Comput. Sci. **128**(6), 127–144 (2005)
17. Lowe, G.: Breaking and fixing the Needham-Schroeder public-key protocol using FDR. In: TACAS (1996)
18. Lowe, G.: Casper: a compiler for the analysis of security protocols. J. Comput. Secur. **6**(1–2), 53–84 (1998)
19. Mills, H.D., Linger, R.C., Hevner, A.R.: Principles of Information Systems Analysis and Design. Academic Press, New York (1986)
20. Needham, R., Schroeder, M.: Using encryption for authentication in large networks of computers. Commun. ACM **21**(12), 993–999 (1978)
21. Nogueira, S., Sampaio, A., Mota, A.: Test generation from state based use case models. Formal Aspects of Comput. (2014)
22. O'Halloran, C.: A calculus of information flow. In: ESORICS (1990)
23. O'Halloran, C.: Category theory and information flow applied to computer security. DPhil Thesis, University of Oxford (1993)
24. O'Halloran, C.: Assessing Safety Critical COTS Systems (1999)
25. Prowell, S.J., Poore, J.H.: Sequence-based software specification of deterministic systems. Softw. Practi. Experience **28**(3), 329–344 (1998)
26. REF 2014. Automated software design and verification. http://impact.ref.ac.uk/CaseStudies/CaseStudy.aspx?Id=4907
27. Roscoe, A.W.: Model-checking CSP. In: A Classical Mind, pp. 353–378. Prentice Hall International (UK) Ltd., Hertfordshire (1994)
28. Roscoe, A.W.: Modelling and verifying key-exchange protocols using CSP and FDR. In: CSFW (1995)
29. Roscoe, A.W.: The Theory and Practice of Concurrency. Prentice Hall, Englewood Cliffs (1997)
30. Roscoe, A.W.: CSP is expressive enough for π. In: Reflections on the Work of CAR Hoare (2010)
31. Roscoe, A.W.: Understanding Concurrent Systems. Springer, Heidelberg (2010)

32. Roscoe, A.W., Broadfoot, P.J.: Proving security protocols with model checkers by data independence techniques. J. Comput. Secur. (1999)
33. Roscoe, A.W., Gardiner, P.H.B., Goldsmith, M.H., Hulance, J.R., Jackson, D.M., Scattergood, J.B.: Hierarchical compression for model-checking CSP or how to check 10^{20} dining philosophers for deadlock. In: TACAS (1995)
34. Roscoe, A.W., Goldsmith, M.: The perfect spy for model-checking crypto-protocols. In: DIMACS (1997)
35. Roscoe, A.W., Goldsmith, M.H., Cox, A.D.B., Scattergood, J.B.: Formal Methods in the Development of the H1 Transputer. In: WOTUG (1991)
36. Roscoe, A.W., Hopcroft, P.J.: Theories of programming and formal methods. Chapter Slow Abstraction via Priority (2013)
37. Sampaio, A., Nogueira, S., Mota, A., Isobe, Y.: Sound and mechanised compositional verification of input-output conformance. Softw. Testing Verification Reliab. **24**(4), 289–319 (2014)
38. Tretmans, J.: Test Generation with Inputs, Outputs, and Quiescence. In: TACAS (1996)
39. Tudor, N.J., Botham, J.: Proving properties of automotive systems of systems under ISO 26262 using automated formal methods. In: System Safety and Cyber Security (2014)
40. Zakiuddin, I., Moffat, N., O'Halloran, C., Ryan, P.: Chasing events to certify a critical system. Technical report (1998)

Information Flow, Distributed Systems, and Refinement, by Example

Joshua D. Guttman[1,2(✉)]

[1] The MITRE Corporation, Bedford, MA, USA
[2] Worcester Polytechnic Institute, Worcester, MA, USA
guttman@wpi.edu

1 Introduction

Non-interference is one of the foundational notions of security stretching back to Goguen and Meseguer [3]. Roughly, a set of activities C is non-interfering with a set D if any possible behavior at D is compatible with anything that could have occurred at C. One also speaks of "no information flow" from C to D in this case. Many hands further developed the idea and its variants (e.g. [12,15]), which also flourished within the process calculus context [1,2,6,13]. A.W. Roscoe contributed a characteristically distinctive idea to this discussion, in collaboration with J. Woodcock and L. Wulf. The idea was that a system is secure for flow from C to D when, after hiding behaviors at the source C, the destination D experiences the system as *deterministic* [8,11]. In the CSP tradition, a process is deterministic if, after engaging in a sequence t of events, it can refuse an event a, then it always refuses the event a after engaging in t [9].

One advantage of this approach via determinism is that it disposed of the so-called "refinement paradox" of non-interference (for which C. Morgan [7] cites J. Jacob [6], who does not use the term). Namely, a system might display non-interference, but refine to a system that caused impermissible information flows. Refinement does not preserve ignorance, in Morgan's words. However, if the system is already deterministic to the destination, no refinement can provide the destination with information about the behavior of the source.

Unfortunately, non-interference is too strong a property to be desirable except rarely. One rarely would design a system that has the activities C, D when C should not interfere with D in any way at all. One would instead like to design systems in which there are at least clear limitations on how that interference may occur. For instance, perhaps there is a responsible intermediary M such that C may influence M and M may then decide what information to make visible to the destination D. Thus, writing "may influence directly" as $\rightsquigarrow$, we have $C \rightsquigarrow M \rightsquigarrow D$, although $C \not\rightsquigarrow D$. In this case, the "may-influence" relation is not transitive. One may view this intransitive non-interference as a kind of declassification, one in which the permissible intermediaries are trusted to decide what information may reach the destination. From this point of view, it is a kind of "who" declassification, in which the policy identifies which domains M are permitted to choose what information to allow to pass from C to D [14].

© Springer International Publishing AG 2017
T. Gibson-Robinson et al. (Eds.): Roscoe Festschrift, LNCS 10160, pp. 88–103, 2017.
DOI: 10.1007/978-3-319-51046-0_5

A second advantage of Roscoe's determinism idea turned out to be its surprising and attractive applicability to intransitive non-interference, developed with M. Goldsmith [10]. Non-interference given an intransitive "may-influence" relation meant that, *hiding* the behavior of the sensitive source C, and *fixing* the behavior of the permissible intermediary M, the destination D again experiences the system as deterministic.

However, suppose we have explicit specifications of what we would like to permit D to learn about C? For instance, the buyer should be able to learn what the president had for breakfast, so as to replenish the larder, but not who she vetted for the court opening. This is called "what" declassification, since the content determines what D may learn and what not. The determinism point of view does not seem to provide an explanation of "what" declassification, which would be attractive.

We think it also attractive to recast the notions in a context that makes the graph structure of distributed systems explicit, and allows us to use the graph structure as a guide to information flow properties [4]. In this paper, we aim to explain, largely by example, three aspects of information flow in distributed systems that are governed by "what" declassification policies:

1. How to define policies bounding "what" declassification, i.e. upper bounds on information flow, and also functionality goals expressed as lower bounds on information flow;
2. How to represent distributed systems as directed graphs in which the nodes are processing elements and the arcs are message channels, in which these policies are meaningful;
3. How to ensure that these conclusions are preserved when a system is refined using a surprisingly simple but still useful principle.

Functionality goals as lower bounds on information flow are new in this paper, as is the simple refinement principle.

2   An Example System

We will consider a system EpiDB with very simple, but nevertheless useful, behavior. We do not focus on the realism of EpiDB, as we will use it simply to stimulate intuition for the information flow considerations at hand. EpiDB is suggested by a related unpublished demonstration system written by two colleagues.

2.1   The EpiDB idea

EpiDB serves as a database for epidemiological information. Imagine that healthcare providers deposit two kinds of records into the system. First, we have a table of *disease records*, that say of a particular person that they had a particular disease during a period of time. Second, we have a table of *personal encounter records*, that say of an unordered pair of people that they had an encounter on a particular date, or that they encounter each other habitually, possibly because they belong to the same family or school class.

EpiDB will be used by public health analysts who seek to understand the propagation of diseases through this population. Thus, an analyst A asks a query about a person p_1, a disease d, and a time t_0. If that query is permitted from A, and p_1 had the disease d at a time t_1 near t_0, then the system will return a set of tuples (p_2, e_2, t_2) such that p_2 encountered p_1 at time e_2, and had disease d at time t_2, where e_2 and t_2 are near t_0. For simplicity, we will choose a parameter ϵ, and take "ϵ-near" to mean that $|t' - t| < \epsilon$. Thus, the query takes a sort of join on the two tables, containing the disease and personal encounter records, restricted to times near t_0.

If the query is permitted from A but p_1 did not have the disease d near t_0, it returns a distinctive value *unsick* denying the diagnosis. If the query is impermissible from A, it returns a distinctive value *imperm* denying permission. Perhaps some analysts are responsible only for certain diseases, and if they start querying for sexually transmitted diseases instead of influenza (e.g.), they are letting their curiosity get the better of them. Alternatively, some analysts may be authorized to ask about some patients but not others, or some time periods. In this example system, we will assume that permission is independent of the contents of the database, and does not change as it operates.

If the database's state consists of the tables of disease records with contents T^d and personal encounter records with contents T^e, then we will write $\mathsf{ans}(A, q, T^d, T^e)$ for the result when query $q = (p_1, d, t_0)$ is received on c, where:

$$\mathsf{ans}(c, q, T^d, T^e) = \begin{cases} unsick & \text{if not sick } \epsilon\text{-near } t_0 \\ imperm & \text{if not permitted} \\ \{(p_2, e_2, t_2) \colon \exists t_1 \,.\, (p_1, d, t_1) \in T^d, \ (p_2, d, t_2) \in T^d, \\ \qquad\qquad (\{p_1, p_2\}, e_2) \in T^e, \\ \qquad\qquad \text{and } t_1, t_2, e_2 \text{ are } \epsilon\text{-near } t_0\} \end{cases}$$

To simplify the statement of information flow upper and lower bounds, we will assume one type of coordination between the analysts and the data provider. Namely, we will assume that the data provider remains up-to-date, while the analysts are not concerned with very recent events. Thus, we will assume that if an analyst ever makes a query q about a time t, and a provider ever deposits a record r concerning a related time $t' < t + 2\epsilon$, then in fact the system received r before q. As a consequence, no query ever has a result that would have been altered by records received subsequently. In particular, the analyst can never detect the order of arrival of records by a sequence of queries.

2.2   Simplest EpiDB system

Thus, the simplest version of our system EpiDB takes the form shown in Fig. 1, in which a provider PR delivers data into the database E itself, which can be queried by an analyst A_1. We assume that E starts empty, so that its contents at any time is just what PR has delivered over channel 3.

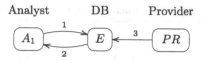

Fig. 1. Schematic system EpiDB

We regard the whole graph as the system, rather than simply the node E, partly because in subsequent steps there are additional nodes, but also because the security and functionality goals of the system are about A_1 and PR. In particular, A_1 is authorized to learn certain aspects of the behavior of PR. A_1 can learn which records PR has submitted that are relevant to a permissible query. If PR submits records that are not related to any permissible query of A_1, then EpiDB is obliged to ensure that they can have no effect on what A_1 observes on channels $1, 2$.

We do not need to specify the behavior of A_1 and PR, since the goals should hold regardless of their actions. Thus, we regard them as always willing to send or receive any message on their outgoing or incoming channels.

By contrast, E has a specification. We can describe it as a state machine where the state includes two sets of tuples, representing the tables T^d, T^e. An additional state component records the not-yet-processed query (p_1, d, t_0) or else $\perp$ if every query has already received a response. A new record r_d, r_e may be deposited at any moment, even between receiving a query and answering it, so this state component remembers any as-yet unanswered query. We do, however, maintain the upper bound t of the times mentioned in all queries we have received; we refuse to receive a new record whose time does not exceed $t + 2\epsilon$. We record this maximum query time in the state component m, and we require that when a record r is received, its time is greater than $m + 2\epsilon$. We write time(q) or time(r) for the last component of q, r, which is its time component.

We give the labeled transition relation in Fig. 2. Notice that E does not accept a new query until it has answered the previous one, and restored $\perp$ to the first state component. Also, channel 2 carries a *set* of records (p_2, e_2, t_2), or else a symbol *unsick, imperm*.

2.3   The Intended Information Flow

EpiDB is intended to limit information flow from the provider PR to the analyst A_1. In particular, the access control system is intended to limit flow to information for which A_1 is authorized. The remainder of the system is intended to maximize flow subject to authorization, and relevance to the queries A_1 asks.

For definiteness, we will assume that each analyst A has been assigned:

persons(A): A set of persons of interest for A;
diseases(A): A set of diseases A is authorized to consider;
start(A): an earliest time about which to query; and
finish(A): a most recent time about which to query.

Pre-State	Label (channel, message)	Post-State
$(\bot, T^d, T^e, m)$	$(1, q)$	(q, T^d, T^e, m')
(q, T^d, T^e, m)	$(2, a)$	$(\bot, T^d, T^e, m)$
(x, T^d, T^e, m)	$(3, r_d)$	$(x, T^d \cup \{r_d\}, T^e, m)$
(x, T^d, T^e, m)	$(3, r_e)$	$(x, T^d, T^e \cup \{r_e\}, m)$

where $a = \mathsf{ans}(A_1, q, T^d, T^e)$, $m' = \max(m, \mathsf{time}(q))$
q is a non-$\bot$ query, x is any value,
and r_d, r_e are respectively a disease record and an encounter record,
with $\mathsf{time}(r_d), \mathsf{time}(r_e) > m + 2\epsilon$

Fig. 2. Labeled transition relation for E

Since A will be able to learn about disease records within ϵ of the time t_0 in a query, we will write $\mathsf{Int}(A) = [\mathsf{start}(A) - \epsilon, \mathsf{finish}(A) + \epsilon]$ to define the the interval of disease records A is authorized to learn about.

The analyst A who queries p, d, t will learn whether p had disease d at time t' near t, as long as $p \in \mathsf{persons}(A)$, $d \in \mathsf{diseases}(A)$, and $t' \in \mathsf{Int}(A)$. Or more precisely, A learns whether PR has registered this fact in the relevant portion of its run. The set of permissible queries creates a region R_0 of the space of disease records that A can learn about directly.

The relevant portion of PR's run also contains a set of encounter records of the form $(\{p, p'\}, e)$, and these records create an *adjacency* relation between records $r_d \in R_0$ and other disease records involving p', d, and a nearby time t'. We will refer to the set of disease records adjacent to R_0 as R_1.

Essentially, the authorization mechanism entails that A should learn nothing about what disease records and encounter records PR has submitted, except as they help to determine R_0 and R_1. In particular, PR messages that provide encounter records not connected to R_0 should be invisible to A. Moreover, given a set of encounter records, PR messages that provide disease records not in R_0 or R_1 are also invisible.

In particular, A's observations as a consequence of a single query must remain unchanged, regardless of variation in PR's messages containing encounter records unconnected to R_0 and regardless of variation in disease records not in $R_0 \cup R_1$. A query imposes no ordering requirement on PR's messages.

By submitting a sequence of queries, A can learn conjunctions of the conclusions returned by the individual queries. But by the timing constraints, A cannot exclude any particular order in which the records may have arrived. In particular, a record can have been absent from an earlier response if it is found in a later response.

Thus, the purpose of the EpiDB system is essentially a *what*-declassification, where the regions R_0, R_1 for each permissible query q determine what aspects of the sensitive PR runs should be "declassified" and made available to the analyst A asking q.

Later (Sect. 5) we will refine the schematic version of EpiDB from Figs. 1 and 2 into a more complex system with separate components that guide an efficient and reliable implementation.

3   Information Flow in the Frame Model

In this section, we will summarize the key notions of [4]. Systems (or *frames*), represented as directed graphs, have *executions*; the local portions of an execution are called *local runs*; and an observer who sees one local run is trying to infer information at a source, by determining what local runs at that source are *compatible* with the observations. An information flow specification, which we call a *blur*, is a specific kind of closure condition on the set of compatible local runs at the information source.

3.1   Frames and Executions

We formalize systems such as EpiDB by structures we call *frames*. A frame $\mathcal{F}$ consists of a directed graph, the nodes (or locations) of which are processing elements each defined by a labeled transition system, and the arcs of which carry messages. An *execution* of a frame $\mathcal{F}$ is a partially ordered set of events, where each event e has a channel chan(e) and a message msg(e). The events associated with a single node n must be linearly ordered, and moreover must form a possible trace of lts(n). However, events on two channels that are not attached to a common node may be unordered, unless some causal sequence of events connects them. We will use the words "node" and "location" synonymously.

Definition 1. *Let* $\mathcal{LO}, \mathcal{CH}, \mathcal{DA}, \mathcal{ST}, \mathcal{EV}$ *be domains that we will call* locations, channels, data, states, *and* events, *resp.*

1. *A labeled transition relation is a ternary relation* $\rightsquigarrow \subseteq \mathcal{ST} \times \mathcal{EV} \times \mathcal{ST}$. *A labeled transition system is a pair* $(\rightsquigarrow, s_0)$ *of a labeled transition relation and an "initial state"* $s_0 \in \mathcal{ST}$. LTS *is the set of labeled transition systems.*
2. *When* $\ell \in \mathcal{LO}$, *we define* chans(ℓ) = $\{c \in \mathcal{CH} \colon$ sndr(c) = ℓ *or* rcpt(c) = $\ell\}$.
3. *A frame is a structure* $\mathcal{F}$ *containing the domains and functions shown in Table 1 satisfying the following properties:*
   (a) *For all* $e_1, e_2 \in \mathcal{EV}$, *if* chan($e_1$) = chan($e_2$) *and* msg($e_1$) = msg($e_2$), *then for all* $\ell \in \mathcal{LO}$ *and* $s, s' \in \mathcal{ST}$, $s \overset{e_1}{\rightsquigarrow}_\ell s'$ *iff* $s \overset{e_2}{\rightsquigarrow}_\ell s'$.
   (b) *For all* $s, s' \in \mathcal{ST}$, $e \in \mathcal{EV}$, *and* $\ell \in \mathcal{LO}$, $s \overset{e}{\rightsquigarrow}_\ell s'$ *implies* chan(e) $\in$ chans(ℓ).
   where we let $(\rightsquigarrow_\ell, \mathsf{initial}(\ell))$ = lts(ℓ).

The *histories* of an LTS $(\rightsquigarrow, s_0)$ are all finite or infinite alternating sequences $h = \langle s_0, e_0, s_1, \ldots, s_i, e_i, s_{i+1}, \ldots \rangle$ starting with s_0, such that $(s_j, e_j, s_{j+1}) \in \rightsquigarrow$ whenever e_j is well defined. In particular, s_{j+1} is well defined whenever e_j is, so that h does not end with an event e_j. A *trace of* $(\rightsquigarrow, s_0)$ is a finite or

Table 1. Signature of frames

$$\mathcal{LO}, \mathcal{CH}, \mathcal{DA}, \mathcal{ST}, \mathcal{EV}$$
sndr: $\mathcal{CH} \to \mathcal{LO}$ rcpt: $\mathcal{CH} \to \mathcal{LO}$
chan: $\mathcal{EV} \to \mathcal{CH}$ msg: $\mathcal{EV} \to \mathcal{DA}$
lts: $\mathcal{LO} \to$ LTS

infinite sequence of events $tr = \langle e_0, e_1 \ldots \rangle$ such that there is a history h where tr enumerates the events in h.

An execution is a partially ordered set of events that—when projected onto chans(ℓ)—always yields a trace for ℓ.

Definition 2. $\mathcal{A} = (E, \preceq)$ *is an* execution *for a frame* $\mathcal{F}$, *written* $\mathcal{A} \in \mathsf{Exc}(\mathcal{F})$, *iff* $E \subseteq \mathcal{EV}$ *and* $\preceq$ *is a well-founded partial ordering on* E, *and, for all* $\ell \in \mathcal{LO}$, *letting* $tr_\mathcal{A}(\ell)$ *be the set* $\{e \in E \colon \mathsf{chan}(e) \in \mathsf{chans}(\ell)\}$,

1. $tr_\mathcal{A}(\ell)$ *is linearly ordered by* $\preceq$; *and*
2. $tr_\mathcal{A}(\ell)$ *ordered by* $\preceq$ *is a trace of* $\mathsf{lts}(\ell)$.

When $\mathcal{LO}$ is finite, the "well-founded" condition is redundant. If $\mathcal{A} = (E, \preceq)$ is an execution, and $\preceq'$ is a partial order that is stronger than $\preceq$, i.e. $\preceq \subseteq \preceq'$, then $\mathcal{A}' = (E, \preceq')$ is also an execution. The weakest partial order is generated from the sequential traces of the individual locations, and extended to events at other locations when they share an event on some channel that connects them. However, any strengthening of this order determines another execution based on the same set E of events.

Our notion of execution ignores what states the locations ℓ reach after engaging in the events $tr_\mathcal{A}(\ell)$, and thus ignores the effects of nondeterminism. A similar theory can be developed including the resulting states, which would let us talk about refusals as well as traces, but we will postpone that opportunity for now.

We have here a synchronous notion of communication; a message m passes over channel c only if both endpoints can take a transition with label c, m. Thus, the sender learns that the recipient is willing to accept m over c now. Information flows over channels in both directions.

3.2   Local Runs and Compatibility

We can now define what an observer with access to a particular set of channels sees, or what a source of information does. We will assume that the observer or the source has access to a set of channels $C \subseteq \mathcal{CH}$. Often C is of the form $C = \mathsf{chans}(\ell)$ for some $\ell \in \mathcal{LO}$ or $C = \bigcup_{\ell \in L} \mathsf{chans}(\ell)$ for some $L \subseteq \mathcal{LO}$, but this is not always the case.

A local run at C is just the result of restricting the events in some execution to the channels C.

Definition 3. *Let* $\mathcal{B} = (E, R)$ *be a partially ordered set of events, and* $C \subseteq \mathcal{CH}$.

1. *The* restriction $\mathcal{B} \upharpoonright C$ *is* (B_0, R_0), *where*
   $B_0 = \{e \in E : \mathsf{chan}(e) \in C\}$, *and*
   $R_0 = R \cap (B_0 \times B_0)$.
2. $\mathcal{B}$ *is a* C-run *of* $\mathcal{F}$ *iff for some* $\mathcal{A} \in \mathsf{Exc}(\mathcal{F})$, $\mathcal{B} = \mathcal{A} \upharpoonright C$.
3. C-$\mathsf{runs}(\mathcal{F}) = \{\mathcal{B} : \mathcal{B} \text{ is a } C\text{-run of } \mathcal{F}\}$.

We write C-runs *when* $\mathcal{F}$ *is understood, and, when* C *is understood, we speak of* local runs.

$\mathcal{B}_2$ *extends* $\mathcal{B}_1$, *when* $\mathcal{B}_1 = (E_1, \preceq_1)$ *and* $\mathcal{B}_2 = (E_2, \preceq_2)$ *are p.o. sets, iff* $E_1 \subseteq E_2$; $\preceq_1 = \preceq_2 \cap (E_1 \times E_1)$; *and* $\{e : \exists e_1 \in E_1 \cdot e \preceq_2 e_1\} \subseteq E_1$.

Fix some frame $\mathcal{F}$. What an observer at D knows is that some $\mathcal{B} \in D$-$\mathsf{runs}(\mathcal{F})$ occurred, since she observed some $\mathcal{B}$. She wants to consider what local runs are still possible at some source $D \subseteq \mathcal{CH}$. These are the members of D-$\mathsf{runs}(\mathcal{F})$ that are restrictions of executions that also restrict to $\mathcal{B}$.

Definition 4. *Let* $C, D \subseteq \mathcal{CH}$ *and* $\mathcal{D} \in D$-runs.

1. *A local run* $\mathcal{B} \in C$-runs *is compatible with* $\mathcal{D}$ *iff, for some* $\mathcal{A} \in \mathsf{Exc}$, $\mathcal{A} \upharpoonright C = \mathcal{B}$ *and* $\mathcal{A} \upharpoonright D = \mathcal{D}$.
2. $J_{C \lhd D}(\mathcal{D}) = \{\mathcal{B} \in C\text{-}\mathsf{runs} : \mathcal{B} \text{ is compatible with } \mathcal{D}\}$.

We use the letter J to indicate that these $\mathcal{B}$ can occur jointly with $\mathcal{D}$. The subscripts indicate that information would flow from C to D if $J_{C \lhd D}(\mathcal{D})$ fails to have suitable closure properties. The subscript D adjacent to the argument $\mathcal{D}$ is meant to remind that $\mathcal{D} \in D$-runs, as a kind of type-annotation; the left-most subscript C is a reminder of the type of the local runs in the result.

3.3   Blurs to Limit Information Flow

Generally speaking, when $J_{C \lhd D}(\mathcal{D})$ is "large" for all $\mathcal{D} \in D$-runs, then there is little flow from C to D. The observations at D leave open many possibilities for what could have happened at C. We can make precise what the observer at D cannot learn by considering *closure operators* on sets of local C-runs. We think of the observer's vision as blurred insofar as she cannot distinguish a local C-run from other members of a closed set. Thus, the relation of coarsening on closure operators represents the observer's loss of resolution as information flow decreases.

Generally speaking, a closure operator obeys three properties. Each set in *included* in its closure; closure is *idempotent*; and closure is *monotonic* with respect to the inclusion relation. We found that information flow respects the graph structure of frames when we strengthen the montonicity property somewhat [4]. We call operators that satisfy these strengthened conditions *blur operators*.

Definition 5. *A function* ϕ *on sets is a* blur operator *iff it satisfies:*

Inclusion: *For all sets* S, $S \subseteq \phi(S)$;
Idempotence: ϕ *is idempotent, i.e. for all sets* S, $\phi(\phi(S)) = \phi(S)$; *and*

Union: ϕ *commutes with unions: If* $\{S_a\}_{a\in I}$ *is a family indexed by* I, *then*

$$\phi(\bigcup_{a\in I} S_a) = \bigcup_{a\in I} \phi(S_a).$$

S *is* ϕ-*blurred iff* ϕ *is a blur operator and* $S = \phi(S)$.

Observe that $\bigcup_{a\in I} \phi(S_a) \subseteq \phi(\bigcup_{a\in I} S_a)$ is equivalent to monotonicity, so that the *union* property is effectively monotonicity plus a converse. The *union* property ensures that ϕ is determined by its action on singletons. Since $S = \bigcup_{a\in S}\{a\}$, $\phi(S) = \bigcup_{a\in S} \phi(\{a\})$.

Blur operators form a lattice under pointwise inclusion, which provides a way to compare the flow of information in different situations. Thus, ϕ allows at least as much information flow as ψ if $\phi(S) \subseteq \psi(S)$ for every S.

The EpiDB Blur. In the case of EpiDB, we are interested in a blur ϕ on the local runs at channel 3, i.e. $C = \{3\}$. Since, by the *union* property, we only need to define $\phi(\{\mathcal{B}\})$ for singletons of a $\mathcal{B} \in C$-runs, we must say which local runs $\mathcal{B}'$ should be indistinguishable from $\mathcal{B}$ for the observer on channels $1, 2$, i.e. A_1. However, Sect. 2.3 already makes clear which $\mathcal{B}'$ this should be. Analyst A_1 has permissions defined in terms of persons(A_1), diseases(A_1), and Int(A_1).

Define $R_0(\mathcal{B})$ to be the set of disease records (p, d, t) delivered in $\mathcal{B}$ such that $p \in$ persons(A_1), $d \in$ diseases(A_1), and $t \in$ Int(A_1). Define $R_1(\mathcal{B})$ to be the set of disease records (p_1, d, t_1) in $\mathcal{B}$ such that there is an encounter record $(\{p, p_1\}, e)$ in $\mathcal{B}$ with t, e, t_1 successively ϵ-near. Then

$$\phi(\{\mathcal{B}\}) = \{\mathcal{B}' : R_0(\mathcal{B}) = R_0(\mathcal{B}') \text{ and } R_1(\mathcal{B}) = R_1(\mathcal{B}')\}$$

We can also express this more operationally: $\phi(S)$ is closed under

1. permutations;
2. adding:
   (a) records submitted elsewhere in $\mathcal{B}$;
   (b) encounter records not connecting $R_0(\mathcal{B})$ to any disease record in $\mathcal{B}$;
   (c) disease records $r_d = (p, d, t)$ such that
       i. $p \notin$ persons(A_1), $d \notin$ diseases(A_1), or $t \notin$ Int(A_1), and
       ii. r_d is not connected to $R_0(\mathcal{B})$ by an encounter record;
3. omitting records of the same kinds.

Limited Flow. The blur notion suggests a *restricted information flow* notion, and moreover the latter respects the graph structure. Specifically, limiting what information flows to a *cut set* in the graph guarantees the same limit applies to observers beyond that cut set.

Definition 6. *Let* obs, src $\subseteq \mathcal{CH}$ *and* $\phi\colon \mathcal{P}(\text{src-runs}) \to \mathcal{P}(\text{src-runs})$.
   $\mathcal{F}$ ϕ-*limits* src-to-obs *flow iff* ϕ *is a blur operator, and, for every* $\mathcal{B} \in$ obs-runs $J_{\text{src}\triangleleft\text{obs}}(\mathcal{B})$ *is* ϕ-*blurred.*

This notion respects the graph structure of the frame $\mathcal{F}$. First, since effectively information can flow in either direction over a channel, we consider the undirected graph $\mathsf{ungr}(\mathcal{F}) = (V, E)$ where the vertices V are the locations, $V = \mathcal{LO}$, and where an undirected edge (ℓ_1, ℓ_2) exists iff, for some $c \in \mathcal{CH}$, $\mathsf{sndr}(c) = \ell_1$ and $\mathsf{rcpt}(c) = \ell_2$ or vice versa. Now, for $C_0, C_1, C_2 \subseteq \mathcal{CH}$, let us say that C_1 is a *cut between* C_0 and C_1 iff, for every path p through $\mathsf{ungr}(\mathcal{F})$ that starts at a $c_0 \in C_0$ and ends at a $c_2 \in C_2$, p traverses some $c_1 \in C_1$. Now:

Theorem 1 (Cut-Blur Principle, [4]). *Let* $\mathsf{src}, \mathsf{cut}, \mathsf{obs} \subseteq \mathcal{CH}$, *where* cut *is a cut between* src *and* obs *in* $\mathcal{F}$.

If $\mathcal{F}$ ϕ-*limits* src-*to*-cut *flow, then* $\mathcal{F}$ ϕ-*limits* src-*to*-obs *flow.*

There is also a two-frame version of the same idea. Here, $\mathcal{F}_2$ agrees with $\mathcal{F}_1$ on the portion of the graph that lies from src to cut, and on the LTS of those locations. As long as $\mathcal{F}_2$ does not exercise possibilities at cut that $\mathcal{F}_1$ does not, then ϕ-limited flow is preserved. We write $\mathcal{CH}_i, \mathcal{LO}_i, C\text{-runs}_i$, etc. for the channels, locations, local runs etc. of $\mathcal{F}_i$.

Theorem 2 ([4]). *Let* $\mathsf{src}, \mathsf{cut} \subseteq \mathcal{CH}_1$ *in* $\mathcal{F}_1$.

Let $\mathcal{F}_2$ *be a frame, with* $\mathsf{src}, \mathsf{cut} \subseteq \mathcal{CH}_2$, *and such that, if* p *is any path in* $\mathsf{ungr}(\mathcal{F}_1)$ *starting at some* $c_0 \in \mathsf{src}$ *and traversing no arc in* cut, *and* p *reaches* $c \in \mathcal{CH}_1$, *then:*

1. $c \in \mathcal{CH}_2$, $\mathsf{sndr}_1(c) \in \mathcal{LO}_2$, *and* $\mathsf{rcpt}_1(c) \in \mathcal{LO}_2$;
2. $\mathsf{sndr}_2(c) = \mathsf{sndr}_1(c)$, *and* $\mathsf{rcpt}_2(c) = \mathsf{rcpt}_1(c)$;
3. $\mathsf{lts}_1(\mathsf{sndr}_1(c)) = \mathsf{lts}_2(\mathsf{sndr}_2(c))$ *and* $\mathsf{lts}_1(\mathsf{rcpt}_1(c)) = \mathsf{lts}_2(\mathsf{rcpt}_2(c))$.

Let $\mathsf{obs} \subseteq \mathcal{CH}_2$ *be such that* cut *is a cut between* src *and* obs *in* $\mathcal{F}_2$. *If* $\mathsf{cut}\text{-runs}_2 \subseteq \mathsf{cut}\text{-runs}_1$, *and* $\mathcal{F}_1$ ϕ-*limits* src-*to*-cut *flow, then* $\mathcal{F}_2$ ϕ-*limits* src-*to*-obs *flow.*

In fact, the cut-blur principle is a corollary of this; when we equate $\mathcal{F}_2 = \mathcal{F}_1$, the assumptions necessarily hold.

This principle is useful for "localizing" the enforcement of ϕ-limiting to the portion of the system lying between src and cut. It says that we can freely vary the structure of the remainder of the system, just so long as we do not force cut to engage in new local behaviors. For instance, if we consider $\mathsf{cut} = \{1, 2\}$ and $\mathsf{src} = \{3\}$ in either Fig. 1 or 4, it says that we can freely expand the node A_1 into multiple nodes and arcs, as long as cut remains a cut. The assumption that $\mathsf{cut}\text{-runs}_2 \subseteq \mathsf{cut}\text{-runs}_1$ is immediate here, since we assume that A_1 may attempt any sequence of communications anyway.

4   Questions and Answers

We would now like a corresponding way to specify functionality goals, i.e. *lower* bounds on information flow between a source and an observer. For instance, if A_1 is permitted to submit a query $q = (p, d, t)$ over channel 1, then A_1 really should be able to learn from the system what the answer is, as of the time of this interaction. Thus, the system is guaranteeing that a local run over channels $1, 2$ can always extend to one in which A_1 submits query q and receives a symbol or set S of records over channel 2. And this answer tells A_1 whether PR has submitted a nearby disease record, and, in the stream of records PR has submitted on channel 3, what other disease records are adjacent via encounter records.

Thus, the response is compatible with a set of local PR runs, and serves to notify A_1 that no other type of run remains possible. We will call a classification like this a *question about* a set of channels such as the PR's channel set $\{3\}$.

Definition 7. *A family of sets Q is a* question about *a set of channels $C \subseteq CH$ in $\mathcal{F}$ iff $\bigcup Q = C$-runs$(\mathcal{F})$.*

In our example, we can regard each permitted query $q = (p, d, t)$ as determining a question Q about PR's channel 3. Namely, two $\mathcal{B}, \mathcal{B}' \in \{3\}$-runs belong to the same $X \in Q$ iff either:

- in both $\mathcal{B}$ and $\mathcal{B}'$, p is not sick with d at t, or else
- in both p is sick, with the same sick acquaintances and the same timings.

We can regard an impermissible query as determining a question also, but it is the trivial, singleton family $\{\{3\}$-runs$\}$. Thus, each query q determines a question Q_q about channel 3.

An observer at D may want to determine which member of this family Q obtains. That is, the observer would like to extend the current local run so that the system's behavior will determine an $A \in Q$ that must have been found at C. This may require D to engage in certain events that "ask about" Q, after which the system's behavior will lead to the information. Naturally, the events that pose the question must be within the power of the observer at D.

Definition 8. *$\mathcal{F}$ answers Q for $D \subseteq CH$ iff (i) Q is a question about C in $\mathcal{F}$, and (ii), for every $\mathcal{D} \in D$-runs, there is an extension $\mathcal{D}'$ of $\mathcal{D}$ and a family $\mathcal{R}$ of finite extensions of $\mathcal{D}'$ such that:*

1. *For all $\mathcal{A} \in$ Exc, if $\mathcal{A} \restriction C = \mathcal{D}$, then there exists an extension $\mathcal{A}'$ of $\mathcal{A}$ such that $\mathcal{A}' \restriction C = \mathcal{D}'$;*
2. *for every $\mathcal{E} \in \mathcal{R}$, there exists a $X \in Q$ such that $J_{C \lhd D}(\mathcal{E}) \subseteq X$; and*
3. *for every extension $\mathcal{E}$ of $\mathcal{D}'$, there exists a $\mathcal{E}_0 \in \mathcal{R}$ such that either $\mathcal{E}$ extends $\mathcal{E}_0$ or $\mathcal{E}_0$ extends $\mathcal{E}$.*

The first of these clauses ensures that the observer can always request the system to answer Q. The second ensures that an observation in $\mathcal{R}$ selects some answer to the question, although there may be more than one right answer. The second says that the observations that determine an answer *bar* the tree of all extensions of $\mathcal{D}'$, so that any sufficiently long extension will have selected an answer.

Evidently, EpiDB answers the question Q_q for each q. The extension $\mathcal{D}'$ to a local A_1-run $\mathcal{D}$ consists in waiting for an answer on channel 2 to a previous, unanswered question (if any), and then submitting q on channel 1. The family $\mathcal{R}$ is then the set of local runs in which $\mathcal{D}'$ is extended by a symbol or set of records.

Of course, if a frame ϕ-blurs flow from C, then an answerable question about C can never be more informative than a ϕ-blurred question:

Lemma 1. *Let Q be a question about C in $\mathcal{F}$. Suppose that $\mathcal{F}$ answers Q for $D \subseteq C\mathcal{H}$, and that $\mathcal{F}$ ϕ-limits C-to-D flow.*

Then there is a Q' such that Q is a coarsening of Q', $\mathcal{F}$ answers Q' for D, and for every $X \in Q'$, X is ϕ-blurred.

Indeed, Q' can be chosen so that a pair of D-runs that can receive the same answer in Q can receive the same answer in Q'.

Proof. For each choice of $\mathcal{D}'$ and $\mathcal{R}$, collect the sets $J_{C \triangleleft D}(R)$ for $R \in \mathcal{R}$; let Q' be the resulting collection. Since $\mathcal{F}$ ϕ-limits C-to-D flow, each $J_{C \triangleleft D}(R)$ is ϕ-blurred.

To preserve "can receive the same answer," coarsen that Q' by taking unions:

In particular say that $R, R' \in \mathcal{R}$ are Q-*similar*, which we will write $R \sim_Q R'$, if there is an $X \in Q$ such that $J_{C \triangleleft D}(R) \subseteq X$ and $J_{C \triangleleft D}(R') \subseteq X$. Define

$$Q'_{\mathcal{R}} = \{ \bigcup_{R' \sim_Q R} J_{C \triangleleft D}(R') : R \in \mathcal{R} \}.$$

The *union* property of blurs ensures that the resulting sets are ϕ-blurred.

Now let Q' collect $Q'_{\mathcal{R}}$ from each choice of $\mathcal{D}'$ and $\mathcal{R}$. $\square$

In our EpiDB example, the questions Q_q are already ϕ-blurred.

5   Refining EpiDB

Although the simple presentation of EpiDB in Figs. 1 and 2 makes it clear why it will meet its information flow goals—both upper bounds and lower bounds—they are very far from a reasonable implementation. A reasonable implementation should have a number of different properties:

- It should be implemented via a number of virtual machines, so that its components can be responsive under high loads;
- It should separate an index from the actual archive that stores the data, to allow fast retrieval despite large quantities of data;
- It should separate critical services such as authorization from more vulnerable components that must service potentially malicious connections from analysts and providers.

All of these considerations militate for breaking the component E in Fig. 1 into a collection of cooperating components that interact via message channels. This decomposition fits the frame model very naturally, since the connections among these components are easy to define statically.

Step 1: Separating Authorization. A natural thing to do first is to identify a distinct component that uses the credentials of A_1 and the query q to make an authorization decision. For instance, these credentials could be certificates used in a bilateral TLS handshake. The authorization service can emit a cryptographic token that will be consulted by components in later expansions. Figure 3 shows the resulting frame graph. Now the state of AR reflects whether authorization has been requested by the current query, and if so, the value of the resulting token. The behavior of the system on its channels $1, 2, 3$ is actually unchanged: In particular, given a local run $\mathcal{D}$ on channels $1, 2$, the set of compatible local runs on channel 3, $J_{\{3\} \lhd \{1,2\}}(\mathcal{D})$ is the same for the two systems.

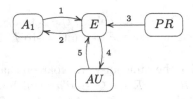

Fig. 3. EpiDB with authorization service separated

Since the information flow of the system is defined solely in terms of $J_{\lhd}(\cdot)$, any desired upper and lower bounds on flow are necessarily preserved.

A Refined EpiDB Architecture. After several stages of refinement, we obtain a system of the form shown in Fig. 4. It breaks down the database into components with specialized responsibilities:

QC is a *query controller*. It accepts queries from A_1, passes requests to the index controller IC, which extracts records from the archive controller AC that are accumulated at QC. It returns the resulting sets to A_1.

IC is an *index controller*. It maintains an association between keys p_i naming people and a list of disease record numbers for those people. It has a similar association from people to encounter records. When given a person and a table name, it passes a list of record numbers to AC for retrieval.

AC is an *archive controller*. It maintains a store of records for each table, organized by record number.

IG is an *ingress controller*. It maintains the maximum record number used so far. It receives new records from the provider PR, assigns the next record number, and sends the record and number to AC. It notifies IC of the new association of this record number with the relevant p_is.

AU is the *authorization service*. QC contacts AU for each new query, obtaining a signed authorization token that accompanies QC's messages to IC. These tokens also appear in the system audit logs, if an audit subsystem is added.

The self-loop channels $8, 9$ allow QC and AC to signal certain internal events. The only other channel needing explanation is 6. At the beginning of processing any query, QC uses channel 6 to request the current maximum record number from AC, which maintains this. QC then limits all records retrieved to ones below this maximum. Hence, even when new records are being deposited by PR

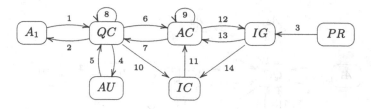

Fig. 4. Refined architecture for EpiDB

and IG concurrently, the query elicits consistent information reflecting the state of the database at the time of that maximum record number. Channel 12 is used only to propagate the maximum query time (shown as m in Fig. 2) to the ingress controller.

Again, the functional correctness criterion for this system is just that the same local runs should be possible on its two external interfaces, and with the same compatibility relations $J_{\{3\}\lhd\{1,2\}}(\mathcal{D})$.[1] The practical requirement for the system designer to meet is that the index and archive controllers IC, AC should cooperate to maintain the database accurately, which is well understood.

The Interface-Preserving Refinement Principle. This refinement strategy is simple and easily formalized. When $\mathcal{F}_1$, $\mathcal{F}_2$ are frames, we write $J^i_{C\lhd D}(\cdot)$ for the compatibility function in $\mathcal{F}_i$.

Theorem 3. *Suppose that $\mathcal{F}_1$ and $\mathcal{F}_2$ are two frames, and $C, D \subseteq C\mathcal{H}_1 \cap C\mathcal{H}_2$. If $D\text{-runs}_1 = D\text{-runs}_2$, and for all $\mathcal{D} \in D\text{-runs}_i$, $J^1_{C\lhd D}(\mathcal{D}) = J^2_{C\lhd D}(\mathcal{D})$, then:*

1. *$\mathcal{F}_1$ ϕ-limits C-to-D flow iff $\mathcal{F}_1$ ϕ-limits C-to-D flow;*
2. *$\mathcal{F}_1$ answers $\mathcal{Q}$ for D iff $\mathcal{F}_2$ answers $\mathcal{Q}$ for D.*

This follows directly from the forms of the definitions.

However, it is useful. For instance, it immediately follows that the properties of the system are preserved in case the system serves more than one analyst. In Fig. 5, we present an augmented system containing multiple analysts. However, since the behaviors on the interfaces 1, 2 and 3 are unaffected, Theorem 3 immediately entails that the augmented system continues to meet its goals for A_1. By symmetry, it meets the same goals for the other A_i.

As another example, the system we have described has no audit mechanism built in. However, having designed the system and established its information flow properties, we can add nodes and channels to perform audit without changing the local runs and compatibility functions for the interfaces 1, 2 and 3. This provides a clear argument for orthogonality of design that has sometimes eluded secure systems methodology.

---

[1] By an interface, we just mean a set of channels, often but not necessarily near each other in the graph.

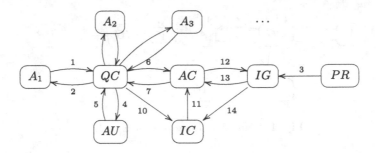

Fig. 5. EpiDB augmented with multiple analysts. Channels 8, 9 omitted as clutter

6 Conclusion

We have discussed the frame model, and illustrated how to use it to establish *what*-declassification policies, or information flow upper bounds. The same ideas lead to a natural approach for showing lower bounds, i.e. that a system really answers questions which may be posed on one of these interfaces.

However, the frame model gives an abstraction of a possible system: How can one determine that an actual system displays the structure and behavior of a given frame as designed? In particular, two central items are needed. First, the active components of the actual system should correlate with the nodes of the frame. The behaviors of each component should conform to the LTS of the correlated node. Second, the message-passing activity of the system should occur along channels identified in the frame. There should be no other interactions, whether between components of the system or between components and the external world.

Similarly, to build a real system using a frame as specification, one needs, first, a way to build local programs that conform to an LTS specification, and various familiar ideas such as reactive programming and event-handling libraries appear helpful. In any case, the programming here is purely sequential and independent of any shared state interactions.

How then to establish, second, that the components interact with each other, and only with each other, as specified in the graph? This requires cryptographic support, both for secrecy to ensure that messages between components canot leak to the external world, and for authenticity to ensure that a component cannot receive a message off a channel unless its peer transmitted onto the channel. A protocol is needed also to ensure that message passing approximates the synchronous semantics the model uses.

Indeed, there is an additional role for cryptography, which is to provide attestation, i.e. digitally signed evidence that a node is genuine and under the control of the expected code. The Trusted Platform Modules were intended as an anchor for this sort of evidence, and user-level trusted execution environments (TEEs) such as Intel's Software Guard Extensions provide a simpler framework for achieving attestations [5]. TEEs provide symmetric cryptographic support to protect a thread and local memory, encrypting pages as they leave the processor's cache. Moreover, the processor provides digital signatures that attest to the code in control of the TEE. These attestations allow components to validate one another, to ensure that they are affiliated in the pattern stipulated in their model. The attestations also allow an external party to decide to believe this also, before making a decision as to whether to deliver data into the system, or accept it from the system. Thus, in addition to hardware support, we need to be able to use cryptographic protocols in the right way; another area in which A.W. Roscoe has also made his contributions.

Acknowledgments. I am grateful to Paul D. Rowe and John D. Ramsdell, with whom I discussed many of these ideas. In particular, John Ramsdell worked out the successive frame versions summarized in the figures.

References

1. Focardi, R., Gorrieri, R.: The compositional security checker: a tool for the verification of information flow security properties. IEEE Trans. Softw. Eng. **23**(9), 550–571 (1997)
2. Focardi, R., Gorrieri, R.: Classification of security properties. In: Focardi, R., Gorrieri, R. (eds.) FOSAD 2000. LNCS, vol. 2171, pp. 331–396. Springer, Heidelberg (2001). doi:10.1007/3-540-45608-2_6
3. Goguen, J.A., Meseguer, J.: Security policies and security models. In: IEEE Symposium on Security and Privacy (1982)
4. Guttman, J.D., Rowe, P.D.: A cut principle for information flow. In: IEEE Computer Security Foundations. IEEE Computer Society Press, July 2015
5. Intel: Intel Software Guard Extensions (Intel SGX) (2016). https://software.intel.com/en-us/sgx
6. Jacob, J.: Security specifications. In: IEEE Symposium on Security and Privacy, pp. 14–23. IEEE Computer Society (1988)
7. Morgan, C.: *The Shadow Knows*: refinement of ignorance in sequential programs. In: Uustalu, T. (ed.) MPC 2006. LNCS, vol. 4014, pp. 359–378. Springer, Heidelberg (2006). doi:10.1007/11783596_21
8. Roscoe, A.W.: CSP and determinism in security modelling. In: IEEE Security and Privacy, pp. 114–127. IEEE (1995)
9. Roscoe, A.W.: The Theory and Practice of Concurrency. Prentice-Hall, Upper Saddle River (1997)
10. Roscoe, A.W., Goldsmith, M.H.: What is intransitive noninterference? In: 12th IEEE Computer Security Foundations Workshop, pp. 228–238. IEEE CS Press, June 1999
11. Roscoe, A.W., Woodcock, J.C.P., Wulf, L.: Non-interference through determinism. J. Comput. Secur. **4**, 27–53 (1996)
12. Rushby, J.: Noninterference, transitivity, and channel-control security policies. SRI International, Computer Science Laboratory (1992)
13. Ryan, P.Y.A.: A CSP formulation of noninterference and unwinding. IEEE CSFW **3**, 19–30 (1990)
14. Sabelfeld, A., Sands, D.: Declassification: dimensions and principles. J. Comput. Secur. **17**(5), 517–548 (2009)
15. Sutherland, D.: A model of information. In: 9th National Computer Security Conference. National Institute of Standards and Technology (1986)

Abstractions for Transition Systems with Applications to Stubborn Sets

Henri Hansen[✉]

Department of Mathematics, Tampere University of Technology, Tampere, Finland
henri.hansen@tut.fi

Abstract. *Partial order reduction* covers a range of techniques based on eliminating unnecessary transitions when generating a state space. On the other hand, *abstractions* replace sets of states of a system with abstract representatives in order to create a smaller state space. This article explores how stubborn sets and abstraction can be combined. We provide examples to provide intuition and expand on some recent results. We provide a classification of abstractions and give some novel results on what is needed to combine abstraction and partial order reduction in a sound way.

1 Introduction

The term *partial order reduction* refers to methods that combat state explosion by eliminating unnecessary transitions. This article focuses on *stubborn sets* [20]. The theory as presented here, mostly applies to also *ample* [17] and *persistent* [9] sets. We use the term "stubborn set method" or "partial order reduction" to mean any method that attempts to reduce the size of a state space by exploring some subset of enabled transitions in each state of a state.

The term *abstraction* [3] refers to methods that eliminate some features of a system, by mapping the states of a to a smaller set. The goal of abstraction is to preserve counterexamples to specifications while bringing down the complexity of model checking. Abstractions can be thought of as equivalence relations over states and an abstract state space is generated by expanding the relevant transitions that are enabled in the equivalence class. In this sense abstraction includes also methods such as symmetry [5]. Abstractions have been combined with partial order reduction methods both in the early literature and more recently. Significant synergistic benefits between abstraction and reduction was gained with a relaxed zone abstraction of timed automata [11]. In [1], partial order reduction was combined with an abstraction that replaces bisimilar states with a common representative. We discuss the result in this article.

We take the view in this article that *transitions* of systems are inherently *deterministic*, i.e., each transition has a unique outcome. We use the term *firing* for the execution of a single transition. Abstraction may then result in *nondeterminism*, because an abstraction may not distinguish between two states from which a given transition is fired, while still differentiating between the states that result when the transition is fired.

© Springer International Publishing AG 2017
T. Gibson-Robinson et al. (Eds.): Roscoe Festschrift, LNCS 10160, pp. 104–123, 2017.
DOI: 10.1007/978-3-319-51046-0_6

The interpretation of the transitions from a semantic standpoint is done by associating transitions with *actions*. Several transitions may be associated with she same action, and this gives rise to the concept of *operational* (non) determinism, which refers to whether the external behavior of the system is deterministic. The relationship between operational determinism and abstraction is a complicated one, and we provide some insights on the issue in this article.

This article is organized so that we first explore a general theory of transition systems in Sect. 2, which gives the ground theory and semantic models, and also some results regarding determinism. Section 3 defines abstractions and abstract state spaces, and we prove that general abstractions behave monotonously only with linear time semantic models that are not significantly stronger than traces and divergence traces. Then, a state-of-the art version of stubborn sets for preservation of safety properties and some divergence properties are given in Sect. 4. We also discuss some static relations of transitions that can be used for the computation of stubborn sets.

Section 5 provides results about how stubborn sets can be combined with abstraction. We provide a few theorems for certain classes of abstractions, to show how relations for computing the stubborn sets generalize for the abstract state spaces. We also provide some examples that show that the results do not apply for abstractions in general.

The last section provides some concluding remarks and outlines future work.

2   Theoretical Preliminaries

We consider a system where transitions operate on a collection of n variables with domains $X_1, \ldots, X_n$. The domains will in most cases be numerable, but this need not be the case in general. For example, in the case of timed automata, clocks can assume non-negative real values. We denote the set of syntactically possible states by $X = X_1 \times \cdots \times X_n$.

A *transition* is a pair (g, e), where $g : X \to \{true, false\}$ is called a *guard* and $e : X \to X$ is called an *effect*. The set of transitions of the system is denoted with $\mathcal{T}$.

The *initial value* of a system is denoted $\hat{x} \in X$. We call the tuple $(X, \mathcal{T}, \hat{x})$ a *system description*, or simply a *system*.

The execution semantics of a system are defined over *labeled transition systems (LTSs)*.

Definition 1 (LTS-unfolding). *An LTS is a 4-tuple $(S, \mathcal{T}, \Delta, \hat{s})$, where S is a set of states, $\Delta \subseteq S \times \mathcal{T} \times S$ is a set of semantic transitions, and $\hat{s} \in S$ is the initial state.*

Given a system $M = (X, \mathcal{T}, \hat{x})$, the LTS-unfolding of the system M is given as $L = (S, \mathcal{T}, \Delta, \hat{s})$ where

- *$\hat{s} = \hat{x}$.*
- *Δ and S are defined as the minimal sets such that*

1. $\hat{x} \in S$, and
2. whenever $(g,e) = t$ and $t \in T$, $x \in S$ and $g(x) = true$, then $e(x) \in S$ and $(x, t, e(x)) \in \Delta$.

We refer to the LTS-unfolding of the system as the concrete state space *of M.*

Given an LTS, we define the following notation for convenience. We write $s \xrightarrow{t} s'$, when $(s, t, s') \in \Delta$. $s \xrightarrow{t}$ means that $\exists s' : s \xrightarrow{t} s'$. $s \xcancel{\xrightarrow{t}}$ means that $s \xrightarrow{t}$ does not hold. For a sequence $t_1 t_2 \cdots t_n \in T^*$, $s \xrightarrow{t_1 \cdots t_n} s'$ means that $\exists s_0, \ldots, s_n$ such that $s = s_0 \wedge s' = s_n$ and, for $0 < i \leq n$, $s_{i-1} \xrightarrow{t_i} s_i$. When we write $s_0 \xrightarrow{t_1 \cdots t_n} s_n$, we let s_i for $0 < i \leq n$, denote the state such that $s_0 \xrightarrow{t_1 \cdots t_i} s_i$. The set $en(s) = \{t \in T \mid s \xrightarrow{t}\}$ refers to transitions enabled at s and $dis(s) = T \setminus en(s)$ refers to actions disabled at s.

Because an effect of a transition is a function, a concrete state space is always *deterministic*, i.e., if $s \xrightarrow{t} s'$ and $s \xrightarrow{t} s''$, then $s' = s''$.

The properties of the system are determined as behaviours interpreted over a set of symbols Σ, called *actions* or *events*. We assume that a mapping $l : T \to \Sigma \cup \{\epsilon\}$ is given and fixed, and extended to Σ^* in the usual manner by concatenating, i.e., for $l(t_1 \cdots t_n) = l(t_1) l(t_2) \cdots l(t_n)$, and ϵ denotes the empty string. We write $s \xRightarrow{\sigma} s'$ when there are transitions $t_1, \ldots, t_n$ such that $s \xrightarrow{t_1 \cdots t_n} s'$ $l(t_1 \cdots t_n) = \sigma$.

In keeping with tradition, when there is some $t \in T$ such that $l(t) = a$ and $s \xrightarrow{t} s'$, we also write $s \xrightarrow{a} s'$, except when $a = \epsilon$, when we write $s \xrightarrow{\tau} s'$. We refer to such transitions as τ-transitions or invisible transitions. We write $\sigma \leq \rho$ if σ is a prefix of ρ and $\sigma < \rho$ if it is a proper prefix.

A *semantic model* is an equivalence or pre-order relation for systems or LTSs. For the purpose of this article, we consider semantics over LTSs. Two systems are considered equivalent if and only if their concrete state spaces are equivalent.

There are several semantic models which can be considered, we shall consider only a few most relevant. Note that we restrict this study to linear time properties. The sets of *traces, divergence traces, failures*, and *stable failures* of an LTS are defined as:

$\mathsf{Tr}(L) = \{\sigma \in \Sigma^* \mid \hat{s} \xRightarrow{\sigma}\}$

$\mathsf{Divtr}(L) = \{\sigma \in \Sigma^* \mid \exists s : \hat{s} \xRightarrow{\sigma} s \wedge s \xrightarrow{\tau^\omega}\}$

$\mathsf{Mindiv}(L) = \{\sigma \in \mathsf{Divtr}(L) \mid \forall \rho < \sigma : \rho \notin \mathsf{Divtr}(L)\}$

$\mathsf{Fail}(L) = \{(\sigma, F) \in \Sigma^* \times 2^\Sigma \mid \exists s : \hat{s} \xRightarrow{\sigma} s \wedge \forall a \in F : \neg(s \xRightarrow{a})\}$

$\mathsf{Sfail}(L) = \{(\sigma, F) \in \Sigma^* \times 2^\Sigma \mid \exists s : \hat{s} \xRightarrow{\sigma} s \wedge \forall a \in F \cup \{\tau\} : \neg(s \xrightarrow{a})\}$

$\mathsf{CSP}(L) = \mathsf{Sfail}(L) \cup \{(\sigma, X) \mid \exists \rho : \rho \leq \sigma \wedge \rho \in \mathsf{Divtr}(L) \wedge X \in 2^\Sigma\}$

The CSP-set is known as the *failures-divergences*-model, which is named like this as it is commonly associated with the process-algebra CSP [18]. It preserves Sfail up to minimal divergence traces, and all divergence traces are extended with maximal behaviour in terms of Sfail. It is also worth to mention the so called CFFD-equivalence [24], which preserves infinite traces, Sfail, and Divtr. It also preserves, under suitable interpretation, all linear temporal logic properties of a system. A comprehensive survey of different semantic models and epistemological considerations behind them can be found in [26].

Let L_1 and L_2 be LTSs. We write $L_1 \sqsubseteq_{\mathsf{Tr}} L_2$ if and only if $\mathsf{Tr}(L_1) \subseteq (L_2)$. For the other semantic sets $L_1 \sqsubseteq_X L_2$ is defined analogously. We also write $L_1 \sqsubseteq_{X,Y} L_2$ to mean $L_1 \sqsubseteq_X L_2 \wedge L_1 \sqsubseteq_Y L_2$ If $L_1 \sqsubseteq_X L_2$ and $L_2 \sqsubseteq_X L_1$, we say that L_1 and L_2 are X-equivalent, and write $L_1 \equiv_X L_2$. We also write $M_1 \sqsubseteq_X M_2$ if and only $L_1 \sqsubseteq_X L_2$, where L_1 and L_2 are concrete state spaces of M_1 and M_2. We abuse the notation slightly by writing $\mathsf{Tr}(s) = \{\sigma \mid s \overset{\sigma}{\Rightarrow}\}$ and $s \sqsubseteq_X s'$ for states analogously.

We distinguish between determinism of the transition system, and *operational determinism*, i.e. determinism from the point of view of the actions it performs. Operational determinism, also known as *determinacy* [12,16] is defined as follows.

Definition 2. *An LTS $L = (S, T, \Delta, \hat{s})$ is operationally deterministic if and only if for all traces σ, if $\hat{s} \overset{\sigma}{\Rightarrow} s_1$ and $\hat{s}.\overset{\sigma}{\Rightarrow} s_2$, then*

1. *For each $a \in \Sigma$, $s_1 \overset{a}{\Rightarrow}$ if and only if $s_2 \overset{a}{\Rightarrow}$, and*
2. *$s_1 \overset{\tau^\omega}{\longrightarrow}$ if and only if $s_2 \overset{\tau^\omega}{\longrightarrow}$.*

Except for the treatment of divergences, all the semantic equivalences between trace + divergence trace equivalence and divergence sensitive branching bisimulation collapse into one equivalence for operationally deterministic LTSs [6,12].

The following theorem is evident.

Theorem 1. *For every LTS L, there exists an operationally deterministic L_D such that $L \equiv_{\mathsf{Tr},\mathsf{Divtr}} L_D$.*

For trace equivalence the theorem is well-known, and for finite LTSs a simple variant of the block-splitting algorithm produces exactly the equivalent LTS. For divergence traces, it is sufficient to store a local τ-loop in diverging states.

We provide a significant strengthening of [12, Corollary 1]. The following lemma applies in the absence of divergences.

Lemma 1. *Assume there are no divergences and $L_1 \equiv_{\mathsf{Fail}} L_2$. Then L_1 is operationally deterministic if and only if L_2 is.*

Proof. Let $\hat{s}_1 \overset{\sigma}{\Rightarrow} s_1$ in L_1. Now, there must be a state s_2 of L_2 such that $\hat{s}_2 \overset{\sigma}{\Rightarrow} s_2$, due to trace equivalence, which is implied by Fail-equivalence. Assume that L_1 is operationally deterministic and denote by $F_1 = \{a \in \Sigma \mid \neg(s_1 \overset{a}{\Rightarrow})\}$ and $F_2 = \{a \in \Sigma \mid \neg(s_2 \overset{a}{\Rightarrow})\}$. Firstly, assume $a \notin F_1$. If $\neg(s_2 \overset{a}{\Rightarrow})$, $F_2 \neq F_1$, which contradicts Fail-equivalence. Secondly, assume $a \in F_1$. Then σa is not a trace of L_1 because L_1 is operationally deterministic, so that $a \in F_2$ must also hold. This implies F_2 must be the same for every such state and hence L_2 is operationally deterministic. □

Theorem 2. *Let $L_1 \equiv_{\mathsf{Divtr},\mathsf{Sfail}} L_2$. Then L_1 is operationally deterministic if and only if L_2 is.*

Proof. Assume L_1 is operationally deterministic. Let $\hat{s}_1 \overset{\sigma}{\Rightarrow} s_1$ in L_1 and $\hat{s}_2 \overset{\sigma}{\Rightarrow} s_2$ in L_2. If s_1 is not diverging, s_2 cannot be diverging either due to Divtr-equivalence. Lemma 1 guarantees then that s_1 and s_2 must agree on failures.

If s_1 is diverging, then $\sigma \in \mathsf{Divtr}(L_1)$, and $(\sigma, X) \notin \mathsf{Sfail}(L_1)$ for any X. Thus s_2 must also be diverging, or there would be $(\sigma, X) \in \mathsf{Sfail}(L_2)$ for some X, which would contradict equivalence.   □

Theorem 2 is strong enough for the purpose of this article, but we conjecture that a stronger theorem would hold. In process-algebra terms, with a reasonable set of operators, if $\equiv_P$ is a "reasonable" congruence and $L_1 \equiv_P L_2$ for any nondeterministic L_1 and L_2, then P is not stronger than $\mathsf{Tr}, \mathsf{Divtr}$. We leave the exact formulation of "reasonable" and research of the theory for future research.

(a) Operationally deterministic   (b) Operationally nondeterministic

Fig. 1. Two CSP-equivalent processes

The failures/divergences theory associated with CSP considers divergence as *chaos*, or maximally nondeterministic behaviour. Neither Theorem 1 nor 2 holds for CSP-equivalence, the counterexample to the latter is shown in Fig. 1. An operationally deterministic LTS may be CSP-equivalent with a nondeterministic one. It should be noted, however, that the interpretation of operational determinism we use is different from the one usually associated with CSP, as it is customary to assume that diverging processes are not deterministic in the context of CSP.

A system is *specified* in terms of some semantic model P by giving a set $\mathcal{L}$, or, alternatively, an LTS that has the requires semantics. We say that the system M satisfies the specification if $P(L) \subseteq \mathcal{L}$ where L is the concrete state space of M. If M does not satisfy the specification, then there exists some behaviour that is not in $\mathcal{L}$. For example, if we specify in terms of traces, then $\hat{s} \overset{\sigma}{\Rightarrow}$ such that $\sigma \notin \mathcal{L}$. The execution $\hat{s} \xrightarrow{t_1 \cdots t_n} s$ such that $l(t_1 \cdots t_n) = \sigma$ is called a (concrete) *counterexample*. Similarly, a counterexample with respect to Divtr or Sfail is execution of L that diverges or has a stable failure not specified by $\mathcal{L}$.

3   Abstraction

Definition 3. *Let $M = (X, \mathcal{T}, \hat{x})$ be a system and X' be any set. An* abstraction *of the system α is a mapping $\alpha : X \to X'$, and an* abstract unfolding *or α-unfolding of M is the LTS $L^\alpha = (S^\alpha, \mathcal{T}, \Delta^\alpha, \hat{s}^\alpha)$, which is the minimal LTS satisfying*

1. $S^\alpha \subseteq X'$.
2. $\hat{s}^\alpha = \alpha(\hat{x}) \in S^\alpha$.

3. $(x_1, t, x_2) \in \Delta^\alpha$ only if $x_1 \in S^\alpha$, and $\exists x, y \in X : \alpha(x) = x_1$ and $g(x) = true$, $y = e(x)$ and $\alpha(y) = x_2$.
4. If $x_1 \in S^\alpha$, $\exists x, y \in X : \alpha(x) = x_1$ and $g(x) = true$, $y = e(x)$ and $\alpha(y) = x_2$, and $x_2 \neq x_1$ or $l(t) \in \Sigma$, then $(x_1, t, x_2) \in \Delta^\alpha$.

We refer to the α-unfolding as an *abstract state space*. Please note that as per the definition, L^α is not required to preserve such τ-transitions of L that firing the transition results in the same abstract state, though it is allowed to do so.

We use otherwise the same notation for abstract state spaces, but to avoid confusion we write $\xrightarrow{t}_\alpha$ and $\Rightarrow_\alpha$ for transitions and executions. An abstract unfolding gives rise to a different semantic sets than the concrete unfolding. For example, if $\mathcal{L}$ is a specification in terms of traces and given an abstraction α, an *abstract counterexample* is an execution $\hat{s}^\alpha \xrightarrow{t_1 \cdots t_n}_\alpha$ such that $l(t_1 \cdots t_n) \notin \mathcal{L}$.

If α is the identity mapping on X, then L^α is simply the unfolding of the system. Each α with range X' induces an equivalence relation for the states of the concrete state space, such that $s, s' \in S$ are equivalent if $\alpha(s) = \alpha(s')$. We denote by $X_\alpha = \{[s]_\alpha \mid s \in S\}$ where $[s]_\alpha = \{x \in X : \alpha(x) = \alpha(s)\}$. We mostly use this notation and write $[s]_\alpha$ for the states of L^α.

If α_1 and α_2 are abstractions, we write $\alpha_1 \prec \alpha_2$ iff for every $s \in X$ we have $[s]_{\alpha_1} \subseteq [s]_{\alpha_2}$. We say in such a case that α_1 is a *refinement* of α_2, and α_2 is said to be *coarser* than α_1. The identity mapping on X is a refinement of every abstraction, and a mapping that maps the whole of X into a single element set is the coarsest possible abstraction.

It is possible that the abstract unfolding is nondeterministic: if there are two states u, v such that $\alpha(u) = \alpha(v)$, and (u, t, w_1) and (v, t, w_2) are two (concrete) transitions, it may still be that $\alpha(w_1) \neq \alpha(w_2)$. To complicate matters further, it may be that $\alpha_1 \prec \alpha_2$ such that L^{α_1} is nondeterministic and L^{α_2} is deterministic. Consider Fig. 2. The fist LTS is a concrete state space, and we have two abstractions, $\alpha_1 \prec \alpha_2$. L^{α_1} is nondeterministic, while L^{α_2} is deterministic.

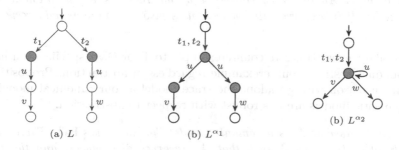

(a) L (b) L^{α_1} (b) L^{α_2}

Fig. 2. Determinism may be both destroyed and introduced

We give here some properties of abstractions that can be used firstly, to overcome the limitation imposed by Theorem 3, and secondly, to deduce some important properties later when we combine abstractions with reductions.

Definition 4. *Let $M = (X, T, \hat{x})$, where $X = X_1 \times \cdots \times X_n$. Let $\mathcal{A}$ be a collection of abstractions for M. We say that $\mathcal{A}$*

- respects divergences *if and only if for every $\alpha \in \mathcal{A}$, $[s]_\alpha \xrightarrow{\tau}_\alpha [s]_\alpha$ implies that there is some $s' \in [s]_\alpha$ such that $s' \xrightarrow{\tau^\omega}$,*
- preserves divergences *if and only if for every $\alpha \in \mathcal{A}$ if there are $s_0, \ldots, s_{n-1} \in [s]_\alpha$ and $s_0 \xrightarrow{\tau} s_1 \xrightarrow{\tau} \cdots \xrightarrow{\tau} s_{n-1} \xrightarrow{\tau} s_0$, then $[s]_\alpha \xrightarrow{\tau}_\alpha [s]_\alpha$,*
- *is* monotonous with respect to *the semantic model P if and only if for every $\alpha_1, \alpha_2 \in \mathcal{A}$, if $\alpha_1 \prec \alpha_2$, then $L^{\alpha_1} \sqsubseteq_P L^{\alpha_2}$,*
- preserves *the semantic model P if and only if for every $\alpha \in \mathcal{A}$, $s \in S$ $\alpha(s) \equiv_P s$,*
- respects *the semantic model P if and only if for every $\alpha \in \mathcal{A}$, $s_1, s_2 \in S$, $s_1 \sqsubseteq_P \alpha(s_1)$.*
- *is a collection of* 1-simulations *if and only if for every $\alpha \in \mathcal{A}$, $s_1, s_2, s_3 \in S$, and $t \in T$, if $s_1 \xrightarrow{t} s_2$, $\alpha(s_1) = \alpha(s_3)$ and $s_3 \xrightarrow{t}$, then there exists $s_4 \in S$ such that $s_3 \xrightarrow{t} s_4$ and $\alpha(s_3) = \alpha(s_4)$,*
- preserves (operational) determinism *if and only if for every $\alpha_1, \alpha_2 \in \mathcal{A}$ such that $\alpha_1 \prec \alpha_2$, L^{α_2} is (operationally) deterministic if L^{α_1} is (operationally) deterministic,*
- respects enabling *if and only if, for every $\alpha \in \mathcal{A}$, if $[s]_\alpha = [s']_\alpha$, then $en(s) = en(s')$,*
- $\mathcal{A}$ respects stability *if and only if, for every $\alpha \in \mathcal{A}$, if $[s]_\alpha = [s']_\alpha$, then either (1) neither s, s' or $[s]_\alpha$ is stable, or (2) there exist stable states $s_1, s'_1 \in [s]_\alpha$ such that $s \xRightarrow{\epsilon} s_1$, $s' \xRightarrow{\epsilon} s'_1$ and $en(s_1) = en(s'_1) = en([s]_\alpha)$,*
- separable *if and only if, for every $\alpha \in \mathcal{A}$ where $\alpha : X \to X'$, $X' = X'_1 \times \cdots X'_n$, and there exists $\alpha_1, \ldots \alpha_n$, $\alpha_i : X_i \to X'_i$ for $i = 1, \ldots, n$, such that for $x = (x_1, \ldots, x_n) \in X$, $\alpha(x) = (\alpha_1(x_1), \ldots, \alpha_n(x_n))$.*

From these definitions, the following proposition is self-evident.

Proposition 1. *An arbitrary collection of abstractions is monotonous with respect to* Tr. *If it preserves divergences, it is also monotonous with respect to* Divtr.

As a corollary, every concrete counterexample to Tr or Divtr specification has a corresponding abstract counterexample regardless of abstraction. Proposition 1 is the main reason why we adopt the trace model as our canonical model, as other semantic models are less robust with respect to abstraction.

Theorem 3. *Assume P is a semantic model that preserves* Fail. *There exists a family of abstractions $\mathcal{A}$ such that $\mathcal{A}$ preserves divergences, and there are $\alpha_1, \alpha_2 \in \mathcal{A}$, $\alpha_1 \prec \alpha_2$ and some L such that $L^{\alpha_1} \not\sqsubseteq_P L^{\alpha_1}$.*

Proof. Theorem 2 and the example in Fig. 2 prove this.   □

Theorem 3 together with Theorem 2 mean that except for Tr and Divtr, abstraction *in general* is not guaranteed to preserve counterexamples.

Proposition 2. *If A is a collection of 1-simulations that preserves and respects divergences and respects stability, then A preserves operational determinism.*

Proof. Assume L is operationally deterministic. Then there exists a D-relation as described in [12, Definition 8] on the states of L. Denote this D-relation with $\sim$. It is simple to show that if α is a 1-simulation that preserves and respects divergences and stability, then $\alpha(s_1) = \alpha(s_2)$ implies $s_1 \sim s_2$.   □

Theorem 4. *Assume A respects stability and preserves divergences. Then A is monotonous with respect to* CSP.

Proof. Let $\alpha, \beta \in A$ and A respects stability, and $\alpha \prec \beta$. Let $(\sigma, A) \in \mathsf{Sfail}(L^\alpha)$. Then there is a stable state $[s]_\alpha$ such that $[\hat{s}]_\alpha \overset{\sigma}{\Rightarrow}_\alpha [s]_\alpha$, and $A \cap en(s) = \emptyset$. Then $[\hat{s}]_\beta \overset{\sigma}{\Rightarrow} [s]_\beta$ holds, and either $[s]_\beta$ is diverging or it is stable and $en([s]_\beta) = en([s]_\alpha)$, so that $(\sigma, A) \in \mathsf{Sfail}(L^\beta)$ □

Example 1. Consider the mapping $h(s)$ which returns a representative of s in the equivalence class under a strong bisimulation relation. The quotient L^h where $S^h = \{h(s) \mid s \in S\}$ and Δ^h is Δ restricted to S^h. L^h is strongly bisimilar to L. When A consists of strong bisimulations the abstractions preserve virtually all reasonable semantic models. Such abstractions were used in [1].

Example 2. In *Predicate abstraction*, a set of predicates over states is defined, and an abstract state consists of the set of states which agree on the truth value of all predicates. Predicate abstraction is used for example in the so-called CEGAR approach [2]. Predicate abstraction is not separable or monotonous in general, nor does it respect enabling or stability.

   The abstractions described in [2], however, do result in A that respects enabledness, because the coarsest abstraction h has the property that for every guard g, $h(s) = h(s')$ if and only if $g(s) = g(s')$.

Example 3. *Data abstraction* or *value abstraction* is a general term for abstractions that replace the set of values of a variable with a smaller set. Data abstractions are easily expanded into separable sets of abstractions, where each variable is abstracted separately.

4   Stubborn Set Reductions

4.1   State-of-the Art for Finite Traces

In this section we start with definition of stubborn sets that is as such applicable to any LTSs.

Definition 5 (Reduced LTS). *Given an LTS $(S, \mathcal{T}, \Delta, \hat{s})$, a function $T : S \mapsto 2^{\mathcal{T}}$ is a reduction function. We define the reduced LTS of L by T, as $L_T = (S_T, \mathcal{T}, \Delta_T, \hat{s})$, where S_T and Δ_T are minimal subsets of S and Δ, respectively, that satisfy the following conditions:*

- $\hat{s} \in S_T$, and
- if $s \in S_T$, $s \xrightarrow{t} s'$ and $t \in T(s)$, then $s' \in S_T$ and $(s, t, s') \in \Delta_T$.

By definition, a reduced LTS is a sub-LTS of the original LTS. For the remainder of this section we shall refer to L_T an L as the reduced and full LTSs, respectively. The properties preserved in the reduction depend on the properties of the reduction function. The term *stubborn set* in this article is a collective term for the sets produced by reduction functions. We describe the stubborn set reduction functions by giving various conditions.

Such conditions can be given towards one of two goals. The first goal, adopted in most of the literature on partial order reduction, is to provide a set of conditions sufficient for preserving the semantics of the system in the fullest. In the case of traces, this would mean that the reduced LTS should be trace-equivalent to the original. That is, the reduced LTS should satisfy $\mathsf{Tr}(L) = \mathsf{Tr}(L_T)$. We will explore such conditions in what follows, but they will be of secondary importance.

The second goal, one which we shall be primarily aiming for, is the preservation of the existence of a counterexample. For example, with traces, given a specification $\mathcal{L}$, the reduction should satisfy $\mathsf{Tr}(L) \cap \mathcal{L} \neq \emptyset$ if and only if $\mathsf{Tr}(L_T) \cap \mathcal{L} \neq \emptyset$.

We introduce the conditions incrementally to make them more understandable. The first two (or their equivalents in the case for abstract state spaces) are common to all versions. We also give a third condition, which is more restrictive, but it is used in practical analysis. Every condition is given for a state s.

D1. For every $t \in T(s)$ and $t_1, \ldots, t_k \notin T(s)$, if $s \xrightarrow{t_1 \cdots t_k t} s'$, then $s \xrightarrow{t t_1 \cdots t_k} s'$.

N. There exists $t \in T(s)$ such that for every $t_1, \ldots, t_k \notin T(s)$, if $s \xrightarrow{t_1 \cdots t_k}$ and $s \xrightarrow{t} s'$, then $s' \xrightarrow{t_1 \cdots t_k}$. Such a transition is called a *neutral transition*.

D2. For every $t \in T(s)$ and every $t_1, \ldots, t_k \notin T(s)$, if $s \xrightarrow{t}$, then $s' \xrightarrow{t_1 \cdots t_k t}$.

The classical stubborn sets are defined using **D1** and **D2**; **D1** and **D2** clearly imply **N**. We give our theoretical treatment for **N** as it theoretically has the potential to overcome the optimality result of [22]. The conditions above are not sufficient for preservation of properties such as traces. This stems from two issues. The first one is that they allow the reduction to ignore permutations of transitions in such a way that the order of symbols in the trace is not preserved.

The trace-preserving version requires the concept of *visible transition*. A transition t is visible if and only if $l(t) \neq \epsilon$, i.e., if its occurrence in an execution has an effect on the trace.

V. If there is some visible transition $t \in T(s)$ such that $t \in en(s)$, then $T(s)$ contains all visible transitions, including the disabled ones.

But for preserving counterexamples, we do not need to be quite as strict. Assume $\hat{s} \xrightarrow{\sigma} s$ and $\sigma \rho \notin \mathcal{L}$. Let $u_1, \ldots, u_n \in \mathcal{T}$ such that $\rho = l(u_1 \cdots u_n)$. We define the following conditions:

Va. If $u_i \in T(s)$ for some i and $u_j \notin T(s)$ for $1 \leq j < i$, then for some prefix of $\rho' \leq l(u_i u_1 \cdots u_{i-1} u_{i+1} \cdots u_n)$, $\sigma \rho' \notin \mathcal{L}$.

Vb. If $u_i \notin T(s)$ for each i, then there is a neutral transition $t \in T(s)$ such that for some prefix $\rho' \leq l(t u_1 \cdots \cdots u_n)$, $\sigma \rho' \notin \mathcal{L}$.

Verbally, the condition **Va** states that if we take a transition that is a part of a counterexample, then commuting the said transition to the front of the execution will also result in a counterexample. **Vb** states that if we explore a neutral transition and ignore transitions remaining of a counterexample, we can still continue and find a counterexample. Note that **V** trivially implies **Va** by forcing all visible transitions in the stubborn set and **Vb** is implied when the stubborn set contains only τ-transitions.

We still need to solve the so-called ignoring problem, where neutral transitions are taken indefinitely. Such a scenario is possible if the system contains, for example, a cycle consisting of neutral transitions. To ensure progress, the literature suggests rather crude rules such as those requiring that the stubborn set contains all transitions if a cycle is closed. We forgo such rules for a more nuanced approach.

We need to define the set of *interesting* transitions at a state s. If we set out to preserve all traces, the set of interesting transitions will be the set of visible transitions in every state. When we set out to preserve only the existence of counterexamples, we can choose the set of interesting transitions in several ways, as long as it has the property that all possible ways of completing a counterexample will contain at least one interesting transition.

We say that a set U of transitions is *interesting* at state s for every relevant execution $\hat{s} \stackrel{\sigma}{\Rightarrow}_T s \xrightarrow{t_1 \cdots t_n}$ there is some $1 \leq i \leq n$ such that $t_i \in U$. Note that "relevant execution" may mean one of several things. If the reduction must preserve all traces, then $U = \{t \mid l(t) \in \Sigma\}$, the set of visible transitions must be interesting. If it must preserve counterexamples of some type, then the set must guarantee that every counterexample that visits s, requires the firing of at least one interesting transition at s.

We say that a set $W \subseteq \mathcal{T}$ is *closed under enabling* at state s, if for every $t \in W$, $s \xrightarrow{t_1 \cdots t_n t}$ implies that either $s \xrightarrow{t}$ or $t_i \in W$ for some $1 \leq i \leq n$.

S. There exists a set W that is closed under enabling at s and contains all interesting transitions, and for every $u \in W \cap en(s)$ there exists a sequence $s \xrightarrow{t_1 \cdots t_n} s'$ of neutral transitions such that $u \in T(s')$.

The proof of the following theorem was given in [13].

Theorem 5. *Let $\mathcal{L}$ be a trace specification. If T is a reduction function that satisfies conditions **D1**, **N**, **Va**, **Vb**, and **S**. Then L_T has a trace $\sigma \notin \mathcal{L}$ if and only if L some trace $\rho \notin \mathcal{L}$.*

Proof. If L_T has an illegal trace, then L trivially has an illegal trace, because all traces of L_T are traces of L. The other direction is by induction on the unexplored part of an illegal trace. Let s be a state of L_T. The situation where

$\hat{s} \overset{\sigma}{\Rightarrow}_T s$ and $\sigma \notin \mathcal{L}$ is the trivial base case. Let $\sigma\rho \notin \mathcal{L}$ be some trace of L_T and let $\hat{s} \overset{\sigma}{\Rightarrow}_T s$ be such that $s \overset{\rho}{\Rightarrow}$. Let $u_1, \ldots, u_n \in \mathcal{T}$ be transitions such that $s \xrightarrow{u_1 \cdots u_n}$ and $l(u_1 \cdots u_n) = \rho$.

Firstly, assume $u_i \in T(s)$ for some $1 \leq i \leq n$, and without loss of generality, assume i is chosen as the minimal such i. Let s_i be such that $s \xrightarrow{u_1 \cdots u_i} s_i$ and Now, **D1** guarantees that u_i must be enabled and that $s \xrightarrow{u_i u_1 \cdots u_{i-1}} s_i$. Then $s \overset{u_i}{\longrightarrow}_T s'$ holds for some state. **Va** then guarantees that some prefix of $s' \xrightarrow{u_1 \cdots u_{i-1} u_{i+1} \cdots u_n}$ completes the illegal trace, and we have an inductive step.

Secondly, assume that $t_i \notin T(s)$ for every $1 \leq i \leq n$. Then **N** guarantees there is a neutral transition $t \in T$ such that $s \overset{t}{\rightarrow}_T s'$ and $s' \xrightarrow{u_1 \cdots u_n}$. **Vb** then guarantees that some prefix of $l(tu_1 \cdots u_n)$ will complete the illegal trace, so that $\sigma l(t) \rho' \notin \mathcal{L}$, where ρ' is some prefix of ρ. If the prefix is shorter than ρ, this constitutes an inductive step.

If $\rho = \rho'$, we need to employ **S**. Note that because $s \xrightarrow{u_1 \cdots u_n}$ completes an illegal trace, it is guaranteed that u_i is interesting in s for some $1 \leq i \leq n$. Let u_k be interesting. Let W be the set stipulated by **S** that is closed under enabling. Because it W is closed under enabling, then some $u_i \in W$ such that u_i is enabled at s and $i < k$. Then there exists $s_0 \overset{t_1}{\rightarrow}_T s_1 \overset{t_2}{\rightarrow}_T \cdots \overset{t_m}{\rightarrow}_T s_m$ of neutral transitions such that $s_0 = s$ and $u_i \in T(s_m)$. **N** guarantees that in each of these states s_l, as long as $u_j \notin T(s_l)$ for $1 \leq j \leq n$, $s_{l+1} \xrightarrow{u_1 \cdots u_n}$ holds, and **Vb** guarantees some prefix $u_1 \cdots u_n$ of completes the illegal trace from s_{l+1}. If $u_j \in T(s_l)$ for some $1 \leq j \leq n$ and $1 \leq l < m$, the first inductive case materializes. At the latest in s_m this happens, because $u_i \in T(s_m)$. $\qquad\square$

4.2 Stable Failures, Divergences, and Branching Time

The condition **S**, **Va** and **Vb** are sufficient for finite counterexamples, but not in general for infinite traces; we cannot just extend **Va** to infinite traces. Consider the language over $\Sigma = \{a, b\}$ that contains all infinite traces such that either a or b (but not both) can appear infinitely many times. Counterexamples consist of infinite sequences where both a and b appear infinitely many times. Consider Fig. 3(a). We label the transitions directly with elements of Σ. **Va** and **Vb** are satisfied by exploring only a in the initial state, because if ρ is an infinite counterexample of any kind, then $a\rho$ is also. This holds no matter how many finite steps we have taken, both a and b are needed to complete counterexamples, i.e., every counterexample contains at least an a-transition, so that $\{a\}$ is interesting and it is immediately chosen as the stubborn set. It is also neutral with respect to b. **V** would be sufficient with **S** to preserve traces, and this implies for finite systems that infinite traces are preserved.

Consider then Fig. 3(b) and the requirement that $\text{Divtr} \subseteq \{\epsilon\}$. Counterexamples to this include any divergences after any visible transitions. In the initial state $\{\tau_1, \tau_2\}$ is a stubborn set that satisfies **V** in addition to all the conditions in Theorem 5. Because $a\tau_1^\omega$ is a counterexample, τ_1 is interesting because it is needed before any counterexample is finished. τ_2 is neutral, as $\overset{a}{\rightarrow}$ is the only

(a) Infinite trace   (b) Divergence trace

Fig. 3. Counterexamples to infinite properties

execution consisting of transitions that are not in the stubborn set, and it is preserved.

The best conditions for preserving *all* divergence traces all require conditions such as the following. It has recently been discussed in [23].

L. For every visible transition t, every infinite execution $s_0 \xrightarrow{t_1}_T s_1 \xrightarrow{t_2}_T \cdots$ in the reduced state space contains a state s_i such that $t \in T(s_i)$.

For finite state spaces, this is called a *cycle condition* because all infinite executions are cyclic. We shall not explore their use in this article.

For CSP-semantics the problem in Fig. 3 does not manifest, because CSP does not require us to preserve *all* divergences, only minimal ones, which then are extended with otherwise maximal behaviour. The traditional stubborn sets as described, for example, in [21,23], require the conditions **V** and a condition called **I**, which unfortunately loses its meaning when we use the condition **N**.

IN. $T(s)$ contains either a neutral τ-transition or all τ-transitions.

Lemma 2. *If T is a reduction function that satisfies* **D1**, **N** *and* **IN** *in every state of L_T, and if $s \xrightarrow{\tau^\omega}$, then $s \xrightarrow{\tau^\omega}_T$.*

Proof. Let s be a state of L_T and let $s \xrightarrow{t_1 t_2 \cdots}$ be a diverging execution starting from s. If none of t_i is in $T(s)$, then **IN** guarantees there is a neutral τ-transition t and s' such that $s \xrightarrow{t}_T s'$ and $s' \xrightarrow{t_1 t_2 \cdots}$. On the other hand, if $t_i \in T(s)$ for some i, we choose the minimal i such that this holds. then let $s \xrightarrow{t_1 t_2 \cdots t_i} s_i$. **D1** guarantees that $s \xrightarrow{t_i}_T s'$ for some s' such that $s' \xrightarrow{t_1 t_2 \cdots t_{i-1} t_{i+1} \cdots}$.

This gives an infinite sequence of τ-transitions in L_T whenever a state is diverging.   □

Unfortunately **D1**, **N** and **IN** are not enough, even with **V**, to preserve stable failures, as is witnessed by Fig. 4, but **D1**, **D2**, **V** and **IN** are. In the presence of **D2** all transitions are neutral, so **IN** is equivalent to **I**. Various solutions that use conditions more restrictive than **N** have been used in practice with good empirical results when preserving traces or CSP [8,14].

For completeness we restate the important results that are well-known about preservation of the semantic models discussed earlier, as well as one for branching properties. We need two further conditions.

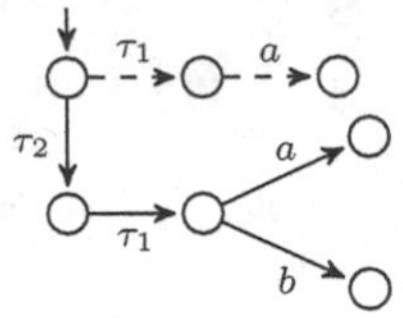

Fig. 4. Counterexample to stable failures

D0. $en(s) \cap T(s) = \emptyset$ if and only if $en(s) = \emptyset$.
 B. $en(s) \subseteq T(s)$ or $T(s) \cap en(s)$ contains a single invisible transition.

Theorem 6. *Assume T satisfies* **D1** *at every state of L_T. Then the following hold:*

1. *If T satisfies* **D0** *and* **D2** *at every state of L_T, then L_T contains all reachable states s of L such that $en(s) = \emptyset$.*
2. *If all visible transitions are interesting and T satisfies* **N**, **IN**, *and* **V** *at every state of L_T, then $L_T \equiv_{\mathsf{Mindiv}} L$.*
3. *If all visible transitions are interesting and T satisfies* **D2**, **S**, **IN**, *and* **V** *at every state of L_T, then $L_T \equiv_{\mathsf{CSP}} L$.*
4. *If all visible transitions are interesting and T satisfies* **D0**, **D2**, **V**, *and* **L** *at every state of L_T, then $L_T \equiv_{\mathsf{Sfail,Divtr}} L$.*
5. *If L is deterministic and $T(s)$ satisfies* **D2**, **V**, **B**, *and* **S** *in every state of L_T, then L_T is branching bisimilar to L.*

Mostly the theorem was proven in [21], albeit with a slightly different set of rules which, nevertheless, for deterministic transition systems are implied by the given conditions. The second statement of the theorem is novel, and follows from Lemma 2.

4.3   Considerations for Computing Stubborn Sets

Various methods for actually computing stubborn sets as defined in the earlier parts of this section have been proposed. Most commonly they include a form of *dependency relation*, or *dependency graph*, such as in [8,10,14]. Several authors discuss strategies based on shared variables and they range from forbidding changes of variables [4] to more nuanced approaches such as using write-up sets [19], analysis of guards [15]. It was proven in [22] that the classic stubborn sets are optimal in a model-theoretic sense with respect to symmetric dependency relations such as those used in [7]. We discuss some relations that can be defined by the rather coarse level of analysis [7], based on so-called effect sets. Unfortunately, these sets do not make it possible to employ the theoretical benefits afforded by the use of condition **N** instead of **D2**.

Definition 6. *Let L be an LTS. We define the following relations.*

- *A left dependency relation $\rightsquigarrow$ over T is any relation such that if either $t \rightsquigarrow u$ or for every state s, if $s \xrightarrow{ut} s_2$ then there is a state s_3 such that $s_1 \xrightarrow{u} s_3$ and $s_3 \xrightarrow{t} s_2$. We write $t \not\rightsquigarrow u$ when $t \rightsquigarrow u$ does not hold.*
- *A dependency relation $\leftrightharpoons$ over T is any relation such that if either $t \leftrightharpoons u$ or for every state s, if $s \xrightarrow{u} s_1$ and $s \xrightarrow{t} s_2$ then there is a state s_3 such that $s_1 \xrightarrow{t} s_3$ and $s_2 \xrightarrow{u} s_3$. We write $t \not\leftrightharpoons u$ when $t \leftrightharpoons u$ does not hold.*

The following lemma is given for the left-dependency and dependency relations

Lemma 3. *Let $s_0, s_n \in S$, $t, t_1, \ldots, t_n \in T$ and $s_0 \xrightarrow{t_1 \cdots t_n} s_n$*

- *If $t \not\rightsquigarrow t_i$ for $1 \leq i \leq n$, and $s_n \xrightarrow{t} s'_n$ for some s'_n then there is a state s'_0 such that $s_0 \xrightarrow{t} s'_0$ and $s'_0 \xrightarrow{t_1 \cdots t_n} s'_n$.*
- *If $t \not\leftrightharpoons t_i$ for $1 \leq i \leq n$, and $s_0 \xrightarrow{t}$ then $s_n \xrightarrow{t}$.*

Recall that a *guard* is a binary function $X \rightarrow \{true, false\}$. Recall that transitions are of the form (g, e), where g is a guard.

Definition 7. *Let G be a set of guards. A guard relation for state s is a relation $\hookrightarrow$ over $T \times G \cup G \times T$ that has the following properties.*

1. *If $t = (g, e) \in T$ and $g(s) = false$, then $t \hookrightarrow g_i$ if $g_i \in G$ such that $g_i(s) = false$ and for all $x \in X$, $g(x) = true$ implies $g_i(x) = true$.*
2. *If $g \in G$ and $g(s) = false$, then $g \hookrightarrow t$ if $t \in T$ and there exists some states s_1 and s_2 such that $s_1 \xrightarrow{t} s_2$, $g(s_1) = false$ and $g(s_2) = true$.*

The following lemma is useful in calculation of stubborn sets:

Lemma 4. *Let $U \subseteq T$ be a set of transitions and G be a set of guards. The set U is closed under enabling at state s if there exists a guard relation $\hookrightarrow$ for s and a subset $G' \subseteq G$ such that*

1. *For every $t \in dis(s) \cup U$, there is some $g \in G'$ such that $t \hookrightarrow g$.*
2. *For every $g \in G'$ and $t \in T$, if $g \hookrightarrow t$ then $t \in U$.*

Lemma 4 was proven, for example, in [14]. Lemmas 3 and 4 are useful in the computation of stubborn sets; We do not go into details about particular algorithms, they have been discussed in [7,8,10,15,22,25] to name a few. We give the theorem that the computation of stubborn sets is based on.

Theorem 7. *Let $\leftrightharpoons$ be a dependency relation and $\hookrightarrow$ be a guard relation for s. The set $T(s)$ satisfies **D1** and **D2** if there exists a set of guards G such that*

1. *For every $t \in T(s) \cap en(s)$ and $u \in T$, if $t \leftrightharpoons u$ then $u \in T(s)$.*
2. *For every $t \in T(s) \cap dis(s)$, there exists some $g \in G$ such that $t \hookrightarrow g$.*
3. *For every $g \in G$ and $t \in T$, if $g \hookrightarrow t$ then $t \in T(s)$.*

Recall that $X = X_1 \times \cdots \times X_n$. Let $x = (x_1, \ldots, x_n)$ and $y = (y_1, \ldots, y_n)$. We write $\delta(x, y) = \{i \mid x_i \neq y_i\}$ Given a transition $t = (g, e)$ we define the *effect* sets as:

- The *guard set* of t as $Gd(t) = \{i \mid \exists x, y \in X : \delta(x, y) = i \wedge g(x) \neq g(y)\}$,
- the *write set* of t as $Wr(t) = \{i \mid \exists x \in X : i \in \delta(x, e(x))\}$, and
- the *read set* of t as $Rr(t) = \{i \mid \exists x, y \in X : \delta(x, y) = i \wedge \exists j \in Wr(t) : j \in \delta(e(x), e(y))\}$.

The union of these sets, $Vr(t) = Gd(t) \cup Wr(t) \cup Rr(t)$ is called *variable set* of t. Intuitively, the guard set consists of variables whose value has an effect on the guard, the write set is the set of variables whose value is subject to change when the transition is fired, and the read set is the set of variables whose value has an effect on the resulting state, i.e. if a variable in a read set changes its value, then firing the transition will result in some change in some variable in the write set.

Given $t_1, t_2 \in \mathcal{T}$, if we define the relation $\leftrightharpoons^G$ so that $t_1 \not\leftrightharpoons^G t_2$ implies $Wr(t_1) \cap Vr(t_2) = Wr(t_2) \cap Vr(t_1) = \emptyset$, then this will result in a dependency relation. It is also a left dependency relation.

We can define $\hookrightarrow^G$ using the guard of each transition, or, if the guard is given as a conjunction of clauses, for example so that $g = g_1 \wedge \cdots \wedge g_k$, we can use the conjuncts in G and have $g_i \hookrightarrow^G t$ if $Wr(t)$ contains some variable appearing in g_i, for example.

5   Stubborn Sets and Abstraction

As we saw in Sect. 3, abstraction may lead to nondeterminism. We also saw in Sect. 4 that the state-of-the art stubborn sets do not preserve all counterexamples if transitions may be nondeterministic. In this section we discuss some problems with combining stubborn sets and abstractions. We discuss the results of [1], and show that the approach applies only to a narrow class of abstractions.

The proof of Theorem 5 does not require the system is deterministic, but abstraction nevertheless gives rise problem. Consider the following hypothesis: given an abstraction α, the set U satisfies **N** at that state $[s]_\alpha$ in L^α if for every state $s' \in [s]_\alpha$, U satisfies **N** in L. Figure 5(a) and (b) demonstrate a counterexample to the hypothesis; abstractions do not in general satisfy this property. The transition τ_1 is neutral in all the states of the equivalence class (indicated by the gray states).

Firstly we note that we could define a dependency relation $\leftrightharpoons^\alpha$ for the transitions of L^α directly, analogously to Definition 6. Then Theorem 6 would hold for all other parts, except part 5 which assumes transitions are deterministic, and this is not true for L^α in general. The following lemma is trivial, but we state it in any case.

Lemma 5. *If α is separable, then the relations $\leftrightharpoons^G$ and $\hookrightarrow^G$ are dependency and guard relations for L^α.*

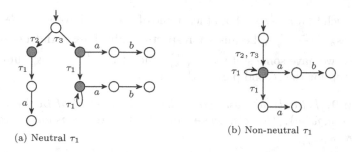

(a) Neutral τ_1

(b) Non-neutral τ_1

Fig. 5. Troublesome cases for abstraction and stubborn sets

This lemma is important in practice, as it applies to several methods that are used in practice. For example in [4], the analysis is carried out using this type of dependency. Thus, all linear time stubborn set methods based on these relations are in fact robust with respect to separable abstractions.

Definition 8. *Let α be an abstraction. The relation $\leftrightharpoons_\alpha$ over $\mathcal{T}$ is an* abstract dependency relation, *or α-dependency, if for every s, if $t, u \in en(s)$ either $t \leftrightharpoons_\alpha u$ or the following hold:*

1. *For for every s' such that $s \xrightarrow{t} s'$ we have $s' \xrightarrow{u}$ (and symmetrically for u), and*
2. *For every state s_1 such that $s \xrightarrow{tu} s_1$ there is a state s_2 such that $s \xrightarrow{ut} s_2$ and $[s_1]_\alpha = [s_2]_\alpha$ (and symmetrically).*

Lemma 6. *Assume $\mathcal{A}$ respects enabledness and $\alpha \in \mathcal{A}$. For every $t_1, \dots, t_n$ such that $t_i \not\leftrightharpoons_\alpha t$ for $1 \leq i \leq n$, if $[s]_\alpha \xrightarrow{t_1 \cdots t_n}_\alpha [s_n]_\alpha$ and $[s]_\alpha \xrightarrow{t}_\alpha [s']_\alpha$, then there is a state $[s'_n]_\alpha$ such that $[s']_\alpha \xrightarrow{t_1 \cdots t_n}_\alpha [s'_n]_\alpha$ and $[s_n]_\alpha \xrightarrow{t}_\alpha [s_n]'$.*

Furthermore, if $\mathcal{A}$ is a collection of 1-simulations, then for every $[s'_n]_\alpha$ such that $[s_n]_\alpha \xrightarrow{t}_\alpha [s'_n]_\alpha$, $[s]_\alpha \xrightarrow{t t_1 \cdots t_n}_\alpha [s'_n]_\alpha$ holds.

Proof. We prove the claims by induction. If $n = 0$, both claims holds trivially. Assume as inductive hypothesis that the first claim holds for $n - 1$. Let $[s_0]_\alpha \xrightarrow{t_1 \cdots t_n}_\alpha [s_n]_\alpha$ and $[s_0]_\alpha \xrightarrow{t}_\alpha [s'_0]_\alpha$. By inductive hypothesis we have $[s'_0]_\alpha \xrightarrow{t_1 \cdots t_{n-1}}_\alpha [s'_{n-1}]_\alpha$ and $[s_{n-1}]_\alpha \xrightarrow{t}_\alpha [s'_{n-1}]_\alpha$. Let s_{n-1} be one of the states in $[s_{n-1}]_\alpha$ such that $s_{n-1} \xrightarrow{t} s'_{n-1}$.

Because α respects enabledness, $s_{n-1} \xrightarrow{t_n} s_n$ for some state s_n. And because $\leftrightharpoons_\alpha$ is an α-dependency relation, we must have $s_n \xrightarrow{t} s'_n$ for some state s'_n and $s'_{n-1} \xrightarrow{t_n} s^*_n$ for some state $s^*_n \in [s'_n]_\alpha$.

Hence $[s_{n-1}]_\alpha \xrightarrow{t_n t}_\alpha [s'_n]_\alpha$ and $[s'_{n-1}]_\alpha \xrightarrow{t_n}_\alpha [s_n]'_\alpha$, finishing the inductive step for the first part of the lemma.

Assume then that α is a 1-simulation and the second claim holds for $n - 1$. Let $[s_n]_\alpha \xrightarrow{t}_\alpha [s'_n]_\alpha$. Then, for every state $s_n \in [s_n]_\alpha$ there exists some state

$s'_n \in [s'_n]_\alpha$ such that $s_n \xrightarrow{t} s'_n$. For at least one of them we have $s_{n-1} \xrightarrow{t_n} s_n \xrightarrow{t} s'_n$, and again, $s_{n-1} \xrightarrow{t} s'_{n-1}$ because α respects enabledness. And because of α-dependency, we have some state $s^*_n \in [s'_n]_\alpha$ such that $s'_{n-1} \xrightarrow{t_n} s^*_n$, finishing the inductive step for the second part of the lemma. □

Definition 9. *Let α be an abstraction. Let G be a set of of Boolean functions $\alpha(X) \to \{true, false\}$. The relation $\hookrightarrow_\alpha$ over $T \times G \cup G \times T$ is an abstract guard relation for $[s]_\alpha$ if*

1. *For every $t \in dis_\alpha([s]_\alpha)$ there exists a guard $g \in G$ such that $g([s]_\alpha) = false$ and $t \hookrightarrow_\alpha g$.*
2. *For every state $g \in G$ and $t \in T$, if there is some states s', s'' such that $s' \xrightarrow{t} s''$, $g([s']_\alpha) = false$ and $g([s'']_\alpha) = true$ then $g \hookrightarrow_\alpha t$.*

Theorem 8. *Assume $\mathcal{A}$ is a collection of 1-simulations and that it respects enabledness. Let $\alpha \in \mathcal{A}$. Let $[s]_\alpha$ be an abstract state. Then the set U satisfies D1 and D2 if there exist some abstract guard relation $\hookrightarrow_\alpha$, a set of guards G, and an abstract dependency relation $\rightleftharpoons_\alpha$ such that*

1. *For every $t \in en_\alpha([s]_\alpha)$ and $u \in T$, if $t \in U$ and $t \rightleftharpoons_\alpha u$ then $u \in U$.*
2. *For every $t \in dis_\alpha([s]_\alpha)$ there is some $g \in G$ such that $t \hookrightarrow_\alpha g$ and for every $[s']_\alpha$.*
3. *For every $g \in G$ and $t \in T$, if $g \hookrightarrow_\alpha t$, then $t \in U$.*

Proof. Because Definition 9 is strictly analogous to Definition 7 and Lemma 4 applies, we skip the proof that U will be closed under enabling. Lemma 6 applied to the first condition proves **D2**. Because α is a 1-simulation, Lemma 6 guarantees that also **D1** holds. □

The restriction that $\mathcal{A}$ must respect both enabledness and determinism is a severe one. The result of [1] merits discussion in light of the weakness of the above theorem. The result of using α-dependency when α is a strong bisimulation is sound, because two states cannot be strongly bisimilar unless they have the same enabled transitions. It does not hold, however, for weaker equivalences. Consider Fig. 6(a). The grey states are branching bisimilar, but not strongly bisimilar. α-dependency would declare the transitions labeled a and τ_2 as independent regardless of what happens after they are fired, because they are not enabled together. In fact, simple as it is, Fig. 6(a) leaves little hope for developing a method that is based on dependencies significantly less restrictive than those that consider the whole equivalence class, i.e., dependency in Definition 6 applied to the whole abstract state space.

The counterexample to abstractions that are not 1-simulations is given in Fig. 6(b). The abstraction equates the gray states in the figure. We can then define an abstract dependency relation that declares a and b independent. c and b are likewise independent. The set $\{a\}$ would satisfy the conditions of Theorem 8 under this abstraction. The abstraction also respects enabledness. In the state that follows the execution of a, $\{c\}$ is a set that likewise satisfies the conditions

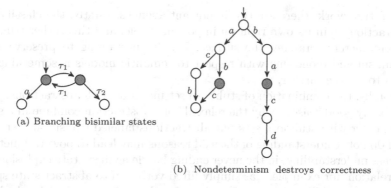

(a) Branching bisimilar states

(b) Nondeterminism destroys correctness

Fig. 6. Counterexamples to α-dependency

of the theorem, and the execution of d is missed. The example leaves open the possibility that forbids possibly nondeterministic transitions (such as c) from being stubborn.

6 Discussion and Future Work

As this article is to appear in a collection to honor professor Bill Roscoe, I break the convention and write in first person. I do so out of respect for the community and the person, as I hope to explain in a more personal manner what has been written here. I also wish to express my gratitude and sense of honor to have been invited to write this article.

The main theorem in [11] states that for timed automata, relaxing zone abstractions and applying an abstract dependency very similar to the one in Theorem 8 will preserve the existence of counterexamples. In fact, it not only does this, but sometimes it is able to reduce away abstract counterexamples that are spurious. When I started writing this article, I started with a hypothesis stronger than Theorem 8, one that would replicate the same powerful results.

A series of counterexamples, given in the previous sections, emerged while I was trying to prove a similar result, and in the end, the result was not significantly stronger than the main theorem of [1]. Instead of this article providing groundbreaking results as I had hoped, it thus is more of a document of how such a result does not hold for the abstract dependency relation as defined here. I hope that a careful analysis of the counterexamples to weaker hypothesis might prove fruitful in the pursuit of a more general theorem, one that may still be out there. I am still haunted by the intuition that there is a hidden diamond amid the ashes of this failed theorem.

For other parts, the results in this article are mostly re-stated facts that have been known separately with a couple of minor improvements to existing results. I hope my analysis may serve as a starting point for a more careful analysis of properties of abstractions and how they combine with the myriad other methods.

For future work, there are two important avenues. Firstly, the classification of abstractions is in its own right an important topic, and this rather truncated treatment merely scratches the surface. Results pertaining to preservation of determinism and monotony with respect to semantic models is something that we plan to pursue further.

Secondly, the combination of stubborn set methods with abstractions. There are probably good reasons why the relaxed zone abstraction combine in a synergistic manner with stubborn sets but abstractions labeled transition systems in general do not. Understanding of the said reasons may lead to powerful methods, or at least understanding, in the never ending battle against state explosion. The guard relation, for example, was simply lifted verbatim to abstract state spaces. It remains a possibility that some version of such a relation might be the key to unlock a more powerful theory.

Acknowledgements. I wish to thank the editors for inviting me to submit an article, Antti Valmari for pioneering the field and his eagerness to discuss the topic after all these years, Xu Wang for discussions we have had over the years about the merits and pitfalls of various approaches, and Dragan Bosnacki for providing some insights on the matter. I am grateful to Bill Roscoe, for asking me one instrumental question about partial order reduction years ago. Answering that question led me to write a few articles, and, in a way, also this one.

References

1. Bošnački, D., Scheffer, M.: Partial order reduction and symmetry with multiple representatives. In: Havelund, K., Holzmann, G., Joshi, R. (eds.) NFM 2015. LNCS, vol. 9058, pp. 97–111. Springer, Heidelberg (2015). doi:10.1007/978-3-319-17524-9_8
2. Clarke, E., Grumberg, O., Jha, S., Lu, Y., Veith, H.: Counterexample-guided abstraction refinement. In: Emerson, E.A., Sistla, A.P. (eds.) CAV 2000. LNCS, vol. 1855, pp. 154–169. Springer, Heidelberg (2000). doi:10.1007/10722167_15
3. Clarke, E.M., Grumberg, O., Long, D.E.: Model checking and abstraction. ACM Trans. Programm. Lang. Syst. (TOPLAS) **16**(5), 1512–1542 (1994)
4. Clarke, E.M., Grumberg, O., Peled, D.: Model Checking. MIT press, Cambridge (1999)
5. Emerson, E.A., Sistla, A.P.: Symmetry and model checking. In: Courcoubetis, C. (ed.) CAV 1993. LNCS, vol. 697, pp. 463–478. Springer, Heidelberg (1993). doi:10.1007/3-540-56922-7_38
6. Engelfriet, J.: Determinancy → (observation equivalence = trace equivalence). Theor. Comput. Sci. **36**, 21–25 (1985)
7. Geldenhuys, J., Hansen, H., Valmari, A.: Exploring the scope for partial order reduction. In: Liu, Z., Ravn, A.P. (eds.) ATVA 2009. LNCS, vol. 5799, pp. 39–53. Springer, Heidelberg (2009). doi:10.1007/978-3-642-04761-9_4
8. Gibson-Robinson, T., Hansen, H., Roscoe, A.W., Wang, X.: Practical partial order reduction for CSP. In: Havelund, K., Holzmann, G., Joshi, R. (eds.) NFM 2015. LNCS, vol. 9058, pp. 188–203. Springer, Heidelberg (2015). doi:10.1007/978-3-319-17524-9_14

9. Godefroid, P. (ed.): Partial-Order Methods for the Verification of Concurrent Systems. LNCS, vol. 1032. Springer, Heidelberg (1996). doi:10.1007/3-540-60761-7
10. Hansen, H., Kwiatkowska, M., Qu, H.: Partial order reduction for model checking Markov decision processes under unconditional fairness. In: Quantitative Evaluation of Systems (QEST 2011), pp. 203–212. IEEE (2011)
11. Hansen, H., Lin, S.-W., Liu, Y., Nguyen, T.K., Sun, J.: Diamonds are a girl's best friend: partial order reduction for timed automata with abstractions. In: Biere, A., Bloem, R. (eds.) CAV 2014. LNCS, vol. 8559, pp. 391–406. Springer, Heidelberg (2014). doi:10.1007/978-3-319-08867-9_26
12. Hansen, H., Valmari, A.: Operational determinism and fast algorithms. In: Baier, C., Hermanns, H. (eds.) CONCUR 2006. LNCS, vol. 4137, pp. 188–202. Springer, Heidelberg (2006). doi:10.1007/11817949_13
13. Hansen, H., Valmari, A.: Safety property-driven stubborn sets. In: Larsen, K.G., Potapov, I., Srba, J. (eds.) RP 2016. LNCS, vol. 9899, pp. 90–103. Springer, Heidelberg (2016). doi:10.1007/978-3-319-45994-3_7
14. Hansen, H., Wang, X.: Compositional analysis for weak stubborn sets. In: 2011 11th International Conference on Application of Concurrency to System Design (ACSD), pp. 36–43. IEEE (2011)
15. Laarman, A., Pater, E., van de Pol, J., Hansen, H.: Guard-based partial-order reduction. Int. J. Softw. Tools Technol. Transfer 18(4), 427–448 (2016)
16. Milner, R. (ed.): A Calculus of Communicating Systems. LNCS, vol. 92. Springer, Heidelberg (1980). doi:10.1007/3-540-10235-3
17. Peled, D.: All from one, one for all: on model checking using representatives. In: Courcoubetis, C. (ed.) CAV 1993. LNCS, vol. 697, pp. 409–423. Springer, Heidelberg (1993). doi:10.1007/3-540-56922-7_34
18. Roscoe, A.W.: The Theory and Practice of Concurrency. Prentice-Hall, Upper Saddle River (1997)
19. Valmari, A.: A stubborn attack on state explosion. In: Clarke, E.M., Kurshan, R.P. (eds.) CAV 1990. LNCS, vol. 531, pp. 156–165. Springer, Heidelberg (1991). doi:10.1007/BFb0023729
20. Valmari, A.: Stubborn sets for reduced state space generation. In: Rozenberg, G. (ed.) ICATPN 1989. LNCS, vol. 483, pp. 491–515. Springer, Heidelberg (1991). doi:10.1007/3-540-53863-1_36
21. Valmari, A.: Stubborn set methods for process algebras. In: Proceedings of the DIMACS Workshop on Partial Order Methods in Verification (1997)
22. Valmari, A., Hansen, H.: Can stubborn sets be optimal? Fundamenta Informaticae 113(3–4), 377–397 (2011)
23. Valmari, A., Hansen, H.: Stubborn set intuition explained. In: International Workshop on Petri Nets and Software Engineering 2016, pp. 213–232 (2016)
24. Valmari, A., Tienari, M.: Compositional failure-based semantic models for basic lotos. Formal Aspects Comput. 7(4), 440–468 (1995)
25. Valmari, A., Vogler, W.: Fair testing and stubborn sets. In: Bošnački, D., Wijs, A. (eds.) SPIN 2016. LNCS, vol. 9641, pp. 225–243. Springer, Heidelberg (2016). doi:10.1007/978-3-319-32582-8_16
26. Glabbeek, R.J.: The linear time — branching time spectrum II. In: Best, E. (ed.) CONCUR 1993. LNCS, vol. 715, pp. 66–81. Springer, Heidelberg (1993). doi:10.1007/3-540-57208-2_6

A Hybrid Relational Modelling Language

He Jifeng and Li Qin[✉]

Shanghai Key Laboratory of Trustworthy Computing,
International Research Center of Trustworthy Software,
East China Normal University, Shanghai, China
qli@sei.ecnu.edu.cn

Abstract. Hybrid systems are usually composed by physical components with continuous variables and discrete control components where the system state evolves over time according to interacting laws of discrete and continuous dynamics. Combinations of computation and control can lead to very complicated system designs. We treat more explicit hybrid models by proposing a hybrid relational calculus, where both clock and signal are present to coordinate activities of parallel components of hybrid systems. This paper proposes a hybrid relational modelling language with a set of novel combinators which support complex combinations of both testing and signal reaction behaviours to model the physical world and its interaction with the control program. We provide a denotational semantics (based on the hybrid relational calculus) to the language, and explore healthiness conditions that deal with time and signal as well as the status of the program. A number of small examples are given throughout the paper to demonstrate the usage of the language and its semantics.

Keywords: Formal language and semantics · Unifying theories of programming · Relation calculus · Hybrid systems

1 Introduction

Hybrid system is an emergent area of growing importance, emphasising a systematic understanding of dynamic systems that combine digital and physical effects. Combinations of computation and control can lead to very complicated system designs. They occur frequently in automotive industries, aviation, factory automation and mixed analog-digital chip design.

The basic conceptional definition of a hybrid system includes a direct specification of its behaviours associated with both continuous and discrete dynamics and their non-trivial interactions [dSS00,Bra95]. The states of hybrid systems evolve over time according to interacting laws of discrete and continuous dynamics. For

This work was supported by Shanghai Knowledge Service Platform Project (No. ZF1213), Doctoral Fund of Ministry of Education of China (No. 20120076130003) and the NSFC-Zhejiang Joint Fund for the Integration of Industrialization and Informatization (No. U1509219).

T. Gibson-Robinson et al. (Eds.): Roscoe Festschrift, LNCS 10160, pp. 124–143, 2017.
DOI: 10.1007/978-3-319-51046-0_7

discrete dynamics, the hybrid system changes state instantaneously and discontinuously; while during continuous transitions, the system state is a continuous function of continuous time and varies according to a differential equation.

Hybrid system modelers mix discrete time reactive systems with continuous time ones. Systems like Simulink treat explicit models made of *Ordinary Differential Equations*, while others like Modelica provide more general implicit models defined by *Differential Algebraic Equations*. A variety of models for hybrid systems have been developed, such as hybrid automata [ACH93, Hen96, Tav87], phase transition system [MMP91], declarative control [Koh88], extended state transition system [ZH04], and hybrid action systems [RRS03, Ben98]. Platzer proposed a logic called Differential Dynamic Logic for specifying properties of hybrid systems [Pla08, Pla10]. His hybrid systems analysis approach has also been implemented in the verification tool KeYmaera for hybrid systems. We refer the readers to [CPP06] for an overview of languages and tools related to hybrid systems modeling and analysis.

There are a number of specification languages developed for hybrid systems. Inspired by the work in [He94], Zhou et al. [ZWR96] presented a hybrid variant of *Communicating Sequential Processes* (HCSP) [Hoa85] as a language for describing hybrid systems. They gave a semantics in *the extended duration calculus* [ZH04]. Rönkkö et al. [RRS03] extended *the guarded command language* [Dij76] with differential relations and gave a weakest-precondition semantics in higher-order logic with built in derivatives. Rounds and Song [RS03] developed a hybrid version of the π-*calculus* [Mil99] as a modelling language for embedded systems. Modelling languages for hybrid systems further include *SHIFT* [Des96] for networks of hybrid automata, and *R-Charon* for reconfigurable systems [Kra06].

Rather than addressing the formal verification of hybrid systems using simulation based approaches or model checking, this paper focuses on a general framework. It uses a simple hybrid modelling language to model non-trivial interactions between hybrid dynamics. This language captures the defining features of the hybrid systems such as monitoring physical variables over continuous time, asynchronous reacting to control signals, etc. Following the *UTP* approach advocated in [HH98], we build a mathematical theory of the *hybrid relations* as the foundation of the hybrid modelling languages. This is a presentation within predicate calculus of Tarski's theory of relations [Tar41], enriched with his fixed point theory [Tar55]. We show that the hybrid relational calculus is a conservative extension of the classical relational calculus, *i.e.*, all the algebraic laws of the operators remain valid in the new calculus.

The rest of the paper is organised as follows.

The hybrid relational modelling language is proposed in Sect. 2. Its semantical model is provided in Sect. 3 with UTP approaches. Section 3.1 adds continuous variables into the alphabet of relations to record the continuous dynamic behaviors of the hybrid system.

In Sect. 3.2, healthiness conditions placed on hybrid relations are proposed to ensure that the hybrid relations satisfy additional desirable properties related to clocks, signals and intermediate observations between initiation and termination. Sections 3.3 to 3.5 give a denotational semantics to every primitive command and combinator in the hybrid modelling language including the concurrent composition and the novel synchronous constructs **until** and **when** proposed to specify the interactions between components.

The paper ends with Sect. 4 for conclusion and future works.

2   A Hybrid Modelling Language

This section presents a hybrid modelling language, which extends the guarded command language [Dij76] by adding output command, synchronisation constructs and parallel operator. The syntax of the hybrid modelling language is as follows where x is a discrete variable, v is a continuous variable and s is a signal.

$$AP :: = \textbf{skip} \mid \textbf{chaos} \mid \textbf{idle} \mid x := e \mid x \leftarrow v \mid !s \mid \textbf{delay} \mid \textbf{delay}(\delta)$$

$$EQ :: = R(v, \dot{v}) \mid EQ \textbf{ init } (v = e) \mid EQ|EQ$$

$$P :: = AP \mid P \sqcap P \mid P; P \mid P \lhd b(x) \rhd P \mid P\|P \mid \mu X \bullet P(X) \mid$$

$$EQ \textbf{ until } g \mid \textbf{when}(G) \mid \textbf{timer } c \bullet P \mid \textbf{signal } s \bullet P$$

$$g :: = \textbf{I} \mid signal \mid test \mid g \cdot g \mid g + g$$

$$test :: = \textbf{true} \mid v \geq e \mid v \leq e \mid \neg test \mid test \wedge test \mid test \vee test$$

$$G :: = g\& P \mid G\|G$$

AP is a collection of atomic commands. **skip** is an atomic program that terminates immediately without changing any state value. **chaos** is an atomic program that diverges immediately. **idle** is an atomic program that never terminates and does not send out signals. $x := e$ is the conventional assignment which assigns the value of a discrete expression e to a discrete variable x. $x \leftarrow v$ samples the current value of a continuous variable v and assigns it to a discrete variable x. $!s$ emits a signal s. **delay** acts like **skip** but its terminating time is unknown in advance. **delay**(δ) keeps idle and terminates after δ time units.

EQ contains statements for continuous dynamics. $R(v, \dot{v})$ is a differential relation specifying the dynamics of the continuous variable v. $EQ \textbf{ init } v_0$ assigns the initial value v_0 to the continuous variable v governed by EQ. $EQ|EQ$ is a conjunction of two dynamics.

P lists all combinators in the hybrid language. The first line includes classic sequential composition operators, parallel composition operators and recursion operator. The first two structures in the second are new hybrid structures specifying the interactions between the continuous and discrete components of the hybrid system. They will be introduced in detail in Sect. 3.5. The last two operations of P are hiding operators for timers and signals.

The last three lines of the syntax comprise the structure of a guard command language for G which is a core element of the new hybrid structures. The guard condition g can be a signal, a value test and their combination. The notation $\mathbf{I}$ stands for a guard condition which will always be triggered immediately. $g\&P$ is a reactive structure that will execute P when g is triggered. $G\|G$ stands for a guarded choice operator.

Example 1 (Temperature control system). Consider a simple hybrid system controlling the temperature of a room. We use a continuous variable θ to record the room temperature and a discrete variable $H : \{on, off\}$ to denote the status of the heater. When the room temperature is below 19 degrees, the heater will be turned on and when the temperature exceeds 20, the heater will be turned off. Let Δ be the changing rate of the temperature, the specification of such system in our modelling language is as follows.

$$H := off; (\dot{\theta} = -\Delta \ \mathbf{init} \ \theta = 25) \ \mathbf{until} \ (\theta \leq 19);$$

$$\mathbf{when} \ \begin{pmatrix} \theta \leq 19 \ \& \ (H := on; (\dot{\theta} = \Delta) \ \mathbf{until} \ \theta \geq 20) \ \| \\ \theta \geq 20 \ \& \ (H := off; (\dot{\theta} = -\Delta) \ \mathbf{until} \ \theta \leq 19) \end{pmatrix}^*$$

where P^* stands for the recursive program $\mu X \bullet (P; X)$.

3   Semantical Model

The semantics of the hybrid language is defined based on the UTP theory. We will first choose the alphabet and healthiness conditions for the hybrid programs and provide the denotational semantics for every command and combinator. We refer the readers to [HH98] for the basic notations of UTP theory. And for the lack of space, we omit all proofs of the theorems in this section.

3.1   Alphabet

The hybrid programs studied in this paper are formalised with hybrid relations with an enlarged alphabet including continuous variables.

Definition 1 (Hybrid Relation).
A hybrid relation is a pair $(\alpha P, P)$, where P is a predicate containing no free variables other than in αP. Its alphabet αP contains sets of input and output discrete variables and a set $\mathbf{con}\alpha P$ of continuous variables.

$$\alpha P \ = \ \mathbf{in}\alpha P \ \cup \ \mathbf{out}\alpha P \ \cup \ \mathbf{con}\alpha P$$

The input variable set $\mathbf{in}\alpha P =_{df} \{st, t, pos\} \cup PVar \cup ClockVar$
where
$st, st' \in \{term, stable, div\}$ represent the program status at its start and finish time respectively. The meanings of program status $term, stable, div$ are introduced in Sect. 3.2.

$t, t' \in Time$ (of the type non-negative real numbers) are discrete variables denoting the start and end time instances of the observation one makes during the execution of the program.

$pos : \mathbb{N}$ (of the type nature numbers) is a variable introduced to facilitate the mechanism for describing the dependency of the signals. Its value will be recorded in the clock of each signal when it is emitted. The detailed usage will be demonstrated later associated with the clock variables.

$PVar$ denotes the set of discrete program variables.

$ClockVar$ denotes the set of clock variables

$$ClockVar =_{df} \{s.\textbf{clock} \mid s \in \textbf{InSignal} \cup \textbf{OutSignal}\}$$

where **InSignal** and **OutSignal** stand for the sets of input signals and output signals respectively with the constraint $\textbf{InSignal} \cap \textbf{OutSignal} = \emptyset$.
A clock variable $s.\textbf{clock}$ is a sequence of pairs with the type $Time \times \mathbb{N}$. For a pair (τ, p) as an entry of the sequence, τ stands for the time instant at which s occurs, while p denotes its emitting position in the queue of the dependent signals that are observed at the same instant. For example, if the emission of s_2 depends on the emission of s_1 at time τ, then we have $(\tau, m) \in s_1.\textbf{clock}$ and $(\tau, n) \in s_2.\textbf{clock}$ with $m < n$.

The output alphabet contains the dashed variables from input alphabet.

$$\textbf{out}\alpha P = \{x' \mid x \in \textbf{in}\alpha P\}$$

The continuous variables in $\textbf{con}\alpha P$ are mappings from time to corresponding physical status of the physical components, *i.e.*, of the type $Time \rightarrow Real$. The set $\textbf{con}\alpha P = \textbf{own}\alpha P \cup \textbf{env}\alpha P$ is divided into two sets: $\textbf{own}\alpha P$ and $\textbf{env}\alpha P$ where the former comprises those continuous variables owned by the relation, and the latter denotes the set of variables that are accessible by P but managed by the environment. The set $\textbf{own}\alpha P = \textbf{phy}\alpha P \cup \textbf{timer}\alpha P$ includes a special subset $\textbf{timer}\alpha P$ to specify the timers owned by P.
A refinement order can be defined over hybrid relations as follows.

Definition 2 (Refinement).
Let P and Q be hybrid relations with the same alphabet A. We will use the notation $P \sqsupseteq Q$ to abbreviate the formula $\forall x, y, ..., u, v \bullet (P \Rightarrow Q)$ where $x, y, ..., u, v$ are all the variables of the alphabet A.

3.2   Healthiness Conditions

In this section, we will introduce healthiness conditions one by one and show that every healthiness condition obtains a subset of the previous domain and the healthy programs form a complete lattice w.r.t. the refinement order.

Time.
To describe the dynamical behaviour of physical components we will focus on

those hybrid relations in which the termination time is not before its initial time. As a result, we require a hybrid relation P to meet the following healthiness condition:

$(\mathbf{HC1})P = P \wedge (t \leq t')$

A hybrid relation is called **HC1**-healthy if it satisfies the condition **HC1**. We introduce a function **H1** to turn a hybrid relation into a **HC1**-healthy hybrid relation:

$\mathbf{H1}(P) =_{df} P \wedge (t \leq t')$

It is trivial to show that **H1** is monotonic and idempotent.

Signals.

Signals are means of communications and synchronisations between different components and between a program with its environment. In general, a signal, denoted by its name, has two types of status, *i.e.*, either presence or absence. A signal is present if it is received by a program from its environment, or it is emitted as the result of an output command.

For any signal s, we use a clock variable $s.\mathbf{clock}$ to record the time instants at which s has been present. As usual, we adopt $s.\mathbf{clock}$ and $s.\mathbf{clock}'$ to represent the values at the start time t and the finish time t' correspondingly. $s.\mathbf{clock}$ has to be a subset of $s.\mathbf{clock}'$ since the latter may be added some time instants of $[t, t']$ at which the signal s is present. Consequently, we require a hybrid relation P to meet the following healthiness condition:

$(\mathbf{HC2})P = P \wedge \mathbf{inv}(s)$

where $\mathbf{inv}(s) =_{df} (s.\mathbf{clock} \subseteq s.\mathbf{clock}') \wedge (s.\mathbf{clock}' \subseteq (s.\mathbf{clock} \cup [t, t'] \times \mathbb{N}))$

$\mathbf{H2}(P) =_{df} P \wedge \mathbf{inv}(s)$

It is trivial to prove that the order in which **H1** and **H2** are composed is irrelevant, *i.e.*, $\mathbf{H1} \circ \mathbf{H2} = \mathbf{H2} \circ \mathbf{H1}$. With this fact, we can define a composite mapping $\mathbf{H12} =_{df} \mathbf{H1} \circ \mathbf{H2}$. And it can be proved that **HC1** and **HC2**-healthy hybrid relations are closed under choice, conditional and sequential composition.

Theorem 1.

(1) $\mathbf{H12}(P) \sqcap \mathbf{H12}(Q) = \mathbf{H12}(P \sqcap Q)$
(2) $\mathbf{H12}(P) \triangleleft b \triangleright \mathbf{H12}(Q) = \mathbf{H12}(P \triangleleft b \triangleright Q)$
(3) $\mathbf{H12}(P); \mathbf{H12}(Q) = \mathbf{H12}(\mathbf{H12}(P); \mathbf{H12}(Q))$

For simplicity, we will confine ourselves to **HC1** *and* **HC2**-*healthy hybrid relations in the next section.*

Intermediate Observation and Divergence.

In this section, we add logical variables st and st' to the input alphabet and the output alphabet of a hybrid relation to describe the program status before it starts, and the status it completes respectively. These variables range over the set $\{term, stable, div\}$, where

$st = term$ indicates the predecessor of the hybrid program terminates successfully. As a result, the control passes to the current hybrid program.

$st = stable$ indicates its predecessor is waiting for ignition. Therefore, the hybrid program can not start its execution because its predecessor has not finished yet.

$st = div$ indicates the behaviour of the predecessor becomes chaotic, and it can not be rescued by the execution of the current hybrid program.

Here we propose an order $<$ over the set of program status:

$$div < stable < term$$

This order can be adopted to define the merge mechanism for the parallel composition operator in Sect. 3.5.

Example 2 (Atomic Hybrid Relations).

Let $PVar$ be a set of discrete data variables, and

$$A =_{df} \{st, t, pos\} \cup PVar \cup \{s.\textbf{clock} \mid s \in \textbf{OutSignal}\}$$

(1) The hybrid relation **skip** does nothing, and terminates immediately.

$$\textbf{skip} =_{df} II_A \lhd (st \neq div) \rhd \textbf{H12}(\perp_A)$$

where II_A is the identity relation over set A and $\perp_A =_{df} true$.

(2) **chaos** represents the worst hybrid program, and its behaviour is totally unpredictable.

$$\textbf{chaos} =_{df} \textbf{H12}(\perp_A) \lhd st = term \rhd \textbf{skip}$$

(3) **delay** behaves like hybrid program **skip** except its termination time is unknown in advance.

$$\textbf{delay} =_{df} \textbf{H12}(II_{A\backslash\{t\}}) \lhd st = term \rhd \textbf{skip}$$

From Theorem 1 it follows that these atomic hybrid programs are **HC1** and **HC2** healthy. Note that the above atomic hybrid relations have no constraints to the continuous variables.   □

The healthiness conditions relevant to st are proposed to capture the intermediate observation (**HC3**) and divergence (**HC4**) features of hybrid programs.

A hybrid program P remains idle until its sequential predecessor terminates successfully. This constraint requires P to satisfy the following healthiness condition:

(**HC3**) $P = P \lhd st = term \rhd \textbf{skip}$

We can prove that all atomic hybrid programs of Example 2 are **HC3**-healthy.

$$\textbf{H3}(P) =_{df} P \lhd st = term \rhd \textbf{skip}$$

A **HC3**-healthy program has **skip** as its left unit and **chaos** as its left zero.

Theorem 2 (Left unit and left zero).

(1) $\textbf{skip}; \textbf{H3}(P) = \textbf{H3}(P)$

(2) $\textbf{chaos}; \textbf{H3}(P) = \textbf{chaos}$

Once a hybrid program enters a divergent state, its future behaviour becomes uncontrollable. This requires it to meet the following healthiness condition:

(**HC4**) $P = P;\textbf{skip}$

$\textbf{H4}(P) =_{df} P;\textbf{skip}$

HC4-healthy programs are closed under choices, conditional and sequential composition.

Theorem 3.

(1) $\textbf{H4}(P) \sqcap \textbf{H4}(Q) = \textbf{H4}(P \sqcap Q)$
(2) $\textbf{H4}(P) \lhd b \rhd \textbf{H4}(Q) = \textbf{H4}(P \lhd b \rhd Q)$
(3) $\textbf{H4}(P); \textbf{H4}(Q) = \textbf{H4}(P; Q)$ *provided that Q is* **HC3**-*healthy.*

The composition order of **H3** and **H4** is irrelevant, *i.e.*, $\textbf{H4} \circ \textbf{H3} = \textbf{H3} \circ \textbf{H4}$. Define $\textbf{H} =_{df} (\textbf{H1} \circ \textbf{H2} \circ \textbf{H3} \circ \textbf{H4})$. We can prove that **H** is monotonic and idempotent and $\textbf{H} = \textbf{H3} \circ \textbf{H4}$.

The mapping **H** distributes over non-deterministic choice, conditional and sequential composition.

Theorem 4.

(1) $\textbf{H}(P) \sqcap \textbf{H}(Q) = \textbf{H}(P \sqcap Q)$
(2) $\textbf{H}(P) \lhd b \rhd \textbf{H}(Q) = \textbf{H}(P \lhd b \rhd Q)$
(3) $\textbf{H}(P); \textbf{H}(Q) = \textbf{H}(\textbf{H}(P); \textbf{H}(Q))$

The distributivity of **H** over parallel operators will be shown in Sect. 3.5. To summarize, the healthy hybrid program domain is closed under these composition operators.

Theorem 5.
The domain of healthy hybrid programs $\mathbb{P} =_{df} \{P \mid P = \textbf{H}(P)\}$ *and the refinement order* $\sqsupseteq$ *forms a complete lattice* $L =_{df} (\mathbb{P}, \sqsupseteq)$.

3.3   Atomic Commands

The definitions of atomic commands **skip**, **chaos** and **delay** are already given in *Example 2*. One can verify that they are all healthy w.r.t. the mapping **H**.
Let e be an expression with only discrete variables. Assignment $x := e$ assigns the value of e to the discrete variable x instantaneously. It supports the discrete state change of the hybrid programs.

$$(x := e) =_{df} \textbf{H}(\mathit{II}_{\textbf{in}\alpha}[e/x])$$

Let v be a continuous variable in **own**α. Assignment $x \leftarrow v$ assigns the current value of v to the discrete variable x instantaneously. It provides a direct way in the language for sampling the value of a continuous variable to a discrete program variable.

$$(x \leftarrow v) =_{df} \textbf{H}(\mathit{II}_{\textbf{in}\alpha \setminus \{x\}} \wedge x' = v(t'))$$

The output command !s emits signal s, and then terminates immediately. Its execution does not take time.

$$!s =_{df} \mathbf{H}(\Pi_{\mathbf{ina}}[(s.\mathbf{clock} \cup \{(t,\ pos)\})/s.\mathbf{clock}])$$

The program **idle** never terminates, and keeps stable status forever.

$$\mathbf{idle} =_{df} \mathbf{H}(\Pi_B \wedge \mathbf{time-passing} \wedge st' = stable)$$

where

$$B =_{df} \{s.\mathbf{clock} \mid s \in \mathbf{OutSignal}\}$$

$$\mathbf{time-passing} =_{df} \bigwedge_{c \in \mathbf{timer}\alpha} \forall \tau \in [t, t') \bullet (\dot{c}(\tau) = 1)$$

Let $\delta \geq 0$. The delay command $\mathbf{delay}(\delta)$ suspends the execution δ time units.

$$\mathbf{delay}(\delta) =_{df} \mathbf{H} \left(\begin{array}{l} \Pi_B \wedge \mathbf{time-passing} \wedge \\ \left(\begin{array}{l} (t' - t) < \delta \wedge st' = stable\ \vee \\ (t' - t) = \delta \wedge \Pi_{\{pos\} \cup PVar} \wedge st' = term \end{array} \right) \end{array} \right)$$

Notice that the difference between **delay** and $\mathbf{delay}(\delta)$ is that the end time t' of **delay** is unspecified (arbitrarily after its start time).

3.4   Dynamics of Continuous Variables

Let v be a continuous variable used to model the status of a physical device. The continuous transitions of v governed by the physical laws can usually be specified by a hybrid relation $R(v, \dot{v})$, whose dynamic behaviour over an interval $[t, t']$ is described by

$$R =_{df} \forall \tau \in [t, t') \bullet R(v, \dot{v})(\tau)$$

Let e be an expression with only discrete variables. The hybrid relation $R\ \mathbf{init}\ (v = e)$ sets the value of e as the initial value of continuous variable v.

$$R\ \mathbf{init}\ (v = e) =_{df} R \wedge (v(t) = e)$$

Let R_1 and R_2 be hybrid relations of distinct variables v and w. Their composition $R_1 \mid R_2$ is simply defined as the conjunction of R_1 and R_2:

$$R_1 \mid R_2 =_{df} R_1 \wedge R_2$$

Differential equation $\dot{v} = f(v)$ and differential-algebraic equation $(F(v, \dot{v}, t) = 0)$ are both seen as a special kind of hybrid relations over continuous variable v.

Example 3. Let v be a continuous variables over continuous time c. A differential-algebraic equation $F(v, \dot{v}, c) = 0$ can be treated as a hybrid relation where

$$DF =_{df} (t \leq t') \wedge \forall \tau : [t, t') \bullet (F(v(\tau), \dot{v}(\tau), \tau) = 0) \qquad \square$$

The refinement order defined for hybrid relations in Sect. 3.1 can be applied to the relation R.

Definition 3.
Assume that $R_1(v, \dot{v})$ and $R_2(v, \dot{v})$ are equipped with the same alphabet (say $\{v\}$), we define

$$R_1 \sqsupseteq R_2 =_{df} \forall t, t', \forall v \bullet (R_1 \Rightarrow R_2)$$

It means that if a continuous variable v is a solution of R_1, then it is also a solution of R_2. In other terms, R_1 can be considered as a refinement of R_2 since any continuous evolvement it allows for the continuous variable v is also allowed by R_2.

3.5 Combinators

Let P and Q be hybrid programs, the combinators of the hybrid language include the classic sequential operators, parallel operators and recursion operators. Besides, it has two hybrid reactive structures specifying the interactions between the continuous and discrete components of the system. In this section, we will give the definitions of the combinators.

Sequential Operators.
The sequential programming operators, including nondeterministic choice $P \sqcap Q$, conditional choice $P \lhd b \rhd Q$ and sequential composition $P; Q$ can be defined by the same predicates as in [HH98] but over the enriched alphabet for hybrid relations satisfying healthiness conditions. For lack of space, we only give the definition of $P; Q$ for example.

Definition 4 (Sequential Composition).
Let P and Q be hybrid relations with $\mathbf{out}\alpha P = \{x' \mid x \in \mathbf{in}\alpha Q\}$, $\mathbf{own}\alpha P = \mathbf{own}\alpha Q$ and $\mathbf{env}\alpha P = \mathbf{env}\alpha Q$. The sequential composition $P; Q$ is defined by the following predicate:

$$P; Q =_{df} \exists m \bullet P[m/x'] \wedge Q[m/x]$$

with $\alpha(P; Q) =_{df} \mathbf{in}\alpha P \cup \mathbf{out}\alpha Q \cup \mathbf{con}\alpha P$.

The sequential composition operator enjoys the same set of algebraic laws as its counterpart given in [HH98].

Parallel Operators.
Before we get to the definition of the parallel composition of hybrid programs, we first revisit two notions of parallel composition operators that will be employed in the definition.

Definition 5 (Disjoint Parallel Operator).
Let P and Q be hybrid relations with disjoint $\mathbf{out}\alpha$ and $\mathbf{own}\alpha$. The notation $P \mid Q$ represents the following hybrid relation

$$P \mid Q =_{df} P \wedge Q$$

with $\mathbf{in}\alpha(P \mid Q) =_{df} \mathbf{in}\alpha P \cup \mathbf{in}\alpha Q$, $\mathbf{own}\alpha =_{df} \mathbf{own}\alpha P \cup \mathbf{own}\alpha Q$ and $\mathbf{env}\alpha =_{df} (\mathbf{env}\alpha P \setminus \mathbf{own}\alpha Q) \cup (\mathbf{env}\alpha Q \setminus \mathbf{own}\alpha P)$.

The operator $\mid$ is symmetric and associative. It distributes over conditional, and has $II_\emptyset$ as its unit. Moreover, $\mid$ and ; satisfy the mutual distribution law.

For programs whose $\mathbf{out}\alpha$ and $\mathbf{own}\alpha$ are overlapped, we employ a parallel by merge operator to merge the results of the parallel components.

Definition 6 (Merge Mechanism).
A merge mechanism M is a pair $(x : \mathbf{Val}, op)$, where x is a variable of type $\mathbf{Val}$, and op is a binary operator over $\mathbf{Val}$.

Definition 7 (Parallel by Merge).
Let P and Q be hybrid relations with the shared output x' and its merge mechanism $M = (x : \mathbf{Val}, op)$. We define their parallel composition by merge, denoted $P \parallel_M Q$, as follows:

$$P \parallel_M Q =_{df} \exists m, n : \mathbf{Val} \bullet \begin{pmatrix} P[m/x'] \; \wedge \; Q[n/x'] \; \wedge \\ x' \; = \; op(m, n) \end{pmatrix}$$

with $\mathbf{in}\alpha(P \parallel_M Q) =_{df} \mathbf{in}\alpha P \cup \mathbf{in}\alpha Q$, $\mathbf{own}\alpha(P \parallel_M Q) =_{df} \mathbf{own}\alpha P \cup \mathbf{own}\alpha Q$
and $\mathbf{env}\alpha(P \parallel_M Q) =_{df} (\mathbf{env}\alpha P \setminus \mathbf{own}\alpha Q) \cup (\mathbf{env}\alpha Q \setminus \mathbf{own}\alpha P)$.

With the above notions of parallel operator, we can define the semantics of general parallel composition $P \parallel Q$. We need to merge the program status st and the pos variables from both components.

For st, we select the merge operator for the program status as the greatest lower bound, *i.e.*, **glb** (remember that we have the order $div < stable < term$).

For pos, we select the merge operator as **max** which selects the greater value.

Definition 8 (Parallel Operator for Hybrid Programs).

Let P and Q be hybrid programs satisfying the following conditions:
$PVar(P) \cap PVar(Q) = \emptyset$, $\mathbf{own}\alpha(P) \cap \mathbf{own}\alpha(Q) = \emptyset$,
$\mathbf{timer}\alpha(P) \cap \mathbf{env}\alpha(Q) = \emptyset$, $\mathbf{timer}\alpha(Q) \cap \mathbf{env}\alpha(P) = \emptyset$ *and*
$\mathbf{OutSignal}(P) \cap \mathbf{OutSignal}(Q) = \emptyset$
The parallel composition $P \parallel Q$ is equipped with the following alphabet:
$PVar =_{df} PVar(P) \cup PVar(Q)$, $\mathbf{phy}\alpha =_{df} \mathbf{phy}\alpha(P) \cup \mathbf{phy}\alpha(Q)$,
$\mathbf{timer}\alpha =_{df} \mathbf{timer}\alpha(P) \cup \mathbf{timer}\alpha(Q)$,
$\mathbf{env}\alpha =_{df} (\mathbf{env}\alpha(P) \setminus \mathbf{own}\alpha(Q)) \cup (\mathbf{env}\alpha(Q) \setminus \mathbf{own}\alpha(P))$,
$\mathbf{InSignal} =_{df} (\mathbf{InSignal}(P) \setminus \mathbf{OutSignal}(Q)) \cup (\mathbf{InSignal}(Q) \setminus \mathbf{OutSignal}(P))$,
$\mathbf{OutSignal} =_{df} \mathbf{OutSignal}(P) \cup \mathbf{OutSignal}(Q)$.
The dynamic behaviour of $P \parallel Q$ is described by

$$P \parallel Q =_{df} (((P; \mathbf{delay}) \parallel_M Q) \vee (P \parallel_M (Q; \mathbf{delay}))); \mathbf{skip}$$

where the merge mechanism M is defined by

$$M =_{df} ((st, pos) : \begin{pmatrix} (\{term, stable, div\}, \mathbb{N}), \\ (\mathbf{glb}, \mathbf{max}) \end{pmatrix}$$

The **delay** commands are used to synchronise the end time of the two components and the successive **skip** command makes the program satisfy **HC4**. The merge mechanism M merges the status of the parallel components with a greatest lower bound operator. For example, if st' of P is *term* and st' of Q is *stable*, then the st' of $P \parallel Q$ is *stable*. It also merges the pos' for the output signals to be the greater one, *i.e.* if pos' of P is m and pos' of Q is n, then the pos' of $P\|Q$ is $\mathbf{max}(m, n)$.

With the definition of the merge mechanism M, we can obtain that the domain of healthy hybrid relations is closed w.r.t. parallel composition.

Theorem 6.
If P and Q is healthy hybrid relations, i.e., $P = \mathbf{H}(P)$ and $Q = \mathbf{H}(Q)$, then so does $P\|_M Q$, i.e., $P\|_M Q = \mathbf{H}(P\|_M Q)$.

The parallel composition is symmetric and associative, and distributes over conditional and nondeterministic choices. Furthermore, it has **skip** and **chaos** as its unit and zero respectively. Moreover, the parallel composition has a true concurrent semantics: parallel components proceed independently and simultaneously.

Theorem 7.

(1) $(x := e; P) \parallel Q \;=\; (x := e); (P \parallel Q)$
(2) $(\mathbf{delay}(\delta); P) \parallel (\mathbf{delay}(\delta); Q) \;=\; \mathbf{delay}(\delta); (P \parallel Q)$
(3) $\mathbf{delay}(\epsilon) \parallel \mathbf{delay}(\delta) \;=\; \mathbf{delay}(\mathbf{max}(\epsilon, \delta))$

Guard Condition.
This subsection focusses on the guard conditions that will appear in the new hybrid structures **when** and **until** which will be defined in the next section.
In our hybrid language, the guard condition supports the following form: (1) value test: monitoring the value changing of a continuous variable. (2) signal: monitoring the emission of a signal. (3) their combinations via operator $\cdot$ and $+$.
Like the hybrid automata, our language supports a transition when the value of a continuous variable exceeds a given bound. In addition, our language can support the reactions to receiving certain signals from the environment.

Example 4 (Gear shifting). Consider a car-driving control system. For a manual transmission car, its accelerating process can be divided into 4 shifting modes depending on the running gears. Assume that the proper speed interval for shifting from gear 1 to gear 2 is 20 kph to 30 kph. The car will change gear from 1 to 2 when (1) the current speed lies in the interval, **and** (2) the driver pushes the gear lever from 1 to 2. Let signal $gear\_up$ means the driver pushes the gear lever, the specification of the shifting can be written as follows.

$$\mathbf{when}\ ((20 < v \leq 30) \cdot gear\_up\ \&\ Gear_2)$$

where v is a continuous variable representing the speed of the car; $Gear_2$ represents the specification for the running mode of the car with gear 2. The guard condition involves both value testing and signal reception. $\qquad\square$

To specify the reactive behaviours, we need to define the trigger condition of the guards. We introduce the following function **fired** to specify the status of a guard g over time interval:

g.**fired** : $Interval \rightarrow Time \rightarrow Bool$

where for any $\tau \in [t, t']$, g.**fired**$([t, t'])(\tau) = true$ indicates g is fired at the time instant τ. In other terms, given a time instant τ within the time interval $[t, t']$, the function tells us whether the guard g is fired at τ.

This function is defined by induction as follows:

1. **I** is ignited immediately after it starts its execution.
   I.**fired**$([t, t'])(\tau) =_{df} (\tau = t)$
2. s is fired whenever an input signal s is received.
   s.**fired**$([t, t'])(\tau) =_{df} \exists n \in \mathbb{N} \bullet (\tau, n) \in s$.**clock**$'$
3. $test$ is fired whenever the value of expression $test$ is true at that time instant.
   $test$.**fired**$([t, t'])(\tau) =_{df} test(\tau)$
4. the composite guard $g_1 \cdot g_2$ is fired only when both g_1 and g_2 are fired simultaneously.
   $(g_1 \cdot g_2)$.**fired** $=_{df} g_1$.**fired** $\wedge$ g_2.**fired**
5. the composite guard $g_1 + g_2$ is fired when either g_1 or g_2 is fired.
   $(g_1 + g_2)$.**fired** $=_{df} g_1$.**fired** $\vee$ g_2.**fired**

Two guards are identical if they have the same firing function:
$(g = h) =_{df} (g$.**fired** $= h$.**fired**$)$

From the above definitions and the properties of predicate combinators we conclude that both guard combinators $\cdot$ and $+$ are idempotent, symmetric and associative, and furthermore $\cdot$ distributes over $+$.

Theorem 8.

*(1) $(Guard, +, \cdot,$ **true**, **false**$)$ forms a Boolean algebra.*
*(2) $g +$ **true** $=$ **true**.*
*(3) $g \cdot$ **false** $=$ **false**.*

We say g is weaker than h (denoted by $g \leq h$), if the ignition of h can awake g immediately:
$g \leq h =_{df} h = (h \cdot g)$
From Theorem 8(1) it follows that $\leq$ is a partial order. Then we have
$g \leq h$ iff $g = (g + h)$.
In order to specify the blocking behaviour of the **when** construct, we need to define a trigger condition for the guard condition so that it is fired at the endpoint of a time interval and before that it remains unfired. To identify such cases we introduce the boolean function g.**triggered** : $Interval \rightarrow Bool$.

$$g.\textbf{triggered}([t, t']) =_{df} \begin{pmatrix} g.\textbf{fired}([t, t'])(t') \wedge \\ \forall \tau \in [t, t') \bullet \neg g.\textbf{fired}([t, t'])(\tau) \end{pmatrix}$$

To specify those cases when the guard g remains inactive we introduce the boolean function $g.\mathbf{inactive} : Interval \to Bool$.

$$g.\mathbf{inactive}([t, t']) =_{df} \forall \tau \in [t, t'] \bullet \neg g.\mathbf{fired}([t, t'])(\tau)$$

Note that $g.\mathbf{triggered} \neq \neg g.\mathbf{inactive}$. For example, let g be $(c = 3)$ where c is a timer. For the interval $[0, 4]$, we have both $g.\mathbf{triggered} = \mathbf{false}$ and $g.\mathbf{inactive} = \mathbf{false}$ since $g.\mathbf{fired}([0, 4])(3) = \mathbf{true}$.

The corresponding boolean functions for the composition of guards have the following properties.

Theorem 9.

(1) $(g_1 + g_2).\mathbf{triggered} = \begin{pmatrix} g_1.\mathbf{triggered} \wedge (g_2.\mathbf{triggered} \vee g_2.\mathbf{inactive}) \vee \\ g_2.\mathbf{triggered} \wedge (g_1.\mathbf{triggered} \vee g_1.\mathbf{inactive}) \end{pmatrix}$

(2) $(g_1 + g_2).\mathbf{inactive} = g_1.\mathbf{inactive} \wedge g_2.\mathbf{inactive}$

When Statement.
With the boolean functions **triggered** and **inactive** defined above, we can define the semantics of the **when** construct.

The program $\mathbf{when}(g_1 \& P_1 [.... [g_n \& P_n)$ waits for one of its guards to be fired, then selects a program P_i with the ignited guard to be executed. It is much like the conventional guarded choice construct except that its guards refer to continuous variables and signals whose status change through time.

In detail, the behaviour of $\mathbf{when}(g_1 \& P_1 [.... [g_n \& P_n)$ can be interpreted as follows.

(1) It will keep waiting $(st' = stable)$ when every guard is inactive in its execution interval $[t, t']$.
(2) It will execute P_i when g_i is triggered during its execution interval $[t, t']$. If more than one guard is triggered, the triggered branches are selected nondeterministically.

Definition 9.
$\mathbf{when}(g_1 \& P_1 [.... [g_n \& P_n) =_{df}$

$\mathbf{H}(st' = stable \wedge II_B \wedge \mathbf{time-passing} \wedge (g_1 + ... + g_n).\mathbf{inactive})) \vee$

$\displaystyle\bigvee_{1 \le i \le n} \mathbf{H} \begin{pmatrix} st' = term \wedge II_{PVar \cup B} \wedge \mathbf{time-passing} \wedge \mathbf{update}(pos, g_i) \wedge \\ g_i.\mathbf{triggered} \wedge (g_1 + .. + g_n).\mathbf{triggered} \end{pmatrix} ; P_i$

where

$B =_{df} \{s.clock \mid s \in \mathbf{OutSignal}\}$

$\mathbf{update}(pos, g) =_{df} (pos' = pos) \lhd g \cap Signal = \emptyset \rhd (pos' > \mathbf{max}(pos, \mathbf{index}(g))$

$\mathbf{index}(g) =_{df} \mathbf{max}(\{0\} \cup \{\pi_2(\mathbf{last}(s.clock')) \mid s \in g\})$

The **update**(pos, g) makes sure that the variable pos' records the maximum index of the signals emitted at the same time so far.

From Theorem 4 we conclude that **when**$(g_1\&P_1 [\!| ... [\!| g_n\&P_n)$ lies in the complete lattice L introduced in Theorem 5 whenever all guarded programs P_i are elements of L. In other words, the healthy hybrid relation domain is closed w.r.t. the **when** construct.

Some interesting algebraic laws of the **when** statement are listed below:

Theorem 10.

(1) The guards of the same guarded branch can be composed by + operator.
   when$(g_1\&P [\!| g_2\&P [\!| G)$ = **when**$((g_1 + g_2)\&P [\!| G)$
*(2) The effect of **true** guard is equivalent to the guard **I**.*
   when$(\textbf{true}\&P [\!| G)$ = **when**$(\textbf{I}\&P [\!| G)$
*(3) The successive program of the **when** construct can be distributed to every branch of the **when** construct.*
   when$(g_1\&P_1 [\!| ... [\!| g_n\&P_n); Q$ = **when**$(g_1\&(P_1; Q) [\!| ... [\!| g_n\&(P_n; Q))$
*(4) The previous assignment can be distributed to every branch of the **when** construct.*

$(x := e);$ **when**$(g_1\&P_1 [\!| ... [\!| g_n\&P_n)$

$\qquad\qquad$ = **when**$(g_1[e/x]\&(x := e; P_1) [\!| ... [\!| g_n[e/x]\&(x := e; P_n))$

(5) The branches with the same guard can be combined with nondeterministic choice.
   when$(g\&P [\!| g\&Q [\!| G)$ = **when**$(g\&(P \sqcap Q) [\!| G)$
(6) A branch with conditional choice can be divided into two branches.

   when$(g\&(P \lhd b \rhd Q) [\!| G)$ = **when**$((b \cdot g)\&P [\!| (\neg b \cdot g)\&Q [\!| G)$

Until Statement.

The statement R **until** g specifies a hybrid program where the change of the continuous variables is governed by the hybrid relation R until the guard condition g is triggered. It is suitable to specify the behaviour of the control plant which evolves accordingly until receiving control signals from the controlling device.

Definition 10.

Let $R(v, \dot{v})$ be a hybrid relation specifying the dynamics of the continuous variable v. Let g be a guard. Assume that all the signals of g are included in the alphabet of R, then

$$\alpha(R \textbf{ until } g) =_{df} \alpha R$$

*and the behaviour of R **until** g is described by*

$$R \textbf{ until } g =_{df} \textbf{H} \left(\left\{ \begin{array}{l} \left(\begin{array}{l} st' = stable \ \wedge \ II_B \ \wedge \ R \ \wedge \\ \textbf{time-passing} \ \wedge \ g.\textbf{inactive} \end{array} \right) \vee \\ \left(\begin{array}{l} st' = term \ \wedge \ II_{PVar\cup B} \ \wedge \ \textbf{update}(pos, g) \ \wedge \ R \ \wedge \\ \textbf{time-passing} \ \wedge \ g.\textbf{triggered} \end{array} \right) \end{array} \right. \right)$$

where $B =_{df} \{s.\textbf{clock} \mid s \in \textbf{OutSignal}\}$.

The R **until** g statement will keep stable when the guard g is inactive during the execution interval where the continuous variables evolve as the hybrid relation R specifies. It will terminate when the guard g is triggered.

Theorem 11.
The **until** *constructor is monotonic with respect to its hybrid relation component.*
If $R1 \sqsupseteq R2$ *then* $(R1 \textbf{ until } g) \sqsupseteq (R2 \textbf{ until } g)$.

Example 5 (Bouncing ball). Consider the bouncing ball system. Let q be a continuous variable indicating the distance between the ball and the floor. The dynamics of the ball in its falling phase can be specified as follows.

$$Fall =_{df} ((q \geq 0 \wedge \ddot{q} = -g) \textbf{ init } \dot{q} = 0) \textbf{ until } q = 0$$

where g is the acceleration imposed by gravity.

When the ball hits the ground at time τ, its velocity $\dot{q}$ will change to $-r\dot{q}(\tau)$ instantaneously where r is a restitution coefficient ranging over $(0, 1]$. In order to set the initial value of $\dot{q}$ for the bouncing-back phase, we use the sampling assignment $x \leftarrow \dot{q}$ to copy the value of $\dot{q}(\tau)$ to a discrete variable x after $Fall$.

The dynamics of the ball in its bouncing-back phase can be specified as follows.

$$Bounce =_{df} ((q \geq 0 \wedge \ddot{q} = -g) \textbf{ init } \dot{q} = -rx) \textbf{ until } \dot{q} = 0$$

In summary, the bouncing ball system with the initial height $h_0 > 0$ from the ground can be specified as

$$BBall =_{df} (q \leftarrow h_0); (Fall; (x \leftarrow \dot{q}); Bounce)^*.$$

Note that when $r < 1$, the initial position of the ball in the falling phase is decreased for each iteration. It results to **Zeno behaviour** when the execution time is large enough and the time cost for each iteration becomes significantly close to 0. In this case, the process can perform infinite transitions within a very small time interval, which is considered as **chaos** in our model. To avoid the Zeno behaviour, we let the system stop bouncing when the speed of the ball is smaller than a small enough value δ.

$$Non\_Zeno\_BBall =_{df} (q \leftarrow h_0); (Fall; (x \leftarrow \dot{q}); (Bounce \lhd x \geq \delta \rhd \textbf{idle}))^* \qquad \square$$

Signal Hiding.
Let P be a program, and s an output signal of P. The signal hiding operator **signal** $s \bullet P$ makes the signal s a bounded signal name of P which cannot be observed by P's environment. Through signal hiding operator, the scope of a signal can be set by the designers so that only the parallel components can react to a signal. It is helpful when modeling a distributed hybrid system where each component has limited communication capacity.

Definition 11 (Signal Hiding).
The signal hiding statement **signal** $s \bullet P$ *behaves like* P *except that* s *becomes invisible to its environment.*

signal $s \bullet P =_{df} \exists s.\textbf{clock}' \bullet P[\epsilon/s.\textbf{clock}]$

with $\alpha(\textbf{signal } s \bullet P) =_{df} \alpha(P) \setminus \{s.\textbf{clock}, s.\textbf{clock}'\}$

where ϵ *denotes the empty sequence.*

Timer Declarations.

Let P be a hybrid program, and c a timer of P. The timer declaration operator **timer** $c \bullet P$ declares P as the region of permitted use of timer c. A timer c is a special continuous variable with its derivation $\dot{c} = 1$.

Definition 12 (Timer declaration).

The timer declaration statement set c to be a local timer of P starting from 0.

$$\textbf{timer } c \bullet P =_{df} \exists c \bullet P[0/c[t]]$$

with $\alpha(\textbf{timer } c \bullet P) =_{df} \alpha(P) \setminus \{c\}$

The timer declaration operator facilitates the modeling of time-out mechanism which is one of the common reaction mechanisms in hybrid systems.

Example 6. Consider a control requirement that a program will execute P when a signal s is received within $3\,\text{s}$, otherwise, it will execute Q. This requirement can be specified with the time-out mechanism as follows.

$$\textbf{timer } c \bullet \textbf{when}((c < 3) \cdot s \;\&\; P \;\|\; (c \geq 3) \;\&\; Q) \qquad\qquad \Box$$

Theorem 12.

*The **delay** command can be rewritten as the following time-out form.*

$$\textbf{delay}(\delta) = \textbf{timer } c \bullet \textbf{idle until } (c \geq \delta)$$

Recursion.

Based on the conclusion in Sect. 3.2 and the combinators defined in above subsections, the healthy hybrid programs form a complete lattice L and is closed w.r.t. all above combinators. In this sense, we can obtain the semantics of recursive programs in this domain.

Definition 13 (Recursion).

A recursive program is defined as the weakest fixed point, denoted as $\mu X.F(X)$, of the equation $X = F(X)$ in the complete lattice L.

The notation $\nu X.F(X)$ is used to stand for the strongest fixed point of the above equation. The fixed points μF and νF are subject to the following laws:

Theorem 13.

(1) $Y \sqsupseteq \mu X.F(X)$ *whenever* $Y \sqsupseteq F(Y)$
(2) $\nu X.F(X) \sqsupseteq Y$ *whenever* $F(Y) \sqsupseteq Y$
(3) *If* $F(X) \sqsupseteq G(X)$ *for all* X, *then* $\mu X.F(X) \sqsupseteq \mu X.G(X)$ *and* $\nu X.F(X) \sqsupseteq \nu X.G(X)$.

For simplicity we will use the notation P^* to stand for the recursive program $\mu X.(P; X)$.

Theorem 14.

If $P \sqsupseteq Q$ then $P^* \sqsupseteq Q^*$

Following the concept of *approximation chain* explored in [HH98], we are going to show that under some conditions the strongest and weakest fixed points of the equation $X = P; X$ are in fact the same.

Theorem 15.

If there exists $l > 0$ such that $P[term, term/st, st'] \sqsupseteq (t' - t) \geq l$, then

(1) $\mu X.(P; X) = \nu X.(P; X)$
(2) $P^* \sqsupseteq S$ whenever $(P; S) \sqsupseteq S$

This theorem provides us a verification approach for the iterative program in which each iteration takes some time to finish. In other terms, it does not consider the programs with Zeno behaviours. According to this theorem, to prove that the non-Zeno iterative program satisfy a given specification, it is sufficient for us to prove its single iteration does not violate the specification.

For the systems that contains Zeno behaviour, we need to change the specification to make an approximation for avoiding the Zeno behaviour by setting a lower bound to the interval for each iteration. It can be reviewed in Example 5.

4   Conclusion

This paper proposes a hybrid modelling language, where the discrete transitions are modelled by assignment and output as zero time actions, while the continuous transitions of physical world are described by differential equations and synchronous constructs. We adopt a signal-based interaction mechanism to synchronise the activities of control programs with physical devices. A rich set of guard compositions allows us to construct sophisticated firing conditions of the transition of physical devices.

Compared with hybrid automata and HCSP, our language enriches the interaction mechanisms between processes via supporting asynchronous reactions to more complicated guards allowing combinations of testing and signals inspired by *Esterel* language. Besides, our language is equipped with true concurrency semantics of parallel composition and the communications between components are not restricted to fixed channels. In our language, the physical state of the system can be observed by all control programs and the signals can be exchanged between them with engineered protocols. It can specify the coordination control patterns in many modern control scenarios in which a set of physical objects are controlled by a network of control components.

In the future we plan to work on a proof system for hybrid program based on the algebraic laws obtained from the UTP semantics of the hybrid language. Besides the conventional sequential combinators, the proof system will focus on verification of parallel programs. We also intend to carry out non-trivial case studies with multiple physical objects and network of control components using the hybrid language and the proof system.

References

[dSS00] van der Schaft, A.J., Schumacher, J.M.: An Introduction to Hybrid Dynamical Systems. Springer, Verlag (2000)

[Bra95] Branicky, M.S.: Studies in hybrid systems: modeling, analysis, and control. Ph.D. Thesis, EECS Department, Massachusetts Institute of Technology (1995)

[ACH93] Alur, R., Courcoubetis, C., Henzinger, T.A., Ho, P.-H.: Hybrid automata: an algorithmic approach to the specification and verification of hybrid systems. In: Grossman, R.L., Nerode, A., Ravn, A.P., Rischel, H. (eds.) HS 1991-1992. LNCS, vol. 736, pp. 209–229. Springer, Heidelberg (1993). doi:10.1007/3-540-57318-6_30

[Ben98] Benveniste, A.: Compositional and uniform modelling of hybrid systems. IEEE Trans. Autom. Control 43(4), 579–584 (1998)

[BCP10] Benveniste, A., Cailland, B., Pouzet, M.: The fundamentals of hybrid system modelers. In: CDC, pp. 4180–4185. IEEE (2010)

[BG92] Berry, G., Gonthier, G.: The esterel synchronous programming language: design, semantics and implementation. Sci. Comput. Program. 19(2), 87–152 (1992)

[Ber96] Berry, G.: Constructive semantics of Esterel: from theory to practice (abstract). In: Wirsing, M., Nivat, M. (eds.) AMAST 1996. LNCS, vol. 1101, pp. 225–225. Springer, Heidelberg (1996). doi:10.1007/BFb0014318

[CPP06] Carloni, L.P., Passerone, R., Pinto, A.: Languages and tools for hybrid systems design. Found. Trends Electron. Des. Autom. 1(1/2), 1–193 (2006)

[Des96] Deshpande, A., Göllü, A., Varaiya, P.: SHIFT: a formalism and a programming language for dynamic networks of hybrid automata. In: Antsaklis, P., Kohn, W., Nerode, A., Sastry, S. (eds.) HS 1996. LNCS, vol. 1273, pp. 113–133. Springer, Heidelberg (1997). doi:10.1007/BFb0031558

[Dij76] Dijkstra, E.W.: A Discipline of Programming. Prentice-Hall, Englewood Cliffs (1976)

[He94] Jifeng, H.: From CSP to hybrid systems. In: Roscoe, A.W. (ed.) a classical mind: essays in honour of C.A.R. Hoare, pp. 171–189 (1994)

[He03] Jifeng, H.: A clock-based framework for constructions of hybrid systems. In: The Proceedings of ICTAC 2013 (2013)

[Hen96] Henzinger, T.A.: The theory of hybrid automata. In: LICS, pp. 278–292. IEEE Computer Society (1996)

[Hoa85] Hoare, C.A.R.: Communicating Sequential Processes. Prentice Hall, Upper Saddle River (1985)

[HH98] Hoare, C.A.R., Jifeng, H.: Unifying Theories of Programming. Prentice Hall, Englewood Cliffs (1998)

[Koh88] Kohn, W.: A declarative theory for rational controllers. In: Proceedings of 27th CDC, pp. 130–136 (1988)

[Kra06] Kratz, F., Sokolsky, O., Pappas, G.J., Lee, I.: R-Charon, a modeling language for reconfigurable hybrid systems. In: Hespanha, J.P., Tiwari, A. (eds.) HSCC 2006. LNCS, vol. 3927, pp. 392–406. Springer, Heidelberg (2006). doi:10.1007/11730637_30

[MMP91] Maler, O., Manna, Z., Pnueli, A.: Prom timed to hybrid systems. In: Bakker, J.W., Huizing, C., Roever, W.P., Rozenberg, G. (eds.) REX 1991. LNCS, vol. 600, pp. 447–484. Springer, Heidelberg (1992). doi:10.1007/BFb0032003

[Mil99] Milner, R.: Communicating and Mobile Systems: the π-calculus. Cambridge University Press, New York (1999)

[Pla08] Platzer, A.: Differential dynamic logic: automated theorem proving for hybrid systems. Ph.D. thesis, Department of Computing Science, University of Oldenburg (2008)

[Pla10] Platzer, A.: Logical analysis of hybrid systems. In: Kutrib, M., Moreira, N., Reis, R. (eds.) DCFS 2012. LNCS, vol. 7386, pp. 43–49. Springer, Heidelberg (2012). doi:10.1007/978-3-642-31623-4_3

[RRS03] Ronkko, M., Ravn, A.P., Sere, K.: Hybrid action systems. Theoret. Comput. Sci. **290**(1), 937–973 (2003)

[RS03]   Rounds, W.C., Song, H.: The Ö-calculus: a language for distributed control of reconfigurable embedded systems. In: Maler, O., Pnueli, A. (eds.) HSCC 2003. LNCS, vol. 2623, pp. 435–449. Springer, Heidelberg (2003). doi:10.1007/3-540-36580-X_32

[Sim]   Simulink. www.mathworks.com/products/simulink/

[Tar41] Tarski, A.: On the calculus od relations. J. Symbolic Logic **6**(3), 73–89 (1941)

[Tar55] Tarski, A.: A lattice-theoretical fixpoint theorem and its applications. Pac. J. Math. **5**, 285–309 (1955)

[Tav87] Tavermini, L.: Differential automata and their discrete simulations. Non-Linear Anal. **11**(6), 665–683 (1987)

[ZH04]   Chen, Z.C., Hansen, M.R.: Duration Calculus: A Formal Approach to Real-time Systems. Springer, Heidelberg (2004)

[ZWR96] Chaochen, Z., Ji, W., Ravn, A.P.: A formal description of hybrid systems. In: Alur, R., Henzinger, T.A., Sontag, E.D. (eds.) HS 1995. LNCS, vol. 1066, pp. 511–530. Springer, Heidelberg (1996). doi:10.1007/BFb0020972

What Makes Petri Nets Harder to Verify: Stack or Data?

Ranko Lazić[1]([✉]) and Patrick Totzke[2]

[1] Department of Computer Science, DIMAP, University of Warwick, Coventry, UK
R.S.Lazic@warwick.ac.uk
[2] LFCS, School of Informatics, University of Edinburgh, Edinburgh, UK

Abstract. We show how the yardstick construction of Stockmeyer, also developed as counter bootstrapping by Lipton, can be adapted and extended to obtain new lower bounds for the coverability problem for two prominent classes of systems based on Petri nets: ACKERMANN-hardness for unordered data Petri nets, and TOWER-hardness for pushdown vector addition systems.

1 Introduction

Unordered Data Petri Nets. (UDPN [15]) extend Petri nets by decorating tokens with data values taken from some countable data domain $\mathbb{D}$, broadly in the vein of coloured Petri nets [13]. These values act as pure names: they can only be compared for equality or non-equality upon firing transitions. Such systems can model for instance distributed protocols where process identities need to be taken into account [24]. UDPNs also coincide with the natural generalisation of Petri nets in the framework of sets with atoms [3]. In spite of their high expressiveness, UDPNs fit in the large family of Petri net extensions among the *well-structured* ones [1,8]. As such, they still enjoy decision procedures for several verification problems, prominently safety through the *coverability* problem.

UDPNs have an interesting position in the taxonomy of well-structured Petri net extensions (see Fig. 1). Indeed, all their extensions forgo the decidability of the *reachability* problem (whether a target configuration is reachable) and of the *place boundedness* problem (whether the number of tokens in a given place can be bounded along all runs): this is the case of ν-*Petri nets* [24] that allow to create fresh data values, of *ordered data Petri nets* [15] that posit a dense linear ordering on $\mathbb{D}$, and of *unordered data nets* [15] that allow to perform 'whole-place' operations, which move and/or duplicate all the tokens from a place to another. By contrast, it is currently open whether reachability is decidable for UDPNs, but recent results on computing their coverability trees [11] and on linear combinations of unordered data vectors [12] suggest to conjecture decidability.

Supported by the EPSRC, grants EP/M011801/1 and EP/M027651/1, and by the Royal Society, grant IE150122.

© Springer International Publishing AG 2017
T. Gibson-Robinson et al. (Eds.): Roscoe Festschrift, LNCS 10160, pp. 144–161, 2017.
DOI: 10.1007/978-3-319-51046-0_8

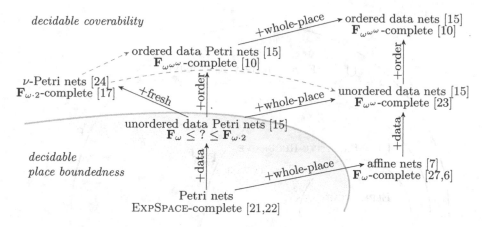

Fig. 1. A short taxonomy of some well-structured extensions of Petri nets. The complexities refer to the coverability problems, and can be taken as proxies for expressiveness; the new lower bound in this paper is displayed in blue, and the exact complexity for UDPNs remains open. Place boundedness is decidable below the yellow line and undecidable above. As indicated by the dashed arrows, freshness can be enforced using a dense linear order or whole-place operations. (Color figure online)

The Power of Well-Structured Systems. This work is part of a general programme that aims to understand the expressive power and algorithmic complexity of well-structured transition systems (WSTS), for which the complexity of the coverability problem is a natural proxy. Besides the intellectual satisfaction one might find in classifying the worst-case complexity of this problem, we hope indeed to gain new insights into the algorithmics of the systems at hand, and into their relative 'power'. A difficulty is that the generic *backward* algorithm [1,8] developed to solve coverability in WSTS relies on well-quasi-orders (wqos), for which complexity analysis techniques are not so widely known.

Nevertheless, in a series of recent papers, the exact complexity of coverability for several classes of WSTSs has been established. These complexities are expressed using ordinal-indexed *fast-growing* complexity classes $(\mathbf{F}_\alpha)_\alpha$ [25], e.g. TOWER complexity corresponds to the class $\mathbf{F}_3$ and is the first non elementary complexity class in this hierarchy, ACKERMANN corresponds to $\mathbf{F}_\omega$ and is the first non primitive-recursive class, HYPER-ACKERMANN to $\mathbf{F}_{\omega^\omega}$ and is the first non multiply-recursive class, etc.; see Fig. 2. To cite a few of these complexity results, coverability is $\mathbf{F}_\omega$-complete for reset Petri nets and affine nets [6,27], $\mathbf{F}_{\omega\cdot2}$-complete for ν-Petri nets [17], $\mathbf{F}_{\omega^\omega}$-complete for lossy channel systems [4,26] and unordered data nets [23], and even higher complexities appear for timed-arc Petri nets and ordered data Petri nets ($\mathbf{F}_{\omega^{\omega^\omega}}$-complete [10]) and priority channel systems and nested counter systems ($\mathbf{F}_{\varepsilon_0}$-complete [5,9]); see the complexities in violet in Fig. 1 for the Petri net extensions related to UDPNs.

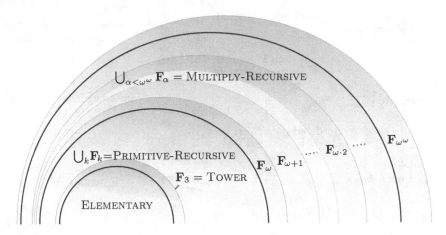

Fig. 2. Some complexity classes beyond ELEMENTARY. The two new lower bounds in this paper are $\mathbf{F}_3$ (Sect. 3) and $\mathbf{F}_\omega$ (Sect. 7), whereas the best known upper bound for UDPN coverability is $\mathbf{F}_{\omega \cdot 2}$ [17].

New Lower Bound for UDPNs. In this paper, we tackle the huge gap in what is known about the worst-case complexity of the coverability problem for UDPNs: between the TOWER, i.e. $\mathbf{F}_3$, lower bound established in [15] and the $\mathbf{F}_{\omega \cdot 2}$ upper bound that holds even for the more general class of ν-Petri nets [17]. Our main result is an increased $\mathbf{F}_\omega$ lower bound, making it known that coverability for UDPNs cannot be decided in primitive recursive time or space.

For this ACKERMANN lower bound, we follow the pattern of Stockmeyer's yardstick construction [28] and Lipton's classical proof of EXPSPACE-hardness for Petri nets [21], in that we design an 'object-oriented' implementation of the Ackermann function in UDPNs. By this, we mean that the implementation provides an interface with increment, decrement, zero, and max operations on larger and larger *counters* up to an Ackermannian value. This allows then the simulation of a Minsky machine working in Ackermann space.

The difficulty is that the bootstrapping implementation in UDPNs of the hierarchy of counters requires an iteration operator on 'counter libraries'—of the kind employed recently in the context of channel systems with insertion errors to obtain $\mathbf{F}_\omega$-hardness [16] and in the context of ν-Petri nets to obtain $\mathbf{F}_{\omega \cdot 2}$-hardness [17]—but UDPNs have fundamentally unordered configurations as well as no basic mechanism for creating fresh data values. To overcome that obstacle—and this is the key technical idea in the paper—we enrich the interfaces of the counter implementations by a *local freshness test*: verifying that a given data value is distinct from all data values that the implementation (and, recursively, the implementations of all lesser counters in the hierarchy) currently employs internally; see Sects. 5 and 6.

Pushdown Vector Addition Systems. Motivations for considering extensions of Petri nets by a pushdown stack include verifying procedural programs with unbounded integer variables [2] and optimising two-variable queries on XML documents with unbounded data at leaf nodes [14]. The boundedness problem, as well as the coverability and counter-boundedness problems in the restricted setting of pushdown vector addition systems (PVAS) of dimension 1, have recently been shown decidable [18–20]. However, the coverability and reachability problems are interreducible for PVASs in general [14, 20], and the whether they are decidable remains a challenging open question.

Partly in order to introduce the bootstrapping technique that is the basis of our $\mathbf{F}_\omega$ lower bound for UDPN coverability, we present a proof that the reachability problem for PVASs (also the coverability and boundedness problems) is $\mathbf{F}_3$-hard; this TOWER lower bound means that the latter problems cannot be decided in elementary time or space.

Outline. In the two sections, we introduce the bootstrapping technique using pushdown vector addition systems and obtain TOWER-hardness of their reachability problem. The four sections that follow develop the more involved ACKER-MANN-hardness of the coverability problem for unordered data Petri nets. The latter lower bound still leaves a gap to the best known $\mathbf{F}_{\omega \cdot 2}$ upper bound, and we finish with some remarks about that in the concluding section.

2 Pushdown Vector Addition Systems

It is convenient for our purposes to formalise PVASs as programs that operate on non-negative counters and a finite-alphabet stack. More precisely, we define them as finite sequences of commands which may be labelled, where a command is one of:

- an increment of a counter ($x := x + 1$),
- a decrement of a counter ($x := x - 1$),
- a push (push a),
- a pop (pop a),
- a nondeterministic jump to one of two labelled commands (goto L or L'),
- or termination (halt).

Initially, all counters have value 0 and the stack is empty. Whenever a decrement of a counter with value 0 or an erroneous pop is attempted, the program aborts. In every program, halt occurs only as the last command.

Example 2.1. We display in Fig. 3 a PVAS fragment, which will be useful in the next section. It is shown diagramatically, where multiple outgoing edges from a node are to be implemented by the nondeterministic jumps.

The reachability problem for PVASs can now be stated as follows:

Input: A PVAS $\mathcal{P}$.
Question: Does $\mathcal{P}$ have a computation which reaches the halt command with all counters being 0 and the stack being empty?

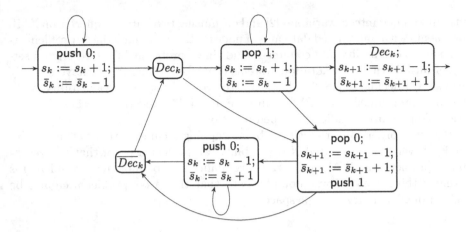

Fig. 3. PVAS procedure Dec_{k+1}. The calls of procedures Dec_k and $\overline{Dec_k}$ use the stack in the standard manner. The latter is the variant of Dec_k that decrements s_k exactly tower(k) times, i.e. with s_k and $\bar{s}_k$ swapped.

3 TOWER-Hardness

Theorem 3.1. *The reachability problem for PVASs is* TOWER-*hard.*

Proof. We reduce from the tower(n)-bounded halting problem for *Minsky programs* with n commands, where:

– for $k \in \mathbb{N}$, the 'tetration' operation is defined by

$$\text{tower}(0) = 1 \text{ and } \text{tower}(k+1) = 2^{\text{tower}(k)} \ ;$$

– the Minsky programs are defined like PVASs, except that they have no stack, have only deterministic jumps (goto L), but can test counters for zero (if $x = 0$ then L else L').

The following problem is TOWER-hard [25, Sect. 2.3.2 and Theorem 4.1]:

> **Input**: A Minsky program $\mathcal{M}$ with n commands.
> **Question**: Can $\mathcal{M}$ reach the halt command by a computation during which all counter values are at most tower(n)?

Given such a Minsky program $\mathcal{M}$, we construct in time polynomial in n a PVAS $\mathcal{P}(\mathcal{M})$ that simulates $\mathcal{M}$ as long as its counters do not exceed tower(n). Similarly to Stockmeyer's yardstick construction [28] and Lipton's proof of EXPSPACE-hardness for Petri nets [21], the idea is to bootstrap the ability to simulate zero tests of counters that are bounded by tower(1), tower(2), ..., tower(n).

More precisely, for each counter x of $\mathcal{M}$, $\mathcal{P}(\mathcal{M})$ have a pair of counters x and $\bar{x}$, on which it maintains the invariant $x + \bar{x} = \text{tower}(n)$. Thus, every increment of x in $\mathcal{M}$ is translated to $x := x + 1$; $\bar{x} := \bar{x} - 1$ in $\mathcal{P}(\mathcal{M})$, and similarly for decrements.

For every zero test of x in $\mathcal{M}$, $\mathcal{P}(\mathcal{M})$ uses auxiliary counters s_n and $\bar{s}_n$, for which it also maintains $s_n + \bar{s}_n = \text{tower}(n)$. Moreover, we assume that $s_n = 0$ at the start of each zero-test simulation. The simulation begins by $\mathcal{P}(\mathcal{M})$ transferring some part of $\bar{x}$ to s_n (while preserving the invariants). It then calls a procedure Dec_n that decrements s_n exactly $\text{tower}(n)$ times. For the latter to be possible, x must have been 0. Otherwise, or in case not all of $\bar{x}$ was transferred to s_n, the procedure can only abort. When Dec_n succeeds, the initial values of x and $\bar{x}$ are reversed, so to finish the simulation, everything is repeated with x and $\bar{x}$ swapped.

The main part of the construction is implementing Dec_k for $k = 1, 2, \ldots, n$. Assuming that Dec_k which decrements s_k exactly $\text{tower}(k)$ times and maintains $s_k + \bar{s}_k = \text{tower}(k)$ has been implemented for some $k < n$, Dec_{k+1} consists of performing the following by means of s_k, $\bar{s}_k$ and Dec_k, cf. Fig. 3:

- push exactly $\text{tower}(k)$ zeros onto the stack;
- keep incrementing the $\text{tower}(k)$-digit binary number that is on top of the stack until no longer possible, and decrement s_{k+1} for each such increment;
- pop $\text{tower}(k)$ ones that are on top of the stack, and decrement s_{k+1} once more.

Following the same pattern: starting with all counters having value 0, $\mathcal{P}(\mathcal{M})$ can initialise each auxiliary counter $\bar{s}_k$ to $\text{tower}(k)$, and each $\bar{x}$ to $\text{tower}(n)$; also provided $\mathcal{M}$ reaches its halt command, $\mathcal{P}(\mathcal{M})$ can empty all its counters, as required.

$\square$

4   Unordered Data Petri Nets

This extension of classical Petri nets is by decorating tokens with data values taken from some countably infinite data domain $\mathbb{D}$. These values act as pure names: they can only be compared for equality or non-equality upon firing transitions. We recall the definition from [23,24].

A multiset over set X is a function $M : X \to \mathbb{N}$. The set $X^\oplus$ of all multisets over X is ordered pointwise, and the union of $M, M' \in X^\oplus$ is $(M \oplus M') \in X^\oplus$ with $(M \oplus M')(\alpha) \stackrel{\text{def}}{=} M(\alpha) + M'(\alpha)$ for all $\alpha \in X$. If $M \geq M'$ holds then the difference $(M \ominus M')$ is defined as the unique $M'' \in X^\oplus$ with $M = M' \oplus M''$.

Definition 4.1. *An unordered data Petri net (UDPN) over domain $\mathbb{D}$ consists of finite sets P, T, Var of places, transitions and variables, respectively, and a flow function $F : (P \times T) \cup (T \times P) \to Var^\oplus$ that assigns each place $p \in P$ and transition $t \in T$ a finite multiset of variables.*

A marking is a function $M : P \to \mathbb{D}^\oplus$. Intuitively, $M(p)(\alpha)$ denotes the number of tokens of type α in place p. A transition $t \in T$ is enabled in marking M with mode σ if $\sigma : Var \to \mathbb{D}$ is an injection such that $\sigma(F(p,t)) \leq M(p)$ for all $p \in P$. *There is a step* $M \to M'$ *between markings* M *and* M' *if there exists* t *and* σ *such that* t *is enabled in* M *with mode* σ, *and for all* $p \in P$,

$$M'(p) = M(p) \ominus \sigma(F(p,t)) \oplus \sigma(F(t,p)) \ .$$

For notational convenience we will sometimes write that a marking M *has tokens* $\langle n_1, n_2, \ldots, n_k \rangle$ *of type* α *in places* $\langle p_1, p_2, \ldots, p_k \rangle$ *if* $M(p_i)(\alpha) = n_i$ *holds for all* $1 \le i \le k$. *Similarly, we write that a transition* t *takes (resp. puts)* $\langle n_1, n_2, \ldots, n_k \rangle$ *tokens of type* α *in places* $\langle p_1, p_2, \ldots, p_k \rangle$ *if for all* $1 \le i \le k$ *it holds that* $F(p_i, t)(\alpha) = n_i$ *(resp.* $F(t, p_i)(\alpha) = n_i$).

Notice that UDPN are a generalization of ordinary P/T nets, which have only one type of token, i.e. $\mathbb{D} = \{\bullet\}$. See Fig. 4 for a depiction of an UDPN in the usual Petri net notation.

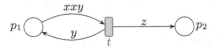

Fig. 4. An UDPN with places p_1, p_2, variables x, y, z and a single transition t. The transition t takes $\langle 2, 0 \rangle$ tokens of type x and $\langle 1, 0 \rangle$ tokens of type y in places $\langle p_1, p_2 \rangle$. It puts 1 token of type z onto p_2 and 1 token of type y onto p_1.

The *Coverability Problem* for UDPN is the following decision problem where $\xrightarrow{*}$ denotes the transitive and reflexive closure of the step relation.

Input: An UDPN (P, T, Var, F) and two markings $I, F : P \to \mathbb{D}^\oplus$.

Question: Does there exist a marking $F' \ge F$ such that $I \xrightarrow{*} F'$?

The following example shows that three places and a simple addressing mechanism are enough to simulate ordinary Petri nets with an arbitrary number of places. This suggests that UDPN are more succinct than Petri nets and indeed, as we shall see in Sect. 6, UDPN can be used to design more involved addressing mechanisms. This will allow us to push the classical approach of [21] to simulate bounded counter machines from a double exponential bound to an Ackermannian bound.

Example 4.2. Given a Petri net with places $P = \{p_0, \ldots, p_{n-1}\}$, we build a UDPN with three places a, $\bar{a}$, and v and variables $Var = \{x_0, \ldots, x_{n-1}\}$.

The intuition is for a and $\bar{a}$ to maintain an *addressing* mechanism for the original places in P, while v maintains the actual token counts of the original net. The places a and $\bar{a}$ hold $n - 1$ different data values such that all reachable configurations are of the form $\bigoplus_{i=0}^{n-1} M_i$ where $M_i(a) = i$ and $M_i(\bar{a}) = n - 1 - i$ for all $0 \le i < n$.

Each partial marking M_i represents a marking of the place p_i in the original net by holding in $M_i(v)$ the number of tokens in place p_i. Each transition of the

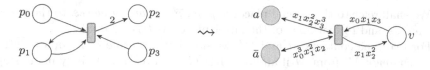

Fig. 5. Simulation of a Petri net transition (left) by a UDPN (right).

original net translates into a UDPN transition where the flows of the variables with places a and $\bar{a}$ identify uniquely the places of the original net, while the flows with place v update the token counts accordingly.

Figure 5 shows how a transition of a Petri net with 4 places (on the left) is simulated with this construction (on the right).

5   Counter Libraries in UDPNs

To present our lower bound construction, we indirectly describe UDPNs in terms of sequential programs. For this purpose we will now develop a simple but convenient language for programming with UDPNs.

Routines, Libraries, and Programs. Let a *library* mean a sequence of named routines

$$\ell_1 : R_1, \ldots, \ell_K : R_K$$

where $\ell_1, \ldots, \ell_K$ are pairwise distinct labels. In turn, a *routine* is a sequence of commands $c_1, \ldots, c_{K'}$, where the last command $c_{K'}$ is return and each c_i for $i < K'$ is one of the following:

- a UDPN transition,
- a nondeterministic jump goto G for a nonempty subset G of $\{1, \ldots, K'\}$, or
- a subroutine invocation call ℓ'.

When a library contains no subroutine calls, we say it is a *program*. The denotation of a program L is a UDPN $\mathcal{N}(L)$ constructed so that:

- The places of $\mathcal{N}(L)$ are all the places that occur in transition commands of L, and four special places p, $\bar{p}$, p', $\bar{p}'$. Places $\langle p, \bar{p} \rangle$ are used to store the pair of numbers $\langle i, K - i \rangle$ where $\ell_i : R_i$ is the routine being executed, and then places $\langle p', \bar{p}' \rangle$ to store the pair of numbers $\langle i', K' - i' \rangle$ where i' is the current line number in routine R_i and K' is the maximum number of lines in any $R_1, \ldots, R_K$.
- Each transition of $\mathcal{N}(L)$ either executes a transition command $c_{i'}$ inside some R_i ensuring that $\langle p, \bar{p} \rangle$ contains $\langle i, K - i \rangle$ and modifying the contents of $\langle p', \bar{p}' \rangle$ from $\langle i', K' - i' \rangle$ to $\langle i' + 1, K' - (i' + 1) \rangle$, or similarly executes a nondeterministic jump command.

We shall refer to the special places p, $\bar{p}$, p', $\bar{p}'$ as *control places*, to the rest as *tape places*, and to markings of the latter places as *tape contents*.

For two tape contents M and M', we say that a routine $\ell_i : R_i$ in a program L *can compute* M' from M if and only if $\mathcal{N}(L)$ can reach in finitely many steps M' with the control at the last line of R_i from M with the control at the first line of R_i. When $\ell_i : R_i$ cannot compute any M' from M, we say that it *cannot terminate* from initial tape content M.

Note that there are two sources of nondeterminism in routine computations: choosing how to instantiate the variables in the commands that are UDPN transitions, and resolving the destinations of the jump commands. The computations can also become blocked, which happens if they reach a UDPN transition that is disabled due to insufficient tokens being available in the current tape content.

Interfaces and Compositions of Libraries. For a library L, let us write $\Lambda_{\text{in}}(L)$ and $\Lambda_{\text{out}}(L)$ for the set of all routine labels that are invoked in L and provided by L, respectively. We say that libraries L_0 and L_1 are *compatible* if and only if $\Lambda_{\text{in}}(L_0)$ is contained in $\Lambda_{\text{out}}(L_1)$. In that case, we can compose them to produce a library $L_0 \circ L_1$ in which tape contents of L_1 persist between successive invocations of its routines, as follows:

- $\Lambda_{\text{in}}(L_0 \circ L_1) = \Lambda_{\text{in}}(L_1)$ and $\Lambda_{\text{out}}(L_0 \circ L_1) = \Lambda_{\text{out}}(L_0)$.
- $L_0 \circ L_1$ has an additional place w used to store the name space of L_0 (i.e., for each name manipulated by L_0, one token labelled by it) and an additional place $\bar{w}$ for the same purpose for L_1.
- For each routine $\ell : R$ of L_0, the corresponding routine $\ell : R \circ L_1$ of $L_0 \circ L_1$ is obtained by ensuring that the transition commands in R (resp., L_1) maintain the name space stored on place w (resp., $\bar{w}$), and then inlining the subroutine calls in R.

Example 5.1. Suppose that in L_1 the routine with label ℓ_1 consists only of the transition command $a\,\bigcirc \xrightarrow{\;y\;} \square \xrightarrow{\;y\;} \bigcirc b$ followed by **return**. Suppose further that L_0 has a routine with label ℓ_0 and commands $a\,\bigcirc \xrightarrow{\;x\;} \square \xrightarrow{\;x\;} \bigcirc c$ followed by **call** ℓ. Then the corresponding routine ℓ_0 in the composition $L_0 \circ L_1$ is

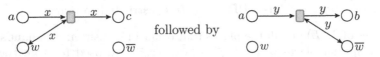

$$\text{followed by}$$

Notice that, in the above definition of $\mathcal{N}(L_0 \circ L_1)$, the places of $\mathcal{N}(L_0)$ and $\mathcal{N}(L_1)$ are not duplicated: a transion command in L_0 may operate on some place which is also used in L_1. The name space places w and $\bar{w}$ and the way transition commands translate into actual UDPN transitions in $\mathcal{N}(L_0 \circ L_1)$ ensure that the commands of the two libraries do not interfere. However, this relies on an additional mechanism for preventing the same name to be used by both L_0 and L_1—unless disjointness of corresponding places is guaranteed—and that is what the local freshness checks developed in the sequel provide.

Counter Libraries. We aim to write programs that simulate bounded two-counter Minsky machines. For this purpose we will now focus on libraries that provide the necessary operations to manipulate a pair of counters. Letting Γ denote the set of labels of operations

$$\Gamma \stackrel{\text{def}}{=} \{init, fresh, eq, i.inc, i.dec, i.iszero, i.ismax : i \in \{1,2\}\},$$

we regard L to be a *counter* library if and only if $\Lambda_{\text{out}}(L) = \Gamma$ and $\Lambda_{\text{in}}(L) \subseteq \Gamma$.

When L is also a program, and N is a positive integer, we say that L is *N-correct* if and only if the routines behave as expected with respect to the bound N and correctly implement a freshness test on a special tape place ν. Namely, for every tape content M that can be computed from the empty tape content by a sequence σ of operations from Γ, provided *init* occurs only as the first element of σ, every routine in $\Gamma \setminus \{init\}$ either does not terminate or computes a unique tape content from M. If n_i is the difference between the numbers of occurrences in σ of *i.inc* and *i.dec*, we must have for both $i \in \{1,2\}$:

- *i.inc* can terminate from M if and only if $n_i < N - 1$;
- *i.dec* can terminate from M if and only if $n_i > 0$;
- *eq* can terminate from M (and compute M) if and only if $n_1 = n_2$;
- *i.iszero* can terminate from M (and compute M) if and only if $n_i = 0$;
- *i.ismax* can terminate from M (and compute M) if and only if $n_i = N - 1$.

Moreover, N-correctness requires that L behaves with respect to *fresh* and ν so that:

- only transition commands in the routines *init* and *fresh* use the place ν;
- if M is computed from the empty tape content by *init*, then M has no tokens on place ν;
- for every tape content A that has one token of type α on place ν and is otherwise empty, and for every tape content M computed by a sequence σ as above, we have that *fresh* can terminate from $M \oplus A$ (and compute $M \oplus A$) if and only if α is not in the support of $M(p)$ for all places $p \neq \nu$.

We also need a notion of correctness for counter libraries that may not be programs, i.e. may invoke operations on another pair of counters (which we call *auxiliary*). Given a counter library L, and given a function $F : \mathbb{N}^+ \to \mathbb{N}^+$, we say that L is $F - correct$ if and only if, for all N-correct counter programs C, the program $L \circ C$ is $F(N)$-correct.

We now present two example counter libraries, which will be used in our later constructions.

Example 5.2 (An Enumerated Counter Program). For every positive integer N, one can implement a pair of N-bounded counters by manipulating the values and their complements directly as follows. Let $Enum(N)$ be the counter program which uses four places $e_1, \bar{e}_1, e_2, \bar{e}_2$ and such that for both $i \in \{1,2\}$:

- routine *init* chooses a datum β, and puts $N - 1$ tokens onto $\bar{e}_1$ and $N - 1$ tokens onto $\bar{e}_2$, all carrying β;

- routine *fresh* takes one token from e_1 or $\bar{e}_1$, and checks it for inequality with the token on ν;
- routine *eq* guesses $n \in \{0, \ldots, N-1\}$, takes $\langle n, N-1-n, n, N-1-n \rangle$ tokens from places $\langle e_1, \bar{e}_1, e_2, \bar{e}_2 \rangle$, and then puts them back;
- routine *i.inc* moves a token from $\bar{e}_i$ to e_i;
- routine *i.dec* moves a token from e_i to $\bar{e}_i$;
- routine *i.iszero* takes $N-1$ tokens from place $\bar{e}_i$ and then puts them back;
- routine *i.ismax* takes $N-1$ tokens from place e_i and then puts them back.

It is simple to verify that $Enum(N)$ is computable in space logarithmic in N, and that:

Lemma 5.3. *For every N, the counter program $Enum(N)$ is N-correct.*

Example 5.4 (A Counter Library for Doubling). Let *Double* be a counter library which uses four places b_1, $\bar{b}_1$, b_2, $\bar{b}_2$, is such that:

- routine *init* first initialises the auxiliary counters (call *init*), then chooses a datum β and checks that it is fresh with respect to the auxiliary counters (call *fresh*), and finally puts one token carrying β onto both $\bar{b}_1$ and $\bar{b}_2$;
- routine *fresh* checks that the given datum (on the special place ν) is both fresh with respect to the auxiliary counters, and distinct from the datum on b_1 or $\bar{b}_1$ (equivalently, b_2 or $\bar{b}_2$), see Fig. 6 for the code that implements this;
- routine *eq* first calls *eq* on the auxiliary counters, then either takes $\langle 1, 0, 1, 0 \rangle$ or $\langle 0, 1, 0, 1 \rangle$ tokens from places $\langle b_1, \bar{b}_1, b_2, \bar{b}_2 \rangle$, and finally puts them back;

and for both $i \in \{1, 2\}$:

- routine *i.inc* calls *i.inc*, or calls *i.ismax* and moves a token from $\bar{b}_i$ to b_i;
- routine *i.dec* calls *i.dec*, or calls *i.iszero* and moves a token from b_i to $\bar{b}_i$;
- routine *i.iszero* calls *i.iszero*, takes a token from $\bar{b}_i$ and puts it back;
- routine *i.ismax* calls *i.ismax*, takes a token from b_i and puts it back.

Given a correct program C that provides counters bounded by N, the library *Double* essentially uses two extra bits (each represented by a pair $\langle b_i, \bar{b}_i \rangle$ of places) to implement a program *Double* $\circ$ *C*, where the bound on the provided counters is $2N$.

Lemma 5.5. *The counter library Double is $\lambda x.2x$-correct.*

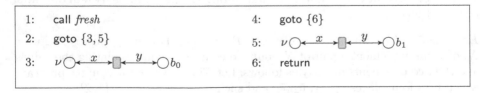

Fig. 6. The routine *fresh* of the counter library *Double*. Here, the numbers on the left of the commands are line numbers to be referenced in goto commands.

Proof. When the control reaches the end of the *init* routine, $Double \circ C$ has as tape content a marking $M \oplus M_C$, where M_C is a marking of $\mathcal{N}(C)$ representing two 0-valued counters with bound N, and M has $\langle 0, 1, 0, 1 \rangle$ tokens of some type β on places $\langle b_1, \bar{b}_1, b_2, \bar{b}_2 \rangle$. So by adding two new most significant bits, this tape content represents two 0-counters with bound $2N$. Notice that all routines apart from *init* preserve the invariant that tape contents have exaxtly two tokens of type β on the places $b_1, \bar{b}_1, b_2, \bar{b}_2$. We can easily check that those routines satisfy the respective correctness criteria.

For example, take the routine *eq* and let $n_1, n_2 \in \mathbb{N}$ denote the values of the counters represented by the current tape content M. If $n_1 = n_2$, then $M \oplus M_C$ has $\langle 1, 0, 1, 0 \rangle$ or $\langle 0, 1, 0, 1 \rangle$ tokens on places $\langle b_1, \bar{b}_1, b_2, \bar{b}_2 \rangle$ and the numbers n_1', n_2' represented by M_C are the same. Since C is N-correct, the command call *eq* terminates. Moreover, one of the two operations to take $\langle 1, 0, 1, 0 \rangle$ or $\langle 0, 1, 0, 1 \rangle$ from $\langle b_1, \bar{b}_1, b_2, \bar{b}_2 \rangle$ is possible. So *eq* terminates. Conversely, if $n_1 \neq n_2$, then either the content of places $\langle b_1, \bar{b}_1, b_2, \bar{b}_2 \rangle$ is $\langle 0, 1, 1, 0 \rangle$ or $\langle 1, 0, 0, 1 \rangle$, or the values represented by the auxiliary counters are not equal. In the first case, the commands to take $\langle 1, 0, 1, 0 \rangle$ or $\langle 0, 1, 0, 1 \rangle$ are disabled; in the latter case, the command call *eq* does not terminate, by the correctness assumption on C.

In a similar fashion we can see that the routine *fresh* (see Fig. 6) is correct: suppose the current tape content is $M \oplus M_C$ and A is the tape content that has one token α on place ν and is otherwise empty. If α is different from β (used on places $b_i, \bar{b}_i$) and also different from all data values in the configuration of C, then the routine must terminate without changing the tape content. If $\alpha = \beta$ then then both commands in lines 3 and 5 will block. If α appears in M_C then the command call *fresh* in line 1 must block. □

6 Bootstrapping Counter Libraries

The most complex part of our construction is an operator $-^*$ whose input is a counter library L. Its output L^* is also a counter library which behaves like an arbitrary number of copies of L composed in sequence. Namely, for every N-correct counter program C, the counter operations provided by $L^* \circ C$ behave in the same way as those provided by

$$\overbrace{L \circ \cdots \circ L}^{N} \circ Enum(1).$$

Hence, when L is F-correct, we have that L^* is F'-correct, where $F'(x) = F^x(1)$.

The main idea for the definition of L^* is to combine a distinguishing of name spaces as in the composition of libraries with an arbitrarily wide indexing mechanism like the one employed in Example 4.2. The key insight here is that a whole collection of 'addressing places' $\langle a_i, \bar{a}_i \rangle_i$ as used in Example 4.2 can be simulated by adding one layer of addressing. We will use the routine *fresh* to set up this addressing mechanism during initialisation, recursively.

Let us write here I, I' for the two N-bounded auxiliary counters and number the copies of L by $0, \ldots, N-1$, writing $\ell_1 : R_1$ up to $\ell_K : R_K$ for the routines of L

and K' for the maximum number of commands in a routine. Since L is a counter library, it has $K = |\Gamma'| = 11$ routines, and we assume without loss of generality that $\ell_1 = init$ and $\ell_2 = fresh$. The net for L^* can maintain the control and the tape of each copy of L in the implicit composition as follows.

- To record that the program counter of the ith copy of L is currently in routine $\ell_j : R_j$ at line j', $\langle i, N - 1 - i, j, K - j, j', K' - j' \rangle$ tokens carrying a separate name α_i are kept on special places $\langle w, \overline{w}, p, \overline{p}, p', \overline{p}' \rangle$.
- The current height i of the stack of subroutine calls is kept in one of the auxiliary counters, and we have that:
  • for all $i' < i$, the program counter of the i'th copy of L is at some subroutine invocation call ℓ' such that the program counter of the $(i' + 1)$th copy of L is in the routine named ℓ';
  • for all $i' > i$, there are $\langle i', N - 1 - i', 0, 0, 0, 0 \rangle$ tokens carrying $\alpha_{i'}$ on places $\langle w, \overline{w}, p, \overline{p}, p', \overline{p}' \rangle$.
- For every name manipulated by the ith copy of L, $\langle i, N - 1 - i \rangle$ tokens carrying it are kept on special places $\langle w', \overline{w}' \rangle$.

Table 1. A glossary of tape places in L^*. Not listed are places that are internally used in transition commands of L, nor the control places of $\mathcal{N}(L^* \circ C)$.

$w, \overline{w}$	Contain the addressing mechanism for recording the current control information of the L_i
$w', \overline{w}'$	Contain the name spaces of the L_i, where the multiplicities of tokens identify the indices i
$p, \overline{p}$	Identify the currently active routines of the L_i
$p', \overline{p}'$	Identify the currently active commands of the L_i
f	Temporarily stores a guessed datum for comparison
ν	Stores the datum to be checked for freshness

To define L^*, its places are all the places that occur in L, plus nine special places w, $\overline{w}$, w', $\overline{w}'$, p, $\overline{p}$, p', $\overline{p}'$ and f. Table 1 summarises how those places are used. All routines of the library L^* end in the same sequence of commands, which we will just call *the simulation loop*. This uses I' and place f repeatedly to identify numbers j' and j'' such that there are exactly $\langle I, N - 1 - I, j', K - j', j'', K' - j'' \rangle$ tokens carrying α_I on $\langle w, \overline{w}, p, \overline{p}, p', \overline{p}' \rangle$, and then advance the Ith copy of L by performing its command c at line j'' in routine $\ell_{j'} : R_{j'}$ of L as follows.

- If c is a UDPN transition, use I' and place f to maintain the Ith name space, i.e. to ensure that all names manipulated by c have $\langle I, N - 1 - I \rangle$ tokens on places $\langle w', \overline{w}' \rangle$.
- If c has put a datum β on place ν, invoke routine *fresh* of the auxiliary counters.

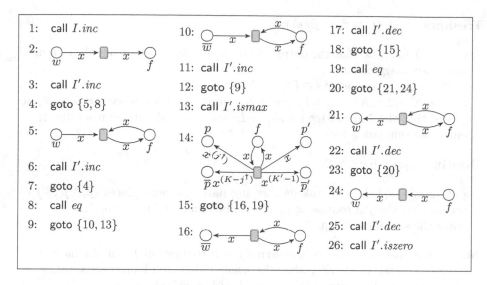

```
1:   call I.inc                                    17:  call I'.dec
2:                                                 18:  goto {15}
3:   call I'.inc                                   19:  call eq
4:   goto {5,8}                                    20:  goto {21,24}
5:
6:   call I'.inc                                   22:  call I'.dec
7:   goto {4}                                      23:  goto {20}
8:   call eq
9:   goto {10,13}                                  25:  call I'.dec
                                                   26:  call I'.iszero
10:
11:  call I'.inc
12:  goto {9}
13:  call I'.ismax
14:
15:  goto {16,19}
16:
21:
24:
```

Fig. 7. Performing a call $\ell_{j\dagger}$ provided $I < N - 1$. At the beginning, I' is assumed to be zero, and the same is guaranteed at the end.

– If c is a nondeterministic jump **goto** G, choose $j^\ddagger \in G$ and ensure that there are $\langle j^\ddagger, K' - j^\ddagger \rangle$ tokens carrying α_I on places $\langle p', \overline{p}' \rangle$.
– If c is a subroutine invocation **call** $\ell_{j\dagger}$ and $I < N - 1$, put $\langle j^\dagger, K - j^\dagger, 1, K' - 1 \rangle$ tokens carrying α_{I+1} on places $\langle p, \overline{p}, p', \overline{p}' \rangle$, and increment I. Example code that implements this can be found in Fig. 7.
– If c is a subroutine invocation **call** ℓ', $I = N - 1$ and ℓ' is not an increment or a decrement (of the trivial counter program $Enum(1)$), simply increment the program counter by moving a token carrying α_I from place $\overline{p}'$ to place p'. When ℓ' is an increment or a decrement, L^* blocks.
– In the remaining case, c is **return**. Remove the tokens carrying α_I from places $\langle p, \overline{p}, p', \overline{p}' \rangle$. If $I > 0$, move a token carrying α_{I-1} from $\overline{p}'$ to place p' and decrement I. Otherwise, exit the loop and return.

The code of this simulation loop is used (inlined) in the actual code for the routines R_j^* of L^*, which simulate the routines of the outmost copy L_0 as follows.

Initialization ($\ell_j = \ell_1 = init$):

– call $init$ to initialise the auxiliary counters;
– for each $i \in \{0, \ldots, N - 1\}$, put $\langle i, N - 1 - i \rangle$ tokens carrying a fresh name α_i onto places $\langle w, \overline{w} \rangle$ (this uses the auxiliary counters, their *fresh* routine, and place f);
– put $\langle 1, K - 1, 1, K' - 1 \rangle$ tokens carrying name α_0 onto places $\langle p, \overline{p}, p', \overline{p}' \rangle$ to record that the first routine ($init$) of L_0 should be simulated from line 1;
– enter the simulation loop.

Freshness test ($\ell_j = \ell_2 = fresh$):

- call *fresh* to check that the datum β on place ν is distinct from all data used in the auxiliary counters;
- verify that $\beta \neq \alpha_i$ for all $i \in \{0, \ldots, N-1\}$;
- put $\langle 2, K-2, 1, K'-1 \rangle$ tokens carrying name α_0 onto places $\langle p, \overline{p}, p', \overline{p}' \rangle$ to record that the 2nd routine (*fresh*) of L_0 should be simulated from line 1;
- enter the simulation loop.

Routines $\ell_j : R_j^*$ for $j > 2$:

- put $\langle 2, K-j, 1, K'-j \rangle$ tokens carrying name α_0 onto places $\langle p, \overline{p}, p', \overline{p}' \rangle$ to record that the jth routine of L_0 should be simulated from line 1;
- enter the simulation loop.

Notice that these routines do not actually call routines of L but simulate them internally and terminate only after the whole simulation loop terminates.

Observe that L^* is computable from L in logarithmic space.

Lemma 6.1. *For every function $F : \mathbb{N} \to \mathbb{N}$ and F-correct counter library L, the counter library L^* is $\lambda x. F^x(1)$-correct.*

Proof. Recall that for any $N \in \mathbb{N}$, the program $L^N \circ Enum(1)$, the N-fold composition of L with itself and the trivial 1-bounded counter program, is $F^k(1)$-correct by our assumption on L and Lemma 5.3.

We need to show that $L^* \circ C$ is $F^N(1)$-correct for every N-correct counter program C. We argue that, after initialisation and with respect to termination/nontermination of the counter routines $\Gamma \setminus \{init\}$, the program $L^* \circ C$ behaves just as $L^N \circ Enum(1)$.

Fix $k \leq \{1, \ldots, N\}$. We say a tape content M of $L^k \circ Enum(1)$ is *represented* by a tape content $M^\dagger$ of $L^* \circ C$ if, for all $i \in \{0, \ldots, k-1\}$,

1. there is a unique name α_{N-k+i} that labels $\langle N-k+i, k-i-1 \rangle$ tokens on places $\langle w, \overline{w} \rangle$ in $M^\dagger$, and
2. the restriction M_i of M to the names in the name space to the ith copy of L equals the restriction $M^\dagger_{N-k+i}$ of $M^\dagger$ to the names that label $\langle N-k+i, k-i-1 \rangle$ tokens on places $\langle w', \overline{w}' \rangle$ and to the places of L.

Let us now look at how the code of the simulation loop in L^* acts on representations of tape contents of $L^k \circ Enum(1)$.

For two tape contents M and M' of $L^k \circ Enum(1)$, we say that the simulation loop $\langle j, j' \rangle - computes$ M' from M if from a tape content (of $L^* \circ C$) that represents M, where the stack height stored in the first auxiliary counter is $N-k$ and there are $\langle j, K-j, j', K'-j' \rangle$ tokens carrying α_{N-k} on places $\langle p, \overline{p}, p', \overline{p}' \rangle$, the net $\mathcal{N}(L^* \circ C)$ can reach, by simulating a single command and without reducing the stack height below $N-k$, a tape content that represents M'.

The following claim can be shown by induction on $k \leq N$.

Claim. For two tape contents M, M' of $L^k \circ Enum(1)$, command j' of routine $\ell_j{:}R_j$ computes M' from M in $L^k \circ Enum(1)$, if and only if, the simulation loop in $L^* \circ C$ $\langle j, j' \rangle$-computes M' from M.

This in particular (for $k = N$) implies that, after correct initialisation and with respect to termination of routines other than *init*, $L^* \circ C$ bahaves just like $L^N \circ Enum(1)$. Notice that if $L^* \circ C$ computes a *fresh* command within the *init* routine of $L^N \circ Enum(1)$, the simulation loop ensures that the new datum is also distinct from all values used in the auxiliary counters of L^*. It remains to show that, for any tape content M that is computed from the empty tape content by the *init* routine of $L^N \circ Enum(1)$, there is a tape content of $L^* \circ C$ that represents M and that is computed from the empty tape content by the *init* routine of $L^* \circ C$.

To see this, observe that the first command of *init* in $L^* \circ C$ calls the initialisation routine of C, providing the auxiliary counters. By the assumption that C is N-correct, this allows to place exactly $\langle i, N-1-i \rangle$ tokens carrying a fresh name α_i onto places $\langle w, \overline{w} \rangle$ for each $i \in \{0, \ldots, N-1\}$. Thus, after these commands, the tape content of $L^* \circ C$ represents the empty tape content of $L^N \circ Enum(1)$. The rest of the initialisation routine contains the code of the simulation loop, so the conclusion follows from the claim above, where $k = N$. □

7 ACKERMANN-**Hardness**

We work with a hierarchy of functions A_i, defined as follows for all k and x in $\mathbb{N}$:

$$A_1(x) \stackrel{\text{def}}{=} 2x \quad \text{and} \quad A_{k+2}(x) \stackrel{\text{def}}{=} A_{k+1}^x(1).$$

The *Ackermann* function is then defined as $A_\omega(x) \stackrel{\text{def}}{=} A_{x+1}(x)$, and by [25, Sect. 2.3.2 and Theorem 4.1], we have that the next problem is ACKERMANN-complete (cf. Sect. 3) and that the class ACKERMANN is closed under primitive recursive reductions:

Input: A 2-counter Minsky program $\mathcal{M}$ with n commands.
Question: Can $\mathcal{M}$ reach the halt command by a computation during which both counter values are less than $A_\omega(n)$?

Theorem 7.1. *The coverability problem for UDPNs is* ACKERMANN-*hard.*

Proof. Suppose $\mathcal{M}$ is a 2-counter Minsky program with n commands. By Lemmas 5.3, 5.5 and 6.1, we have that the counter program

$$Acker(n) \stackrel{\text{def}}{=} (\cdots (Double \overbrace{\,^*)^* \cdots)^*}^{n} \circ Enum(n)$$

is $A_\omega(n)$-correct.

Since the star operator is computable in logarithmic space and increases the number of places by adding a constant, we have that $Acker(n)$ is computable in time elementary in n, and that its number of places is linear in n.

It remains to simulate $\mathcal{M}$ by a one-routine library that uses the two $A_\omega(n)$-bounded counters provided by the counter program $Acker(n)$. The resulting one-routine program can terminate if and only if its UDPN can cover the marking in which the two line-number places point to the last command.   □

8   Conclusion

We have shown that the reachability, coverability and boundedness problems for pushdown vector addition systems are $\mathbf{F}_3$-hard. Whether they are decidable remains unknown, in the case of reachability even with only one counter, i.e. in dimension 1. The best known lower bound for the latter problem is NP [20].

For unordered data Petri nets, we have advanced the state-of-the-art lower bound of the coverability (and thus also reachability) problem from $\mathbf{F}_3$ [15] to $\mathbf{F}_\omega$. A gap therefore remains to the best known $\mathbf{F}_{\omega \cdot 2}$ upper bound [17]. We conjecture $\mathbf{F}_\omega$-completeness, which would complement nicely the $\mathbf{F}_{\omega \cdot 2}$-completeness [17] and $\mathbf{F}_{\omega^\omega}$-completeness [23] results for the extensions of UDPN by fresh name generation and whole-place operations, respectively. However, the tightening from $\mathbf{F}_{\omega \cdot 2}$ to $\mathbf{F}_\omega$ membership seems a considerable challenge for the following reason: by providing UDPNs with an initial supply of N fresh names on some auxiliary place, they can operate for N steps indistinguishably from ν-Petri nets, and so the classical backward coverability algorithm [1,8] cannot terminate for UDPNs in only Ackermann many iterations.

References

1. Abdulla, P.A., Čerāns, K., Jonsson, B., Tsay, Y.-K.: Algorithmic analysis of programs with well quasi-ordered domains. Inform. Comput. **160**(1–2), 109–127 (2000)
2. Atig, M.F., Ganty, P.: Approximating Petri net reachability along context-free traces. In: FSTTCS. LIPIcs, vol. 13, pp. 152–163. LZI (2011)
3. Bojańczyk, M., Klin, B., Lasota, S.: Automata theory in nominal sets. Logic. Meth. Comput. Sci. **10**(3:4), 1–44 (2014)
4. Chambart, P., Schnoebelen, P.: The ordinal recursive complexity of lossy channel systems. In: LICS, pp. 205–216. IEEE Press (2008)
5. Decker, N., Thoma, D.: On freeze LTL with ordered attributes. In: Jacobs, B., Löding, C. (eds.) FoSSaCS 2016. LNCS, vol. 9634, pp. 269–284. Springer, Heidelberg (2016). doi:10.1007/978-3-662-49630-5_16
6. Figueira, D., Figueira, S., Schmitz, S., Schnoebelen, P.: Ackermannian and primitive-recursive bounds with Dickson's Lemma. In: LICS, pp. 269–278. IEEE Press (2011)
7. Finkel, A., McKenzie, P., Picaronny, C.: A well-structured framework for analysing Petri net extensions. Inform. Comput. **195**(1–2), 1–29 (2004)
8. Finkel, A., Schnoebelen, P.: Well-structured transition systems everywhere! Theor. Comput. Sci. **256**(1–2), 63–92 (2001)
9. Haase, C., Schmitz, S., Schnoebelen, P.: The power of priority channel systems. Logic. Meth. Comput. Sci. **10**(4:4), 1–39 (2014)

10. Haddad, S., Schmitz, S., Schnoebelen, P.: The ordinal recursive complexity of timed-arc Petri nets, data nets, and other enriched nets. In: LICS, pp. 355–364. IEEE Press (2012)
11. Hofman, P., Lasota, S., Lazić, R., Leroux, J., Schmitz, S., Totzke, P.: Coverability trees for Petri nets with unordered data. In: Jacobs, B., Löding, C. (eds.) FoSSaCS 2016. LNCS, vol. 9634, pp. 445–461. Springer, Heidelberg (2016). doi:10.1007/978-3-662-49630-5_26
12. Hofman, P., Leroux, J., Totzke, P.: Linear combinations of unordered data vectors. arXiv:1610.01470 [cs.LO] (2016)
13. Jensen, K.: Coloured Petri Nets - Basic Concepts, Analysis Methods and Practical Use - Volume 1. Monographs in Theoretical Computer Science. An EATCS Series, 2nd edn. Springer, Heidelberg (1996)
14. Lazić, R.: The reachability problem for vector addition systems with a stack is not elementary. arXiv:1310.1767 [cs.FL] (2013)
15. Lazić, R., Newcomb, T., Ouaknine, J., Roscoe, A.W., Worrell, J.: Nets with tokens which carry data. Fund. Inform. 88(3), 251–274 (2008)
16. Lazić, R., Ouaknine, J., Worrell, J.: Zeno, Hercules, and the Hydra: Safety metric temporal logic is Ackermann-complete. ACM Trans. Comput. Logic 17(3), 1–27 (2016). Article 16
17. Lazić, R., Schmitz, S.: The complexity of coverability in ν-Petri nets. In: LICS, pp. 467–476. ACM (2016)
18. Leroux, J., Praveen, M., Sutre, G.: Hyper-Ackermannian bounds for pushdown vector addition systems. In: CSL-LICS, pp. 63:1–63:10. ACM (2014)
19. Leroux, J., Sutre, G., Totzke, P.: On boundedness problems for pushdown vector addition systems. In: Bojańczyk, M., Lasota, S., Potapov, I. (eds.) RP 2015. LNCS, vol. 9328, pp. 101–113. Springer, Heidelberg (2015). doi:10.1007/978-3-319-24537-9_10
20. Leroux, J., Sutre, G., Totzke, P.: On the coverability problem for pushdown vector addition systems in one dimension. In: Halldórsson, M.M., Iwama, K., Kobayashi, N., Speckmann, B. (eds.) ICALP 2015. LNCS, vol. 9135, pp. 324–336. Springer, Heidelberg (2015). doi:10.1007/978-3-662-47666-6_26
21. Lipton, R.: The reachability problem requires exponential space. Technical report 62. Yale University (1976)
22. Rackoff, C.: The covering and boundedness problems for vector addition systems. Theor. Comput. Sci. 6(2), 223–231 (1978)
23. Rosa-Velardo, F.: Ordinal recursive complexity of unordered data nets. Technical report TR-4-14. Universidad Complutense de Madrid (2014)
24. Rosa-Velardo, F., de Frutos-Escrig, D.: Decidability and complexity of Petri nets with unordered data. Theor. Comput. Sci. 412(34), 4439–4451 (2011)
25. Schmitz, S.: Complexity hierarchies beyond Elementary. ACM Trans. Comput. Theor. 8(1), 1–36 (2016)
26. Schmitz, S., Schnoebelen, P.: Multiply-recursive upper bounds with Higman's lemma. In: Aceto, L., Henzinger, M., Sgall, J. (eds.) ICALP 2011. LNCS, vol. 6756, pp. 441–452. Springer Berlin Heidelberg, Berlin, Heidelberg (2011). doi:10.1007/978-3-642-22012-8_35
27. Schnoebelen, P.: Revisiting Ackermann-hardness for lossy counter machines and reset Petri nets. In: Hliněný, P., Kučera, A. (eds.) MFCS 2010. LNCS, vol. 6281, pp. 616–628. Springer, Heidelberg (2010). doi:10.1007/978-3-642-15155-2_54
28. Stockmeyer, L.J.: The complexity of decision procedures in Automata Theory and Logic, Ph.D. thesis. MIT, Project MAC TR-133 (1974)

Analysing Lock-Free Linearizable Datatypes Using CSP

Gavin Lowe[(✉)]

Department of Computer Science, University of Oxford, Oxford, UK
gavin.lowe@cs.ox.ac.uk

Abstract. We consider how we can use the process algebra CSP and the model checker FDR in order to obtain assurance about the correctness of concurrent datatypes. In particular, we perform a formal analysis of a concurrent queue based on a linked list of nodes. We model the queue in CSP and analyse it using FDR. We capture two important properties using CSP, namely linearizability and lock-freedom.

1   Introduction

Many concurrent programs are designed so that threads interact only via a small number of concurrent datatypes. Code outside of these concurrent datatypes can be written in pretty-much the same way as the corresponding sequential code; only the code of the datatypes themselves needs to be written in a way that takes concurrency into account.

Modern concurrent datatypes are often designed to be *lock-free*. No locks (or lock-like mechanisms) are used. This means that threads should not be indefinitely blocked by other threads, even if a thread is permanently de-scheduled. Many clever lock-free datatypes have been designed, e.g. [9,16,24,25]. However, these datatypes tend to be complex, and less obviously correct than traditional lock-based datatypes. Clearly we need techniques for gaining greater assurance in their correctness.

In this paper we use CSP [20] and the model checker FDR [7] to analyse the lock-free queue of [16]. The queue is based on a linked list of nodes. More precisely, we analyse the version of the queue given in [9], which simplifies the presentation by assuming the presence of a garbage collector (although our CSP model will include that garbage collection); by contrast, the version in [16] performs explicit de-allocation of nodes by threads.

CSP has been used to analyse concurrent programs on a number of previous occasions, e.g. [13,23,28]. However, to the best of our knowledge, this is the first model of a dynamic data structure. Further, we include a mechanism—akin to garbage collection—that reclaims nodes when they become free, allowing them to be re-used. This extends the range of behaviours that our model captures to include behaviours with an unbounded number of enqueue and dequeue operations (on a bounded-length queue).

© Springer International Publishing AG 2017
T. Gibson-Robinson et al. (Eds.): Roscoe Festschrift, LNCS 10160, pp. 162–184, 2017.
DOI: 10.1007/978-3-319-51046-0_9

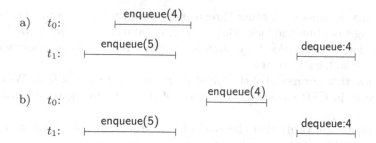

Fig. 1. Two timelines of executions: (a) a linearizable execution; (b) an unlinearizable execution. Time runs from left to right; each horizontal line indicates the duration of a method call, labelled with the name of the method and (for a dequeue) the value returned; the identities of threads are at the left.

A concurrent datatype is said to be *linearizable* [10] if:

- Each method call appears to take place atomically: different method calls do not interfere with one another. The order in which method calls appear to take place is consistent with a sequential execution.
- Each call appears to take place at some point between the call's invocation and response; this point is referred to as the *linearization point*. Put another way, if one call ends before another begins, then the former should appear to take place before the latter.

For example, consider Fig. 1, which displays timelines of two possible executions of a concurrent queue. In execution (a), threads t_0 and t_1 perform concurrent enqueues of 4 and 5, and then t_1 performs a dequeue, obtaining 4. This execution is linearizable. The two enqueues appear to have taken place atomically, with the 4 being enqueued before the 5. Alternatively, if the dequeue had obtained 5, the execution would still have been linearizable. The second clause, above, allows the two enqueues to appear to take place in either order.

By contrast, execution (b) is not linearizable. Here the enqueue of 5 finishes before the enqueue of 4. Hence we would expect that the subsequent dequeue would obtain 5; the second clause above enforces this.

In this paper we use FDR to show that our model of the lock-free queue is indeed a linearizable queue. We believe that CSP allows such linearizable specifications to be captured in a very elegant way. Our method of capturing the specification is modular: it can easily be adapted to other linearizable specifications. Our method does not require the user to identify the linearization points.

Linearizability is a safety property: it specifies that no method call returns a "bad" result; however, it does not guarantee that the system makes progress. The property of *lock freedom* guarantees progress. Formally, a concurrent datatype is lock-free if, in every state, it guarantees that some method call finishes in a finite number of steps [9]. Unsurprisingly, a datatype that uses locks in a meaningful way is not lock-free: if one thread acquires a lock, but is permanently de-scheduled, other threads may perform an unbounded number of steps trying to obtain the lock. But further, a datatype may fail to be lock-free even if it doesn't use locks, for example if threads repeatedly interfere with one another and so have to re-try.

We show that our model of the lock-free queue is indeed lock-free. We capture the property in CSP using a combination of deadlock freedom and divergence freedom.

Finally, we also verify that the model is free from null-pointer references, and dangling references (where deallocated objects are accessed).

FDR has recently been extended with a form of symmetry reduction [8]. We use this symmetry reduction in our analysis. The model will contain a large amount of symmetry: it will be symmetric in the type of identities of nodes, the type of identities of threads, and the type of data, in the sense that applying any permutation over one of these types to any state of the model will produce another state of the model. The symmetry reduction factors the model by this symmetry. We show that this gives a significant speed up in checking time, and hence an increase in the size of system that we can analyse.

One additional benefit of our approach is that it is easy to adapt the model in order to consider variants in the design of the datatype. We briefly illustrate how such changes in the model can explain a couple of non-obvious aspects of the datatype.

To summarise, our main contributions are as follows:

- A technique for modelling and analysing concurrent datatypes;
- A generic modular technique for capturing linearizability;
- A straightforward technique for capturing lock freedom;
- A technique for modelling reference-linked data structures, including a mechanism for recycling of nodes;
- An investigation into the performance improvements provided by symmetry reduction;
- An instructive case study in the application of CSP-based verification.

The rest of the paper is structured as follows. We present the lock-free queue datatype in Sect. 2. We present the CSP model in Sect. 3, and describe our analysis using FDR in Sect. 4. We sum up and discuss prospects for this line of work in Sect. 5.

1.1 Related Work

A number of other papers have considered the verification of linearizability, using either model checking or other verification techniques. However, we are not aware of other examples of the verification of lock freedom.

Vechev et al. [27] study linearizabilty using the SPIN model checker, using two different approaches. One approach uses bounded-length runs, at the end of which it is checked whether the run was linearizable, by considering all relevant re-orderings of the operations. The other approach requires linearization points to be identified by the user. Like us, they model a garbage collector. The approach suffers from state-space explosion issues: for a concurrent set based on a linked list, applicability is limited to two threads and two keys, even when linearization points are provided.

Liu et al. [12] also study linearizability in the context of refinement checking, in their case, using the model checker PAT. They capture linearizability but not liveness properties. They describe experiments using symmetry reduction and partial order reduction to improve the efficiency of the search. By way of comparison, we (with Tom Gibson-Robinson) have built a CSP model corresponding to one of their examples, in a similar style to the model of this paper; our experiments suggest that FDR is several hundred times faster on these models (on similar architectures).

Burckhardt et al. [2] analyse for linearizability as follows. They randomly pick a small number of threads to perform a small number of operations, typically three threads each performing three operations. They then use the CHESS model checker to generate all behaviours caused by interleaving these operations, and test whether each corresponds to a sequential execution of the same operations. They uncover a large number of bugs within the .NET Framework 4.0.

Černý et al. [3] show that linearizability is decidable for a class of linked-list programs that invoke a fixed number of operations in parallel. Their restrictions exclude the example of this paper: they assume a *fixed* head node, no tail reference, and that threads traverse the list monotonically; however, it is not clear how essential these restrictions are. Their approach shows that a program is a linearizable version of its own sequential form, rather than a linearizable version of a more abstract specification, such as a queue. In practice, their approach is limited to a pair of operations in parallel, because of the state space explosion.

Vafeiadis [26] uses abstract interpretation to verify linearizability, by considering candidate linearization points. The technique works well on some examples, but does not always succeed, and works less well on examples with more complex abstractions. Colvin et al. [5] and Derrick et al. [6] prove linearizability by verifying a simulation against a suitable specification, supported by a theorem prover. These approaches give stronger guarantees than our own, but require much more effort on the part of the verifier.

1.2   CSP

In this section we give a brief overview of the syntax for the fragment of CSP that we will be using in this paper. We then review the relevant aspects of CSP semantics, and the use of the model checker FDR in verification. For more details, see [20].

CSP is a process algebra for describing programs or *processes* that interact with their environment by communication. Processes communicate via atomic *events*. Events often involve passing values over channels; for example, the event c.3 represents the value 3 being passed on channel c. Channels may be declared using the keyword **channel**; for example, **channel** c : Int declares c to be a channel that passes an Int. The notation {|c|} represents the set of events over channel c.

The simplest process is STOP, which represents a deadlocked process that cannot communicate with its environment. By contrast, **div** is a divergent process that performs an unbounded number of internal τ events.

The process a $\rightarrow$ P offers its environment the event a; if the event is performed, the process then acts like P. The process c?x $\rightarrow$ P is initially willing to input a value x on channel c, i.e. it is willing to perform any event of the form c.x; it then acts like P (which may use x). Similarly, the process c?x:X $\rightarrow$ P is willing to input any value x from set X on channel c, and then act like P. Within input constructs, we use "_" as a wildcard: c?_ indicates an input of an arbitrary value. The process c!v $\rightarrow$ P outputs value v on channel c. Inputs and outputs may be mixed within the same communication, for example c?x!v $\rightarrow$ P.

The process P $\square$ Q can act like either P or Q, the choice being made by the environment: the environment is offered the choice between the initial events of P and Q. By contrast, P $\sqcap$ Q may act like either P or Q, with the choice being made internally, not under the control of the environment. $\square$ x:X $\bullet$ P(x) is an indexed external choice, with the choice being made over the processes P(x) for x in X. The process **if** b **then** P **else** Q represents a conditional. The process b & P is a guarded process, that makes P available only if b is true; it is equivalent to **if** b **then** P **else** STOP.

The process P [| A |] Q runs P and Q in parallel, synchronising on events from A. The process || x:X $\bullet$ [A(x)] P(x) represents an indexed parallel composition, where, for each x in X, P(x) is given alphabet A(x); processes synchronize on events in the intersection of their alphabets. The process P ||| Q interleaves P and Q, i.e. runs them in parallel with no synchronisation. ||| x:X $\bullet$ P(x) represents an indexed interleaving.

The process P \ A acts like P, except the events from A are hidden, i.e. turned into internal τ events.

A *trace* of a process is a sequence of (visible) events that a process can perform. We say that P is refined by Q in the traces model, written P $\sqsubseteq_T$ Q, if every trace of Q is also a trace of P. FDR can test such refinements automatically, for finite-state processes. Typically, P is a specification process, describing what traces are acceptable; this test checks whether Q has only such acceptable traces.

Traces refinement tests can only ensure that no "bad" traces can occur: they cannot ensure that anything "good" actually happens; for this we need the stable failures or failures-divergences models. A *stable failure* of a process P is a pair (tr, X), which represents that P can perform the trace tr to reach a stable state (i.e. where no internal events are possible) where X can be refused, i.e., where none of the events of X is available. We say that P is refined by Q in the stable failures model, written P $\sqsubseteq_F$ Q, if every trace of Q is also a trace of P, and every stable failure of Q is also a stable failure of P.

We say that a process *diverges* if it can perform an infinite number of internal (hidden) events without any intervening visible events. If P $\sqsubseteq_F$ Q and Q is divergence-free, then if P can stably offer an event a, then so can Q; hence such tests can be used to ensure Q makes useful progress.

2 The Lock-Free Queue

In this section we present the lock-free queue. Our presentation is based on that from [9]. The code, in Scala, is in Fig. 2.

The lock-free queue uses *atomic references*[1]. An atomic reference encapsulates a standard reference, say to an object of class A, and provides get and set operations. In addition, it provides an atomic compare-and-set (CAS) operation, which can be thought of as an atomic implementation of the following:

```
def compareAndSet(expected: A, update: A) : Boolean = {
  if(expected == current){ current = update; true} else false
}
```

A thread passes in two values: expected, which the thread believes the atomic reference holds; and update, the value the thread wants to update it to. If the current value is indeed as expected, it is updated. The thread receives an indication as to whether the operation was successful. This operation can be used to allow concurrent threads to interact safely in a lock-free way.

The lock-free queue is built as a linked list of Nodes: each node holds a value field, of (polymorphic) type T; nodes are linked together using next fields which are atomic references to the following node.

The lock-free queue employs two shared variables, both atomic references (lines 9–10 of Fig. 2): head is a reference to a dummy header node; and tail is normally a reference to the last node in the linked list, but will temporarily refer to the penultimate node when an item has been partially enqueued.

The main idea of the algorithm, which gives it its lock-free property, is as follows: if one thread partially enqueues an item, but is de-scheduled and leaves the queue in an inconsistent state with tail not referring to the final node, then other threads try to tidy up by advancing tail; one will succeed, and so progress is made, and eventually a thread will complete its operation.

The enqueue operation starts by creating a node to store the new value[2]. It then reads tail and the following node into local variables myTail and myNext. As an optimization, it re-reads tail, in case it has changed, retrying if it has. Otherwise, in the normal case that myNext is **null**, it attempts a CAS operation on myTail.next (line 19), to set it to the new node. If this succeeds, the value is correctly enqueued. It then attempts to advance the tail reference to the new node, and returns regardless of whether this is successful: if the CAS fails, some other thread has already advanced tail. If myNext is not **null** (line 23), it means

---

[1] http://docs.oracle.com/javase/7/docs/api/java/util/concurrent/atomic/Atomic Reference.html.

[2] The Scala code ignores the possibility of new nodes not being available, but we will need to consider this possibility in our CSP models.

```
1   class LockFreeQueue[T]{
2     // We build linked lists from Nodes of the following type
3     class Node(val value: T, val next: AtomicReference[Node])
4
5     // initial dummy header
6     private val firstNode =
7       new Node(null.asInstanceOf[T], new AtomicReference[Node](null))
8     // Atomic references to head and tail nodes
9     private val head = new AtomicReference(firstNode)
10    private val tail = new AtomicReference(firstNode)
11
12    /** Add value to the queue */
13    def enqueue(value: T) : Unit = {
14      val node = new Node(value, new AtomicReference[Node](null))
15      while(true){
16        val myTail = tail.get; val myNext = myTail.next.get
17        if(myTail == tail.get) // in case it has been changed (optimization)
18          if(myNext == null){
19            if(myTail.next.compareAndSet(null, node)){
20              tail.compareAndSet(myTail, node); return
21            } // else re-try
22          }
23          else // myNext != null, try to advance tail
24            tail.compareAndSet(myTail, myNext) // and retry
25        // else retry
26    } }
27
28    /** Dequeue and return a value if the queue is non-empty; else return null */
29    def dequeue : T = {
30      while(true){
31        val myHead = head.get; val myTail = tail.get; val myNext = myHead.next.get
32        if(myHead == head.get) // in case it has been changed (optimization)
33          if(myHead == myTail){
34            if(myNext == null) return null // empty queue, return null
35            else // new item partially enqueued
36              tail.compareAndSet(myTail, myNext) // try to advance tail; retry
37          }
38          else{ // non-empty queue; try to remove node from queue
39            if(head.compareAndSet(myHead, myNext)) return myNext.value
40            // else myNext.value already taken; retry
41          }
42        // else Head changed; retry
43    } } }
```

Fig. 2. The lock-free queue in Scala.

that a value has been partially enqueued, with tail not advanced to the last node: it attempts to so-advance tail, and retries.

The dequeue operation starts by reading head, tail and the node after head into local variables myHead, myTail, and myNext. It then re-reads head, in case it has changed, retrying if it has. Otherwise, if the head and tail are equal, and myNext is **null** (line 34), the queue is empty, and the operation returns the special value **null** to indicate this. Alternatively, if head and tail are equal but myNext is non-**null** (line 35), there is a partially enqueued item, so it tries to advance tail and retries. Otherwise, the queue is non-empty (line 38). It tries to advance the head to myNext using a CAS operation; if the CAS succeeds, it returns the value in myNext; otherwise, another thread has taken the value in myNext, so the operation retries.

Note that an individual enqueue or dequeue operation is not guaranteed to terminate: it may repeatedly find partially enqueued items, and so repeatedly retry. However, if this happens infinitely often then infinitely many other operations will terminate, so the data structure is still lock-free.

3   The CSP Model

In this section we present our CSP model of the lock-free queue.[3] In Sect. 3.1 we model the nodes of the list, and the atomic references head and tail. In Sect. 3.2 we model the program threads that perform the enqueueing and dequeueing operations. In Sect. 3.3 we describe the technique for re-cycling nodes, which identifies nodes that have been removed from the linked list and that have no relevant references to them, and frees them up, making them available for reuse. We put the system together in Sect. 3.4.

Our model is parameterized by three types (see Fig. 3): the type NodeIDType of node identities; the type T of data held in the queue; and the type ThreadID of thread identities. The type NodeIDType contains a distinguished value Null, which models the **null** reference; we write NodeID for the set of "proper" nodes. We will consider larger values for these types in Sect. 4.5. The models will be symmetric in the types NodeID, T and ThreadID.

```
datatype NodeIDType = Null | N0 | N1 | N2    -- node identities
NodeID = diff(NodeIDType, {Null})            -- real nodes
datatype T = A | B                            -- data values
datatype ThreadID = T0 | T1                   -- thread identities
```

Fig. 3. The basic types of the model.

3.1   Nodes, Head, Tail, and the Constructor

The CSP model of the nodes of the linked list is presented in Fig. 4. We declare channels corresponding to actions by threads upon nodes. The event initNode.t.n.v

[3] The CSP script is available from http://www.cs.ox.ac.uk/people/gavin.lowe/ LockFreeQueue/LockFreeQueueLin.csp.

-- Channels used by nodes.
channel initNode : ThreadID . NodeIDType . T
channel getValue : ThreadID . NodeIDType . T
channel getNext : ThreadID . NodeIDType . NodeIDType
channel CASnext : ThreadID . NodeIDType . NodeIDType . NodeIDType . Bool
channel removeNode : ThreadID . NodeIDType
channel free : NodeID
channel noFreeNode : ThreadID

-- A node process, with identity me, currently free.
FreeNode :: (NodeIDType) $\rightarrow$ Proc
FreeNode(me) =
  initNode?_!me?value $\rightarrow$ Node(me, value, Null, false)
  $\square$ $\square$ e : diff (alphaNode(me), {|initNode,free,noFreeNode|}) • e $\rightarrow$ **div**

-- A node process, identity me, holding datum value and next pointer next;
-- removed indicates whether the node has been removed from the list.
Node :: (NodeIDType, T, NodeIDType, Bool) $\rightarrow$ Proc
Node(me, value, next, removed) =
  getValue?_!me.value $\rightarrow$ Node(me, value, next, removed)
  $\square$ getNext?_!me.next $\rightarrow$ Node(me, value, next, removed)
  $\square$ CASnext?_!me?expected?new!(expected=next) $\rightarrow$
     Node(me, value, **if** expected=next **then** new **else** next, removed)
  $\square$ not(removed) & removeNode?_!me $\rightarrow$ Node(me, value, next, true)
  $\square$ removed & free.me $\rightarrow$ FreeNode(me)
  $\square$ noFreeNode?_ $\rightarrow$ Node(me, value, next, removed)

-- Alphabet of node me.
alphaNode(me) = {| free.me, initNode.t.me, removeNode.t.me, noFreeNode.t,
           getValue.t.me, getNext.t.me, CASnext.t.me | t $\leftarrow$ ThreadID |}
-- All nodes
AllNodes = $\parallel$ id : NodeID • [alphaNode(id)] FreeNode(id)

Fig. 4. Model of the nodes.

represents thread t initialising node n to hold v; getValue.t.n.v represents t reading value v from n; getNext.t.n.n1 represents t obtaining the value n1 of n's next field; CASnext.t.n.expected.new.res represents t performing a CAS on n's next field, trying to change it from expected to new, with res giving the boolean result; removeNode.t.n represents t marking n as removed from the linked list; free.n represents n being recycled; and noFreeNode.t represents t failing to obtain a new node.

A free node (process FreeNode) can be initialised with a particular value and with its next field Null. Our model also allows the node to perform various events corresponding to a thread incorrectly accessing this node, after which it diverges; later we verify that the system cannot diverge, and so verify that no such event can occur.

An initialised node can: (1) have its value field read by a thread; (2) have its next field read by a thread; (3) have a CAS operation performed on its next field by a thread: if the expected field matches the current value of next, the value is updated to the new field and the result is true; otherwise next is unchanged and the result is false; (4) be marked as removed from the linked list (if not so already); (5) be freed up, if already marked as removed from the linked list; (6) signal that no free node is available (all nodes will synchronize on this event, so it will be available only if all nodes are in this state).

We combine the nodes in parallel with the natural alphabets.

Figure 5 gives the CSP model of the atomic reference variables, head and tail, together with a "constructor" process Constructor that initialises these variables and the dummy header node. The type AtomicRefID gives identities of these atomic references. Event getNode.t.ar.n represents thread t reading the value n of atomic reference ar. Event CAS.t.ar.expected.new.res represents t performing a CAS operation on ar, trying to change it from expected to new, with res giving the boolean result. Event initAR.h represents the two atomic references being initialised to refer to initial dummy header node h.

```
datatype AtomicRefID = Head | Tail −− The IDs of atomic references
−− Channels used by Head and Tail
channel getNode : ThreadID . AtomicRefID . NodeIDType
channel CAS : ThreadID . AtomicRefID . NodeIDType . NodeIDType . Bool
channel initAR : NodeID


−− An atomic reference to node
AtomicRefNode :: (AtomicRefID, NodeIDType) → Proc
AtomicRefNode(me, node) =
    getNode?t!me.node → AtomicRefNode(me, node)
    □ CAS?t!me?expected?new!(expected=node) →
        AtomicRefNode(me, if expected=node then new else node)


−− The atomic reference variables
HeadAR = initAR?h → AtomicRefNode(Head, h)
TailAR = initAR?h → AtomicRefNode(Tail, h)


AllARs = HeadAR [| {|initAR|} |] TailAR


−− The constructor
Constructor = initAR?h → initNode?_!h?_ → RUN({|beginEnqueue, beginDequeue|})
```

Fig. 5. Model of the head and tail atomic references, and the constructor.

The model of an atomic reference is similar in style to the model of a node, but simpler. The constructor chooses an initial dummy header node h, initialises the two atomic references to refer to it, initialises h to hold a nondeterministic initial value, and then allow begin events to occur; the effect of the last step is to block other threads until the construction is complete.

3.2   Enqueueing and Dequeueing Threads

Figures 6 and 7 give the models of the threads. In order to later capture the requirements, we include additional events to signal the start or end of an enqueue or dequeue operation, including the end of a dequeue operation that failed because the queue was empty, or an enqueue operation that failed because the queue was full (i.e. there was no free node). We also include events on channel releaseRefs to represent a thread releasing its references (before re-trying).

```
−− events to signal the start or end of operations
channel beginEnqueue, endEnqueue, endEnqueueFull, endDequeue : ThreadID . T
channel beginDequeue, endDequeueEmpty : ThreadID
channel releaseRefs : ThreadID −− a thread releases its references

−− A thread, which enqueues or dequeues.
Thread(me) =
  beginEnqueue.me?value → Enqueue(me, value)
  □ beginDequeue.me → Dequeue(me)
```

Fig. 6. Model of a thread.

Each Thread process represents a thread that repeatedly performs enqueue or dequeue operations. The process Enqueue(me, value) represents a thread with identity me trying to enqueue value. It starts by trying to initialise a node to hold value; if this fails, as indicated by the noFreeNode event, it signals that the queue is full. The process Enqueue' corresponds to the **while** loop in the enqueue function of Fig. 2. Most of the definition is a direct translation of the Scala code from that figure: the reader is encouraged to compare the two. If the enqueue succeeds, this is signalled with an endEnqueue event. If the enqueue fails, and the thread has to retry, it releases the references it held, so these can potentially be recycled. The dequeue operation is modelled in a very similar way.

3.3   Recycling Nodes

We now describe our mechanism for recycling nodes in the model. While the mechanism is very similar to memory management techniques in implementations, the intention is different: our aim is to increase the coverage of our

```
-- An enqueueing thread
Enqueue :: (ThreadID, T) → Proc
Enqueue(me, value) =
  initNode.me?node!value → Enqueue'(me, value, node)
  □ noFreeNode.me → endEnqueueFull.me.value → Thread(me)

Enqueue' :: (ThreadID, T, NodeIDType) → Proc
Enqueue'(me, value, node) =
  getNode.me.Tail?myTail → getNext.me.myTail?myNext →
  getNode.me.Tail?myTail' →
  if myTail=myTail' then -- in case it's been changed (optimization)
    if myNext=Null then
      CASnext.me.myTail.Null.node?result →
      if result then -- enqueue succeeded, so advance tail
        CAS.me.Tail.myTail.node?_ → endEnqueue.me.value → Thread(me)
      else -- CASnext failed; retry
        releaseRefs.me → Enqueue'(me, value, node)
    else -- myNext≠Null, try to advance tail
      CAS.me.Tail.myTail.myNext?_ →
      releaseRefs.me → Enqueue'(me, value, node)
  else -- Tail changed; retry
    releaseRefs.me → Enqueue'(me, value, node)

-- A dequeuing thread
Dequeue :: (ThreadID) → Proc
Dequeue(me) =
  getNode.me.Head?myHead → getNode.me.Tail?myTail →
  getNext.me.myHead?myNext → getNode.me.Head?myHead' →
  if myHead=myHead' then -- in case it's been changed (optimization)
    if myHead=myTail then
      if myNext=Null then endDequeueEmpty.me → Thread(me) -- empty queue
      else -- new item partially enqueued
        CAS.me.Tail.myTail.myNext?_ → -- try to advance tail; retry
        releaseRefs.me → Dequeue(me)
    else -- non-empty queue; try to remove node from queue
      CAS.me.Head.myHead.myNext?result →
      if result then
        getValue.me.myNext?value → removeNode.me.myHead →
        endDequeue.me.value → Thread(me)
      else -- myNext.value already taken; retry
        releaseRefs.me → Dequeue(me)
  else releaseRefs.me → Dequeue(me) -- Head changed; retry
```

Fig. 7. Model of a thread (continued).

HPs :: (ThreadID, NodeIDType, NodeIDType, NodeIDType, Bool) → Proc
HPs(me, h, t, n, enq) =
　　beginEnqueue.me?_ → HPs(me, h, t, n, true)
　　□ beginDequeue.me → HPs(me, h, t, n, false)
　　□ getNode.me.Tail?t' → HPs(me, h, if enq then t' else Null, n, enq)
　　□ getNode.me.Head?h' → HPs(me, if enq then Null else h', t, n, enq)
　　□ getNext.me?_:NodeID?n' → HPs(me, h, t, if enq then Null else n', enq)
　　□ (□ e : releaseEvents(me) • e →
　　　　　HPs(me, Null, Null, Null, if e=(releaseRefs.me) then enq else false))
　　□ free?_:diff(NodeID, {t, h, n}) → HPs(me, h, t, n, enq)

−− The events on which me releases all its hazard pointers.
releaseEvents(me) = {|endEnqueue.me, endEnqueueFull.me, endDequeue.me,
　　　　　　　　endDequeueEmpty.me, releaseRefs.me|}

−− All hazard pointer processes, synchronizing on free events.
alphaHP(me) = union(releaseEvents(me),
　　{| beginEnqueue.me, beginDequeue.me, getNode.me, getNext.me, free |})
HazardPointers = || me ← ThreadID • [alphaHP(me)] HPs(me,Null,Null,Null,false)

Fig. 8. The hazard pointers.

model, capturing executions with an arbitrary number of enqueue and dequeue operations.

We use a technique inspired by *hazard pointers* [17]. The idea (as an implementation technique) is that each thread has a few pointer variables, known as hazard pointers: no node referenced by such a pointer should be recycled. When a thread removes a node from a data structure, it can add the node to a list of removed nodes. The thread intermittently reads the hazard pointers of all threads, and recycles any removed node that is not referenced by a hazard pointer.

In the lock-free list, the hazard pointers should be each thread's myTail during an enqueue operation, and its myHead and myNext during a dequeue operation. It is obvious that it would be hazardous to recycle any of these nodes, since fields of each are accessed by the thread. Our subsequent analysis shows that these are sufficient hazard pointers.

Figure 8 gives the relevant part of the CSP model. The process HPs(me, h, t, n, enq) records the hazard pointers of thread me; the parameters h, t and n store the thread's myHead, myTail and myNext variables, where relevant; the parameter enq records whether the thread is enqueueing; these are updated by synchronizing with the relevant events of the thread. The hazard pointer parameters are reset to Null when the thread releases the references. This process allows any node other than its hazard pointers to be freed. All HPs processes synchronize on the free events, so a node can be freed when it is not referenced by *any* hazard pointer.

3.4 The Complete System

We combine the system together in parallel in Fig. 9.

```
-- All threads
AllThreads0 = ||| id : ThreadID • Thread(id)
AllThreads = AllThreads0 [| {|beginEnqueue, beginDequeue|} |] Constructor

-- synchronisation set between Threads and HazardPointers.
HPSyncSet = union( {| beginEnqueue, beginDequeue, getNode, getNext |},
                   Union({ releaseEvents(t) | t ← ThreadID }) )
-- synchronisation set between Threads/HazardPointers and Nodes/AtomicRefs
syncSet = union( {| initNode.t.n, getValue.t.n, getNext.t.n, CASnext.t.n |
                    t ← ThreadID, n ← NodeID |},
                 {| getNode, CAS, free, removeNode, noFreeNode, initAR |} )
-- Put components together in parallel
System0 = (AllThreads [| HPSyncSet |] HazardPointers)
          [| syncSet |] (AllNodes ||| AllARs)

-- Prioritise releaseRefs, free and removeNode over all other events.
PriEvents = {|releaseRefs, free, removeNode|}
System1 = prioritise (System0, < PriEvents, diff (Events, PriEvents) >)
System = System1 \ union(syncSet, {|releaseRefs|})
```

Fig. 9. The complete system.

We prioritise releaseRefs, free and removeNode events over all other events, for two reasons. Firstly, we want to ensure that nodes are recycled as soon as possible, so a thread does not fail to obtain a new node when there is one waiting to be recycled. Secondly, this acts as a form of partial-order reduction, and markedly reduces the size of the state space. This prioritisation is sound since forcing these events to occur does not disable any of the standard events on nodes (on channels getValue, getNext and CASnext).

We then hide other events: in the resulting process System, the only visible events are the begin and end events.

4 Analysis

We now describe our FDR analysis of the model. In Sect. 4.1 we show that the datatype is a linearizable queue. In Sect. 4.2 we show that the queue is lock-free, and also that no thread attempts to access a freed node (i.e. there are no dangling pointers). In Sect. 4.3 we show that no node attempts to de-reference a null reference. In Sect. 4.4 we discuss the use of symmetry reduction in the checks. In Sect. 4.5 we discuss our results. Finally, in Sect. 4.6 we discuss how the model can be adapted to alternative designs, and so understand why some details of the datatype are as they are.

4.1 A Linearizable Queue

Recall that a datatype is linearizable if each method call appears to take place atomically at some point between the call's invocation and response; these points are called linearization points. We prove that our model is a linearizable queue by building a suitable specification in two steps: first we build a specification of a queue, where the events correspond to the linearization points; and then we ensure that these events occur between the corresponding begin and end events. (Alur et al. [1] have proposed a similar technique.)

Our specification (Fig. 10) introduces events to correspond to the linearization points. The process QueueSpec models a queue, based on these events, where the parameter q records the sequence of values currently in the queue. A dequeue attempt succeeds when the queue is non-empty; otherwise it signals that the queue is empty. An enqueue may succeed or fail, depending upon the queue's current length. An enqueue is guaranteed to succeed when $\#q+2*card(ThreadID)-1 < card(NodeID)$, since a free node will always be available in this case. When $\#q+1 < card(NodeID) \leq \#q+2*card(ThreadID)-1$, an enqueue may either succeed or fail, depending upon how many deleted nodes are still referenced by hazard pointers of other threads.

We then ensure that the events of QueueSpec occur between the corresponding begin and end events. The process Linearizer(me) does this for events of thread me. We combine the components together in parallel, hiding the events of QueueSpec. The resulting specification requires that each trace (of begin and end events) is linearizable: each operation appears to happen atomically at the point of the corresponding (hidden) linearization event; the results of these operations are consistent with an execution of a sequential queue (as enforced by the QueueSpec process); each linearization event occurs between the corresponding begin and end events (as enforced by the corresponding Linearizer process).

Note that we carry out the check in the stable failures model. On the assumption that System is divergence-free, this also ensures liveness properties: that the relevant events eventually become available (if not preempted by other events). We discharge the divergence-freedom assumption below.

Spec is nondeterministic. Each state that is reachable after a particular trace tr corresponds to a state of Queue that represents a possible linearization that is consistent with tr. FDR normalises the specification: each state of the normalised specification corresponds to the *set* of states that the original specification can reach after a particular trace, i.e. the set of linearizations that are consistent with the visible trace so far.

```
channel enqueue, dequeue : ThreadID . T
channel dequeueEmpty, enqueueFull : ThreadID

QueueSpec = Queue(<>)
Queue(q) =
  ( if q ≠ <> then dequeue?t!head(q) → Queue(tail(q))
    else dequeueEmpty?t → Queue(q) )
  □
  if #q+2*card(ThreadID)−1 < card(NodeID) then enqueue?t?x → Queue(q^<x>)
  else if #q+1 < card(NodeID) then
      enqueue?t?x → Queue(q^<x>) ⊓ enqueueFull?t → Queue(q)
  else enqueueFull?t → Queue(q)

Linearizer (me) =
  beginEnqueue. me ? value → (
    enqueue. me . value → endEnqueue. me . value → Linearizer(me)
    □ enqueueFull. me → endEnqueueFull. me . value → Linearizer(me) )
  □
  beginDequeue. me → (
    dequeueEmpty. me → endDequeueEmpty. me → Linearizer(me)
    □ dequeue. me ? value → endDequeue. me . value → Linearizer(me) )

AllLinearizers  =  ||| id : ThreadID • Linearizer (id )
specSyncSet = {| enqueue, dequeue, dequeueEmpty, enqueueFull |}
Spec = ( AllLinearizers  [| specSyncSet |] QueueSpec) \ specSyncSet
assert Spec ⊑_F System
```

Fig. 10. Testing for linearizability.

4.2   Lock-Freedom and Dangling Pointer Freedom

Recall that a concurrent datatype is said to be lock-free if it always guarantees that some method call finishes in a finite number of steps, even if some (but not all) threads are permanently desscheduled. A failure of lock freedom can occur in two ways:

- One or more threads perform an infinite sequence of events without an operation ever finishing;
- A thread reaches a state where it is unable to perform any event, so if all other threads are permanently descheduled, the system as a whole makes no progress.

The former type of failure of lock freedom is easy to capture: a violation of this property would involve an unbounded number of events without an end event, which would represent a divergence of SystemE, below.

−− System with only end events visible
SystemE = System \ {| beginEnqueue, beginDequeue|}
assert SystemE :[divergence free]

In order to capture the latter type of failure, we need to be able to model the permanent descheduling of threads. We do this via a process Scheduler that allows all but one thread to be descheduled: the descheduling of thread t is captured by the event dies.t; the regulator allows events of a thread only if it has not been descheduled. We then check that the resulting system is deadlock free.

−− Alphabet of thread t
alpha(t) =
{| initNode.t, getValue.t, getNext.t, CASnext.t, getNode.t, removeNode.t,
    CAS.t, beginEnqueue.t, endEnqueue.t, endEnqueueFull.t, endDequeue.t,
    beginDequeue.t, endDequeueEmpty.t |}

channel dies: ThreadID −− A particular thread dies

−− A regulator for the lock freedom property.
Scheduler(alive) =
  (□ t: alive, e: alpha(t) • e → Scheduler(alive))
  □ card(alive) > 1 & dies?t:alive → Scheduler(diff(alive,{t}))

SchedulerSyncSet = Union({alpha(t) | t ← ThreadID})
SystemLF0 = System0 [| SchedulerSyncSet |] Scheduler(ThreadID)
SystemLF = prioritise(SystemLF0, <PriEvents , diff(Events,PriEvents)>)
            \ union(syncSet, {|releaseRefs, beginEnqueue, beginDequeue|})
assert SystemLF :[deadlock free]

Recall that dereferencing a dangling pointer (i.e. referencing a node that has been freed) leads to a divergence. The above divergence-freedom check therefore also ensures freedom from such dangling pointer errors. This check also guarantees that System is divergence-free, giving the liveness properties mentioned at the end of the last subsection.

4.3 Null Reference Exceptions

Finally, we check that no thread ever tries to de-reference the Null reference: we hide all other events and check that no event can occur.

nullRefs =
  {|initNode.t.Null,getValue.t.Null,getNext.t.Null,CASnext.t.Null | t ← ThreadID|}
  assert STOP ⊑$_T$ System0 \ diff(Events,nullRefs)

4.4   Using Symmetry Reduction

Each of the above refinement checks can be run either with or without symmetry reduction. In order to use symmetry reduction, the refinement assertion is labelled with

: [symmetry reduce]: diff(NodeIDType,{|Null|}), T, ThreadID

This tells FDR to perform symmetry reduction in the types of real node identities (excluding Null), data and thread identities. The script uses no constant from these types, other than within the definition of the types; it is shown in [8] that the model is symmetric in the types under this condition, and so the symmetry reduction is sound.

4.5   Results

As noted at the start of Sect. 3, the model is parameterized by three types: the type NodeID of "proper" nodes; the type T of data; and the type ThreadID of thread identities. We have used FDR to check the above assertions, for various sizes of these types. All the checks we tried succeeded.

Parameters	Check	No sym. red. #states	No sym. red. time	Sym. red. #states	Sym. red. time
2, 2, 3	lin. queue	207K	0.5s	9.3K	0.5s
2, 2, 3	divergences	150K	0.9s	6.7K	0.4s
2, 2, 3	lock freedom	406K	0.5s	18K	0.4s
2, 2, 3	null refs	150K	0.5s	6.7K	0.2s
3, 3, 4	lin. queue	5465M	7196s	6.7M	55s
3, 2, 4	divergences	234M	647s	1.1M	22s
3, 2, 4	lock freedom	1354M	1015s	5.2M	28s
3, 3, 4	null refs	1454M	1679s	2.1M	10s
3, 3, 5	lin. queue	—	—	109M	1520s
3, 3, 6	divergences	—	—	98M	1638s
3, 3, 6	lock freedom	—	—	584M	3265s
3, 3, 6	null refs	—	—	98M	460s

Fig. 11.   Results of analyses. The "Parameters" column shows the sizes of ThreadID, T and NodeID, respectively. In the "Check" column, "lin. queue" represents the check for being a linearizable queue (Sect. 4.1), "divergences" represents the divergences-based check (Sect. 4.2), "lock freedom" represents the deadlock-based check (Sect. 4.2), and "null refs" represents the check for null reference exceptions (Sect. 4.3).

Figure 11 gives information about some of the checks we carried out, including the number of states and the time taken (on a 32-core machine, with two 2 GHz Intel(R) Xeon(R) E5-2650 0 CPUs, with 128 GB of RAM, FDR version 3.4.0). Figures are given both without and with symmetry reduction.

The first block of entries is for our standard test case: here the checks are effectively instantaneous, either with or without symmetry reduction. The second block of entries is indicative of the maximum sizes of parameters that can be checked without symmetry reduction. Here, symmetry reduction gives significant reductions in both the number of states and the checking time. The third block is indicative of the maximum sizes of parameters that can be checked with symmetry reduction.

4.6 Alternative Designs

It is straightforward to adapt the above model so as to consider alternative designs for the lock-free queue: this can help us understand some of the details of the original design from [16].

For example, if an enqueue finds that myNext $\neq$ null, it attempts to advance tail via a CAS operation (line 23 of Fig. 2). To investigate why this is necessary, we can remove the corresponding event from the definition of Enqueue. FDR then finds that the datatype is no longer lock-free. It finds a divergence of SystemE which corresponds to the following trace of System0

<beginEnqueue.T0.A, beginEnqueue.T1.A, initNode.T1.N2.A, initNode.T0.N1.A,
  getNode.T1.Tail.N0, getNext.T1.N0.Null, getNode.T0.Tail.N0,
  getNode.T1.Tail.N0, CASnext.T1.N0.Null.N2.true, getNext.T0.N0.N2,
  getNode.T0.Tail.N0, releaseRefs.T0, getNode.T0.Tail.N0 >,

after which the last four events can be repeated indefinitely. Thread T1 partially enqueues node N2, but fails to advance Tail to it. As a result, thread T0 repeatedly reads N0 from Tail, finds that its next reference is non-null, and retries.

A similar behaviour explains why the dequeue operation attempts to advance tail if myNext $\neq$ Null (line 36 of Fig. 2).

5 Conclusions

In this paper we have used CSP and its model checker FDR to analyse a lock-free queue. Novel aspects include the modelling of a dynamic datatype with a mechanism for recycling nodes. We have shown how to capture linearizable specifications and lock-freedom using CSP refinement checks.

We should be clear about the limitations of our analysis. We have verified the datatype for the small values of the parameters listed in Fig. 11 and a few others. This does not necessarily imply that the datatype is correct for larger parameters. However, the analyses should certainly give us great confidence in its correctness—more confidence than standard testing. It seems likely that any error in such a datatype would manifest itself for small values of the parameters.

– If there is a flaw caused by one thread's execution being interfered with by other threads, then it is likely that the actions of the interfering threads could have been performed by a single thread, and so such a flaw would manifest itself in a system of just two threads. One approach to formalise this argument would be *counter abstraction* [14,15,18], which counts the number of processes in each state, but in an abstracted domain.

– The enqueue and dequeue operations affect just the first two and last two nodes in the list. Hence any flaw is likely to manifest itself when there are at most two nodes in the list, and so will be captured by a system with $2 + \#\mathsf{ThreadID}$ nodes (since each enqueueing thread can hold a node that it has not yet enqueued).

– The implementation is data independent: it performs no operations on the data itself. Any flaw concerning data values (of type T) must manifest itself in an inappropriate value being dequeued, since this is the only part of the specification that cares about data values. One can create a corresponding flaw when T contains just two values A and B, by renaming the incorrectly dequeued value to A, and every other value to B. (Lazić and Roscoe have developed a general theory of data independence, formalising arguments like this; however, there results are not applicable here, because our Spec process does not satisfy their **Norm** property [19, Sect. 15.2].)

It might be interesting to try and formalise some of these ideas, although these are very challenging problems.

I believe that concurrent data structures are a very good target for CSP-style model checking. The algorithms are small enough that they can be accurately modelled and analysed using a model checker such as FDR. The requirements are normally clear. Yet the algorithms are complex enough that it is not obvious that they are correct.

Translating from executable code to a CSP model is straightforward. Indeed, I believe that there are good prospects for performing this translation automatically.

It also seems straightforward to produce the corresponding specifications. In particular, CSP seems well suited for capturing linearizability. The components of the specification correspond to the different aspects of the requirements: QueueSpec captures the queue behaviour, and each Linearizer captures that the actions of a particular thread are linearized. Adapting this to a different linearizable specification requires only replacing the QueueSpec, and adapting the events of Linearizer appropriately. It is interesting that this specification uses parallel composition and hiding: this creates a much clearer structure than the corresponding sequential process.

Building on the work in this paper, Chen [4] and Janssen [11] have studied a number of other concurrent datatypes, including several implementations of a set based on a linked list, a stack, a combining tree, an array-based queue, and a lock-based hash set. Some of these datatypes made use of a potentially unbounded sequence counter. However, this counter can be captured in a finite model using the observation that (in most cases) the counter is actually used as a *nonce*: the exact value of the counter is unimportant; what matters is whether the value changes between two reads. Hence we can use the technique of Roscoe and Broadfoot [21] (developed for the analysis of security protocols) for simulating an unbounded supply of nonces within a finite model.

Our approach does not require identifying the linearization points (the points at which the operations seem to take effect). However, we suspect that when there are identifiable linearization points, our check can be made more efficient: the implementation events corresponding to the linearization events can be renamed to the corresponding specification events, and those events left visible in the specification; this will often reduce the size of the search. However, it is not always possible to identify linearization points at the time they are performed; for example, for an unsuccessful dequeue the linearization point is the read of **null** for myNext (line 31 of Fig. 2), but only if the subsequent re-read of head (line 32) gives an unchanged value: one can only be sure that the read of myNext was a linearization point at a *later* point in the trace.

We proved that the queue is lock-free. A related condition is *wait freedom*. A datatype is wait-free if each method call terminates within a finite number of steps. The queue we have studied is not wait-free: for example, an enqueue operation will not terminate if the CAS operation in line 19 of Fig. 2 repeatedly fails: however, this would imply that other threads are repeatedly successfully enqueueing other items. Surprisingly, it turns out to be impossible to capture wait freedom using a CSP refinement check. Roscoe and Gibson-Robinson have shown [22] that every finite- or infinite-traces-based property that can be captured by a CSP refinement check can also be captured by the combination of a finite-traces refinement check and satisfaction of a *deterministic* Büchi automaton. It is reasonably straightforward to show that capturing the infinite-traces wait freedom property requires a *nondeterministic* Büchi automaton.

Acknowledgements. This work has benefited from my working with Bill Roscoe for over 25 years. It would have been impossible without his contributions to CSP and FDR. Many of the techniques used in this paper are based on his ideas.

I would like to thank Tom Gibson-Robinson for useful discussions on this work, in particular concerning our joint work on adding symmetry reduction to FDR, and for producing the CSP model that allowed comparison with the work of [12]. I would also like to thank Ke Chen and Ruben Janssen for more general discussions concerning CSP model checking of concurrent datatypes.

References

1. Alur, R., McMillan, K., Peled, D.: Model-checking of correctness conditions for concurrent objects. In: Proceedings of the 11th Annual IEEE Symposium on Logic in Computer Science, LICS 1996 (1996)
2. Burckhardt, S., Dern, C., Musuvathi, M., Tan, R.: Line-Up: a complete and automatic linearizability checker. In: Proceedings of the 2010 ACM SIGPLAN Conference on Programming Language Design and Implementation (PLDI 2010), pp. 330–340 (2010)

3. Černý, P., Radhakrishna, A., Zufferey, D., Chaudhuri, S., Alur, R.: Model checking of linearizability of concurrent list implementations. In: Touili, T., Cook, B., Jackson, P. (eds.) CAV 2010. LNCS, vol. 6174, pp. 465–479. Springer, Heidelberg (2010). doi:10.1007/978-3-642-14295-6_41
4. Chen, K.: Analysing concurrent datatypes in CSP. Master's thesis. University of Oxford (2015)
5. Colvin, R., Dohery, S., Groves, L.: Verifying concurrent data structures by simulation. Electron. Notes Theor. Comput. Sci. **137**, 93–110 (2005)
6. Derrick, J., Schellhorn, G., Wehrheim, H.: Mechanically verified proof obligations for linearizability. ACM Trans. Programm. Lang. Syst. **33**(1), 4:1–4:43 (2011)
7. Gibson-Robinson, T., Armstrong, P., Boulgakov, A., Roscoe, A.W.: Failures Divergences Refinement (FDR) Version 3 (2013)
8. Gibson-Robinson, T., Lowe, G.: Symmetry reduction in CSP model checking. Submitted for publication (2016)
9. Herlihy, M., Shavit, N.: The Art of Multiprocessor Programming, 1st edn. Morgan Kaufmann, San Francisco (2012)
10. Herlihy, M., Wing, J.: Linearizability: a correctness condition for concurrent objects. ACM Trans. Program. Lang. Syst. **12**(3), 463–492 (1990)
11. Janssen, R.: Verification of concurrent datatypes using CSP. Master's thesis. University of Oxford (2015)
12. Liu, Y., Chen, W., Liu, Y.A., Sun, J., Zhang, S.J., Dong, J.S.: Verifying linearizability via optimized refinement checking. IEEE Trans. Softw. Eng. **39**(7), 1018–1039 (2013)
13. Lowe, G.: Implementing generalised alt – a case study in validated design using CSP. In: Communicating Process Architectures, pp. 1–34 (2011)
14. Mazur, T., Lowe, G.: Counter abstraction in the CSP/FDR setting. In: Proceedings of the Seventh International Workshop on Automated Verification of Critical Systems (AVoCS 2007). Electronic Notes on Theoretical Computer Science, vol. 250, pp. 171–186 (2007)
15. Mazur, T., Lowe, G.: CSP-based counter abstraction for systems with node identifiers. Sci. Comput. Program. **81**, 3–52 (2014)
16. Michael, M., Scott, M.: Simple, fast, and practical non-blocking and blocking concurrent queue algorithms. In: Proceedings of the Fifteenth Annual ACM Symposium on Principles of Distributed Computing, pp. 267–275 (1996)
17. Michael, M.M.: Safe memory reclamation for dynamic lock-free objects using atomic reads and writes. In: Proceedings of Principles of Distributed Computing (PODC 2002) (2002)
18. Pnueli, A., Jessie, X., Zuck, L.D.: Liveness with $(0, 1, \infty)$-counter abstraction. In: Proceedings of the 14th International Conference on Computer Aided Verification (CAV 2002), pp. 107–122 (2002)
19. Roscoe, A.W.: The Theory and Practice of Concurrency. Prentice Hall, Upper Saddle River (1998)
20. Roscoe, A.W.: Understanding Concurrent Systems. Springer, London (2010)
21. Roscoe, A.W., Broadfoot, P.J.: Proving security protocols with model checkers by data independence techniques. J. Comput. Secur. **7**(2,3), 147–190 (1999)
22. Roscoe, A.W., Gibson-Robinson, T.: The relationship between CSP. FDR and Büchi automata, Draft paper (2016)
23. Roscoe, A.W., Hopkins, D.: SVA, a tool for analysing shared-variable programs. In: Proceedings of AVoCS 2007, pp. 177–183 (2007)
24. Shalev, O., Shavit, N.: Split-ordered lists: lock-free extensible hash tables. J. ACM **53**(3), 379–405 (2006)

25. Sundell, H., Tsigas, P.: Lock-free deques and doubly linked lists. J. Parallel Distrib. Comput. **68**(7), 1008–1020 (2008)
26. Vafeiadis, V.: Automatically proving linearizability. In: Touili, T., Cook, B., Jackson, P. (eds.) CAV 2010. LNCS, vol. 6174, pp. 450–464. Springer, Heidelberg (2010). doi:10.1007/978-3-642-14295-6_40
27. Vechev, M., Yahav, E., Yorsh, G.: Experience with model checking linearizability. In: Păsăreanu, C.S. (ed.) SPIN 2009. LNCS, vol. 5578, pp. 261–278. Springer, Heidelberg (2009). doi:10.1007/978-3-642-02652-2_21
28. Welch, P., Martin, J.: A CSP model for Java multithreading. In: Proceedings of the International Symposium on Software Engineering for Parallel and Distributed Systems, pp. 114–122. IEEE (2000)

Discrete Random Variables
Over Domains, Revisited

Michael Mislove[✉]

Department of Computer Science, Tulane University, New Orleans, LA 70118, USA
mislove@tulane.edu

Abstract. We revisit the construction of discrete random variables over domains from [15] and show how Hoare's "normal termination" symbol ✓ can be used to achieve a more expressive model. The result is a natural model of flips of a coin that supports discrete and continuous (sub)probability measures. This defines a new random variables monad on **BCD**, the category of bounded complete domains, that can be used to augment semantic models of demonic nondeterminism with probabilistic choice. It is the second such monad, the first being Barker's monad for randomized choice [3]. Our construction differs from Barker's monad, because the latter requires the source of randomness to be shared across multiple users. The monad presented here allows each user to access a source of randomness that is independent of the sources of randomness available to other users. This requirement is useful, e.g., in models of crypto-protocols.

Keywords: Domain random variable · Sequential domain monoids · Continuous random variables

1 Introduction and Related Work

About ten years ago, the author presented a model for finite random variables over domains [15]. That model was based on work of Varacca [21,22], whose *indexed valuations* monads for probabilistic choice enjoy distributive laws over the standard power domains at the price of weakening one of the laws for probabilistic choice [11]. The model in [15] is arcane, but it nevertheless inspired an attempt to extend the ideas to a model that would support continuous probability measures over domains [9], an approach that was unfortunately flawed [16,17]. Here we present an improved construction for the model described in [15] that has the advantage of supporting all sub-probability measures – including both discrete and continuous – over sequences of flips of a random coin, yielding a new model for computational processes that involve probabilistic choice.

The last assertion can be understood by considering a natural model for sequences of coin tosses, the full binary tree, $\mathbb{CT} = \{0,1\}^* \cup \{0,1\}^\omega$. The root represents the starting point, and the nth level $\mathcal{C}_n$ of n-bit words represents

M. Mislove—Work partially supported by AFOSR Grant FA9550-13-1-0135-1.

© Springer International Publishing AG 2017
T. Gibson-Robinson et al. (Eds.): Roscoe Festschrift, LNCS 10160, pp. 185–202, 2017.
DOI: 10.1007/978-3-319-51046-0_10

the possible outcomes of n flips of the coin. A probability distribution over this family is then a probability measure on $\mathbb{C}T$. Endowed with the prefix order, $\mathbb{C}T$ is a domain whose set of maximal elements is a Cantor set, $\mathcal{C}$, and so this model is called the *Cantor tree*. If we endow $\mathcal{C}_n$ with a probability distribution μ_n representing the chances for a specific sequence of outcomes of n flips of the coin, and if $\pi_{m,n}\colon \mathcal{C}_n \longrightarrow \mathcal{C}_m$ satisfies $\pi_{m,n}\,\mu_n = \mu_m$ for $m \leq n$, then the sequence $\mu_n \longrightarrow_w \mu$ has a limit μ in the weak topology which is concentrated on $\mathcal{C}$. Likewise, any such measure μ gives rise to an associated sequence of measures, $\pi_n\,\mu$, where $\pi_n\colon \mathcal{C} \longrightarrow \mathcal{C}_n$ is the natural projection. Everything appears to be fine, until one tries to construct a monad based on these ideas, and then the construction falters when one tries to define a Kleisli lift (for details, see [16,17]).

In more detail, the flaw in the definition of the Kleisli lift in [9] was its use of concatenation of strings, which is not monotone in its first argument. Our remedy is to replace the Cantor tree $\mathbb{C}T$ with a domain monoid where composition is Scott continuous. Our construction yields a new monad on domains using a *domain monoid* $\mathbb{M}\{0,1\} = \{x\checkmark, x\bot \mid x \in \{0,1\}^*\}\cup\{0,1\}^\omega$. This domain monoid utilizes an idea first devised by Hoare that appears prominently in models of CSP [5]: a $\checkmark$-symbol that denotes normal termination. Algebraically, $\checkmark$ is an identity for multiplication, and making strings ending in $\checkmark$ maximal makes the multiplication in the monoid Scott continuous. Adding infinite strings requires a least element $\bot$ with strings ending in $\bot$ denoting terms that might diverge.

Probability is introduced by applying the sub-probability monad, $\mathbb{V}$; then monoid structure on $\mathbb{M}\{0,1\}$ then induces an affine domain monoid structure on $\mathbb{V}\mathbb{M}\{0,1\}$ where multiplication is convolution, induced by the monoid multiplication on $\mathbb{M}\{0,1\}$ with $\delta_\checkmark$ the identity. Moreover, since $\mathbb{M}\{0,1\}$ is a tree, it follows that $\mathbb{V}\mathbb{M}\{0,1\}$ is a bounded complete domain (cf. Corollary 1). The remainder of the construction follows along lines similar to those in [9]. However, restricting to random variables defined only on antichains as in [3,9] is not necessary for our construction, and this simplifies things somewhat.

1.1   The Plan of the Paper

The next section begins with a review of some background material from domain theory and other areas we need, including a result about the probability monad on the category of compact Hausdorff spaces and continuous maps and on the subcategory of compact monoids and continuous monoid homomorphisms. We also introduce our new "sequential domain monoid" construction, which is inspired by sequential composition from the process calculus world, and which forms a monad $\mathbb{M}$ on various categories of domains. Then we show that following $\mathbb{M}$ with the subprobability monad $\mathbb{V}$ yields a monad that supports convolution of subprobability measures as a Scott-continuous operation. While the facts that $\mathbb{M}$ and $\mathbb{V}\mathbb{M}$ are monads are not necessary to show the main results of the paper, we include them to show that our constructions are canonical. In any case, Sect. 3 contains the main results of the paper, where we give the construction of our new monad, CRV, of random variables, and the paper concludes with a summary and comments about future work.

2   Background

2.1   Domains

Most of the results we need about domain theory can be found in [1] or [8]; we give specific references for those that appear elsewhere.

To start, a *poset* is a partially ordered set. A subset $S \subseteq P$ is *directed* if each finite subset of S has an upper bound in S, and P is *directed complete* if each of P's directed subsets has a least upper bound. A directed complete partial order is called a *dcpo*. The relevant maps between dcpos are the monotone maps that also preserve suprema of directed sets; these maps are usually called *Scott continuous*. The resulting category is denoted DCPO.

These notions can be presented in a purely topological fashion: a subset $U \subseteq P$ of a poset is *Scott open* if (i) $U = \uparrow U \equiv \{x \in P \mid (\exists u \in U)\ u \leq x\}$ is an upper set, and (ii) if $\sup S \in U$ implies $S \cap U \neq \emptyset$ for each directed subset $S \subseteq P$. It is routine to show that the family of Scott-open sets forms a topology on any poset; this topology satisfies $\downarrow x \equiv \{y \in P \mid y \leq x\} = \overline{\{x\}}$ is the closure of a point, so the Scott topology is always T_0, but it is T_1 iff P is a flat poset. In any case, a mapping between dcpos is Scott continuous in the order-theoretic sense iff it is a monotone map that is continuous with respect to the Scott topologies on its domain and range. The category DCPO is Cartesian closed.

If P is a poset, and $x, y \in P$, then x *approximates* y iff for every directed set $S \subseteq P$, if $\sup S$ exists and if $y \leq \sup S$, then there is some $s \in S$ with $x \leq s$. In this case, we write $x \ll y$ and we let $\downarrow y = \{x \in P \mid x \ll y\}$. A *basis* for a poset P is a family $B \subseteq P$ satisfying $\downarrow y \cap B$ is directed and $y = \sup(\downarrow y \cap B)$ for each $y \in P$. A *continuous poset* is a poset that has a basis, and a dcpo P is a *domain* if P is a continuous dcpo. An element $k \in P$ is *compact* if $x \ll x$, and P is *algebraic* if $KP \equiv \{k \in P \mid k \ll k\}$ forms a basis. Domains are sober spaces in the Scott topology (cf. [14]).

We let DOM denote that category of domains and Scott continuous maps; this is a full subcategory of DCPO, but it is not Cartesian closed. Nevertheless, DOM has several Cartesian closed full subcategories. For example, there are the full subcategories SDOM of Scott domains, and BCD, its continuous analog: a *Scott domain* is an algebraic domain P for which KP is countable, and every non-empty subset of P has a greatest lower bound, or equivalently, every subset of P with an upper bound has a least upper bound. A domain is *bounded complete* if every non-empty subset has a greatest lower bound; BCD denotes the category of bounded complete domains and Scott-continuous maps.

Domains also have a Hausdorff refinement of the Scott topology which will play a role in our work. The *weak lower topology* on a poset P has the sets of the form $O = P \backslash \uparrow F$ as a basis, where $F \subset P$ is a finite subset. The *Lawson topology* on a domain P is the common refinement of the Scott- and weak lower topologies on P. This topology has the family

$$\{U \backslash \uparrow F \mid U \text{ Scott open \& } F \subseteq P \text{ finite}\}$$

as a basis. The Lawson topology on a domain is always Hausdorff. A domain is *coherent* if its Lawson topology is compact. We denote the closure of a subset

$X \subseteq P$ of a domain in the Lawson topology by $\overline{X}^\Lambda$, and Coh denotes the category of coherent domains and Scott-continuous maps. While the subcategory of Coh of coherent domains is Cartesian, and the subcategory of coherent domains having least elements is closed under arbitrary products, the category Coh is not Cartesian closed.

Example 1. This example is used extensively in [3,9]. Let $\mathcal{C}$ denote the middle third Cantor set from the unit interval. This is a Stone space, and so it can be realized as a projective limit of finite spaces $\mathcal{C} \simeq \varprojlim_{\alpha \in A} \mathcal{C}_\alpha$. Since $\mathcal{C}$ is second countable, we can define a countable family of finite spaces $\mathcal{C}_n$ for which $\mathcal{C} \simeq \varprojlim_n \mathcal{C}_n$. Indeed, we can take $\mathcal{C} = \{0,1\}^\omega$ and $\mathcal{C}_n = \{0,1\}^n$ for each n.

From a domain-theoretic perspective, $\mathbb{CT} = \bigcup_n \mathcal{C}_n \cup \mathcal{C} = \{0,1\}^* \cup \{0,1\}^\omega$, the finite and infinite words over $\{0,1\}$ in the prefix order. The finite words form the set of compact elements, $K\mathbb{CT}$, and so $\mathbb{CT}$ is an algebraic domain. It is called the *Cantor Tree*, and it can be viewed as the state space of the outcomes of flipping a coin: the root is the starting point, and with 0 denoting *Tails* and 1 *Heads*, the outcomes as we work our way up the tree give all possible results of flipping a coin some number of times. For example, the family $\mathbb{CT}_n = \bigcup_{m \leq n} \mathcal{C}_m$ gives the finite tree of possible outcomes of n flips of the coin.

As we commented in the introduction, $\mathbb{CT}$ is alluring as a model for the outcomes of tossing a coin, but it does not work well as a computational model. In particular, viewing $\mathbb{CT}_n$ as the possible outcomes of n tosses of a coin, the "obvious" mechanism to compose one sequence of tosses with another is concatenation, the operation used in [9]. But concatenation is not monotone in its first argument, and this undermines the approach. We define an alternative model of coin flips below as the family $\mathbb{M}\{0,1\}$. This is the heart of our model for probabilistic choice.

There is one technical result we will need, which comes from [8]:

Lemma 1. *If $f \colon B \longrightarrow E$ is a monotone map from a basis for a domain D into a dcpo E, then $\hat{f} \colon D \longrightarrow E$ defined by $\hat{f}(x) = \sup f(\downarrow x \cap B)$ defines the largest Scott-continuous map below f. Moreover, if for each $x \in D$ there is a directed set $B_x \subseteq \downarrow x \cap B$ with $x = \sup B_x$ and $\sup \hat{f}(B_x) = f(x)$, then $\hat{f}$ extends f.*

Proof. This is Lemma IV-9.23 of [8].

2.2 $\mathbb{M}\{0,1\}$ as a Domain Monoid

In this section we define a domain monoid $\mathbb{M}\{0,1\}$ based on the finite and infinite words over $\{0,1\}$.

Proposition 1. *We define $\mathbb{M}\{0,1\} \equiv (\{x\checkmark, x\bot \mid x \in \{0,1\}\}^* \cup \{0,1\}^\omega, \leq)$, where $\leq$ is defined by:*

- *If $x \in \{0,1\}^*\checkmark, y \in \mathbb{M}\{0,1\}$, then $x \leq y$ iff $x = y$;*
- *If $x \in \{0,1\}^*\bot, y \in \mathbb{M}\{0,1\}$, then $x \leq y$ iff $(\exists m \leq n < \omega)\, x \in \{0,1\}^m\bot, y \in \{0,1\}^n\bot \cup \{0,1\}^n\checkmark \cup \{0,1\}^\omega$ and $x_i \leq y_i$ for all $i \leq m$; and*
- *If $x \in \{0,1\}^\omega, y \in \mathbb{M}\{0,1\}$, then $x \leq y$ iff $x = y$.*

Then $\mathbb{M}D$ *is a bounded complete algebraic domain whose set of compact elements is* $K\mathbb{M}\{0,1\} = \{x\checkmark, x\bot \mid x \in \{0,1\}^*\}$.

Proof. It is routine to show that the partial order defined above endows $\mathbb{M}\{0,1\}$ with a tree structure whose root is $\bot$ and whose leaves (=maximal elements) are $\{x\checkmark \mid x \in \{0,1\}^*\} \cup \{0,1\}^\omega$. It's then obvious that the elements $x\checkmark$ and $x\bot$ are compact for x finite, and that each infinite word x satisfies $x = \sup_n x_1 \cdots x_n \bot$.

Theorem 1. *Endowed with the Lawson topology,* $(\mathbb{M}\{0,1\}, \leq, \cdot)$ *is a compact ordered monoid under the multiplication given by:*

$$x \cdot y = \begin{cases} x'y, & \text{if } x = x'\checkmark \in \{0,1\}^*\checkmark, \\ x, & \text{if } x \in \{0,1\}^*\bot \cup \{0,1\}^\omega. \end{cases}$$

Proof. Proposition 1 implies $\mathbb{M}\{0,1\}$ is a bounded complete algebraic domain, which implies it is coherent. If $x_1 < x_2 \in \mathbb{M}\{0,1\}$, then $x_1 \in \{0,1\}^*\bot$, so $x_1 \cdot y_1 = x_1 < x_2 \leq x_2 \cdot y_2$ for any $y_1 \leq y_2$. On the other hand, if x_1 is maximal, then $x_1 = x_2$. If $x_1 \in \{0,1\}^*\checkmark$, then $x_1 \cdot y_1 = x'y_1 \leq x'y_2 = x_1 \cdot y_2$, if $y_1 \leq y_2$. And if $x_1 \in \{0,1\}^\omega$, then $x_1 \cdot y_1 = x_1 = x_1 \cdot y_2$. It follows that the multiplication is monotone. By definition, $\checkmark$ is an identity for the multiplication. So it only remains to prove multiplication is jointly Lawson continuous.

It's straightforward to show multiplication is Scott continuous in each variable separately, which implies it is jointly Scott continuous. For Lawson continuity, it's sufficient to show that, given $z \in K\mathbb{M}\{0,1\}$, $A = \{(x,y) \mid x \cdot y \in \uparrow z\}$ is Scott compact. But $z \in K\mathbb{M}\{0,1\}$ implies $z = z'\checkmark$ or $z = z'\bot$, for a finite $z' \in \{0,1\}^*$. From this if follows that there are only finitely many ways to write z' is a concatenation of a prefix $p \in \{0,1\}^*$ and a suffix $s \in \{0,1\}^*$, and then

$$z = \begin{cases} p\checkmark \cdot s\bot & \text{if } z \in \{0,1\}^*\bot, \\ z = p\checkmark \cdot s\checkmark & \text{if } z \in \{0,1\}^\checkmark. \end{cases}$$

Then $z \leq x \cdot y$ implies there is some factorization $z = p\checkmark \cdot s\bot$ or $z = p\checkmark \cdot s\bot$ with $p\checkmark = x$ and either $s\checkmark \leq y$ or $s\bot \leq y$. Then A is a finite union of sets of the form $\uparrow(p\checkmark, s'\checkmark)$ or $\uparrow(p\checkmark, s\bot)$.

2.3   The Subprobability Monad

Probability on Comp and Dom. It is well known that the family of probability measures on a compact Hausdorff space is the object level of a functor which defines a monad on Comp, the category of compact Hausdorff spaces and continuous maps (Theorem 2.13 of [7]). As outlined in [10], this monad gives rise to two related monads:

1. On Comp, it associates to a compact Hausdorff space X the free *barycentric algebra* over X, the name deriving from the counit $\epsilon \colon \mathsf{Prob}(S) \longrightarrow S$ which assigns to each measure μ on a probabilistic algebra S its barycenter $\epsilon(\mu)$ (cf. Theorem 5.3 of [13], which references [20]).

2. A *compact affine monoid* is a compact monoid S for which there also is a continuous mapping $\cdot\colon [0,1] \times S \times S \longrightarrow S$ satisfying the property that translations by elements of S are affine maps (cf. Sect. 1.1ff. of [10]). On the category CompMon of compact monoids and continuous monoid homomorphisms, Prob gives rise to a monad that assigns to a compact monoid S the free compact affine monoid over S (cf. Corollary 7.4 of [10]).

Remarkably, these results have analogs in domain theory. Before we describe them, we first review some basic facts about (sub)probability measures on domains. Most of these results can be found [11].

Definition 1. *A* valuation *on a dcpo D is a mapping $\mu\colon \Sigma(D) \longrightarrow [0,1]$, where $\Sigma(D)$ denotes the Scott-open subsets of D, satisfying:*

Strictness: $\mu(\emptyset) = 0$.
Monotonicity: $U \subseteq V$ *Scott-open imlies* $\mu(U) \leq \mu(V)$.
Modularity: $\mu(U \cup V) + \mu(U \cap V) = \mu(U) + \mu(V)$, $\forall U, V \in \Sigma(D)$,
Continuity: *If* $\{U_i\}_{i \in I} \subseteq \Sigma(D)$ *is* $\subseteq$-*directed, then* $\sup_i \mu(U_i) =$ $\mu(\bigcup_i U_i)$.

If $\mu(D) = 1$, then μ is normalized. *We let $\mathbb{V}(D)$ denote the family of valuations on D under the pointwise order: $\mu \sqsubseteq \nu$ iff $\mu(U) \leq \nu(U)$ for all $U \in \Sigma(D)$; $\mathbb{V}_1(D)$ denotes the family of normalized valuations.*

It was first shown by Sahib-Djarhomi [19] that $\mathbb{V}(D)$ is a dcpo if D is one. The main result describing the domain structure of $\mathbb{V}(D)$ is the following:

Theorem 2 (*Splitting Lemma [11]*). *Let D be a domain with basis B. Then $\mathbb{V}(D)$ is a domain with a basis consisting of the simple measures with supports in B. Moreover, for simple measures $\mu = \sum_{x \in F} r_r \delta_x$ and $\nu = \sum_{y \in G} s_y \delta_y$, the following are equivalent:*

- $\mu \leq \nu$ (*respectively, $\mu \ll \nu$*).
- *There are non-negative* transport numbers $\langle t_{x,y} \rangle_{(x,y) \in F \times G}$ *satisfying:*
    1. $r_x = \sum_{y \in G} t_{x,y}$ $\forall x \in F$,
    2. $\sum_{x \in F} t_{x,y} \leq s_y$ $\forall y \in G$,
    3. $t_{x,y} > 0$ *implies* $x \leq y$ (*respectively, $x \ll y$*) $\forall (x,y) \in F \times G$.
    Moreover, if μ and ν are probability measures, then we can refine (ii) above to
    (ii') $\sum_{x \in F} t_{x,y} = s_y$ $\forall y \in G$.

It is well-known that each Borel subprobability measure on a domain D gives rise to a unique valuation in the obvious way. Conversely, it was shown by Alvarez-Manilla, Edalat and Sahib-Djarhomi [2] that the converse holds, so we can identify the family of Borel subprobability measures on D with the family of valuations, including the order structure. Throughout this paper, we will refer to (sub)probability measures, rather than valuations, but the order structure is the one defined from valuations; for coherent domains, using the traditional functional-analytic approach to defining measures, the order can be realized as: For $\mu, \nu \in \mathbb{V}(D)$, $\mu \leq \nu$ iff $\int_D f d\mu \leq \int_D f d\nu$ for all $f\colon D \longrightarrow \mathbb{R}_+$ *monotone* and Lawson continuous.

Now for the analogs of (i) and (ii) at the start of this subsection:

Proposition 2. *Let D be a domain. Then*

1. $\mathbb{V}$ *defines a monad on* DCPO.
2. $\mathbb{V}$ *defines an endofunctor on* Coh, *the category of coherent domains and Scott-continuous maps.*
3. *If D is a domain with a Scott-continuous multiplication $\cdot\colon D \times D \longrightarrow D$ under which D is a topological semigroup, then there is a Scott-continuous convolution operation $*\colon \mathbb{V}(D) \times \mathbb{V}(D) \longrightarrow \mathbb{V}(D)$ defined by $(\mu * \nu)(U) = (\mu \times \nu)\{(x, y) \in D \times D \mid x \cdot y \in U\}$. Under this operation, $\mathbb{V}(D)$ is an affine topological semigroup.*

Proof. The result in (i) is contained in [11], and (ii) is from [12]. For (iii), it is well-known that the family of simple subprobability measures $\{\sum_{x \in F} r_x \delta_x \mid \sum_{x \in F} r_x \leq 1 \ \& \ F \subseteq S \text{ finite}\}$ is a semigroup under convolution if S is a semigroup. Since the operation $*$ is nothing more than $\mathbb{V}(\cdot)$, it is Scott-continuous on $\mathbb{V}(D \times D)$ if D is a domain semigroup. And since the simple measures contain a basis for $\mathbb{V}(D \times D)$, it follows that convolution is associative on all of $\mathbb{V}(D \times D)$. Thus $(\mathbb{V}(D), *)$ is a domain semigroup. The fact that $\mathbb{V}$ defines a monad on Dom means the only thing left to show is that each component of the unit $\eta\colon 1_{\mathsf{Coh}} \longrightarrow \mid \mid \circ \mathbb{V}$ is a semigroup homomorphism. Since $\eta_D(d) = \delta_d$, this amounts to showing that $\delta_x * \delta_y = \delta_{x \cdot y}$ for each $x, y \in D$, for D a domain semigroup. But given $x, y \in D$, and $U \in \Sigma(D)$, we have

$$(\delta_x * \delta_y)(U) = \delta_x \times \delta_y(\{(r, s) \in D \times D \mid r \cdot s \in U\})$$

$$= \begin{cases} 1 & \text{iff } x \cdot y \in U \\ 0 & \text{otherwise} \end{cases} = \delta_{x \cdot y}(U).$$

The final claim that $\mathbb{V}(D)$ is an affine semigroup is clear.

Remark 1. There is a wealth of material on the semigroup of probability measures on a compact or locally compact (semi)group, but the assumption is invariably that the (semi)group is Hausdorff. The results above show that basic facts still hold if one generalizes to subprobability measures over domain semigroups endowed with the Scott topology. It turns out that, if the domain D is coherent and the multiplication $\cdot\colon D \times D \longrightarrow D$ is Lawson continuous, then one can retrieve the "classic" result, extended to subprobability measures.

$\mathbb{V}(D)$ is in BCD if D is a Tree Domain. Our next goal is to show that $\mathbb{V}\mathbb{M}\{0, 1\}$ is in BCD. Then, using a function space construction, if E is in BCD, we can define a monad of random variables over BCD. We begin with the following result; it is stated in [12], although no proof is provided; we include one here for completeness sake:

Lemma 2. *If T is a finite tree, then $\mathbb{V}(T)$ is closed under finite infima. Hence $\mathbb{V}(T) \in BCD$.*

Proof. We prove that if $\mu, \nu \in \mathbb{V}(T)$, then $\mu \wedge \nu \in \mathbb{V}(T)$. We proceed by induction on $|T|$: the case that $|T| = 1$ is obvious, since $\mathbb{V}(\{*\}) \simeq [0,1]$. So suppose the result holds for $|T| \leq n$, and let T be a tree with $n + 1$ elements. If $T' = T \setminus \{\perp_T\}$, then T' is a forest of k trees, $T' = \bigcup_{i \leq k} T_i'$. The inductive hypothesis implies $\mathbb{V}(T_i')$ is closed under finite infima for each i. So, if $\mu, \nu \in \mathbb{V}(T)$, then $\mu|_{T_i'} \wedge \mu|_{T_i'} \in \mathbb{V}(T_i')$ for each $i \leq k$, and since the T_i's are pairwise disjoint, it follows that $\mu|_{T'} \wedge \nu|_{T'} \in \mathbb{V}(T')$. So, for any open sets $U, V \subseteq T'$, we have

$$\mu \wedge \nu \, (U \cup V) + \mu \wedge \nu \, (U \cap V) = \mu \wedge \nu \, (U) + \mu \wedge \nu \, (V).$$

The only remaining case to show $\mu \wedge \nu \in \mathbb{V}(T)$ is when $U = T$ or $\nu = T$; without loss of generality, we assume $U = T$. In that case,

$$\mu \wedge \nu \, (U \cup V) + \mu \wedge \nu \, (U \cap V) = \mu \wedge \nu \, (T) + \mu \wedge \nu \, (V) = \mu \wedge \nu \, (U) + \mu \wedge \nu \, (V).$$

Corollary 1. *If $T \simeq \mathrm{bilim}_n T_n$ is a the bilimit of finite trees, then $\mathbb{V}(T)$ is in BCD. In particular, $\mathbb{V} \mathbb{M}\{0, 1\} \in$ BCD.*

Proof. If $T \simeq \mathrm{bilim}_n T_n$ with each T_n a finite tree, then the continuity of the functor $\mathbb{V}$ implies $\mathbb{V}(T) \simeq \lim_n \mathbb{V}(T_n)$, and since BCD is closed under limits, the result follows. The final claim follows from our remark in the proof of Proposition 1.

2.4   Domains of Partial Maps

In the last subsection we alluded to a "function space construction" that we'd need in our random variables model. We address that issue in this subsection, where we give some results about partial maps defined on the non-empty Scott-closed subsets of a domain. The results are needed for our analysis of sub-probabilities on domains.

To begin, recall that the *support* of a finite positive Borel measure μ on a topological space X is the smallest closed set $C \subseteq X$ satisfying $\mu(C) = \mu(X)$. For measures on a domain D, we let $\mathrm{supp}_\Sigma \, \mu$ denote the support of μ with respect to the Scott topology, and $\mathrm{supp}_\Lambda \, \mu$ denote the support of μ with respect to the Lawson topology. The appropriate domain for the random variables we plan to study is $\mathrm{supp}_\Sigma \, \mu$, the smallest Scott-closed subset X satisfying $\mu(D \setminus X) = 0$, where μ is the measure assigned to the domain of the random variable.

Recall that the lower power domain over a domain D is the family $\Gamma(D)$ of non-empty Scott-closed subsets of D ordered by inclusion; in fact, $\mathcal{P}_L(D) = (\Gamma(D), \subseteq)$ is the free sup-semilattice domain over D. $\mathcal{P}_L(D)$ defines a monad on every Cartesian closed category of domains; in fact, $\mathcal{P}_L(D)$ is bounded complete for any domain D. This leads us to an important construction that we need, one which we believe should be useful in applications of domains; although we have made only a cursory effort at best to locate the result, we find it surprising that we have been unable to find it in the literature.

Proposition 3. *Let D and E both be BCD. Let*

$$[D \rightharpoonup E] \stackrel{def}{=} \{f \colon C \longrightarrow E \mid C \in \mathcal{P}_L(D)\}$$

denote the family of Scott-continuous partial maps defined on non-empty Scott-closed subsets of D. *We order* $[D \rightharpoonup E]$ *by*

$$f \leq_L g \quad \textit{iff} \quad dom\ f \subseteq dom\ g\ and\ f \leq g|_{dom\ f}.$$

Then $[D \rightharpoonup E]$ *is a bounded complete domain.*

Proof (Outline). The proof can be broken down into three claims:

1. $[D \rightharpoonup E]$ *is a dcpo:* Given $\mathcal{F} \subseteq [D \rightharpoonup E]$ directed, one first shows $\sup \mathcal{F} \in [C \longrightarrow E]$, where $C = \bigsqcup_{f \in \mathcal{F}} dom\ f$, the Scott-closure of the union of the Scott-closed sets $\{dom\ f \mid f \in \mathcal{F}\}$. This is done by noting that $X = \bigcup_{f \in \mathcal{F}} dom\ f$ is a directed union of Scott-closed subsets of the domain D, so it is a lower set that has a basis, which implies X is a continuous poset. Then $F \colon X \longrightarrow E$ by $F(x) = \sup\{f(x) \mid x \in dom\ f \in \mathcal{F}\}$ is well-defined because $\mathcal{F}$ is directed, so the same is true of those $f \in \mathcal{F}$ for which $x \in dom\ f$. In fact, F is Scott-continuous, because, given $Y \subseteq X$ directed for which $x = \sup Y \in X$ exists, then $x \in dom\ f$ for some $f \in \mathcal{F}$. Since $f \colon dom\ f \longrightarrow E$ is Scott-continuous, we have $f|_{\downarrow x} \colon \downarrow x \longrightarrow E$ is Scott-continuous. Thus $F|_{\downarrow x} = \sup\{f|_{\downarrow x} \mid f \in \mathcal{F}\ \&\ x \in dom\ f\}$ is the supremum of a directed family of Scott-continuous functions on $\downarrow x$, so it also is Scott-continuous on $\downarrow x$. Thus $F(\sup Y) = \sup F(Y)$ since $Y \subseteq \downarrow \sup Y = \downarrow x$. Then this continuous map extends continuously to the round ideal completion of X, and one argues this extension satisies $F = \sup \mathcal{F}$, so $[D \rightharpoonup E]$ is a dcpo.
2. *Next show* $[D \rightharpoonup E]$ *is a domain:* The set $[D \rightharpoonup E] = \bigcup_{C \in \Gamma(D)}[C \longrightarrow E]$ is the directed union of domains $[C \longrightarrow E]$ for $C \in \Gamma(D)$, and each of these domains has a basis, $\mathcal{B}_C \subseteq [C \longrightarrow E]$. We let $\mathcal{B} = \bigcup_{C \in \Gamma(D)} \mathcal{B}_C$ be the (directed) union of these function families. It follows that $\mathcal{B}$ is a basis for $[D \rightharpoonup E]$.
3. *Finally, validate the category claims.* If D, E are both in BCD, then given $f, g \in [D \rightharpoonup E]$, we can define $f \wedge g$ by $dom\ f \wedge g = dom\ f \cap dom\ g$, and for $x \in dom\ f \wedge g$, we let $(f \wedge g)(x) = f(x) \wedge g(x)$. That $f \wedge g$ is the inf of f and g follows from the fact that $h \leq f, g$ implies $dom\ h \subseteq dom\ f \cap dom\ g$, and then the result is clear.

2.5   Domain Random Variables

With the results of the previous subsection in hand, we're now ready to begin our construction of domain random variables. We start with a lemma that will underpin our main result.

Lemma 3. *Let* D *be a domain and let* $\mu, \nu \in \mathbb{V}(D)$. *Then* $\mu \sqsubseteq \nu$ *implies* $supp_\Sigma\, \mu \subseteq supp_\Sigma\, \nu$. *Moreover, if* $\{\mu_i\}_{i \in I} \subseteq \mathbb{V}(D)$ *is directed with* $\sup_i \mu_i = \mu$, *then* $\sup_i supp_\Sigma\, \mu_i = supp_\Sigma\, \mu$.

Proof. For the first claim, $\mu \sqsubseteq \nu$ iff $\mu(U) \leq \nu(U)$ for each Scott-open set U. So, $\mu(U) = 0$ if $\nu(U) = 0$, and it follows that $\text{supp}_\Sigma \, \mu \subseteq \text{supp}_\Sigma \, \nu$. For the second claim, since $(\Gamma(D), \subseteq)$ (the family of Scott-closed subsets of D) is a domain, the first result implies $\sup_i \text{supp}_\Sigma \, \mu_i \subseteq \text{supp}_\Sigma \, \mu$. Conversely, $A = D \backslash \sup_i \text{supp}_\Sigma \, \mu_i$ is Scott-open, and $\mu(A) > 0$ would violate $\sup_i \mu_i = \mu$. So $\mu(A) = 0$, which implies $\text{supp}_\Sigma \, \mu \subseteq D \backslash A = \sup_i \text{supp}_\Sigma \, \mu_i$.

We now define domain random variables based on a given domain D.

Definition 2. *Let D be a domain. A* domain random variable *on D is a mapping $X \colon \text{supp}_\Sigma \, \mu \longrightarrow E$ where μ is a subprobability measure on D and $X \colon \text{supp}_\Sigma \longrightarrow E$ is a Scott-continuous map. Given domains D and E, we define*

$$RV(D, E) \overset{def}{=} \{(\mu, X) \in \mathbb{V}(D) \times [\text{supp}_\Sigma \, \mu \longrightarrow E]\} \quad where$$
$$(\mu, X) \leq (\nu, Y) \quad iff \quad \mu \sqsubseteq \nu \ \& \ X \leq Y|_{\text{supp}_\Sigma \, \mu}$$

Proposition 4. *If D and E are domains, then*

- *$RV(D, E)$ is a dcpo.*
- *If D and E are in a CCC of domains, then $RV(D, E)$ is a domain.*
- *If $\mathbb{V}(D), D$ and E are all in a CCC C of domains, then so is $RV(D, E)$.*

Proof. The fact that the relation $\leq$ on $RV(D, E)$ is well defined follows from part (i) of Lemma 3. The proof of the first statement is straightforward, using part (ii) of Lemma 3. For the second part, first note that Proposition 3 implies $\mathbb{V}(D) \times [D \rightharpoonup E]$ is a domain since $\mathbb{V}(D)$ is one. The first part implies $RV(D, E) \subseteq \mathbb{V}(D) \times [D \rightharpoonup E]$ is closed under directed suprema. Moreover, for $(\mu, X) \in RV(D, E)$,

$$\downarrow(\mu, X) \supseteq \{(\mu', X') \mid \mu' \ll \mu \ \& \ X' \ll X|_{\text{supp}_\Sigma \, \mu'} \text{ in } [\text{supp}_\Sigma \, \mu' \longrightarrow E]\},$$

and that the right-hand set is directed with supremum (μ, X). This implies $RV(D, E)$ is a domain. The third statement is then clear.

Theorem 3. *Fix a domain D. Then $RV(D, -)$ is the object level of a continuous endofunctor on DCPO that leaves each CCC of domains that contains $\mathbb{V}(D)$ invariant.*

Proof. Given a Scott-continuous map $f \colon E \longrightarrow F$ between domains E and F, define $RV(D, f) \colon RV(D, E) \longrightarrow RV(D, F)$ by $RV(D, f)(\mu, X) = (\mu, f \circ X)$. The third part of Proposition 4 then implies that $RV(D, -)$ is an endofunctor on any CCC of domains that contains D and $\mathbb{V}(D)$. This endofunctor is continuous because its components are.

3   A Monad of Continuous Random Variables

The development so far has been about domain theory with only a passing reference to a particular model of computation. We now focus more narrowly to obtain a monad of continuous random variables designed to model the prototypical source of randomness, the tosses of a fair (and also an unfair) coin. Such a model underlies the work in [3,9], for example, where the focus is on measures μ on the Cantor tree for which $\mathrm{supp}_\Lambda\, \mu$ is an antichain. We begin with a discussion around such a model.

3.1   Modeling Coin Flips

We have chosen the sequential domain $\mathbb{M}\{0,1\}$ because it provides a model for a series of coin flips that might occur during a computation. Our intuitive view is that a random choice of some element of from a semantic domain D would consist of a coin flip followed by a choice of the element from D based on the outcome. So, it is essentially a two-step process: the random process flips the coin resulting in a 0 (tails) or a 1 (heads), and then successfully terminates, adding a $\checkmark$ to the outcome, and then a random variable X is applied to this result to select the element of D. Note that a sequence of coin flips followed by a choice is a process that iterates the coin flips a prescribed number of times, represented by $x_1\checkmark \cdot x_2\checkmark \cdots x_n\checkmark = x_1\cdots x_n\checkmark$, followed by the application of the random variable X.

3.2   The Inevitability of Nondeterminism

Our choice of $\mathbb{M}\{0,1\}$ to model coin flips naturally leads to the question of how to combine sequences of coin flips by two processes combined under sequential composition. The multiplication operation is used here, but it raises an additional issue.

Example 2. Suppose we have processes, P and Q, both of which employ probabilistic choice, and that we want to form the sequential composition $P; Q$. Let's assume P can flip a fair coin 0, 1 or 2 times, and on each toss, if there is a 0, then an action a is executed, while if there is a 1, then action b is executed, and control then is passed to Q. Likewise, suppose Q can toss a fair coin 0, 1 or 2 times and if the result is a 0, it executes an action c, while if a 1 appears, an action d is executed, and again, Q terminates normally after each execution. In our approach based on $\mathbb{M}\{0,1\}$, if we represent P as (μ, X), and Q as (ν, Y). then the composition $P; Q = (\mu * \nu, X \odot Y)$, where $*$ represents a convolution operator on measures, and $\odot$ an appropriate operation on the random variable components.

Consider now the value of $X \odot Y$ on the outcome of two 0s. This outcome could arise in any of three ways:

- P could terminate without making any coin tosses, and Q could toss its coin twice, then normally terminate. This would produce the value $X \odot Y(00) = cc\checkmark$;
- P could toss its coin once, pass control, and Q could toss its coin once, and terminate. This would produce $X \odot Y(00) = ac\checkmark$;
- P could toss its coin twice, pass control to Q, which terminates normally without tossing its coin. This would produce $X \odot Y(00) = aa\checkmark$.

Since we have no way of knowing which of the three possibilities occurred, we must allow $X \odot Y$ to account for all three possibilities. This means $X \odot Y(00)$ must contain all three outcomes. The traditional way of representing such multiple outcomes is through a model of nondeterministic choice, i.e., a power domain.

Notation 1. Throughout the remainder of the paper, we assume the semantic domains D where random variables take their values are bounded complete domains, and the inf-operation models probabilistic choice. Thus, such domains support a Scott-continuous nondeterministic choice operator– the inf-operation – which we denote by $\oplus_D$.

3.3   Constructing a Monad

We now focus more narrowly by restricting random variables to be defined on a particular probability space, namely, $\mathbb{M}\{0,1\}$. This amounts to restricting the functor to $RV(\mathbb{M}\{0,1\}, -)$. However, this restriction is not enough to define a monad – we must restrict the measures on $\mathbb{M}\{0,1\}$ that are allowed. We do this by restricting the simple measures that are allowed, and then taking the smallest subdomain of $\mathbb{V}\mathbb{M}\{0,1\}$ containing them.

Definition 3. *We say a simple measure $\sum_{x \in F_\mu} r_x \delta_x$ on $\mathbb{M}\{0,1\}$ is normal if $F_\mu \subseteq \{0,1\}^* \checkmark$. We denote the set of normal simple measures by $\mathbb{V}_N\mathbb{M}\{0,1\}$.*

Since each normal measure is concentrated on a subset of $\{0,1\}^* \checkmark \subseteq \operatorname{Max}\mathbb{M}\{0,1\}$, the suprema of a directed set of normal simple measures is another such. However, the following will be useful:

Proposition 5. *Let $\mu_n \in \mathbb{V}_N\mathbb{M}\{0,1\}$ be a sequence of normal measures. Then the following are equivalent:*

1. *$\mu_n \longrightarrow \mu$ in the weak topology on $\mathbb{V}\mathbb{M}\{0,1\}$.*
2. *$\mu_n \longrightarrow \mu$ in the Lawson topology on $\mathbb{V}\mathbb{M}\{0,1\}$.*
3. *The sequence $\{\inf_{m \geq n} \mu_m \mid n \geq 1\}$ satisfies $\mu = \sup_n (\inf_{m \geq n} \mu_m)$.*

Proof. From Corollary 1 we know $\mathbb{V}\mathbb{M}\{0,1\} \in \mathsf{BCD}$, and hence it is a coherent domain. The equivalence of (i) and (ii) is then Corollary 15 of [4], while the equivalence of (ii) and (iii) is Proposition VII-3.10 of [8].

Theorem 4. *If $\mu \in \mathbb{V}\mathbb{M}\{0,1\}$ is concentrated on $\{0,1\}^\omega$, then there are normal simple measures $\mu_n \in \mathbb{V}_N\mathbb{M}\{0,1\}$ with $\mu_n \longrightarrow \mu$ in the weak topology.*

Proof. Define $\phi_n \colon \{0,1\}^\omega \longrightarrow \{0,1\}^n \checkmark$ by $\phi_n(x_1 \cdots) = x_1 \cdots x_n \checkmark$. This is Lawson continuous between compact Hausdorff spaces (in the relative topologies), and then Proposition 2 of [6] implies $\mathsf{Prob}\,\{0,1\}^\omega \simeq \lim_n (\mathsf{Prob}\,\{0,1\}^n \checkmark, \phi_n)$. But the same argument *verbatim* shows $\mathbb{V}(\{0,1\}^\omega) \simeq \lim_n (\mathbb{V}(\{0,1\}^n \checkmark), \phi_n)$. Since $\mathbb{V}\mathbb{M}\{0,1\}$ is a coherent domain and all the measures $\mu, \phi_n \mu$ are concentrated on $\operatorname{Max}\mathbb{V}\mathbb{M}\{0,1\}$, the relative Lawson topology agrees with the weak topology on these measures.

Definition 4. *If D is a dcpo, we define the family of* random variables *on D to be*

$$CRV(D) \stackrel{def}{=} RV(\mathbb{M}\{0,1\}, D) = \{(\mu, X) \in \mathbb{VM}\{0,1\} \times [supp_\Sigma \, \mu \longrightarrow D]\}.$$

Theorem 5. *If D is a dcpo, then so is $CRV(D)$. Moreover, if D is in BCD, then so is $CRV(D)$. Finally, CRV extends to a continuous endofunctor on BCD.*

Proof. Proposition 4 implies $CRV(D)$ is a dcpo if D is one. Together with Corollary 1, it also implies $CRV(D)$ is in BCD if D is, since $\mathbb{VM}\{0,1\} \in$ BCD.

As for the final claim, If $f: D \longrightarrow E$, then define $CRV \, f: CRV(D) \longrightarrow CRV(E)$ by $CRV \, f(\mu, X) = (\mu, f \circ X)$. It's clear that this makes CRV a functor, and the comments above show it's an endofunctor on BCD. It's also continuous because its components are. $\qquad\blacksquare$

In the general theory we often couch the discussion in terms of sub-probability measures, with the implicit assumption that any mass unallocated is associated with nontermination. Since we have an explicit nontermination symbol in the current situation, this is a convenient place to describe the relationship between sub-probability measures and probability measures on the same domain.

Notation 2. If D is a domain, we let

$$PRV(D) = \{(\mu, X) \in \mathsf{Prob}\,\mathbb{M}\{0,1\} \times [\text{supp}_\Sigma \, \mu \longrightarrow D]\},$$

We call $PRV(D)$ the family of *probabilistic random variables over D*.

Proposition 6. *If D is a domain in BCD, then the mapping*

$$(\mu, X) \mapsto (\mu \oplus (1 - ||\mu||)\delta_\perp, X): CRV(D) \longrightarrow PRV(D)$$

is a closure operator on $CRV(D)$, and its image, $PRV(D)$, also is a domain in BCD. Moreover, a basis for $PRV(D)$ is the family $\{(\mu, X) \in PRV(D) \mid \mu \text{ is simple}\}$.

Proof. It's straightforward to show that the mapping $\mu \mapsto \mu + (1 - ||\mu||)\delta_\perp$ is a closure operator on $\mathbb{VM}\{0,1\}$, and clearly its image is $\mathsf{Prob}\,\mathbb{M}\{0,1\}$, which is a dcpo. It follows from Corollary I-2.5 of [8] that $\mathsf{Prob}\,\mathbb{M}\{0,1\}$ is a domain, and that $\mu \ll \nu \in VD$ implies $\mu + (1 - ||\mu||)\delta_\perp \ll \nu + (1||\nu||)\delta_\perp$. This last point implies $\mathsf{Prob}\,\mathbb{M}\{0,1\}$ has a basis of simple measures. It now follows that $(\mu, X) \mapsto (\mu + (1 - ||\mu||)\delta_\perp, X)$ is a closure operator on $CRV(D)$; note that $X(\perp)$ is well-defined since D is bounded complete. Thus, the image of $CRV(D)$ is $PRV(D)$, and the same result from [8] applies to finish the proof. $\qquad\blacksquare$

The Structure of $\mathbb{VM}\{0,1\}$. Since $\mathbb{M}\{0,1\} = \{x\checkmark, x\perp \mid x \in \{0,1\}^*\} \cup \{0,1\}^\omega$, we can exploit the structure of $\mathbb{M}\{0,1\}$, and the structure this induces on $\mathbb{VM}\{0,1\}$, as follows:

Definition 5. *For each $n \geq 1$, we let $\mathbb{M}_n = \cup_{k \leq n}\{x\checkmark, x\bot \mid x \in \{0,1\}^k\}$. We also define $\pi_n \colon \mathbb{M}\{0,1\} \longrightarrow \mathbb{M}_n$ by $\pi_n(x) = \begin{cases} x & \text{if } x \in \mathbb{M}_n, \\ x_1 \cdots x_n \bot & \text{if } x \notin \mathbb{M}_n. \end{cases}$*

If $m \leq n$, let $\pi_{m,n} \colon \mathbb{M}_n \longrightarrow \mathbb{M}_m$ by $\pi_{m,n}(x) = \begin{cases} x & \text{if } x \in \mathbb{M}_m, \\ x_1 \cdots x_m \bot & \text{if } x \in \mathbb{M}_n \backslash \mathbb{M}_m. \end{cases}$

Note that $\pi_m = \pi_{m,n} \circ \pi_n$ for $m \leq n$.

Proposition 7. $\mathbb{M}\{0,1\} \simeq \mathrm{bilim}\,(\mathbb{M}_n, \pi_{m,n}, \iota_{m,n})$*, where $\iota_{m,n} \colon \mathbb{M}_m \hookrightarrow \mathbb{M}_n$ is the inclusion. Moreover, $\mathbb{V}\mathbb{M}\{0,1\} = \mathrm{proj}\lim_n (\mathbb{V}\mathbb{M}_n, \mathbb{V}\pi_{m,n})$.*

Proof. It's straightforward to verify that $\iota_{m,n} \colon \mathbb{M}_m \longrightarrow \mathbb{M}_n \colon \pi_{m,n}$ forms an embedding–projection pair for $m \leq n$, and then it follows that $\mathbb{M}\{0,1\} = \mathrm{bilim}\,(\mathbb{M}_n, \pi_{m,n}, \iota_{m,n})$. This implies $\mathbb{M}\{0,1\} \simeq \mathrm{proj}\lim_n (\mathbb{M}_n, \pi_{m,n})$ in the Scott topologies, and the same argument as in the proof of Theorem 1 shows this also holds for the Lawson topology. Then the same argument we used in the proof of Theorem 4 implies $\mathrm{Prob}\,\mathbb{M}\{0,1\} \simeq \lim_n (\mathrm{Prob}\,\mathbb{M}_n, \mathrm{Prob}\,\pi_{m,n})$ and $\mathbb{V}\mathbb{M}\{0,1\} \simeq \mathrm{proj}\lim_n (\mathbb{V}\mathbb{M}_n, \mathbb{V}\pi_{m,n})$.

Corollary 2. *If D is a domain, we define:*

- $CRV_n(D) = \{(\mathbb{V}\pi_n\,\mu, X|_{supp_\Sigma\,\mathbb{V}\pi_n\,\mu}) \mid (\mu, X) \in CRV(D)\}$, *and*
- $\varPi_n \colon CRV(D) \longrightarrow CRV_n(D)$ *by* $\varPi_n(\mu, X) = (\mathbb{V}\pi_n\,\mu, X|_{supp_\Sigma\,\mathbb{V}\pi_n\,\mu})$.

Then $CRV_n(D) \subseteq CRV(D)$ and $\mathbf{1}_{CRV(D)} = \sup_n \varPi_n$.

Proof. This follows from Propositions 3 and 7.

For CRV to define a monad, we have to show how to lift a mapping $h \colon D \longrightarrow CRV(E)$ to a mapping $h^\dagger \colon CRV(D) \longrightarrow CRV(E)$ satisfying the laws listed in Lemma 4 below. Corollary 2 reduces the problem to showing the following:

Given $h \colon D \longrightarrow CRV(E)$, let $h_n = \varPi_n \circ h \colon D \longrightarrow CRV_n(D)$. Then there is a mapping $h_n^\dagger \colon CRV_n(D) \longrightarrow CRV_n(E)$, satisfying the monad laws listed in Lemma 4 below for each n.

Since $CRV_n(E)$ has two components, we let $h_n^\dagger = (h_{n,1}, h_{n,2})$. Using this notation, we note the following:

If $(\sum_{x \in F} r_x \delta_x, X) \in CRV_n(D)$, then for each $x \in F$

$$h_{n,1}(X(x)) = \sum_{y \in G_x} s_y \delta_y \in \mathbb{V}\mathbb{M}_n,$$

where G_x denotes the set on which the simple measure $h_{n,1}X(x)$ is concentrated for each $x \in F$. Moreover,

$$h_{n,1}(\sum_{x \in F} r_x \delta_x, X) = \sum_{x \in F} r_x(\delta_x * \sum_{y \in G_x} s_y \delta_y)$$

$$= \sum_{x \in F} \sum_{y \in G_x} r_x s_y \delta_{x \cdot y}.$$

This implies $\text{supp}_{\Sigma} h_{n,1}(\sum_{x \in F} r_x \delta_x) = \bigcup_{x \in F} \downarrow x \cdot G_x = \bigcup_{x \in F \& y \in G_x} \downarrow (x \cdot y)$.

Definition 6. *We define* $h_n^{\dagger} = (h_{n,1}, h_{n,2}) \colon CRV_n(D) \longrightarrow CRV_n(E)$, *where*
- $h_{n,1}(\sum_{x \in F} r_x \delta_x, X) = \sum_{x \in F} r_x(\delta_x * h_{n,1}(X(x)))$
  $= \sum_{x \in F} r_x(\delta_x * \sum_{y \in G_x} s_y \delta_y)$, *and*
- $h_{n,2}(\sum_{x \in F} r_x \delta_x, X) \colon \text{supp}_{\sum_{x \in F} r_x(\delta_x * \sum_{y \in G_x} s_y \delta_y)} \longrightarrow E$ *by*
  $h_{n,2}(\sum_{x \in F} r_x \delta_x, X)(z)$
  $\qquad = \wedge \{h_{n,2}(X(x'))(y') \mid z \leq x' \cdot y', x' \leq x \in F, y' \leq y \in G_x\}$

Lemma 4. *Given* $h \colon D \longrightarrow CRV(E)$, *the mapping* $h_n^{\dagger} \colon CRV_n(D) \longrightarrow CRV_n(E)$ *satisfies the monad laws:*
(1) If $\eta_D \colon D \longrightarrow CRV(D)$ *is* $\eta_D(d) = (\delta_{\checkmark}, \chi_d)$, *then*
  $\eta_D^{\dagger} \colon CRV_n(D) \longrightarrow CRV_n(D)$ *is the identity;*
(2) $h_n^{\dagger} \circ \eta_D = h_n$; *and*
(3) If $k \colon CRV(E) \longrightarrow CRV(P)$ *and* $k_n = \Pi_n \circ k$, *then* $(k_n^{\dagger} \circ h_n)^{\dagger} = k_n^{\dagger} \circ h_n^{\dagger}$.

Proof. (1) Note that $\eta_D(D) \subseteq CRV_n(D)$ for each $n \geq 1$, so $\Pi_n \circ \eta_D = \eta_D$. Then $(\eta_D^{\dagger})_1(\sum_{x \in F} r_x \delta_x, X) = \sum_{x \in F} r_x(\delta_x * \delta_{\checkmark}) = \sum_{x \in F} r_x \delta_x$, and $(\eta_D^{\dagger})_2(\sum_{x \in F} r_x \delta_x, X)(z) = \wedge\{(\eta_D)_2(X(x'))(y') \mid z \leq x' \cdot y', x' \leq x \in F, y' \leq \checkmark\}$

$$= \begin{cases} \chi_{X(z)}(\checkmark) & \text{if } z \in \{0,1\}^* \checkmark \\ \chi_{X(z)}(\bot) & \text{if } z \in \{0,1\}^* \bot \end{cases} = X(z).$$

(2) If $h_{n,1}(d) = \sum_{x \in F} r_x \delta_x$, then
$h_{n,1}(\delta_{\checkmark}, \chi_d) = \sum_{x \in F} r_x(\delta_x * \delta_{\checkmark}) = \sum_{x \in F} r_x \delta_x$. Likewise,
$h_{n,2}(\delta_{\checkmark}, \chi_d)(z)$
$\qquad = \wedge\{h_{n,2}(\chi_d(x'))(y') \mid z \leq x' \cdot y', x' \leq \checkmark, y' \leq y \in G_{\checkmark}\}$

$$= h_{n,2}(d)(y') = \begin{cases} h_{n,2}(d)(z) & \text{if } \bot < z \\ h_{n,2}(d)(\bot) & \text{if } z = \bot \end{cases} = h_{n,2}(\eta_D(d)).$$

(3) $k_n^{\dagger} \circ h_n^{\dagger}(\sum_{x \in F} r_x \delta_x, X)$
$= k_n^{\dagger}(h_{n,1}(\sum_{x \in F} r_x \delta_x, X), h_{n,2}(\sum_{x \in F} r_x \delta_x, X))$
$= (k_{n,1}(h_{n,1}(\sum_{x \in F} r_x \delta_x, X), h_{n,2}(\sum_{x \in F} r_x \delta_x, X)),$
$\qquad k_{n,2}(h_{n,1}(\sum_{x \in F} r_x \delta_x, X), h_{n,2}(\sum_{x \in F} r_x \delta_x, X))).$
Now, $k_{n,1}(h_{n,1}(\sum_{x \in F} r_x \delta_x, X), h_{n,2}(\sum_{x \in F} r_x \delta_x, X))$
$= k_{n,1}(\sum_{x \in F} r_x(\delta_x * (\sum_{y \in G_x} s_y \delta_y)), h_{n,2}(\sum_{x \in F} r_x \delta_x, X))$
$= k_{n,1}(\sum_{x \in F} \sum_{y \in G_x} r_x s_y \delta_{x \cdot y}, h_{n,2}(\sum_{x \in F} r_x \delta_x, X))$
$= \sum_{x \in F \& y \in G_x} r_x s_y(\delta_{x \cdot y} * k_{n,1}(h_{n,2}(\sum_{x \in F} r_x \delta_x, X)(x \cdot y))).$
On the other hand,
$(k_n^{\dagger} \circ h_n)^{\dagger}(\sum_{x \in F} r_x \delta_x, X)$

$$= ((k_n^\dagger \circ h_n)_1(\textstyle\sum_{x\in F} r_x\delta_x, X), (k_n^\dagger \circ h_n)_2(\textstyle\sum_{x\in F} r_x\delta_x, X))$$
$$= (\textstyle\sum_{x\in F} r_x(\delta_x * k_n^\dagger \circ h_{n,1}(X(x)),$$
$$\quad (k_n^\dagger \circ h_n)_2(\textstyle\sum_{x\in F} r_x\delta_x, X))$$
$$= (\textstyle\sum_{x\in F} r_x(\delta_x * (k_n^\dagger)_1(\textstyle\sum_{y\in G_x} s_y\delta_y, h_{n,2}(\textstyle\sum_{x\in F} r_x\delta_x, X)),$$
$$\quad (k_n^\dagger \circ h_n)_2(\textstyle\sum_{x\in F} r_x\delta_x, X))$$
$$= (\textstyle\sum_{x\in F} r_x(\delta_x * (\textstyle\sum_{y\in G_x} s_y(\delta_y * k_{n,1}(h_{n,2}(\textstyle\sum_{x\in F} r_x\delta_x, X)(x\cdot y)))),$$
$$\quad (k_n^\dagger \circ h_n)_2(\textstyle\sum_{x\in F} r_x\delta_x, X)))$$

We conclude that
$$(k_n^\dagger \circ h_n^\dagger)_1(\textstyle\sum_{x\in F} r_x\delta_x, X)$$
$$\quad = k_{n,1}(h_{n,1}(\textstyle\sum_{x\in F} r_x\delta_x, X), h_{n,2}(\textstyle\sum_{x\in F} r_x\delta_x, X))$$
$$\quad = \textstyle\sum_{x\in F \,\&\, y\in G_x} r_x s_y(\delta_{x\cdot y} * k_{n,1}(h_{n,2}(\textstyle\sum_{x\in F} r_x\delta_x, X)(x\cdot y))))$$
$$\quad = \textstyle\sum_{x\in F} r_x(\delta_x * (\textstyle\sum_{y\in G_x} s_y(\delta_y * k_{n,1}(h_{n,2}(\textstyle\sum_{x\in F} r_x\delta_x, X)(x\cdot y))))$$
$$\quad = (k_n^\dagger \circ h_n)_1(\textstyle\sum_{x\in F} r_x\delta_x, X),$$

which shows the first components of $k_n^\dagger \circ h_n^\dagger$ and $(k_n^\dagger \circ h_n)^\dagger$ agree. A similar (laborious) argument proves the second components agree as well.

Theorem 6. *The functor CRV defines a monad on BCD.*

Proof. This follows from Lemma 4 and Corollary 2.

Remark 2. As noted earlier, if M is a compact monoid, convolution satisfies $(\mu * \nu)(A) = (\mu \times \nu)\{(x, y) \in M \times M \mid xy \in A\}$, so it is a mapping $*\colon \mathsf{Prob}(M) \times \mathsf{Prob}(M) \longrightarrow \mathsf{Prob}(M)$. Our use of $*$ in Theorem 6 is of a different character, since we are integrating along a measure μ to obtain a measure $\widehat{f}(\mu, X) = \int_x df \circ X(x) * \mu(x)$, where $f\colon CRV(D) \longrightarrow \mathbb{VM}\{0, 1\}$.

3.4   CRV and Continuous Probability Measures

An accepted model for probabilistic choice is a probabilistic Turing machine, a Turing machine equipped with an second infinite tape containing a random sequence of bits. As a computation unfolds, the machine can consult the random tape from time to time and use the next random bit as a mechanism for making a choice. The source of randomness is not usually defined, and in a sense, it's immaterial. But it's common to assume that the same source is used throughout the computation – i.e., there's a single probability measure that's governing the sequence of random bits written on the tape.

In the models described in [9] and in [3], the idea of the random tape is captured by the Cantor tree $\mathbb{CT} = \bigcup_n \mathcal{C}_n \cup \mathcal{C}$, where the "single source of randomness" arises naturally as a measure μ on the Cantor set (at the top). That measure μ can be realized as $\mu = \sup_n \phi_n \mu$, where $\phi_n\colon \mathcal{C} \longrightarrow \mathcal{C}_n$ is the natural projection. As a concrete example, one can take μ to be Haar measure on $\mathcal{C}$ regarded as an infinite product of two-point groups, and then μ_n is the normalized uniform measure on $\mathcal{C}_n \simeq 2^n$. Then the possible sequence of outcomes of coin tosses on a particular computation are represented by a single path through the tree $\mathbb{CT}$, and the results at the nth-level are governed by the distribution

$\phi_n \, \mu$. The outcome at that level is used to define choices in the semantic domain D via a random variable $X \colon \mathcal{C}_n \longrightarrow D$ for each n.

The same ideas permeate our model CRV, but our structure is different. The mappings $\phi_n \colon \mathbb{CT} \longrightarrow \mathcal{C}_n$ are replaced in our model by the mappings

$$\pi_n \colon \mathbb{M}\{0,1\} \longrightarrow \mathbb{M}_n \text{ given by } \pi_n(x) = \begin{cases} x & \text{if } x \in \mathbb{M}_n \\ x_1 \cdots x_n \bot & \text{if } |x \notin \mathbb{M}_n \end{cases}$$

described in Definition 5. Then $\mathbb{M}_n$ is a retract of $\mathbb{M}\{0,1\}$ under π_n.

To realize *any* measure μ concentrated on $\mathcal{C} \subseteq \mathbb{M}\{0,1\}$, and the measures μ_n, we define new projections $\rho_n \colon \mathcal{C} \longrightarrow \mathcal{C}_n \checkmark$ from the Cantor set of maximal elements of $\mathbb{M}\{0,1\}$ to the n-bit words ending with $\checkmark$ in the obvious fashion. These mappings are continuous, but their images $\mu_n = \rho_n \, \mu$ are incomparable (since the set $\mathcal{C}_n \checkmark \subseteq \operatorname{Max} \mathbb{M}\{0,1\}$ for each n). Nevertheless, Proposition 5 implies the sequence $\rho_n \, \mu \longrightarrow \mu$ in $\mathbb{M}\{0,1\}$ in the Lawson topology. From a computational perspective, we can consider the related measures $\pi_m \mu = \nu_m$, then $\nu_m \le \mu_n$ for each m and each $n \ge m$. But $\mu = \sup_m \nu_m$ since $\mathbf{1}_{\mathbb{M}\{0,1\}} = \sup_m \pi_m$, and then $\nu_m \le \mu_n$ for $n \ge m$ implies $\mu_n \longrightarrow \mu$ in the Scott topology, since $\nu_m \ll \mu$ for each m.

4 Summary and Future Work

We have constructed a new monad for probabilistic choice using domain theory. The model consists of pairs (μ, X), where $\mu \in \mathbb{VM}\{0,1\}$ and $X \colon \operatorname{supp}_\Sigma \mu \longrightarrow D$ is a Scott-continuous random variables that defines the choices in the semantic domain D. The fact that CRV forms a monad relies crucially on the convolution operation on $\mathbb{VM}\{0,1\}$ that arises from the monoid operation on $\mathbb{M}\{0,1\}$, and the new order on $\mathbb{M}\{0,1\}$, rather than the prefix order on the set of finite and infinite words over $\{0,1\}$.

Our construction is focused on bounded complete domains, in order to utilize the inf-operation to define the Kleisli lift – in particular, in the random variable component of a pair (μ, X). One fault that was identified in the monad $\mathbb{V}$ is its lack of a distributive law over and of the power domains, which model nondeterministic choice. But here we see that we must assume the domain of values for our random variables already must support nondeterminism, since it arises naturally when one composes random variables (cf. Subsect. 3.2).

With all the theory, one might rightfully ask for some examples. An obvious target would be the models of CSP, starting with the seminal paper [5]. Morgan, McIver and their colleagues [18] have developed an extensive theory of CSP with probabilistic choice modeled by applying the sub-probability monad $\mathbb{V}$ to CSP models. It would be interesting to compare the model developed here, as applied, e.g., to the model in [18].

Acknowledgement. The author wishes to thank Tyler Barker for some very helpful discussions on the topic of monads of random variables.

References

1. Abramsky, S., Jung, A.: Domain Theory. In: Handbook of Logic in Computer Science, pp. 1–168. Clarendon Press, Oxford (1994)
2. Alvarez-Manilla, M., Edalat, A., Saheb-Djahromi, N.: An extension result for continuous valuations. J. Lond. Math. Soc. **61**(2), 629–640 (2000)
3. Barker, T.: A Monad for Randomized Algorithms. Tulane University Ph.D. dissertation (2016)
4. van Breugel, F., Mislove, M., Ouaknine, J., Worrell, J.: Domain theory, testing and simulations for labelled Markov processes. Theor. Comput. Sci. **333**, 171–197 (2005)
5. Brookes, S.D., Hoare, C.A.R., Roscoe, A.W.: A theory of communicating sequential processes. J. ACM **31**, 560–599 (1984)
6. Fedorchuk, V.: Covariant functors in the category of compacta, absolute retracts, and Q-manifolds. Russ. Math. Surv. **36**, 211–233 (1981)
7. Fedorchuk, V.: Probability measures in topology. Russ. Math. Surv. **46**, 45–93 (1991)
8. Gierz, G., Hofmann, K.H., Lawson, J.D., Mislove, M., Scott, D.: Continuous Lattices and Domains. Cambridge University Press, Cambridge (2003)
9. Goubault-Larrecq, J., Varacca, D.: Continuous random variables. In: LICS 2011, pp. 97–106. IEEE Press (2011)
10. Hofmann, K.H., Mislove, M.: Compact affine monoids, harmonic analysis and information theory. In: Mathematical Foundations of Information Flow, AMS Symposia on Applied Mathematics, vol. 71, pp. 125–182 (2012)
11. Jones, C.: Probabilistic nondeterminism, Ph.D. thesis. University of Edinburgh (1988)
12. Jung, A., Tix, R.: The troublesome probabilistic powerdomain. ENTCS **13**, 70–91 (1998)
13. Keimel, K.: The monad of probability measures over compact ordered spaces and its Eilenberg-Moore algebras, preprint (2008). http://www.mathematik. tu-darmstadt.de/~keimel/Papers/probmonadfinal1.pdf
14. Mislove, M.: Topology, domain theory and theoretical computer science. Topol. Appl. **89**, 3–59 (1998)
15. Mislove, M.: Discrete random variables over domains. Theor. Comput. Sci. **380**, 181–198 (2007). Special Issue on Automata, Languages and Programming
16. Mislove, M.: Anatomy of a domain of continuous random variables I. Theor. Comput. Sci. **546**, 176–187 (2014)
17. Mislove, M.: Anatomy of a domain of continuous random variables ll. In: Coecke, B., Ong, L., Panangaden, P. (eds.) Computation, Logic, Games, and Quantum Foundations. The Many Facets of Samson Abramsky. LNCS, vol. 7860, pp. 225–245. Springer, Heidelberg (2013). doi:10.1007/978-3-642-38164-5_16
18. Morgan, C.A., McIver, K., Seidel, J.W.: Saunders: a probabilistic process algebra including demonic nondeterminism. Formal Aspects Comput. **8**, 617–647 (1994)
19. Saheb-Djahromi, N.: CPOs of measures for nondeterminism. Theor. Comput. Sci. **12**, 19–37 (1980)
20. Swirszcz, T.: Monadic functors and convexity. Bulletin de l'Académie Polonaise des Sciences, Série des sciences math. astr. et phys. **22**, 39–42 (1974)
21. Varacca, D.: Two denotational models for probabilistic computation, Ph.D. thesis. Aarhus University (2003)
22. Varacca, D., Winskel, G.: Distributing probabililty over nondeterminism. Math. Struct. Comput. Sci. **16**(1), 87–113 (2006)

A Demonic Lattice of Information

Carroll Morgan[⊠]

University of New South Wales, and Data61, Sydney, Australia
carroll.morgan@unsw.edu.au

Abstract. Landuaer and Redmond's *Lattice of Information* was an early and influential formalisation of the pure structure of security [8]: a partial order was defined for information-flow from a hidden state. In modern terms we would say that more-security *refines* less-security. For Landauer, the deterministic case [op. cit.], the refinement order is a lattice.

Very recently [3,9] a similar approach has been taken to purely probabilistic systems and there too a refinement order can be defined; but it is not a lattice [12].

In between deterministic and probabilistic is demonic, where behaviour is not deterministic but also not quantifiable. We show that our own earlier approach to this [15,16] fits into the same pattern as deterministic and probabilistic, and illustrate that with results concerning compositionality, testing, soundness and completeness. Finally, we make some remarks about source-level reasoning.

1 A *Deterministic* Lattice of Information — The Original

1.1 Historical Introduction and Intuition

Landauer and Redmond proposed in 1993 *A Lattice of Information* [8] for deterministic channels that accept hidden input and produce visible output. The "information" in Landauer's title is what the channel's output tells an observer about the input that we are trying to hide from her.[1]

Definition 1. *Deterministic channel* _____ Given non-empty *input space* $\mathcal{I}$ and *output space* $\mathcal{O}$, a *deterministic channel* is a total function from $\mathcal{I}$ to $\mathcal{O}$. For channel $C: \mathcal{I} \to \mathcal{O}$, an input i in $\mathcal{I}$ produces an output $C(i)$ in $\mathcal{O}$. □

With "deterministic" we emphasise that for any input i the channel C always outputs the same output o, that is $o = C(i)$.

Take for the input space $\mathcal{I}$ the letters $\{A, B, E, W\}$, and let the output space $\mathcal{O}^1$ be $\{\text{VOWEL}, \text{CONS}\}$ for "vowel" or "consonant"; then define channel $C^1: \mathcal{I} \to \mathcal{O}^1$ in the obvious way. Define another channel $C^2: \mathcal{I} \to \mathcal{O}^2$ where $\mathcal{O}^2$ is $\{\text{EARLY}, \text{LATE}\}$ for "early" or "late" in the alphabet. These two channels $C^{1,2}$

---

[1] We use the feminine she/her consistently for adversaries. Plural we/us is used for the designers or users of programs, or the readers of this article; and neuter "it" or plural "they" is used for third parties.

© Springer International Publishing AG 2017
T. Gibson-Robinson et al. (Eds.): Roscoe Festschrift, LNCS 10160, pp. 203–222, 2017.
DOI: 10.1007/978-3-319-51046-0_11

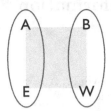

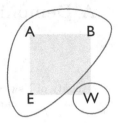

(a) VOWEL/CONS partition for C^1 (b) EARLY/LATE partition for C^2

Fig. 1. Partitions induced on $\mathcal{I}$ by the channels C^1 and C^2

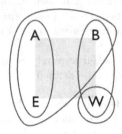

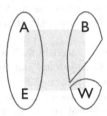

(a) Both cookie-cutters applied   (b) The meet is finer than both.

Fig. 2. Induced partitions

have different output spaces $\mathcal{O}^{1,2}$ (but the same input space) because they are observing different things. We compare them therefore only wrt. the information they release about their inputs: the precise values of their outputs will be seen to be irrelevant.

Each channel induces a partition on $\mathcal{I}$ via the kernels of the functions $C^{1,2}$, as shown in Fig. 1, where the partitions' cells show just which elements of $\mathcal{I}$ can be distinguished by an observer who sees the output of the channel: two input elements can be distinguished by an observer just when they are not in the same cell. Thus Fig. 1(a) shows that B, W cannot be distinguished by an observer of C^1's output, because they are both consonants; but Fig. 1(b) shows that B, W can be distinguished by C^2, because B is early but W is late.

In general we write $\mathbb{E}\mathcal{I}$ for the set of partitions of $\mathcal{I}$; clearly $\mathbb{E}\mathcal{I}$ is a subset of the powerset $\mathbb{P}\mathcal{I}$ of $\mathcal{I}$, and there is partial order that relates two partitions in $\mathbb{E}\mathcal{I}$ just when one can be formed from the other by dividing cells into smaller pieces (or, in the opposite direction, by merging cells). It is a lattice because both meet (greatest lower bound) and join (least upper bound) are defined. The meet can be visualised by thinking of partitions as "cookie cutters", with set $\mathcal{I}$ being the "dough" and *both* partitions

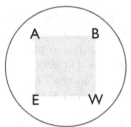

Fig. 3. The join is coarser than both $C^{1,2}$.

applied, one on top of the other: the pieces formed by both cookie-cuts together determine the cells of the meet, shown for C^1 and C^2 in Fig. 2. It is the least informative channel that reveals as much about the input as each of $C^{1,2}$ does: for example the meet must distinguish A, B because C^1 does, and it must distinguish B, W because C^2 does. Complementarily, the join is the most informative channel that reveals no more than $C^{1,2}$ and is shown in Fig. 3: in this case it is the channel that reveals nothing.[2] Note that none of these constructions –neither the partial order, nor the meet/join– require details of output sets $\mathcal{O}^{1,2}$; only the partitions induced by the channels are important.

In software engineering the refinement order relates specifications S to implementations P just when P is as good as or better than S according to precise criteria set by the user. The available criteria are determined carefully, even "legally", beforehand and can be seen as the terms of reference available for writing contracts between user and supplier. Normally, program-refinement is written $S \sqsubseteq P$, that specification S is *refined by* implementation P. Since here our focus is on security, we consider "revealing less" to be better than "revealing more", so that we would write (exhaustively) for the examples above

$$\text{Fig. 2(b)} \sqsubseteq \text{Fig. 1(a)} \qquad\qquad \text{Fig. 1(a)} \sqsubseteq \text{Fig. 3}$$
$$\text{Fig. 2(b)} \sqsubseteq \text{Fig. 1(b)} \qquad\qquad \text{Fig. 1(b)} \sqsubseteq \text{Fig. 3}$$
$$\text{Fig. 2(b)} = \text{Fig. 1(a)} \sqcap \text{Fig. 1(b)} \qquad \text{Fig. 3} = \text{Fig. 1(a)} \sqcup \text{Fig. 1(b)}.$$

This shows (unfortunately) that the mathematical term "partition refinement" (finer cells) and the computer-science term "program refinement" (fewer distinctions made, less information revealed, better for the user) go exactly in opposite directions. We follow the Computer-Science convention.

1.2 Definition of Secure Refinement for Channels

The definition of secure refinement for deterministic channels is that for $S\colon \mathcal{I} \to \mathcal{O}^S$ and $P\colon \mathcal{I} \to \mathcal{O}^P$ we have $S \sqsubseteq P$ just when there is a refinement-function $R\colon \mathcal{O}^S \to \mathcal{O}^P$ such that $P = R \circ S$. The relation ($\sqsubseteq$) is reflexive and transitive (obviously), and it is antisymmetric. Note that channels can be in refinement even when their output spaces differ.

The intuition for its definition is that having such an R means that P's output cannot tell you anything you do not already know, at least implicitly, from the output of S: that is if you know o^S (i.e. $S(i)$), then you do not need to run P to know o^P as well (i.e. $P(i)$) — it is simply $R(o^S)$, i.e. determined by the result o^S you already have, precisely because $P = R \circ S$.

---

[2] Although both C^1 and C^2 distinguish A, W, their join cannot. Because C^2 does not distinguish A, B, the join cannot; it can't distinguish B, W because C^1 does not: by transitivity therefore the join must regard A, W as equal. The same applies to E, W.

An equivalent formulation of refinement is to see S, P, R as Boolean matrices, with for example $S_{i,o} = \textit{true}$ just when $S.i = o$, as in Fig. 4.[3] Because the channels S, P are deterministic (and total) the corresponding matrices have exactly one *true* in each row, and the induced cells are given by the matrix columns, with *true* entries identifying members of the cell corresponding to that column. Similarly because R represents a function, it too has exactly one *true* in each row. With matrices the formulation of refinement is that if channel S is a Boolean $\mathcal{I} \times \mathcal{O}^S$ matrix and channel P is a Boolean $\mathcal{I} \times \mathcal{O}^P$ matrix then $S \sqsubseteq P$ just when there is a Boolean $\mathcal{O}^S \times \mathcal{O}^P$ matrix R such that $P = SR$.[4]

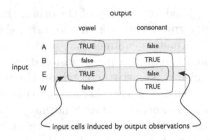

Fig. 4. Matrix representation of a deterministic channel

Figure 5 shows how the meet of $C^{1,2}$ in Fig. 2(b) is refined in this style, i.e by a matrix R by a matrix to C^1. Notice that the column-labels $0, 1, 2$ of the meet (and the rows of the refinement matrix, in the middle) have no external significance: this emphasises that it is the partition of the input cells, alone, that indicates the information flow induced by a channel. Figure 6 uses a different matrix R' to refine the same meet to C^2 instead.

	0	1	2
A	TRUE	false	false
B	false	TRUE	false
E	TRUE	false	false
W	false	false	TRUE

$\times$

	vowel	consonant
0	TRUE	false
1	false	TRUE
2	false	TRUE

$=$

	vowel	consonant
A	TRUE	false
B	false	TRUE
E	TRUE	false
W	false	TRUE

The column labels 0,1,2 for the matrix representing $C^1 \sqcap C^2$ are chosen arbitrarily.

Fig. 5. Refinement of $C^1 \sqcap C^2$ to C^1.

	0	1	2
A	TRUE	false	false
B	false	TRUE	false
E	TRUE	false	false
W	false	false	TRUE

$\times$

	early	late
0	TRUE	false
1	TRUE	false
2	false	TRUE

$=$

	early	late
A	TRUE	false
B	TRUE	false
E	TRUE	false
W	false	TRUE

Fig. 6. Refinement of $C^1 \sqcap C^2$ to C^2.

---

[3] For matrix M indexed by r, c we write $M_{r,c}$ for the value in row r and column c.
[4] We write SR for the matrix multiplication of S and R.

1.3   Testing, Soundness and Completeness

In Sect. 1.2 the refinement function, eqv. matrix, is a witness to the refinement $S \sqsubseteq P$, showing not only that the partition cells induced by S can be merged to form the cells of P, but actually how to do it; the existence of such an R is in fact refinement's definition. In principle this gives a method for constructing implementations P from specifications S, a "security by design" approach where suitable matrices R guide the programmer's efforts.

The complementary problem however is how a customer should convince a court that $S \not\sqsubseteq K$, that when he bought S but got K he was cheated.[5] It's not practical to go through all the (infinitely many) potential R matrices and show the court, for each one, that $P \neq SR$.[6] Just as R provides a witness for $(\sqsubseteq)$, we need a witness for $(\not\sqsubseteq)$ too.

In this deterministic setting a witness for $(\not\sqsubseteq)$ is a subset ι of $\mathcal{I}$ such that some cell of K is a subset of ι but no cell of S is a subset of ι. Intuitively this means that there is a "Could we have let slip that i is an ι?" test that K would *fail* by revealing some cell $\kappa \subseteq \iota$, since K cannot release κ unless $i \in \kappa$. Because no cell σ of S satisfies $\sigma \subseteq \iota$, that slip was excluded by the specification.

These two witnesses, refinement matrix R for $(\sqsubseteq)$ and subset ι of $\mathcal{I}$ for $(\not\sqsubseteq)$, are related by "soundness" and "completeness". *Soundness* says that whenever $S \sqsubseteq X$, i.e. there exists a suitable witness R for refinement, then there cannot be any refuting witness ι that (inconsistently) would establish $S \not\sqsubseteq X$. In intuitive terms, it is that if a software engineer follows sound practices then he will never lose a court case. *Completeness* says that whenever $S \not\sqsubseteq X$, i.e. there is no refinement witness R, then there exists a refuting witness ι of that; we do not have to try (and reject) every single R.

Another way of looking at soundness and completeness in practical terms is as follows. On the one hand we want $(\sqsubseteq)$ to be weak, since the weaker it is the more implementation strategies are available to the engineer and the less he will charge for his work. But it cannot be *too* weak, e.g. the universal relation, since then he could build faulty implementations: this is soundness. On the other hand, we want $(\sqsubseteq)$ to be strong, since the stronger it is the less likely it is that implementations will disappoint their customers. But it cannot be *too* strong, e.g. the identity, since in that case the engineer will have so few design options that his products will be expensive or even impracticable. This is completeness.

And finally, we can think of witness R as a method of construction, whereas ι is a method of testing. Follow R and our implementation P is guaranteed at least as secure as the specification S (soundness); but if we simply dream-up (i.e. cobble together) a product without such an R, and in fact there turns out not to be one, then there will be a test ι that S will pass but K will fail (completeness). And we might meet that ι in a courtroom.

---

[5] The mnemonics are S for Specification and P for an imPlementation (or Program) that is supposed to refine S, and K for a "Kludge" that, as an example, in fact does not refine S. In uncommitted cases, neither P nor K, we will use X.

[6] In the probabilistic case Sect. 2, there would be infinitely many R's to check: it would literally take forever.

2 A Probabilistic Partial Order (Not Lattice) of Information

The probabilistic analogue of the deterministic case Sect. 1 is communication channels with probabilistic transmission [17]. Here the input is a message to be sent and the output is the message received, chosen from a distribution determined by the input. The traditional representation of such channels is stochastic matrices where, real numbers in each row i give for each column o the probability that input i will result in output o. Deterministic channels are special cases of probabilistic channels, where *true* is probability 1 and *false* is probability 0.

As shown elsewhere [1–3,5,9–11,13,14] and mentioned above, there is a probabilistic analogue of secure refinement $S \sqsubseteq P$ that can be formulated as a generalisation of Sect. 1.2: the refinement matrix R is now stochastic, representing a "probabilistic merge" of S-outputs to P-outputs mediated by R such that again $P = SR$. This relation (between matrices) is reflexive and transitive (obviously). But it is not antisymmetric: for that we quotient to *abstract channels* where all-zero columns are removed, similar columns are merged and the order of (the remaining) columns is ignored [14].[7] Unfortunately the resulting abstracted partial order is not a lattice [12] but, aside from that, it shares many structural properties with deterministic refinement. In particular there are probabilistic analogues of soundness and completeness, with tests based on "gain functions" over $\mathcal{I}$ which are more general than the subsets of $\mathcal{I}$ that suffice for deterministic channels [3,9].[8]

3 A Demonic Lattice of Information

3.1 Basic Structure

With Sects. 1 and 2 as motivating examples, we now treat our main topic: the demonic case, where observations are not necessarily wholly determined by the inputs, but we have no quantitative information about possible variations. This was earlier proposed in [15,16], but the probabilisitic model Sect. 2 was not known (we believe) at that time.

Definition 2. *Demonic channel: matrix formulation* ——————— A demonic channel from $\mathcal{I}$ to $\mathcal{O}$ is a Boolean matrix with $\mathcal{I}$-indexed rows and $\mathcal{O}$-indexed columns in which each row has at least one *true* element.   □

Whereas deterministic channels induce partitions on their input-space $\mathcal{I}$, demonic channels induce more generally simply sets of subsets of $\mathcal{I}$, i.e. like

---

[7] The identity matrix is stochastic, and the product of two stochastic matrices is stochastic. Matrix columns are *similar* just when each is a multiple of the other. Column order can then be ignored by representing the matrix as a set of (the remaining) columns.

[8] The completeness property was called the *Coriaceous Conjecture* in [3]. It was proved in [1,9] and, it turns out, earlier by [4].

partitions but allowing the cells to overlap. The overlaps occur just for those i-rows containing more than one *true*: those shared i's "belong" more to than one o-column, i.e. to more than one cell.[9] We now give a more abstract definition in those terms.

Definition 3. *Secure refinement for demonic channels: matrix formulation*
——————— A demonic "specification" channel $S: \mathcal{I} \twoheadrightarrow \mathcal{O}^S$ is secure-refined by an "implementation" channel $P: \mathcal{I} \twoheadrightarrow \mathcal{O}^P$ just when there is a demonic matrix $R: \mathcal{O}^S \twoheadrightarrow \mathcal{O}^P$ such that $P = SR$ where R is also a demonic channel.[10] We write $S \sqsubseteq P$ for that.   □

The similarity between the three models is striking: in each case refinement is post-multiplication by a matrix of the same kind.

Demonic (secure-) refinement is reflexive and transitive but, as we observe in the example below, and as in the probabilistic case Sect. 2, the relation is not anti-symmetric: so far, we have only a pre-order.

Each column of the refinement matrix R makes a cell in P by taking the union of the S-cells that have *true* in that column. With that insight, we can rephrase Definition 3 as

$$S \text{ is (demonic/secure) refined by } P \text{ iff for every cell of } P \atop \text{there is a set of cells of } S \text{ of which it is the union.} \tag{1}$$

Put still another way, every cell of the more-refined P must be "justified" as the union of some set of cells in the less-refined S. An example of anti-symmetry's failure is then that $X = \{\{i_0\}, \{i_1\}, \{i_0, i_1\}, \{i_0, i_1, i_2\}\}$ and $Y = \{\{i_0\}, \{i_1\}, \{i_0, i_1, i_2\}\}$ refine each other: to refine X to Y ignore the cell $\{i_0, i_1\}$ in X; to refine Y back to X merge the $\{i_0\}$ and $\{i_1\}$ in Y to replace the $\{i_0, i_1\}$ in X. Using matrices with 1 for *true* and 0 for *false*, with matrices we would have for X to Y the refinement

$$
\begin{array}{cccc}
 & X & R & Y \\
\hline
\begin{matrix} i_0 \\ i_1 \\ i_2 \end{matrix} &
\begin{pmatrix} 1 & 0 & 1 & 1 \\ 0 & 1 & 1 & 1 \\ 0 & 0 & 0 & 1 \end{pmatrix} &
\begin{pmatrix} 1 & 0 & 0 \\ 0 & 1 & 0 \\ 0 & 0 & 1 \\ 0 & 0 & 1 \end{pmatrix} = &
\begin{pmatrix} 1 & 0 & 1 \\ 0 & 1 & 1 \\ 0 & 0 & 1 \end{pmatrix} \quad ,
\end{array}
$$

where for example the third column of R shows that X's cells $\{i_0, i_1\}$ and $\{i_0, i_1, i_2\}$ are merged to a single cell $\{i_0, i_1, i_2\}$, and so $\{i_0, i_1\}$ is "lost". For

---

[9] We continue to call them "cells", as for partitions, in spite of the possible overlaps.
[10] We write $\mathcal{X} \twoheadrightarrow \mathcal{Y}$ for matrices (of any element-type) with $\mathcal{X}$-indexed rows and $\mathcal{Y}$-indexed columns. For deterministic matrices $\mathcal{I} \twoheadrightarrow \mathcal{O}$ is isomorphically functions $\mathcal{I} \to \mathcal{O}$.

the other direction Y to X we would have the matrices

$$
\begin{array}{ccc}
Y & R' & X \\
\hline
\end{array}
$$

$$
\begin{array}{c}
i_0 \\
i_1 \\
i_2
\end{array}
\begin{pmatrix} 1\,0\,1 \\ 0\,1\,1 \\ 0\,0\,1 \end{pmatrix}
\begin{pmatrix} 1\,0\,1\,0 \\ 0\,1\,1\,0 \\ 0\,0\,0\,1 \end{pmatrix}
=
\begin{pmatrix} 1\,0\,1\,1 \\ 0\,1\,1\,1 \\ 0\,0\,0\,1 \end{pmatrix}
\quad ,
$$

where the third column of R' "creates" $\{i_0, i_1\}$ from $\{i_0\}$ and $\{i_1\}$.

We achieve anti-symmetry via the usual closure construction.

Definition 4. *Union-closure for anti-symmetry* _____ Say that a subset of $\mathbb{P}\mathcal{I}$ is *union closed* just when the union of each of its subsets is also an element of it. Define the *union closure* of some subset X of $\mathbb{P}\mathcal{I}$ to be the smallest union-closed subset of $\mathbb{P}\mathcal{I}$ that contains X, well defined because $\mathbb{P}\mathcal{I}$ is union-closed, and any intersection of union-closed sets is again union-closed. Write $X^\cup$ for the union-closure of X. □

Note that all union-closed subsets of $\mathbb{P}\mathcal{I}$ contain $\emptyset$, and so are non-empty.[11]

Lemma 1. *Anti-symmetry on union-closed sets* _____ Take refinement ($\sqsubseteq$) as in Definition 3. If $X, Y : \mathbb{P}\mathcal{I}$ are union-closed, with both $X \sqsubseteq Y$ and $Y \sqsubseteq X$, then in fact $X = Y$.

Proof. Any element of Y must be the union of some subset of X and hence an element of $X^\cup$, which latter equals X again, because of its union-closure. □

Definition 5. *Demonic-refinement domain for information hiding* _____
Let $\mathbb{U}\mathcal{I}$ be the union-closed subsets of $\mathbb{P}\mathcal{I}$ that cover $\mathcal{I}$: it is the abstract model for demonic information-hiding. The refinement relation ($\sqsubseteq$) is as defined above (Definition 3) for $\mathbb{P}\mathcal{I}$; but on $\mathbb{U}\mathcal{I}$ it is (also) antisymmetric, thus a partial order. □

Note that reflexivity and transitivity of ($\sqsubseteq$) on $\mathbb{U}\mathcal{I}$ are inherited, since $\mathbb{U}\mathcal{I} \subseteq \mathbb{P}\mathcal{I}$.

Lemma 2. $\mathbb{U}\mathcal{I}$ *is a lattice* _____ On $\mathbb{U}\mathcal{I}$ the refinement relation (Definition 3) is simply ($\supseteq$). Thus for $X, Y : \mathbb{U}\mathcal{I}$, both therefore union-closed, their join $X \sqcup Y$ is simply $X \cap Y$, because it is union-closed as well and ($\supseteq$) is a lattice. Their meet however needs explicit union closure: we define $X \sqcap Y$ to be $(X \cup Y)^\cup$.

Proof. Omitted. □

---

[11] For any subset I of $\mathcal{I}$ we have $\emptyset \subseteq I$ and so $\emptyset = \cup\emptyset \in I^\cup$ also.

3.2   Spies in Action: An Example of Demonic Nondeterminism

Recall the channels from Fig. 1. We can see that the union-closure of C^1 from Fig. 1(a) is $\{\emptyset, \mathsf{AE}, \mathsf{BW}, \mathsf{AEBW}\}$, where we write AE for $\{\mathsf{A}, \mathsf{E}\}$ etc. The union-closure of C^2 is $\{\emptyset, \mathsf{W}, \mathsf{ABE}, \mathsf{AEBW}\}$. Therefore from Lemma 2 the join $C^1 \sqcup C^2$ is $\{\emptyset, \mathsf{AEBW}\}$ as in Fig. 3, and the meet $C^1 \sqcap C^2$ is

$$\{\emptyset, \mathsf{W}, \mathsf{AE}, \mathsf{BW}, \mathsf{ABE}, \underline{\mathsf{AEW}}, \mathsf{AEBW}\}, \tag{2}$$

where the underlined $\underline{\mathsf{AEW}}$ has been added by union-closure (Lemma 2). We note however that (2) is *not* simply the union-closure of the meet Fig. 2(b) in the deterministic lattice: that would instead be $\{\mathsf{B}, \mathsf{W}, \mathsf{AE}\}^{\cup}$, that is

$$\{\emptyset, \mathsf{B}, \mathsf{W}, \mathsf{AE}, \underline{\mathsf{BW}}, \underline{\mathsf{ABE}}, \underline{\mathsf{AEW}}, \underline{\mathsf{ABEW}}\}. \tag{3}$$

In fact in $\mathbb{U}\mathcal{I}$ we have $(3) \sqsubseteq (2)$ by discarding $\{\mathsf{B}\}$ from the former.

Thus in this case $\mathbb{U}\mathcal{I}$ admits a more-refined, that is a more *secure* meet (2) than the (3) admitted by $\mathbb{E}\mathcal{I}$; that is because (2) describes behaviour that no deterministic channel can realise, as we now discuss.

Suppose that $C^{1,2}$ are real spies, named *Ms. Vowel* and *Mrs. Early*, and our adversary M sends them into the field to discover the value of our hidden letter i. The mission however is so dangerous that she knows that only one of the spies will return: she just don't know beforehand which it will be. That is the nondeterminism. How do we describe this situation in $\mathbb{U}\mathcal{I}$?

In $\mathbb{U}\mathcal{I}$ this mission is in fact $C^1 \sqcap C^2$, as in (2) and, as we remarked above, it is a strict refinement of the deterministic (3) where both spies return. The following lemma shows that (2) cannot be deterministic.

Lemma 3. *Characterisation of determinism within* $\mathbb{U}\mathcal{I}$ —— For input space $\mathcal{I}$, the (union-closures of the) deterministic subset $\mathbb{E}\mathcal{I}$ of its demonic channels $\mathbb{U}\mathcal{I}$ comprise exactly those that are complement-closed. That is, any X in $\mathbb{U}\mathcal{I}$ is in fact $Y^{\cup}$ for some Y in $\mathbb{E}\mathcal{I}$ iff X is intersection- and complement-closed.

Proof. "Only if" is trivial. If X in $\mathbb{U}\mathcal{I}$ is complement-closed, then it is also intersection-closed. For each i in $\mathcal{I}$ let X_i be the intersection of all elements (subsets of $\mathcal{I}$) of X that contain i. By intersection-closure of X each X_i is itself in X: in fact it is the smallest element of X that contains i.

Now for any two $i \neq i'$ we have that X_i and $X_{i'}$ are either equal or disjoint: if they had a proper overlap then either X_i or $X_{i'}$, or both, could be made smaller.

The sets X_i are the cells of the partition of which X is the union-closure: they are pairwise disjoint, non-empty, and cover $\mathcal{I}$. □

Lemma 3 shows that (2) cannot be deterministic, because it can reveal BW if Ms. Vowel returns (and says CONS); and it can also reveal ABW if Mrs. Early returns (saying EARLY). But this mission can never reveal B, that is the intersection $\mathsf{BW} \cap \mathsf{ABW}$, since for that both spies would have to return.

Now we consider an intriguing further possibility, where the spies report by radio instead of in person, using Booleans agreed beforehand (a one-time pad):

for Ms. Vowel "*true*" encodes VOWEL etc. On this even more dangerous mission M knows that both spies will be captured, but she knows also that exactly one will send a report back to her by radio, either *true* or *false*. But she won't know which spy it was. Here the demonic channel is

$$\{\emptyset, \mathrm{BW}, \mathrm{ABE}, \mathcal{I}\} \tag{4}$$

which, by Lemma 3 again, is also properly demonic. This use of encoding, we should remark, underscores our abstraction from output values: from our point of view "Ms. Consonant" would be exactly the same spy as Ms. Vowel, and Mrs. Late would have the same utility as Mrs. Early.

3.3   Testing, Soundness and Completeness

The methodological concerns of Sect. 1.3 apply to demonic channels too: if we suspect that $S \not\sqsubseteq K$, how can we prove the refinement's failure in court?

Our earlier technique, for testing deterministic channels, does not work for
† demonic channels. Let S be $\{\emptyset, \{i_0, i_1\}, \{i_2\}, \{i_0, i_1, i_2\}\}$ and K, not a refinement, be $\{\emptyset, \{i_0, i_1\}, \{i_1, i_2\}, \{i_0, i_1, i_2\}\}$. We know that $S \not\sqsubseteq K$ because $\{i_1, i_2\}$ in K is not the union of any cells in S. But no deterministic test ι in the style of Sect. 1.3 shows $S \not\sqsubseteq K$, because every cell of K is a superset of some cell of S. Thus deterministic tests are too weak, not complete for demonic channels. Strangely, every cell of K's being a superset of come cell of S, in a sense more demonic, is still *not* sufficient for refinement.[12]

In this section we synthesise a complete test-suite for demonic channels.

By definition we have $S \not\sqsubseteq K$ just when there is some cell κ in K that is not the union of any set of cells $\sigma_{1,\ldots,N}$ drawn from S — which, in turn, is just when there is further some single element i of $\mathcal{I}$ such that every i-containing cell σ of S is *not* a subset of κ. That is we have $S \not\sqsubseteq K$ just when

$$\begin{array}{l} \text{there are } i, \kappa \text{ with } i \in \kappa \in K \text{ such that for every } \sigma \text{ in } S \\ \text{we have } i \in \sigma \Rightarrow \sigma \not\subseteq \kappa. \end{array} \tag{5}$$

Our preliminary definition of the "suite" of demonic tests is therefore that they are pairs (i, ι) with $i \in \iota \subseteq \mathcal{I}$. A demonic channel X passes such a test just when every cell χ in X with $i \in \chi$ satisfies $\chi \not\subseteq \iota$.[13]

For *soundness* of the (preliminary) test suite, argue the contrapositive by assuming that we have $S \sqsubseteq P$ and a test (i, ι) that P fails, so that there is some cell π in P with $i \in \pi \subseteq \iota$. But $\pi = \cup_n \sigma_n$ for some $\sigma_{1,\ldots,N}$, and so $i \in (\cup_n \sigma_n) \subseteq \iota$ whence, for some n, we have $i \in \sigma_n \subseteq \iota$ with $\sigma_n \in S$. That is, there is a cell σ_n of S that fails the test, and so S fails as a whole.

For *completeness* of the test suite, suppose $S \not\sqsubseteq K$ and appeal to (5) above to choose i, κ; then set $\iota := \kappa$. The test (i, ι) itself is passed by S, by (5); but it is

---

[12] They are trivially sound, however, since weakening a test suite trivially preserves its soundness: with fewer tests, there will be fewer failures.

[13] In fact $i \in \iota$ is not necessary, since a pair (i, ι) with $i \notin \iota$ would be a test passed by every cell, vacuously sound for all channels. Allowing it would make no difference.

failed by K because we do not have $i \in \iota \Rightarrow \iota \not\subseteq \iota$ — the antecedent is true but the consequent is trivially false. For example the test that shows

$$\{\emptyset, \{i_0, i_1\}, \{i_2\}, \{i_0, i_1, i_2\}\} \quad \not\subseteq \quad \{\emptyset, \{i_0, i_1\}, \{i_1, i_2\}, \{i_0, i_1, i_2\}\},$$

the example from (†) above, is $(i_1, \{i_1, i_2\})$ — the cells σ on the left that satisfy $i_1 \in \sigma$ are $\{i_0, i_1\}$ and $\{i_0, i_1, i_2\}$ and, for both, we have $\sigma \not\subseteq \{i_1, i_2\}$. The cell $\kappa := \{i_1, i_2\}$ on the right however satisfies $i_1 \in \kappa$ but not of course $\kappa \not\subseteq \{i_1, i_2\}$.

For our preferred definition of demonic testing we reformulate the above in terms of two subsets of $\mathcal{I}$, rather than an element i and a subset ι, because that will be more convenient for source-level reasoning over programs.[14]

Definition 6. *Tests for demonic refinement* _____ A test for demonic refinement over space $\mathcal{I}$ is a pair (α, β) of subsets of $\mathcal{I}$. A demonic channel X passes the test (α, β) just when all its cells pass the test; a cell χ of X passes the test just when $\chi \subseteq \alpha \Rightarrow \chi \subseteq \beta$. □

The top of the $\mathbb{U}\mathcal{I}$ lattice is the reveal-nothing channel $\{\emptyset, \mathcal{I}\}$, and it passes every non-trivial test; the bottom of the lattice is the reveal-everything channel $\mathbb{P}\mathcal{I}$ which fails them all.[15]

Lemma 4. *Equivalence of testing suites* _____ The test suite of Definition 6 is equivalent in power to the preliminary test suite (i, ι) discussed at (5).

Proof. We show that $S \not\subseteq K$ can be established by an (α, β)-test iff it can be established by an (i, ι)-test.

if — Any (i, ι)-test can be expressed as an (α, β)-test by setting $\alpha := \iota$ and $\beta := (\mathcal{I} - \{i\})$. To see that, let χ be an arbitrary cell and reason

$$i \in \chi \Rightarrow \chi \not\subseteq \iota$$
iff $\quad \chi \not\subseteq (\mathcal{I} - \{i\}) \Rightarrow \chi \not\subseteq \iota$
iff $\quad \chi \subseteq \iota \Rightarrow \chi \subseteq (\mathcal{I} - \{i\})$
iff $\quad \chi \subseteq \alpha \Rightarrow \chi \subseteq \beta$. $\qquad\qquad$ "set $\alpha, \beta := \iota, (\mathcal{I} - \{i\})$"

Thus (α, β)-tests are at least as discriminating as (i, ι)-tests.
only if — If $S \not\subseteq K$ is established by (α, β), then for all cells σ in S we have $\sigma \subseteq \alpha \Rightarrow \sigma \subseteq \beta$; and for some cell κ in K we have $\kappa \subseteq \alpha \wedge \kappa \not\subseteq \beta$. Now reason

$$\kappa \subseteq \alpha \wedge \kappa \not\subseteq \beta$$
iff $\quad \kappa \subseteq \alpha \wedge i \in \kappa \qquad\qquad$ "for some $i \notin \beta$"
hence $\quad \kappa$ fails test (i, α),

---

[14] Subsets of $\mathcal{I}$, rather than individual elements, are more easily turned into predicates for source-level reasoning over a state space of typed variables: if you add another variable, a subset remains a subset but a point is no longer a point.

[15] Non-trivial tests make at least one distinction. Tests (α, β) are trivial when $\alpha \subseteq \beta$ (passed by every cell), and when α, β are disjoint (passed only by cell $\emptyset$.) In general (α, β) is equivalent to $(\alpha, \alpha \cap \beta)$.

Also for example (α', β') is weaker than (α, β) when $\alpha' \subseteq \alpha$ and $\beta \subseteq \beta'$. Compare Footnote 22 below.

and for a contradiction

if σ fails test (i, α) "for the same $i \notin \beta$ as above"

then $i \in \sigma \wedge \sigma \subseteq \alpha$

hence $i \in \sigma \wedge \sigma \subseteq \beta$ "assumption σ passes test (α, β)"

hence $i \in \beta$,

which contradicts $i \notin \beta$, and so in fact σ cannot fail test (i, α).

Thus test (i, α) establishes $S \not\sqsubseteq K$, as required.

$\square$

Although $\mathbb{UI}$ is restricted to union-closed subsets of $\mathcal{I}$, we can give an "abridged" representation of demonic channels in which union-closure is taken implicitly. In abridged form the non-refinement example from (†) becomes

$$\{\{i_0, i_1\}, \{i_2\}\} \quad \not\sqsubseteq \quad \{\{i_0, i_1\}, \{i_1, i_2\}\},$$

and the (α, β)-test for this non-refinement is $(\{i_1, i_2\}, \{i_0, i_2\})$. In fact we have

Lemma 5. *Testing abridged representations* _____ For any subset X of $\mathbb{PI}$ and subsets α, β of $\mathcal{I}$, we have that X passes the test (α, β) iff the channel $X^{\cup}$ passes that same (α, β).

Proof. If $X^{\cup}$ passes the test then so does X, because $X \subseteq X^{\cup}$.

If $X^{\cup}$ fails the test (α, β) then for some $\chi_1, \cdots, _N$ in X we have $\cup(\chi_1, \cdots, _N) \subseteq \alpha$ but $\cup(\chi_1, \cdots, _N) \not\subseteq \beta$. From the latter we have $\chi_n \not\subseteq \beta$ for some n; but from the former we still have $\chi_n \subseteq \alpha$ for that n. Because that χ_n from X fails the test, so does X itself. $\square$

From here on, we will use abridged representations if convenient. In fact, among abridged representations of a channel there is a smallest one where no cell is the union of any other cells (except itself). We call that the "reduced" representation of the channel, and note that all deterministic channels $\mathbb{EI}$ are reduced.

Definition 7. *Reduced demonic channels* _____ A subset X of $\mathbb{PI}$ is a *reduced* channel just when $\cup X = \mathcal{I}$ and no cell χ in X is the union $\cup\chi_1, \cdots, _N$ of any other cells in X except trivially $\cup\{\chi\}$. Note that $\emptyset$ is excluded from an abridged representation, since it is $\cup\{\}$ (as well as $\cup\{\emptyset\}$.) $\square$

We say that a reduced Y with $X = Y^{\cup}$ is a *reduction* of X.

Lemma 6. *Uniqueness of reductions* _____ Any demonic channel X in $\mathbb{UI}$ has a unique reduction, a unique reduced channel Y in $\mathbb{PI}$ such that $X = Y^{\cup}$.

Proof. Existence of a reduction of X is trivial: keep removing superfluous cells in X until no more are superfluous.

For uniqueness we argue from Lemma 5 and the soundness of testing that two reductions Y, Y' of the same X must satisfy $Y \sqsubseteq Y'$ and $Y' \sqsubseteq Y$, so that any cell γ of Y is expressible as a union $\cup\gamma'_1, \cdots, _N$ of cells γ'_n from Y'.

In turn, each of those γ'_n's must be a union of cells $\cup\gamma_{n, (1, \cdots, _M)}$ back in Y, so that $\gamma = \cup\gamma_{(1, \cdots, N), (1, \cdots, M)}$.

Because Y is reduced, each $\gamma_{(1, \cdots, N), (1, \cdots, M)}$ must be just γ itself. Thus γ is in Y'. $\square$

3.4 Justifying Refinement's Definition

The tests of Definition 6 justify a refinement failure $S \not\sqsubseteq K$ by guaranteeing that there is a test that S passes but K fails. The utility of a discriminating test is that, if you can find it, it proves the failure with a single witness. But the tests (α, β) are hardly an obvious, intuitive choice themselves.

To justify refinement's definition to both client and vendor, we appeal to a more primitive notion of correctness that we take as self-evidently desirable for security (of demonic channels): that if K can reveal its input is some i *exactly* but S never can, then K cannot be a refinement of S.

Definition 8. *Primitive refinement of channels* _____ We say that S is *primitively refined* by P just when there is no singleton cell $\{i\}$ in P that is not also in S. We write it $S \preccurlyeq P$.   □

Put more simply, Definition 8 says that $S \preccurlyeq P$ unless there is a particular i that P can reveal but S cannot. "I might not know any theory; but I know that if S guarantees never to leak my password, then P can't either."[16]

It's the simplicity of ($\preccurlyeq$), in everyday terms, that is its justification. But it is however too simple for general use: Definition 8 does not justify ($\sqsubseteq$) directly. If S leaks the last character of a password, but K leaks the last two characters, then probably $S \not\sqsubseteq K$ — but we will still have $S \preccurlyeq K$ because neither leaks the password exactly.

Therefore to justify ($\sqsubseteq$) using Definition 8 we must do more: for that, we recognise that channels will probably not be used alone: larger channels can be made from a collection of smaller ones. In particular, we define

Definition 9. *Channel composition* _____ The composition of two channels $C^{1,2}$ over the same input $\mathcal{I}$ but outputs $\mathcal{O}^{1,2}$ respectively a new channel of type $\mathcal{I} \to (\mathcal{O}^1 \times \mathcal{O}^2)$ defined

$$(C^1 \| C^2).i \ := \ (C^1.i, C^2.i).$$

□

Thus an adversary with access to two channels $C^{1,2}$ acting on the same input can be considered to be using a single channel $C^1 \| C^2$: she observes its composite output (o^1, o^2) where $o^{1,2} := C^{1,2}.i$ respectively.

We now give two desirable principles that should apply to ($\sqsubseteq$) in general:[17]

robustness If $S \sqsubseteq P$ then we should have primitive refinement even in the context of an arbitrary (other) channel C, that is $(S\|C) \preccurlyeq (P\|C)$.

necessity If $S \not\sqsubseteq P$ then for there must be some (other) channel C that justifies the failure, i.e. such that $(S\|C) \not\preccurlyeq (P\|C)$.

---

[16] Just to be clear: a security breach releasing some large number N of passwords usually means in our terms that there are N singleton cells, not that there is just one cell with N passwords in it. The former means that each of N people has his password leaked exactly. The latter means instead that someone's password is leearned to be one of those N.

[17] Together they are an equivalence because $S \sqsubseteq P$ iff $(S\|C) \preccurlyeq (P\|C)$ for all C.

From the two principles above we can derive two others:

safety If $S \sqsubseteq P$ then $S \preccurlyeq P$, from applying *robustness* with the identity context.

monotonicity If $S \sqsubseteq P$ then $(S\|C) \sqsubseteq (P\|C)$ for any (other) channel C — for, if not, by *necessity* there would be (still another) channel D such that $(S\|C)\|D \not\preccurlyeq (P\|C)\|D$, that is by associativity $S\|(C\|D) \not\preccurlyeq P\|(C\|D)$; and that, by robustness wrt. channel $C\|D$, implies $S \not\sqsubseteq P$.

We note that the basic principles rest on two informal notions: that ($\not\preccurlyeq$) reasonably captures "is clearly broken" in the sense a layman might understand it, and that ($\|C$) describes "contexts" in which laymen would expect our channels reasonably to be able to operate. In particular, robustness emphasises that checking channels' security properties individually is not enough: two adversaries could have one channel each and, if they combined their results, they would in fact be acting like a single adversary using the channels' composition, probably a more powerful attack than is possible with either channel alone.

Once those notions ($\preccurlyeq$) and ($\|C$) are fixed, robustness and necessity determine refinement ($\sqsubseteq$) uniquely. That is, justification of ($\preccurlyeq$) and ($\|C$) and robustness and necessity are collectively a justification of ($\sqsubseteq$) and, further, it is the only relation that can be justified that way. This process is called *compositional closure*, that ($\sqsubseteq$) is the compositional closure under ($\|$) of ($\preccurlyeq$).

The derived principles have direct significance for everyday use when a system $C_1\| \cdots \|C_N$ might be composed of many subsystems C_n: safety says that if a vendor establishes $S \sqsubseteq P$ through his software-development safe practices then, because (as well) he has established $S \preccurlyeq P$, his client will be happy; and monotonicity says that the vendor can use stepwise refinement [19] on his C_n's separately to modularise his software-development process that ultimately produces the whole system $C_1\| \cdots \|C_N$. We now have

Theorem 1. *Refinement is justified* _____ Definition 5 of refinement satisfies robustness and necessity wrt. Definition 8 (primitive refinement) and Definition 9 (composition).

Proof.

Robustness

Assume that $S \sqsubseteq P$ but suppose for a contradiction that $S\|C \not\preccurlyeq P\|C$. In that case there must be π, γ from P, C respectively and input i such that the intersection $\pi \cap \gamma$ is $\{i\}$ for some i in $\mathcal{I}$, indicating than when the observation of $P\|C$ is (π, γ) an adversary would know that the input was i exactly, and furthermore that that does not occur with any σ from S. Now because $S \sqsubseteq P$ we have $\pi = \cup\sigma_{1,\dots,N}$ for some $\sigma_{1,\dots,N}$ each in S, so that

$$(\sigma_1 \cap \gamma) \cup \cdots \cup (\sigma_N \cap \gamma) \quad = \quad \{i\} \quad \text{also,}$$

and so for at least one n we must have $\sigma_n \cap \gamma = \{i\}$, contradicting "furthermore" at (†) above. Thus $S\|C \preccurlyeq P\|C$ as desired.

Necessity

If $S \not\sqsubseteq K$ then by Sect. 3.3 (completeness and Definition 6) there is an (α, β)
%   test that S passes but K fails. Choose therefore a cell κ in K such that $\kappa \subseteq \alpha$
but $\kappa \not\subseteq \beta$, and choose an element k in $\kappa - \beta$.
Define channel $C{:}\,\mathcal{I} \to Bool$ so that

$$C.i \quad := \quad i = k \vee i \notin \alpha, \tag{6}$$

and form channel $K\|C$ which for input k can give[18] output $(\kappa, true)$. In that
case the adversary reasons

$$\begin{array}{ll}
& i \in \kappa \wedge (i = k \vee i \notin \alpha) \\
\text{implies} & i \in \alpha \wedge (i = k \vee i \notin \alpha) \qquad\qquad\qquad\qquad\qquad\qquad\qquad \text{``}\kappa \subseteq \alpha\text{''} \\
\text{hence} & i = k,
\end{array}$$

so that she deduces that i is k exactly.
Now we show that $S\|C$ can never reveal that $i = k$ exactly. If $S\|C$ is given
(the same) input k then it will produce output $(\sigma, true)$ for some σ. Now
assume for a contradiction that the adversary can deduce that i is k exactly
in this case also. Write $\overline{\alpha}$ for $\mathcal{I} - \alpha$ and reason

$$\begin{array}{lll}
\text{implies} & \sigma \cap (\{k\} \cup \overline{\alpha}) = \{k\} & \text{``assumption for contradiction''[19]} \\
\text{implies} & \sigma \cap (\{k\} \cup \overline{\alpha}) \cap \overline{\alpha} = \{k\} \cap \overline{\alpha} & \text{``}(\cap\overline{\alpha})\text{ both sides''} \\
\text{implies} & \sigma \cap \overline{\alpha} = \emptyset & \text{``}k \in \alpha\text{''} \\
\text{iff} & \sigma \subseteq \alpha & \\
\text{implies} & \sigma \subseteq \beta & \text{``assumption that }S\text{ passes test }(\alpha, \beta)\text{''} \\
\text{implies} & k \in \beta, & \text{``}k \in \sigma\text{''}
\end{array}$$

which contradicts that k was chosen from $\kappa - \beta$ at (%) above.
So we conclude that if $S \not\sqsubseteq K$ then there is an input k and a channel C such
that running $K\|C$ on k can reveal k exactly but $S\|C$ on k can never reveal
k exactly, that is that $S\|C \not\preceq K\|C$.

$\square$

Corollary 1. *Refinement is sound and monotonic* _____ Definition 5 of refinement satisfies soundness and monotonicity wrt. Definition 8 (primitive refinement) and Definition 9 (composition).

Proof. Immediate from Theorem 1. $\square$

---

[18] It's "can" rather than "must" because K is nondeterministic: it might not select cell κ for input k; but because $k \in \kappa$, it can.

[19] The left-hand side is the possibilities the observer deduces for the input i when she sees that $i \in \sigma$ and that $C.i = true$. The equality therefore says that she concludes the only possible input value is k.

4 "Weakest Pre-tests" and Source-Level Reasoning

For eventual source-level reasoning, where e.g. leakage via channels is made a primitive imperative-programming statement, we can imagine asking what security guarantees we must have *before* a program runs in order to be sure that running the program has not leaked "too much" information *afterwards*.

Suppose that in our letters example it's especially important that the spies never learn that our i is exactly A, because A is information about an especially important person. For us the other people B, E, W are not so important.

Let our program (i.e. channel) be X with typical cell-names χ. To express "X never reveals that i is A" using a test in the style of Definition 6, we could write $\chi \subseteq \{A\} \Rightarrow \chi \subseteq \emptyset$ for all $\chi \in X$. We can see by inspection from Fig. 2 that both the "one spy returns" channel and the "radio spies" channel pass that test (because all of their cells χ do).

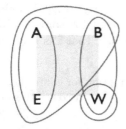
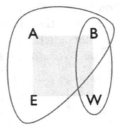

(a) Only one spy returns.   (b) A Boolean radio message is received.

Fig. 7. Ms. Vowel and Mrs. Early in action

So now we complicate things by imagining that, as a result of previous missions, M has some "a priori" knowledge about our i, knowledge that we would also like to express as a test. For example we could say that she knows *before* she sends Vowel and Early that i cannot be E, expressing that with the test $\chi \subseteq \mathcal{I} \Rightarrow \chi \subseteq \{ABW\}$. Could she ever learn from her spies that actually $i = A$? The general "weakest pre-test" question for protecting A is[20].

What security criterion must our i satisfy *before* the spies are sent in order to ensure that M cannot not learn $i = A$ once the spies have reported?

Obviously the pre-test $i \neq A$ would be strong enough — if you don't want A to be leaked, don't put it in your database. But can we do better?

The effect that M's a-priori knowledge, expressed as a cell μ say, has on her spies' output cells is simply that each cell χ becomes $\chi \cap \mu$ — she learns χ from the channel, and she knew μ already. Thus to convert our post-test $\chi \subseteq \{A\} \Rightarrow \chi \subseteq \emptyset$ on χ to a pre-test on μ alone, we replace χ by $\chi \cap \mu$, to give

$$(\chi \cap \mu) \subseteq \{A\} \quad \Rightarrow \quad (\chi \cap \mu) \subseteq \emptyset , \quad \text{and then} \tag{7}$$

---

[20] This is obviously by analogy with weakest preconditions [6].

instantiate that for every χ in the (abridged) channel Fig. 7(a) — we can do that because we know the channel's construction and so we know what χ's it can produce. If we take $\chi = \{W\}$, we get $(\{W\} \cap \mu) \subseteq \{A\} \Rightarrow (\{W\} \cap \mu) \subseteq \emptyset$, which is equivalent to $\mu \subseteq ABE \Rightarrow \mu \subseteq ABE$, that is just *true*. For all four cells it's

$$
\begin{array}{llll}
\mu \subseteq ABE \;\Rightarrow \mu \subseteq ABE & true & \text{when } \chi = W & \text{(done just above)} \\
\mu \subseteq ABW \Rightarrow \mu \subseteq BW & — & \text{when } \chi = AE & \\
\mu \subseteq AE \;\;\Rightarrow \mu \subseteq AE & true & \text{when } \chi = BW & \\
\mu \subseteq AW \;\Rightarrow \mu \subseteq W & — & \text{when } \chi = ABE, &
\end{array}
\tag{8}
$$

where in each case we get a test again, but of "pre-cell" μ rather than "post-cell" χ, because $\chi \cap \mu \subseteq \iota$ can be written $\mu \subseteq \iota \cup \overline{\chi}$. Thus our overall pre-test for Fig. 7(a) and the post-test $\chi \subseteq \{A\} \Rightarrow \chi \subseteq \emptyset$ is the conjunction

$$
\mu \subseteq ABW \Rightarrow \mu \subseteq BW \quad \text{and} \quad \mu \subseteq AW \Rightarrow \mu \subseteq W
\tag{9}
$$

that we get by discarding the *true*'s from (8).

Thus a single post-test can generate a conjunction of pre-tests, which conjunctions we take therefore as our general form of test.[21] In this case however the first conjunct of (9) implies the second, and so we end up with only the first one.[22] To cast it back into everyday language, we rewrite (9) equivalently as $E \notin \mu \Rightarrow A \notin \mu$, that is that

if M believes i is not E, she must also believe it's not A.

Under those conditions, her one-spy-returns attack will never reveal that $i = A$.

In the case of the "radio spies" Fig. 7(b) we get only the second conjunct (because the case $\chi = AE$ of (8) is missing), which as we have just seen is weaker than the first and so we can withstand "M's knowing more". That is, in Fig. 7(b) we are secure against M's knowing beforehand that $i \neq B$ as at (\$) above; but in Fig. 7(a) we are not. That's not surprising, since Fig. 7(a) $\sqsubset$ Fig. 7(b) and therefore we expect to be less at risk from the radio spies.

For source-level reasoning we could e.g. write channels as primitive statements leak c in $\Phi(o,i)$ where Φ is a formula in state variables i and bound variable c is the emitted value: in state i the channel can emit any o satisfying Φ. As a special case we'd write leak Exp(i) for the deterministic case, when Φ is c = Exp(i) for some expression Exp in i. A modality $K\Psi(i)$ would express that the current cell χ satisfied $\chi \subseteq \{i : \mathcal{I} | \Psi(i)\}$, and our tests would then be of the form $(\forall c \bullet K\Psi(i, c) \Rightarrow K\Omega(i, c))$ where the universal quantifier would if necessary express wt-generated conjunctions (which distribute through subsequent wt's).

---

[21] Starting again, from *conjunctions* of post-tests, will just generate conjunctions of conjunctions of pre-tests, so we do not have to expand our expressiveness any further. Furthermore, every member of $U\mathcal{I}$ is characterised uniquely by a conjunction of such tests: every conjunction of tests "is" union-closed (easy); and for every union-closed set there is a conjunction of tests that only it satisfies (sneaky).

[22] In (9) here the (α', β') on the right is weaker than (α, β) on the left because we have $\alpha' \subseteq \alpha$ and $\alpha' \cap \beta \subseteq \beta'$. Compare Footnote 15 above.

With all that, expressing our "weakest pre-test" approach at the source level (and making reference to variables implicit) would give in general

$$\text{wt}(\texttt{leak c in } \Phi(\texttt{c}), \; \mathsf{K}\Psi \Rightarrow \mathsf{K}\Omega)$$
$$= \quad (\forall c \bullet \mathsf{K}(\Phi \Rightarrow \Psi) \Rightarrow \mathsf{K}(\Phi \Rightarrow \Omega)),$$

and for the deterministic case $(\forall c \bullet \mathsf{K}(\mathit{Exp} = c \Rightarrow \Psi) \Rightarrow \mathsf{K}(\mathit{Exp} = c \Rightarrow \Omega))$.

The pre-test $\mathsf{E} \notin \mu \Rightarrow \mathsf{A} \notin \mu$ that we discovered at (†) above, to constrain M's prior knowledge, would be therefore be rendered at the source level as

$$\mathsf{K}(i \neq \mathsf{E}) \Rightarrow \mathsf{K}(i \neq \mathsf{A}) \qquad \begin{array}{l} \text{If } M \text{ knows } i \text{ is not } \mathsf{E}, \\ \text{then she also knows it's not } \mathsf{A}. \end{array}$$

Looking further ahead, we remark that for *updates* to the hidden state i the weakest pre-test is particularly simple, because updates leak nothing: if for example statement S is some assignment i:= Exp(i), then the weakest pre-test is given by[23]

$$\text{wt}(S, \; \mathsf{K}\Psi \Rightarrow \mathsf{K}\Omega) \quad = \quad \mathsf{K}(\text{wp}(S, \Psi)) \Rightarrow \mathsf{K}(\text{wp}(S, \Omega)), \qquad (10)$$

where wp is conventional weakest-precondition [6]; and this applies even when S is a demonic assignment (like a choice from a set). Non-leaking statements generate no pre-conjunctions. Conventional pre-and postconditions are embedded as "half tests" $\mathsf{K}(\mathit{true}) \Rightarrow \mathsf{K}\Omega$, equivalently just $\mathsf{K}\Omega$, and are respected by (10).

5   Conclusion

We have located a demonic model of information flow "in between" Landuaer and Redmond's deterministic model [8] and a more recent probabilistic model [3,9]. Originally presented *ab initio* as "The Shadow" [15], it is now more clearly structured; and as a result its properties can be divided into those inherent in demonic choice, and those shared with other models of information flow.

The deterministic model is a restriction (not an abstraction) of the demonic model: they give the same level of detail, but the latter describes more situations than the former. For example collaboration of the Spies (Sect. 3.2) cannot be expressed at all in the deterministic mode. The demonic model is however an abstraction (not a restriction) of the probabilistic: they can describe the same systems, but the latter gives a more detailed (i.e. quantitative rather than only qualitative) description. For the Spies, we are abstracting from the probabilities that one or the other might return, and the prior probability on the secret letter A, B, E, W.

All three systems have the the same structural definition of secure refinement, particularly evident when we use the matrix formulation: one channel P is a secure refinement of another channel S just when P can be obtained via post-multiplication by a so-called refinement matrix. This is in fact channel cascade,

---

[23] We assume here that S is everywhere terminating.

if the refinement matrix is for that purpose considered to be a channel from S-observables to P-observables.

The deterministic- and the demonic systems are lattices wrt. the refinement order; but the probabilistic system is not [12]: it is however a partial order if properly quotiented.

All three systems have a complementary testing semantics, one that provides a witness to any refinement failure. All three systems can justify their refinement order by general principles, robustness and necessity (Sect. 3.4) whereby the refinement relation is reduced to a more primitive form that is accepted "by the layman". (In the probabilistic case, the reduction is to the more primitive *Bayes Vulnerability*, the probability of guessing the secret in one try [5, 9].)

Finally, we mention that these systems show how the notion of security has become more sophisticated over the decades. Originally a system was said to be secure or insecure, an absolute black-or-white judgement, based on whether is suffered from "interference" or not [7]. Later it was realised that this criterion is too strong, since almost no useful system can be wholly interference-free: even a password-based login system releases information when a login attempt fails.

That led to the idea comparing two programs' information flow, particularly comparing a specification with an implementation: refinement holds just when the implementation cannot leak except when the specification can. In the probabilistic case, the comparison is even more sophisticated: the implementation must leak *no more than* the specification does.

Our aim is to enable this kind of refinement-based reasoning at the source-code level, based on "information-flow aware" assertions like those proposed in Sect. 4. From those it should be possible to construct an algebra of program transformations that preserve security- and functional characteristics during the program-development process in which specifications are manipulated to become implementations.

Finally, in the longer term we would like to add a fourth layer above the three mentioned here: one where probability, demonic choice and secrecy are handled all at once.

References

1. Alvim, M.S., Chatzikokolakis, K., McIver, A., Morgan, C., Palamidessi, C., Smith, G.: Additive and multiplicative notions of leakage, and their capacities. In: IEEE 27th CSF 2014, pp. 308–322. IEEE (2014)
2. Alvim, M.S., Chatzikokolakis, K., McIver, A., Morgan, C., Palamidessi, C., Smith, G.: Axioms for information leakage. Proc. CSF **2016**, 77–92 (2016)
3. Alvim, M.S., Chatzikokolakis, K., Palamidessi, C., Smith, G.: Measuring information leakage using generalized gain functions. In: Proceedings of 25th IEEE (CSF 2012), pp. 265–279, June 2012
4. Blackwell, D.: Comparison of experiments. In: Proceedings Second Berkeley Symposium on Mathematical Statistics and Probability, pp. 93–102 (1951)
5. Bordenabe, N.E., Smith, G.: Correlated secrets in information flow. Proc. CSF **2016**, 93–104 (2016)
6. Dijkstra, E.W.: A Discipline of Programming. Prentice-Hall, New Jersey (1976)
7. Goguen, J.A., Meseguer, J.: Unwinding and inference control. In: Proceedings of IEEE Symposium on Security and Privacy, pp. 75–86. IEEE Computer Society (1984)
8. Landauer, J., Redmond, T.: A lattice of information. In: Proceedings of 6th IEEE CSFW 1993, pp. 65–70, June 1993
9. McIver, A., Meinicke, L., Morgan, C.: Compositional closure for Bayes risk in probabilistic noninterference. In: Abramsky, S., Gavoille, C., Kirchner, C., Meyer auf der Heide, F., Spirakis, P.G. (eds.) ICALP 2010. LNCS, vol. 6199, pp. 223–235. Springer, Heidelberg (2010). doi:10.1007/978-3-642-14162-1_19
10. McIver, A., Meinicke, L., Morgan, C.: A Kantorovich-Monadic powerdomain for information hiding, with probability and nondeterminism. In: Proceedings LICS 2012 (2012)
11. McIver, A., Meinicke, L., Morgan, C.: Hidden-Markov program algebra with iteration. Mathematical Structures in Computer Science (2014)
12. McIver, A., Morgan, C., Meinicke, L., Smith, G., Espinoza, B.: Abstract channels, gain functions and the information order. In: FCS 2013 (2013). http://prosecco.gforge.inria.fr/personal/bblanche/fcs13/fcs13proceedings.pdf
13. McIver, A., Morgan, C., Rabehaja, T.: Abstract hidden Markov models: a monadic account of quantitative information flow. In: Proceedings LICS 2015 (2015)
14. McIver, A., Morgan, C., Smith, G., Espinoza, B., Meinicke, L.: Abstract channels and their robust information-leakage ordering. In: Abadi, M., Kremer, S. (eds.) POST 2014. LNCS, vol. 8414, pp. 83–102. Springer, Heidelberg (2014). doi:10.1007/978-3-642-54792-8_5
15. Morgan, C.: *The shadow knows*: refinement of ignorance in sequential programs. In: Uustalu, T. (ed.) MPC 2006. LNCS, vol. 4014, pp. 359–378. Springer, Heidelberg (2006). doi:10.1007/11783596_21
16. Morgan, C.C., Knows, T.S.: Refinement of ignorance in sequential programs. Sci. Comput. Program. **74**(8), 629–653 (2009). Treats Oblivious Transfer
17. Shannon, C.E.: A mathematical theory of communication. Bell Syst. Tech. J. **27**(379–423), 623–656 (1948)
18. Smith, G.: On the foundations of quantitative information flow. In: Alfaro, L. (ed.) FoSSaCS 2009. LNCS, vol. 5504, pp. 288–302. Springer, Heidelberg (2009). doi:10.1007/978-3-642-00596-1_21
19. Wirth, N.: Program development by stepwise refinement. Commun. ACM **14**(4), 221–227 (1971)

A Brief History of Security Protocols

Peter Y.A. Ryan[✉]

University of Newcastle, Newcastle upon Tyne, UK
`peter.ryan@uni.lu`

Abstract. The universe seethes with protocols, from the interactions of elementary particles (Feynman diagrams) to the power plays of nation states. Security protocols allow remote entities to interact safely, and as such they form the glue that holds the information society together. In this chapter we give an overview of the evolution of security protocols, from the Needham-Schroeder Secret Key protocol to quantum and post-quantum cryptography, and the tools and techniques used to understand and analyse them with particular emphasis on the major and seminal role played by Bill Roscoe in this history.

1 Introduction

Protocols are the rules governing the interaction of entities and as such they can be found everywhere, from the interactions of elementary particles, through the ordering of wine from the sommellier in a fancy restaurant, to the power plays between nations. In this chapter I will focus on a particular type of protocol: security protocols, also often known as cryptographic protocols. These first arose with the emergence of networked computing but have now become pervasive across the internet. Every time you place an order on Amazon or initiate an e-banking transaction you are invoking security protocols, probably without even being aware of it.

The information society depends critically on such protocols: without them the formation of remote trust relationships would not be possible. It is therefore essential that they are designed and verified with great care. It was realised very early on that their design and analysis is immensely challenging; in the words of the late Roger Needham: "Crypto protocols are three line programs that people still manage to get wrong." In this chapter I provide a brief, rather biased and far from exhaustive, outline of the rich panorama of security protocols and the techniques and tools to analyse and verify them, with particular emphasis on the significant contributions made by Bill Roscoe to this field.

2 Security Protocols

Security protocols enable people or entities to interact safely and securely in a potentially hostile environment, such as the internet. Thus, for example, you want to be sure that the party that you are interacting with really is who you

T. Gibson-Robinson et al. (Eds.): Roscoe Festschrift, LNCS 10160, pp. 223–245, 2017.
DOI: 10.1007/978-3-319-51046-0_12

think they are, e.g. that you are really passing your credit card details to Amazon and not to some cyber-criminal. You will typically want to be confident that your information is not leaked to entities eavesdropping on the communications channels. Furthermore, it may be important to guarantee that information exchanged is not altered in transit.

The above requirements are usually referred to as *authentication, confidentiality/secrecy* and *integrity/authenticity*, but other, often even more subtle, properties may be required in some contexts, for example for digital contracts we may require *non-repudiation*, that nobody can deny their actions, and *fairness*, i.e. that no party gains an advantage over others. Already making such requirements mathematically precise is very challenging, let alone designing and proving protocols to guarantee them.

Describing a basic protocol is typically fairly straightforward: for each role you specify the expected sequence of sends and receives of messages required for a successful execution of the protocol. Where the challenges arise is in precisely formulating the security goals and in accurately modelling the attacker's capabilities.

3   Cryptographic Primitives and Notation

Crypto protocols are built out of crypto primitives: encryption, digital signatures, hashes etc. We will not go into details as to how these work and formal definitions here, but rather just indicate the properties they provide and introduce some notation.

Encryption of a plaintext M under a key k is denoted by $\{M\}_k$. Decryption of a ciphertext C using key k is denoted by $\mathcal{D}_k(C)$. Of course, any self-respecting encryption algorithm should satisfy:

$$\forall M \in \mathcal{P}, \ \forall k \in \mathcal{K} : \mathcal{D}_{k^{-1}}(\{M\}_k) = M$$

where k^{-1} denotes the inverse key to k. For symmetric algorithms we often have $k = k^{-1}$, see the discussion later. We will typically assume that the plaintext can only be extracted by someone possessing the appropriate (decryption) key.

The digital signature on the message M computed using the signing key sk, corresponding to the public/verification key pk is denoted: $Sig_{sk}(M)$. There will be a verification algorithm that, given the verification key pk and the signature returns 1 or 0 according to whether the signature is valid or not. We assume that a valid signature cannot be generated for a given text M without possession of the signing key.

The cryptographic hash applied to a message M is denoted $Hash(M)$, or $Hash_k(M)$ in the case of a keyed hash. We assume that it is straightforward to compute such a hash given M but infeasible to compute the pre-image M given $Hash(M)$. Furthermore, computing collisions, i.e. finding M and M' such that:

$$Hash(M) = Hash(M')$$

is deemed intractable.

An important notion is that of so-called *nonces*: a node A generates a fresh, hard to guess (high entropy) value N_A and sends off a message containing this value. When A receives back a message containing N_A or values that are function of N_A, then A can be confident that the received message was generated after her creation of N_A. In other words, she can place an upper bound on the age of the incoming message.

3.1 Symmetric Cryptography

For almost the entire history of cryptography it was (implicitly) assumed that for two parties to communicate securely over open channels they would have to have previously shared some secret key material. The key used to encrypt is identical to the key used to decrypt, or if not precisely identical it is trivial to derive one from the other. The Caesar cipher for example involves shifting each letter forward by c places in the alphabet to encrypt, and shifting forward by $-c \bmod 26$ to decrypt. Modern block ciphers such as AES and stream ciphers fall in this class, now usually referred to as *symmetric crypto*.

A consequence of this is that for large networks of users key distribution is a serious problem. Suppose that we have a network of N nodes and we want to allow any pair to be able to communicate securely, then we need to distribute $N - 1$ keys to each node, resulting in $\mathcal{O}(N^2)$ keys. In an open system like the internet where the community of users is unbounded key distribution is effectively impossible.

3.2 Public Key/Asymmetric Cryptography

In the 1960s this assumption that secure communication is only possible with a prior shared secret was overthrown by Diffie and Hellman, [11], triggering a revolution in cryptography with the development of *public key cryptography*, often also referred to as *asymmetric cryptography*. The key idea is to tease the encryption and decryption keys apart in such a way as to ensure that deriving the secret key from the public key be intractable. This means that the encryption key, usually referred to as the *public key*, can be published openly while keeping the decryption key secret. This of course is impossible with conventional algorithms and involves the introduction of new concepts such as so-called *hard* problems and one-way functions, easy to compute in one direction but intractable in the other, and trapdoor functions, which are easy to compute with knowledge of a secret trapdoor but intractable without. The resulting revolution in cryptography is arguably comparable to that in astronomy brought about by Copernicus or in physics with Einstein's theory of relativity.

Later, Rivest, Shamir and Adelman, [23], proposed the RSA algorithm which relies on the assumed hardness of factorising the products of large primes. A little later El Gamal published an algorithm based on the difficulty of taking discrete logs, [14]. We outline the latter to illustrate:

We work in a group $\mathcal{G}$ of large prime order q with generator g. Anne generates a random value $x \in \{0, \cdots, q - 1\}$ and computes $h_A := g^x$, which she makes public. To encrypt a message m for Anne, Bob randomly chooses $r \in \{0, \cdots, q-1\}$ and computes the pair:

$$(\alpha, \beta) := (g^r, m \cdot h_A^r)$$

Anne can now decrypt this knowing x:

$$m = \beta / \alpha^x$$

Besides encryption, public key crypto gives rise to the idea of *digital signatures*: allowing the possessor of a secret key to prove that he is the originator of a digital document. Anyone with access to the corresponding verification key can verify the signature, but only the person possessing the signing key should be able to generate a signature on a given document that will verify against the verification key.

It is probably fair to say that the time was ripe for such ideas: on the one hand people were getting increasingly concerned about key distribution problems and on the other ideas of computational complexity and hard problems were in the air.

As a historical aside: similar ideas were proposed in secret at GCHQ a few years earlier by James Ellis, Clifford Cox and Malcolm Williamson. It seems though that GCHQ did not realise the full significance or potential of these ideas, nor did they come up with the important idea of digital signatures.

4   Key Distribution and Establishment

We now outline some representative examples of key establishment protocols, starting with one that employs only symmetric crypto.

4.1   Needham-Schroeder Secret Key Protocol

Already, using just symmetric crypto we can alleviate the key distribution problem, but at the cost of having to introduce trusted third parties responsible for generating and distributing new session keys on demand. Suppose that we have N nodes and a trusted server S. Suppose further that at setup time each node A is provided with a distinct key that it shares with S, denoted K_{AS}.

Now suppose that Anne decides that she would like to set up a secure channel with Bob. To do this she initiates the following Needham-Schroeder Symmetric Key protocol:

$$
\begin{aligned}
&A \rightarrow S : A, B, N_A \\
&S \rightarrow A : \{B, N_A, k_{AB}, \{A, K_{AB}\}_{K_{BS}}\}_{K_{AS}} \\
&A \rightarrow B : \{A, K_{AB}\}_{K_{BS}} \\
&B \rightarrow A : \{N_B\}_{K_{AB}} \\
&A \rightarrow B : \{N_B - 1\}_{K_{AB}}
\end{aligned}
\tag{1}
$$

In the first step Anne signals to S her desire to communicate with Bob, enclosing a nonce N_A. In the second step S responds to her by sending a nested encryption: the inner part is encrypted under the key K_{BS}, the outer layer is encrypted with the key shared with K_{AS}. Thus A is able to strip off the outer layer and reveal N_A, K_{AB} and B, where K_{AB} is a fresh key that S has just generated. A should confirm that the identity B revealed at this point agrees with the one she included in her request; if it does not it indicates that her request was corrupted and so S will have encrypted the inner layer under a key other than that shared with B. She should also check that the N_A agrees with that she supplied. If either check fails she should abandon the protocol immediately.

Assuming that all this checks out, Anne now forwards on the third step the inner encrypted term to Bob. On receipt Bob can decrypt this to reveal K_{AB} and A and concludes that S has provided the key K_{AB} for him to communicate with Anne. Of course there should be suitable redundancy in the plaintexts such that decrypting a message with the wrong key will reveal what will be evident as garbage. The last two exchanges are designed to allow the parties to confirm that they share K_{AB}.

The protocol was analysed by the authors using the BAN-logic (Burroughs-Abadi-Needham), which we will discuss shortly, and was deemed secure, although the analysis did identify the impossibility of proving freshness of the third message to Bob. This is indicative of the attack we describe in the next section. The protocol is secure within the scope of its assumptions, in particular that keys are not compromised, but flawed if we step outside this assumption. This is rather the pattern in the design and analysis of crypto protocols: proof within a given threat model only to later find that the protocol is flawed if the assumptions are relaxed, or the requirement strengthened.

Denning-Sacco Attack. If we allow for the possibility that past session keys get compromised then the NSSK protocol is found to be flawed. This might occur due to leakage of keys or to an attacker succeeding in breaking out the key after cryptanalysis of past ciphertexts. Now of course such breaches will happen and the flaw lies not with the protocol but with the storage of keys or weaknesses of the crypto algorithm. Any past traffic encrypted under the broken key is of course compromised. The difficulty with the protocol is that its design allows the attacker Yves, Y, to exploit such a compromise further: he can fool the responder in the protocol, Bob in our example, to accept an old, compromised key as fresh by simple replaying the third message to Bob:

$$Y \rightarrow B : \{A, K_{AB}\}_{K_{BS}}$$
$$B \rightarrow Y : \{N_B\}_{K_{AB}} \tag{2}$$
$$Y \rightarrow B : \{N_B - 1\}_{K_{AB}}$$

This flaw was identified by Denning and Sacco, [10], Now, unless Bob is assiduously recording the messages of all past runs and checking them against new runs, he has no way of knowing that this is not a freshly generated message from S, via A. He assumes therefore that Anne has recently requested a fresh session key to talk to him and now Yves will be able to impersonate Anne, breaching the confidentiality and authenticity of their communications.

Freshness. This attack is significant as it illustrates the importance of the notion of freshness in crypto protocols. Like groceries, crypto keys go stale over time. There are essentially two ways to provide guarantees of freshness: timestamps and nonces.

Timestamps work by cryptographically binding an indication of the time of creation to a term or value. This is rather tricky to get right: you need rather well synchronised clocks across the network, you need to know that timestamps are generated by a reliable entity and have not been altered in transit etc. One fix of the NSSK protocol takes the form of the Kerberos protocol, [20] which uses timestamps to counter the Denning-Sacco attack.

Another way to fix NSSK without introducing timestamps is to redesign it, in particular altering the flow of the messages. This is what happens, for example, with the Yahalom protocol[1], the details of which we omit, but simply remark that here Anne sends a request to Bob, with a nonce N_A, and Bob forward this to S along with N_A and a nonce of his own N_B. Both nonces are included in the response from S, so providing both Anne and Bob with freshness guarantees for the key material provided.

Nonces arguably provide a more robust mechanism to guarantee freshness than timestamps, in that the entity obtaining the guarantee is much more self-reliant: it just has to rely on the quality of the mechanism generating its nonces. On the other hand, nonces do require a two way exchange while timestamps only require one way communication.

4.2 NSPK

We've seen that, with protocols like NSSK, we can alleviate the key distribution problem to some extent using only symmetric crypto, but we still have to distribute $\mathcal{O}(N)$ keys in advance and we need trusted servers. To do better than this we need to venture into the realms of public key crypto. Given a Public Key Infrastructure (PKI) we can build protocols using PK primitives. We start by illustrating with an early, rather simple protocol again due to Needham and Schroder:

$$A \rightarrow B : \{A, N_A\}_{K_B}$$
$$B \rightarrow A : \{N_A, N_B\}_{K_A} \tag{3}$$
$$A \rightarrow B : \{N_B\}_{K_B}$$

The intuition behind the design is that only B can extract N_A from the first message, and so when A gets the second message back and decrypts it to find

---

[1] Invented by Raphael Yahalom and communicated to Roger Neeedham and published along with the BAN-logic proof in [7].

N_A buried inside she can be sure that it came from B. Similarly, only A can extract N_B from the second message, so when B gets the third message and decrypts it to reveal N_B he can be sure that it came from A. Note furthermore that the nonces give them both freshness guarantees on the messages that they receive.

The protocol was analysed by the authors using the BAN logic and given a clean bill of health. Exactly how to interpret this analysis is rather delicate and indeed people have fallen into pitfalls as a result. Some years ago I reviewed a paper that proposed using the $N_A \oplus N_B$ as a new session key. At first glance this seems plausible, the argument above suggests that the nonces should only be known to A and B. However there is a problem, that was only uncovered about 17 years after the protocol and the BAN proof was published

Lowe's Attack. In 1995, [17], Lowe published the now famous attack on NSPK:

$$A \rightarrow Y : \{A, N_A\}_{K_Y}$$
$$Y \rightarrow B : \{A, N_A\}_{K_B}$$
$$B \rightarrow A : \{N_A, N_B\}_{K_A} \tag{4}$$
$$A \rightarrow Y : \{N_B\}_{K_Y}$$
$$Y \rightarrow Y : \{N_B\}_{K_B}$$

The upshot of this is that Anne believes, correctly, that she has been interacting with Yves, but Bob has been misled into believing that he has been interacting with Anne, and hence he might conclude that N_A and N_B are secrets known only to Anne and him.

This tale is very instructive and it is worth asking how come the protocol was given a clean bill of health and yet is so badly flawed. Indeed some have argued that Lowe's scenario is not really an attack given that the authors of the protocol never claimed that the secrecy of N_A and N_B would be guaranteed.

- The NSPK authors were not explicit about what security properties the protocol was intended to achieve. They described it as an authentication protocol, and indeed it does achieve a weak form of authentication even in the presence of Lowe's scenario: Anne must indeed be involved in the execution for it to occur. If Bob's concern is just to know that Anne as alive and responsive online then the protocol achieves this.
- Lowe's scenario violates one of the assumptions of the BAN logic: that recognised players in the protocol are honest. Yves is a recognised player with a recognised PK but he does not play by the rules.

The lesson here is that the interpretation of the outcome of an analysis is very delicate. It is not enough to claim that a protocol is secure, you must make precise exactly what flavour of security property you are claiming and under what assumptions about the system and the attacker's capabilities.

5   Diffie-Hellman Based Key Establishment Protocols

Using public key crypto primitives we can design endless protocols to provide authenticated key establishment. Many of these are based on the Diffie-Hellman mechanism, [11]. We work in a group $\mathcal{G}$ of large prime order q with generator g. A and B generate fresh random values $x, y \in \{0, \cdots, q-1\}$ respectively. They each raise g to their secret values and exchange the resulting values:

$$A \to B : X := g^x$$
$$B \to A : Y := g^y$$

Now A computes the shared secret $K_A := Y^x = g^{yx}$ and B computes $K_B := X^y = g^{xy}$. Due to the commutativity of exponentiation, and assuming the messages are not corrupted in transit, we should have $K_A = K_B$.

This allows two parties with no prior shared secret to establish a fresh shared secret by communicating over open channels. Its security depends on the assumed difficulty of taking discrete logs in appropriately chosen groups. An eavesdropper on the channel sees the X and Y terms but without being able to extract either x or y he is unable to compute the key. It does not of itself provide any authentication: you have a secure channel, but you can't be sure who is at the other end.

5.1   Authenticating Key Establishment

In this section we overview some of the more interesting and representative of the Authenticated DH-based Key Establishment (AKE) protocols.

Explicit Authentication. A crucial challenge in public key crypto is how to ensure that public keys are correctly bound to the rightful owner, i.e. the person holding the corresponding secret key. If you want to send a message for Anne's eyes only you want to be sure that the PK you use to encrypt the message is indeed the one for which Anne holds the secret key. Achieving such assurance is usually achieved with a Public Key Infrastructure (PKI): a trustworthy way of binding PKs to identities. For this we use Certificate Authorities (CAs) who issue signed certificates linking PK and identities. Using such a PKI to support the authentication there are two main styles of AKE:

– Explicitly authenticated.
– Implicitly authenticated via key confirmation.

Station to Station. The Station-to-station (STS) protocol is a classic instance of the former: the messages are digitally signed to provide authentication of the resulting session key.

$$A \to B : g^x$$
$$B \to A : g^y, \{(Sig_B(g^y, g^x))\}_K$$
$$A \to B : \{(Sig_A(g^x, g^y))\}_K$$

where again $K = g^{xy}$. The protocol is thus DH at its core with some extra constructs to authenticate the exchanges. On receiving Anne's DH term, and having generated is own y value, Bob can already compute the key K. He signs both the DH terms and encrypts this with K and sends this, along with his DH term g^y, back to Anne. Anne can now compute K, decrypt the term using K, and verify Bob's signature. She now signs the DH terms, signs and encrypts under K and sends this back to Bob.

5.2   Implicit Authentication

A different approach is not to sign the messages but rather to fold long-term key values into the computation of the session key. The key establishment phase is followed by a *key confirmation* phase in which the parties exchange values that allow then to confirm, or not, that they have computed the same key, from which they can infer that the other party (or parties) are indeed whom they thought. A prime example of this style of protocol is the MTI family, [18], of which we mention one to illustrate:

Let $y_A = g^{x_A}$ denote Anne's PK, and $y_B = g^{x_B}$ Bob's PK, with corresponding secret keys x_A and x_B respectively. They now run DH style protocol:

$$A \to B : t_A := g^x$$
$$B \to A : t_B := g^y$$

and compute their keys: $K_A = t_B^{x_A} \cdot y_B^{r_A} = g^{r_B \cdot x_A + x_B \cdot r_A}$ and $K_B = t_A^{x_B} \cdot y_A^{r_B} = g^{r_A \cdot x_B + x_A \cdot r_B}$.

Key Confirmation. Various techniques have been proposed for key confirmation but we will just illustrate with one: hash key confirmation:

$$A \to B : Hash(1, k_{AB})$$
$$B \to A : Hash(2, k_{AB})$$
(5)

Anne computes the hash of a fixed, agreed value such as 1 concatenated with her key and sends this to Bob. Bob computes the hash on his key and checks that these values agree, in which case he is convinced that he ran the protocol with Alice. He now sends the hash applied to 2 concatenated with his key value back to Alice for her to check that this agrees with the value she computes.

5.3   Password Authenticated Key Establishment

If we do not have access to a PKI, we need other ways to authenticate an AKE. One approach is to assume that Anne and Bob previously exchanged a low entropy secret such as a password π and to use this to authenticate a typically DH based key establishment. This is usually done by again folding π into the calculation of K, followed by some form of key establishment. The challenge in the design of such protocols is to avoid giving the attacker the means to launch off-line dictionary attacks: the low entropy nature of the shared secret means that brute force search is feasible if the attacker has a way to confirm guesses.

To illustrate, a naive attempt might be to use a DH protocol but then compute the key as (a function of) $g^{x \cdot y \cdot \pi}$, followed by key confirmation. This fails immediately to an active attacker: suppose Yves masquerades as Bob. He gets g^x from Anne and sends g^y to Anne who replies with something like $Hash(1, g^{x \cdot y \cdot \pi}))$. Yves can now use this value to test guesses at π at his leisure.

A simple PAKE is PPK, [6],

$$A \rightarrow B : X := h(\pi) \cdot g^x$$
$$B \rightarrow A : Y := h(\pi) \cdot g^y$$

With $K_A = (Y/h(\pi))^x$ and $K_B = (X/h(\pi))^y$. As long as they indeed share the same password the $h(\pi)$ terms cancel in the key computation and both derive $K = g^{x \cdot y}$. If not, the attacker has to deal with a non-zero term raised to an unknown, high-entropy value created by the honest party which masks the correct key value and so foils off-line dictionary search.

6   HISPs

If we have access to an authenticated *out of bands channel* we can take yet another approach to designing a AKE. These are channels that typically do not provide any secrecy but are assumed to provide authentication. An example is a visual channel between a mobile device and a server. Suppose that a user wants to establish a secure channel between his mobile device and a nearby printer, and assume that he can see the display on both and can compare short strings displayed on them. We can design a protocol that will establish a fresh key between the devices whose authenticity is guaranteed with high probability if the codes displayed on the two devices match. More precisely, if another device attempts a man-in-the middle attack it has only a slim chance of injecting a fake DH terms that will give rise to matching codes. The probability of success of such an attack falls off exponentially with the length of codes, so there is a tradeoff between the level of security and usability.

A naive design would fall prey to the fact that the space of possible codes is rather small for short codes, say six digits, so it would be feasible for a NITM to quickly search over DH terms to find one that yields a match. This is countered by requiring the devices first to crypto commit the DH terms and then compete the protocol. Due to space constraints we do not go into details here but just remark that again Bill played a major role in the development of such protocols, [25].

More recently, [28], Bill observed that an attacker could attempt repeated man-in-the-middle (MitM) attacks by disguising a failed attack by aborting the protocol as soon as he knows of the failure, but before the honest party has enough information to establish that it was an attack. The honest party might attribute such events to network failures so allowing the attacker to launch many attempts before taking counter-measures. Bill introduced a new class of protocols known as *Auditable* HISPs to counter such a strategy. This requires a new *delay* primitive, a form of crypto commitment that can be prised open without the opening key but it takes some lower bounded amount of time to do so. Thus, even if an attacker attempting a MitM attack aborts, the honest party will in due course be able to detect the attempted attack when the relevant delay term is opened.

7   Analysis Frameworks and Tools

We have not said much yet about the tools and techniques that have been developed for the analysis of security protocols. We turn our attention to this in this section.

7.1   BAN-Logic

The BAN-logic, due to Burrows, Abadi and Needham, [7], is one of the earliest frameworks proposed for the analysis of security protocols. It is described as a logic of authentication and is designed to allow the analyst to reason about the way the honest parties' beliefs evolve as the protocol unfolds. Accordingly a number of postulates are provided asserting for example:

$$\frac{A \mid\equiv A \underset{\longleftrightarrow}{k} B, A \lhd \{X\}_k,}{A \mid\equiv B \mid\sim X}$$

which can be interpreted as: if A believes ($\mid\equiv$) that the key k is good for communication with B ($A \underset{\longleftrightarrow}{k} B$) (i.e. is known only to A and B) and A receives ($\lhd$) a message X encrypted under K, then A can be confident that X originated ($\mid\sim$) from B. This assumes that agents recognise their own messages and this postulate is appropriate for symmetric, non-malleable encryption. Informally this is justified by observing that if K is indeed known only to A and B then, aside from A, only B could have constructed the ciphertext.

To analyse a protocol you first formulate the initial beliefs of the parties as statements of the logic, for example regarding shared secrets and keys, the association of public keys to identities etc. Then there is a so-called *idealisation* step in which the protocol transitions are mapped into the logic. Then you apply the postulates to the initial predicates and try to derive the goals of the protocol. A typical goal for an AKE might be:

$$A \mid\equiv A \underset{\longleftrightarrow}{k} B$$

i.e., at the end of a successful run of the protocol A believes that the session key k is "good" for communication with B. Or even:

$$B \mid\equiv A \mid\equiv A \underset{\longleftrightarrow}{k} B$$

i.e., that B believes that A believes that k is good to communicate with him.

7.2   Getting Off the BAN-Wagon

The BAN-logic was seminal and ground breaking and in the words of the late Roger Needham (the "N" of "BAN") "....it has a number of scalps under its belt." However it has a number of limitations:

- What exactly is meant by "authentication" is not explicit.
- There is no explicit model of the attacker's capabilities, these are implicitly buried in the choice of inference rules.
- There is no clear semantics of notion of "belief", "freshness" etc.
- Recognised agents are assumed "honest".
- The idealisation process is informal and error-prone.

Considerable effort was invested in providing a more formal semantics and a degree of automation to the BAN-logic but certain limitations remain intrinsic to the approach. It was a feeling of unease with the BAN-logic that prompted me, while at the Defence Research Agency, to submit a project proposal to explore the application of mainstream formal methods, in particular process algebra and model-checking to the analysis of security protocols. The project was in collaboration with the University of Oxford and the spin-off company Formal Systems, as well as Royal Holloway. Bill's contributions were the main driver in the success of the project.

Soon after the start of the project, Gavin Lowe found the attack on the NSPK protocol. This showed up clearly the deficiencies of the BAN-logic and demonstrated the power of the process algebra and model-checking approach. As a consequence of the success of the approach virtually all work on BAN-logic and related belief logics ceased and the application of model-checkers and theorem provers is now mainstream for the modelling and analysis of security protocols.

7.3   The Dolev-Yao Model

Roughly contemporaneous with the BAN-logic another seminal approach to the analysis of security protocols was proposed: the Dolev-Yao model, [12]. Here, in contrast to the BAN-logic, the capabilities of the attacker are modelled explicitly: we assume that the attacker has complete control over the communications network, constrained only by the cryptography. Thus the attacker can eavesdrop, intercept, delay, reroute, replay etc. messages at will. He can also inject fake messages, up to the constraints of the cryptography. An inference system specifies exactly what terms attacker is able to construct given the knowledge and terms that he already possesses. Thus he can de-concatenate or concatenate terms, compute hashes. He can extract plaintext only if he possesses the decryption key and he can construct a signature on a term only if he possesses the signing key and so on.

This is usually referred to as the assumption of *perfect cryptography*, in other words we assume the cryptography works exactly as specified and we treat the algebra of terms as a free algebra. We do not concern ourselves with how terms are actually formed as bit strings but rather we handle everything symbolically.

The symbolic approach has the advantage of simplicity and lends itself well to automation, in particular using established formal methods tools. It is clear however that it is an approximation to reality. It is not true for example that:

$$m \neq m' \wedge k \neq k' \Rightarrow \{m\}_K \neq \{m'\}_k$$

It may be true that the attacker cannot derive a sensitive value exactly, but he may still be able to derive some information about the value. Also, while we can include known algebraic properties of the crypto primitives in the inference rules of the model, there is always the possibility that we may miss some critical structure in the underlying crypto primitives. Thus it can be argued that while an analysis in the Dolev-Yao model can provide good assurance of the correctness of a protocol it cannot provide a full proof. To take proper account of the characteristics of the crypto algorithms we need to turn to another approach, the so-called *provable security* or computational approaches, that we discuss below.

It is also worth remarking that the distinction between the symbolic and the computational approaches to the analysis of protocols is somewhat analogous to that between access control models, e.g. Bell-Lapadula [2] and information flow properties such as non-interference, [15]. The former has the advantage of simplicity but is a rough approximation to reality. Terms like *read* and *write* as used in the Bell-Lapadula model have at best an approximate semantics. Access control models regulate overt channels but fail to capture covert channels, ways that information can flow outside the explicit channels of the model. It was such observations that prompted the development of information flow models such as *non-interference*, [15].

7.4   Process Algebra and Model-Checking

The Dolev-Yao model is incorporated in the process algebra approach as the basis for the model of the attacker. The set of inference rules are coded up and an algorithm that forms the transitive closure of the information available to the attacker is implemented (this requires a extension to the basic FDR model-checker). "Honest" agents can be modelled straightforwardly in CSP, and the attacker can be equipped with a recognised identity, credentials etc. (or equivalently we can think of "honest" agents being corrupted by the attacker acquiring keys and credentials).

The security goals can be captured quite directly as CSP specifications. Thus, for example, a secrecy property can be captured by stating that certain sensitive terms not become known to the attacker, i.e. never show up in the attacker's knowledge base. Similarly authentication properties can be encoded by requiring that for all traces if a message M appears apparently from an agent A then earlier in the trace A sent M.

Once we have a model of the system S, including the model of the attacker, and we have a specification process P, we can perform the analysis by using FDR to check if S is a refinement of P. If the check fails it returns a trace that violates the refinement and that embodies an attack scenario against the protocol. We thus have a very powerful, automated tool for finding flaws in protocol designs.

The difficulty is, as always with model-checkers, that in order for the refinement checks to go through we need to keep the state space of the system modest. A naive encoding of the system will quickly lead to exponential explosion of the size of the state space and so great skill and ingenuity is required to keep the state space to a manageable size while at the same time performing meaningful checks. This where the skill and ingenuity of Bill and others in Oxford really comes to the fore.

It is well known that the analysis of security protocols is undecidable, and hence model-checking analysis, while very effective at finding flaws, cannot typically prove a protocol secure, any more than testing a system can guarantee the absence of bugs. Various ingenious techniques have been developed by Bill and others to push the envelop, e.g. data independence, [22], inductive techniques, [9], nonce recycling [24] etc.

7.5 Provable Security

In parallel with the development of the symbolic approaches described above, that emerged from the formal methods community, the cryptographic community have been developing their own, very different style of analysis, often referred to as *Provable Security* or the *computational* approach. Here the idea is to provide reduction style proofs showing that if an attack exists on the protocol then this can be used as an oracle to break the underlying "hard" problem. The security property is typically formulated as an indistinguishability game: that an attacker with polynomially bound computing power can distinguish between instances with different sensitive information with a probability only negligibly better than random guessing.

For example, the secrecy of an encryption algorithm can be formulated by a game along the following lines:

The attacker Y chooses two messages of the same length, m_H and m_T and submits these to the Challenger C. C flips a coin and encrypts m_b, where b is the outcome of the coin flip, and returns $\{m_b\}_K$ to Y. Y now has to guess at b, let's call his guess b'. Y wins the game when he guesses right and loses when he guesses wrong. We define Y's advantage Adv_Y as:

$$Adv_Y := Prob[b = b'] - 1/2$$

We deem the algorithm to be secure if Adv_Y is a negligible function of the security parameter, usually taken to be the key length. By negligible we mean that this falls off faster than any polynomial.

The idea is that if the algorithms leaks essentially no information about the plaintext then Y's guesses should be scarcely better than random. More precisely, we can drive the advantage down as small as we like by suitable choice of the size of the security parameter. Turning this around: if the algorithm leaks even the slightest information about the plaintext then Y will be able to exploit this to win the game. The fact that Y is allowed to choose the messages means that he is free to choose a pair for which information leakage is maximised, so neatly sidestepping the need to quantify over all pairs of plaintexts.

Some encryption algorithms, e.g. the one-time-pad provide *perfect*, unconditional security, regardless of the computational power of the attacker. For such algorithms we require that the advantage be strictly zero.

Similar, but more elaborate games are formulated to capture the security properties of protocols as opposed to algorithms. Arguably such proofs are more compelling than symbolic style analysis as they take more faithful account of the nature of cryptographic algorithms and also take account of probabilities and the computational resources of the adversary. However, they too have their share of downsides: the proofs are typically very long and complex and error prone. At any point in time there are probably only a handful of people with the expertise and time to carefully check such proofs. Some experts, [16], have severely criticised the whole approach. And of course such proofs are only as good as the underlying hardness assumptions.

A challenge is to understand how the symbolic and computational approaches are related, and in particular how the approximations of the symbolic approach might be justified using computational techniques. A first step in this direction was taken by Abadi et al. [1] which presented conditions under which the approximations of the symbolic approach are justified for some primitives.

Provable security proofs are typically extremely complex and hard to check so a way to cryptographically justify the approximations of the symbolic approach would help get the best of both worlds: the automation and clarity of the symbolic along with the rigorous foundations of the cryptographic/computational.

8 Composability and Refinement

One of the sources of the special challenges posed by the design and analysis of secure systems is the fact that, contrary to safety-critical systems, security properties typically do not compose or refine. That is to say, you can have two systems, for instance protocols, that each individually satisfy a security property and yet when they are composed in a seemingly sensible way fail to satisfy the property. Similarly, you can have a system that satisfies a secrecy property, non-interference say, and yet a conventional (trace) refinement fails to satisfy the property.

The canonical example of the latter is a stream cipher: suppose that we have an excellent such cipher that generates a key stream that is effectively indistinguishable from random as far as the attacker is concerned and so is deemed secure. A perfectly satisfactory refinement of such a device is one that generates only one key stream, but this is manifestly insecure. In essence the problem is that classical, safety refinement is all about reducing non-determinism in behaviour. This is clearly appropriate for a safety-critical system, but secrecy properties rely on uncertainty.

Bill has made significant contributions here too: co-inventing the idea of secrecy as *low-determinism*, [26]. Here a system is deemed not to leak information to a low (classification) environment if the system is deterministic from the low point of view. This means that whatever sensitive activities may be going on behind the interface cannot affect low's observations, and hence cannot convey any sensitive information to low. The beauty of this approach is that it is preserved by refinement and is rather easy to automatically check (FDR has been equipped with a determinism button).

Another of Bill's contributions to the area of information flow is to identify a number of ways that information may be abstracted from the attacker (environment) view, and how to formalise these in CSP. The most obvious way is to simply hide events from view, but here care has to be taken: in CSP hidden events are assumed to occur eagerly, i.e. as soon as enabled. This may not be appropriate for events under the control of the sensitive process that may block or delay their occurence in a way that leaks information. To handle this Bill proposed, besides the usual *eager hiding* operator, a *lazy hiding* operator. Besides hiding events we can merge their identity: low sees the occurence of an event but does not know which of a certain set it is. A further abstraction operator is to mask an event by adding spurious, fake events. Thus, when the environment sees an event it does not know if this is a genuine or fake occurence, Full details can be found in [27].

8.1 Universal Composability

Canetti's notion of *universal composability* (UC), [8], is an elaboration of provable security that seeks to address the issue of composability of crypto primitives and protocols. If two protocols are shown to satisfy properties in the UC model then it will be possible to safely compose them to give a secure result. This allows for a more modular approach to the design and analysis of security-critical systems, but it does come at a price: designs that satisfy UC are typically more complex than ones satisfying conventional characterisations of security. It is often not clear if this complexity is strictly necessary for security or arises as an artefact of the model.

9   Quantum Computing

There is much activity currently in the area of quantum computing. We know that, for certain classes of problem at least, we can obtain an exponential speed up over classical computers. We know in theory how to build and even program a quantum computer and we know of a few algorithms, [31], that can solve problems believed to be intractable with a classical computer. Interestingly, these problems are also the main hard problems on which much of public key cryptography is based: factorisation of products of large primes and taking discrete logarithms. Nobody, as far as is publicly known, has yet constructed a quantum computer of any scale and serious engineering obstacles remain, but if a large scale quantum computer is constructed then much of contemporary cryptography will come crashing down.

One response to the threat posed by quantum computing is to develop quantum cryptography. While quantum phenomena threaten conventional cryptography on the one hand, they also open up new possibilities for quantum based information assurance. In the next section we outline the basics of quantum crypto.

Another response to the threat is to explore so-called *post-quantum* cryptography. Here the idea is to identify hard problems Peterefficient solution on a quantum computer. We outline these in Sect. 11.

10   Quantum Crypto

In 1984 Bennett and Brassard. [4], proposed the idea of performing key establishment where the security is based on the postulates of quantum mechanics rather than on the assumed hardness of certain classes of problem. Thus, in principle, quantum crypto offers the possibility of unconditional secrecy, i.e. guaranteed even in the presence of an attacker with unbounded computational power. Due to space constraints we omit the full details but rather just give a high-level indication of the techniques.

Key establishment is carried out over a quantum channel: Anne sends a stream of photons, each of which she prepares in an independently chosen state from amongst the four possible conjugate coding states: ($\uparrow$) 0° ($\nearrow$) 45° ($\rightarrow$) 90° ($\searrow$) 135°. Typically these will be linear polarisations of photons.

Bob, at the other end of the quantum channel measures each photon in one of the two possible conjugate measurement frames, chosen at random for each photon: the horizontal ($\oplus$) or diagonal ($\otimes$) basis. We take the convention that in the $\oplus$ basis, a 0° photon encodes a 1 and a 90° photon encodes a 0, while in the $\otimes$ basis, 45° encodes a 1 and 135° a 0.

We will not go into the details of the "operational semantics" arising from the quantum mechanics, except to remark that when the polarization of a photon is measured with the "correct" basis the state will collapse to the correct Eigenstate with 100% probability. If the "wrong" basis is used, the wave function will collapse into either of the Eigenstates with 50% probability. Thus, for example, if a $\uparrow$ photon is measured in the $\oplus$ basis it will collapse to the $\uparrow$ state. If a $\nearrow$ photon is measured in the $\oplus$ basis it will collapse to a $\uparrow$ state with 50% probability and a $\rightarrow$ state with 50% probability, and similarly for the other combinations. More generally, if the angle between the photon state and an Eigenstate is θ, then the probability that it will collapse to this Eigenstate is given by $cos^2(\theta)$.

The design is such that if Y attempts to eavesdrop on the quantum channel, i.e. attempts to measure the states of the photons, he will inevitably perturb the state of many. After the quantum phase there follows a series of classical exchanges between Anne and Bob, typically in the clear but authenticated:

- Key Sifting: For roughly half the photons Bob will have chosen the wrong measurement frame, resulting in a random bit. They need to identify these and bin them.
- Quantum Error Rate Estimation: Now Anne and Bob need get an estimate of how much noise/eavesdropping occurred. Note that they cannot distinguish noise from eavesdropping. For this they agree a random sample of the surviving photons on which they compare classical bits. From this they can derive an estimate of the error rate. For BB'84, if this is below 11% they can proceed, if above they abort.

- Information Reconciliation: They now discard the sample set and perform error correction of the remaining bits.
- Secrecy Amplification: they now distill the resulting bit stream to eliminate any information that may have flowed to the attacker from eavesdropping on the quantum or classical channels.
- Key Confirmation: Finally, to confirm that Anne and Bob indeed share the same distilled key and to authenticate the key, they perform a final key confirmation.

They now have a secret key that can be used for secure communication in a One-Time-Pad (Vernam) encryption mode to provide unconditional secrecy Alternatively, the key can be used for encryption under a suitable block cipher such as AES, but in this case the security properties are no longer unconditional.

So far we have not said anything about authentication of the protocol, so in a sense we have a quantum equivalent of DH in the classical world. To authenticate the key-establishment we could use digital signatures, but of course this provides only conditional guarantees, i.e. that depend on the assumed hardness of certain problems. QKE usually strives for unconditional guarantees, depending only on the postulated of quantum mechanics. Consequently, authentication is usually provided by assuming that Anne and Bob share a secret bit string beforehand. Chunks of this string are used in a one-time fashion in Message Authentication Codes based on universal hash functions. This means that each authentication burns plenty of bits and hence runs of the protocol have to generate enough fresh key to replenish that burnt up in authentication as well as provide a surplus of fresh key for subsequent communication.

Since the original BB'84 protocol many new protocols have been proposed, for example based on entanglement, Ekert'92 [13], rather than the *prepare and measure* approach of BB'84. A further development of this approach is the notion of device independent QKE, [32], in which the device that provides Anne and Bob with entangled pairs need not be trusted. A further, rather amazing proposal is *counter-factual* QKE, [21], in which key is derived from photons that are not even transmitted.

Quantum cryptography has its proponents and opponents. Proponents claim that in the face of the possibility of efficient classical algorithms and quantum computers to solve supposedly hard problems, and intelligence agencies' undermining of security standards, e.g. [5], the time is ripe for unconditionally secure cryptography. Opponents argue that although in theory providing perfect secrecy, in practice all implementations have been found to be flawed. Assumptions underlying the proofs of security turn out to be false in actual implementations. For example it proves extremely hard to generate single photon pulses, and an attacker can potentially exploit multi-photon pulses. Current technology means that quantum channels can only operate over limited distances and favourable conditions and typically only in a point to point fashion. In any case the theory is fascinating and the technology will doubtless continue to improve.

11 Post-quantum Crypto

Shor's algorithm gives an exponential speed up on factoring and taking discrete logs, but for many other problems believed to be hard there is no known quantum algorithm giving such a speed up. There is now a very active research community exploring the use of such problems to design cryptographic algorithms and protocols. Amongst the problems studies are: Lattice based, multivariate equations, hash-based, code-based and supersingular elliptic curve isogeny. For some of these there are known reductions to problems known to be HP-hard, such as the Shortest Vector Problem. Whether these problems are really hard, in the classical context let alone the quantum is not of course proven. How to characterise the class of problems for which efficient quantum algorithms exist is not known, but it appears that the key observation is that quantum algorithms are particularly good at finding hidden periodicity.

12 Voting Protocols

An area that has seen intense activity over the past decade or so is that of secure voting schemes. With pressure in many democracies to move to digital elections, and even to internet-based elections this has become an urgent issue. While digital technologies can bring advantages they also bring many new, poorly understood threats. The crypto and security communities have been active in developing protocols to make computer aided voting more secure, in particular the so-called *end-to-end verifiable* schemes that provide voters with the means to confirm to their own satisfaction that their vote is accurately included in the tally and yet not provide any proof to third party as to how they voted.

At an abstract level, voting protocols can be viewed as instances of secure, distributed computation, but in fact they turn out to present special challenges of their own. The difficulties arise at the edges, with the creation of the encrypted inputs, i.e. votes. Ideally we want to avoid the need to trust any of the technology and in particular the devices that encrypt the vote's choice. We need to encrypt the vote in a way that gives the voter assurance that the vote is correctly encrypted and yet, in order to avoid coercion or vote buying threats, provides no way to convince a third party of this. This is usually handled by some form of cut-and-chose protocol: the device is required to produce n encryptions of the voter's choice and all but one is chosen at random for audit. If the $n-1$ audited encryptions are shown to be correct this provides evidence that the remaining encryption is also correct. A sequential version of this, in which the voter is given the choice to cast or audit a ballot an unbounded number of times is referred to as *Benaloh challenges*, [3].

A more sophisticated approach, [19], that leads to a higher level of assurance, is to have the voter perform an interactive zero-knowledge proof of the correctness of the encryption in the booth. In order to mask the vote the device also provides fake transcripts of proofs for the alternative votes. Only the voter knows which was the genuine, interactive proof. This very elegant approach was implemented in a commercial system called *VoteHere* but this ultimately failed, due presumably to the complexity of the ceremony from the voter's point of view.

As if all this were not challenging enough, we have the additional requirement that if something goes wrong it is important to be able to identify the culprit. Without this we have the danger of users seeking to discredit the system or the election crying foul when in fact the system has performed perfectly correctly. Consider the following scenario: a voter inputs a vote for Trump and opts to audit this. On audit the encryption indeed shows a vote to Trump but the voter complains that he input a vote for Clinton. It is now hard to establish whether it is the system or the voter that is at fault.

One approach that resolves this issue, at least regarding the ballot audit step, is *Prêt à Voter*, [29]. In this scheme each ballot form has an independent, random permutation of the candidate list. The encryption is now not of the vote but of the order in which the candidates are listed on the ballot. In the booth the voter marks the ballot and detaches and discards the candidate list leaving only an indication of the position marked (or perhaps a ranking vector) and the encryption of the candidate order. The beauty of this approach is that ballot auditing can now be performed on blank ballots rather than encrypted votes. The correctness of the encryption of the vote follows from the correct construction of the ballot, i.e. that the order of the candidates printed on the form is consistent with the order buried in the ciphertext. Thus we can audit blank forms and there can be no dispute: the ballot is either correctly formed or it is not. Furthermore the audit can be performed entirely independent of the voter or the vote, hence there is no privacy issue.

Such schemes are appealing, at least in theory, in that they hold out the possibility of avoiding any reliance on the correctness of the technology: the guiding principle is that of auditability and any corruption or malfunction of any component is detectable. The problem is that understanding the arguments on which this assurance is based is far from straightforward: voters have to be convinced that their vote is correctly encrypted, that this encryption is accurately included in the tally and is correctly handled and decrypted. This fine for someone with a PhD in modern crypto but a bit hard to swallow for the average voter or indeed voting official or politician.

A different approach to providing voter verifiability is to provide voters with secret tracker numbers: votes are posted in the clear alongside their associated tracker, allowing voters to confirm in a very direct, intuitive fashion that their vote is accurately included in the tally. The drawback with doing this in a naive way is that it opens up coercion and vote-buying possibilities: if the voter is able to simply check her vote then so is a coercer. However we notice that such a coercion attack is only effective if the coercer demands the tracker before the vote/tracker pairs are posted to the bulletin board. If he asks for the tracker after posting the voter has the possibility to provide a alternative tracker that points to whatever vote the coercer required.

The above observation provides the key idea behind the *Selene* scheme, [30], Here some rather simple crypto under the bonnet ensures:

- Each voter gets a unique tracker.
- The trackers are committed to the voters but not revealed to them until after the vote/tracker pairs have been posted. Furthermore this is done in such a way as to provide high assurance that it is the correct, assigned tracker but in a way that the voter can deny if pressed further by the coercer.

Selene thus provides a very simple, understandable way for voters to verify their vote while providing a good level of mitigation against coercion and vote buying. It still does not provide sufficient levels of security to be used critical, binding elections, but then no existing internet based voting system currently provides adequate security for such elections.

13   Socio-Technical Aspects of Security

I would like to finish by mentioning an important but until recently largely neglected aspect of protocol design and analysis: the human aspects. All security critical systems involve humans and the humans typically have a critical role to play in both contributing to and undermining the security. Many of the major security breaches that regularly hit the headlines are due to attackers manipulating the humans rather than any exploitation of failures of the purely technical aspects, the crypto algorithms and protocols etc. Users are fooled into visiting fake web sites and revealing credentials, or are subjected to *social engineering* attacks in which they reveal passwords, or they simply pick up a free USB stick from a bowl in the lobby bearing the company logo but carrying malware etc. Attackers exploit the frailties of human nature but also very often poorly-designed user interfaces.

An interesting question in itself is: why have the socio-technical aspects been so neglected by the information security community when it is clear that they are so critical? The answer I suspect is that for techie folk these aspects are hard to deal with: it is fiendishly difficult to model and understand how humans behave in arbitrary contexts. However, things are changing: people are starting to model *ceremonies* rather than just protocols. Such ceremonies take account of the role of the human in the unfolding of the protocol. For many years now the SOUPS workshop has been addressing issues of usable security, and more recently the STAST workshop the Socio-Technical Aspects of Security and Trust.

14   Conclusions

Security protocols are essential to enable safe, secure interactions and establish trust relations. As such they lie at the heart of the information society. They have seen a rich and rapid evolution over the last few decades. Their design and analysis is one of the most formidable challenges in computing science. In this chapter we have attempted to give a overview of the rich diversity of protocols, security goals and tools and techniques for their analysis. Bill has played a major role in the development of analysis tools and, more recently, in the design of protocols, in particular of HISPs.

Acknowledgements. This chapter is based on a Taft Lecture delivered at the University of Cincinnati. I thank Jintai Ding for the invitation and the Taft Foundation for supporting the visit. I also thank the EPSRC and Luxembourg FNR for funding my research in these areas over many years. Above all though I thank Bill Roscoe for his insights, guidance and friendship over the years.

References

1. Abadi, M., Rogaway, P.: Reconciling two views of cryptography. In: Leeuwen, J., Watanabe, O., Hagiya, M., Mosses, P.D., Ito, T. (eds.) TCS 2000. LNCS, vol. 1872, pp. 3–22. Springer, Heidelberg (2000). doi:10.1007/3-540-44929-9_1
2. Elliott Bell, D., Lapadula, L.J.: Secure computer systems: mathematical foundations. Technical report. Mitre Corporation, Bedford, MA, USA (1973)
3. Benaloh, J.: Simple verifiable elections. In: 2006 on Electronic Voting Technology Workshop Proceedings of the USENIX/Accurate Electronic Voting Technology Workshop, EVT 2006, Berkeley, CA, USA, p. 5. USENIX Association (2006)
4. Bennett, C.H., Brassard, G.: Quantum public key distribution reinvented. SIGACT News **18**(4), 51–53 (1987)
5. Bernstein, D.J., Lange, T., Niederhagen, R.: Dual EC: a standardized back door. Cryptology ePrint Archive, Report 2015/767 (2015). http://eprint.iacr.org/2015/767
6. Boyko, V., MacKenzie, P., Patel, S.: Provably secure password-authenticated key exchange using Diffie-Hellman. In: Preneel, B. (ed.) EUROCRYPT 2000. LNCS, vol. 1807, pp. 156–171. Springer, Heidelberg (2000). doi:10.1007/3-540-45539-6_12
7. Burrows, M., Abadi, M., Needham, R.: A logic of authentication. Proc. Royal Soc. Lond. **426**, 233–271 (1989)
8. Canetti, R.: Universally composable security: a new paradigm for cryptographic protocols. Cryptology ePrint Archive, Report 2000/067 (2000). http://eprint.iacr.org/2000/067
9. Creese, S.J., Roscoe, A.W.: Data independent induction over structured networks. In: International Conference on Parallel and Distributed Processing Techniques and Applications. CSREA Press, Las Vegas (2000)
10. Dorothy, E., Denning, D.E., Sacco, G.M.: Timestamps in key distribution protocols. Commun. ACM **24**(8), 533–536 (1981)
11. Diffie, W., Hellman, M.: New directions in cryptography. IEEE Trans. Inf. Theor. **22**(6), 644–654 (2006)
12. Dolev, D., Yao, A.C.: On the security of public key protocols. Technical report, Stanford, CA, USA (1981)
13. Ekert, A.K.: Quantum cryptography based on Bell's theorem. Phys. Rev. Lett. **67**, 661–663 (1991)
14. ElGamal, T.: A public key cryptosystem and a signature scheme based on discrete logarithms. In: Blakley, G.R., Chaum, D. (eds.) CRYPTO 1984. LNCS, vol. 196, pp. 10–18. Springer, Heidelberg (1985). doi:10.1007/3-540-39568-7_2

15. Goguen, J.A., Meseguer, J.: Security policies and security models. In: 1982 IEEE Symposium on Security and Privacy, Oakland, CA, USA, 26–28 April 1982, pp. 11–20 (1982)
16. Koblitz, N., Menezes, A.J.: Another look at provable security. J. Cryptol. **20**(1), 3–37 (2007)
17. Lowe, G.: Breaking and Fixing the Needham-Schroeder Public-key Protocol Using FDR. Springer, Heidelberg (1996)
18. Matsumoto, T., Takashima, Y., Imai, H.: On seeking smart public-key-distribution systems. Trans. Inst. Electron. Commun. Eng. Jpn. **E69**(2), 99–106 (1986). Section E
19. Neff, C.A.: Practical high certainty intent verification for encrypted votes (2004)
20. Neuman, B.C., Ts'o, T.: Kerberos: an authentication service for computer networks. Commun. Mag. **32**(9), 33–38 (1994)
21. Noh, T.-G.: Counterfactual quantum cryptography. Phys. Rev. Lett. **103** (2009). 230501
22. Ranko, L., David, N.: A unifying approach to data-independence. Technical report, Oxford, UK (2000)
23. Rivest, R.L., Shamir, A., Adleman, L.: A method for obtaining digital signatures and public-key cryptosystems. Commun. ACM **21**(2), 120–126 (1978)
24. Roscoe, A.W., Broadfoot, P.J.: Proving security protocols with model checkers by data independence techniques. J. Comput. Secur. **7**(2–3), 147–190 (1999)
25. Roscoe, A.W., Nguyen, L.H.: Efficient group authentication protocols based on human interaction. In: Proceedings of ARSPA (2006)
26. Roscoe, A.W., Woodcock, J.C.P., Wulf, L.: Non-interference through determinism. In: Gollmann, D. (ed.) ESORICS 1994. LNCS, vol. 875, pp. 31–53. Springer, Heidelberg (1994). doi:10.1007/3-540-58618-0_55
27. Roscoe, A.W.: Understanding Concurrent Systems, 1st edn. Springer-Verlag New York Inc., New York (2010)
28. Roscoe, A.W.: Detecting failed attacks on human-interactive security protocols (2016)
29. Ryan, P.Y.A.: A variant of the Chaum voter-verifiable scheme. In: Proceedings of the 2005 Workshop on Issues in the Theory of Security, WITS 2005, pp. 81–88. ACM, New York (2005)
30. Ryan, P.Y.A., Rønne, P.B., Iovino, V.: Selene: voting with transparent verifiability and coercion-mitigation. In: Financial Cryptography and Data Security - FC 2016 Workshops, pp. 176–192 (2016)
31. Shor, P.W.: Polynomial-time algorithms for prime factorization and discrete logarithms on a quantum computer. SIAM J. Comput. **26**(5), 1484–1509 (1997)
32. Vazirani, U., Vidick, T.: Fully device-independent quantum key distribution. Phys. Rev. Lett. **113** (2014). 140501

More Stubborn Set Methods
for Process Algebras

Antti Valmari[✉]

Department of Mathematics, Tampere University of Technology,
P.O. Box 553, FI-33101 Tampere, Finland
Antti.Valmari@tut.fi

Abstract. Six stubborn set methods for computing reduced labelled transition systems are presented. Two of them preserve the traces, and one is tailored for on-the-fly verification of safety properties. The rest preserve the tree failures, fair testing equivalence, or the divergence traces. Two methods are entirely new, the ideas of three are recent and the adaptation to the process-algebraic setting with non-deterministic actions is new, and one is recent but slightly generalized. Most of the methods address problems in earlier solutions to the so-called ignoring problem. The correctness of each method is proven, and efficient implementation is discussed.

1 Introduction

Stubborn set methods reduce the number of states that are constructed during state space-based verification of concurrent systems. That is, they alleviate the state explosion problem. They are the "s" of a group that we call *aps set methods*, whose other members are ample sets [1, Chap. 10] and persistent sets [5]. The similarities and differences of the three are discussed in [19].

The first publication on stubborn sets [13] used Petri nets and shared variable programs. Application of the ideas to process algebras proved difficult, because originally stubborn sets assumed deterministic transitions, and actions in process algebras are not necessarily deterministic. Therefore, it took four years before the first successful application to process algebras came out [14]. To the best knowledge of the present author, ample and persistent sets are restricted to deterministic transitions/actions even today. In particular, [8] uses deterministic transitions.

After winning the difficulties with non-determinism, existing stubborn set methods for linear-time safety and liveness properties were carried over to process algebras, yielding a method that preserves the traces and another that preserves the traces, stable failures, and divergence traces. Preserving the minimal divergence traces proved much simpler than preserving all divergence traces. Therefore, a natural method for the failures–divergences semantics of CSP [11] was obtained as a byproduct. A method for mainstream branching-time logics was

© Springer International Publishing AG 2017
T. Gibson-Robinson et al. (Eds.): Roscoe Festschrift, LNCS 10160, pp. 246–271, 2017.
DOI: 10.1007/978-3-319-51046-0_13

developed in [4]. It was generalized to non-deterministic actions and the above-mentioned results were summarized in [15], titled "Stubborn Set Methods for Process Algebras".

These and other early publications focused on finding conditions that suffice to guarantee that the reduction preserves the desired properties. Most conditions formalize various aspects of the idea that some enabled action or transition a need not be fired now (and is thus left out of the aps set), because there is an enabled action or transition b (in the aps set) such that whatever relevant information may be obtained by firing a now, may also be obtained by firing b now and postponing the firing of a (or, in some cases, without ever firing a). However, if a is postponed also in the state reached by firing b and so on, it may be that a is never fired and the property is not preserved. This is known as the *ignoring problem*. Most methods contain a condition that has been designed to solve the ignoring problem.

Until 2010 [2], little attention was paid to how the conditions for the ignoring problem affect reduction results. Today this seems a significant omission, because there are simple examples where established conditions work remarkably badly, at least unless some so far unwritten guidelines are obeyed in their use ([2,19,20], and Sect. 4).

Since 2015, the present author has been involved in a series of publications that aim at improving the solutions to the ignoring problem or otherwise develop stubborn set methods further [6,16,19,20]. The present publication adapts these results into the process-algebraic setting (except [20]), improves various details, and presents some novel results. In particular, Sect. 8 and Method 4 are new.

Section 2 presents the process-algebraic framework and the basic facts on stubborn sets in it. To see the ignoring problem in appropriate light, an old method that preserves the stable failures is recalled in Sect. 3. Two new trace-preserving methods heavily based on [16,19] are presented in Sects. 5 and 4. Section 6 presents and slightly improves a method [20] that preserves so-called fair testing equivalence [10], and develops a new method for tree failures. An idea towards on-the-fly verification [6] is the topic of Sect. 7. Section 8 introduces a new method for detecting divergence traces.

2   System Models and Basic Stubborn Sets

The *invisible action* is denoted with τ. The empty sequence is denoted with ε. We assume that $\tau \neq \varepsilon$.

A *labelled transition system* (abbreviated *LTS*) is a 4-tuple $(S, \Sigma, \Delta, \hat{s})$ such that $\tau \notin \Sigma$, $\varepsilon \notin \Sigma$, $\Delta \subseteq S \times (\Sigma \cup \{\tau\}) \times S$, and $\hat{s} \in S$. The elements of S, Σ, and Δ are called *states*, *visible actions*, and *transitions*, and $\hat{s}$ is the *initial state*. If L, L', L_1 and so on are LTSs, then, unless otherwise stated, $L = (S, \Sigma, \Delta, \hat{s})$, $L' = (S', \Sigma', \Delta', \hat{s}')$, $L_1 = (S_1, \Sigma_1, \Delta_1, \hat{s}_1)$ and so on.

The notation $s - a_1 \cdots a_n \rightarrow s'$ means that there are s_0, ..., s_n such that $s = s_0$, $s_n = s'$, and $(s_{i-1}, a_i, s_i) \in \Delta$ for $i \in \{1, \ldots, n\}$. By $s - a_1 \cdots a_n \rightarrow$ we mean that there exists s' such that $s - a_1 \cdots a_n \rightarrow s'$, and $s - a_1 a_2 \cdots \rightarrow$ denotes an infinite path that starts at s and has the labels a_1, a_2, ... The set of *enabled actions* of a state s is $\mathrm{en}(s) = \{a \in \Sigma \cup \{\tau\} \mid s -a\rightarrow\}$. State s is *stable* if and only if $\neg(s - \tau \rightarrow)$, that is, $\tau \notin \mathrm{en}(s)$. It is a *deadlock* if and only if $\neg(s -a\rightarrow)$ for every $a \in \Sigma \cup \{\tau\}$, that is, $\mathrm{en}(s) = \emptyset$.

The notation $s =a_1 \cdots a_n \Rightarrow s'$ means that there are b_1, ..., b_m such that the removal of every τ from $b_1 \cdots b_m$ yields $a_1 \cdots a_n$, and $s -b_1 \cdots b_m \rightarrow s'$. Like with "$-\cdots\rightarrow$", $s =a_1 \cdots a_n \Rightarrow$ means that $s =a_1 \cdots a_n \Rightarrow s'$ for some s'. A *trace* of s is any $\sigma \in \Sigma^*$ such that $s =\sigma\Rightarrow$. A *stable failure* of s is any $(\sigma, A) \in \Sigma^* \times 2^{\Sigma}$ such that there is s' such that $s =\sigma\Rightarrow s'$ and s' *refuses* $A \cup \{\tau\}$, that is, $\mathrm{en}(s') \cap (A \cup \{\tau\}) = \emptyset$. State s *diverges*, denoted with $s - \tau^\omega \rightarrow$, if and only if there are s_1, s_2, ... such that $s - \tau \rightarrow s_1 - \tau \rightarrow s_2 - \tau \rightarrow \cdots$. A *divergence trace* of s is any $\sigma \in \Sigma^*$ such that there is s' such that $s =\sigma\Rightarrow s' - \tau^\omega \rightarrow$. A trace, stable failure, and divergence trace of an LTS is a trace, etc., of its initial state.

State s' is *reachable from* s if and only if there is $\sigma \in (\Sigma \cup \{\tau\})^*$ such that $s -\sigma\rightarrow s'$. That s' is *reachable* means that s' is reachable from $\hat{s}$. The *reachable part* of L is $(S', \Sigma, \Delta', \hat{s})$, where S' is the set of the reachable states of L and $\Delta' = \Delta \cap (S' \times (\Sigma \cup \{\tau\}) \times S')$.

The *parallel composition* of L_1, ..., L_N is denoted with $L_1 \| \cdots \| L_N$. It means the reachable part of $(S, \Sigma, \Delta, \hat{s})$, where $S = S_1 \times \cdots \times S_N$, $\Sigma = \Sigma_1 \cup \cdots \cup \Sigma_N$, $\hat{s} = (s_1, \ldots, s_N)$, and $(s_1, \ldots, s_n) -a\rightarrow (s'_1, \ldots, s'_n)$ if and only if either $a = \tau$, $(s_i, \tau, s'_i) \in \Delta_i$ for some $i \in \{1, \ldots, n\}$, and $s'_i = s_i$ for the remaining $i \in \{1, \ldots, n\}$; or $a \neq \tau$, $(s_i, a, s'_i) \in \Delta_i$ when $a \in \Sigma_i$, and $s'_i = s_i$ when $a \notin \Sigma_i$.

The *hiding* of A in L is denoted with $L \setminus A$. It means $(S, \Sigma', \Delta', \hat{s})$, where $\Sigma' = \Sigma \setminus A$ and $(s, a, s') \in \Delta'$ if and only if there is b such that $(s, b, s') \in \Delta$ and either $a = \tau$ and $b \in A$, or $a = b \notin A$.

We restrict ourselves to systems of the form

$$L = (L_1 \| \cdots \| L_N) \setminus H,$$

where $L_1, \ldots, L_N$ are LTSs and $H \subseteq \Sigma_1 \cup \cdots \cup \Sigma_N$. To simplify discussion on stubborn sets, we consider a modified system of the form

$$\bar{L} = (\bar{L}_1 \| \cdots \| \bar{L}_N) \setminus (\{\tau_1, \ldots, \tau_N\} \cup H),$$

where the τ_i are new distinct action names and each $\bar{L}_i$ has been obtained from L_i by changing the labels of its τ-transitions to τ_i. More formally, for $i \in \{1, \ldots, N\}$ we have:

- $\tau_i \notin \Sigma_1 \cup \cdots \cup \Sigma_N \cup \{\varepsilon, \tau, \tau_1, \ldots, \tau_{i-1}\}$,
- $\bar{S}_i = S_i$,
- $\bar{\Sigma}_i = \Sigma_i \cup \{\tau_i\}$,
- $\bar{\Delta}_i = \{(s, a, s') \in \Delta_i \mid a \neq \tau\} \cup \{(s, \tau_i, s') \mid (s, \tau, s') \in \Delta_i\}$, and
- $\hat{\bar{s}}_i = \hat{s}_i$.

By the definitions of parallel composition and hiding, $\bar{L}$ is the same LTS as L.

We denote the set of actions of $\bar{L}_1 \| \cdots \| \bar{L}_N$ by Acts, and split it to two sets according to whether the actions correspond to visible or invisible actions of $L = \bar{L}$:

- $\mathsf{Acts} = \Sigma_1 \cup \cdots \cup \Sigma_N \cup \{\tau_1, \ldots, \tau_N\} \cup H$,
- $\mathsf{Vis} = (\Sigma_1 \cup \cdots \cup \Sigma_N) \setminus H$, and
- $\mathsf{Inv} = \{\tau_1, \ldots, \tau_N\} \cup H$.

When discussing stubborn sets, visible actions refer to the elements of Vis, and invisible actions to the elements of Inv. We can now write

$$L = (\bar{L}_1 \| \cdots \| \bar{L}_N) \setminus \mathsf{Inv}.$$

If $a_1 \cdots a_n \in \mathsf{Acts}^*$, then by $\mathsf{Vis}(a_1 \cdots a_n)$ we mean the sequence that is obtained by removing all elements of Inv from $a_1 \cdots a_n$.

Given $\bar{L}_1, \ldots, \bar{L}_N$, and Inv, a stubborn set method constructs a *reduced LTS* $L_r = (S_r, \mathsf{Vis}, \Delta_r, \hat{s})$. At the heart of the method is a function $\mathcal{T}(s)$ that, for any $s \in S$, computes a subset of Acts. The set $\mathcal{T}(s)$ is called *stubborn set*. The set S_r is the smallest set such that (1) $\hat{s} \in S_r$ and (2) if $s \in S_r$, $a \in \mathcal{T}(s)$, and $(s, a, s') \in \Delta$, then $s' \in S_r$. We have $(s, a, s') \in \Delta_r$ if and only if $s \in S_r$ and there is $b \in \mathcal{T}(s)$ such that $(s, b, s') \in \Delta$ and either $a = \tau$ and $b \in \mathsf{Inv}$, or $a = b \in \mathsf{Vis}$.

By r-states, r-paths, r-stable failures, and so on we refer to states, paths, stable failures, and so on of the reduced LTS. For added clarity, we often refer to entities in the full LTS by f-states, f-paths, f-stable failures, and so on. We often use the subscript r or f in path notation. For instance, if $\hat{s} -\sigma\rightarrow_r s$, $s - \tau \rightarrow_f$, but $\neg(s - \tau \rightarrow_r)$, then $(\sigma, \emptyset)$ is an r-stable failure but not necessarily an f-stable failure (not necessarily, because there may be another state s' such that $\hat{s} -\sigma\rightarrow_f s'$ but $\neg(s' - \tau \rightarrow_f)$).

The set $\mathcal{T}(s)$ depends on the properties that we want to be preserved during reduced LTS construction. For instance, in Sects. 4 and 5 of the present publication, the reduced LTS has precisely the same traces as the full LTS, and in Sect. 3 it has precisely the same stable failures. To preserve a certain property, a set of conditions is stated that $\mathcal{T}(s)$ must satisfy. Then an algorithm is developed that constructs sets that satisfy the conditions.

At this stage, we introduce the following conditions. Most of the methods in this publication use at least four of them.

D0 If $\mathsf{en}(s_0) \neq \emptyset$, then $\mathcal{T}(s_0) \cap \mathsf{en}(s_0) \neq \emptyset$.
D1 If $a \in \mathcal{T}(s_0)$, $a_i \notin \mathcal{T}(s_0)$ for $1 \leq i \leq n$, and $s_0 -a_1 \cdots a_n a \rightarrow_f s'_n$, then there is s'_0 such that $s_0 -a \rightarrow_r s'_0 -a_1 \cdots a_n \rightarrow_f s'_n$.
D2r If $a \in \mathcal{T}(s_0)$, $a_i \notin \mathcal{T}(s_0)$ for $1 \leq i \leq n$, $s_0 -a_1 \cdots a_n \rightarrow_f s_n$, and $s_0 -a \rightarrow_r$, then $s_n -a \rightarrow_f$.
D2b If $a \in \mathcal{T}(s_0)$, $a_i \notin \mathcal{T}(s_0)$ for $1 \leq i \leq n$, $s_0 -a_1 \cdots a_n \rightarrow_f$, and $s_0 -a \rightarrow_r s'_0$, then $s'_0 -a_1 \cdots a_n \rightarrow_f$.
D2rb If $a \in \mathcal{T}(s_0)$, $a_i \notin \mathcal{T}(s_0)$ for $1 \leq i \leq n$, $s_0 -a_1 \cdots a_n \rightarrow_f s_n$, and $s_0 -a \rightarrow_r s'_0$, then there is s'_n such that $s_n -a \rightarrow_f s'_n$ and $s'_0 -a_1 \cdots a_n \rightarrow_f s'_n$.
V If $\mathcal{T}(s_0) \cap \mathsf{en}(s_0) \cap \mathsf{Vis} \neq \emptyset$, then $\mathsf{Vis} \subseteq \mathcal{T}(s_0)$.
I If $\mathsf{en}(s_0) \cap \mathsf{Inv} \neq \emptyset$, then $\mathcal{T}(s_0) \cap \mathsf{en}(s_0) \cap \mathsf{Inv} \neq \emptyset$.

D0 says that if the state has enabled actions, then its stubborn set must contain at least one. It prevents us from choosing $\mathcal{T}(\hat{s}) = \emptyset$ and thus constructing a reduced LTS consisting of just the initial state and no transitions, if the full LTS is bigger. More generally, **D0** guarantees that if a state has at least one future, then at least one future of the state is investigated by the stubborn set method. Most, but definitely not all, methods in this publication use **D0**.

All methods in this publication use **D1**. It says that for any path that starts at s_0 and contains at least one occurrence of an element of $T(s_0)$, the first such occurrence can be *moved to the front*. The first transition of the resulting path is in the reduced LTS.

When no element of $T(s_0)$ occurs in a non-empty path, some variant of **D2** is often used to prove the existence of a transition in the reduced LTS that, informally speaking, can be *added to the front* of the path. Different methods in this publication use different variants. Clearly **D2rb** implies **D2r** and **D2b**. **D1** and **D2r** imply **D2b**, but not necessarily **D2rb**, because only **D2rb** rules out the possibility of $s_0' -a_1 \cdots a_n \rightarrow_f s_n'$ and $s_0 -a \rightarrow_r s_0'' -a_1 \cdots a_n \rightarrow_f s_n''$ such that $s_n -a \rightarrow_f s_n'$ but $\neg(s_n -a \rightarrow_f s_n'')$. The letter "D" reflects the fact that **D0**, **D1**, and **D2r** guarantee that the reduced LTS has precisely the same deadlocks as the full LTS.

V guarantees that when a visible action is moved to the front by **D1**, the actions that it jumps over are invisible. This is because they are not in $T(s_0)$, but by **V**, the visibility of a, and $s_0 -a \rightarrow$, every visible action is in $T(s_0)$.

I is like **D0** applied to invisible actions. Not surprisingly, it will be used for preserving divergence traces in Sect. 8. We will see in Sect. 3 that it is also used for preserving stable failures, to avoid concluding that (σ, A) is a stable failure when it is not.

Let $s = (s_1, \ldots, s_N)$ be any state of the system. Let $\mathsf{en}_i(s) = \{a \mid \exists s_i' : (s_i, a, s_i') \in \bar{\Delta}_i\}$. Let $\mathsf{dis}(s, a)$ be a function such that if $a \notin \mathsf{en}(s)$, then it returns an $i \in \{1, \ldots, N\}$ such that $a \in \Sigma_i$ but $a \notin \mathsf{en}_i(s)$. (One option is to return the smallest such i.) Sets that satisfy a desired subset of the above-mentioned conditions can be computed with the aid of the following *leads to -relation*.

Definition 1. *For $a \in$ Acts and $b \in$ Acts, we define $a \leadsto_s b$, if and only if $a \neq b$ and either*

1. *$a \notin \mathsf{en}(s)$ and $b \in \mathsf{en}_{\mathsf{dis}(s,a)}(s)$, or*
2. *$a \in \mathsf{en}(s)$ and there is $j \in \{1, \ldots, N\}$ such that $a \in \Sigma_j$ and $b \in \mathsf{en}_j(s)$.*

Let $\mathsf{cls}(s, u)$ denote the reflexive transitive closure of u with respect to "$\leadsto_s$", and $\mathsf{cls}(s, A) = \bigcup_{u \in A} \mathsf{cls}(s, u)$. Let $a \in \mathsf{cls}(s, u)$ and $s -a_1 \cdots a_n \rightarrow_f s'$, where $a_1 \notin \mathsf{cls}(s, u), \ldots, a_n \notin \mathsf{cls}(s, u)$. If $a \notin \mathsf{en}(s)$, then item 1 of Definition 1 guarantees that $a_i \notin \mathsf{en}_{\mathsf{dis}(s,a)}(s)$ for $1 \leq i \leq n$. So $\bar{L}_{\mathsf{dis}(s,a)}$ does not move when a_i occurs, yielding $a \notin \mathsf{en}(s')$. If $a \in \mathsf{en}(s)$, then item 2 tells that no $\bar{L}_j$ that participates a can start moving during $s -a_1 \cdots a_n \rightarrow_f s'$. So a is concurrent with $a_1 \cdots a_n$. These imply that $\mathsf{cls}(s, u)$ satisfies **D1** and **D2rb**. **V** can be made to hold by adding $a \leadsto_s b$ for every $a \in \mathsf{en}(s) \cap \mathsf{Vis}$ and $b \in \mathsf{Vis} \setminus \{a\}$. **D0** is ensured by choosing an enabled u. If $\mathsf{cls}(s, u)$ does not satisfy **I**, $\mathsf{cls}(s, a)$ may be added to it for some enabled invisible a, that is, $T(s) = \mathsf{cls}(s, u) \cup \mathsf{cls}(s, a)$.

Depending on the choice of u, $\mathsf{cls}(s,u)$ may contain unnecessary enabled actions. A better result is obtained by traversing the directed graph $G_s = (\mathsf{Acts}, \text{"}\leadsto_s\text{"})$ in depth-first order and recognizing its strong components using Tarjan's algorithm [12] (please see [3] for an optimization). In the sequel, we will need variants of this theme. Therefore, let $\mathsf{gsc}(s,c,A,B)$ ("good strong component") denote an algorithm that traverses G_s starting from c without entering actions in A until it finds a strong component such that it contains an enabled action, it and strong components that are reachable from it do not contain actions from B, and no other strong component reachable from it contains enabled actions. (Actions in A are not treated as reachable.) It may also reply that such a component does not exist.

The idea of A is that it is a "$\leadsto_s$"-closed set whose actions have already been included in the stubborn set. So, to save effort, it is not entered. It is often reasonable to disfavour enabled visible actions, because if any is taken, $\mathbf{V}$ tends to make the stubborn set big. This is facilitated with B.

The gsc algorithm is an adaptation of the esc algorithm used in many earlier publications. We have $\mathsf{esc}(s,c) = \mathsf{gsc}(s,c,\emptyset,\emptyset)$. The esc algorithm has been implemented in the ASSET tool [17]. The experiments reported in [6,16,17,20] suggest that it runs very quickly.

The Petri net $a \;[\!]\!\!-\!\!\bigodot\!\!-\!\![\!]\; a_1$ satisfies **D2r** but not **D2b**. This is why it is reasonable to have three variants of **D2**, although the "$\leadsto_s$"-relation in the present publication does not exploit their differences.

While claims that aps set methods preserve the desired properties are based on theorems and proofs, claims that some design choice tends to yield better reduction results than some other are mostly based on engineering intuition and experiments. Unfortunately, for the following reason, experiments are unreliable and theorems on performance are difficult to obtain. Consider

$$\overset{u}{\underset{\text{o}}{\text{ }}}\!\!\!\!\!\overset{c}{\leadsto}\text{o} \;\|\; \overset{v}{\leadsto}\text{o}\overset{c}{\leadsto}\text{o} \;\|\; \text{o}\overset{u}{\leadsto}\text{o} \tau_3 \;\|\; v \to \bar{L}'_4 \;\|\cdots\|\; v \to \bar{L}'_N,$$

where $v \to \bar{L}'_i$ denotes the LTS obtained from $\bar{L}'_i$ by adding a new initial state and a v-transition from it to $\hat{\widetilde{s}}$. Assume that the $\bar{\Sigma}'_i$ do not contain c, u, and v. The computation of $\mathsf{gsc}(\hat{s},c,\emptyset,\emptyset)$ starts with traversing either the edge $c \leadsto_{\hat{s}} u$ or the edge $c \leadsto_{\hat{s}} v$. In the former case, because $\bar{L}_3$ disables u, the traversal continues $u \leadsto_{\hat{s}} \tau_3$ and yields $\{\tau_3\}$. We get a reduced LTS with only one transition, that is, $\hat{s} - \tau_3 \to_\mathsf{r} \hat{s}$. In the latter case, $\{v\}$ is obtained. Firing v switches on $\bar{L}'_4 \|\cdots\| \bar{L}'_N$. If subsequent calls of gsc only use elements of $\bar{\Sigma}'_4 \cup \cdots \cup \bar{\Sigma}'_N$ as their starting points, a copy of the reduced LTS of $\bar{L}'_4 \|\cdots\| \bar{L}'_N$ is obtained, which may be arbitrarily big. This means that reduction results may dramatically depend on implementation details and even on the order in which the component LTSs and their transitions are listed in the input of a verification tool.

Reduction results may also depend on the choice of the function dis. (It is not known how to quickly optimize it.) It is also possible to improve the definition of the "$\leadsto_s$"-relation at the cost of more complicated definition and implementation. In the above example, $u \leadsto_{\hat{s}} \tau_3$ was intuitively unnecessary.

Indeed, in case 1, $a \leadsto_s b$ is unnecessary if there is no path in $\bar{L}_{\mathsf{dis}(s,a)}$ of the form $s_i -b\sigma a\rightarrow$, where $\sigma \in \mathsf{Acts}^*$.

As a consequence, numerical results of an experiment may depend on details that are not central to the main ideas of a publication and, therefore, are not reported in it. This makes it hard to meaningfully compare published experimental results.

3   Stable Failures

Most of this publication deals with the so-called "ignoring problem". To appreciate the problem, this section discusses a situation where it does not arise. The main result of this section is from [15]. It will reveal that visible actions may be ignored only in states from which stable states cannot be reached.

We prove now that five conditions mentioned earlier guarantee together that all stable states are preserved in the reduction, and so are also the traces that lead to them.

Lemma 2. *Assume that the reduced LTS satisfies **D0**, **D1**, **D2r**, **V**, and **I**. If s is an r-state and $s -a_1 \cdots a_n\rightarrow_f s'$ where s' is f-stable, then there is a permutation $b_1 \cdots b_n$ of $a_1 \cdots a_n$ such that $s -b_1 \cdots b_n\rightarrow_r s'$ and $\mathsf{Vis}(b_1 \cdots b_n) = \mathsf{Vis}(a_1 \cdots a_n)$.*

Proof. Assume that s_n is an r-state and $s_n -a_1 \cdots a_n\rightarrow_f s'$, where s' is f-stable. If $n = 0$, the claim is obvious.

From now on $n > 0$. We show that $\{a_1, \ldots, a_n\} \cap \mathcal{T}(s_n) \neq \emptyset$. Because $n > 0$, we have $s_n -a_1\rightarrow_f$. By **D0**, $\mathcal{T}(s_n)$ contains an enabled action. Assume first that $\mathcal{T}(s_n)$ contains an enabled invisible action a. If $\{a_1, \ldots, a_n\} \cap \mathcal{T}(s_n) = \emptyset$, then $s' -a\rightarrow_f$ by **D2r**. This contradicts the f-stability of s' and thus yields the claim. In the opposite case, $\mathcal{T}(s_n)$ contains an enabled visible action. By **V**, $\mathcal{T}(s_n)$ contains all visible actions. By **I**, all enabled actions, and in particular a_1, are visible. So $a_1 \in \mathcal{T}(s_n)$.

So there is $i \in \{1, \ldots, n\}$ such that $a_i \in \mathcal{T}(s_n)$ but $a_j \notin \mathcal{T}(s_n)$ when $1 \leq j < i$. By **D1**, there is s_{n-1} such that $s_n -a_i\rightarrow_r s_{n-1} -a_1 \cdots a_{i-1}a_{i+1} \cdots a_n\rightarrow_f s'$. If $a_i \in \mathsf{Vis}$, then the a_j are invisible by **V** and the minimality of i. Therefore, $\mathsf{Vis}(a_i a_1 \cdots a_{i-1}a_{i+1} \cdots a_n) = \mathsf{Vis}(a_1 \cdots a_n)$. This claim obviously holds also if $a_i \in \mathsf{Inv}$. By the induction assumption, there is a permutation $b_1 \cdots b_{n-1}$ of $a_1 \cdots a_{i-1}a_{i+1} \cdots a_n$ such that $s_{n-1} -b_1 \cdots b_{n-1}\rightarrow_r s'$ and $\mathsf{Vis}(b_1 \cdots b_{n-1}) = \mathsf{Vis}(a_1 \cdots a_{i-1}a_{i+1} \cdots a_n)$. So $s_n -a_i\rightarrow_r s_{n-1} -b_1 \cdots b_{n-1}\rightarrow_r s'$ has the same trace as $s_n -a_1 \cdots a_n\rightarrow_f s'$.   □

Theorem 3. *Assume that the reduced LTS satisfies **D0**, **D1**, **D2r**, **V**, and **I**. Then*

1. *An r-state is r-stable if and only if it is f-stable.*
2. *An r-stable r-state r-refuses precisely the same actions as it f-refuses.*
3. *Each r-state has precisely the same r-stable failures as f-stable failures.*

4. The reduced and full LTSs have precisely the same stable states.
5. The reduced and full LTSs have precisely the same stable failures.

Proof. If an r-state is not r-stable, then trivially it is not f-stable either. If it is r-stable, then **I** implies that it is also f-stable. Item 1 has been proven.

To prove 2, assume that s is r-stable. By 1, s is also f-stable. If $s -a\rightarrow_r$, then trivially $s -a\rightarrow_f$. If $s -a\rightarrow_f$, then by **D0** and the r-stability of s, $s -b\rightarrow_r$ for some $b \in$ Vis. By **V**, $s -c\rightarrow_r$ for every $c \in$ en$(s) \cap$ Vis. By the f-stability of s, $a \in$ Vis. So $s -a\rightarrow_r$.

If (σ, A) is an f-stable failure of an r-state s, then there is an f-path $s =\sigma\Rightarrow_f s'$ such that s' is f-stable and f-refuses A. By Lemma 2, $s =\sigma\Rightarrow_r s'$, and by 1 and 2, s' r-refuses A. So (σ, A) is an r-stable failure of s. If (σ, A) is an r-stable failure of s, then $s =\sigma\Rightarrow_r s'$ where s' r-refuses $A \cup \{\tau\}$. By 2, this path demonstrates that (σ, A) is an f-stable failure of s.

Because $\hat{s}$ is an r-state, 4 follows from Lemma 2 and 1, and 5 follows from 3. □

Although item 4 of Theorem 3 is elegant, often we would rather not have it. This is because any theorem of the form "the reduced LTS contains at least these states" works against the purpose of making the reduced LTS small, when the states are unimportant for the properties that we want to preserve during reduction. Leaving **I** out liberates us from (or deprives us of, depending on our goal) 4, as can be seen from the example ⏧a⏧ ‖ ⏧τ⏧, where $a \in$ Vis. In it, without **I**, we could have $\mathcal{T}(\hat{s}) = \{a\}$ and thus lose the stable state s that has $\hat{s} - \tau \rightarrow_f s$.

Unfortunately, without **I**, an r-stable failure need not be an f-stable failure. This is illustrated by ⏧a ‖ ⏧τ, where $a \in$ Vis. We could have $\mathcal{T}(\hat{s}) = \{a\}$, yielding only one state $\hat{s}$ and only one transition $\hat{s} -a\rightarrow_r \hat{s}$ in the reduced LTS. Then $(\varepsilon, \emptyset)$ would be an r-stable failure although it is not an f-stable failure.

In this example, we could also have $\mathcal{T}(\hat{s}) = \{\tau\}$. Then we would only get $\hat{s} - \tau \rightarrow_r \hat{s}$ and lose the trace a. This means that the conditions listed in Sect. 2 do not suffice for preserving all traces. By Lemma 2, this can only happen if no stable state is reachable after the trace.

The trace a was lost because action a was not taken in any r-state, although a is relevant for preserving the traces. We say that a was *ignored*. The *ignoring problem* is that from some state on, a stubborn set method may ignore an action that is relevant for the interesting property at that state. In the next two sections we adapt two recent solutions to the ignoring problem, with the goal of preserving all traces.

4 Visibility-Driven Stubborn Sets

We start this section by presenting another example of the ignoring problem that was introduced towards the end of the previous section. Then we recall the solution used in the trace-preserving method of [15]. With a couple of examples we illustrate that there is room for improvement. Then we present an improved method.

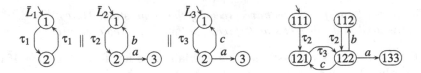

Fig. 1. An example with $\mathsf{Vis} = \{a, b, c\}$ and $\mathsf{Inv} = \{\tau_1, \tau_2, \tau_3\}$

Figure 1 left shows a parallel composition of three LTSs, and right shows the reduced LTS that the new algorithm in this section will yield. We use an obvious indexing scheme for denoting the states. For instance, the initial state is 111. Assume that stubborn sets are constructed by trying $\mathsf{esc}(s, \tau_1)$, $\mathsf{esc}(s, \tau_2)$, $\mathsf{esc}(s, \tau_3)$, $\mathsf{esc}(s, a)$, $\mathsf{esc}(s, b)$, and $\mathsf{esc}(s, c)$ until a set satisfying **D0**, **D1**, **D2rb**, and **V** is found or the list is exhausted. This method chooses $\mathcal{T}(111) = \{\tau_1\}$, yielding $111 - \tau_1 \rightarrow_r 211$. In 211, the method again chooses $\{\tau_1\}$. We get $211 - \tau_1 \rightarrow_r 111$. Because 111 has already been investigated, the method terminates without ever trying other actions of the system. So we have the ignoring problem.

In the trace-preserving stubborn set method in [15], the ignoring problem was solved as follows. The reduced LTS was computed in depth-first order. Tarjan's algorithm [12] was applied on top of the computation, to recognize *terminal* strong components of the reduced LTS. (A strong component is terminal if and only if every transition that starts at a state in it also ends at a state in it.) Let the *root* of a strong component be the state in it that depth-first search enters first (and, as a consequence, backtracks from last).

Whenever the search is about to backtrack from a terminal strong component, the algorithm checks whether every enabled action of its root occurs somewhere within the component. If not, the algorithm extends the stubborn set of the root (keeping **D0**, **D1**, **D2rb**, and **V** valid) such that it contains at least one new enabled action. Instead of backtracking, the algorithm continues the depth-first search via the resulting new transitions. This implements the following condition:

Sen For every r-reachable s'' and every $a \in \mathsf{en}(s'')$, there is an r-path from s'' to some s' such that $a \in \mathcal{T}(s')$.

In our example, the algorithm first constructs the cycle $111 - \tau_1 \rightarrow_r 211 - \tau_1 \rightarrow_r 111$ and backtracks to 111. Then the algorithm detects that it is about to backtrack from the root 111 of the terminal strong component $\{111, 211\}$. Because τ_2 and τ_3 are enabled in 111 but have not been fired in the component, the algorithm adds either $\mathsf{cls}(111, \tau_2) = \{\tau_2\}$ or $\mathsf{cls}(111, \tau_3) = \{\tau_3\}$ to the stubborn set of 111. Let us assume that it chooses $\{\tau_2\}$. We get $111 - \tau_2 \rightarrow_r 121$.

Because of the order in which the esc-sets are tried, the algorithm uses $\mathsf{esc}(121, \tau_1)$ and constructs $121 - \tau_1 \rightarrow_r 221 - \tau_1 \rightarrow_r 121$. Intuitively, this seems a bad choice indeed. Therefore, we suggest a simple but (as far as we know) novel heuristic. We state it in a form that can also be used later in this publication.

Method 4. *Consider a stubborn set construction algorithm that tries* gsc(s, c, A, B) *for each c in some set of actions* $\{c_1, \ldots, c_n\}$ *until a suitable stubborn set is found or the set is exhausted. Assume that s' was first found by firing $s -d \to_r s'$, and* gsc(s, c_i, A, B) *was used as the original stubborn set or extension in s that contains d. At s', try the elements in the order* $c_i, c_{i+1}, \ldots, c_n, c_1, \ldots, c_{i-1}$.

In our example, because 121 was first found via $\tau_2 \in$ esc$(111, \tau_2)$, Method 4 uses τ_2 as the first starting point of the esc-algorithm in 121. Item 1 of Definition 1 draws attention to what $\bar{L}_2$ can execute next, that is, a and b. Because b is enabled in 121 but a is not, we have $b \leadsto_{121} a \leadsto_{121} \tau_3$. Because $121 - \tau_3 \to_f$ and there is no x such that $\tau_3 \leadsto_{121} x$, we have esc$(121, \tau_2) = \{\tau_3\}$. So the method constructs $121 - \tau_3 \to_r 122$. Then the method chooses $\mathcal{T}(122) =$ esc$(122, \tau_2) = \{a, b, c\}$. One of the resulting states is 133. There the method constructs $133 - \tau_1 \to_r 233 - \tau_1 \to_r 133$, because only τ_1 is enabled.

Taking τ_1 in 133 made the reduced LTS grow unnecessarily in the sense that it did not eventually lead to an occurrence of a visible action and thus did not contribute to the traces. For this reason, the following alternative condition was suggested in [15], but it was also pointed out that it is difficult to implement:

SV For every r-reachable s'' and every $a \in$ Vis, there is an r-path from s'' to some s' such that $a \in \mathcal{T}(s')$.

If a terminal strong component contains an r-occurrence of a visible action, then Vis $\subseteq \mathcal{T}(s')$ by **V**, where s' is a state where a visible action r-occurs. So the condition holds for the component.

In the opposite case, it is not easy to see whether each $a \in$ Vis can be thought of as having been taken into account within the component. It may be that a was not encountered when computing the stubborn sets of the states of the component, but for some s' in the component, all enabled actions in cls(s', a) are in $\mathcal{T}(s')$. Then cls$(s', a) \cup \mathcal{T}(s')$ could replace $\mathcal{T}(s')$, making **SV** hold for a while not changing the reduced LTS. Let us replace b by τ_2 in our example, and consider $113 - \tau_1 \to_r 213 - \tau_1 \to_r 113$. This cycle could have arisen from computing $\mathcal{T}(s) =$ esc$(s, \tau_1) = \{\tau_1\}$ for $s \in \{113, 213\}$, not explicitly encountering a; but it could also have arisen from first computing esc$(s, a) = \{a\}$ (because $\bar{L}_3$ keeps a disabled) and then expanding the set to esc$(s, a) \cup$ esc(s, τ_1).

The condition **SV** could be easily made to hold by adding cls(r, Vis) to the stubborn set of the root r of the terminal strong component, if no visible action occurs in the component. The problem with this approach is that it may introduce more enabled actions than necessary, even if $|\text{Vis}| = 1$. Consider $\overset{\tau_1}{\circ}\overset{}{\to}\overset{u}{\circ} \| \overset{\tau_2}{\circ}\overset{}{\to}\overset{v}{\circ} \| \bar{L}_3$, where a is visible, u and v are not, and $\bar{L}_3$ is ready to execute each of them. With it, cls(s, a) contains unnecessarily both τ_1 and τ_2.

In [19], a way of combining the advantages of **Sen** and **SV** was found. We now describe an adaptation of it to the preservation of traces. In it, the following condition replaces both **SV** and **D0**:

S From each r-reachable s'' there is an r-path to some s' that has a set $\text{VIS}(s')$ such that

1. $\text{Vis} \subseteq \text{VIS}(s')$,
2. if $a \notin \text{en}(s')$, $a \in \text{VIS}(s')$, $a_1 \notin \text{VIS}(s')$, $\ldots$, $a_n \notin \text{VIS}(s')$, and $s' - a_1 \cdots a_n \rightarrow_f \dot{s}$, then $a \notin \text{en}(\dot{s})$, and
3. for every $a \in \text{en}(s') \cap \text{VIS}(s')$, there is an r-path from s' to some s such that $a \in \mathcal{T}(s)$.

Let us discuss the intuition of this rather complicated condition. Item 2 says that disabled actions in $\text{VIS}(s')$ remain disabled until an action in $\text{VIS}(s')$ occurs. By item 1, this implies that to enable a disabled visible action, an enabled action in $\text{VIS}(s')$ must occur. Item 3 promises that no enabled action in $\text{VIS}(s')$ is ignored. So for every visible action that can occur in the future, a step towards its occurrence will be taken. If a visible action can occur immediately, that is, is enabled in s', then item 3 promises that it is not ignored.

Because explicit activity against ignoring is only needed in the roots of the terminal strong components, the condition has been formulated so that $\text{VIS}(s')$ need not be computed in every r-state. It suffices that from each r-state, a state where $\text{VIS}(s')$ is computed is r-reachable.

Let "$\rightsquigarrow_s$" be any relation that satisfies item 1 (but not necessarily item 2) of Definition 1. A set satisfying items 1 and 2 of **S** can be obtained by computing the reflexive transitive closure of Vis with respect to "$\rightsquigarrow_{s'}$". This means that $\text{en}(s') \cap \text{VIS}(s')$ can be constructed efficiently with techniques that we are already familiar with, and that then $\text{VIS}(s') \subseteq \text{cls}(s', \text{Vis})$. Item 3 will be established in the sequel by recognizing the terminal strong components and extending the stubborn sets of their roots.

By choosing $s' = s''$ and $\text{VIS}(s') = \text{Acts}$ we see that **Sen** implies **S**. The opposite does not necessarily hold. We can choose $\text{VIS}(133) = \{a, b, c\}$, because $\bar{L}_2$ and $\bar{L}_3$ disable all visible actions. So **S** allows leaving τ_1 out from the stubborn set, avoiding the construction of 233 and the transitions $133 - \tau_1 \rightarrow_r 233 - \tau_1 \rightarrow_r 133$. In this sense, **S** is better than **Sen**.

Let us now prove that this method indeed preserves all traces, and after that discuss its implementation. We first prove a lemma that will be used in the proofs of four theorems.

Lemma 5. *Assume that the reduced LTS satisfies **D1**, **D2b**, and **V**. Let s_n be an r-state and $s_n - a_1 \cdots a_n \rightarrow_f s'_n$. If there is an r-path from s_n to an r-state s such that $\neg(s - a_1 \cdots a_n \rightarrow_f)$ or $\{a_1, \ldots, a_n\} \cap \mathcal{T}(s) \neq \emptyset$, then there are $m \in \mathbb{N}$, $b_1, \ldots, b_m$, r-states s_{n-1} and z_m, an f-state s'_{n-1}, and $i \in \{1, \ldots, n\}$ such that*

- *$s_n - b_1 \cdots b_m \rightarrow_r z_m - a_i \rightarrow_r s_{n-1} - a_1 \cdots a_{i-1} a_{i+1} \cdots a_n \rightarrow_f s'_{n-1}$,*
- *if the reduced LTS satisfies **D2rb**, then $s'_n - b_1 \cdots b_m \rightarrow_f s'_{n-1}$,*
- *$s_n - b_1 \cdots b_m \rightarrow_r z_m$ is a prefix of the r-path from s_n to s,*
- *$\text{Vis}(b_1 \cdots b_m a_i a_1 \cdots a_{i-1} a_{i+1} \cdots a_n) = \text{Vis}(a_1 \cdots a_n b_1 \cdots b_m)$, and*
- *if any of $a_1, \ldots, a_n$ is visible, then $b_1, \ldots, b_m$ are invisible.*

Proof. Let the r-path from s_n to s be $z_0 - b_1 \rightarrow_r \cdots -b_M \rightarrow_r z_M$, where $z_0 = s_n$ and $z_M = s$. Let $z_0' = s_n'$, so $z_0 - a_1 \cdots a_n \rightarrow_f z_0'$. Let $m \in \{0, \ldots, M\}$ be the smallest such that $m = M$ or $\{a_1, \ldots, a_n\} \cap \mathcal{T}(z_m) \neq \emptyset$. By m applications of **D2b**, there are f-states $z_1', \ldots, z_m'$ such that $z_j - a_1 \cdots a_n \rightarrow_f z_j'$ for $1 \leq j \leq m$. If **D2rb** is obeyed, then also $z_0' - b_1 \rightarrow_f \cdots -b_m \rightarrow_f z_m'$. We choose $s_{n-1}' = z_m'$.

If $m = M$, then $s = z_M - a_1 \cdots a_n \rightarrow_f z_M'$. The assumption on s yields $\{a_1, \ldots, a_n\} \cap \mathcal{T}(z_m) \neq \emptyset$. So $\{a_1, \ldots, a_n\} \cap \mathcal{T}(z_m) \neq \emptyset$ both if $m < M$ and if $m = M$.

Let $i \in \{1, \ldots, n\}$ be the smallest such that $a_i \in \mathcal{T}(z_m)$. There is an f-state z' such that $z_m - a_1 \cdots a_i \rightarrow_f z' -a_{i+1} \cdots a_n \rightarrow_f z_m'$. By **D1**, there is an r-state s_{n-1} such that $z_m - a_i \rightarrow_r s_{n-1} - a_1 \cdots a_{i-1} \rightarrow_f z' -a_{i+1} \cdots a_n \rightarrow_f z_m'$.

If each one of $a_1, \ldots, a_n$ is invisible, then $\mathsf{Vis}(b_1 \cdots b_m a_i a_1 \cdots a_{i-1} a_{i+1} \cdots a_n) = \mathsf{Vis}(a_1 \cdots a_n b_1 \cdots b_m)$. Otherwise, there is $v \in \{1, \ldots, n\}$ such that a_v is visible. The minimality of m yields $a_v \notin \mathcal{T}(z_j)$ for $0 \leq j < m$. By **V**, $b_1, \ldots, b_m$ are invisible. If $a_i \in \mathsf{Vis}$, then by **V** and the minimality of i, $a_1, \ldots, a_{i-1}$ are invisible. These yield $\mathsf{Vis}(b_1 \cdots b_m a_i a_1 \cdots a_{i-1} a_{i+1} \cdots a_n) = \mathsf{Vis}(a_1 \cdots a_n b_1 \cdots b_m)$. $\qquad \square$

Theorem 6. *Assume that the reduced LTS satisfies **D1**, **D2b**, **V**, and **S**. Then each r-state has precisely the same r-traces as f-traces.*

Proof. Every r-trace of every r-state is trivially an f-trace of the state.

To prove the other direction, let s_n be any r-state. We prove by induction that for any f-path $s_n - a_1 \cdots a_n \rightarrow_f s_n'$ of length n that starts at s_n, there is an r-path that starts at s_n and has the same trace.

If none of $a_1, \ldots, a_n$ is visible, then the r-path of length 0 that consists solely of s_n has the required trace ε. When $n = 0$, this case applies.

The case remains where there is $v \in \{1, \ldots, n\}$ such that $a_v \in \mathsf{Vis}$. Our next goal is to prove that there is an r-path from s_n to some s such that $\{a_1, \ldots, a_n\} \cap \mathcal{T}(s) \neq \emptyset$. Consider the r-path from $s'' = s_n$ to the s' whose existence is promised by **S**. If at least one state s along the path has $\{a_1, \ldots, a_n\} \cap \mathcal{T}(s) \neq \emptyset$, then the claim obviously holds. In the opposite case, repeated application of **D2b** implies $s' -a_1 \cdots a_n \rightarrow_f$. Because $a_v \in \mathsf{Vis}$ and $\mathsf{Vis} \subseteq \mathsf{VIS}(s')$ by item 1 of **S**, there is a smallest $i \in \{1, \ldots, v\}$ such that $a_i \in \mathsf{VIS}(s')$. Item 2 of **S** yields $a_i \in \mathsf{en}(s')$. Item 3 yields an r-path from s' to some r-state s such that $a_i \in \mathcal{T}(s)$.

The assumptions of Lemma 5 hold such that a_v is visible. It yields $s_n - b_1 \cdots b_m a_i \rightarrow_r s_{n-1} - a_1 \cdots a_{i-1} a_{i+1} \cdots a_n \rightarrow_f s_{n-1}'$ such that it has the same trace as $s_n - a_1 \cdots a_n \rightarrow_f s_n'$. By the induction assumption, s_{n-1} has an r-path with the trace $\mathsf{Vis}(a_1 \cdots a_{i-1} a_{i+1} \cdots a_n)$. This path preceded by $s_n - b_1 \cdots b_m a_i \rightarrow_r s_{n-1}$ implies the claim. $\qquad \square$

Before suggesting an implementation of this method, let us discuss the rationale for it. If $\mathsf{cls}(s, \mathsf{Vis}) \subseteq \mathcal{T}(s)$ holds for any s that is r-reachable from s'', then **S** holds for s''. This can be seen by letting $s' = s$ and $\mathsf{VIS}(s') = \mathsf{cls}(s', \mathsf{Vis})$ in the definition of **S**. Because $\mathsf{cls}(s, \mathsf{Vis})$ may be big, our algorithm uses it only as a last resort. If an enabled visible action is taken to $\mathcal{T}(s)$, then by **V** and its implementation via the "$\rightsquigarrow_s$"-relation, $\mathsf{cls}(s, \mathsf{Vis}) \subseteq \mathcal{T}(s)$. Therefore, the algorithm tries to avoid taking enabled visible actions. Even so, it prefers visible actions as start-ing points, in an attempt to avoid firing actions that do not eventually lead to the occurrence of visible actions and thus do not contribute towards preserving additional traces.

Let $V(s) = \text{en}(s) \cap \text{Vis}$. When a stubborn set is computed for an r-state s for the first time, $\text{gsc}(s, v, \emptyset, V(s))$ is tried for each $v \in \text{Vis}$ in the order of Method 4 until a set is obtained or Vis is exhausted. In the latter case, $\text{cls}(s, \text{Vis})$ is used. We have $\text{gsc}(s, v, \emptyset, V(s)) \subseteq \text{cls}(s, \text{Vis})$.

If the terminal strong component condition calls for extending the stubborn set of s, then $V'(s) = \text{en}(s) \cap \text{VIS}(s)$ is computed as mentioned above. Then $\text{gsc}(s, c, \emptyset, V(s))$ is tried for each $c \in V'(s) \setminus A$, where A is the set of actions a such that there is $\sigma \in \text{Acts}^*$ such that $s -\sigma a\rightarrow_r$. If $V(s) \cap A$ becomes non-empty, then $\mathcal{T}(s)$ need not be extended further. If $V'(s)$ has been exhausted and an extension is still needed, $\text{cls}(s, \text{Vis})$ is used. These are correct by the remarks made above.

The stubborn set is extended in a stepwise manner, to benefit from the facts that an extension may put some $a \in V'(s)$ into A and s may cease to be the root of any terminal strong component. Each of these makes it unnecessary to consider a in s.

The algorithm is *visibility-driven* in the sense that it only uses subsets of $\text{cls}(s, \text{Vis})$. We saw above that this helps avoiding firing unproductive actions, such as τ_1 in our example. If $\text{cls}(s, \text{Vis}) \cap \text{en}(s) = \emptyset$, then nothing is fired, even if this violates **D0**. Figure 1 right shows the reduced LTS that the algorithm constructs in our example.

5   Traces and Always May-Stabilizing Systems

In this section we will present an alternative method for computing trace-preserving reduced LTSs that does not need any condition for solving the ignor-ing problem. It is thus free from the implementation problems and growth of reduced LTS size that such conditions cause. The method is from [16], but its adaptation to process algebras is novel work. In particular, [16] used determinis-tic transitions and always may-terminating systems instead of the always may-stabilizing LTSs that we now define.

Definition 7. *An LTS is always may-stabilizing if and only if from every reach-able state, a stable state is reachable.*

Method 8

1. Choose an action name stop that is not in Acts.
2. Add to each $\bar{L}_i$ a new state and zero or more transitions labelled stop from selected states to the new state. The resulting LTSs are called $L_i^\#$. This is done manually. We will later discuss it in more detail. The added transitions are called *stop-branches*.
3. Compute a reduced LTS $L^\#$ of $(L_1^\# \parallel \cdots \parallel L_N^\#) \setminus \text{Inv}$ obeying **D0**, **D1**, **D2r**, **D2b**, and **V**.

4. If $L^\#$ is not always may-stabilizing, then go back to Step 2, to add more stop-branches. As explained in [16], the test can be performed efficiently with graph-theoretical algorithms either on-the-fly or as a post-processing step.
5. Otherwise let L' be computed by removing all stop-transitions from $L^\#$. It has precisely the same traces as the original system.

Even when not using Method 8, it may be necessary to make a model always may-stabilizing, to ensure that non-progress errors of a certain type are caught. For instance, assume that Client i and the server of a mutual exclusion system communicate via request$_i$, grant$_i$, and release$_i$. A server that just runs around the cycle request$_1$ grant$_1$ release$_1$ request$_2$ grant$_2$ release$_2$ is clearly unacceptable, because Client 2 cannot get service if Client 1 never requests. However, to catch the error, it is necessary to model that Client 1 may refrain from requesting. This can be done by adding a τ-transition from its initial state to a deadlock. This was discussed in [16]. In this section this is irrelevant, because traces do not suffice for catching non-progress errors. It will become relevant in Sect. 6.

If this does not make the model always may-stabilizing, a stop-branch may be added to each component LTS that generates new work to do (for instance, sends messages for transmission) just before where it generates the work. By using a common label for the stop-branches, potentially numerous states are avoided where some but not all LTSs have taken the stop-branch.

Compared to Sect. 3, we have dropped **I** and added **D2b**. As a consequence, it is possible that $L^\#$ is always may-stabilizing even if the model is not. Fortunately, this affects neither the set of traces nor Sect. 6. The important thing is that $L^\#$ can be made always may-stabilizing by making the model always may-stabilizing, so that step 5 can be reached. The following theorem promises this.

Theorem 9. *Assume that the reduced LTS satisfies **D1** and **D2r**. If the full LTS is always may-stabilizing, then also the reduced LTS is always may-stabilizing.*

Proof. Let the *distance to stability* of each f-state s be the shortest length of any f-path from s to an f-stable state (∞, if no such path exists). By the assumption, every f-state has finite distance to stability.

To derive a contradiction, assume that there is an r-state such that there is no r-path from it to an r-stable r-state. Let s_0 be such an r-state with minimal distance to stability, and let this distance be n. By this choice, there are an f-stable f-state s_n and actions $a_1, \ldots, a_n$ such that $s_0 -a_1 \cdots a_n \to_f s_n$.

Because s_0 has an r-path (of length 0) to itself, s_0 is not r-stable. That is, $\mathcal{T}(s_0)$ contains an enabled invisible action a. If none of $a_1, \ldots, a_n$ is in $\mathcal{T}(s_0)$, then by **D2r** a is enabled at s_n, contradicting the assumption that s_n is f-stable. So there is a smallest $i \in \{1, \ldots, n\}$ such that $a_i \in \mathcal{T}(s_0)$. By **D1** there is an r-state s_0' such that $s_0 -a_i \to_r s_0' -a_1 \cdots a_{i-1} a_{i+1} \cdots a_n \to_f s_n$. This contradicts the minimality of n. $\qquad\square$

We still have to prove that if step 5 is reached, the correct traces are obtained.

Theorem 10. *Assume that the reduced LTS satisfies **D0**, **D1**, **D2b**, and **V**. If the reduced LTS is always may-stabilizing, then each r-state has precisely the same r-traces as f-traces.*

Proof. Every r-trace of every r-state is trivially an f-trace of the state.

To prove the other direction, assume that the reduced LTS is always may-stabilizing. Let s_n be any r-state. We prove by induction that for any f-path $s_n -a_1 \cdots a_n \to_f s'_n$ of length n that starts at s_n, there is an r-path that starts at s_n and has the same trace.

If none of $a_1, \ldots, a_n$ is visible, then the r-path of length 0 that consists solely of s_n has the required trace ε. When $n = 0$, this case applies.

The case remains where $a_v \in \mathsf{Vis}$ for some $v \in \{1, \ldots, n\}$. There is an r-path from s_n to an r-stable r-state s. If $\mathcal{T}(s)$ contains no enabled actions, then $\neg(s -a_1 \cdots a_n \to_f)$. Otherwise, let $a \in \mathcal{T}(s)$ such that $s -a \to_r$. Because s is r-stable, a is visible. By **V**, $a_v \in \mathcal{T}(s)$. So the assumptions of Lemma 5 hold both when $\mathcal{T}(s)$ does and when it does not contain enabled actions.

Lemma 5 yields $s_n -b_1 \cdots b_m a_i \to_r s_{n-1} -a_1 \cdots a_{i-1} a_{i+1} \cdots a_n \to_f s'_{n-1}$ such that $b_1, \ldots, b_m$ are invisible and the path has the same trace as $s_n -a_1 \cdots a_n \to_f s'_n$. By the induction assumption, s_{n-1} has an r-path that yields the trace $\mathsf{Vis}(a_1 \cdots a_{i-1} a_{i+1} \cdots a_n)$. This path preceded by $s_n -b_1 \cdots b_m a_i \to_r s_{n-1}$ implies the claim. $\square$

Theorem 11. *The LTS L' yielded by Method 8 has precisely the same traces as the original system.*

Proof. Let $\overset{\downarrow}{\circ}_{\{\mathsf{stop}\}}$ be the LTS with one state, no transitions, and the alphabet $\{\mathsf{stop}\}$. For any LTS L, let $\lfloor L \rfloor_{\mathsf{stop}} = (L \parallel \overset{\downarrow}{\circ}_{\{\mathsf{stop}\}}) \setminus \{\mathsf{stop}\}$, read as "block stop in L". Clearly each $\bar{L}_i$ is strongly bisimilar to $\lfloor L_i^{\#} \rfloor_{\mathsf{stop}}$. So $(\bar{L}_1 \parallel \cdots \parallel \bar{L}_N) \setminus \mathsf{Inv}$ and thus also the original system are strongly bisimilar to

$$\left(\lfloor L_1^{\#} \rfloor_{\mathsf{stop}} \parallel \cdots \parallel \lfloor L_N^{\#} \rfloor_{\mathsf{stop}} \right) \setminus \mathsf{Inv}.$$

Blocking stop-transitions in each component is strongly bisimilar to blocking them after the parallel composition. So the original system is strongly bisimilar to

$$\lfloor L_1^{\#} \parallel \cdots \parallel L_N^{\#} \rfloor_{\mathsf{stop}} \setminus \mathsf{Inv}$$
$$= \left(((L_1^{\#} \parallel \cdots \parallel L_N^{\#}) \parallel \overset{\downarrow}{\circ}_{\{\mathsf{stop}\}}) \setminus \{\mathsf{stop}\} \right) \setminus \mathsf{Inv}$$
$$= \left(((L_1^{\#} \parallel \cdots \parallel L_N^{\#}) \parallel \overset{\downarrow}{\circ}_{\{\mathsf{stop}\}}) \setminus \mathsf{Inv} \right) \setminus \{\mathsf{stop}\}$$
$$= \left(((L_1^{\#} \parallel \cdots \parallel L_N^{\#}) \setminus \mathsf{Inv}) \parallel \overset{\downarrow}{\circ}_{\{\mathsf{stop}\}} \right) \setminus \{\mathsf{stop}\}$$
$$= \lfloor (L_1^{\#} \parallel \cdots \parallel L_N^{\#}) \setminus \mathsf{Inv} \rfloor_{\mathsf{stop}}.$$

By Theorem 10, $L^{\#}$ has precisely the same traces as $(L_1^{\#} \parallel \cdots \parallel L_N^{\#}) \setminus \mathsf{Inv}$. As a consequence, $\lfloor L^{\#} \rfloor_{\mathsf{stop}}$ has precisely the same traces as $\lfloor (L_1^{\#} \parallel \cdots \parallel L_N^{\#}) \setminus \mathsf{Inv} \rfloor_{\mathsf{stop}}$ and thus the original system. $\square$

6   Failures, Tree Failures, and Fair Testing

The sets of traces and stable failures catch illegal deadlocks, but no other *non-progress errors*, that is, errors where something that should happen actually never happens. We will discuss a process-algebraic adaptation of the standard approach to non-progress errors in Sect. 8. There is, however, a surprising result that allows to catch all so-called *may-progress errors* with the methods that we already have. It is presented in this section.

The standard approach to progress requires that in all futures, eventually the awaited thing happens. May-progress only requires that in all futures always, there is a future where eventually the awaited thing happens. It is a strictly weaker notion. Sometimes it is actually more appropriate than classical progress. Even when it is not, it can be used as an incomplete approach that catches some but not all non-progress errors, and never gives false alarms.

Fair testing equivalence [10] preserves a wide range of may-progress properties, and is the weakest congruence that preserves "in all futures always, there is a future where eventually a occurs". Theorem 14 tells how it can be preserved during LTS reduction. It has been slightly modified from [20]. Theorem 12 presents a related result that is new, but intended to appear in the journal version of [20] that is currently in preparation.

A *tree failure* of an LTS consists of a trace and a set of non-empty finite sequences of visible actions such that after executing the trace, the LTS may be in a (not necessarily stable) state where it *refuses* the set, that is, the LTS cannot execute any sequence in the set to completion. The set cannot contain ε, because it cannot be refused. To preserve tree failures, we first present a condition that implies **V**. It is adapted from [1] to the present framework, and its name is from there. Its implementation is obvious.

C2 If $T(s_0) \cap \mathsf{en}(s_0) \cap \mathsf{Vis} \neq \emptyset$, then $T(s_0) = \mathsf{Acts}$.

The following theorem lets us harness any trace-preserving method to preserve tree failures, with the small adaptations possibly needed to establish **C2** and **D2rb**. A counter-example in [20] demonstrates that **V** cannot replace **C2** in the theorem.

Theorem 12. *Assume that the reduced LTS satisfies **D0**, **D1**, **D2rb**, and **C2**, and for every r-state s, the set of the r-traces of s is the same as the set of the f-traces of s. Then for every r-state s, the set of the r-tree failures of s is the same as the set of the f-tree failures of s.*

Proof. Assume first that (σ, K) is an r-tree failure of the r-state s. That is, there is an r-state s' such that $s = \sigma \Rightarrow_r s'$ and s' r-refuses K. For any $\rho \in \mathsf{Vis}^*$, if $s' = \rho \Rightarrow_f$, then by the assumption $s' = \rho \Rightarrow_r$. As a consequence, s' f-refuses K and (σ, K) is an f-tree failure of s.

Assume now that (σ, K) is an f-tree failure of the r-state s_n. There is an f-path $s_n - a_1 \cdots a_n \rightarrow_f s'_n$ such that $\mathsf{Vis}(a_1 \cdots a_n) = \sigma$ and s'_n f-refuses K.

If $n = 0$, then $s_n = s'_n$ and $\sigma = \varepsilon$. Because s'_n f-refuses K, $s_n = s'_n$ r-refuses K. So s_n has the r-tree failure $(\varepsilon, K) = (\sigma, K)$.

From now on $n > 0$. We discuss first the case where there is $v \in \{1, \ldots, n\}$ such that a_v is visible and $a_1, \ldots, a_{v-1}$ are invisible. So $s_n = a_v \Rightarrow_f$. By the assumption, there is s such that $s_n = \varepsilon \Rightarrow_r s - a_v \rightarrow_r$. So $a_v \in T(s)$ and Lemma 5 can be applied. It yields $s_n -b_1 \cdots b_m a_i \to_r s_{n-1} -a_1 \cdots a_{i-1} a_{i+1} \cdots a_n \to_f s'_{n-1}$ and $s'_n -b_1 \cdots b_m \to_f s'_{n-1}$ such that $b_1, \ldots, b_m$ are invisible. Because s'_n f-refuses K, also s'_{n-1} f-refuses K. So s_{n-1} has the f-tree failure (σ', K), where $\sigma' = \sigma$ if a_i is invisible and otherwise $\sigma = a_i \sigma'$. By the induction assumption, s_{n-1} has it also as an r-tree failure. This implies that (σ, K) is an r-tree failure of s_n.

The case remains where $a_1, \ldots, a_n$ are invisible. That implies $\sigma = \varepsilon$. If there is no r-path from s_n to any state s with an enabled visible action in $T(s)$, then s_n r-refuses Vis^+. So it r-refuses K and has (ε, K) as an r-tree failure. Otherwise, let $s_n = \varepsilon \Rightarrow_r s -a \to_r$, where $a \in \mathsf{Vis}$. By **C2**, $\{a_1, \ldots, a_n\} \subseteq T(s) = \mathsf{Acts}$. Because $n > 0$, this implies that Lemma 5 can be applied. The lemma promises that $s_n -b_1 \cdots b_m \to_r z_m$ is a prefix of $s_n = \varepsilon \Rightarrow_r s$, implying that $b_1, \ldots, b_m$ are invisible. So, similarly to the previous case, s'_{n-1} f-refuses K and s_{n-1} has the f-tree failure (ε, K). By the induction assumption, s_{n-1} has the r-tree failure (ε, K). This implies that also s_n has it. $\square$

Fair testing equivalence is obtained by weakening the equivalence that compares the alphabets and tree failures. For $\rho \in \Sigma^*$ and $K \subseteq \Sigma^*$, we let $\rho^{-1} K$ denote $\{\pi \mid \rho \pi \in K\}$. A *prefix* of K is any ρ such that $\rho^{-1} K \neq \emptyset$.

Definition 13. *The LTSs L_1 and L_2 are fair testing equivalent if and only if*

1. *$\Sigma_1 = \Sigma_2$,*
2. *if (σ, K) is a tree failure of L_1, then either (σ, K) is a tree failure of L_2 or there is a prefix ρ of K such that $(\sigma \rho, \rho^{-1} K)$ is a tree failure of L_2, and*
3. *item 2 holds with the roles of L_1 and L_2 swapped.*

The first part of 2 does not follow from the second, when $K = \emptyset$. We have a similar theorem as above, but now **V** suffices.

Theorem 14. *Assume that the reduced LTS satisfies **D0**, **D1**, **D2rb**, and **V**, and for every r-state s, the set of the r-traces of s is the same as the set of the f-traces of s. Then the reduced LTS is fair testing equivalent to the full LTS.*

Proof. The proof is similar to the proof of Theorem 12 with two differences.

First, when $n > 0$ and a_v is visible, application of the induction assumption yields what is promised in item 2 of Definition 13.

Second, the treatment of the case where $n > 0$ but none of $a_1, \ldots, a_n$ is visible is different. If s_n r-refuses K, then (ε, K) is an r-tree failure of s_n. Otherwise, there is $\kappa \in K$ such that $s_n = \kappa \Rightarrow_r$ but $\neg(s'_n = \kappa \Rightarrow_f)$. There is an r-path $z_0 -b_1 \cdots b_M \to_r z_M$ such that $z_0 = s_n$ and $\mathsf{Vis}(b_1 \cdots b_M) = \kappa$. If $\{a_1, \ldots, a_n\} \cap T(z_j) = \emptyset$ for $0 \le j < M$, then **D2rb** yields $s'_n -b_1 \cdots b_M \to_f$, contradicting $\neg(s'_n = \kappa \Rightarrow_f)$. So $\{a_1, \ldots, a_n\} \cap T(z_m) \neq \emptyset$ for some minimal $m \in \{0, \ldots, M-1\}$. Therefore, Lemma 5 can be applied. Let $\pi = \mathsf{Vis}(b_1 \cdots b_m)$. So s'_{n-1} and s_{n-1} have $(\varepsilon, \pi^{-1} K)$ as an f-tree failure. By the induction assumption, s_{n-1} has some $(\rho, \rho^{-1}(\pi^{-1} K))$ as an r-tree failure. This implies that s_n has the r-tree failure $(\pi \rho, (\pi \rho)^{-1} K)$. $\square$

The method for mainstream branching-time logics in [4, 8] relies on a very strong condition: either the ample set contains only one enabled transition and it is invisible, or it contains all enabled transitions. Its adaptation to non-determinism requires even more [15]. These seriously restrict the reduction results that may be obtained. Although Milner's observation equivalence (a.k.a. weak bisimilarity) [7] preserves less information than mainstream branching-time logics, no method is known that exploits this difference. These facts had made the present author believe that powerful aps set methods for proper branching-time properties are not possible. The perhaps most often used example of a proper branching-time property is "in all futures always, there is a future where eventually φ holds". Theorem 14 says, in bold contradiction with the belief, that very little is needed to preserve it! By Theorem 12, even more can be preserved at little extra cost.

Aps set methods that support the standard approach to progress only work well when no explicit fairness assumptions are needed. Integrating a fairness assumption into the property makes too many actions visible, and a series of counter-examples presented in the hopefully forthcoming journal versions of [16, 19] makes fairness-preserving aps set methods seem a distant goal. As a consequence, the method in [20] and this section is perhaps the first aps set method that can, in a useful sense, verify progress properties whose standard treatment needs fairness assumptions.

It is perhaps worth mentioning also that there are no congruences strictly between fair testing and trace equivalences [18].

7 Automata-Theoretic Visibility

In this section we discuss an alternative to the standard notion of visibility that introduces fewer "$\leadsto_s$"-pairs and thus facilitates better reduction results. The results of this section are adapted from [6].

In automata-theoretic model checking, the system under verification is put in parallel with an automaton that keeps track of some information on the executed sequence of actions, and eventually accepts or rejects the sequence. In this section, we apply this idea to *safety properties*, that is, properties whose counter-examples are *finite* sequences of actions.

So we assume that in addition to the system, the verification model contains an automaton $(Q, \mathsf{Vis}, \Lambda, \hat{q}, F)$, where $\Lambda \subseteq (Q \setminus F) \times \mathsf{Vis} \times Q$, $\hat{q} \in Q$, and $F \subseteq Q$. Its acceptance condition is the same as with finite automata (and not the same as with Büchi automata). It synchronizes with every visible action of the system. (We will later see that it could equally well synchronize with every action.) Transitions out from acceptance states are banned, because they are irrelevant for the verification criterion mentioned below.

Let $q \in Q$ and $\sigma \in \mathsf{Vis}^*$. We say that σ is *accepted in* q if and only if there is a path from q to some $q' \in F$ such that its sequence of actions is σ. The goal of the verification is to find out whether the system can execute any sequence of visible actions that is accepted in $\hat{q}$. For that purpose, a reduced LTS of the parallel composition of the system and the automaton is constructed. Its states are elements of $S_1 \times \cdots \times S_N \times Q$ and its initial state is $(\hat{s}_1, \ldots, \hat{s}_N, \hat{q})$. For brevity, we write them as $S \times Q$ and $(\hat{s}, \hat{q})$. It has a transition from (s, q) to (s', q') if and only if $\mathcal{T}((s, q))$ contains an enabled action a such that $s - a \rightarrow_f s'$ and either $a \in \mathsf{Vis}$ and $(q, a, q') \in \Lambda$, or $a \in \mathsf{Inv}$ and $q' = q$.

Even without stubborn sets, the use of an automaton reduces LTS size in two ways. First, it facilitates *on-the-fly verification*: when an accepting path has been found, the construction of the LTS can be stopped, potentially saving a huge number of states (but only if the system is incorrect). Second, it makes it easy to avoid constructing many states that are certainly irrelevant for the verification question. For instance, assume that we are checking "if the first visible action is a, then the second visible action is b and the third is c". If a trace begins with b or c, then it cannot lead to a violation of the property. The construction of such traces can be prevented simply by not having any transition of the form $(\hat{q}, b, q')$ or $(\hat{q}, c, q')$ in Λ.

On the other hand, the approach may also make the number of states grow, because the same state s of the system may occur in two reachable states (s, q_1) and (s, q_2) of the parallel composition. In practice, this has not been a significant problem.

The goal of this section is to obtain a third kind of improvement: the condition **V** can be replaced by two strictly weaker conditions, yielding smaller stubborn sets and better LTS reduction. The method works with every solution to the ignoring problem that has been presented in this publication. In this section, we use a variant of the **S** condition. The computation of stubborn sets obeys **D1** and **D2b** on the system, and the following three conditions that also consider the automaton:

V1 If $a \in \mathcal{T}((s_0, q_0)) \cap \mathsf{en}(s_0) \cap \mathsf{Vis}$, $a_i \in \mathsf{Vis} \setminus \mathcal{T}((s_0, q_0))$ for $1 \leq i \leq n$, $\sigma \in \mathsf{Vis}^*$, and $a_1 \cdots a_n a \sigma$ is accepted at q_0, then also some prefix of $a a_1 \cdots a_n \sigma$ is accepted at q_0.

V2 If $a \in \mathcal{T}((s_0, q_0)) \cap \mathsf{en}(s_0) \cap \mathsf{Vis}$, $a_i \in \mathsf{Vis} \setminus \mathcal{T}((s_0, q_0))$ for $1 \leq i \leq n$, and $a_1 \cdots a_n$ is accepted at q_0, then also some prefix of $a a_1 \cdots a_n$ is accepted at q_0.

SA From each r-reachable (s'', q'') there is an r-path to some (s', q') that has a set $A \subseteq \mathsf{Acts}$ such that
1. every σ that is accepted in q' contains at least one element of A,
2. if $a \notin \mathsf{en}(s')$, $a \in A$, $a_1 \notin A$, $\ldots$, $a_n \notin A$, and $s' - a_1 \cdots a_n \rightarrow_f \dot{s}$, then $a \notin \mathsf{en}(\dot{s})$, and
3. for every $a \in \mathsf{en}(s') \cap A$, there is an r-path from (s', q') to some (s, q) such that $a \in \mathcal{T}((s, q))$.

V1 has been designed to guarantee that in proofs of theorems, whenever **D1** is applied to a path that yields an accepted sequence of visible actions, also the resulting path yields an accepted sequence of visible actions. **V2** has been designed to work similarly with **D2b**, and **SA** protects against ignoring, similarly to **S**. This implies that the proof of Theorem 6 applies with small changes. As a consequence, the reduced LTS contains a reachable state where the automaton accepts if and only if the full LTS contains such a state. A similar result holds for Theorems 10 and 11.

To efficiently construct sets that satisfy **V1** and **V2**, let next(q) be defined as $\{a \mid \exists q' : (q, a, q') \in \Lambda\}$. We let $a \leadsto_{(s,q)} a_1$ if and only if $a \leadsto_s a_1$ or the following conditions hold:

1. $a \in \mathsf{en}(s) \cap \mathsf{next}(q)$, and
2. there is a path $(q, a_1, \ldots, a_n, q_n)$ in the automaton such that $q_n \in F$ and there is no path of the form $(q, a, q'_0, b_1, \ldots, b_k, q'_k)$ in the automaton such that $0 \leq k \leq n$, $q'_k \in F$, and either
   - $k < n$ and $i \in \{1, \ldots, k\}$ is the smallest such that $a_i = a$; and $b_1 = a_1$, $\ldots$, $b_{i-1} = a_{i-1}$, $b_i = a_{i+1}$, $\ldots$, $b_k = a_{k+1}$, or
   - $b_1 = a_1 \neq a$, $\ldots$, $b_k = a_k \neq a$.

Condition 2 may look like cheating: it is complicated and has been designed so that it is obvious that its use implies **V1** and **V2**. However, it is not cheating, because *it only talks about the automaton*. There are common situations where it is easy to see that condition 2 does not hold. They can be exploited to improve LTS reduction. We will now discuss two.

First, consider the mutual exclusion property, where e_1, e_2, ℓ_1 and ℓ_2 model Clients 1 and 2 entering and leaving the critical section. Consider any accepted sequence of actions that starts with e_2. If e_1 is added or moved to its front, the result starts with $e_1 e_2$. It violates mutual exclusion and is thus accepted. As a consequence, for any path $(q, a_1, \ldots, a_n, q_n)$ where $a_1 = e_2$ that satisfies the first line of condition 2 above, there is a path of the form $(q, e_1, q'_0, e_2, q'_1)$ such that $q'_1 \in F$. So condition 2 does not hold, and, unlike **V**, we need not introduce $e_1 \leadsto_{(s,q)} e_2$, although both e_1 and e_2 are visible.

Second, consider the property "after the first occurrence of a, there is no c until b has occurred". To not lose such counter-examples as aac, the automaton must allow more than one a, although only the first a is relevant. This can be implemented by adding a self-loop (q, a, q) to each $q \notin F$ after the first a-transition. If $a'_1 \cdots a'_{n'}$ is accepted in q, then, by the nature of the property, it remains accepted if all instances of a are removed from it, resulting in $a_1 \cdots a_n$. After that, $(q, a, q, a_1, \ldots, a_n, q_n)$ is a path that makes condition 2 fail. So, unlike **V**, no pair of the form $a \leadsto_{(s,q)} a_1$ need be added, although $a \in \mathsf{Vis}$.

As a matter of fact, the reasoning in this example makes the distinction between visible and invisible actions unnecessary. If each accepted sequence of actions remains accepted when i-actions are arbitrarily added to or removed from it, then treating i as invisible is equivalent to treating i as visible and having a self-loop (q, i, q) for each $q \in Q \setminus F$. By the reasoning, no pair of the form $i \leadsto_{(s,q)} a_1$ need be added.

On the other hand, a cannot be made invisible in the example, because its first occurrence is important. The example illustrates *relaxed visibility*: an action becomes unimportant at some point of a counter-example, after which it is treated as if it were invisible [9].

It is also worth pointing out that the automata are typically small. Therefore, it is realistic to pre-compute for each $q \in Q$, $a \in \mathsf{next}(q)$, and $b \in \mathsf{next}(q)$, whether condition 2 holds. We leave the development of good algorithms for this purpose as a research topic for the future.

8   Divergence Traces

In this section we present a new idea for reducing the amount of work involved in preserving divergence traces. We first discuss earlier methods and their disadvantages, then present a theorem underlying the new method, then present the method itself, briefly discuss its implementation, and finally illustrate it with a tiny example.

An example in [15] demonstrates that the conditions presented until now do not suffice for preserving divergence traces. Therefore, a new condition was presented. We show a slight variant of it.

L If $s_0 -a_1 \rightarrow_r s_1 -a_2 \rightarrow_r \cdots$, then for every $a \in \mathsf{Vis}$ there is $i \in \mathbb{N}$ such that $a \in T(s_i)$.

As a matter of fact, there must be infinitely many such i. This can be seen by applying the condition to $s_{i+1} -a_{i+2} \rightarrow_r \cdots$.

If an r-state s is an f-deadlock, we can pretend that $T(s) = \mathsf{Acts}$ and thus contains all visible actions. Therefore, **D0** and **L** imply **SV**.

Let **D3** be like **D2b**, but apply to infinite f-paths $s_0 -a_1 a_2 \cdots \rightarrow_f$. We show now that **D0**, **D1**, **D3**, **V**, **I**, and **L** guarantee that all divergence traces are preserved. If a first $a_i \in T(s_0)$ exists, **D1** moves it to the front. If $a_i \in \mathsf{Vis}$, then $a_1, \ldots, a_{i-1}$ are invisible by **V**, so the trace does not change. If $a_i \in \mathsf{Inv}$, obviously the trace does not change either. If no a_i is in $T(s_0)$, then either **D0** and **V** (if $a_1 \in \mathsf{Vis}$) or **I** (if $a_1 \in \mathsf{Inv}$) guarantee that $T(s_0)$ contains an enabled invisible a. **D3** yields $s_0 -a \rightarrow_r s_0' -a_1 a_2 \cdots \rightarrow_f$, which does not change the trace. Infinite repetition of this reasoning implies the existence of an infinite r-path $s_0 = s^0 -b_1 \rightarrow_r s^1 -b_2 \rightarrow_r \cdots$ whose trace $\mathsf{Vis}(b_1 b_2 \cdots)$ is a prefix of $\mathsf{Vis}(a_1 a_2 \cdots)$. To derive a contradiction, assume that it is a proper prefix, that is, there is $v \in \mathbb{N}$ such that $a_v \in \mathsf{Vis}$ and $\mathsf{Vis}(b_1 b_2 \cdots) = \mathsf{Vis}(a_1 \cdots a_{v-1})$. By **L**, $a_v \in T(s^j)$ for infinitely many j. For each such j, **D1** moves a_i to the front for some $i \in \{1, \ldots, v\}$. But this can happen at most v times, so we have a contradiction.

If S_r is finite, then **D3** follows from **D2b**, and **L** is equivalent to the claim that for every visible a, every cycle in the reduced LTS has a state s such that $a \in T(s)$. In [1], this was ensured—in our terminology—by constructing the reduced LTS in depth-first order and ensuring that when any $s -a \rightarrow_r s'$ is constructed, either s' is not in the depth-first search stack or—in our setting— $\mathsf{Vis} \subseteq T(s)$. (The condition in [1] corresponds to $T(s) = \mathsf{Acts}$. It includes also the invisible actions and is thus strictly worse than $\mathsf{Vis} \subseteq T(s)$. Because the equivalent of $T(s)$ in [1] cannot contain disabled actions, $\mathsf{Vis} \subseteq T(s)$ cannot be formulated naturally in the formalism of [1].)

In [2, Fig. 4] it was pointed out that this condition works badly on a variant of the dining philosophers' system. In [19] it was demonstrated that in the case of cyclic non-interacting LTSs, the condition may lead to the construction of all reachable states. Intuition and both examples suggest that it is better to ensure $\mathsf{Vis} \subseteq \mathcal{T}(s')$ instead. Unfortunately, it is not known whether this is the case more generally. **L** allows distributing the $a \in \mathsf{Vis}$ to the stubborn sets of all states in the cycle. However, the cycle detection condition does not justify the use of other states than s and s', because in addition to the detected cycle $s' -a_1 \to_r s_1 -a_2 \to_r \cdots -a_n \to_r s -a \to_r s'$ there may be another cycle $s' -b_1 \to_r z_1 -b_2 \to_r \cdots -b_m \to_r s -a \to_r s'$ such that it is not detected separately and none of $s_1, \ldots, s_{n-1}$ is in it. Examples of this are easy to construct. This observation makes it reasonable to ask: is it certain that both the use of s and the use of s' are correct. By the following lemma, it is.

Lemma 15. *Consider a directed graph and depth-first search that starts in its vertex v_0. Any cycle that is reachable from v_0 contains an edge (v, v') such that when the search investigates the edge, v' is in depth-first search stack.*

Proof. Let v be the first state in the cycle that the search backtracks from, and let (v, v') be the edge in the cycle that starts at v. (If there are more than one such edge, any can be chosen.) At the time when the search backtracks from v, it has investigated all edges that start at v, including (v, v'). So v' is not unfound. It has not already been backtracked from, because otherwise v would not be the first. The only remaining possibility is that it is in the depth-first search stack. $\square$

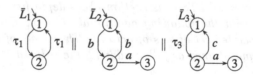

Fig. 2. An example with $\mathsf{Vis} = \{a, b, c\}$ and $\mathsf{Inv} = \{\tau_1, \tau_3\}$

That $\mathsf{Vis} \subseteq \mathcal{T}(s')$ holds can be ensured by replacing the original stubborn set $\mathcal{T}(s')$ with $\mathcal{T}(s') \cup \mathsf{cls}(s', \mathsf{Vis})$.

The example in Fig. 2 has the divergence traces ε, b, ba, and infinitely many others. Assume that a reduced LTS is obtained with the method described above. To represent both ε, a, and ba, it must contain at least three instances of the $\tau_1 \tau_1$-cycle, one where $\bar{L}_2$ stays in state 1, one where $\bar{L}_2$ stays in state 2, and one where $\bar{L}_2$ stays in state 3. We now develop a new method where one $\tau_1 \tau_1$-cycle suffices. Let $\mathsf{ens}(s_0, \ldots, s_{m-1})$ be defined as $\bigcup_{j=0}^{m-1} (\mathcal{T}(s_j) \cap \mathsf{en}(s_j))$.

Theorem 16. *Assume that the reduced LTS obeys **D1** and **D2rb**. Assume further that $s_0 -b_1 \to_r s_1 -b_2 \to_r \cdots -b_m \to_r s_0$, where $b_1, \ldots, b_m$ are invisible. If $s_0 -a_1 \cdots a_n \to_f s_0'$ where $\{a_1, \ldots, a_n\} \cap \mathsf{ens}(s_0, \ldots, s_{m-1}) = \emptyset$, then $s_0' - \tau^\omega \to_f$.*

Proof. Let $j \bmod m = j - m\lfloor j/m \rfloor$. For $j \geq m$, let $s_j = s_{j \bmod m}$ and $b_{j+1} = b_{(j \bmod m)+1}$. We prove by induction that for $j \in \mathbb{N}$ there are s'_j such that $s_j - a_1 \cdots a_n \to_f s'_j$ and, if $j > 0$, we also have $s'_{j-1} - b_j \to_f s'_j$.

The case $j = 0$ is given in the assumptions. We now prove the induction step from j to $j+1$. If any of $a_1, \ldots, a_n$ is in $\mathcal{T}(s_j)$, then by **D1** and the induction assumption, $a_i \in \mathsf{en}(s_j)$, where i is the smallest such that $a_i \in \mathcal{T}(s_j)$. So $a_i \in \mathcal{T}(s_{j \bmod m}) \cap \mathsf{en}(s_{j \bmod m})$. Because this contradicts the assumptions of the theorem, we conclude that $\{a_1, \ldots, a_n\} \cap \mathcal{T}(s_j) = \emptyset$. Now **D2rb** yields an s'_{j+1} such that $s_{j+1} - a_1 \cdots a_n \to_f s'_{j+1}$ and $s'_j - b_{j+1} \to_f s'_{j+1}$.

So $s'_0 - b_1 \to_f s'_1 - b_2 \to_f \cdots$. Because $b_1, b_2, \ldots$ are invisible, we have $s'_0 - \tau^\omega \to_f$. $\square$

This theorem justifies the following method for reducing the work involved in preserving divergence traces. The condition **DV0** in the method is explained later in this section. Until then, please assume that **D0** is used instead.

The method does not try to exploit the theorem in all possible situations; it only exploits it when it is easy. Information on the divergence caused by $s_0 - b_1 \to_r \cdots - b_m \to_r s_0$ is propagated when actions outside $\mathsf{ens}(s_0, \ldots, s_{m-1}) \to$ occur, and dropped when inside actions occur. If $s'_0 - a_2 \to_r s''_0$ has already been constructed when $s_0 - a_1 \to_r s'_0$ is constructed, then it may be that the information never reaches s''_0. Fortunately, this does not mean that the method gives wrong answers; it only means that the savings are not obtained. If the information never reaches s''_0, then **I** is applied in it in the usual way, leading to the detection of a divergence.

Method 17. *The reduced LTS construction obeys depth-first order, **DV0**, **D1**, **D2rb**, **V**, and **L**, with the following additional activity. Each r-state has an initially empty associated set of sets of actions. These sets of actions are called div-sets. They are maintained as follows during the reduced LTS construction:*

1. *Whenever a cycle $s_0 - b_1 \to_r s_1 - b_1 \to_r \cdots - b_m \to_r s_0$ is detected where $b_1, \ldots, b_m$ are invisible, then $\mathsf{ens}(s_0, \ldots, s_{m-1})$ is added to each r-state of the cycle.*
2. *Whenever an r-transition $s - a \to_r s'$ is constructed, those div-sets of s are copied to s' that do not contain a.*

*For each r-state s, when the algorithm is about to backtrack from it, the algorithm checks whether it has any div-set. If it has none, then, before backtracking, the algorithm ensures that **I** is obeyed (this may imply extending $\mathcal{T}(s)$, obtaining new r-states, and entering them). If it has any, then the algorithm adds $s - \tau \to_r s$ before backtracking.*

To maximize the benefit, it seems reasonable to try to avoid firing enabled actions in the div-sets. The use of Method 4 automatically disfavours some of them. It may be possible to improve the results by modifying the order in which the starting points of the gsc-algorithm are chosen. This idea has not yet been studied.

We will soon see an example where the algorithm enters an r-state s_0 such that it inherits a div-set and $\mathsf{cls}(s_0, \mathsf{Vis})$ contains no enabled actions. In such a situation, no visible action can become enabled, and it is already known that s_0 diverges. Therefore, no new information on traces or divergence traces can be obtained by continuing the analysis from s_0. To exploit this, we replace **D0** by a condition that only differs from **D0** by allowing $T(s_0)$ to not contain enabled actions in such a situation.

DV0 If $\mathsf{cls}(s_0, \mathsf{Vis}) \cap \mathsf{en}(s_0) \neq \emptyset$, then $T(s_0) \cap \mathsf{en}(s_0) \neq \emptyset$.

An abstract version of the condition could be formulated using the formulation of **S** as a model. However, the concrete version shown above is much simpler, so we chose to present it instead.

Let $V(s) = \mathsf{en}(s) \cap \mathsf{Vis}$. In r-states with div-sets, **DV0** may be implemented by trying $\mathsf{gsc}(s_0, v, \emptyset, V(s))$ for each $v \in \mathsf{Vis}$ and then $\mathsf{cls}(s_0, \mathsf{Vis})$, similarly to Sect. 4. In r-states without div-sets, after trying the last $\mathsf{gsc}(s_0, v, \emptyset, V(s))$ in vain, it is reasonable to try $\mathsf{gsc}(s_0, c, \emptyset, V(s))$ for each enabled invisible c. This is because **I** forces to take an enabled invisible action if there are any. (Trying $\mathsf{gsc}(s_0, c, \emptyset, V(s))$ may yield enabled actions that are all outside $\mathsf{cls}(s_0, \mathsf{Vis})$, but this is correct, because **DV0** does not require that $T(s_0) \cap \mathsf{cls}(s_0, \mathsf{Vis}) \cap \mathsf{en}(s_0) \neq \emptyset$.) If also these attempts are unsuccessful, $\mathsf{cls}(s_0, \mathsf{Vis})$ is computed. If it violates **I**, $\mathsf{gsc}(s_0, c, \mathsf{cls}(s_0, \mathsf{Vis}), \emptyset)$ is computed for an arbitrary enabled invisible c, and the result is added to the stubborn set.

When **L** forces to extend the stubborn set of s_0, $\mathsf{cls}(s_0, \mathsf{Vis})$ is used.

Because many r-states are likely to share div-sets, it is reasonable to store the div-sets outside the r-states and only have a list of pointers to them in each r-state. Because implementing a single pointer is simpler than implementing a list of pointers, and because it is not known whether more than one div-set on an r-state brings significant additional benefit, it may also be reasonable to only implement a single pointer.

Consider Method 17 on the example in Fig. 2. It first constructs $111 - \tau_3 \rightarrow_r 112$, because $\mathsf{gsc}(111, x, \emptyset, \mathsf{en}(s) \cap \mathsf{Vis})$ yields $\{\tau_3\}$ for any $x \in \{a, b, c\}$. Then it constructs $112 - \tau_1 \rightarrow_r 212 - \tau_1 \rightarrow_r 112$, because gsc fails with visible actions and τ_3, but succeeds with τ_1. The method detects that this is a divergence cycle, and thus adds the div-set $\{\tau_1\}$ to 112 and 212. From then on, all new r-states get the same div-set, because there is no "$\leadsto_s$"-path from a, b, or c to τ_1 in any state, and **I** is no longer obeyed thanks to the existence of a div-set in the state. Furthermore, because of $112 - c \rightarrow_f 111$, also $\hat{s} = 111$ inherits a div-set. Therefore, unlike with the old method, altogether only one $\tau_1 \tau_1$-cycle is constructed.

9   Conclusions

We discussed many recent or new stubborn set methods for process-algebraic verification that address in particular, but not only, problems related to earlier solutions to the ignoring problem. The methods in Sects. 5 to 7 have been experimented with a bit with good results, using the ASSET tool [17]. The models were always may-terminating, to avoid the need of the **S** condition that ASSET does not implement. To get wider experimental results, a proper implementation of each method would be needed. This means that the research on better solutions to the ignoring problem is progressing well, but not yet ready.

References

1. Clarke, E.M., Grumberg, O., Peled, D.A.: Model Checking. MIT Press, Cambridge (1999). 314 pages
2. Evangelista, S., Pajault, C.: Solving the ignoring problem for partial order reduction. Softw. Tools Technol. Transfer **12**(2), 155–170 (2010)
3. Eve, J., Kurki-Suonio, R.: On computing the transitive closure of a relation. Acta Informatica **8**(4), 303–314 (1977)
4. Gerth, R., Kuiper, R., Peled, D., Penczek, W.: A partial order approach to branching time logic model checking. In: Proceedings of Third Israel Symposium on the Theory of Computing and Systems, pp. 130–139. IEEE (1995)
5. Godefroid, P.: Partial-Order Methods for the Verification of Concurrent Systems: An Approach to the State-Explosion Problem. LNCS, vol. 1032. Springer, Heidelberg (1996)
6. Hansen, H., Valmari, A.: Safety property-driven stubborn sets. In: Larsen, K.G., Potapov, I., Srba, J. (eds.) RP 2016. LNCS, vol. 9899, pp. 90–103. Springer, Heidelberg (2016). doi:10.1007/978-3-319-45994-3_7
7. Milner, R.: Communication and Concurrency. Prentice-Hall, Englewood Cliffs (1989)
8. Peled, D.: Partial order reduction: linear and branching temporal logics and process algebras. In: Peled, D., Pratt, V., Holzmann, G. (eds.) Proceedings of a DIMACS Workshop on Partial Order Methods in Verification. DIMACS Series in Discrete Mathematics and Theoretical Computer Science, vol. 29, pp. 233–257. American Mathematical Society (1997)
9. Peled, D., Valmari, A., Kokkarinen, I.: Relaxed visibility enhances partial order reduction. Formal Meth. Syst. Des. **19**, 275–289 (2001)
10. Rensink, A., Vogler, W.: Fair testing. Inf. Comput. **205**(2), 125–198 (2007)
11. Roscoe, A.W.: Understanding Concurrent Systems. Springer, Heidelberg (2010)
12. Tarjan, R.E.: Depth-first search and linear graph algorithms. SIAM J. Comput. **1**(2), 146–160 (1972)
13. Valmari, A.: Error detection by reduced reachability graph generation. In: Proceedings of the 9th European Workshop on Application and Theory of Petri Nets, pp. 95–122 (1988)
14. Valmari, A.: Alleviating state explosion during verification of behavioural equivalence. Department of Computer Science, University of Helsinki, Report A-1992-4, Helsinki, Finland (1992). 57 pages
15. Valmari, A.: Stubborn set methods for process algebras. In: Peled, D., Pratt, V., Holzmann, G. (eds.) Proceedings of a DIMACS Workshop on Partial Order Methods in Verification. DIMACS Series in Discrete Mathematics and Theoretical Computer Science, vol. 29, pp. 213–231. American Mathematical Society (1997)
16. Valmari, A.: Stop it, and be stubborn! In: Haar, S., Meyer, R. (eds.) 15th International Conference on Application of Concurrency to System Design, pp. 10–19. IEEE Computer Society (2015). doi:10.1109/ACSD.2015.14

17. Valmari, A.: A state space tool for concurrent system models expressed in C++. In: Nummenmaa, J., Sievi-Korte, O., Mäkinen, E. (eds.) SPLST 2015, Symposium on Programming Languages and Software Tools. CEUR Workshop Proceedings, vol. 1525, pp. 91–105 (2015)
18. Valmari, A.: The congruences below fair testing with initial stability. In: Desel, J., Yakovlev, A. (eds.) 16th International Conference on Application of Concurrency to System Design (The proceedings to officially appear when IEEE Computer Society condescends to publish it. Based on earlier experience, it may take more than half a year)
19. Valmari, A., Hansen, H.: Stubborn set intuition explained. In: Cabac, L., Kristensen, L.M., Rölke, H. (eds.) Proceedings of the International Workshop on Petri Nets and Software Engineering 2016. CEUR Workshop Proceedings, vol. 1591, pp. 213–232 (2016)
20. Valmari, A., Vogler, W.: Fair testing and stubborn sets. In: Bošnački, D., Wijs, A. (eds.) SPIN 2016. LNCS, vol. 9641, pp. 225–243. Springer International Publishing, Cham (2016). doi:10.1007/978-3-319-32582-8_16

A Branching Time Model of CSP

Rob van Glabbeek[1,2(✉)]

[1] Data61, CSIRO, Sydney, Australia
[2] Computer Science and Engineering,
University of New South Wales, Sydney, Australia
rvg@unsw.edu.au

Abstract. I present a branching time model of CSP that is finer than all other models of CSP proposed thus far. It is obtained by taking a semantic equivalence from the linear time – branching time spectrum, namely divergence-preserving coupled similarity, and showing that it is a congruence for the operators of CSP. This equivalence belongs to the bisimulation family of semantic equivalences, in the sense that on transition systems without internal actions it coincides with strong bisimilarity. Nevertheless, enough of the equational laws of CSP remain to obtain a complete axiomatisation for closed, recursion-free terms.

1 Introduction

The process algebra CSP—*Communicating Sequential Processes*—was presented in BROOKES, HOARE & ROSCOE [4]. It is sometimes called *theoretical* CSP, to distinguish it from the earlier language CSP of HOARE [10]. It is equipped with a denotational semantics, mapping each CSP process to an element of the failures-divergences model [4,5]. The same semantics can also be presented operationally, by mapping CSP processes to states in a labelled transition system (LTS), and then mapping LTSs to the failures-divergences model. OLDEROG & HOARE [13] shows that this yields the same result. Hence, the failures-divergences model of CSP can alternatively be seen as a semantic equivalence on LTSs, namely by calling two states in an LTS equivalent iff they map to the same element of the failures-divergences model.

Several other models of CSP are presented in the literature, and each can be cast as a semantic equivalence on LTSs, which is a congruence for the operators of CSP. One such model is called *finer* than another if its associated equivalence relation is finer, i.e., included in the other one, or more discriminating. The resulting hierarchy of models of CSP has two pillars: the divergence-strict models, most of which refine the standard failures-divergences model, and the stable models, such as the model based on stable failures equivalence from BERGSTRA, KLOP & OLDEROG [2], or the stable revivals model of ROSCOE [16].

Here I present a new model, which can be seen as the first branching time model of CSP, and the first that refines all earlier models, i.e. both pillars mentioned above. It is based on the notion of coupled similarity from PARROW & SJÖDIN [14]. What makes it an interesting model of CSP—as opposed to, say,

© Springer International Publishing AG 2017
T. Gibson-Robinson et al. (Eds.): Roscoe Festschrift, LNCS 10160, pp. 272–293, 2017.
DOI: 10.1007/978-3-319-51046-0_14

strong or divergence-preserving weak bisimilarity—is that it allows a complete equational axiomatisation for closed recursion-free CSP processes that fits within the existing syntax of that language.

2 CSP

CSP [4,5,11] is parametrised with a set Σ of *communications*. In this paper I use the subset of CSP given by the following grammar.

$$P, Q ::= STOP \mid \mathbf{div} \mid a \to P \mid P \sqcap Q \mid P \sqcup Q \mid P \rhd Q \mid$$
$$P \|_A Q \mid P \backslash A \mid f(P) \mid P \triangle Q \mid P \Theta_A Q \mid p \mid \mu p.P$$

Here P and Q are CSP expressions, $a \in \Sigma$, $A \subseteq \Sigma$ and $f : \Sigma \to \Sigma$. Furthermore, p ranges over a set of *process identifiers*. A CSP *process* is a CSP expression in which each occurrence of a process identifier p lays within a recursion construct $\mu p.P$. The operators in the above grammar are *inaction, divergence, action prefixing, internal, external* and *sliding choice, parallel composition, concealment, renaming, interrupt* and *throw*. Compared to [15,17], this leaves out

- successful termination (*SKIP*) and sequential composition (;),
- infinitary guarded choice,
- prefixing operators with name binding, conditional choice,
- relational renaming, and
- the version of internal choice that takes a possibly infinite set of arguments.

The operators $STOP$, $a \to$, $\sqcap, \sqcup$, $\backslash A$, $f(\_)$ and recursion stem from [4], and $\mathbf{div}$ and $\|_A$ from [13], whereas $\rhd$, $\triangle$ and Θ_A were added to CSP by ROSCOE [15,17]. The operational semantics of CSP is given by the binary transition relations $\xrightarrow{\alpha}$ between CSP processes. The transitions $P \xrightarrow{\alpha} Q$ are derived by the rules in Table 1. Here a, b range over Σ and α, β over $\Sigma \overset{\cdot}{\cup} \{\tau\}$, and relabelling operators f are extended to $\Sigma \overset{\cdot}{\cup} \{\tau\}$ by $f(\tau) = \tau$. The transition labels α are called *actions*, and τ is the *internal action*.

3 The Failures-Divergences Model of CSP

The process algebra CSP stems from BROOKES, HOARE & ROSCOE [4]. It is also called *theoretical* CSP, to distinguish it from the language CSP of HOARE [10]. Its semantics [5] associates to each CSP process a pair $\langle F, D \rangle$ of *failures* $F \subseteq \Sigma^* \times \mathscr{P}(\Sigma)$ and *divergences* $D \subseteq \Sigma^*$, subject to the conditions:

$$(\varepsilon, \emptyset) \in F \tag{N1}$$

$$(st, \emptyset) \in F \Rightarrow (s, \emptyset) \in F \tag{N2}$$

$$(s, X) \in F \wedge Y \subseteq X \Rightarrow (s, Y) \in F \tag{N3}$$

$$(s, X) \in F \wedge \forall c \in Y. \, (sc, \emptyset) \notin F \Rightarrow (s, X \cup Y) \in F \tag{N4}$$

$$\forall Y \in \mathscr{P}_{fin}(X). \, (s, Y) \in F \Rightarrow (s, X) \in F \tag{N5}$$

$$s \in D \Rightarrow st \in D \tag{D1}$$

$$s \in D \Rightarrow (st, X). \tag{D2}$$

Table 1. Structural operational semantics of CSP

$$\mathbf{div} \xrightarrow{\tau} \mathbf{div} \qquad (a \to P) \xrightarrow{a} P \qquad P \sqcap Q \xrightarrow{\tau} P \qquad P \sqcap Q \xrightarrow{\tau} Q$$

$$\frac{P \xrightarrow{a} P'}{P \square Q \xrightarrow{a} P'} \qquad \frac{P \xrightarrow{\tau} P'}{P \square Q \xrightarrow{\tau} P' \square Q} \qquad \frac{Q \xrightarrow{a} Q'}{P \square Q \xrightarrow{a} Q'} \qquad \frac{Q \xrightarrow{\tau} Q'}{P \square Q \xrightarrow{\tau} P \square Q'}$$

$$\frac{P \xrightarrow{a} P'}{P \triangleright Q \xrightarrow{a} P'} \qquad \frac{P \xrightarrow{\tau} P'}{P \triangleright Q \xrightarrow{\tau} P' \triangleright Q} \qquad P \triangleright Q \xrightarrow{\tau} Q \qquad \frac{P \xrightarrow{\alpha} P'}{f(P) \xrightarrow{f(\alpha)} f(P')}$$

$$\frac{P \xrightarrow{\alpha} P' \;(\alpha \notin A)}{P \|_A Q \xrightarrow{\alpha} P' \|_A Q} \qquad \frac{P \xrightarrow{a} P' \;\; Q \xrightarrow{a} Q' \;(a \in A)}{P \|_A Q \xrightarrow{a} P' \|_A Q'} \qquad \frac{Q \xrightarrow{\alpha} Q' \;(\alpha \notin A)}{P \|_A Q \xrightarrow{\alpha} P \|_A Q'}$$

$$\frac{P \xrightarrow{\alpha} P' \;(\alpha \notin A)}{P \backslash A \xrightarrow{\alpha} P' \backslash A} \qquad \frac{P \xrightarrow{a} P' \;(a \in A)}{P \backslash A \xrightarrow{\tau} P' \backslash A} \qquad \frac{P \xrightarrow{\alpha} P' \;(\alpha \notin A)}{P \ominus_A Q \xrightarrow{\alpha} P' \ominus_A Q} \qquad \frac{P \xrightarrow{a} P' \;(a \in A)}{P \ominus_A Q \xrightarrow{a} Q}$$

$$\frac{P \xrightarrow{\alpha} P'}{P \triangle Q \xrightarrow{\alpha} P' \triangle Q} \qquad \frac{Q \xrightarrow{\tau} Q'}{P \triangle Q \xrightarrow{\tau} P' \triangle Q'} \qquad \frac{Q \xrightarrow{a} Q'}{P \triangle Q \xrightarrow{a} Q'} \qquad \mu p.P \xrightarrow{\tau} P[\mu p.P/p]$$

Here $\varepsilon \in \Sigma^*$ is the empty sequence of communications and st denotes the concatenation of sequences s and $t \in \Sigma^*$. If $\langle F, D \rangle$ is the semantics of a process P, $(s, \emptyset) \in F$, with $s \notin D$, tells that P can perform the sequence of communications s, possibly interspersed with internal actions. Such a sequence is called a *trace* of P, and Conditions N1 and N2 say that the set of traces of any processes is non-empty and prefix-closed. A failure $(s, X) \in F$, with $s \notin D$, says that after performing the trace s, P may reach a state in which it can perform none of the actions in X, nor the internal action. A communication $x \in \Sigma$ is thought to occur in cooperation between a process and its environment. Thus $(s, X) \in F$ indicates that deadlock can occur if after performing s the process runs in an environment that allows the execution of actions in X only. From this perspective, Conditions N3 and N4 are obvious.

A divergence $s \in D$ is a trace after which an infinite sequence of internal actions is possible. In the failures-divergences model of CSP divergence is regarded *catastrophic*: all further information about the process' behaviour past a divergence trace is erased. This is accomplished by *flooding*: all conceivable failures (st, X) and divergences st that have s as a prefix are added to the model (regardless whether P actually has a trace st).

A CSP process P from the syntax of Sect. 2 has the property that for any trace s of P, with $s \notin D$, the set $next(s)$ of actions c such that sc is also a trace of P is finite. By (N3–4), $(s, X) \in F$ iff $(s, X \cap next(s)) \in F$. It follows that if $(s, X) \notin F$, then there is a finite subset Y of X, namely $X \cap next(s)$, such that $(s, Y) \notin F$. This explains Condition (N5).

In BROOKES & ROSCOE [5] the semantics of CSP is defined denotationally: for each n-ary CSP operator Op, a function is defined that extracts the failures and divergences of $Op(P_1, \ldots, P_n)$ out of the failures and divergences of the argument processes $P_1, \ldots, P_n$. The meaning of a recursively defined CSP process $\mu p.P$ is obtained by means of fixed-point theory. Alternatively, the failures and divergences of a CSP process can be extracted from its operational semantics:

Definition 1. Write $P \Longrightarrow Q$ if there are processes $P_0, \ldots, P_n$, with $n \geq 0$, such that $P = P_0$, $P_i \xrightarrow{\tau} P_{i+1}$ for all $0 \leq i < n$, and $P_n = Q$.

Write $P \xrightarrow{\alpha} Q$ if there are processes P', Q' with $P \Longrightarrow P' \xrightarrow{\alpha} Q' \Longrightarrow Q$.

Write $P \xrightarrow{\hat{\alpha}} Q$ if either $\alpha \in \Sigma$ and $P \xRightarrow{\alpha} Q$, or $\alpha = \tau$ and $P \Longrightarrow Q$.

Write $P \xRightarrow{s} Q$, for $s = a_1 a_2 \ldots a_n \in \Sigma^*$ with $n \geq 0$, if there are processes $P_0, \ldots, P_n$ such that $P = P_0$, $P_i \xrightarrow{\hat{a_i}} P_{i+1}$ for all $0 \leq i < n$, and $P_n = Q$.

Let $I(P) = \{\alpha \in \Sigma \cup \{\tau\} \mid \exists Q. P \xrightarrow{\alpha} Q\}$.

Write $P\Uparrow$ if there are processes P_i for all $i \geq 0$ with $P \xRightarrow{s} P_0 \xrightarrow{\tau} P_1 \xrightarrow{\tau} \ldots$.

$s \in \Sigma^*$ is a *divergence trace* of a process P if there is a Q with $P \xRightarrow{s} Q\Uparrow$.

The *divergence set* of P is $\mathscr{D}(P) := \{st \mid s \text{ is a divergence trace of } P\}$.

A *stable failure* of a process P is a pair $(s, X) \in \Sigma^* \times \mathscr{P}(\Sigma)$ such that $P \xRightarrow{s} Q$ for some Q with $I(Q) \cap (X \cup \{\tau\}) = \emptyset$. The *failure set* of a process P is $\mathscr{F}(p) = \{(s, X) \mid s \in \mathscr{D}(P) \text{ or } (s, X) \text{ is a stable failure of } P\}$.

The semantics $[\![P]\!]_{\mathscr{F}\mathscr{D}}$ of a CSP process P is the pair $\langle \mathscr{F}(P), \mathscr{D}(P) \rangle$.

Processes P and Q are *failures-divergences equivalent*, notation $P \equiv_{FD} Q$, iff $[\![P]\!]_{\mathscr{F}\mathscr{D}} = [\![Q]\!]_{\mathscr{F}\mathscr{D}}$. Process P is a *failures-divergences refinement* of Q, notation $P \sqsupseteq_{FD} Q$, iff $\mathscr{F}(P) \subseteq \mathscr{F}(Q) \wedge \mathscr{D}(P) \subseteq \mathscr{D}(Q)$.

The operational semantics of Sect. 2 (then without the operators $\triangleright$, $\triangle$ and Θ_A) appears, for instance, in [13], and was created after the denotational semantics. In OLDEROG & HOARE [13] it is shown that the semantics $[\![P]\!]$ of a CSP process defined operationally through Definition 1 equals the denotational semantics given in [5]. The argument extends smoothly to the new operators $\triangleright$, $\triangle$ and Θ_A [17]. This can be seen as a justification of the operational semantics of Sect. 2.

In BROOKES, HOARE & ROSCOE [4] a denotational semantics of CSP was given involving failures only. Divergences were included only implicitly, namely by thinking of a trace s as a divergence of a process P iff P has all failures (st, X). So the semantics of **div** or $\mu X.X$ is simply the set of all failure pairs. As observed in DE NICOLA [6], this approach invalidates a number of intuitively valid laws, such as $P \,\square\, \mathbf{div} = \mathbf{div}$. The improved semantics of [5] solves this problem.

In HOARE [11] a slightly different semantics of CSP is given, in which a process is determined by its failures, divergences, as well as its *alphabet*. The latter is a superset of the set of communications the process can ever perform. Rather than a parallel composition $\|_A$ for each set of synchronising actions $A \subseteq \Sigma$, this approach has an operator $\|$ where the set of synchronising actions is taken to be the intersection of the alphabets of its arguments. Additionally, there is an operator $\|\|$, corresponding to $\|_\emptyset$. This approach is equally expressive as the one of [5], in the sense that there are semantics preserving translations in both directions. The work reported in this paper could just as well have been carried out in this *typed* version of CSP.

4   A Complete Axiomatisation

In [4–6,11,15,17] many algebraic laws $P = Q$, resp. $P \sqsubseteq Q$, are stated that are *valid* w.r.t. the failures-divergences semantics of CSP, meaning that $P \equiv_{FD} Q$, resp. $P \sqsubseteq_{FD} Q$. If Th is a collection of equational laws $P = Q$ then $Th \vdash R = S$ denotes that the equation $R = S$ is derivable from the equations in Th using reflexivity, symmetry, transitivity and the rule of congruence, saying that if Op is an n-ary CSP operator and $P_i = Q_i$ for $i = 1, \ldots, n$ then $Op(P_1, \ldots, P_n) = Op(Q_1, \ldots, Q_n)$. Likewise, if Th is a collection of inequational laws $P \sqsubseteq Q$ then $Th \vdash R \sqsubseteq S$ denotes that the inequation $R \sqsubseteq S$ is derivable from the inequations in Th using reflexivity, transitivity and the rule saying that if Op is an n-ary CSP operator and $P_i \sqsubseteq Q_i$ for $i = 1, \ldots, n$ then $Op(P_1, \ldots, P_n) \sqsubseteq Op(Q_1, \ldots, Q_n)$.

Definition 2. An equivalence $\sim$ on process expressions is called a *congruence* for an n-ary operator Op if $P_i \sim Q_i$ for $i = 1, \ldots, n$ implies $Op(P_1, \ldots, P_n) \sim Op(Q_1, \ldots, Q_n)$. A preorder $\preceq$ is a *precongruence* for Op, or Op is *monotone* for $\preceq$, if $P_i \preceq Q_i$ for $i = 1, \ldots, n$ implies $Op(P_1, \ldots, P_n) \preceq Op(Q_1, \ldots, Q_n)$.

If $\sim$ is a congruence for all operators of CSP (resp. $\preceq$ is a precongruence for all operators of CSP) and Th is a set of (in)equational laws that are valid for $\sim$ (resp. $\preceq$) then any (in)equation $R = S$ with $Th \vdash R = S$ (resp. $R \sqsubseteq S$ with $Th \vdash R \sqsubseteq S$) is valid for $\sim$ (resp. $\preceq$).

$\equiv_{FD}$ is a congruence for all operators of CSP. This follows immediately from the existence of the denotational failures-divergences semantics. Likewise, $\sqsubseteq_{FD}$ is a precongruence for all operators of CSP [4–6,11,13,15,17].

Definition 3. A set Th of (in)equational laws—an *axiomatisation*—is *sound and complete* for an equivalence $\sim$ (or a preorder $\preceq$) if $Th \vdash R = S$ iff $R \sim S$ (resp. $Th \vdash R \sqsubseteq S$ iff $R \preceq S$). Here "$\Rightarrow$" is *soundness* and "$\Leftarrow$" completeness.

In DE NICOLA [6] a sound and complete axiomatisation of $\sqsubseteq_{FD}$ for recursion-free CSP, and no process identifiers or variables, is presented. It is quoted in Table 2. As this axiomatisation consist of a mix of equations and inequations, formally it is an inequational axiomatisation, where an equation $P = Q$ is understood as the conjunction of $P \sqsubseteq Q$ and $Q \sqsubseteq P$. This mixed use is justified because $\equiv_{FD}$ is the *kernel* of $\sqsubseteq_{FD}$: one has $P \equiv_{FD} Q$ iff $P \sqsubseteq_{FD} Q \wedge Q \sqsubseteq_{FD} P$.

In [6], following [4,5], two parallel composition operators $\|$ and $\|\|$ were considered, instead of the parametrised operator $\|_A$. Here $\| = \|_\Sigma$ and $\|\| = \|_\emptyset$. In Table 2 the axioms for these two operators are unified into an axiomatisation of $\|_A$. Additionally, I added axioms for sliding choice, renaming, interrupt and throw—these operators were not considered in [6]. The associativity of parallel composition (Axiom **P0**) is not included in [6] and is not needed for completeness. I added it anyway, because of its importance in equational reasoning.

The soundness of the axiomatisation of Table 2 follows from $\sqsubseteq_{FD}$ being a precongruence, and the validity of the axioms—a fairly easy inspection using the denotational characterisation of $[\![\_]\!]$. To obtain completeness, write $\square_{i \in I} P_i$, with

Table 2. A complete axiomatisation of $\sqsubseteq_{FD}$ for recursion-free CSP

$\bot$	$\mathbf{div} \sqsubseteq P$
I1	$P \sqcap P = P$
I2	$P \sqcap Q = Q \sqcap P$
I3	$P \sqcap (Q \sqcap R) = (P \sqcap Q) \sqcap R$
I4	$P \sqcap Q \sqsubseteq P$
E1	$P \,\square\, P = P$
E2	$P \,\square\, Q = Q \,\square\, P$
E3	$P \,\square\, (Q \,\square\, R) = (P \,\square\, Q) \,\square\, R$
E4	$P \,\square\, STOP = P$
E5	$P \,\square\, \mathbf{div} = \mathbf{div}$
D1	$P \,\square\, (Q \sqcap R) = (P \,\square\, Q) \sqcap (P \,\square\, R)$
D2	$P \sqcap (Q \,\square\, R) = (P \sqcap Q) \,\square\, (P \sqcap R)$
D3	$(a \to P) \,\square\, (a \to Q) = a \to (P \sqcap Q)$
D4	$(a \to P) \sqcap (a \to Q) = a \to (P \sqcap Q)$
SC	$P \triangleright Q = (P \,\square\, Q) \sqcap Q$
P0	$P \|_A (Q \|_A R) = (P \|_A Q) \|_A R$
P1	$P \|_A Q = Q \|_A P$
P2	$(P \sqcap Q) \|_A R = (P \|_A R) \sqcap (Q \|_A R)$
P3	$P \|_A \mathbf{div} = \mathbf{div}$

P4 If $P = \square_{i \in I} (a_i \to P_i)$ and $Q = \square_{j \in J} (b_j \to Q_j)$ then :

$$P \| Q = \square_{a_i \notin A} (a_i \to (P_i \|_A Q)) \,\square$$
$$\square_{a_j = b_j \in A} (a_i \to (P_i \|_A Q_j)) \,\square$$
$$\square_{b_j \notin A} (b_j \to (P \|_A Q_j))$$

H1	$(P \sqcap Q) \backslash A = (P \backslash A) \sqcap (Q \backslash A)$	
H2	$(P \,\square\, a \to Q) \backslash A = ((P \,\square\, Q) \backslash A) \sqcap (Q \backslash A)$	
H3	$(\square_{i \in I} (b_i \to P_i)) \backslash A = (\square_{i \in I} (b_i \to (P_i \backslash A)))$	if $\forall i \in I. b_i \notin A$
H4	$\mathbf{div} \backslash A = \mathbf{div}$	
R1	$f(P \sqcap Q) = f(P) \sqcap f(Q)$	
R2	$f(P \,\square\, Q) = f(P) \,\square\, f(Q)$	
R3	$f(a \to P) = f(a) \to f(P)$	
R4	$f(STOP) = STOP$	
R5	$f(\mathbf{div}) = \mathbf{div}$	
T1	$(P \sqcap Q) \,\Theta_A\, R = (P \,\Theta_A\, R) \sqcap (Q \,\Theta_A\, R)$	
T2	$(P \,\square\, Q) \,\Theta_A\, R = (P \,\Theta_A\, R) \,\square\, (Q \,\Theta_A\, R)$	
T3	$(a \to P) \,\Theta_A\, Q = a \to (P \,\Theta_A\, Q)$	if $a \notin A$
T4	$(a \to P) \,\Theta_A\, Q = a \to Q$	if $a \in A$
T5	$STOP \,\Theta_A\, Q = STOP$	
T6	$\mathbf{div} \,\Theta_A\, Q = \mathbf{div}$	
U1	$(P \sqcap Q) \,\triangle\, R = (P \,\triangle\, R) \sqcap (Q \,\triangle\, R)$	
U2	$(P \,\square\, Q) \,\triangle\, R = (P \,\triangle\, R) \,\square\, (Q \,\triangle\, R)$	
U3	$(a \to P) \,\triangle\, Q = (a \to (P \,\triangle\, Q)) \,\square\, Q$	
U4	$STOP \,\triangle\, P = P$	
U5	$\mathbf{div} \,\triangle\, P = \mathbf{div}$	

$I = \{i_1, \ldots, i_n\}$ any finite index set, for $P_{i_1} \,\Box\, P_{i_2} \,\Box\, \ldots \Box\, P_{i_n}$, where $\Box_{i \in \emptyset} P_i$ represents $STOP$. This notation is justified by Axioms **E2**–**4**. Furthermore, $\sqcap_{j \in J} P_j$, with $J = \{j_1, .., j_m\}$ any finite, nonempty index set, denotes $P_{j_1} \sqcap P_{j_2} \sqcap \ldots \sqcap P_{j_m}$. This notation is justified by Axioms **I2** and **I3**. Now a *normal form* is a defined as a CSP expression of the form **div** or $\sqcap_{j \in J} R_j$, with $R_j = \left(\Box_{k \in K_j} (a_{kj} \to R_{kj}) \right)$ for $j \in J$, where the subexpressions R_{kj} are again in normal form. Here J and the K_j are finite index sets, J nonempty.

Axioms $\perp$ and **I4** derive $P \sqcap \mathbf{div} = \mathbf{div}$. Together with Axioms **D1**, **SC**, **P1**–**4**, **H1**–**4**, **R1**–**5**, **T1**–**6** and **U1**–**5** this allows any recursion-free CSP expression to be rewritten into normal form. In [6] it is shown that for any two normal forms P and Q with $P \sqsubseteq_{FD} Q$, Axioms $\perp$, **I1**–**4**, **E1**–**5** and **D1**–**4** derive $\vdash P = Q$. Together, this yields the completeness of the axiomatisation of Table 2.

5   Other Models of CSP

Several alternative models of CSP have been proposed in the literature, including the readiness-divergences model of OLDEROG & HOARE [13] and the stable revivals model of ROSCOE [16]. A hierarchy of such models is surveyed in ROSCOE [17]. Each of these models corresponds with a preorder (and associated semantic equivalence) on labelled transition systems. In [7] I presented a survey of semantic equivalences and preorders on labelled transition systems, ordered by inclusion in a lattice. Each model occurring in [17] correspond exactly with with one of the equivalences of [7], or—like the stable revivals model—arises as the meet or join of two such equivalences.

In the other direction, not every semantic equivalence or preorder from [7] yields a sensible model of CSP. First of all, one would want to ensure that it is a (pre)congruence for the operators of CSP. Additionally, one might impose sanity requirements on the treatment of recursion.

The hierarchy of models in [17] roughly consist of two hierarchies: the stable models, and the divergence-strict ones. The failures-divergences model could be seen as the centre piece in the divergence-strict hierarchy, and the stable failures model [15], which outside CSP stems from BERGSTRA, KLOP & OLDEROG [2], plays the same role in the stable hierarchy. Each of these hierarchies has a maximal (least discriminating) element, called $\mathcal{FL}^\Downarrow$ and $\mathcal{FL}$ in [17]. These correspond to the ready trace models $RT^\downarrow$ and RT of [7].

The goal of the present paper is to propose a sensible model of CSP that is strictly finer than all models thus far considered, and thus unites the two hierarchies mentioned above. As all models of CSP considered so far have a distinctly linear time flavour, I here propose a branching time model, thereby showing that the syntax of CSP is not predisposed towards linear time models. My model can be given as an equivalence relation on labelled transition system, provided I show that it is a congruence for the operators of CSP. I aim for an equivalence that allows a complete axiomatisation in the style of Table 2, obtained by replacing axioms that are no longer valid by weaker ones.

One choice could be to base a model on strong bisimulation equivalence [12]. Strong bisimilarity is a congruence for all CSP operators, because their operational semantics fits the tyft/tyxt format of [9]. However, this is an unsuitable equivalence for CSP, because it fails to abstract from internal actions. Even the axiom **I1** would not be valid, as the two sides differ by an internal action.

A second proposal could be based on weak bisimilarity [12]. This equivalence abstracts from internal activity, and validates **I1**. The default incarnation of weak bisimilarity is not finer than failures-divergences equivalence, because it satisfies **div** = $STOP$. Therefore, one would take a divergence-preserving variant of this notion: the *weak bisimulation with explicit divergence* of BERGSTRA, KLOP & OLDEROG [2]. Yet, some crucial CSP laws are invalidated, such as **I3** and **D1**. This destroys any hope of a complete axiomatisation along the lines of Table 2.

My final choice is *divergence-preserving coupled similarity* [7], based on coupled similarity for divergence-free processes from PARROW & SJÖDIN [14]. This is the finest equivalence in [7] that satisfies **I3** and **D1**. In fact, it satisfies all of the axioms of Table 2, except for the ones marked red: ⊥, **I4**, **E1**, **E5**, **D2–4**, **SC**, **P2**, **P3**, **H2**, **U2**, **U3** and **U5**.

Divergence-preserving coupled similarity belongs to the bisimulation family of semantic equivalences, in the sense that on transition systems without internal actions it coincides with strong bisimilarity.

In Sect. 6 I present divergence-preserving coupled similarity. In Sect. 7 I prove that it is a congruence for the operators of CSP, and in Sect. 8 I present a complete axiomatisation for recursion-free CSP processes without interrupts.

6   Divergence-Preserving Coupled Similarity

Definition 4. A *coupled simulation* is a binary relation $\mathscr{R}$ on CSP processes, such that, for all $\alpha \in \Sigma \cup \{\tau\}$,

- if $P \mathscr{R} Q$ and $P \xrightarrow{\alpha} P'$ then there exists a Q' with $Q \xRightarrow{\hat{\alpha}} Q'$ and $P' \mathscr{R} Q'$,
- and if $P \mathscr{R} Q$ then there exists a Q' with $Q \Longrightarrow Q'$ and $Q' \mathscr{R} P$.

It is *divergence-preserving* if $P \mathscr{R} Q$ and $P\!\!\Uparrow$ implies $Q\!\!\Uparrow$. Write $P \sqsupseteq^\Delta_{CS} Q$ if there exists a divergence-preserving coupled simulation $\mathscr{R}$ with $P \mathscr{R} Q$. Two processes P and Q are *divergence-preserving coupled similar*, notation $P \equiv^\Delta_{CS} Q$, if $P \sqsupseteq^\Delta_{CS} Q$ and $Q \sqsupseteq^\Delta_{CS} P$.

Note that the union of any collection of divergence-preserving coupled simulations is itself a divergence-preserving coupled simulation. In particular, $\sqsupseteq^\Delta_{CS}$ is a divergence-preserving coupled simulation. Also note that in the absence of the internal action τ, coupled simulations are symmetric, and coupled similarity coincides with strong bisimilarity (as defined in [12]).

Intuitively, $P \sqsupseteq^\Delta_{CS} Q$ says that P is "ahead" of a state matching Q, where P' is ahead of P if $P \Longrightarrow P'$. The first clause says that if P is ahead of a state matching Q, then any transition performed by P can be matched by Q— possibly after Q "caught up" with P by performing some internal transitions.

The second clause says that if P is ahead of Q, then Q can always catch up, so that it is ahead of P. Thus, if P and Q are in stable states—where no internal actions are possible—then $P \sqsubseteq^A_{CS} Q$ implies $Q \sqsubseteq^A_{CS} P$. In all other situations, P and Q do not need to be matched exactly, but there do exists under- and overapproximations of a match. The result is that the relation behaves like a weak bisimulation w.r.t. visible actions, but is not so pedantic in matching internal actions.

Proposition 1. $\sqsupseteq^A_{CS}$ *is reflexive and transitive, and thus a preorder.*

Proof. The identity relation Id is a divergence-preserving coupled simulation, and if $\mathscr{R}$, $\mathscr{R}'$ are divergence-preserving coupled simulations, then so is $\mathscr{R}$; $\mathscr{R}' \cup \mathscr{R}'$; $\mathscr{R}$. Here $\mathscr{R}$; $\mathscr{R}'$ is defined by $P \mathscr{R}$; $\mathscr{R}'$ R iff there is a Q with $P\mathscr{R}Q\mathscr{R}'R$.

$\mathscr{R};\mathscr{R}'$ is divergence-preserving: if $P\mathscr{R}Q\mathscr{R}'R$ and $P{\Uparrow}$, then $Q{\Uparrow}$, and thus $R{\Uparrow}$. The same holds for $\mathscr{R}'$; $\mathscr{R}$, and thus for $\mathscr{R}$; $\mathscr{R}' \cup \mathscr{R}'$; $\mathscr{R}$.

To check that $\mathscr{R}$; $\mathscr{R}' \cup \mathscr{R}'$; $\mathscr{R}$ satisfies the first clause of Definition 4, note that if $Q\mathscr{R}'R$ and $Q \stackrel{\alpha}{\Longrightarrow} Q'$, then, by repeated application of the first clause of Definition 4, there is an R' with $R \stackrel{\alpha}{\Longrightarrow} R'$ and $Q'\mathscr{R}'R'$.

Towards the second clause, if $P\mathscr{R}Q\mathscr{R}'R$, then, using the second clause for $\mathscr{R}$, there is a Q' with $Q \Longrightarrow Q'$ and $Q'\mathscr{R}P$. Hence, using the first clause for $\mathscr{R}'$, there is an R' with $R \Longrightarrow R'$ and $Q'\mathscr{R}'R'$. Thus, using the second clause for $\mathscr{R}'$, there is an R'' with $R' \Longrightarrow R''$ and $R''\mathscr{R}'Q'$, and hence $R'' \mathscr{R}'$; $\mathscr{R}$ P'. $\qquad\square$

Proposition 2. *If $P \Longrightarrow Q$ then $P \sqsubseteq^A_{CS} Q$.*

Proof. I show that $Id \cup \{(Q,P)\}$, with Id the identity relation, is a coupled simulation. Namely if $Q \stackrel{\alpha}{\longrightarrow} Q'$ then surely $P \stackrel{\alpha}{\Longrightarrow} Q'$. The second clause of Definition 4 is satisfied because $P \Longrightarrow Q$. Furthermore, if $Q{\Uparrow}$ then certainly $P{\Uparrow}$, so the relation is divergence-preserving. $\qquad\square$

Proposition 3. $P \sqsupseteq^A_{CS} Q$ *iff* $P \sqcap Q \equiv^A_{CS} Q$.

Proof. "$\Rightarrow$": Let $\mathscr{R}$ be the smallest relation such that, for any P and Q, $P \sqsupseteq^A_{CS} Q$ implies $P\mathscr{R}Q$, $(P \sqcap Q)\mathscr{R}Q$ and $Q\mathscr{R}(P \sqcap Q)$. It suffices to show that $\mathscr{R}$ is a divergence-preserving coupled simulation.

That $\mathscr{R}$ is divergence-preserving is trivial, using that $(P \sqcap Q){\Uparrow}$ iff $P{\Uparrow} \vee Q{\Uparrow}$.

Suppose $P^* \mathscr{R} Q$ and $P^* \stackrel{\alpha}{\longrightarrow} P'$. The case that $P^* = P$ with $P \sqsupseteq^A_{CS} Q$ is trivial. Now let Q be $Q^* \sqcap P^*$. Since $P^* \stackrel{\alpha}{\longrightarrow} P'$, surely $Q \stackrel{\alpha}{\Longrightarrow} P'$, and $P' \mathscr{R} P'$. Finally, let $P^* = (P \sqcap Q)$ with $P \sqsupseteq^A_{CS} Q$. Then $\alpha = \tau$ and P' is either P or Q. Both cases are trivial, taking $Q' = Q$.

Towards the second clause of Definition 4, suppose $P^* \mathscr{R} Q$. The case $P^* = P$ with $P \sqsupseteq^A_{CS} Q$ is trivial. Now let Q be $Q^* \sqcap P^*$. Then $Q \Longrightarrow P^*$ and $P^* \mathscr{R} P^*$. Finally, let $P^* = (P \sqcap Q)$ with $P \sqsupseteq^A_{CS} Q$. Then $Q \Longrightarrow Q$ and $Q\mathscr{R}(P \sqcap Q)$.

"$\Leftarrow$": Suppose $P \sqcap Q \sqsupseteq^A_{CS} Q$. Since $P \sqcap Q \stackrel{\tau}{\longrightarrow} P$ there exists a Q' with $Q \Longrightarrow Q'$ and $P \sqsupseteq^A_{CS} Q'$. By Proposition 2 $Q' \sqsupseteq^A_{CS} Q$ and by Proposition 1 $P \sqsupseteq^A_{CS} Q$. $\qquad\square$

7   Congruence Properties

Proposition 4. $\equiv_{CS}^A$ *is a congruence for action prefixing.*

Proof. I have to show that $P \equiv_{CS}^A Q$ implies $(a \to P) \equiv_{CS}^A (a \to Q)$.

Let $\mathscr{R}$ be the smallest relation such that, for any P and Q, $P \sqsubseteq_{CS}^A Q$ implies $P \mathscr{R} Q$, and $P \equiv_{CS}^A Q$ implies $(a \to P) \mathscr{R} (a \to Q)$. It suffices to show that $\mathscr{R}$ is a divergence-preserving coupled simulation.

Checking the conditions of Definition 4 for the case $P \mathscr{R} Q$ with $P \sqsubseteq_{CS}^A Q$ is trivial. So I examine the case $(a \to P) \mathscr{R} (a \to Q)$ with $P \equiv_{CS}^A Q$.

Suppose $(a \to P) \xrightarrow{\alpha} P'$. Then $\alpha = a$ and $P' = P$. Now $(a \to Q) \xrightarrow{\alpha} Q$ and $P \mathscr{R} Q$, so the first condition of Definition 4 is satisfied.

For the second condition, $(a \to Q) \Longrightarrow (a \to Q)$, and, since $Q \equiv_{CS}^A P$, $(a \to Q) \mathscr{R} (a \to P)$. Thus, $\mathscr{R}$ is a coupled simulation.

As $a \to P$ does not diverge, $\mathscr{R}$ moreover is divergence-preserving.   □

Since $STOP \sqsupseteq_{CS}^A (a \to STOP) \triangleright STOP$ but $STOP \not\sqsubseteq_{CS}^A (a \to STOP) \triangleright STOP$, and thus $b \to STOP \not\sqsupseteq_{CS}^A b \to ((a \to STOP) \triangleright STOP)$, the relation $\sqsupseteq_{CS}^A$ is *not* a precongruence for action prefixing.

It is possible to express action prefixing in terms of the throw operator: $a \to P$ is strongly bisimilar with $(a \to STOP) \Theta_{\{a\}} P$. Consequently, $\sqsupseteq_{CS}^A$ is not a precongruence for the throw operator.

Proposition 5. $\equiv_{CS}^A$ *is a congruence for the throw operator.*

Proof. Let $A \subseteq \Sigma$. Let $\mathscr{R}$ be the smallest relation such that, for any P_1, P_2, Q_1, Q_2, $P_1 \sqsupseteq_{CS}^A Q_1$ and $P_2 \equiv_{CS}^A Q_2$ implies $P_1 \mathscr{R} Q_1$ and $(P_1 \Theta_A P_2) \mathscr{R} (Q_1 \Theta_A Q_2)$. It suffices to show that $\mathscr{R}$ is a divergence-preserving coupled simulation.

So let $P_1 \sqsupseteq_{CS}^A Q_1$, $P_2 \equiv_{CS}^A Q_2$ and $(P_1 \Theta_A P_2) \xrightarrow{\alpha} P'$. Then $P_1 \xrightarrow{\alpha} P_1'$ for some P_1', and either $\alpha \notin A$ and $P' = P_1' \Theta_A P_2$, or $\alpha \in A$ and $P' = P_2$. So there is a Q_1' with $Q_1 \xRightarrow{\hat{\alpha}} Q_1'$ and $P_1' \sqsupseteq_{CS}^A Q_1'$. If $\alpha \notin A$ it follows that $(Q_1 \Theta_A Q_2) \xRightarrow{\hat{\alpha}} (Q_1' \Theta_A Q_2)$ and $(P_1' \Theta_A P_2) \mathscr{R} (Q_1' \Theta_A Q_2)$. If $\alpha \in A$ it follows that $(Q_1 \Theta_A Q_2) \xRightarrow{\hat{\alpha}} Q_2$ and $P_2 \mathscr{R} Q_2$.

Now let $P_1 \sqsupseteq_{CS}^A Q_1$ and $P_2 \equiv_{CS}^A Q_2$. Then there is a Q_1' with $Q_1 \Longrightarrow Q_1'$ and $Q_1' \sqsupseteq_{CS}^A P_1$. Hence $Q_1 \Theta_A Q_2 \Longrightarrow Q_1' \Theta_A Q_2$ and $(Q_1' \Theta_A Q_2) \mathscr{R} (P_1 \Theta_A P_2)$.

The same two conditions for the case $P \mathscr{R} Q$ because $P \sqsupseteq_{CS}^A Q$ are trivial. Thus $\mathscr{R}$ is a coupled simulation. That $\mathscr{R}$ is divergence-preserving follows because $P_1 \Theta_A P_2 \Uparrow$ iff $P_1 \Uparrow$.   □

I proceed to show that $\sqsupseteq_{CS}^A$ is a precongruence for all the other operators of CSP. This implies that $\equiv_{CS}^A$ is a congruence for all the operators of CSP.

Proposition 6. $\sqsupseteq_{CS}^A$ *is a precongruence for internal choice.*

Proof. Let $\mathscr{R}$ be the smallest relation such that, for any P_i and Q_i, $P_i \sqsupseteq_{CS}^A Q_i$ for $i = 1, 2$ implies $P_i \mathscr{R} Q_i$ $(i = 1, 2)$ and $(P_1 \sqcap P_2) \mathscr{R} (Q_1 \sqcap Q_2)$. It suffices to show that $\mathscr{R}$ is a divergence-preserving coupled simulation.

So let $P_i \sqsupseteq^A_{CS} Q_i$ for $i = 1, 2$ and $(P_1 \sqcap P_2) \xrightarrow{\alpha} P'$. Then $\alpha = \tau$ and $P' = P_i$ for $i = 1$ or 2. Now $Q_1 \sqcap Q_2 \Longrightarrow Q_i$ and $P_i \mathscr{R} Q_i$.

Now let $P_i \sqsupseteq^A_{CS} Q_i$ for $i = 1, 2$. Then there is a Q'_1 with $Q_1 \Longrightarrow Q'_1$ and $Q'_1 \sqsupseteq^A_{CS} P_1$. By Proposition 2 $P_1 \sqsupseteq^A_{CS} P_1 \sqcap P_2$ and by Proposition 1 $Q'_1 \sqsupseteq^A_{CS} P_1 \sqcap P_2$.

The same two conditions for the case $P \mathscr{R} Q$ because $P \sqsupseteq^A_{CS} Q$ are trivial. Thus $\mathscr{R}$ is a coupled simulation. That $\mathscr{R}$ is divergence-preserving follows because $P_1 \sqcap P_2 \Uparrow$ iff $P_1 \Uparrow \vee P_2 \Uparrow$.   □

Proposition 7. $\sqsupseteq^A_{CS}$ *is a precongruence for external choice.*

Proof. Let $\mathscr{R}$ be the smallest relation such that, for any P_i and Q_i, $P_i \sqsupseteq^A_{CS} Q_i$ for $i = 1, 2$ implies $P_i \mathscr{R} Q_i$ $(i = 1, 2)$ and $(P_1 \square P_2) \mathscr{R} (Q_1 \square Q_2)$. It suffices to show that $\mathscr{R}$ is a divergence-preserving coupled simulation.

So let $P_i \sqsupseteq^A_{CS} Q_i$ for $i = 1, 2$ and $(P_1 \square P_2) \xrightarrow{\alpha} P'$. If $\alpha \in \Sigma$ then $P_i \xrightarrow{\alpha} P'$ for $i = 1$ or 2, and there exists a Q' with $Q_i \overset{\alpha}{\Longrightarrow} Q'$ and $P' \sqsupseteq^A_{CS} Q'$. Hence $Q_1 \square Q_2 \overset{\alpha}{\Longrightarrow} Q'$ and $P' \mathscr{R} Q'$. If $\alpha = \tau$ then either $P_1 \xrightarrow{\tau} P'_1$ for some P'_1 with $P' = P'_1 \square P_2$, or $P_2 \xrightarrow{\tau} P'_2$ for some P'_2 with $P' = P_1 \square P'_2$. I pursue only the first case, as the other follows by symmetry. Here $Q_1 \Longrightarrow Q'_1$ for some Q'_1 with $P'_1 \sqsupseteq^A_{CS} Q'_1$. Thus $Q_1 \square Q_2 \Longrightarrow Q'_1 \square Q_2$ and $(P'_1 \square P_2) \mathscr{R} (Q'_1 \square Q_2)$.

Now let $P_i \sqsupseteq^A_{CS} Q_i$ for $i = 1, 2$. Then, for $i = 1, 2$, there is a Q'_i with $Q_i \Longrightarrow Q'_i$ and $Q'_i \sqsupseteq^A_{CS} P_i$. Hence $Q_1 \square Q_2 \Longrightarrow Q'_1 \square Q'_2$ and $(Q'_1 \square Q'_2) \mathscr{R} (P_1 \square P_2)$.

Thus $\mathscr{R}$ is a coupled simulation. That $\mathscr{R}$ is divergence-preserving follows because $P_1 \square P_2 \Uparrow$ iff $P_1 \Uparrow \vee P_2 \Uparrow$.   □

Proposition 8. $\sqsupseteq^A_{CS}$ *is a precongruence for sliding choice.*

Proof. Let $\mathscr{R}$ be the smallest relation such that, for any P_i and Q_i, $P_i \sqsupseteq^A_{CS} Q_i$ for $i = 1, 2$ implies $P_i \mathscr{R} Q_i$ $(i = 1, 2)$ and $(P_1 \rhd P_2) \mathscr{R} (Q_1 \rhd Q_2)$. It suffices to show that $\mathscr{R}$ is a divergence-preserving coupled simulation.

So let $P_i \sqsupseteq^A_{CS} Q_i$ for $i = 1, 2$ and $(P_1 \rhd P_2) \xrightarrow{\alpha} P'$. If $\alpha \in \Sigma$ then $P_1 \xrightarrow{\alpha} P'$, and there exists a Q' with $Q_1 \overset{\alpha}{\Longrightarrow} Q'$ and $P' \sqsupseteq^A_{CS} Q'$. Hence $Q_1 \rhd Q_2 \overset{\alpha}{\Longrightarrow} Q'$ and $P' \mathscr{R} Q'$. If $\alpha = \tau$ then either $P' = P_2$ or $P_1 \xrightarrow{\tau} P'_1$ for some P'_1 with $P' = P'_1 \rhd P_2$. In the former case $Q_1 \rhd Q_2 \Longrightarrow Q_2$ and $P_2 \mathscr{R} Q_2$. In the latter case $Q_1 \Longrightarrow Q'_1$ for some Q'_1 with $P'_1 \sqsupseteq^A_{CS} Q'_1$. Thus $Q_1 \rhd Q_2 \Longrightarrow Q'_1 \rhd Q_2$ and $(P'_1 \rhd P_2) \mathscr{R} (Q'_1 \rhd Q_2)$.

Now let $P_i \sqsupseteq^A_{CS} Q_i$ for $i = 1, 2$. Then there is a Q'_2 with $Q_2 \Longrightarrow Q'_2$ and $Q'_2 \sqsupseteq^A_{CS} P_2$. By Proposition 2 $P_2 \sqsupseteq^A_{CS} P_1 \rhd P_2$ and by Proposition 1 $Q'_2 \sqsupseteq^A_{CS} P_1 \rhd P_2$.

Thus $\mathscr{R}$ is a coupled simulation. That $\mathscr{R}$ is divergence-preserving follows because $P_1 \rhd P_2 \Uparrow$ iff $P_1 \Uparrow \vee P_2 \Uparrow$.   □

Proposition 9. $\sqsupseteq^A_{CS}$ *is a precongruence for parallel composition.*

Proof. Let $A \subseteq \Sigma$. Let $\mathscr{R}$ be the smallest relation such that, for any P_i and Q_i, $P_i \sqsupseteq^A_{CS} Q_i$ for $i = 1, 2$ implies $(P_1 \|_A P_2) \mathscr{R} (Q_1 \|_A Q_2)$. It suffices to show that $\mathscr{R}$ is a divergence-preserving coupled simulation.

So let $P_i \sqsupseteq^A_{CS} Q_i$ for $i = 1, 2$ and $(P_1 \|_A P_2) \xrightarrow{\alpha} P'$. If $\alpha \notin A$ then $P_i \xrightarrow{\alpha} P'_i$ for $i = 1$ or 2, and $P' = P'_1 \|_A P'_2$, where $P'_{3-i} := P_{3-i}$. Hence there exists a Q'_i

with $Q_i \stackrel{\hat{\alpha}}{\Longrightarrow} Q_i'$ and $P_i' \sqsupseteq_{CS}^A Q_i'$. Let $Q_{3-i}' := Q_{3-i}$. Then $Q_1 \|_A Q_2 \stackrel{\hat{\alpha}}{\Longrightarrow} Q_1' \| Q_2'$ and $(P_1' \| P_2') \mathcal{R} (Q_1' \| Q_2')$. If $\alpha \in A$ then $P_i \stackrel{\alpha}{\longrightarrow} P_i'$ for $i = 1$ and 2. Hence, for $i = 1, 2$, $Q_i \stackrel{\alpha}{\Longrightarrow} Q_i'$ for some Q_i' with $P_i' \sqsupseteq_{CS}^A Q_i'$. Thus $Q_1 \|_A Q_2 \stackrel{\alpha}{\Longrightarrow} Q_1' \|_A Q_2'$ and $(P_1' \|_A P_2') \mathcal{R} (Q_1' \|_A Q_2')$.

Now let $P_i \sqsupseteq_{CS}^A Q_i$ for $i = 1, 2$. Then, for $i = 1, 2$, there is a Q_i' with $Q_i \Longrightarrow Q_i'$ and $Q_i' \sqsupseteq_{CS}^A P_i$. Hence $Q_1 \|_A Q_2 \Longrightarrow Q_1' \|_A Q_2'$ and $(Q_1' \|_A Q_2') \mathcal{R} (P_1 \|_A P_2)$.

Thus $\mathcal{R}$ is a coupled simulation. That $\mathcal{R}$ is divergence-preserving follows because $P_1 \|_A P_2 \Uparrow$ iff $P_1 \Uparrow \vee P_2 \Uparrow$. $\square$

Proposition 10. $\sqsupseteq_{CS}^A$ *is a precongruence for concealment.*

Proof. Let $A \subseteq \Sigma$. Let $\mathcal{R}$ be the smallest relation such that, for any P and Q, $P \sqsubseteq_{CS}^A Q$ implies $(P \backslash A) \mathcal{R} (Q \backslash A)$. It suffices to show that $\mathcal{R}$ is a divergence-preserving coupled simulation.

So let $P \sqsubseteq_{CS}^A Q$ and $P \backslash A \stackrel{\alpha}{\longrightarrow} P^*$. Then $P^* = P' \backslash A$ for some P' with $P \stackrel{\beta}{\longrightarrow} P'$, and either $\beta \in A$ and $\alpha = \tau$, or $\beta = \alpha \notin A$. Hence $Q \stackrel{\beta}{\longrightarrow} Q'$ for some Q' with $P' \sqsubseteq_{CS}^A Q'$. Therefore $Q \backslash A \stackrel{\alpha}{\longrightarrow} Q' \backslash A$ and $(P' \backslash A) \mathcal{R} (Q' \backslash A)$.

Now let $P \sqsubseteq_{CS}^A Q$. Then there is a Q' with $Q \Longrightarrow Q'$ and $Q' \sqsupseteq_{CS}^A P$. Hence $Q \backslash A \Longrightarrow Q' \backslash A$ and $(Q' \backslash A) \mathcal{R} (P \backslash A)$.

To check that $\mathcal{R}$ is divergence-preserving, suppose $(P \backslash A) \Uparrow$. Then there are P_i and $\alpha_i \in A \cup \{\tau\}$ for all $i > 0$ such that $P \stackrel{\alpha_1}{\longrightarrow} P_1 \stackrel{\alpha_2}{\longrightarrow} P_2 \stackrel{\alpha_3}{\longrightarrow} \ldots$. By the first condition of Definition 4, there are Q_i for all $i > 0$ such that $P_i \mathcal{R} Q_i$ and $Q \stackrel{\hat{\alpha}_1}{\Longrightarrow} Q_1 \stackrel{\hat{\alpha}_2}{\Longrightarrow} Q_2 \stackrel{\hat{\alpha}_3}{\Longrightarrow} \ldots$. This implies $Q \backslash A \Longrightarrow Q_1 \backslash A \Longrightarrow Q_2 \backslash A \Longrightarrow \ldots$.

In case $\alpha_i \in \Sigma$ for infinitely many i, then for infinitely many i one has $Q_{i-1} \stackrel{\alpha_i}{\Longrightarrow} Q_i$ and thus $Q_{i-1} \backslash A \stackrel{\tau}{\Longrightarrow} Q_i \backslash A$. This implies that $(Q \backslash A) \Uparrow$.

Otherwise there is an $n > 0$ such that $\alpha_i = \tau$ for all $i \geq n$. In that case $P_n \Uparrow$ and thus $Q_n \Uparrow$. Hence $(Q_n \backslash A) \Uparrow$ and thus $(Q \backslash A) \Uparrow$. $\square$

Proposition 11. $\sqsupseteq_{CS}^A$ *is a precongruence for renaming.*

Proof. Let $f : \Sigma \to \Sigma$. Let $\mathcal{R}$ be the smallest relation such that, for any P and Q, $P \sqsubseteq_{CS}^A Q$ implies $f(P) \mathcal{R} f(Q)$. It suffices to show that $\mathcal{R}$ is a divergence-preserving coupled simulation.

So let $P \sqsubseteq_{CS}^A Q$ and $f(P) \stackrel{\alpha}{\longrightarrow} P^*$. Then $P^* = f(P')$ for some P' with $P \stackrel{\beta}{\longrightarrow} P'$ and $f(\beta) = \alpha$. Hence $Q \stackrel{\beta}{\longrightarrow} Q'$ for some Q' with $P' \sqsubseteq_{CS}^A Q'$. Therefore $f(Q) \stackrel{\alpha}{\longrightarrow} f(Q')$ and $f(P') \mathcal{R} f(Q')$.

Now let $P \sqsubseteq_{CS}^A Q$. Then there is a Q' with $Q \Longrightarrow Q'$ and $Q' \sqsupseteq_{CS}^A P$. Hence $f(Q) \Longrightarrow f(Q')$ and $f(Q') \mathcal{R} f(P)$.

To check that $\mathcal{R}$ is divergence-preserving, suppose $f(P) \Uparrow$. Then $P \Uparrow$, so $Q \Uparrow$ and $f(Q) \Uparrow$. $\square$

Proposition 12. $\sqsupseteq_{CS}^A$ *is a precongruence for the interrupt operator.*

Proof. Let $\mathcal{R}$ be the smallest relation such that, for any P_i and Q_i, $P_i \sqsupseteq_{CS}^A Q_i$ for $i = 1, 2$ implies $P_2 \mathcal{R} Q_2$ and $(P_1 \triangle P_2) \mathcal{R} (Q_1 \triangle Q_2)$. It suffices to show that $\mathcal{R}$ is a divergence-preserving coupled simulation.

So let $P_i \sqsupseteq^\Delta_{CS} Q_i$ for $i = 1, 2$ and $(P_1 \triangle P_2) \xrightarrow{\alpha} P'$. Then either $P' = P'_1 \triangle P_2$ for some P'_1 with $P_1 \xrightarrow{\alpha} P'_1$, or $\alpha = \tau$ and $P' = P_1 \triangle P'_2$ for some P'_2 with $P_2 \xrightarrow{\tau} P'_2$, or $\alpha \in \Sigma$ and $P_2 \xrightarrow{\alpha} P'$.

In the first case there is a Q'_1 with $Q_1 \xRightarrow{\hat{\alpha}} Q'_1$ and $P'_1 \sqsupseteq_{CS} Q'_1$. It follows that $(Q_1 \triangle Q_2) \xRightarrow{\hat{\alpha}} (Q'_1 \triangle Q_2)$ and $(P'_1 \triangle P_2) \mathscr{R} (Q'_1 \triangle Q_2)$.

In the second case there is a Q'_2 with $Q_2 \Longrightarrow Q'_2$ and $P'_2 \sqsupseteq^\Delta_{CS} Q'_2$. It follows that $(Q_1 \triangle Q_2) \Longrightarrow (Q_1 \triangle Q'_2)$ and $(P_1 \triangle P'_2) \mathscr{R} (Q_1 \triangle Q'_2)$.

In the last case there is a Q'_2 with $Q_2 \xRightarrow{\hat{\alpha}} Q'_2$ and $P'_2 \sqsupseteq_{CS} Q'_2$. It follows that $(Q_1 \triangle Q_2) \xRightarrow{\hat{\alpha}} Q'_2$ and $P'_2 \mathscr{R} Q'_2$.

Now let $P_i \sqsupseteq^\Delta_{CS} Q_i$ for $i = 1, 2$. Then, for $i = 1, 2$, there is a Q'_i with $Q_i \Longrightarrow Q'_i$ and $Q'_i \sqsupseteq^\Delta_{CS} P_i$. Hence $Q_1 \triangle Q_2 \Longrightarrow Q'_1 \triangle Q'_2$ and $(Q'_1 \triangle Q'_2) \mathscr{R} (P_1 \triangle P_2)$.

Thus $\mathscr{R}$ is a coupled simulation. That $\mathscr{R}$ is divergence-preserving follows because $P_1 \triangle P_2 \Uparrow$ iff $P_1 \Uparrow \lor P_2 \Uparrow$.   □

8   A Complete Axiomatisation of $\equiv^\Delta_{CS}$

A set of equational laws valid for $\equiv^\Delta_{CS}$ is presented in Table 3. It includes the laws from Table 2 that are still valid for $\equiv^\Delta_{CS}$. I will show that this axiomatisation is sound and complete for $\equiv^\Delta_{CS}$ for recursion-free CSP without the interrupt operator. The axioms **U2** and **U3**, which are not valid for $\equiv^\Delta_{CS}$, played a crucial rôle in reducing CSP expressions with interrupt into normal form. It is not trivial to find valid replacements, and due to lack of space and time I do not tackle this problem here.

The axiom **H5** replaces the fallen axiom **H2**, and is due to [17]. Here the result of hiding actions results in a process that cannot be expressed as a normal form built up from $a \rightarrow$, $\sqcap$ and $\square$. For this reason, one needs a richer normal form, involving the sliding choice operator. It is given by the context-free grammar

$$N \rightarrow D \mid D \rhd I$$
$$I \rightarrow D \mid I \sqcap I$$
$$D \rightarrow STOP \mid \mathbf{div} \mid E \mid \mathbf{div}\,\square\,E$$
$$E \rightarrow (a \rightarrow N) \mid (a \rightarrow N)\,\square\,E \,.$$

Definition 5. A CSP expression is in *head normal form* if it is of the form $([\mathbf{div}\,\square]\,\square_{i \in I}(a_i \rightarrow R_i)) \rhd \sqcap_{j \in J} R_j$, with $R_j = ([\mathbf{div}\,\square]\,\square_{k \in K_j}(a_{kj} \rightarrow R_{kj}))$ for $j \in J$. Here I, J and the K_j are finite index sets, and the parts between square brackets are optional. Here, although $\sqcap_{i \in \emptyset} P_i$ is undefined, I use $P \rhd \sqcap_{i \in \emptyset} P_i$ to represent P. An expression is in *normal form* if it has this form and also the subexpressions R_i and R_{kj} are in normal form.

A head normal form is *saturated* if the **div**-summand on the left is present whenever any of the R_j has a **div**-summand, and for any $j \in J$ and any $k \in K_j$ there is an $i \in I$ with $a_i = a_{kj}$ and $R_i = R_{kj}$.

My proof strategy is to ensure that there are enough axioms to transform any CSP process without recursion and interrupt operators into normal form, and to make these forms saturated; then to equate saturated normal forms that are divergence-preserving coupled simulation equivalent.

Due to the optional presence in head normal forms of a **div**-summand and a sliding choice, I need four variants of the axiom **H5**; so far I have not seen a way around this. Likewise, there are 4×4 variants of the axiom **P4** from Table 2, of which 6 could be suppressed by symmetry (**P4–P13**). There are also 3 axioms replacing **P2** (**P14–P16**).

9 Soundness

Since divergence-preserving coupled similarity is a congruence for all CSP operators, to establish the soundness of the axiomatisation of Table 3 it suffices to show the validity w.r.t. $\equiv^{\Delta}_{CS}$ of all axioms. When possible, I show validity w.r.t. strong bisimilarity, which is a strictly finer equivalence.

Definition 6. Two processes are *strongly bisimilar* [12] if they are related by a binary relation $\mathscr{R}$ on processes such that, for all $\alpha \in \Sigma \cup \{\tau\}$,

– if $P \mathscr{R} Q$ and $P \xrightarrow{\alpha} P'$ then there exists a Q' with $Q \xrightarrow{\alpha} Q'$ and $P' \mathscr{R} Q'$,
– if $P \mathscr{R} Q$ and $Q \xrightarrow{\alpha} Q'$ then there exists a P' with $P \xrightarrow{\alpha} P'$ and $P' \mathscr{R} Q'$.

Proposition 13. *Axiom* **I1** *is valid for* $\equiv^{\Delta}_{CS}$.

Proof. $\{(P \sqcap P, P), (P, P \sqcap P) \mid P \text{ a process}\} \cup Id$ is a divergence-preserving coupled simulation. □

Proposition 14. *Axiom* **I2** *is valid even for strong bisimilarity.*

Proof. $\{(P \sqcap Q, Q \sqcap P) \mid P, Q \text{ processes}\} \cup Id$ is a strong bisimulation. □

Proposition 15. *Axiom* **I3** *is valid for* $\equiv^{\Delta}_{CS}$.

Proof. The relation $\{(P \sqcap (Q \sqcap R), (P \sqcap Q) \sqcap R), ((P \sqcap Q) \sqcap R, P \sqcap (Q \sqcap R)), (Q \sqcap R, (P \sqcap Q) \sqcap R), (P \sqcap Q, P \sqcap (Q \sqcap R)), (R, Q \sqcap R), (P, P \sqcap Q) \mid P, Q, R \text{ processes}\} \cup Id$ is a divergence-preserving coupled simulation. □

Proposition 16. *Axioms* **E2–4** *are valid for strong bisimilarity.*

Proof. The relation $\{(P \square (Q \square R), (P \square Q) \square R) \mid P, Q, R \text{ processes}\} \cup Id$ is a strong bisimulation. So is $\{(P \square Q, Q \square P) \mid P, Q \text{ processes}\} \cup Id$, as well as $\{(P \square STOP, P) \mid P \text{ a process}\} \cup Id$. □

Proposition 17. *Axiom* **S1** *is valid for* $\equiv^{\Delta}_{CS}$.

Proof. $\{(P' \rhd P, P), (P, P' \rhd P) \mid P' \sqsupseteq^{\Delta}_{CS} P\} \cup Id$ is a divergence-preserving coupled simulation. This follows from Proposition 2. □

Proposition 18. *Axiom* **S2** *is valid for* $\equiv^{\Delta}_{CS}$.

Table 3. A complete axiomatisation of $\equiv_{CS}^A$ for recursion-free CSP without interrupt

I1	$P \sqcap P = P$
I2	$P \sqcap Q = Q \sqcap P$
I3	$P \sqcap (Q \sqcap R) = (P \sqcap Q) \sqcap R$
E2	$P \square Q = Q \square P$
E3	$P \square (Q \square R) = (P \square Q) \square R$
E4	$P \square STOP = P$
S1	$P \triangleright P = P$
S2	$P \triangleright (Q \triangleright R) = (P \triangleright Q) \triangleright R$
S3	$(P \triangleright Q) \triangleright R = (P \square Q) \triangleright R$
S4	$(P \sqcap Q) \triangleright R = (P \square Q) \triangleright R$
S5	$STOP \triangleright P = P$
S6	$(P \triangleright Q) \sqcap (R \triangleright S) = (P \square R) \triangleright (Q \sqcap S)$
S7	$(P \triangleright Q) \square (R \triangleright S) = (P \square R) \triangleright (Q \square S)$
D1	$P \square (Q \sqcap R) = (P \square Q) \sqcap (P \square R)$
Prune	$(a \to P) \square a \to (P \sqcap Q) = a \to (P \sqcap Q)$
P0	$P \|_A (Q \|_A R) = (P \|_A Q) \|_A R$
P1	$P \|_A Q = Q \|_A P$
P4–P13	*more axioms for parallel composition follow on the next page*
H1	$(P \sqcap Q) \backslash A = (P \backslash A) \sqcap (Q \backslash A)$
H5	$\left(\square_{i \in I} (a_i \to P_i) \right) \backslash A = \left(\square_{a_i \notin A} (a_i \to (P_i \backslash A)) \right)$ $\triangleright \sqcap_{a_i \in A} (P_i \backslash A)$
H6	$\left(\mathbf{div} \square \square_{i \in I} (a_i \to P_i) \right) \backslash A = \left(\mathbf{div} \square \square_{a_i \notin A} (a_i \to (P_i \backslash A)) \right)$ $\triangleright \sqcap_{a_i \in A} (P_i \backslash A)$
H7	$\left(\left(\square_{i \in I} (a_i \to P_i) \right) \triangleright P' \right) \backslash A = \left(\square_{a_i \notin A} (a_i \to (P_i \backslash A)) \right)$ $\triangleright (P' \backslash A \sqcap \sqcap_{a_i \in A} (P_i \backslash A))$
H8	$\left(\left(\mathbf{div} \square \square_{i \in I} (a_i \to P_i) \right) \triangleright P' \right) \backslash A = \left(\mathbf{div} \square \square_{a_i \notin A} (a_i \to (P_i \backslash A)) \right)$ $\triangleright (P' \backslash A \sqcap \sqcap_{a_i \in A} (P_i \backslash A))$
R0	$f(P \triangleright Q) = f(P) \triangleright f(Q)$
R1	$f(P \sqcap Q) = f(P) \sqcap f(Q)$
R2	$f(P \square Q) = f(P) \square f(Q)$
R3	$f(a \to P) = f(a) \to f(P)$
R4	$f(STOP) = STOP$
R5	$f(\mathbf{div}) = \mathbf{div}$
T0	$(P \triangleright Q) \, \Theta_A \, R = (P \, \Theta_A \, R) \triangleright (Q \, \Theta_A \, R)$
T1	$(P \sqcap Q) \, \Theta_A \, R = (P \, \Theta_A \, R) \sqcap (Q \, \Theta_A \, R)$
T2	$(P \square Q) \, \Theta_A \, R = (P \, \Theta_A \, R) \square (Q \, \Theta_A \, R)$
T3	$(a \to P) \, \Theta_A \, Q = a \to (P \, \Theta_A \, Q)$ if $a \notin A$
T4	$(a \to P) \, \Theta_A \, Q = a \to Q$ if $a \in A$
T5	$STOP \, \Theta_A \, Q = STOP$
T6	$\mathbf{div} \, \Theta_A \, Q = \mathbf{div}$

(continued)

Table 3. (*continued*)

Below $P = \square_{i \in I}(a_i \to P_i)$ and $Q = \square_{j \in J}(b_j \to Q_j)$.

(P4)
$$P \|_A Q = \square_{a_i \notin A}(a_i \to (P_i \|_A Q)) \square$$
$$\square_{a_j = b_j \in A}(a_i \to (P_i \|_A Q_j)) \square$$
$$\square_{b_j \notin A}(b_j \to (P \|_A Q_j))$$

(P5)
$$(\mathbf{div} \,\square\, P) \|_A Q = \mathbf{div} \,\square\, \square_{a_i \notin A}(a_i \to (P_i \|_A Q)) \square$$
$$\square_{a_j = b_j \in A}(a_i \to (P_i \|_A Q_j)) \square$$
$$\square_{b_j \notin A}(b_j \to ((\mathbf{div} \,\square\, P) \|_A Q_j))$$

(P6)
$$(\mathbf{div} \,\square\, P) \|_A (\mathbf{div} \,\square\, Q) = \mathbf{div} \,\square\, \square_{a_i \notin A}(a_i \to (P_i \|_A (\mathbf{div} \,\square\, Q))) \square$$
$$\square_{a_j = b_j \in A}(a_i \to (P_i \|_A Q_j)) \square$$
$$\square_{b_j \notin A}(b_j \to ((\mathbf{div} \,\square\, P) \|_A Q_j))$$

(P7)
$$(P \rhd P') \|_A Q = (\square_{a_i \notin A}(a_i \to (P_i \|_A Q)) \square$$
$$\square_{a_j = b_j \in A}(a_i \to (P_i \|_A Q_j)) \square$$
$$\square_{b_j \notin A}(b_j \to ((P \rhd P') \|_A Q_j))) \rhd P' \|_A Q$$

(P8)
$$((\mathbf{div} \,\square\, P) \rhd P') \|_A Q = (\mathbf{div} \,\square\, \square_{a_i \notin A}(a_i \to (P_i \|_A Q)) \square$$
$$\square_{a_j = b_j \in A}(a_i \to (P_i \|_A Q_j)) \square$$
$$\square_{b_j \notin A}(b_j \to (((\mathbf{div} \,\square\, P) \rhd P') \|_A Q_j)))$$
$$\rhd P' \|_A Q$$

(P9)
$$(P \rhd P') \|_A (\mathbf{div} \,\square\, Q) = ((\mathbf{div} \,\square\, \square_{a_i \notin A}(a_i \to (P_i \|_A (\mathbf{div} \,\square\, Q))) \square$$
$$\square_{a_j = b_j \in A}(a_i \to (P_i \|_A Q_j)) \square$$
$$\square_{b_j \notin A}(b_j \to ((P \rhd P') \|_A Q_j)))$$
$$\rhd P' \|_A (\mathbf{div} \,\square\, Q)$$

(P10)
$$((\mathbf{div} \,\square\, P) \rhd P') \|_A (\mathbf{div} \,\square\, Q) = (\mathbf{div} \,\square\, \square_{a_i \notin A}(a_i \to (P_i \|_A (\mathbf{div} \,\square\, Q))) \square$$
$$\square_{a_j = b_j \in A}(a_i \to (P_i \|_A Q_j)) \square$$
$$\square_{b_j \notin A}(b_j \to (((\mathbf{div} \,\square\, P) \rhd P') \|_A Q_j)))$$
$$\rhd P' \|_A (\mathbf{div} \,\square\, Q)$$

(P11)
$$(P \rhd P') \|_A (Q \rhd Q') = (\square_{a_i \notin A}(a_i \to (P_i \|_A (Q \rhd Q'))) \square$$
$$\square_{a_j = b_j \in A}(a_i \to (P_i \|_A Q_j)) \square$$
$$\square_{b_j \notin A}(b_j \to ((P \rhd P') \|_A Q_j)))$$
$$\rhd (P' \|_A (Q \rhd Q') \sqcap (P \rhd P') \|_A Q')$$

(P12)
$$((\mathbf{div} \,\square\, P) \rhd P') \|_A (Q \rhd Q') = (\mathbf{div} \,\square\, \square_{a_i \notin A}(a_i \to (P_i \|_A (Q \rhd Q'))) \square$$
$$\square_{a_j = b_j \in A}(a_i \to (P_i \|_A Q_j)) \square$$
$$\square_{b_j \notin A}(b_j \to (((\mathbf{div} \,\square\, P) \rhd P') \|_A Q_j)))$$
$$\rhd (P' \|_A (Q \rhd Q') \sqcap ((\mathbf{div} \,\square\, P) \rhd P') \|_A Q')$$

(P13)
$$((\mathbf{div} \,\square\, P) \rhd P') \|_A ((\mathbf{div} \,\square\, Q) \rhd Q') = (\mathbf{div} \square$$
$$\square_{a_i \notin A}(a_i \to (P_i \|_A ((\mathbf{div} \,\square\, Q) \rhd Q'))) \square$$
$$\square_{a_j = b_j \in A}(a_i \to (P_i \|_A Q_j)) \square$$
$$\square_{b_j \notin A}(b_j \to (((\mathbf{div} \,\square\, P) \rhd P') \|_A Q_j)))$$
$$\rhd (P' \|_A ((\mathbf{div} \,\square\, Q) \rhd Q') \sqcap ((\mathbf{div} \,\square\, P) \rhd P') \|_A Q')$$

(*continued*)

Table 3. (*continued*)

Below $P = \square_{i \in I}(a_i \to P_i)$ and $Q = \bigsqcap_{j \in J} Q_j$.

(P14) $\qquad P\|_A Q = \square_{a_i \notin A}(a_i \to (P_i\|_A Q)) \triangleright \bigsqcap_{j \in J}(P\|_A Q_j))$

(P15) $\quad (\textbf{div} \,\square\, P)\|_A Q = (\textbf{div} \,\square\, \square_{a_i \notin A}(a_i \to (P_i\|_A Q))) \triangleright \bigsqcap_{j \in J}((\textbf{div} \,\square\, P)\|_A Q_j))$

Below $P = \bigsqcap_{i \in I} P_i$ and $Q = \bigsqcap_{j \in J} Q_j$.

(P16) $\qquad\qquad P\|_A Q = \bigsqcap_{a_i \notin A}(P_i\|_A Q) \sqcap \bigsqcap_{j \in J}(P\|_A Q_j))$

Proof. $\{(P \triangleright (Q \triangleright R), (P \triangleright Q) \triangleright R), ((P \triangleright Q) \triangleright R, P \triangleright (Q \triangleright R))$ | $P, Q, R \text{ processes}\} \cup Id$ is a divergence-preserving coupled simulation. $\square$

Proposition 19. *Axiom* **S3** *is valid for* $\equiv^{\Delta}_{CS}$.

Proof. $\{((P \triangleright Q) \triangleright R, (P \square Q) \triangleright R), ((P \square Q') \triangleright R, (P \triangleright Q) \triangleright R), (Q \triangleright R, (P \square Q) \triangleright R), (R, Q \triangleright R)$ | $Q' \sqsupseteq^{\Delta}_{CS} Q\} \cup Id$ is a divergence-preserving coupled simulation. $\square$

Proposition 20. *Axiom* **S4** *is valid for* $\equiv^{\Delta}_{CS}$.

Proof. $\{((P \sqcap Q) \triangleright R, (P \square Q) \triangleright R), ((P' \square Q') \triangleright R, (P \sqcap Q) \triangleright R), (P \triangleright R, (P \square Q) \triangleright R), (Q \triangleright R, (P \square Q) \triangleright R), (R, Q \triangleright R)$ | $P' \sqsupseteq^{\Delta}_{CS} P \wedge Q' \sqsupseteq^{\Delta}_{CS} Q\} \cup Id$ is a divergence-preserving coupled simulation. Checking this involves Proposition 2. $\square$

Proposition 21. *Axiom* **S5** *is valid for* $\equiv^{\Delta}_{CS}$.

Proof. The relation $\{(STOP \triangleright P, P), (P, STOP \triangleright P)$ | $P \text{ a process}\} \cup Id$ is a divergence-preserving coupled simulation.
   $\square$

Proposition 22. *Axiom* **S6** *is valid for* $\equiv^{\Delta}_{CS}$.

Proof. $\{((P \triangleright Q) \sqcap (R \triangleright S), (P \square R) \triangleright (Q \sqcap S)), ((P' \square R') \triangleright (Q \sqcap S), (P \triangleright Q) \sqcap (R \triangleright S)), (P \triangleright Q, (P \square R) \triangleright (Q \sqcap S)), (R \triangleright S, (P \square R) \triangleright (Q \sqcap S)), (Q \sqcap S, (P \triangleright Q) \sqcap (R \triangleright S)), (S, (P' \square R') \triangleright (Q \sqcap S)), (S, R \triangleright S), (S, Q \sqcap S)$ | $P' \sqsupseteq^{\Delta}_{CS} P \wedge R' \sqsupseteq^{\Delta}_{CS} R\} \cup Id$ is a divergence-preserving coupled simulation. $\square$

Proposition 23. *Axiom* **S7** *is valid for* $\equiv^{\Delta}_{CS}$.

Proof. $\{((P \triangleright Q) \square (R \triangleright S), (P \square R) \triangleright (Q \square S)), ((P \square R) \triangleright (Q \square S), (P \triangleright Q) \square (R \triangleright S)), (Q' \square (R \triangleright S), (P \square R) \triangleright (Q \square S)), ((P \triangleright Q) \square S', (P \square R) \triangleright (Q \square S)), (Q' \square S', Q' \square (R \triangleright S)), (Q' \square S', (P \triangleright Q) \square S')$, | $Q \Longrightarrow Q' \wedge S \Longrightarrow S'\} \cup Id$ is a divergence-preserving coupled simulation. $\square$

Proposition 24. *Axiom* **D1** *is valid for* $\equiv^{\Delta}_{CS}$.

Proof. $\{(P' \;\square\; (Q \sqcap R), (P \;\square\; Q) \sqcap (P \;\square\; R)), ((P \;\square\; Q) \sqcap (P \;\square\; R), P \;\square\; (Q \sqcap R)), (P' \;\square\; Q, P' \;\square\; (Q \sqcap R)) \mid P \Longrightarrow P'\} \cup Id$ is a divergence-preserving coupled simulation. $\qquad\square$

Proposition 25. *Axiom* **Prune** *is valid for* $\equiv^{\Delta}_{CS}$.

Proof. $\{((a{\rightarrow}P)\square a{\rightarrow}(P\sqcap Q), a{\rightarrow}(P\sqcap Q)), (a{\rightarrow}(P\sqcap Q), (a{\rightarrow}P)\square a{\rightarrow}(P\sqcap Q))\} \cup$ Id is a divergence-preserving coupled simulation. $\qquad\square$

Proposition 26. *Axioms* **P0–1** *and* **P4–10** *are valid for strong bisimilarity. Axioms* **P11–16** *are valid for* $\equiv^{\Delta}_{CS}$.

Proof. Straightforward. $\qquad\square$

Proposition 27. *Axioms* **U4**, **H1**, **R0–5** *and* **T0–6** *are valid for strong bisimilarity. Axioms* **H5–8** *are valid for* $\equiv^{\Delta}_{CS}$.

Proof. Straightforward. $\qquad\square$

Proposition 28. *Axiom* **U1** *is valid for* $\equiv^{\Delta}_{CS}$.

Proof. $\{((P \sqcap Q) \bigtriangleup R', (P \bigtriangleup R) \sqcap (Q \bigtriangleup R)), ((P \bigtriangleup R) \sqcap (Q \bigtriangleup R), (P \sqcap Q) \bigtriangleup R), (P \bigtriangleup R', (P \sqcap Q) \bigtriangleup R') \mid R \Longrightarrow R'\} \cup Id$ is a divergence-preserving coupled simulation. $\qquad\square$

10   Completeness

Let Th be the axiomatisation of Table 3.

Proposition 29. *For each recursion-free CSP process P without interrupt operators there is a CSP process Q in normal form such that* $Th \vdash P = Q$.

Proof. By structural induction on P it suffices to show that for each n-ary CSP operator Op, and all CSP processes $P_1, ..., P_n$ in normal form, also $Op(P_1, ..., P_n)$ can be converted to normal form. This I do with structural induction on the arguments P_i.

– Let $P = STOP$ or **div**. Then P is already in normal form. Take $Q := P$.
– Let $P = a \rightarrow P'$. By assumption P' is in normal form; therefore so is P.
– Let $P = P_1 \sqcap P_2$. By assumption P_1 and P_2 are in normal form. So $P =$
$$\left(([\mathbf{div}\;\square]\;\square_{i \in I}(a_i \rightarrow R_i)) \rhd \textstyle\sqcap_{j \in J} R_j\right) \sqcap \left(([\mathbf{div}\;\square]\;\square_{l \in L}(a_l \rightarrow R_l)) \rhd \textstyle\sqcap_{j \in M} R_j\right)$$
with $R_j = ([\mathbf{div}\;\square]\;\square_{k \in K_j}(a_{kj} \rightarrow R_{kj}))$ for $j \in J \cup M$. With Axiom **S5** I may assume that $J, M \neq \emptyset$. Now Axiom **S6** converts P to normal form.

- Let $P = P_1 \square P_2$. By assumption P_1 and P_2 are in normal form. So $P = \left(([\textbf{div}\;\square]\;\square_{i \in I}(a_i \to R_i)) \rhd \sqcap_{j \in J} R_j\right) \square \left(([\textbf{div}\;\square]\;\square_{l \in L}(a_l \to R_l)) \rhd \sqcap_{j \in M} R_j\right)$ with $R_j = ([\textbf{div}\;\square]\;\square_{k \in K_j}(a_{kj} \to R_{kj}))$ for $j \in J \cup M$. With **S5** I may assume that $J, M \neq \emptyset$. Now Axioms **S7** and **D1** convert P to normal form.
- Let $P = P_1 \rhd P_2$. Axioms **S2–4** and **D1** convert P to normal form.
- Let $P = P_1 \|_A P_2$. Axioms **P1** and **P4–16**, together with the induction hypothesis, convert P to normal form.
- Let $P = P \backslash A$. Axioms **H1** and **H5–8**, together with the induction hypothesis, convert P to normal form.
- Let $P = f(P)$. Axioms **R0–5**, together with the induction hypothesis, convert P to normal form.
- Let $P = P_1 \Theta_A P_2$. Axioms **T0–6**, together with the induction hypothesis, convert P to normal form.

Lemma 1. *For any CSP expression P in head normal form there exists a saturated CSP expression Q in head normal form.*

Proof. Let $P = ([\textbf{div}\;\square]\;\square_{i \in I}(a_i \to R_i)) \rhd \sqcap_{j \in J} R_j$. Then P has the form $S \rhd R$. By Axioms **S1–3** $Th \vdash P = (S \square R) \rhd R$. By means of Axioms **D1** and **S4** the subexpression $S \square R$ can be brought in the form $[\textbf{div}\;\square]\;\square_{l \in L}(a_l \to R_l)$. The resulting term is saturated. $\qquad\square$

Definition 7. A CSP expression $(\square_{i \in I}(b_i \to P_i))$ is *pruned* if, for all $i, h \in I$, $b_i = b_h \wedge P_i \sqsupseteq_{CS}^{\Delta} P_h \Rightarrow i = h$.

Theorem 1. *Let P and Q be recursion-free CSP processes without interrupt operators. Then $P \equiv_{CS}^{\Delta} Q$ iff $Th \vdash P = Q$.*

Proof. "$\Leftarrow$" is an immediate consequence of the soundness of the axioms of Th, and the fact that $\equiv_{CS}^{\Delta}$ is a congruence for all operators of CSP.
    "$\Rightarrow$": Let $depth(P)$ be the length of the longest trace of P—well-defined for recursion-free processes P. If $P \equiv_{CS}^{\Delta} Q$ then $depth(P) = depth(Q)$. Given $P \equiv_{CS}^{\Delta} Q$, I establish $Th \vdash P = Q$ with induction on $depth(P)$.
    By Proposition 29 I may assume, without loss of generality, that P and Q are in normal form. By Lemma 1 I furthermore assume that P and Q are saturated. Let $P = ([\textbf{div}\;\square]\;\square_{i \in I}(a_i \to R_i)) \rhd \sqcap_{j \in J} R_j$ and $Q = ([\textbf{div}\;\square]\;\square_{l \in L}(a_l \to R_l)) \rhd \sqcap_{j \in M} R_j$ with $R_j = ([\textbf{div}\;\square]\;\square_{k \in K_j}(a_{kj} \to R_{kj}))$ for $j \in J \cup M$, where R_i, R_l and R_{kj} are again in normal form.
    Suppose that there are $i, h \in I$ with $i \neq h$, $a_i = a_h$ and $R_i \sqsupseteq_{CS}^{\Delta} R_h$. Then $R_i \sqcap R_h \equiv_{CS}^{\Delta} R_h$ by Proposition 3. Since $depth(R_i \sqcap R_h) < depth(P)$, the induction hypothesis yields $Th \vdash R_i \sqcap R_h = R_h$. Hence Axiom **Prune** allows me to prune the summand $a_i \to R_i$ from $\square_{i \in I}(a_i \to R_i)$. Doing this repeatedly makes $\square_{i \in I}(a_i \to R_i)$ pruned. By the same reasoning I may assume that $\square_{l \in L}(a_l \to R_l)$ is pruned.

Since $P\!\Uparrow \Leftrightarrow Q\!\Uparrow$ and P and Q are saturated, P has the **div**-summand iff Q does. I now define a function $f : I \to L$ such that $a_{f(i)} = a_i$ and $R_i \sqsupseteq^A_{CS} R_{f(i)}$ for all $i \in I$.

Let $i \in I$. Since $P \xrightarrow{a_i} R_i$, by Definition 4 $Q \xRightarrow{a_i} Q'$ for some Q' with $R_i \sqsupseteq^A_{CS} Q'$. Hence either there is an $l \in L$ such that $a_l = a_i$ and $R_l \Longrightarrow Q'$, or there is a $j \in M$ and $k \in K_j$ such that $a_{kj} = a_i$ and $R_{kj} \Longrightarrow Q'$. Since P is saturated, the first of these alternatives must apply. By Proposition 2 $Q' \sqsupseteq^A_{CS} R_l$ and by Proposition 1 $R_i \sqsupseteq^A_{CS} R_l$. Take $f(i) := l$.

By the same reasoning there is a function $g : L \to I$ such that $a_{g(l)} = a_l$ and $R_l \sqsupseteq^A_{CS} R_{g(l)}$ for all $l \in L$. Since $\square_{i \in I}(a_i \to R_i)$ and $\square_{l \in L}(a_l \to R_l)$ are pruned, there are no different $i, h \in I$ (or in L) with $a_i = a_h$ and $R_i \sqsupseteq^A_{CS} R_h$. Hence the functions f and g must be inverses of each other. It follows that $Q = \big([\mathbf{div}\ \square]\ \square_{i \in I}(a_i \to R_{f(i)})\big) \rhd \bigsqcap_{j \in M} R_j$ with $R_i \equiv^A_{CS} R_{f(i)}$ for all $i \in I$. By induction $Th \vdash R_i = R_{f(i)}$ for all $i \in I$.

So in the special case that $I = M = \emptyset$ I obtain $Th \vdash P = Q$.   (*)

Next consider the case $J = \emptyset$ but $M \neq \emptyset$. Let $j \in M$. Since $Q \Longrightarrow R_j$, there is a P' with $P \Longrightarrow P'$ and $R_j \sqsupseteq^A_{CS} P'$. Moreover, there is a P'' with $P' \Longrightarrow P''$ and $P'' \sqsupseteq^A_{CS} R_j$. Since $J = \emptyset$, $P'' = P' = P$, so $P \equiv^A_{CS} R_j$. By (*) above $Th \vdash P = R_j$. This holds for all $j \in J$, so by Axiom **I1** $Th \vdash Q = \big([\mathbf{div}\ \square]\ \square_{i \in I}(a_i \to R_i)\big) \rhd P$. By Axiom **S1** one obtains $Th \vdash P = Q$.

The same reasoning applies when $M = \emptyset$ but $J \neq \emptyset$. So henceforth I assume $J, M \neq \emptyset$. I now define a function $h : J \to M$ with $Th \vdash R_j = R_{h(j)}$ for all $j \in J$.

Let $j \in J$. Since $P \xRightarrow{\tau} R_j$, by Definition 4 $Q \Longrightarrow Q'$ for some Q' with $R_j \sqsupseteq^A_{CS} Q'$, and $Q' \Longrightarrow Q''$ for some Q'' with $Q'' \sqsupseteq^A_{CS} R_j$. There must be an $m \in M$ with $Q'' \Longrightarrow R_m$. By Definition 4 $R_j \Longrightarrow R'$ for some R' with $R_m \sqsupseteq^A_{CS} R'$, and $R' \Longrightarrow R''$ for some R'' with $R'' \sqsupseteq^A_{CS} R_m$. By the shape of R_j one has $R'' = R' = R_j$, so $R_j \equiv^A_{CS} R_m$. By (*) above $Th \vdash R_j = R_m$. Take $h(j) := m$.

By the same reasoning there is a function $e : M \to J$ with $Th \vdash R_m = R_{e(m)}$ for all $m \in M$. Using Axioms **I1–3** one obtains $Th \vdash P = Q$. $\square$

11   Conclusion

This paper contributed a new model of CSP, presented as a semantic equivalence on labelled transition systems that is a congruence for the operators of CSP. It is the finest I could find that allows a complete equational axiomatisation for closed recursion-free CSP processes that fits within the existing syntax of the language. For τ-free system, my model coincides with strong bisimilarity, but in matching internal transitions it is less pedantic than weak bisimilarity.

It is left for future work to show that recursion is treated well in this model, and also to extend my complete axiomatisation with the interrupt operator of ROSCOE [15,17].

An annoying feature of my complete axiomatisation is the enormous collections of heavy-duty axioms needed to bring parallel compositions of CSP processes in head normal form. These are based on the expansion law of MILNER [12], but a multitude of them is needed due to the optional presence of divergence-summands and sliding choices in head normal forms. In the process algebra ACP the expansion law could be avoided through the addition of two auxiliary operators: the left merge and the communication merge [3]. Unfortunately, failures-divergences equivalence fails to be a congruence for the left-merge, and the same problems exists for any other models of CSP [8, Sect. 3.2.1]. In [1] an alternative left-merge is proposed, for which failures-divergences equivalence, and also $\equiv_{CS}^A$, is a congruence. It might be used to eliminate the expansion law **P4** from the axiomatisation of Table 2. Unfortunately, the axiom that splits a parallel composition between a left-, right- and communication merge (Axiom CM1 in [3]), although valid in the failures-divergences model, is not valid for $\equiv_{CS}^A$. This leaves the question of how to better manage the axiomatisation of parallel composition entirely open.

References

1. Aceto, L., Ingólfsdóttir, A.: A theory of testing for ACP. In: Baeten, J.C.M., Groote, J.F. (eds.) CONCUR 1991. LNCS, vol. 527, pp. 78–95. Springer, Heidelberg (1991). doi:10.1007/3-540-54430-5_82
2. Bergstra, J.A., Klop, J.W., Olderog, E.-R.: Failures withoutchaos: a new process semantics for fair abstraction. In: Wirsing, M. (ed.) Formal Description of Programming Concepts - III, Proceedings of the 3th IFIP WG 2.2 working conference, Ebberup 1986, North-Holland, Amsterdam, pp. 77–103 (1987)
3. Bergstra, J.A., Klop, J.W.: Process algebra for synchronous communication. Inform. Control **60**, 109–137 (1984). doi:10.1016/S0019-9958(84)80025-X
4. Brookes, S.D., Hoare, C.A.R., Roscoe, A.W.: A theory of communicating sequential processes. J. ACM **31**(3), 560–599 (1984). doi:10.1145/828.833
5. Brookes, S.D., Roscoe, A.W.: An improved failures model for communicating processes. In: Brookes, S.D., Roscoe, A.W., Winskel, G. (eds.) CONCURRENCY 1984. LNCS, vol. 197, pp. 281–305. Springer, Heidelberg (1985). doi:10.1007/3-540-15670-4_14
6. De Nicola, R.: Two complete Axiom systems for a theory of communicating sequential processes. Inf. Control **64**(1–3), 136–172 (1985). doi:10.1016/S0019-9958(85)80048-6
7. Glabbeek, R.J.: The linear time — branching time spectrum II. In: Best, E. (ed.) CONCUR 1993. LNCS, vol. 715, pp. 66–81. Springer, Heidelberg (1993). doi:10.1007/3-540-57208-2_6
8. van Glabbeek, R.J., Vaandrager, F.W.: Modular specification of process algebras. Theor. Comput. Sci. **113**(2), 293–348 (1993). doi:10.1016/0304-3975(93)90006-F
9. Groote, J.F., Vaandrager, F.W.: Structured operational semantics and bisimulation as a congruence. Inf. Comput. **100**(2), 202–260 (1992). doi:10.1016/0890-5401(92)90013-6
10. Hoare, C.A.R.: Communicating sequential processes. Commun. ACM **21**(8), 666–677 (1978). doi:10.1145/359576.359585
11. Hoare, C.A.R.: Communicating Sequential Processes. Prentice-Hall, Upper Saddle River (1985)

12. Milner, R.: Operational and algebraic semantics of concurrent processes. In: van Leeuwen, J. (ed.) Handbook of Theoretical Computer Science, Chap. 19, pp. 1201–1242. Elsevier Science Publishers B.V., North-Holland (1990). Alternatively see Communication and Concurrency. Prentice-Hall (1989), of which an earlier version appeared as A Calculus of Communicating Systems. LNCS, vol. 92. Springer (1980)

13. Olderog, E.-R., Hoare, C.A.R.: Specification-oriented semantics for communicating processes. Acta Informatica **23**, 9–66 (1986). doi:10.1007/BF00268075

14. Parrow, J., Sjödin, P.: Multiway synchronization verified with coupled simulation. In: Cleaveland, W.R. (ed.) CONCUR 1992. LNCS, vol. 630, pp. 518–533. Springer Berlin Heidelberg, Berlin, Heidelberg (1992). doi:10.1007/BFb0084813

15. Roscoe, A.W.: The Theory and Practice of Concurrency. Prentice-Hall, Upper Saddle River (1997). http://www.comlab.ox.ac.uk/bill.roscoe/publications/68b.pdf.

16. Roscoe, A.W.: Revivals, stuckness and the hierarchy of CSP models. J. Logic Algebraic Program. **78**(3), 163–190 (2009). doi:10.1016/j.jlap.2008.10.002

17. Roscoe, A.W.: Understanding Concurrent Systems. Springer, London (2010). doi:10.1007/978-1-84882-258-0

Virtualization Based Development

Jay Yantchev[✉] and Atanas Parashkevov

VLAB Works™, Adelaide, Australia
{jay.yantchev, atanas.parashkevov}@vlabworks.com

Abstract. Virtualization involves replacing all elements of an embedded development environment, including paper specifications, target hardware, test instruments, and plant and equipment, with software representations, for an all-in-software path to creating working executable versions of an embedded system or of any of its components or sub-systems. A virtualization based development process leverages virtualization in all phases of development. It enables acceleration by allowing development tasks to start earlier and by proceeding at a higher pace and on a wider front, for example through automation of development and test, optimization of design, increased test scope and coverage, and calibration procedures that are not feasible with real hardware implementations. This paper outlines the concepts and some of the applications of virtualization based development, defines the technology, tool and process requirements, and introduces VLAB™ as a tool and operating environment for virtualization based development of embedded software and systems. In order to make these concepts as fully covered and easily understood as possible, we will focus and contain the scope of the paper to their application to the development of automotive controller modules, or ECUs, for modern engine systems control.

1 Introduction

This paper, and the concepts, technologies, and methodologies it describes, are developed in a commercial embedded engineering environment. They address problems of the current practices and seek to provide new practical solutions to development engineers, teams, and projects operating under the pressures, constraints, and imperfections of such commercial environments. The goal is practical commercial improvements rather than prohibitively hard to apply or unsustainable academic methods and perfection. However, this paper hopes that a bridge between the two may be built, that future research and academic effort may formalize further the concepts, technologies and methodologies it outlines, or may find that this is already in place, and allow further improvements in their application and automation.

Though virtualization based development, or VBD, is broadly applicable to any embedded development segment and project, in order to cover the concepts and their application as fully as possible, this paper will focus on the area of development of automotive controller modules, or ECUs, and more specifically to ECUs for modern

---

VLAB Works™ is a company of ASTC, and can be contacted at http://www.vlabworks.com.

T. Gibson-Robinson et al. (Eds.): Roscoe Festschrift, LNCS 10160, pp. 294–318, 2017.
DOI: 10.1007/978-3-319-51046-0_15

engine systems control, or ECMs. Typically, the development of a next generation, advanced ECU involves the joint development effort of a whole supply chain of companies, from a car manufacturing OEM driving the ECU requirements and specifications, through the ECU development and manufacturing supplier, or Tier 1 supplier, to semiconductor companies supplying advanced custom IC components and software companies supplying software modules and stacks. The significance of this is that a new ECU development project involves a development process that spans over multiple unrelated companies, multiple engineering disciplines, and multiple levels of system complexity. The opportunities for improvement are therefore numerous, as are the challenges and complexities in achieving them.

There are other significant fundamentals of the automotive ECU industry. One is the balance between cost of development and cost of volume manufacturing and final product. The manufacturing life time of an ECU module is long, the current norms being in the range of 15 years, the costs of manufacturing are high, the cost of individual modules is relatively high, volumes are high, and all these factors combine to make the total post release costs a significant consideration during development and this in turn puts sufficient value and return to upfront development process costs for improved design, optimized performance, and improved quality. In other words, there is budget for good development processes. Another important fundamental is the long ECU development time frames, driven by the long new vehicle platform introduction timeframes. A typical new generation production ECU development cycle is about 3 to 4 years. In addition, each production development project, which requires that all or most of the new technology, tools, and methodology be trialed in advance and fixed at the start of production development, is preceded by an earlier advanced technology phase, may be over a 2 to 3 year timeframe, in which such trials and preparations take place. In other words, there is time to do things right and time to prepare for that. A final fundamental is the importance of regulatory and market driven requirements for safety, reliability, and robustness of the total end system, the vehicle, of which the ECU is a critical part. These requirements have to be designed into each component, ECU module, and subsystem, and tested at that level as well as within the final integrated vehicle. This puts additional requirements on the design process and on the test, verification, and validation process and coverage.

One other important consideration, characteristic of contemporary automotive electronics industry, which is not so much a fundamental but a recent trend, is the rapidly increasing complexity of ECU function, ECU hardware, and most of all of ECU software. The overall volume and complexity of automotive software today exceeds 100 million lines of code and has surpassed the complexity of full computer desktop stacks. In the last seven years alone, software complexity in automotive applications has grown by a factor of $10\times$ and has surpassed that of most aerospace applications. Much of this automotive code is in safety critical applications and needs to be developed, verified and validated under strict safety requirements such as those imposed by ISO 26262. The regulatory and market trends towards improved fuel efficiency, cleaner environment impact, improved safety, increased complexity of integrated function, some involving all subsystems in the vehicle, such as autonomous driving systems, lead to rapid increase in complexity of the ECUs required to deliver and control these functions. With ECUs, this increased complexity of function tends to be control complexity, a rapid increase in the range of possible operating conditions and behaviors, exceeding our unaided abilities to understand, design, and test. The significance of this to our topic is that this requires development processes capable of handling complexity, including understanding, designing, and testing, within some manageable process for project planning and execution. In other words, the tools, methods, and processes of yesterday, which were a good fit for yesterday and may be just managing today, will not be a good fit for tomorrow.

On the flip side of this trend of rapidly increasing complexity of function and operation is the slow pace of change of development methods, tools, and practices in the automotive industry. Due to the high cost and value in the investments in earlier vehicle models, especially in test, validation, and certification, any change in development process needs to ensure an almost unbroken continuity from previous projects. Processes change slowly because they are not allowed to change within a production development ECU project and because, when they could change from one project to the next, there is the risk of high cost of change from the potential loss of prior development or validation investments in moving from one ECU generation to the next. New development tools, methods, and approaches take a long time to evaluate and even longer to adopt and deploy. In the face of this glacial pace of internal change, significant pressures are required to build up as a force for change or the limits of current practice to be reached, for change to happen at all. It was in circumstances like this, when the current development processes, including methods and tools, of major Tier 1s proved inadequate for the ECU plans and commitments already made to major OEM customers, that the technologies, tools, and methods, described here have been applied in practice, honed for purpose, and prove their effectiveness unequivocally.

Another trend affecting not only the automotive ECU industry, but any other supply chains, is the increased globalization of development teamwork. Supply chain development projects may involve companies in different continents, and each company may involve development teams around the world. This requires means for exchanging and reproducing information, environments, and artefacts, including design prototypes, target hardware, software, test set ups, configuration and automation scripts, test scenarios, test results, debug information, and other execution data and user history to be stored, exchanged, and replicated with ease anywhere in the world.

To help with the trends and challenges outlined above, we describe some concepts, technologies, and processes aiming to deliver improvements and advances in embedded development.

2 Virtualization

Virtualization involves replacing all components of an embedded development and test environment, including textual paper specifications, target hardware, test instruments, and plant and equipment, with software representations, for an all-in-software path to a working and executable build of a new ECU or of any of its components in each interim stage of development.

The task of virtualization is to replace a component in the development process, say an ECU prototype hardware board, with a representation in software, which can be used for some purpose instead of the hardware itself, but which can, unlike the hardware itself, be used for that same purpose with all the flexibilities that software can. For example, copy and multiply freely, store, exchange, link with other software, configure, build, load, run, control, instrument, and also debug and test it in the same way as a software component can be. This is the essential task. The precise type of software representation used, and what the methods and tools for developing such a representation are, are of secondary importance and largely depend on the specific purpose. Provided the benefits of use outweigh the effort and time taken to create it, then the goal of virtualization is achieved.

Target Hardware Virtualization. One of the means for virtualization of an ECU hardware component, such as an MCU, and ASIC or an ECU hardware prototype board, is to use a hardware simulation model. This can, for example, be developed in the system level hardware modeling language SystemC, typically using the TLM library extensions for transaction level interaction between such models, and running on a SystemC/TLM simulator. This is now becoming mainstream and well understood. The model of the hardware may be at different levels of internal functional or interface detail, as well as timing abstraction and accuracy. Depending on the purpose, more or less detailed and complex models may be sufficient.

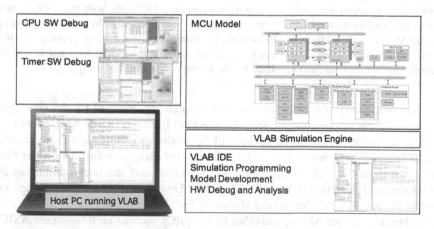

Fig. 1. Virtualization model of a main CPU SoC (MCU) for engine control ECU, and comprising CPU ISS models, and models of memories, of on chip IP blocks, peripheral IO blocks, and interconnects, such as buses, interrupts, and other signals running in VLAB on a PC.

Another means for virtualization of an ECU hardware component is to use an emulation model, which does not model the internal state and operation of the hardware component in any detail, but outwardly fulfills the same function as the hardware component for the intended purpose. For example, Fig. 2, consider testing the operation of low level injection control ECU software running on the main processing module, or MCU, with a microcode programmable Fuel Injection Driver ASIC. It may be sufficient to virtualize the ASIC by emulating it as a simple test bench component with select interfaces and little or no internal function. The outward functional behavior relevant to the planned test scenarios can be programmed in the test scripts via test bench control SW APIs. The Fuel Injection Driver ASIC virtualization can then emulate the necessary interactions with the MCU in the way the test scenarios require. This allows significant simplification in the effort to virtualize the ASIC for these purposes. The complex internal operation of the ASIC and its implementation, which includes a microcode programmable instruction engine, can be abstracted away and much effort and cost saved.

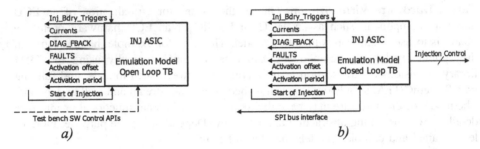

Fig. 2. Virtualization of ECU hardware components, (a) Emulation of an injection ASIC for testing injection control low level software in an open loop testbench, with the ASIC internal function emulated by the test bench scripts via the SW Control API, and (b) Emulation model of the same ASIC with the addition of SPI interface for control by target software running on MCU and external injection control interfaces to an engine model for a closed loop test bench, the injection ASIC internal function emulated by the model component internally.

On the other hand, if the purpose is to develop an environment for the simulation and test of the microcode running on that same Fuel Injection Driver ASIC, then such an ASIC emulation as described above will be inadequate. Instead, a more detailed simulation model is required, involving, among other things, an Instruction Set Simulator (ISS) model, as well as other logic and structure, and accurately simulating the internal state and operation. Such a Fuel Injection Driver ASIC Simulation model will resemble the MCU simulation model shown in Fig. 1.

Fuel Injection Driver ASICs, and other ECU ASICs, such as air flow sensor ASICs, are analog/mixed signal systems, whose system level outward function includes analog functions and interfaces as well as digital ones. However, for ECU software development and test, usually only the digital functions are relevant and require virtualization, using simple abstractions in software. Sometimes, the analog functions and components may need to be included in the virtualization process and represented by software. For example, for simulation of fault injection in the analog connections and sub-systems and of the ASIC fault diagnosis and response. This is required in environments aimed at analyzing the ECU software safety functions, their handling of faults signaled by the ASICs, and the behavior of the overall system in the presence of such faults. Even for such purposes, the analog subsystems can be modelled and virtualized with the help of simple digital functional abstractions, as illustrated in Fig. 3. Very rarely, analog models and simulations are required, usually when the goal of such environments is analysis of the specifications and behavior of the ASIC itself, such as during ASIC or PCB HW design and verification.

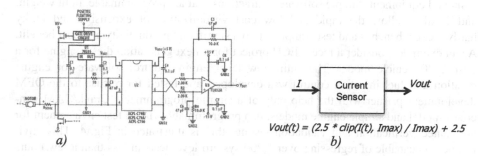

$$Vout(t) = (2.5 * clip(I(t), Imax) / Imax) + 2.5$$

Fig. 3. Virtualization of a current sensor, (a) a sample real current sensor circuit, and (b) the current sensor virtualization as a one line transfer function.

The sample target hardware virtualizations described in this section are usually developed and used for software development and test, or for hardware/software architecture level analysis and validation, or for functional safety analysis. In general, they are not used for verification of the hardware itself. Therefore, it is usually not necessary to represent the details of their internal operation or the details of their signaling interfaces; it suffices to have simpler representations at the minimum level of detail relevant to the overall system function or the operation of the software under test.

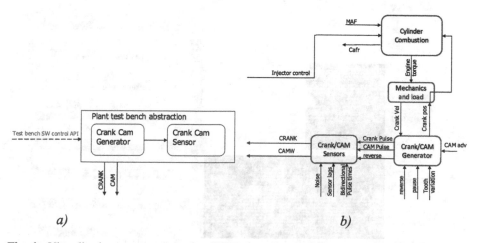

Fig. 4. Virtualization components for ECU low level engine control software testing comprising: (a) an open loop Crank/CAM generator test bench model, and (b) a closed loop engine plant test bench abstraction.

Test Hardware, Plant and Equipment Virtualization. The examples given so far are all of different target hardware components, such as MCU components, peripheral ECU ASIC components, or entire ECU abstractions. The same and wider options are available for the virtualization of other hardware components, such as other operating environment hardware, test and measurement instruments, communications networks, plant and equipment. Simple software abstractions that are programmable, light weight, and flexible, allow the rapid and low cost virtualization of expensive and bulky hardware test benches and test equipment, to a significant productivity and cost benefit. As an example, consider a recent ECU project for a next generation diesel engine for a year 2020 vehicle model. The entire low level engine control software for engine position and fuel injection control was developed and tested for release to the OEM development partner with the help only of a simple programmable Crank/CAM generator model and simple engine models, in a programmable virtual test environment for automated verification and validation testing; this is illustrated in Fig. 4. This environment is capable of regressing over 1,200 system level tests in less than a few hours on a CPU farm no bigger than a desktop box. In addition, alongside the open loop Crank/CAM generator test set up, an equally simple engine virtualization was used for basic closed loop validation of the same software in a virtual test bench for validation and issue analysis and diagnostic.

Test and measurement devices, such as oscilloscopes and logic analyzers, in a hardware test bench are used to observe various hardware signals, such as fuel injection pulses on a the MCU timer IO pins. These functions are easily supported by the native mechanisms for software event or virtual hardware event tracing and logging, Fig. 5 such as an advanced virtualization environment like VLAB provides as part of its base features. Virtual instruments can be attached interactively at the click of the mouse or programmatically by simple API calls. Furthermore, volumes of software or hardware

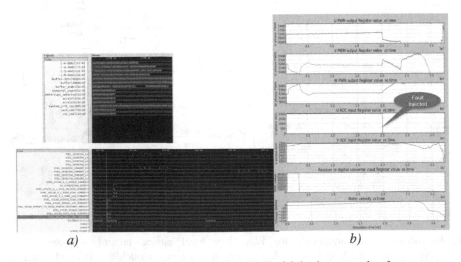

a)   b)

Fig. 5. Virtual oscilloscope tracing and plotting (a) Fuel injection control software events as well as interleaved hardware events and signals, and (b) Motor control system variables, incl calculated PWM and motor velocity in RPM.

events can be logged unobtrusively during execution, and visualized, processed and analyzed by native data analysis and visualization functions of the VLAB virtual environment.

Target Software and System Virtualization. Another means of virtualization of an ECU prototype hardware board, comprise an OS software emulator, running on only an Instruction Set Simulator (ISS) of the CPU subsystem of the main MCU. This type of virtual platform provides an all-in-software environment for running application level tasks - for task debug, task unit test coverage analysis, or for a closed loop ECU software calibration test procedure in conjunction with engine models. The last set up is illustrated in Fig. 6,

Such an environment allows an entire unmodified ECU binary, including the low level and base software, to be loaded and the operation of its application tasks accurately simulated, on a virtual platform comprising only the CPU ISS sub-system platform. None of the peripheral IP and IO blocks in the MCU or any of the ECU ASIC components are required, which reduces the effort to create such platforms and increases the speed of simulation. Speed of closed loop calibration test operation in this virtual environment is very high and bounded by speed of Engine/Plant simulation; it can exceed real time speeds by up to 50× of real time.

The ECU binary software calibration test virtual platform is an example of what we may call a late stage virtualization use case. It is used at the very end of a new ECU development and deployment project, after completing all ECU level development, test, and functional validation activities, as part of the integration with the engine in a vehicle by an OEM of a new ECU supplied by a Tier 1 company. In this case, for commercial reasons between the Tier 1 and the OEM, the OEM will usually not have access to anything more than just the final ECU software binary, no software source code or debug information and no detailed internal hardware specifications are made available from the Tier 1. Even in such a constrained development situation, we can virtualize the ECU environment to a significant commercial benefit, allowing faster than real time calibration procedures, new adaptive optimization algorithms, cheaper all-in-software calibration environments, and calibration test start before availability of the integrated software/hardware ECU module.

Specification Virtualization. At the beginning of an embedded development project, is the System Design phase. The key scope and goal of this phase is to design the intended function of the new embedded system, the "What?" it is supposed to do when completed and installed in its intended operating environment. In the development of a new engine control ECU, this is the phase when the new engine control algorithms and other ECU functions, such as diagnostics support, interactions with other vehicle systems, and any other ECU functions of a more basic or of a more application specific nature, are designed. The primary design goal is to achieve the target system and engine operation key performance indicators, such as fuel efficiency, CO_2 emissions, and others.

The design process may be informal and manual, involving little more than pen and paper, or it may be more formal, with the help of various tools and computer based methodologies. Such examples include the use of algorithm models and system models and simulations, using environments such as the Mathworks® MATLAB®/Simulink®

environment for Model Based Design or MBD. MBD uses a type of virtualization in the form of models and simulations of a certain kind that are suitable for a wider engineering community; this usually includes application or system engineers from a diverse range of domains and disciplines, such as control engineers, who may not be trained or skilled as software engineers. We will skip over the further discussion of MBD itself and leapfrog towards the end of this System Design/Specification phase, whatever the process and methodology for design may be. As we come to the end of this phase, a set of ECU specifications needs to emerge, for use in the subsequent development phases. These include Controller Technical Requirements (CTR) specification documents and Controller Validation Requirements (CVR) specification documents. The CTR document describes the requirements for the new ECU to be developed and the CVR document describes how the new ECU should be tested by the ECU supplier and what should be the results of such tests.

Such ECU specifications, usually developed, provided, and mandated for compliance by the OEM, are large and detailed documents, comprising many hundreds or even thousands of pages, combined. These specifications need to be used both by the OEM engineers creating them, who should know them in a certain way, as they created them, but also, most importantly, by the Tier 1 ECU supplier teams who will need to implement them, and to whom these specifications are new, unknown, and fraught with questions, ambiguities, and unknowns. Written specifications and other human readable materials, whether in paper or electronic form, are very useful to us. We can read a book, understand its concepts and comprehend overall meaning. However, such human readable specifications do little to help with the accurate and comprehensive understanding of the intricate details of the design. This is especially true regarding the intended, or even unintended, dynamic behavior, especially under different or varying operating conditions. In addition, machine readable specifications are required, which can be animated, simulated, or executed for the purpose of trialing, analyzing, or validating our understanding of them, for subsequent implementation, test and validation of the ECU software and hardware module.

If algorithmic models or other system models are available, from an earlier MBD process, they may be used by the implementation teams for the purposes of specification analysis and generation of tests. In general, traditional MBD models, while very useful during the design itself, provide limited help in the transition from design to implementation. They fall short of the needs for describing and understanding the wider requirements for function, interface, and structure. They also fall short of the needs for a shared means for analysis and discussion, between the design team and the implementation team; for example, the different ways in which an implementation may proceed and for feedback from the implementation team back to the system design and specifications team. Such feedback often leads to modification, clarification or elaboration of the specifications, in cases where gaps, contradictions or infeasible requirements are identified by the implementation team during the later implementation phases. These MBD models are developed and used to the extent sufficient to help develop the specifications. However, they may not cover all that an implementation team may require in order to understand the specifications fully, capture all specification requirements, and figure out what is a correct or optimal implementation.

For this purpose, virtualizations of the OEM ECU specifications, both of CTR and CVR, are very useful at the start or in the early implementation phases of development. They provide rapidly developed executable implementations or prototypes of the new specifications; for example, during the Specification Analysis phase at a Tier 1 supplier or, either later on or in parallel, by the OEM software teams who need to develop new applications software to run on the ECU module. The division between an OEM customer and a Tier 1 ECU supplier in this example into separate companies is not an essential one. The same situation arises in a Tier 1 designing and developing a new standard product ECU for multiple customers, where both the ECU System Engineering/Design and the ECU Development Engineering functions are internal to the Tier 1, usually as different departments. Similarly, in an OEM with an internal ECU Development Engineering organization, it will act as an internal Tier 1 ECU supplier.

The virtualization of ECU Specifications takes the form of Executable Specification Models or Virtual Specification Prototypes developed and run in a virtual environment like VLAB. This is done either by the ECU System Engineering/Design team responsible for developing the specifications, or by the ECU Development team responsible for the implementation, test, and supply of the ECU. In either case, they serve the role of a very first prototype realization of the ECU, or a Proto 0, as they are known within the context of contemporary ECU supply chain development project, which involve so called Proto 1, Proto 2, and Proto 3, phases to final manufacturing and release.

In the example given in Fig. 7, a low-level engine control subsystem for a diesel engine is defined in 150 pages of paper specifications. A virtual specification prototype in VLAB, of the integrated software and hardware behavior described in these 150 pages, is implemented in about 3,000 lines of Python/SystemC code, in a fraction of the time and effort required to implement the same specification as prototype software and hardware. The virtual specification prototype implements the same software API

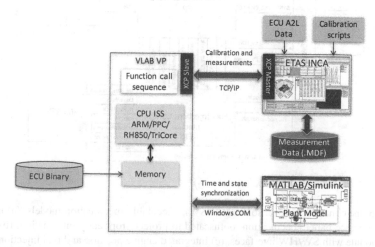

Fig. 6. Virtual platform for ECU software calibration test of unmodified ECU binaries in a closed loop with engine models and INCA™ calibration software.

interfaces and function as the prototype ECU. The application software can therefore link with the virtual specification prototype using the same target tools chain and execute the same as on the prototype ECI. In addition, on the hardware side, the virtual specification prototype senses and generates the same signals as the hardware would. This allows a virtual specification prototype to be used instead of the first hardware/software prototype to validate the analysis and understanding of the system requirements and specifications by the implementation team, saving time, costs, and expensive hardware based trials and tests.

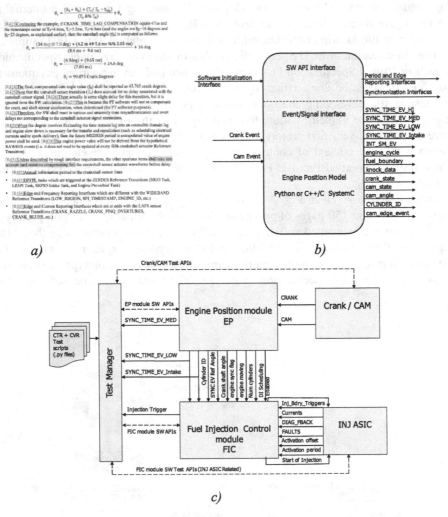

Fig. 7. Engine control low level software (BSW), executable specification models, (a) Example from the reference paper specification, obfuscated to protect proprietary information, (b) Engine position module with SW/HW interfaces, (c) Integrated engine position and fuel injection control sub-system in an open loop test bench, with Crank/CAM generator and an Injection Driver ASIC emulation model.

Test Specifications and Procedures. Once an ECU functional specification, or CTR, has been virtualized and a test bench built around it, as shown in Fig. 7, it is possible to implement all ECU test specifications, or CVR test procedures, as executable test software scripts, as illustrated in Fig. 8. This is akin to virtualizing the paper test specifications, which are in the form of human readable test procedures, as executable test scripts. The entire CVR plan can be implemented, or virtualized, during the Specification Analysis phase, and CVR test cases programmed, run, debugged, and validated in the virtual test environment with the virtual CTR specification prototype.

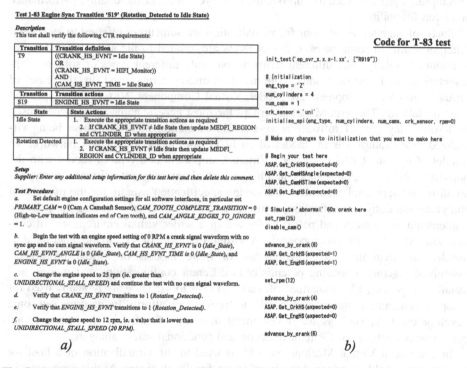

a)   b)

Fig. 8. Virtualization of ECU test procedures, (a) Sample test procedure from ECU CVR test specification document, in English, (b) The same realized as a VLAB Python test script in for a virtual test bench with a virtual specification prototype of the corresponding CTR functional specification.

Types of Virtualizations. The purpose of these examples in this section is not to provide a comprehensive introduction to the technology and methodology of virtualization. Rather, it is to illustrate that the means for virtualization are diverse and that the essential requirement is not that we use any particular rigid approach or a particular type of software representation, but only that a software representation, suitable for the intended purpose, can be developed and used with the desired effect.

For example, for the virtualization of hardware we may use an interface stub, a function emulation model, a detailed specification accurate hardware simulation model, a virtual prototype, or any other software abstraction and simplification of the hardware operation or function, which is suitable for the purpose. can be a valid means for virtualization for embedded development and test.

In the cases described in this section, abstracting away all detail unnecessary for the target purposes of virtualization, thereby simplifying the effort and cost, is of the most importance. This requires a good understanding of the purposes and goals of virtualization as well as a good understanding of the relevant function of the device being virtualized. The goal is to minimize the cost and time and maximize the return on investment in virtualization, which is measured in terms of improvements in the development process, such as improvements in cycle time, costs, quality, performance and even feasibility.

Such software representations for virtualization are sometimes referred to by several different terms. In some cases, different terms are applied to the same type of representation. In other cases, different terms denote truly different types of software representations and virtualizations. The most common terms used in the case of virtualization for development are Model, Virtual Component, Virtual Prototype, and Virtual Platform. The term Model is perhaps the most generic name and is widely used to describe any type of software representation of a component or system being virtualized. For example, as in 'model of an ECU,' or 'model of a CAN network,' or 'model of a Crank/CAM generator.' Virtual Component is a type of model with the purpose of being a building block in a bigger virtual environment. Virtual Prototype is an all-in-software implementation of a design specification usually for the purpose of analyzing the design specification, learning, and evaluating or assessing the possible implementation choices and paths, or for use in a wider virtual environment in conjunction with other virtual components. A Virtual Platform, or VP, on the other hand, is usually an environment comprising one or more models or virtual prototypes, assembled together, operating potentially in different configurations and modes, and usually integrated with simulation software and user tools. They are typically used for complex and multiple purposes, generally to 'provide a platform' for carrying out some development task, such as for development and test of software, architecture and performance analysis, or for fault injection and functional safety analysis.

In contrast, a Virtual Machine, or VM, is used in the virtualization of a host for runtime in the field, as opposed to virtualization for development. At this time, we will not extend our scope to cover such VMs for field runtime use, but will focus on the development phase of a new embedded system.

Virtualization vs. Modeling. There is commonality and overlap between the two concepts and there are differences, though any distinction is not a clear cut one and more a matter of purpose and method. From the point of view of this paper, virtualization is the broader concept and it includes modelling as a special case of virtualization.

In general, the goal of modelling is to create computer based models which are intended to capture faithfully the function, and may be the structure and other important aspects, of a component or system being studied or designed. For existing systems, this is done either in order to study and analyze or to simulate and reproduce their operation. For example, the case of plant models used in a test bench. During new system design, models are used in order to capture and develop a new design, for example a new controller design for a new engine. In Model Based Design, a model-centric development methodology, the starting point and the scope of modeling is to model the system under design at the system level and then perhaps find a path to implement that system design model in the final product.

In the specific case of virtualization during the system design phase, i.e. virtualization of system specifications and designs, the goals and use cases of virtualization overlap with those of modelling in Model Based Design. Virtual specification prototypes and executable specification models are developed for similar or the same purposes as system models in Model Based Design. To model, simulate, and analyze the specification. To serve as a reference for test development and during design implementation. And, for possible design refinement into more detailed models in moving towards implementation.

However, virtualization as defined here, has broader goals and scope than the design phase. Like Model Based Design, virtualization includes modeling and use of design models in the system design phase; however, it extends further than the scope of system design and targets wider application in all end to end phases of the development process and to all elements of the development environment.

Virtualization involves replacing any component or system in the development process with any suitable type of software representation fit for a particular purpose in the development process; the goal is to improve the development process by turning it into a software based process, accelerating and automating any, potentially all, development tasks. Any software representation, however imperfect, of the component or system it replaces, which fits this purpose, is a valid means of virtualization for development. For some purposes, detailed models will be required, such as in the case of virtual platforms of hardware for the purpose of development of very low level, hardware specific, real time software, where the detailed operation of the hardware needs to be modelled in order to simulate and test the interactions between the software and the hardware. In other cases, little more than an empty shell may be sufficient. There is not one starting point for virtualization of development; any task or any phase in the development process may become the target of virtualization in order to accelerate and automate the development and test. For example, the ECU software verification and validation (V&V) test environment of the Integration and Test team may be virtualized for the purpose of automating and parallelizing the test execution of the already developed target software, regardless of the availability models of the system or of the software or the lack thereof such models.

3 Virtualization Based Development

Virtualization-Based Development (or VBD) is a methodology for embedded development that leverages virtualization to establish an all-in-software development environment and a software-based process in all phases, from specification through architecture design, implementation, validation, optimization, to field release and support. Critically, VPD enables the application of modern software tools, methodologies, and processes to embedded development. This in turn allows a significant increase in development productivity, corresponding reduction in costs and cycle time, as well as an increase in the quality, reliability, and predictability of the development process and its resulting artifacts.

The central method of VBD is to look for elements in the embedded development process which are not in software form and hence constrain the development process; devise process improvements which benefit from replacing these elements with software representations; identify the simplest possible virtualizations that support the identified uses; asses the feasibility/costs/benefits as well as the time to implement; deploy and exploit all the scalability, automation, and all other flexibilities of software environments and processes. By turning all elements of the embedded development environment into software, all the tools, methods and processes for software engineering in a desktop environment become available in the embedded development process and can be leveraged alongside the hardware based methods, tools, and processes.

Defined in this way, VBD can be applied either, in a case by case way to the tasks or phases of development, where the greatest improvement can be made, or, in an end to end way replacing or supplementing all hardware based development processes. In the earlier section introducing the concept of virtualization, point examples of virtualization and applications of virtualization were described addressing one or another development task. In this section, we will take an end to end view and will outline how virtualization can be applied in all phases of the end to end development and how VBD processes in different phases integrate into an end to end VBD flow.

We will describe the concept of a VBD flow within a simplified high level ECU development process. To cover some of the complexities inherent in modern ECU development, we will assume that the sample ECU project involves more than one commercial entity. On one side, the *demand side*, an OEM specifying the requirements, commissioning the ECU, and conducting the ECU acceptance tests, system integration and validation tests involving the ECU and the rest of the vehicle engine system. On the other side, the *supply side,* a Tier 1 ECU company designing and implementing the ECU module, including the hardware and software, conducting internally verification and validation tests in preparation for release to the OEM. We will also allow for the possibility that some of the ECU semiconductor hardware, such as custom MCU and ASICs, are co-developed alongside by a third commercial entity, a semiconductor company. The tasks and processes involved in such a large development project involving several companies are on a scale of complexity and detail which cannot be adequately covered in a limited paper such as this one. We will attempt to be close to the true picture in the outline, but in the detail we will at most hope to somewhat approximate and resemble the structure and contents of actual ECU projects of this scale.

First, let us consider the target for development in an ECU development project, the ECU module. As Fig. 9 illustrates, the ECU module comprises integrated hardware and software. Hardware, such as boards with MCU, ASIC, and other electronic and electro-mechanical components, is integrated with software, itself comprising a complex multi-layer stack from the lowest level device drivers and a next layer of hardware abstractions and complex drivers, through OS, middleware, and run time environment layer, to application level tasks and supporting services.

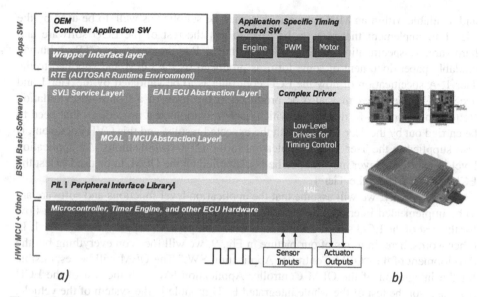

Fig. 9. Engine systems ECU development targets the development of (a) ECU software, and (b) ECU hardware module.

This is complex software. It requires a great deal of effort to develop and test. Much of the complexity of the software arises from the complex and intricate interactions of the software with the hardware, which are required to implement and deliver the complex integrated ECU functions, including sensing and driving complex signals. The rest of the complexity is inherent in the complex algorithms and functions of the ECU itself.

Now, referring back to the discussion on the contrast between Model Based Design, and Virtualization Based Development, we can draw out a helpful illustration. At best, MBD will involve the use of a model to design and validate the system design, followed by a process of refinement of this system design model into a level of detail and structure, from which generation of application level code is possible, either by automated tools or manually. Therefore, the scope and goals of MBD in Engine Control ECU development are limited only to the development of the application software component of the ECU software stack, the box in the top left corner of Fig. 9, labelled "OEM Controller Application SW." The development of the complex remaining layers and components of the ECU software stack are beyond the scope and goals of MBD and are in fact assumed to be somehow made available as the target environment for the application level code generated by MBD. However, in contrast, while MBD is of no help in the development of the rest of the ECU software, hardware, and the integrated ECU module as a whole, the scope and goals of Virtualization Based Development, or VBD, extend to include precisely these activities as well. Any virtualization that allows the development of any of the ECU and ECU software or hardware in an all-in-software environment is within the scope and goals of VBD.

Consider the high level ECU development flow in Fig. 10. The ECU system function is designed and specified by the OEM. If system level models are developed and available within an MBD process, they may be supplied as well, to be used by the Tier 1 to implement these, or, to be used to test the rest of the ECU software and hardware. A specification, a Controller Technical Requirements, or CTR, a human readable paper document of some form, is produced by the OEM and supplied to the Tier 1. A specification of how the ECU controller is to be validated by the Tier 1 and accepted by the OEM may also be produced in the form of a Controller Validation Requirements, or CVR, document, which lists the various test procedures that need to be carried out by the Tier 1, along with the expected results, and this CVR document, is also supplied to the Tier 1 as a supplement to the CTR specifications. An application level test software layer may be specified or supplied by the OEM, to be used to test the ECU deliverable by the Tier 1.

For simplicity, we will assume that the application level functions and software are to be implemented internally by the OEM and we will focus on the development flow for the rest of the ECU software and hardware developed and supplied by the Tier 1. In other words, here, in terms of our picture in Fig. 9, we will focus on everything but the development of the "OEM Controller Application SW." The OEM will be responsible for the integration of the OEM Controller Application SW with the rest of the ECU software, for the test of the whole integrated ECU module in the system of the vehicle, for the validation of the ECU operation against the original system requirements and design, and for any changes and updates to the ECU requirements and specifications as a result of these test and validation activities or due to other changes in the OEM ECU product plans. These are key tasks and responsibilities within the overall end to end ECU flow, but we will leave them at the periphery of our scope in this introduction of VBD and contain the focus of our description to the process inside the Tier 1, from the receipt of a CTR/CVR specification through the development, test, and validation of a new ECU module, and the delivery to the OEM, including any feedback from the OEM test and validation processes.

The two processes, those running at the OEM, and, on the other side of the line, those run by the Tier 1, are illustrated at a high level on Fig. 10. Usually, an ECU development project by an OEM, for a new generation ECU and a new engine, takes 3 to even 4 years elapsed, and involves several hardware and software prototype phases, may be as many as 3 or 4 such phases. In each phase, a new hardware module is designed, implemented, and manufactured, and a new software build is developed, integrated with the hardware, and the two tested together or separately to some extent.

The Tier 1 is responsible for the development and supply of each ECU prototype. In some cases, the sequence of prototypes is planned, as part of an incremental development and test plan, or, in other cases, unplanned prototypes may be required due to implementation issues or unplanned specification changes. A prototype cycle may take 1 to 1.5 or even 2 years, from start to end of validation and feedback from the OEM.

As Fig. 10 illustrates, the ECU prototype development flow is largely sequential. The key elements and dependencies limiting this flow are the limitations of largely paper based, human readable, but machine un-executable, specifications and designs, and the dependencies on hardware availability for the development and test of any software and for the development and validation of any tests. Due to these process limitations and dependencies the overall process suffers from the following:

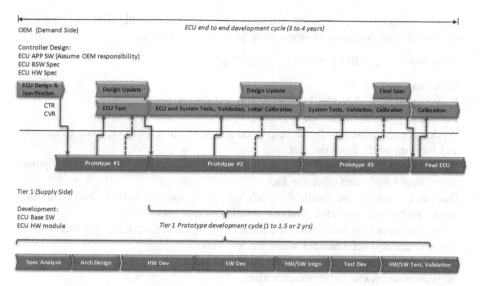

Fig. 10. End to end ECU development process, including OEM, or demand side, processes of ECU design, specification, validation and acceptance, as well as calibration, and Tier 1, or supply side, processes for implementation of these specifications, verification, and delivery to the OEM.

- Working and executable builds of the ECU are available and can be run and tested only very late in the process.
- Testing starts late, which means issues accumulate over a long period of and any essential learnings and feedback from internal and from OEM trials and tests become available very late.
- The cost of identifying, diagnosing, and fixing any functional or design issues is disproportionately high and the timeframes for validation are long.
- Project planning is complex and prone to inaccuracies, as it involves end to end timeframes, risks, and complexities of work flows.

VBD seeks to improve the development process by leveraging virtualization. Virtualization, brings the following new capabilities to the development process:

- Remove from the schedule dependencies due to limitations in availability.
- Replace missing components with executable alternatives.
- Replace human readable but not executable components with executable alternatives.
- Allow essentially unlimited replication and supply of development components for scalability of concurrent execution and engineering.
- Replace manual processes involving hardware and paper with processes involving software which can execute much faster and be automated.
- Increase the level of visibility into the internal operation and structure of the system, the number of points which can be observed and traced.
- Increase the volume and diversity of data that can be collected and analyzed both manually and automatically.

- Allow configurations, operation, and tests which are not possible with real hardware or very difficult to create or impossible to replicate reliably.

As a result, in a VBD process:

- Tasks can start earlier.
- Tasks can be scheduled and completed in a different order.
- Tasks can proceed faster due to scaling of resources and automation.
- Working, executable builds can be created and tested much earlier, more frequently, and independently from the rest.
- Tests can be developed and validated earlier and be available to assist development rather than simply test after the fact.
- Data and feedback are available much earlier, in greater volume and in a form amenable to more complex analysis algorithms and procedures.
- Issues are identified and resolved earlier, development proceeds with much fewer latent issues and accumulates along far less risk.
- Learning happens earlier, and in turn adaptation and improvement of plans and of implementations can occur much earlier.

Figure 11 below illustrates how a VBD process can be applied to an ECU prototype development cycle and the transformation of work flow and time frames this in turn can achieve.

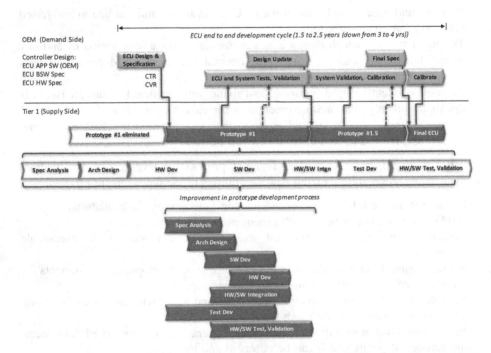

Fig. 11. Improvement in ECU prototype development schedule via VBD, comparing sequential conventional development process above to the concurrent development process possible with VBD.

In the VBD development process, we observe, most notably, that:

– Test development, debug and validation begin as early as the start of the Specification Analysis phase and continue throughout development, in a test driven methodology.
– Software development can begin before hardware development begins and before hardware is available to run the software.
– Hardware development can be delayed, without delaying software development, to allow as much opportunity for test and learning as possible before committing to costly development and manufacture of hardware.
– Software/hardware integration can begin soon after software development begins and proceed well before the hardware development begins.
– Software/hardware tests and validation begins and proceeds early.
– Tasks take less effort due to automation and ongoing issue resolution.
– Some tasks may be extended in time to allow concurrent incremental development with other tasks. For example, test development can start earlier and proceed for longer alongside the software and hardware development and integration to allow the addition of new tests on the way.

In general, significant reductions in prototype cycle time are possible, with a reduction in overall cycle time of 30% to 40%, or even as high as 50%, being a realistic target for actual commercial ECU projects.

At the next level up, the level of the OEM ECU development process, one or more prototype cycles can be eliminated altogether, with the corresponding savings in cycle time and cost. The OEM ECU test and system validation process accelerates by earlier starts in each phase and much more rapid rate of coverage and quality convergence. Consider the example in Fig. 6 (ECU Software Calibration test) where the ECU software calibration test, usually of an average of 3 months or more in duration, can begin and mostly complete, with the final software build before the final ECU hardware is developed or manufactured. The enabler for this acceleration and parallelization of work flow in VBD is virtualization, namely the transformation of the development environment into an all-in-software virtual development environment.

The VBD environment elements and platforms are developed prior or, as shown in Fig. 12, just-in-time alongside the other development tasks. In the case of an agile, iterative, continuous integration and test, development process, the overall development may be broken down into many short iterations, or sprints, each potentially as short as 1 or 2 weeks. New features are added incrementally, one or more at a time in each sprint, in a concurrent engineering process where in parallel the new feature specification is prototyped for reference, new tests are developed and added to the test suite, new software is developed to implement the feature, and new hardware virtualizations are added to support the feature in the virtual development environment. All these tasks proceed in parallel and all coming together at the end of the iteration cycle, where everything is integrated and tested, progress confirmed or corrective feedback and lessons learned derived.

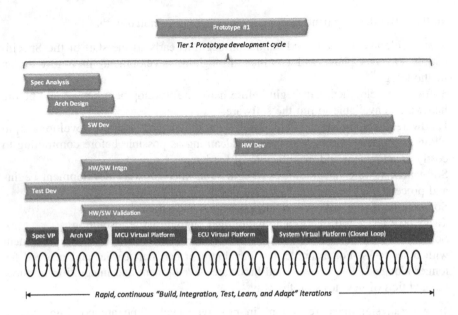

Fig. 12. VBD requires a virtual development environment to be created before or in time with the other tasks.

This is an important point and critical to the feasibility and application of VBD in practice. Virtualization requires time and effort, and there is a cost associated with that. The benefits are overall reduction in ECU development cycle time, in development costs, and improvements in product quality, reliability, and performance. However, effective application of VBD will require that the benefits outweigh the costs of virtualization. Here is one of the key challenges and pre-requisites for the successful deployment and adoption of VBD. The cost and lead time for virtualization need to be reduced as much as possible, the process of virtualization itself to be simplified and automated as much as possible, and the availability and reuse of virtual components increased as much as possible. Good architecture and design of the virtual development environment is key to selecting the rights abstractions and simplifications that are sufficient for the intended uses, on one hand, and, on the other hand, require the least amount of time and cost to create.

Figure 13 below summarizes some key examples and applications of virtualization, for select phases and tasks in the ECU development flow, with a focus on the ECU software development process. For this listing, we revert back to using the picture of the conventional serial waterfall development process. We do this for illustration and to present this from the perspective of someone trying to improve their conventional process towards a VBD process and looking for guidance as to where the opportunities are and what the suitable virtualizations are.

An end to end VBD process for ECU development would involve a wide range of virtualizations. In the example here, Fig. 13, the list includes:

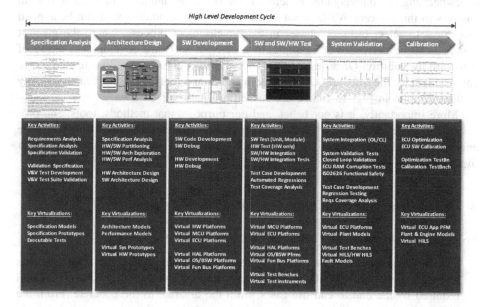

Fig. 13. Key virtualizations and applications of virtualization in the ECU development flow.

- System specifications, requirements and designs, including algorithmic level, but also including concrete software and hardware interfaces.
- Architecture abstractions of systems, software and hardware, for architecture level design exploration and performance analysis, capable of running both without software, as software may not yet be available, and with target compiled software, where such exists.
- Software virtualization and real software in the loop, from target independent application level tasks, through RTOS, middleware, control software, communications protocol software, through to low level target specific driver software, and software APIs and interfaces.
- Hardware virtualizations able to run accurately target compiled software builds, including virtual boards with MCUs, memories, I/O, buses, interconnects, ASICs, analog/mixed signal components, sensors, actuators, and other hardware interfaces, including for debug and test.
- Tests, test procedures, test benches, test scenarios, including fault injection, test instruments, debug and test results, analysis, and visualization.
- Data, signals, events, interactions, concurrency, and time, from system level, for example the event of setting a target RPM value, through CAN messages communicating RPM values, down to software variable values, peripheral register bit settings, interrupt signals of sufficient timing resolution to preserve the order of interrupt events, and waveforms at IO pins at clock cycle edge accuracy.

This is a wide ranging list. The concerns of the reader may be that the overheads and complexities of establishing and operating such environment and process are overwhelming and outweigh the benefits. There is a clear danger of that. There several answers to this concern. VBD is not an all or nothing methodology. It can be applied piecemeal to select tasks or phases in the development process, where the greatest benefit is to be derived. For example, to accelerate software development ahead of hardware availability. Or, to establish an automated regression test and test coverage environment for the software. Or, for fault injection and functional safety analysis. Any of the examples in Fig. 13 can be established profitably on its own.

More importantly, it is our belief, and our purpose, that methods, tools, and processes can be developed to systematically simplify the complexity and reduce the time and effort required to establish a VBD environment and process, which will deliver overall benefits far outweighing any costs.

4   Virtualization Tools and Operating Environments, VLAB

To make virtualization and VBD a practical proposition, we need:

– Virtualization tools, for the rapid and cost effective creation of virtual components and the assembly of virtual platforms, supporting all levels of abstraction and detail required by the end to end use cases, from the abstract to the concrete. From the highest level of embedded system complexity and abstraction, down to the concrete levels of target compiled software images and detailed hardware specifications, where direct interoperation with detailed implementation tools is possible, such as target software toolchains and hardware design implementation environments.
– Virtual operating environments, for the operation of this wide range of virtual components and platforms, and for the user programmable build, configuration, run, command, control, and instrumentation, including the ability to inject faults and simulate failures. Open and interoperable with other tools and environments, such as system simulation tools, software debug and analysis tools, hardware development environments, test tools, hardware in the loop simulations tools, and real hardware.
– Automation tools for the automation of development tasks and processes in the virtual environment, including complete use case pre-integrated solutions, such as for automation of software build, run and debug tasks, automated regression testing, automated test generation and test coverage analysis, or functional safety testing against a specified standard.

VLAB™, short for Virtualization LABoratory, is perhaps the first tool environment which targets this wide, end to end, range of virtualizations, and seeks to enable an end to end virtualization-based development process, with a focus on the embedded software engineer as the target virtualization engineer and user, not the specialist modeling engineer.

VLAB seeks to achieve this by leveraging general purpose software engineering languages and methodologies in the process of virtualization and operation of a virtual environment, not by introducing specialist modeling notations and environments.

- Python is used, for its simple syntax, object orientation and modularization capabilities, to provide a powerful interactive user environment, both for programming and automating the creation and operation of a virtual environment, and for developing virtual components and platforms more rapidly. VLAB contains a full standard Python stack, including not only the standard language and libraries, but also the majority of the popular additional packages for scientific computations, visualization, and software development.
- SystemC is used, at the most basic level, to represent in software the structure, behavior, communications and concurrency, of components and systems, including of hardware systems, VLAB uses the paradigm of SystemC, the industry standard library extensions of SystemC/TLM and SystemC/AMS to the standard C++ language. A programmable SystemC simulator operating in a standard desktop environment, is used to simulate the operation of such virtual components and systems. However, SystemC is a rather low level language for virtualization. VLAB builds on the fundamentals of SystemC by providing many higher level abstractions of the SystemC constructs, most notably in Python. The VLAB environment significantly simplifies the process of virtualization, of creating new virtual components and assembling virtual platforms and environment using Python.
- Any other software library can be imported and linked within VLAB with the rest of the virtual environment, to leverage existing virtualizations in other languages or for data analysis and other computations, e.g. in MATLAB™ and FORTRAN. Also, most significantly, embedded target languages, such as C can be used, including to model software or as target compiled software.

This makes VLAB a very flexible and powerful virtualization, automation, and development tool, and makes it accessible to a very large pool of engineers. It integrates well with industrial scale, production grade, embedded development processes, including the test, verification and validation processes.

At the same time, the use of general purpose programming languages, while an advantage in the adoption by development engineers, presents challenges in the formalization of the underlying concepts and methods. In turn, this limits the opportunities for automation of the process of virtualization and in the application of virtual software representations and models to the automation of design, analysis, test generation, and verification. This is an area we would like to collaborate with and seek help from academic research.

5 Conclusions

We introduced Virtualization Based Design (VBD) as a methodology for converting the embedded system development process into an all-in-software process, with the goals of acceleration and automation. We contrasted VBD to the well-known Model Based Design (MBD) methodology in the area of ECU controller development. The scope of VBD includes MBD but extends further than system design and targets wider application in all phases of the embedded development process and targets all elements of the development environment. Critically, VBD enables the application of modern software tools, methodologies, and processes to embedded and deeply embedded systems in general and to ECU development in particular. We provided a high level overview of VLAB, a software desktop environment that supports end-to-end, industrial scale virtualization of embedded software and system development.

References

1. Broy, M., Kirstan, S., Krcmar, H., Schätz, B., Zimmermann, J.: What is the benefit of a model-based design of embedded software systems in the car industry? In: Software Design and Development: Concepts, Methodologies, Tools, and Applications: Concepts, Methodologies, Tools, and Applications, p. 310 (2013)
2. Why We Model: Using MBD Effectively in Critical Domains. Keynote address at the Modeling in Software Engineering Workshop (MiSE 2013), May 2013
3. Moriyama, Y., et al.: Application of ISS-less technology to Virtual CRAMAS (SILS). Fujitsu Ten Tech. J. **32**, 3–11 (2009)
4. Lantz, J.: Multi-domain model-driven development. In: MAC 2015 (2015)
5. Charette, R.N.: This car runs on code. IEEE Spectr. **46**, 3–11 (2009)
6. VLAB™ documentation and user guides (2016). http://www.vlabworks.com

Author Index

Printed in the United States
By Bookmasters